Defences to Copyright Infringement

Defences to Copyright Infringement

Creativity, Innovation, and Freedom on the Internet

STAVROULA KARAPAPA

Professor of Intellectual Property and Information Law
University of Reading

OXFORD
UNIVERSITY PRESS

UNIVERSITY PRESS

Great Clarendon Street, Oxford, OX2 6DP,
United Kingdom

Oxford University Press is a department of the University of Oxford.
It furthers the University's objective of excellence in research, scholarship,
and education by publishing worldwide. Oxford is a registered trade mark of
Oxford University Press in the UK and in certain other countries

First Edition published in 2020

Impression: 1

Published in the United States of America by Oxford University Press
198 Madison Avenue, New York, NY 10016, United States of America

British Library Cataloguing in Publication Data
Data available

Library of Congress Control Number: 2019953097

ISBN 978–0–19–879563–6

Printed and bound by
CPI Group (UK) Ltd, Croydon, CR0 4YY

Preface

This book is the result of a long-standing interest in defensive rules in copyright law. Although this interest has led me to write on specific defences for copyright infringement in the past, a central aim of this book was to adopt a broader perspective and look into defensive rules more widely, particularly in the light of emergent copy-reliant technologies and modern business models. Indeed, the fourth industrial revolution brings unprecedented challenges to copyright and calls for a critical reflection on whether the applicable copyright defences are actually conducive towards achieving the objectives of EU copyright law. With this book, I attempt to offer legal and teleological insights into how defensive rules should be construed in order to achieve the objectives that EU copyright law means to serve, including, but not limited to, creativity, innovation, and business growth.

The book builds on years of research into the nature and function of defensive rules under EU copyright law. My early research on the private copying exception, which goes back to my doctoral studies at Brunel University, was published with Routledge (Karapapa 2012) and was also discussed in other publications, such as 'A copyright exception for private copying in the United Kingdom' in the European Intellectual Property Review (Karapapa 2013). I am elaborating and closely reflecting on aspects of this research in this book. I have also worked on some aspects of defensive rules from a cross-jurisprudential perspective in the monograph I co-authored with Maurizio Borghi, entitled *Copyright and Mass-Digitization* and published with Oxford University Press in 2013. While working on this monograph, I was attracted by the emergence of copy-reliant technologies—beyond those used in the context of mass digitization initiatives—and was captivated by the fact that, although these technologies can have important public benefits, such as the enhancement of innovation and development of new business models, they are often constrained by copyright norms and the limited availability of copyright exceptions under EU copyright law.

At a broader level, however, what I thought was interesting was that, although the scope of exclusive rights has been gradually enlarged at the legislative and judicial level, certain internal limits to rights have gradually started to shrink. Part of this tension is addressed in my work on the exhaustion principle, which was published with the Intellectual Property Quarterly (Karapapa 2014, 'Reconstructing copyright exhaustion in the online world'). I have also discussed the internal limits of exclusive rights in an article that was published with the European Law Review (Karapapa 2017, 'The requirement for a "new public" in EU copyright law'), taking a particular focus on the concept of the new public in the context of the right of communication to the public. Some of the ideas I expressed in these articles are also reflected in this book.

For the book to be published, I have received support from various people that I want to thank. This book would not have been possible without the support I received from Alex Flach, Gemma Parsons, Natalie Patey, and the team at Oxford University Press. I thank Maurizio Borghi for his generous advice on draft chapters, Lynda O'Brien for editing the manuscript, and various colleagues for insights during early stages of the research—particularly Tanya Aplin, Michael Birnhack, Enrico Bonadio, Ioannis Kokkoris, and Christine Riefa.

Finally, I would like to express my love and gratitude to my husband, Dimitrios, for his unfailing patience and support, and my daughter, Georgia Nicky, whose birth coincided with the writing of this book. It is to her that this book is dedicated.

Table of Contents

Detailed Table of Contents

Table of Cases

UK CASES

EUROPEAN UNION CASES

EUROPEAN COURT OF HUMAN RIGHTS CASES

NATIONAL CASES BY JURISDICTION

Germany

Greece

Hungary

Table of Legislation

NATIONAL LEGISLATION

List of Abbreviations

CDPA	Copyright, Designs, and Patents Act 1988
CVIPA 2002	Copyright (Visually Impaired Persons) Act 2002
EU	European Union
EU Charter	European Union Charter of Fundamental Rights
EUIPO	European Union Intellectual Property Office
NLA	Newspaper Licensing Agency
NLB	National Library for the Blind
OCR	Optical Character Recognition
OHIM	Office for Harmonization in the Internal Market
RNIB	Royal National Institute of Blind People
SCCR	Standing Committee on Copyright and Related Rights
TFEU	Treaty on the Functioning of the European Union
TRIPs	Agreement on Trade-Related Aspects of Intellectual Property Rights
WCT	WIPO Copyright Treaty
WIPO	World Intellectual Property Organization

1

Introduction

Defences against copyright infringement serve as invitations that enable a better understanding of copyright protection, its limits, and its encounter with other legal orders. Unlike other aspects of EU copyright, defences have not yet been subject to comprehensive conceptual analysis, despite the burgeoning literature addressing normative aspects of a particular set of defensive rules, namely copyright exceptions and limitations. Current discussions either focus on instances in which copyright exceptions and limitations should apply or on policy debates on the legal nature and appropriate form of activities permitted by copyright.[1] These discussions bring forward two core legal problems that become particularly prominent in the light of emergent technologies and new business models which rely on the use and re-use of copyright-protected content: the lack of flexibility in the current copyright system that does not allow permitting uses beyond those specifically listed and narrowly drafted in copyright laws,[2] and the very limited entitlement that copyright exceptions and limitations embody in that they are not user rights but are mere defences against allegations of copyright infringement.[3]

---

[1] See e.g. Pascale Chapdelaine, *Copyright User Rights: Contracts and the Erosion of Property* (Oxford: Oxford University Press, 2017); P. Bernt Hugenholtz and Martin Senftleben, 'Fair Use in Europe: In Search of Flexibilities' (2001) Institute for Information Law, Vrije Universiteit, Amsterdam; P. Bernt Hugenholtz, 'Flexible Copyright: Can the EU Author's Rights Accommodate Fair Use' in Ruth L. Okediji (ed.), *Copyright Law in an Age of Limitations and Exceptions* (New York: Cambridge University Press, 2017) 275; also see Robert Burrell and Allison Coleman, *Copyright Exceptions: The Digital Impact* (Cambridge: Cambridge University Press, 2005); Christophe Geiger, ' "Fair Use" through Fundamental Rights in Europe: When Freedom of Artistic Expression allows Creative Appropriations and Opens up Statutory Copyright Limitations' (2018) Center for International Intellectual Property Studies (CEIPI) Research Paper No. 201809.

[2] See in general P. Bernt Hugenholtz and Martin Senftleben, 'Fair Use in Europe: In Search of Flexibilities' (2001) Institute for Information Law, Vrije Universiteit, Amsterdam; Eleonora Rosati, 'Copyright in the EU: In Search of (In)Flexibilities' (2014) 9(7) *Journal of Intellectual Property Law & Practice* 585.

[3] See broadly Pascale Chapdelaine, *Copyright User Rights: Contracts and the Erosion of Property* (Oxford: Oxford University Press, 2017); Niva Elkin-Koren, 'Copyright in a Digital Ecosystem: A User Rights Approach' in Ruth L. Okediji (ed.), *Copyright Law in an Age of Limitations and Exceptions* (New York: Cambridge University Press, 2017) 132; there have been some cases which indicate that certain copyright exceptions are defences but not user rights that could be enforced before the courts: *L'ASBL Association Belge des Consomateurs Test Achats v La SA EMI Recorded Music Belgium et al*, Tribunal of First Instance of Brussels, 27 April 2004, 2004/46/A (Belgium); *L'ASBL Association Belge des Consomateurs Test Achats v La SA EMI Recorded Music Belgium et al*, Brussels Court of Appeal, 9 September 2005, 2004/AR/1649 (Belgium); for a commentary see Natalie Helberger, 'It's not a Right, Silly! The Private Copying Exception in Practice' (7 October 2004) *INDICARE Monitor; Studio Canal*

Defences to Copyright Infringement. Stavroula Karapapa, Oxford University Press (2020). © Stavroula Karapapa.
DOI: 10.1093/oso/9780198795636.001.0001

Indeed, technological developments, such as the emergence of innovative copy-reliant technologies or new services,[4] and the dynamic role of end users on the Internet, challenge existing copyright norms. Although, according to the common sentiment of justice and the laws of jurisdictions outside the European Union,[5] some of these activities should be permitted as they arguably enhance public welfare and have the potential to meet various public policy objectives, the applicable copyright framework in the European Union is too rigid to accommodate novel technologies and modern services that rely on the use and re-use of copyright-protected content, despite recent efforts to enhance the scope of permissible use at the EU level.[6]

By focusing on copyright exceptions and limitations, normative discussions on the future of permissible uses under EU copyright have not addressed defensive claims against copyright infringement from a broader perspective, including the variety of doctrinally established principles and other claims, possibly external to copyright law, that defendants can bring forward to acquit themselves of copyright infringement. In this sense, defensive rules have not yet been discussed as an organic whole. Broadly speaking, defences can include both instances in which defendants can justify infringing liability and escape infringement, and claims that negate infringement altogether. In the context of the fourth industrial revolution, whereby artificial intelligence, big data, digital platforms, and emergent electronic services challenge traditional copyright norms but bear obvious benefits to public welfare, such a holistic approach is essential in order to ascertain the spectrum of permissible use and to draw both positivist and normative conclusions on ways in

---

et al v S. Penguin and Union Federale des Consommateurs Que Choisir, Cour de Cassation, 19 June 2008, No. 07-142777 (France); *Studio Canal et al v S. Penguin and Union Federale des Consommateurs Que Choisir*, Paris Court of Appeal, 4 April 2007, *Gaz. Pal.*, 18 July 2007, No. 199, 23 (France); *Studio Canal et al v S. Penguin and Union Federale des Consommateurs Que Choisir*, Cour de Cassation, 1st civil section, 28 February 2006, No. 549, Bull. 2006 I No. 126, 115 (France) ('*Mulholland Drive*'); Supreme Court (Cour de cassation), 27 November 2008, No. 07-18778 (France) ('*Phil Collins*').

[4] See e.g. Matthew Sag, 'Copyright and Copy-Reliant Technology' (2009) 103 *Northwestern University Law Review* 1607.

[5] An example is the United States, where the fair use standard has in some instances acquitted from infringement activities that would amount to infringement under EU copyright.

[6] See Directive 2001/29/EC of the European Parliament and of the Council of 22 May 2001 on the Harmonisation of Certain Aspects of Copyright and Related Rights in the Information Society, OJ L 167, 22 June 2001, 10–19 (Information Society Directive); Directive (EU) 2012/28 of the European Parliament and of the Council of 25 October 2012 on Certain Permitted Uses of Orphan Works Text with EEA relevance, OJ L 299, 27 October 2012, 5–12 (Orphan Works Directive); Directive (EU) 2017/1564 of the European Parliament and of the Council of 13 September 2017 on Certain Permitted Uses of Certain Works and Other Subject Matter Protected by Copyright and Related Rights for the Benefit of Persons who are Blind, Visually Impaired, or Otherwise Print-Disabled and Amending Directive 2001/29/EC on the Harmonisation of Certain Aspects of Copyright and Related Rights in the Information Society, OJ L 242, 20 September 2017, 6–13 (Directive on Permitted Uses for Disabled Individuals); Directive (EU) 2019/790 of the European Parliament and of the Council of 17 April 2019 on Copyright and Related Rights in the Digital Single Market and Amending Directives 96/9/EC and 2001/29/EC, OJ L 130, 17 May 2019, 92–125 (Digital Single Market Directive).

which the tension between exclusive rights and the public domain can, and should, be resolved.

A question that has not yet been addressed concerns the way in which the various defensive rules compare with each other, how they interact, and whether there are instances of overlap or 'gaps' between defences, i.e. circumstances where a common sentiment of justice would suggest that a defence that is currently not applicable should apply. In other words, how do the available defences operate as a system and how can they be classified in a way that can further our understanding of their normative force, inform policy initiatives on their future reform and/or expansion, particularly in the light of emergent technologies that challenge the contours of copyright protection, and bring forward the tension between private rights and interests for the preservation of a rigorous public domain?

The growing significance of copyright defences

Because emergent technologies, online services, and new business models often rely on the use and re-use of copyright works, defences to copyright infringement have gained increased significance over the past twenty years. These technologies do not merely include the development of technical equipment that enables and facilitates home copying or other engagement with copyright materials by end users, such as smartphones or mobile phone applications, they also extend to a large variety of electronic services that rely on copying copyright-protected materials as part of their operation. Business growth in such copy-reliant technologies and services, but also in the context of online uses of protected materials more broadly, depends on the availability of uses permitted by copyright and on effective defences to copyright infringement.

There is a plethora of modern electronic services that operate on the basis of the use and re-use of content, which is often copyright protected, and many of these have been judicially discussed on a global basis. A notable example is Google Books, a service that involves wholesale copying of copyright-protected books and making portions of them available to the public through a dedicated electronic platform. This service was acquitted of copyright infringement on the basis of the US fair use defence.[7] Initiatives that were spurred on by the effect of the scanning of books that took place within the context of the Google Books project include HathiTrust, a partnership of academic and research institutions which offers a collection of millions of titles digitized from libraries around the world.[8]

---

[7] *Authors Guild, Inc. v Google Inc.*, No. 13-4829-cv (2d Cir. 16 October 2015) (US); in April 2016, the US Supreme Court declined to review the case, leaving the lower court's decision standing. On the history of this case and the broader framework governing mass digitization, see Maurizio Borghi and Stavroula Karapapa, *Copyright and Mass Digitization: A Cross-Jurisdictional Perspective* (Oxford: Oxford University Press, 2013).

[8] *Authors Guild, Inc. v HathiTrust*, No. 11 Civ 6351 (HB), 2012 US Dist (US).

Outside the realm of books, other copy-reliant electronic services to have reached the courts include media monitoring and web scraping services,[9] live Internet streaming platforms,[10] plagiarism detection software,[11] search engines and news aggregators,[12] second-hand stores of used digital goods,[13] and meta-search engines or price comparison websites.[14] There are other innovative services and business models that have been stimulated and enabled by developments in information technology, including mobile applications, cryptocurrencies, and new mega e-stores.

Although these aforementioned technologies, services, and business models challenge traditional copyright norms, they have the potential to make a positive impact on innovation, economic growth, and public welfare through the development of structures that enable creativity, and also have a dynamic effect on market economy. All of these benefits that can result from the development of copy-reliant technologies and services are objectives of copyright protection and are stated in the preambles of various Directives. These broadly involve fostering substantial investment in creativity and innovation, including network infrastructure, that will in turn lead to growth and increased competitiveness in European industry, safeguard employment, and encourage new job creation.[15] They also include the offer of appropriate reward for creativity and investment,[16] and thereby ensure sufficient resources for European cultural creativity and production, and safeguard the independence and dignity of artistic creators and performers.[17] The various EU Directives also mean to serve broader objectives that relate to the development of the Internal Market and

---

[9] See in this regard *Infopaq International A/S v Danske Dagblades Forening*, Case C-5/08, 16 July 2009, ECLI:EU:C:2009:465 (*Infopaq I*); *Infopaq International A/S v Danske Dagblades Forening*, Case C-302/10, 17 January 2012, ECLI:EU:C:2012:16 (*Infopaq II*); *Public Relations Consultants Association Ltd v Newspaper Licensing Agency Ltd* [2013] UKSC 18; [2013] 2 All E.R. 852 (UK); *Public Relations Consultants Association Ltd v Newspaper Licensing Agency Ltd and Others*, Case C-360/13, 5 June 2014, ECLI:EU:C:2014:1195.

[10] *ITV Broadcasting Ltd and Others v TVCatchUp Ltd*, Case C-607/11, 7 March 2013, ECLI:EU:C:2013:147; *C More Entertainment AB v Linus Sandberg*, Case C-279/13, 26 March 2015, ECLI:EU:C:2015:199.

[11] *AV et al v iParadigms*, LLC, 562 Federal Reporter, 3d Series [2009], 630–47 (US).

[12] *Google Inc. v Copiepresse SCRL*, Court of Appeal of Brussels (Cour d'Appel Bruxelles) 5 May 2011, 2007/AR/1730 (Belgium).

[13] *UsedSoft GmbH v Oracle International Corp*, Case C-128/11, 3 July 2012, ECLI:EU:C:2012:407; *Nederlands Uitgeversverbond and Groep Algemene Uitgevers v Tom Kabinet BV*, Case C-263/18, 19 December 2019, ECLI:EU:C:2019:1111; *Capitol Records LLC v ReDigi Inc.*, No. 12 Civ. 95 (RJS) (US).

[14] *Ryanair Ltd v PR Aviation BV*, Case C-30/14, 15 January 2015, ECLI:EU:C:2015:10; *Innoweb BV v Wegener ICT Media BV and Wegener Mediaventions BV*, Case C-202/12, 19 December 2013, ECLI:EU:C:2013:850; *Google Search (Shopping)*, Case AT.39740, Antitrust Procedure, Council Regulation (EC) 1/2003, Art. 7 Regulation (EC) 1/2003, C(2017) 4444 final, 27 June 2017.

[15] Information Society Directive (Directive 2001/29/EC), Recital 4; Digital Single Market Directive (Directive 2019/790), Recitals 2, 5, 8, 18.

[16] Information Society Directive (Directive 2001/29/EC), Recital 10; Digital Single Market Directive (Directive 2019/790), Recital 2.

[17] Information Society Directive (Directive 2001/29/EC), Recital 11.

information society in the European Union and the realization of the fundamental freedoms of the Union through the harmonization of the copyright laws
of the various Member States.[18]

In light of these broad objectives, the Information Society Directive stresses
that 'a fair balance of rights and interests between the different categories of
rightholders, as well as between the different categories of rightholders and users
of protected subject-matter must be safeguarded.'[19] Such a balance, however,
is arguably not achieved under the current legal framework whereby rights are
broadly construed whilst exceptions and limitations are fragmented, narrowly
defined, and do not hold the legal nature of user rights that can be enforced before courts. A fair balance would involve comparison of like with like, namely exclusive rights and fully fledged user rights, at least with regard to defensive rules
that have the potential to achieve the stated aims of copyright protection, including the creation of new works, the development of innovative technologies,
and the enhancement of public welfare. There is a growing body of scholarship
in support of defensive rules that have the legal nature of user rights or of entitlements that are mandatory against possible contractual restriction on behalf of
the copyright holders.[20]

There may be instances where the operation of modern electronic services
and business models may come into conflict with copyright law, thereby making
the permissibility of relevant activities questionable. This is particularly the case
for copy-reliant technologies, which—because of their novel and innovative
character—may not fit squarely with the definition of permitted uses according
to copyright statutes. Indeed, digitization and the Internet have altered the ways
in which copyright works are used and re-used. Distance learning methods may
require transmission of copyright works in ways that traditional copyright exceptions are too limited to cover. The use of bitcoin or cryptocurrencies in content
delivery impacts traditional understanding of what amounts to a commercial
transaction. Libraries and archives can lawfully make copies for preservation purposes, but this privilege cannot safely cover displaying these copies in dedicated
electronic premises or carrying out mega uses of orphan and out-of-commerce
works, without carrying out individual searches on each and every single piece
of work. There is increased impetus for data portability and interoperability

---

[18] Ibid, Recitals 1–3, 6.

[19] Ibid, Recital 31 (affirmed in various cases such as *Funke Medien NRW GmbH v Federal Republic
of Germany*, C-469/17, 29 July 2019, ECLI:EU:C:2019:623 (*Funke Medien*), [32]; *Pelham GmbH,
Moses Pelham, Martin Haas v Ralf Hütter, Florian Schneider-Esleben*, Case C-476/17, 29 July 2019,
ECLI:EU:C:2019:624 (*Pelham*), [32]); Digital Single Market Directive (Directive 2019/790), Recitals 6,
also 21, 61, 70, 75.

[20] See e.g. Pascale Chapdelaine, *Copyright User Rights: Contracts and the Erosion of Property*
(Oxford: Oxford University Press, 2017); Niva Elkin-Koren, 'Copyright in a Digital Ecosystem: A
User Rights Approach' in Ruth L. Okediji (ed.), *Copyright Law in an Age of Limitations and Exceptions*
(New York: Cambridge University Press, 2017) 132.

of content in various devices and mobile applications, especially in light of the Internet of Things, and it is important that there are no geographical or legal restrictions towards the lawful use of such content within the European Union.[21] Many online services, such as media monitoring, price comparison websites, and meta-search engines, operate on the basis of routine extraction and copying of material that may be copyright protected, hence challenging the limits of copyright. The same applies to services employing 'content mining' technologies, such as plagiarism detection, automated language translation, image recognition, or image transformation through tools or filters which enable algorithmic pastiche. Some of these new uses of copyright-protected works, such as data analytics and text mining for non-commercial research, have only recently started to make an appearance in statutes.[22]

All these emergent trends in business and technology call into question the current framework of EU copyright which is rigid and lacks the flexibility that would make allowances for certain uses of copyright works that can ensure a rigorous public domain. What is more, current exceptions and limitations are drafted in technical terms, taking into consideration existing technological trends and not being in a position to accommodate certain uses that align with copyright principles and policy objectives. Examples include the text and data mining and the cross-border teaching exceptions that were introduced in EU copyright years after technologies supporting such uses were made available.[23] In light of emergent technologies which enable new kinds of use and re-use of copyright materials, the expansively drafted exclusive rights, along with the framework of narrowly defined copyright exceptions and limitations and the principle of their strict interpretation,[24] challenge existing norms and cannot offer responses to questions that did not arise at the legislative level. The effect of this is that the scope of defensive rules becomes more and more limited, despite the policy desire to expand the availability of permissible uses at the EU level.[25]

---

[21] Regulation (EU) 2018/302 of the European Parliament and of the Council of 28 February 2018 on Addressing Unjustified Geo-Blocking and Other Forms of Discrimination Based on Customers' Nationality, Place of Residence, or Place of Establishment within the Internal Market and Amending Regulations (EC) No. 2006/2004 and (EU) 2017/2394 and Directive 2009/22/EC, OJ L 60I, 2 March 2018, 1–15.

[22] See e.g. Copyright, Designs and Patents Act 1988 (UK), s. 29A (introduced by the Copyright and Rights in Performances (Research, Education, Libraries and Archives) Regulations, 2014); Digital Single Market Directive (Directive 2019/790), Arts. 3 and 4.

[23] Digital Single Market Directive (Directive 2019/790), Arts 3 and 4.

[24] See in this regard *Infopaq International*, Case C-5/08, 16 July 2009, ECLI:EU:C:2009:465 (*Infopaq I*), [56]; *Infopaq International*, Case C-302/10, 17 January 2012, ECLI:EU:C:2012:16 (*Infopaq II*), [26]; *Stichting Brein v Jack Frederik Wullems*, Case C-527/15, 26 April 2017, ECLI:EU:C:2017:300 (*Filmspeler*), [61]–[62].

[25] See e.g., the discussions preceding the Digital Single Market Directive (Directive 2019/790).

Scope of the book

The central research question this book seeks to address is how the available copyright defences, including doctrinally established principles and statutory exceptions and limitations, impact on the limits of copyright protection and user freedom in the online environment. How do the available defences operate as a system, to what extent are they in a position to accommodate modern uses of copyright works, and how can an understanding of their function in copyright inform law and policy making with a view to designing defensive rules that have the potential to achieve stated objectives of copyright protection, such as creativity, innovation, and business growth on the Internet?[26]

In addressing these questions the book adopts a principle-based approach launched from the proposition that defences are primarily meant to serve as a balancing act, achieved by offering a fair and proportional equilibrium between the protection of authors' rights and the public interest. For this balance to be meaningful, copyright should ensure appropriate remuneration for authors while making allowances for certain activities that enable the preservation of a rigorous public domain. In such a domain, fostering substantial investment in creativity and innovation will in turn lead to growth and increased competitiveness of the European industry, safeguard employment, and encourage new job creation.[27] The viability of these objectives, which are stated as the core aims of EU copyright in many EU Directives,[28] is inextricably premised on a circular logic: the same theoretical principles on which authorship is rewarded via copyright protection ought to form the basis for further creativity and innovation that relies, or is based, on pre-existing works. This premise, which—although straightforward—often escapes attention, becomes more relevant in the online context where new, interactive means of using and re-using copyright works emerge, thereby offering unprecedented opportunities for growth in the creative, technological, and business sector.

In light of the burgeoning debates on the limited availability of uses permitted by copyright, the lack of flexibility in their interpretation, and the weak status of copyright exceptions, which do not currently hold the force of user rights, this book adopts a holistic approach to address defences to infringement as an autonomous

---

[26] These policy objectives are listed in a number of Directives, including the Information Society Directive (Directive 2001/29/EC); the Orphan Works Directive (Directive 2012/28/EU); and the Digital Single Market Directive (Directive 2019/790).

[27] Information Society Directive (Directive 2001/29/EC), Recital 4.

[28] See in this regard the preambles of the Information Society Directive (Directive 2001/29/EC); the Orphan Works Directive (Directive 2012/28/EU); Digital Single Market Directive (Directive 2019/790); Directive 96/9/EC of the European Parliament and of the Council of 11 March 1996 on the Legal Protection of Databases, OJ L 77, 27 March 1996, 20–28 (Database Directive); Directive 2009/24/EC of the European Parliament and of the Council of 23 April 2009 on the Legal Protection of Computer Programs, OJ L 111, 5 May 2009, 16–22 (Computer Programs Directive); Directive 2006/116/EC of the European Parliament and of the Council of 12 December 2006 on the Term of Protection of Copyright and Certain Related Rights, OJ L 372, 27 December 2006, 12–18 (Term Directive).

area of copyright law essential for understanding infringement, but also the very nature of copyright. Subject to examination are statutorily permitted uses, but also the cases where infringement cannot be established because copyright does not subsist in the original work in the first place. This examination attempts to identify areas of overlap in defensive rules and areas that are not currently addressed by the available permitted uses, although the common sentiment of justice and public welfare objectives seem to suggest otherwise. The focus of the book is EU copyright law and doctrine, including references to notable national statutory provisions and case law, and the international norms that influence the scope of EU copyright. A substantial discussion of the ways in which the European Court of Justice has offered authoritative insights into the scope of available defences will also be had. The book argues in favour of a purposive construal of rights and exceptions to rights on the basis of the objectives that copyright law means to serve. In this regard, the book tells the story of copyright from the perspective of copyright defences; it offers positivist and normative insights into law and doctrine and argues towards a principle-based understanding of the scope of available defences that could inform future law and policy making.

Contextualizing permitted uses

Defences against copyright infringement are governed by a number of international, regional, and bilateral instruments on intellectual property, including the Berne Convention,[29] the Agreement on Trade-Related Aspects of Intellectual Property Rights (TRIPs Agreement),[30] and the World Intellectual Property Organization (WIPO) Internet Treaties.[31] Arguably, emphasis at international level has been to strengthen the position of authors and other rightsholders in light of emergent technological challenges, with less emphasis on promotion of access to, and dissemination of, works through a system of copyright exceptions and limitations.[32] In this light, there has been a gradual expansion of the scope of exclusive rights, making defensive claims that are premised on the negation of the elements of infringing liability too difficult to establish. At the same time, copyright exceptions and limitations have received minimal international attention. The Berne Convention lays down a limited list of copyright exceptions, some of which are

---

[29] Berne Convention for the Protection of Literary and Artistic Works (as amended on 28 September 1979) (hereinafter Berne Convention).

[30] Agreement on Trade-Related Aspects of Intellectual Property Rights (1994) (hereinafter TRIPS).

[31] World Intellectual Property Organization (WIPO) Copyright Treaty (1996) (hereinafter WCT); WIPO Performances and Phonograms Treaty (1996) (hereinafter WPPT).

[32] P. Bernt Hugenholtz and Ruth L. Okediji, 'Conceiving an International Instrument on Limitations and Exceptions to Copyright' Final Report, 6–7, <https://www.ivir.nl/publicaties/download/limitations_exceptions_copyright.pdf>, accessed 11 November 2019; Pascale Chapdelaine, *Copyright User Rights: Contracts and the Erosion of Property* (Oxford: Oxford University Press, 2017) 37.

accompanied by a requirement to pay compensation to the copyright holders.[33] Efforts to introduce copyright exceptions for the benefit of the blind, visually impaired, and otherwise print disabled have been made at the international level since 2013 through the Marrakesh Treaty.[34]

Although there are very few copyright exceptions and limitations that are expressly recognized at the international level, the various international instruments do not allow the introduction of such rules to be entirely at the discretion of national legislators. The Berne Convention includes the so-called three-step test, namely the standard by which exceptions and limitations should be construed at the legislative level, and outlines the conditions that contracting states must consider when designing copyright exceptions and limitations.[35] According to the three-step test, it is a matter of legislation in the contracting states to confine copyright exceptions and limitations to (a) certain special cases, which (b) do not conflict with a normal exploitation of the work, and (c) do not unreasonably prejudice the legitimate interests of the copyright holders.[36] Although the Berne version of the three-step test is limited to acts of reproduction and refers to the interests of authors, the test has been reiterated and expanded in other international instruments, namely the TRIPS Agreement[37] and the WIPO Internet Treaties,[38] by being made available to all exclusive rights and taking into account the interests of all relevant rightsholders.[39] Unlike other international intellectual property norms, the three-step test lays down the standard on how legislators should approach copyright exceptions and introduce them into national law. The extent to which the broad wording of the three-step test serves as an efficient guide for legislative interpretation remains uncertain.[40]

---

[33] Berne Convention, Art. 10, 10*bis*, 11*bis*, including certain free uses on quotations, illustrations for teaching, free uses on certain articles and broadcast works, and works seen or heard in connection with current events; and compulsory licenses on broadcasts.

[34] Marrakesh Treaty to Facilitate Access to Published Works for Persons Who Are Blind, Visually Impaired, or Otherwise Print Disabled (2013) (Marrakesh Treaty). This Treaty was signed in 2013 under the auspices of the WIPO and came into effect on 30 September 2016, having as its main goal 'to create a set of mandatory limitations and exceptions for the benefit of the blind, visually impaired, and otherwise print-disabled (VIPs)'. See WIPO website <http://www.wipo.int/treaties/en/ip/marrakesh/ >, accessed 11 November 2019. A detailed analysis of the Marrakesh Treaty is available in Laurence R. Helfer, Molly K. Land, Ruth L. Okediji, and Jerome H. Reichman, *The World Blind Union Guide to the Marrakesh Treaty* (Oxford: Oxford University Press, 2017). Also see Stavroula Karapapa, 'Article 30(3) of the International Convention on the Rights of Disabled Persons' in Ilias Bantekas, Michael Stein, and Dimitrios Anastasiou (eds), *Commentary on the International Convention on the Rights of Disabled Persons* (Oxford: Oxford University Press, 2018) 888.

[35] Berne Convention, Art. 9(2).

[36] Ibid.

[37] TRIPS, Art. 13.

[38] WCT, Art. 10; WPPT, Art. 16.

[39] Stavroula Karapapa, *Private Copying* (London: Routledge, 2012) 99 et seq.; see Sam Ricketson and Jane C. Ginsburg, *International Copyright and Neighbouring Rights: The Berne Convention and Beyond* (Oxford: Oxford University Press, 2006, 2nd edn) 755–878.

[40] There have been national cases where the test has been applied inconsistently, leading to discrepancies and controversy. P. Bernt Hugenholtz and Ruth L. Okediji, 'Conceiving an International Instrument on Limitations and Exceptions to Copyright' Final Report, 21, <https://www.ivir.nl/publicaties/

The test, which arguably sets the balance on the side of copyright holders,[41] has been incorporated into various regional and national laws, including the Information Society Directive.[42] The Directive offers a controversial stipulation of the test, according to which copyright exceptions and limitations 'shall only be applied' when the conditions of the test are met.[43] The recently introduced Directive on Copyright in the Digital Single Market repeats this wording with regard to the copyright exceptions and limitations it incorporates.[44] In this sense, the European version of the three-step test does not merely outline a legislative tool, but provides a standard for judicial interpretation and, effectively, a limit on limitations to copyright.[45] This has resulted in controversy, and opinions on the test vary. Some scholars claim that the three-step test allows for flexibility in the legislative interpretation of the appropriate scope of the exceptions and limitations,[46] whereas others argue that the test can only result in narrow determination of the uses that are permitted by copyright law.[47] Interestingly, numerous Member States have

download/limitations_exceptions_copyright.pdf>, accessed 11 November 2019; Christophe Geiger, 'From Berne to National Law, via the Copyright Directive: The Dangerous Mutations of the Three-Step Test' (2007) 29(12) *European Intellectual Property Review* 486, 489.

[41] Stavroula Karapapa, *Private Copying* (London: Routledge, 2012) 102.

[42] Information Society Directive (Directive 2001/29/EC), Art. 5(5). Also see indicatively Art. 17 of the Estonian Copyright Act of 1992, as last amended in 2003 (RT I 2006, 28, 210—entered into force 30 June 2006) (Estonia); Penultimate paragraph of Art. L. 122-5 of the Intellectual Property Code (consolidated version of 1 August 2019) (France). The same sentence has been inserted in Arts L. 211-13 and L. 342-3 of the Intellectual Property Code regarding the exceptions applicable to related rights and the *sui generis* database right. The French Constitutional Council concluded that the Information Society Directive requires the application of the exceptions to be subordinated to the three-step test. Decision 2006-540 DC, 27 July 2006 (France). For a comment, see Valérie-Laure Benabou, 'Patatras! À Propos de la Décision du Conseil Constitutionnel du 27 Juillet 2006' (2006) 20 *Propriétés Intellectuelles* 240; other examples include Art. 33(2) of the Act No. LXXVI of 1999 on Copyright (Consolidated text (15 March–28 October 2014)) (Hungary); Art. 18(2) of the Latvian Copyright Law (as last amended in 18 December 2014) (Latvia); Art. 9(3) of the Copyright Act (as amended up to Act No. VIII of 2011) (Malta); Art. 75(4) of the Portuguese Code of Copyright and Related Rights (as last amended through Decree n° 100/2017 of 23 August 2017) (Portugal); Art. 33(1) of Law No. 8/1996 on Copyright and Neighbouring Rights (as amended by Law No. 329/2006 and codified in 2006) (Romania); Art. 46 of the Copyright and Related Rights Act (Official Gazette No. 16/2007; No. 68/2008, No. 110/2013, and No. 56/2015) (Slovenia); Art. 31*ter* of the Spanish Copyright Act (Ley 2/2019) (Spain).

[43] Stavroula Karapapa, *Private Copying* (London: Routledge, 2012) 100.

[44] Digital Single Market Directive (Directive 2019/790), Art. 7(2).

[45] Stavroula Karapapa, *Private Copying* (London: Routledge, 2012) 117; P. Bernt Hugenholtz and Ruth L. Okediji, 'Conceiving an International Instrument on Limitations and Exceptions to Copyright' Final Report, 18 et seq., <https://www.ivir.nl/publicaties/download/limitations_exceptions_copyright. pdf>, accessed 11 November 2019.

[46] Andrew F. Christie, 'Maximizing Permissible Exceptions to Intellectual Property Rights' in Annette Kur and Vytautas Mizaras (eds), *The Structure of Intellectual Property Law: Can One Size Fit All?* (Cheltenham: Edward Elgar, 2011) 121; Christophe Geiger et al., 'Declaration A Balanced Interpretation Of The "Three-Step Test" In Copyright Law' (2010) 1 *JIPITEC* 119; Martin Senftleben, 'The International Three-Step Test: A Model Provision for EC Fair Use Legislation' (2010) 1(2) *Journal of Intellectual Property, Information Technology and E-Commerce Law* 67.

[47] See e.g., in this regard Jonathan Griffiths, 'The "Three-Step Test" in European Copyright Law - Problems and Solutions' (2009) *Queen Mary School of Law Legal Studies Research Paper* No. 31/2009, available at <https://ssrn.com/abstract=1476968>, accessed 11 November 2019.

introduced the three-step test as a judicial tool that has to be applied each and every time a defendant raises a defence based on copyright exceptions and limitations.[48]

At the European level, the availability of permitted uses has recently become central to legislative reform and judicial consideration; this follows the long-standing scholarly and policy debate which urges enhancement of permitted uses in the digital environment.[49] At the legislative level, common rules have been set in place to enable digitization and online display of orphan works;[50] the scope of certain permitted uses for the benefit of persons who are blind, visually impaired, or otherwise print-disabled have been enlarged by implementation of the Marrakesh Treaty,[51] and the Directive on Copyright in the Digital Single Market introduced some new copyright exceptions and expanded on the scope of those already available.[52] The new exceptions include text mining, cross-border educational uses, and certain uses of out-of-commerce works. Many of the exceptions available in the Information Society Directive have been subject to judicial interpretation by the Court of Justice of the European Union and there is a large body of rulings that has refined the scope of available defences under EU copyright law,[53] leading to

---

[48] For a critique see Stavroula Karapapa, *Private Copying* (London: Routledge, 2012) 99 et seq.

[49] Legislative initiatives at international, European, and national level have placed their emphasis on the enlargement of the scope of infringement in light of the digital challenge and the Internet. The WIPO Internet Treaties have introduced new rights (in particular the right of communication and making available to the public) and they have also afforded rigorous protection against the circumvention of technological protection measures (see Arts 8, 11, 12 of the WCT; Arts 14, 18, 19 of the WPPT). These treaties, however, which were implemented in Europe through the Information Society Directive (Directive 2001/29/EC), have not introduced any exceptions or limitations and have left this issue at the discretion of the signatory countries (Art. 10 of the WCT; Art. 16 of the WPPT). Although the Information Society Directive attempted to harmonize the area of exceptions and limitations by offering a long list of permitted uses, this list was exhaustive, narrow in scope, and optional for Member States to implement. This has resulted in a minimum degree of harmonization of permitted uses in the various Member States.

[50] Orphan Works Directive (Directive 2012/28/EU).

[51] Directive on Permitted Uses for Disabled Individuals (Directive 2017/1564); also see Regulation (EU) 2017/1563 of the European Parliament and of the Council of 13 September 2017 on the Cross-Border Exchange Between the Union and Third Countries of Accessible Format Copies of Certain Works and Other Subject Matter Protected by Copyright and Related Rights for the Benefit of Persons who are Blind, Visually Impaired or Otherwise Print-Disabled, OJ L 242, 20 September 2017, 1–5.

[52] Digital Single Market Directive (Directive 2019/790).

[53] See e.g., *Infopaq International A/S v Danske Dagblades Forening*, Case C-5/08, 16 July 2009, ECLI:EU:C:2009:465 (*Infopaq I*); *Infopaq International A/S v Danske Dagblades Forening*, Case C-302/10, 17 January 2012, ECLI:EU:C:2012:16 (*Infopaq II*); *Public Relations Consultants Association Ltd v Newspaper Licensing Agency Ltd and Others*, Case C-360/13, 5 June 2014, ECLI:EU:C:2014:1195 (*Meltwater*); *Padawan SL v Sociedad General de Autores y Editores de España (SGAE)*, Case C-467/08, 21 October 2011, ECLI:EU:C:2010:620 (*Padawan*); *Stichting de Thuiskopie v Opus Supplies Deutschland GmbH*, Case C-462/09, 16 June 2011, ECLI:EU:C:2011:397 (*Opus*); *Amazon.com International v Austro-Mechana Gesellschaft zur Wahrnehmung mechanisch-musikalischer Urheberrechte Gesellschaft mbH*, Case C-521/11, 11 July 2013, ECLI:EU:C:2013:515 (*Amazon*); *VG Wort v Kyocera Mita et al*, Cases C-457/11 to C-460/11, 27 June 2013, ECLI:EU:C:2013:426 (*VG Wort*); *ACI Adam BV v Stichting de Thuiskopie*, Case C-435/12, 10 April 2014, ECLI:EU:C:2014:254 (*ACI Adam*); *Johan Deckmyn v Vandersteen et al*, Case C-201/13, 3 September 2014, ECLI:EU:C:2014:2132 (*Deckmyn*); *Technische Universität Darmstadt v Eugen Ulmer KG*, Case C-117/13, 11 September 2014, ECLI:EU:C:2014:2196 (*Darmstadt*); *Pelham GmbH, Moses Pelham, Martin Haas v Ralf Hütter, Florian Schneider-Esleben*, Case C-476/17, 29 July 2019, ECLI:EU:C:2019:624 (*Pelham*); *Funke Medien NRW GmbH v Federal Republic of Germany*, C-469/17, 29 July 2019, ECLI:EU:C:2019:623 (*Funke Medien*).

the harmonization of key concepts, such as the notions of 'work', 'originality', and 'public'.[54] Doctrine has evolved organically through a number of judgments of the court that arguably demonstrate a degree of judicial activism[55] and, on occasion, expand on the scope of copyright's exclusivity.[56]

There are various reasons why the framework of available defences under EU copyright seems rigid and indifferent to flexibility. First, the exceptions and limitations to rights listed in the EU copyright Directives, but most notably in the Information Society Directive and the Directive on Copyright in the Digital Single Market,[57] is a closed list that does not allow room for manoeuvre at the national level.[58] Exceptions are exhaustively enumerated[59] and drafted in narrow terms, with their application being subject to a complex network of satellite conditions. Second, the exceptions and limitations available under EU copyright are subject to the principle of strict interpretation[60] and, in this light, the interpretative freedom at the judicial level is confined. At the same time, the scope of exclusive rights is very broadly drafted in statutory language. For instance, the reproduction right has a wide scope, covering all manifestations of copying,[61] and statutes and case law indicate the existence of broad, yet informal, authorial entitlements

[54]   See in this light, *Infopaq I and II*, Cases C-5/08 and C-302/10 (definition of 'work' and 'originality'); *Levola Hengelo BV v Smilde Foods BV*, Case 310/17, 13 November 2018, ECLI:EU:C:2018:899 (*Levola*) (definition of 'work'); *Nils Svensson and Others v Retriever Sverige AB*, Case C-466/12, 13 February 2014, ECLI:EU:C:2014:76 (definition of 'public').

[55]   See indicatively Eleonora Rosati, *Copyright and the Court of Justice of the European Union* (Oxford, Oxford University Press, 2018); Ana Ramalho, *The Competence of the European Union in Copyright Lawmaking: A Normative Perspective of EU Powers for Copyright Harmonization* (Cham: Springer, 2016).

[56]   E.g., in the aftermath of *Levola* the concept of work as protectable subject matter has been enlarged to the extent that closed copyright systems enumerating specific instances of protected subject matter, such as those available in Cyprus, Ireland, and the United Kingdom, do not align with EU copyright law.

[57]   Information Society Directive (Directive 2001/29/EC); Digital Single Market Directive (Directive 2019/790); Orphan Works Directive (Directive 2012/28/EU); Term Directive (Directive 2006/116/EC); Database Directive (Directive 96/9/EC); Computer Programs Directive (Directive 2009/24/EC).

[58]   Art. 5(3)(o) of the Information Society Directive (Directive 2001/29/EC) allows Member States some discretion to retain copyright exceptions and limitations on 'other cases of minor importance' already available under their national laws. However, the Court of Justice affirmed that 'a Member State cannot, in its national law, lay down an exception or limitation other than those provided for in Art. 5 of Directive 2001/29 [to the phonogram producer's right provided for in Art. 2(c) of that directive]'. See *Pelham GmbH, Moses Pelham, Martin Haas v Ralf Hütter, Florian Schneider-Esleben*, Case C-476/17, 29 July 2019, ECLI:EU:C:2019:624, [65].

[59]   See to that effect Proposal for a European Parliament and Council Directive on the Harmonisation of Certain Aspects of Copyright and Related Rights in the Information Society, Brussels, 10 December 1997, COM(97) 62, OJ C 108, 7 April 1998, 6, Explanatory Memorandum; Information Society Directive (Directive 2001/29/EC), Recital 32; also see *Marc Soulier and Sara Doke v Premier ministre and Ministre de la Culture et de la Communication*, Case C-301/15, ECLI: EU:C:2016:878, [34]; *Land Nordrhein-Westfalen v Dirk Renckhoff*, Case C-161/17, ECLI:EU:C:2018:634, [16]; *Pelham GmbH, Moses Pelham, Martin Haas v Ralf Hütter, Florian Schneider-Esleben*, Case C-476/17, 29 July 2019, ECLI:EU:C:2019:624, [63].

[60]   *VCAST Limited v RTI SpA*, Case C-265/16, 29 November 2017, ECLI:EU:C:2017:913 (*VCAST*), [32]; *ACI Adam and Others*, Case C-435/12, 10 April 2014, EU:C:2014:254 (*ACI Adam*), [22]; *Stichting Brein v Jack Frederik Wullems*, Case C-527/15, 26 April 2017, ECLI:EU:C:2017:300 (*Filmspeler*), [61]–[62]; *Infopaq International*, Case C-5/08, 16 July 2009, ECLI:EU:C:2009:465 (*Infopaq I*), [55]–[56]; *Infopaq International*, C-302/10, 17 January 2012, ECLI:EU:C:2012:16 (*Infopaq II*), [26].

[61]   See e.g. Information Society Directive (Directive 2001/29/EC), Art. 2.

to authorizing or prohibiting *access* to works.[62] This means that defences premised on negations of elements of infringement become more and more narrow in terms of their application. Third, exceptions and limitations are subject to the three-step test twice under EU copyright: firstly at the legislative level and secondly at the judicial level.[63] This has the practical implication that the scope of available exceptions and limitations is subject to dual scrutiny under the conditions of a test that primarily takes into account the interests of copyright holders.[64] Finally, the issue of contractual overridability of exceptions and limitations is not settled at pan-European level; only a few Member States have addressed the relationship of exceptions and restrictive contractual terms,[65] albeit following different approaches in doing so. The Directive on Copyright in the Digital Single Market has expressly addressed the issue of contractual override by reference to some, but not all, copyright exceptions and limitations it introduces.[66] By not offering an indication of the determining factors of such a policy choice more questions are raised than addressed. In this light, the legal nature of exceptions and limitations has not been addressed at the legislative level in a uniform manner across the European Union.

Criticism of the current copyright framework of strong exclusive rights and narrowly drafted exceptions and limitations is burgeoning.[67] Rights are drafted and interpreted in broad terms in line with the objective of achieving a high standard of protection at the EU level,[68] whilst exceptions are very narrowly defined. This is seen as an impediment to creativity, innovation, and economic growth.[69] What is more, it seems that the affirmation that a given activity should be permitted takes

---

[62] Stavroula Karapapa, *Private Copying* (London: Routledge, 2012) 144; Thomas P. Heide, 'Copyright in the EU and U.S.: What "Access Right"' (2001) 48(3) *Journal of the Copyright Society of the U.S.A.*, 363; *VCAST Limited v RTI SpA*, Case C-265/16, 29 November 2017, ECLI:EU:C:2017:913 (*VCAST*), [39].

[63] An example of application at judicial level is *Public Relations Consultants Association Ltd v Newspaper Licensing Agency Ltd and Others*, C-360/13, ECLI:EU:C:2014:1195, [53]–[62]: on-screen copies satisfy both Art. 5(1) and Art. 5(5). However, in *Technische Universität Darmstadt v Eugen Ulmer KG*, C-117/13, ECLI:EU:C:2014:2196, [34] the court appears to imply that legislative scrutiny is sufficient: 'the limitation provided for in Article 5(3)(n) is accompanied by a number of restrictions that guarantee the continuing applicability of such a limitation in special cases which do not conflict with a normal exploitation of the works and do not unreasonably prejudice the legitimate interests of the rightholder'.

[64] Stavroula Karapapa, *Private Copying* (London: Routledge, 2012) 99 et seq.; Christophe Geiger, 'From Berne to National Law, via the Copyright Directive: The Dangerous Mutations of the Three-Step Test' (2007) 29(12) *European Intellectual Property Review* 486.

[65] Belgium, Ireland, Portugal, and the United Kingdom.

[66] Digital Single Market Directive (Directive 2019/790), Art. 7(1).

[67] See indicatively Robert Burrell and Allison Coleman, *Copyright Exceptions: The Digital Impact* (Cambridge: Cambridge University Press, 2005) 276–7.

[68] Information Society Directive (Directive 2001/29/EC), Recital 4.

[69] Ian Hargreaves, *Digital Opportunity: A Review of Intellectual Property and Growth* (2011); European Commission, Communication from the Commission to the European Parliament, the Council, the European Economic and Social Committee and the Committee of the Regions: A Single Market for Intellectual Property Rights, Boosting Creativity and Innovation to Provide Economic Growth, High Quality Jobs and First Class Products and Services in Europe, Brussels, 24 May 2011, COM(2011) 287 final.

numerous years and that policy making and legislative drafting often address technologies and business models that are contemporaneous to law reform, but which lack adaptability to new trends in technology. Even though there is a long list of available exceptions enumerated in the Information Society Directive and the Directive on Copyright in the Digital Single Market, their respective scope is significantly narrow, covering few specifically defined instances. There is a growing body of scholarship which emphasizes the lack of flexibility in the available copyright framework.[70] Because of the lack of such a flexible approach, like the US fair use test, legal uncertainty remains as to the lawfulness and legality of many activities which are emerging as a result of technological advancement. Arguably, such a lack of flexibility has an impact on creativity, innovation, and business growth,[71] but in certain cases it also challenges the common sentiment of justice and reasonableness.[72]

Recent legislative initiatives at the EU level do not seem to have efficiently addressed concerns on the currently fragmented system of copyright exceptions and limitations. The uses permitted under the Orphan Works Directive cover very specific activities and are subject to numerous conditions, challenging the efficacy of the framework of the uses permitted under the Directive. Indeed, the latter has received criticism on various aspects that make its scope of application very limited.[73] The Directive on Copyright in the Digital Single Market added a set of permitted uses in EU copyright and expanded on the scope of already available ones, but its final approval was severely delayed as delegates could not reach a consensus on various aspects. It has also become a source of academic criticism for expanding the availability of exclusive rights, notably through the introduction of a press

---

[70] P. Bernt Hugenholtz and Martin Senftleben, 'Fair Use in Europe: In Search of Flexibilities' (2001) Institute for Information Law, Vrije Universiteit, Amsterdam; P. Bernt Hugenholtz, 'Flexible Copyright: Can the EU Author's Rights Accommodate Fair Use?' in Ruth L. Okediji (ed.), *Copyright Law in an Age of Limitations and Exceptions* (New York: Cambridge University Press, 2017) 275; Eleonora Rosati, 'Copyright in the EU: In Search of (In)Flexibilities' (2014) 9(7) *Journal of Intellectual Property Law & Practice* 585; Robert Burrell and Allison Coleman, *Copyright Exceptions: The Digital Impact* (Cambridge: Cambridge University Press, 2005); also see The Wittem Group, 'European Copyright Code' (2010) 1 Jipitec, Art. 5.5; Jane C. Ginsburg, '"European Copyright Code" – Back to First Principles (with Some Additional Detail)' (2010–11) 58(3) *Journal of Copyright Society of the USA* 265; P. Bernt Hugenholtz, 'The Wittem Group's European Copyright Code' in Tatiana-Eleni Synodinou (ed.), *Codification of European Copyright Law: Challenges and Perspectives* (Alphen aan den Rijn: Kluwer Law International, 2012) 339, 343.

[71] European Commission, Communication from the Commission to the European Parliament, the Council, the European Economic and Social Committee, and the Committee of the Regions: A Single Market for Intellectual Property Rights, Boosting Creativity and Innovation to provide Economic Growth, High Quality Jobs, and First Class Products and Services in Europe, Brussels, 24 May 2011, COM(2011) 287 final.

[72] See, however, *Authors Guild, Inc. v Google Inc.*, No. 13-4829-cv (2d Cir. 16 October 2015) (US); *Authors Guild, et al. v Google, Inc.*, 15–849 (US).

[73] See e.g., Maurizio Borghi, Kris Erickson, and Marcella Favale, 'With Enough Eyeballs All Searches are Diligent: Mobilizing the Crowd in Copyright Clearance for Mass Digitization' (2016) 16(1) *Journal of Intellectual Property* 135.

publishers' right,[74] and for adopting a stringent approach towards online content-sharing service providers through a framework of primary liability, unprecedented at the EU level.[75] Even at the level of copyright exceptions and limitations, however, the Directive did not depart from the rigid approach of other EU instruments as it launched a number of new exceptions and expanded the scope of those already available. A positive feature of the Directive on Copyright in the Digital Single Market is that some copyright exceptions and limitations it introduces are manda-tory against contractual restriction and compulsory for Member States to imple-ment. This means that any contractual terms that aim to restrict the application of a mandatory copyright exception or limitation shall be null and void. However, this is not to say that the relevant exceptions shall have the force of positive user rights that can be invoked before the courts,[76] neither is there clear indication as to what makes certain exceptions mandatory against contractual override and not others.

There is a wealth of academic literature to argue in favour of granting certain permitted uses the status of user rights that can be enforced before the courts, ei-ther by declaring them mandatory against contractual terms or technological re-strictions, or by making them enforceable before the courts. They follow Wesley Hohfeld's theory on jural correlatives which indicates that lawful users can have a claim against copyright holders when the various permissive rules have the status of rights.[77] Despite the scholarly impetus towards the affirmation of certain per-mitted uses as user rights, the so-called copyright exceptions and limitations, ex-emptions from infringement, and user privileges have been judicially affirmed as serving the function of defences in allegations of copyright infringement instead of fully fledged user rights.[78] In this regard, even though they are understood as uses

---

[74] Stavroula Karapapa, 'The Press Publishers' Right in the European Union: An Overreaching Proposal and the Future of News Online' in Enrico Bonadio and Nicola Lucchi (eds), *Non-Conventional Copyright: Do New and Atypical Works Deserve Protection?* (Cheltenham: Edward Elgar, 2018) 316.

[75] Digital Single Market Directive (Directive 2019/790), Arts 15 and 17.

[76] This has not been the case with regard to the exceptions listed in the Information Society Directive and it is currently not clear what the distinctive factor of mandatory and non-mandatory exceptions is, and whether the exceptions listed in the Information Society Directive shall also become mandatory in a future re-evaluation of the Directive.

[77] Wesley N. Hohfeld, 'Some Fundamental Legal Conceptions as Applied in Judicial Reasoning' (1913) 16 *Yale Law Journal*, 30–1; Wesley N. Hohfeld, 'Fundamental Legal Conceptions as Applied to Judicial Reasoning' (2017) 26 *Yale Law Journal* 710.

[78] Indicatively see *Studio Canal et al v S. Penguin and Union Federale des Consommateurs Que Choisir*, Cour de Cassation, 19 June 2008, No. 07-142777 (France); *Studio Canal et al v S. Penguin and Union Federale des Consommateurs Que Choisir*, Paris Court of Appeal, 4 April 2007, *Gaz. Pal.* 18 July 2007, No. 199, 23 (France); *Studio Canal et al v S. Penguin and Union Federale des Consommateurs Que Choisir*, Cour de Cassation, 1st civil section, 28 February 2006, No. 549, Bull. 2006 I No. 126, 115 ('*Mulholland Drive*') (France); Supreme Court (Cour de cassation), 27 November 2008, No. 07-18778 (France) ('*Phil Collins*'); *Fnac Paris v UFC Que Choisir et autres*, Court of Appeal Paris (Cour d'appel Paris), 20 June 2007 (France) ('*Phil Collins*'); *Mr X and UFC Que Choisir v Warner Music France and FNAC Paris*, Paris District Court, 10 January 2006 (France) ('*Phil Collins*'); *L'ASBL Association Belge des Consomateurs Test Achats v La SA EMI Recorded Music Belgium et al*, Tribunal of First Instance of Brussels, 27 April 2004, 2004/46/A (Belgium); *L'ASBL Association Belge des Consommateurs Test Achats v La SA EMI Recorded Music Belgium et al*, Brussels Court of Appeal, 9 September 2005, 2004/AR/1649 (Belgium).

permitted by copyright and special cases where broader interests ought to prevail over copyright protection, they cannot be enforced before the courts. Only very few Member States expressly declare certain copyright exceptions and limitations to be mandatory against contractual override and state that restrictive licensing terms shall be declared null and void.[79] As the relationship of copyright exceptions and limitations to contractual or technological overridability has not been subject to harmonization, there is currently a two-tiered approach to the matter.[80] This can be seen as one of the reasons why exceptions and limitations do not have the normative force of user rights under EU copyright.[81]

Senses of copyright law defences

In a broad sense,[82] the word 'defence' is used to reference any claim that defendants may make in order to persuade the court that they are not liable for copyright infringement. In this sense, a defence covers instances where the defendant denies the elements of copyright infringement, such as claims that the relevant subject matter does not merit protection or that the allegedly offensive behaviour falls outside the scope of exclusive rights. Besides these defensive rules, that function as negations of elements required by the definition of copyright infringement and which acquit defendants on the basis that no infringement took place, defence also broadly covers copyright exceptions and limitations as rules which offer justification for activities of infringement. These are defences resting on the exercise of fundamental human rights or privileges resulting from the fulfilment of public policy objectives, such as library privileges or educational exceptions. A defence may also cover certain uses that are permitted on the basis of grounds that are external to copyright, such as general legal principles or legal provisions originating from different areas of law e.g. e-commerce protection or competition law. This meaning of defence rests on a holistic understanding that covers all claims that have the capacity to rebut infringement; the concept of defence in a broad sense encompasses any liability defeating rule, including denials of the elements of copyright infringement, copyright exceptions and limitations, or other explanations for

---

[79] Belgium, Ireland, Portugal, the United Kingdom.

[80] For most copyright exceptions and limitations, e.g. those included in the Information Society Directive (Directive 2001/29/EC), the relationship between permitted uses and contract is not expressly settled. However, certain exceptions under EU copyright are compulsory against contractual override. See, in particular, the Digital Single Market Directive (Directive 2019/790), Art. 7(1), and the Directive on Permitted Uses for Disabled Individuals (Directive 2017/1564), Art. 3(5).

[81] In other jurisdictions like Canada, however, some exceptions were found to qualify as user rights: see *CCH Canadian Ltd v Law Society of Upper Canada*, 2004 SCC 14 (CCH) (Canada); see in this regard Michael Geist, 'The Canadian Copyright Story: How Canada Improbably Became the World Leader on Users' Rights in Copyright Law' in Ruth L. Okediji (ed.), *Copyright Law in an Age of Limitations and Exceptions* (New York: Cambridge University Press, 2017) 169.

[82] James Goudkamp, *Tort Law Defences* (Oxford: Hart Publishing, 2013).

copyright infringement that find their origin in other areas of law or general legal principles.

When approached in this broad sense, defensive rules can be distinguished on the basis of the function they serve with regard to temporal stages. For instance, defensive rules whose core operation is to focus on the absence of an element of infringement are often found in the definition, and interpretation thereafter, of exclusive rights and their scope. Such rules offer *ex ante* guidance aimed at preventing specifically defined conduct when carried out without authorial permission. By contrast, justification defences, such as those incorporated in copyright exceptions and limitations, become relevant only after an infringing activity or harmful conduct has taken place. In this sense, they bring forward claims relying on further relevant factors, such as public policy objectives, and it is on this basis that the defendant is exempt from liability.

In a more strict sense, the concept of defence covers rules that result in a ruling for the defendant, despite the fact that all the elements of infringement are present. Defendants who bring in relevant claims do not rely on arguments denying the allegations for copyright infringement, but instead they go around these allegations. Most copyright exceptions and limitations are defensive rules that can acquit a defendant of copyright infringement on condition that the conduct in question was carried out for a purpose that the law specifically permits. Copyright exceptions and limitations are rationale-based defences, as is argued in this book, and in this regard they offer a set of permissible justifications, or explanations, for activities that would otherwise amount to copyright infringement. These may be justifications based on fundamental rights or public policy objectives. Exceptions and limitations to copyright permit users to carry out certain activities that would otherwise require permission from the copyright holders, without seeking such authorization. Because they do not focus on defeating the claimant's allegations, but rather bring forward a statutory explanation for a given use, this kind of defence serves as a substantive defensive rule against allegations of copyright infringement. Rules that have the capacity to relieve a defendant of liability, despite the presence of all the elements of copyright infringement, may be found in other legal orders beyond copyright. These include general legal principles or other disciplines, such as competition protection, consumer law, and possibly general commercial law.

Defensive rules that can relieve the defendant of liability, even when all the elements of copyright infringement are present, function as supervening claims and it is these rules that have the ability to operate as defences in a true sense as they have the force to overcome the fact that infringement has taken place. Denials of one or more elements of copyright infringement also serve a defensive function and may be invoked to rebut allegations of infringement without, however, bringing forward a justification for the infringing conduct. For the purposes of this book, however, they need to be systematically analysed and discussed in the context of a broader discussion on defensive rules in order to ascertain what overlaps may occur with other defensive claims and also which aspects of use can promote public policy objectives, but currently remain outside the scope of permissibility under EU copyright.

Classifying copyright law defences

Developing a systemic index of the defences available may be seen as a futile organizational attempt. Rahmatian notes that '[a] proper classification is not really possible; the exceptions are often the result of piecemeal legislation'.[83] It is without doubt that the diversity and the number of available defences under EU copyright law are obstacles towards the development of a satisfactory classification. What is more, numerous defensive rules are purely doctrinal and as such resist strict classification. In such cases, it is not entirely possible to draw a line between normative fiat and deference to judicial reasoning and/or it is likely that these defences may come under more than one category.

There have been very few attempts to classify the available copyright defences. Such efforts have generally been made in US copyright, particularly concerning taxonomies of the various fair use decisions. What was possibly the first attempt to achieve this was made by Alan Latman in 1958,[84] and was followed by classifications made by William Patry,[85] Michael Madison,[86] and Pam Samuelson.[87] The target of such classificatory analysis was often an examination of the predictability of the outcomes of fair use claims.[88] An example of classification includes the typology of the US intellectual property law defences adopted by Gideon Parchomovsky and Alex Stein,[89] who identified three types of defensive rules across intellectual property rights, or, as they called them, three conceptual categories: general, individualized,

---

[83] Andreas Rahmatian, *Copyright and Creativity: The Making of Property Rights in Creative Works* (Cheltenham/Northampton: Edward Elgar, 2011) 141.

[84] Alan Latman, 'Fair Use of Copyrighted Works', Study No. 14, Copyright Law Revision, Studies Prepared for the Subcommittee on Patents, Trademarks and Copyrights, S. Comm. in the Judiciary, 86th Cong. 3, 8–14 (Comm. Print 1960) (where he offers eight categories of fair use cases: incidental uses, criticism and review, parody and satire, scholarly uses, private uses, news, use in adjudicatory purposes, and use for non-profit or governmental purposes).

[85] William Patry, *The Fair Use Privilege in Copyright Law* (Washington, DC: Bureau of National Affairs, 1995, 2nd edn). There are seventeen kinds of uses included in Patry's classification.

[86] Michael J. Madison, 'A Pattern-Oriented Approach to Fair Use' (2004) 45 *William & Mary Law Review* 1525, 1645–65. Madison offers eight categories of fair use cases, including journalism and news reporting, criticism and comment, scholarship and research, reverse engineering, legal and political argument, storytelling, and comparative advertising.

[87] Pamela Samuelson, 'Unbundling Fair Uses' (2009) 77 *Fordham Law Review* 2537, 2540; also see Pamela Samuelson, 'Justifications for Copyright Limitations & Exceptions' in Ruth Okediji (ed.), *Copyright Law in an Age of Limitations and Exceptions* (Cambridge: Cambridge University Press, 2017) 12 et seq.

[88] See e.g. Barton Beebe, 'An Empirical Study of U.S. Fair Use Opinions, 1978–2005' (2008) 156 *University of Pennsylvania Law Review* 549, 609–10.

[89] Gideon Parchomovsky and Alex Stein, 'Intellectual Property Defences' (2013) 113 *Columbia Law Review* 1483.

and class defences. General defences attack the validity of the intellectual property right and, when successful, they do not only offer relief to the actual defendant but also to the public at large. Individualized defences help a defendant to negate infringing liability but leave the plaintiff's right intact in the sense that the plaintiff can assert it against other defendants. Class defences are an in-between category that create immunity for a certain group of users, being, however, more limited than general defences in that they do not invalidate the right of the plaintiff.

At a theoretical and conceptual level, Abraham Drassinower[90] adopted a holistic approach in looking at Canadian copyright defences[91] and drew a distinction between four kinds of copyright defences: of these he regarded only one as a 'properly so-called' copyright exception. According to his classification there are (a) subject matter limitations, (b) scope limitations, (c) miscellaneous exceptions, and (d) exceptions properly so-called. The first two attack either the subject matter or scope of protection, i.e. they target the definition of a *work* or the definition of the *right*. Drassinower argues that there are certain exceptions, notably fair dealing for criticism and review, which are not excused infringement but absent of infringement,[92] and should hence be better regarded as scope limitations. Miscellaneous defences are those that resist internalization within the copyright system as they remain heterogeneous to the purposes of copyright protection, such as the exception on agricultural fairs under Canadian copyright law. Finally, exceptions properly so-called are instances where copyright encounters claims that are recognized in other judicial orders and which remain external to copyright in the sense that they are not capable of integration within it. The encounter with other legal orders has the effect of serving as an actual limit to copyright and, in this regard, exceptions are invitations to understand the relatedness of different juridical orders as aspects of a comprehensive system of rights.[93]

At the European level, attempts to classify the available exceptions and limitations have been very limited.[94] This is partly due to their extensive number, but

---

[90] Abraham Drassinower, 'Exceptions Properly So-Called' in Ysolde Gendreau and Abraham Drassinower (eds), *Langues et Droit d'Auteur/ Language and Copyright* (Montreal: Carswell & Brussels: Bruylant, 2009) 205.

[91] Regarding classifications of copyright defences under Canadian law, Pascale Chapdelaine developed a basic typology of defences as user rights and the various kinds of entitlements that users may acquire on a given work, into (a) user copy owners, (b) service users, and (c) public space users. Pascale Chapdelaine, *Copyright User Rights: Contracts and the Erosion of Property* (Oxford: Oxford University Press, 2017) 191.

[92] Abraham Drassinower, 'Exceptions Properly So-Called' in Ysolde Gendreau and Abraham Drassinower (eds), *Langues et Droit d'Auteur/ Language and Copyright* (Montreal: Carswell & Brussels: Bruylant, 2009) 205, 217.

[93] Abraham Drassinower, 'Exceptions Properly So-Called' in Ysolde Gendreau and Abraham Drassinower (eds), *Langues et Droit d'Auteur/ Language and Copyright* (Montreal: Carswell & Brussels: Bruylant, 2009) 205, 211.

[94] Annette Kur, 'Of Oceans, Islands, and Inland Water - How Much Room for Exceptions and Limitations Under the Three-Step Test?' Max Planck Institute for Intellectual Property, Competition & Tax Law Research Paper Series No. 08-04 (2008); P. Bernt Hugenholtz and Ruth L. Okediji, 'Conceiving an International Instrument on Limitations and Exceptions to Copyright' Final Report, 12 et seq., <https://www.ivir.nl/publicaties/download/limitations_exceptions_copyright.pdf>, accessed 11 November 2019.

mostly because of their diversity in terms of beneficiaries, conditions of application, and theoretical underpinning. At the same time, most scholarly attention focuses on either copyright exceptions and limitations or other aspects of EU copyright law; there has not yet been a uniform attempt to discuss defensive rules as a whole, i.e. one that looks at all instances where a defensive claim can be invoked and which leads to either the affirmation of the absence of infringement or offers a judicial explanation for it.

The value of a classification

This work attempts to offer a measure of conceptual organization for defences to copyright infringement that may foster the development of a fresh understanding on how defensive rules against copyright infringement operate as a system; how they unveil their normative force; what are the instances of gaps or overlap between defences; and how defences should be developed in light of future law reform or possible interpretative expansion.

In order to address these questions, the book adopts a holistic approach and addresses *all* liability defeating rules that are available to combat allegations of infringement. Because of the fragmented framework of copyright exceptions and limitations at the EU level attempts to classify the available defensive rules have the potential to unveil their gaps and overlaps and also to clarify areas on which law and policy-making efforts could focus, especially where normative considerations indicate that the applicability of certain defensive rules should be broader or subject to a more rigorous legal regime. The book investigates how responses may be made to questions not addressed at the legislative level on the basis of law and doctrine. It is often that such questions emerge with regard to modern goods and services, and possible gaps in the law may inhibit innovative activity and business growth. This book discusses copyright law from the perspective of the claims that can be made either to deny allegations of copyright infringement or to explain why a particular activity that amounts to a prima facie act of infringement should be exempt. In this sense, the book does not merely address copyright exceptions and limitations, which are defensive in a strict sense, but covers the spectrum of claims that can be defensive in a practical sense, thereby it offers positivist insight into the way in which the various defensive rules are understood, interpreted, and applied, and draws on normative perspectives as to how to respond to unresolved.

In this regard, the book develops a typology of the various defensive rules available under the current EU copyright framework. Under this framework, there is legislative and doctrinal recognition of a plethora of instances that can have the effect of acquitting a defendant of allegations of copyright infringement—from library privileges, to parody, and to safe harbours for Internet intermediaries. On examining the functions of, and the justifications underpinning, these rules and principles, two main kinds of defence against copyright infringement become apparent. These include denials of the elements of copyright infringement and supervening explanations for carrying out acts restricted by copyright. The latter set of defences often takes the form of copyright exceptions and limitations to infringement, which can then be viewed as grounds offering judicial justification for infringement on the basis of fundamental human rights or as defences construed on the objectives of public policy; they are supervening claims, namely claims that can relieve the defendant from copyright infringement by offering a legislatively permissible rationale on why the defendant is permitted to carry out an activity that would otherwise amount to copyright infringement. Denials of the elements of infringement are instances where the successful negation of an element in which the claimant sues can result in judicial affirmation of the absence of infringement. In this sense, such defensive rules can be seen as the inverse of authorial rights when successfully attacking the scope of exclusive rights, or the negation of a right *in rem*, when challenging the subsistence of copyright in the product of intellect that has allegedly been infringed.

Much can be learned about defensive rules from the way in which they are classified within this system. As already indicated, there are types of defensive rules that affirm the absence of infringement and others that justify it, having a supervening force when successful. Often, denials of the elements of infringement develop a general effect in that they invalidate aspects of authorial entitlement by affirming either that there is no protected subject matter or that the rights in or to the work do not cover the allegedly infringing activity. In this regard, a successful claim can possibly benefit other defendants and have the general result of judicial confirmation that either the allegedly infringed subject matter or (aspects of the) rights of the author in question are part of the public domain. Other defensive rules, notably copyright exceptions and limitations, have a more individualized effect by offering judicial justifications or policy explanations as to why an otherwise infringing activity has taken place.

This book acknowledges that true defences within the copyright system are only those which embody claims with a supervening force. Although all principles developing defensive claims are subject to discussion in order to look into the confines of copyright protection and the breadth of permitted uses, those that qualify as supervening defences against copyright infringement are rules that offer relief from liability despite the fact that all elements of infringement are present. Claims which focus merely on subsistence and scope are typically raised by defendants and hold their significance in the constantly evolving landscape of activities that rely on copying. However, the underlying effect of such claims is to challenge the existence of liability requirements and, in this sense, they can be understood not as defences in a strict sense, but mostly as the inverse of authorial rights and challenges to causation. Defences in the strict sense, however, entail both claims for justified or fair conducts flowing from the exercise of fundamental rights (and possibly incorporated within copyright), and claims for behaviours that are permitted for public policy reasons, i.e. grounds that are indifferent to reasonableness. Most of the activities falling in defences in this strict sense are the so-called copyright exceptions and limitations that may be justified either under the spectrum of fairness, broadly conceived, or reasons of public policy.

It is acknowledged that there are subtle differences between the various defences in terms of the function that they serve with regard to copyright infringement. Such gaps and overlaps ought to be examined in light of the constantly evolving jurisprudence of the Court of Justice of the European Union, which has in recent years taken an active role in the interpretation of copyright doctrine and has developed novel copyright concepts which impact the limits of copyright, such as the requirement of a work being 'the author's own intellectual creation' or the controversial concept of the 'new public' as a constituent of the right of communication to the public.[95]

This book posits that in a strict sense all defences, mostly embodied in the so-called copyright exceptions and limitations, bring forward considerations emerging from the encounter of copyright with other areas of law, such as fundamental rights or public policy. These defences offer an explanation as to why an act that can be primarily seen as an act of copyright infringement is justified by law. In this regard, the book takes the stance that all of these defences are rationale-driven and purpose-oriented. Although a purposive interpretation of defensive claims is welcome and opens the door to considerations of fairness and proportionality, EU copyright has been regularly criticized for adopting a largely case-specific approach with regard to the availability of copyright exceptions at the legislative level and a strict interpretative approach of judicial reasoning.[96] The Directive on Copyright in the Digital Single Market exacerbates such considerations by adding six copyright exceptions to the long list of copyright exceptions and limitations under EU copyright. This approach arguably adds to the fragmentation of permissible use under EU copyright and to the complexity of defensive rules.

It should be noted that the classification offered in this book does not aim to be absolute. It is acknowledged that some defences draw on both fundamental rights and public policy. This could be the case for certain remunerated exceptions such as the private copying exception, or defences available to certain institutional users

---

[95] *Infopaq International A/S v Danske Dagblades Forening*, Case C-5/08, 16 July 2009, ECLI:EU:C:2009:465 (*Infopaq I*); *Infopaq International A/S v Danske Dagblades Forening*, Case C-302/10, 17 January 2012, ECLI:EU:C:2012:16 (*Infopaq II*) (definition of 'work' and 'originality'); *Levola Hengelo BV v Smilde Foods BV*, Case 310/17, 13 November 2018, ECLI:EU:C:2018:899 (*Levola*); *Nils Svensson and Others v Retriever Sverige AB*, Case C-466/12, 13 February 2014, ECLI:EU:C:2014:76 (definition of 'public').

[96] *Infopaq International*, Case C-5/08, 16 July 2009, ECLI:EU:C:2009:465, [56] and [57]; *Football Association Premier League and Others*, Joined Cases C-403/08 and C-429/08, 4 October 2011, ECLI:EU:C:2011:631, [162]; *Public Relations Consultants Association Ltd v Newspaper Licensing Agency Ltd and Others*, Case C-360/13, 5 June 2014, ECLI:EU:C:2014:1195, [23].

such as those available to educational establishments. The logic of classification aims to place defences in categories, but it does not mean to insist on a given classification, particularly in cases where the specimen at issue is a legal doctrine such as the principle of abuse of right, which, depending on the way in which it has organically evolved in national law, may fall under different classifications.[97] In order to avoid oversimplifying the basis on which certain defences are premised, there is the need to retain a degree of flexibility of the taxonomic logic with regard to such kinds of defence.

Methodology

The methodological approach adopted in this work emerges from the attempt to look into the way in which defences available under EU copyright operate as a system. In this regard, the work offers a taxonomy of defences to copyright infringement under EU copyright and an analysis of the way in which defences as a whole can be contextualized.[98] In so doing, the work describes the law and case law which govern various copyright defences, it looks into the gaps and overlaps of the available statutory rules and judicially developed principles, it offers comparisons between defences where appropriate, and it theorizes on conceptual aspects of the available provisions. Subject to discussion are the legal instruments available under EU copyright law, relevant cases from the Court of Justice of the European Union, and the way in which they have been implemented and judicially interpreted in the various Member States.

The design of the taxonomy draws insights from tort law and theory and the way in which the narrative on defences against wrongdoings has been construed in this area of law.[99] While the initial grant of copyright is proprietary in nature,[100] copyright infringement can be viewed as a group of torts.[101] In his remarkably

---

[97] It may be seen as justified on public policy or as an exclusion from the scope of copyright protection in the form of a denial of elements of the alleged infringement.

[98] In this context it is worth noting that defences available to moral rights (that are applicable in some jurisdictions, e.g., the United Kingdom) are not addressed in this work as they are not subject to EU harmonization and remain rather sporadic and limited in their application.

[99] See e.g., James Goudkamp, *Tort Law Defences* (Oxford: Hart Publishing, 2013).

[100] The question of whether intellectual property rights are proprietary or personal in nature has been a longstanding theoretical aspect. See, for example, Adam Mossoff, 'Is Copyright Property?' (2005) 42 *San Diego Law Review* 29; Mark A. Lemley, 'Romantic Authorship and the Rhetoric of Property' (1997) 75 *Texas Law Review* 873; Frank H. Easterbrook, 'Intellectual Property is Still Property' (1990) 13 *Harvard Journal of Law and Public Policy*, 108; Henry E. Smith, 'Intellectual Property as Property: Delineating Entitlements in Information' (2007) 116 *Yale Law Journal* 1742.

[101] However, copyright does not ordinarily fall within the law of torts. See, however, the legal principles developed in US copyright: *Peters v West*, 692 F.3d 629, 633–4 (7th Cir. 2012) (US) ('Fundamentally, proving the basic tort of infringement simply requires the plaintiff to show that the defendant had an actual opportunity to copy the original ... and that the two works share enough unique features to give rise to a breach of the duty not to copy another's work.'); *Lawrence v Dana*, 15 F. Cas. 26, 61 (C.C.D. Mass. 1869) (US) (No. 8,136) ('Rights secured by copyright are property within the meaning

illuminating article,[102] Goold argues that infringement can be understood as a set of five different 'copy-torts', including consumer copying, competitor copying, expressive privacy invasion, artistic reputation injury, and breach of creative control. Drawing parallels from, and understanding copyright by reflective analogy to, tort law helps advance discussions on future policy making on the confines of copyright. The relationship between the plaintiff and the defendant exists because those who cause another harm have a duty to correct that harm.[103] Distinctions of defensive rules as discussed in the seminal work of Goudkamp are particularly useful as they can offer a fresh insight into the way in which defences in copyright law can be understood and classified.[104]

The taxonomic project developed in this book is methodologically construed on the following basis. First, it draws a distinction between defensive rules on the basis of the way in which they attack allegations of copyright infringement, drawing insights from tort law and theory. In this regard, it posits that there are two main kinds of defence in copyright: negations of the elements of infringement, namely arguments supporting the absence of infringement, and rationale-based defences, i.e. defensive rules claiming that there is a judicial justification or public policy explanation for a given conduct. On a second level, defensive rules in each category are subdivided either on the basis of their intrinsic characteristics and function within the copyright system. In particular, denials of elements infringement may attack different aspects of the claimant's entitlement, from the subsistence of copyright to the breadth and scope of exclusive rights or the authorization to carry out a given activity. Defendants who can successfully raise a defence by challenging subject matter or scope do not need to invoke a copyright exception in that their conduct does not amount to infringement. If, however, this is not possible, rationale-based defences may be available to them. This set of defences is clustered on the basis of the kind of justification that is brought forward to explain why an allegedly infringing use should be permitted, which may be premised on a fundamental human right, a public policy objective, or on grounds that are external to copyright such as e-commerce protection, competition law, or general legal principles. A special set of defensive rules on the basis of its legal nature and function within EU copyright is premised on condition that the copyright holders receive fair compensation.

The analysis offered is needed for three main reasons. First, there has not been a systematic attempt to offer a taxonomic index of the available defensive rules

---

of the law of copyright, and whoever invades that property beyond the privilege conceded to subsequent authors commits a tort.')

[102] Patrick Russell Goold, 'Unbundling the "Tort" of Copyright Infringement' (2016) 102 *Virginia Law Review* 1833.

[103] Jules L. Coleman, *The Practice of Principle: In Defence of a Pragmatist Approach to Legal Theory* (Oxford: Oxford University Press, 2001) 13–24.

[104] James Goudkamp, *Tort Law Defences* (Oxford: Hart Publishing, 2013).

under EU copyright law, despite the fact that some classificatory efforts have been made in the European Union and Canada. Secondly, much can be learned about defensive rules from the way in which they are interpreted, applied, and classified. Finally, classificatory analysis and conceptualization may inform the framework of available defences by suggesting that the scope of defences should be expanded, whether certain defensive rules ought to be strengthened e.g., by becoming mandatory against restrictive contractual terms, and whether existing defences are necessary or in compliance with the *acquis communautaire* or international norms.

Outline

This work is divided into two parts. Part A analyses the defensive claims that consist of denials of the elements of infringement. These broadly include claims whereby the defendant argues that one or more elements of copyright infringement are absent or that an exemption applies. Such claims broadly cover arguments that focus on the lack of copyright subsistence requirements, for instance, that the copied work is not original or that it does not fall within the definition of protected subject matter (Chapter 2). If this is successfully argued, there can be no liability for copyright infringement. Similar is the effect of claims attacking allegations of infringement on the basis that a particular conduct falls outside the scope of exclusive rights (Chapter 3). Such claims, which for the purposes of the present work are referred to as 'scope limitations', attack either the statutory or judicial construal of rights and offer an interpretation in the favour of the defendant. It is argued that the temporary copying exception, which is currently available under Article 5(1) of the Information Society Directive, also sets a scope limitation to the reproduction right, despite the fact that it is organically listed within the set of copyright exceptions and limitations within the Directive (Chapter 4). The reason for this is not merely that this is the only compulsory exception for Member States to implement under the Information Society Directive, but also the interpretative guidance offered in historical documents preceding its implementation indicates the fit of the exception as a scope limitation to the reproduction right. [105] A final body of defensive rules premised on the negation of infringing liability because elements of infringement are absent targets the consent of the copyright holders (Chapter 5). Copyright is a system of permissions and if it can be successfully argued that the copyright holder has either expressly or implicitly authorized a particular conduct, the defendant will be acquitted of infringement. Implied consent is becoming more and more relevant in the online context and there have been a number of judicial

---

[105] Proposal for a European Parliament and Council Directive on the Harmonisation of Certain Aspects of Copyright and Related Rights in the Information Society, Brussels, 10 December 1997, COM (97) 628, 29, Art. 5(3).

affirmations of relevant defensive claims,[106] which contribute to the development of an understanding of authorial conduct that can imply permissibility.

Part B focuses on defensive claims with a supervening force; effectively, arguments that can offer either a justification or a public policy explanation for a particular conduct. It is in the sphere of such claims that copyright encounters different legal orders such as human rights, competition law, e-commerce protection, or general legal principles. A possible conflict between copyright and other legal disciplines is regulated either within copyright law or law and doctrine that is extraneous to copyright. In this part of the work, the subject of discussion is primarily copyright exceptions and limitations and also defences that are external to copyright, but which have the potential to serve as defensive rules in allegations of copyright infringement. Copyright exceptions and limitations are broadly discussed in reference to their function in the copyright system and fall within three categories: speech entitlements (Chapter 6), namely defensive rules that aim to enable new, possibly copyright-protected, speech; public policy exceptions (Chapter 7), namely entitlements and privileges that are set in place in order to meet certain public policy objectives; and remunerated uses (Chapter 8), namely a set of activities that are permitted on the basis that copyright holders receive fair compensation. This latter set of permitted use, which is often available under a statutory license, creates property-like entitlements for copyright holders who have an entitlement to fair compensation owing to specific user conduct with regard to protected works. In this regard, although offering a broader scope, the relevant activities do not represent end user rights. Finally, subject to discussion shall be certain defensive rules that are external to copyright law, but which are relevant and useful in combatting allegations of copyright infringement (Chapter 9). These include claims incorporated into the legal framework governing electronic commerce, or general legal principles such as the public interest or the abusive exercise of rights.

---

[106] *Nils Svensson and Others v Retriever Sverige AB*, Case C-466/12, 13 February 2014, ECLI:EU:C:2014:76 (*Svensson*); 'Vorschaubilder I', Supreme Court (Bundesgerichtshof) 29 April 2010, I ZR 69/08 (Germany), available in German at <http://www.bundesgerichtshof.de>, accessed 11 November 2019; 'Vorschaubilder II', Supreme Court (Bundesgerichtshof), 19 October 2011, I ZR 140/10 (Germany); *Kommunikation und Recht*, Jena Court of Appeal (Oberlandesgericht Jena), 2 U 319/07, 27 February 2008, 301 (Germany).

PART A

DENIALS OF THE ELEMENTS OF INFRINGEMENT

Introduction to Part A

In a broad sense, the word 'defence' can be used to refer to any argument made by a defendant with the aim of persuading the court to hold that they are not liable. In this broad sense, defence encompasses denials of one or more of the elements of infringement. For example, the defendant may argue that copyright did not subsist in a work in the first place, or that the act in question does not fall within the copyright holder's exclusive rights, or that the claimant had expressly or impliedly authorized the use. It seems that the availability of this kind of defence becomes more and more limited as the recent jurisprudence of the Court of Justice of the European Union adopts a pro-author stance in interpreting both subsistence requirements and scope of rights. In *Infopaq I*,[1] the court expanded the concept of work as protectable subject matter by holding that an extract of eleven words can qualify for copyright protection, insofar as it is the author's own intellectual creation. Even though there is neither a *de minimis* principle in copyright law nor a restriction of what qualifies as protectable subject matter, the express stipulation that very short extracts can still qualify for protection brings originality, authorship, and the idea/expression principle (and the doctrine of substantiality of taking in some jurisdictions, such as the United Kingdom) into new light.[2] In *Levola*,[3] the court affirmed that copyright can subsist in any subject matter that is capable of being expressed in a precise and objective manner. What is more, rights are very broadly drafted at the EU level and, in particular, through the relevant Directives; their internal limits are subject to judicial interpretation, which, in some instances, impacts the scope of available protection. This includes, for instance, the newly elaborated concept of the 'new public' in the context of the right of communicating works in electronic networks,[4] which may be viewed as having an effect on the scope and applicability of the relevant rights.

---

[1] *Infopaq International A/S v Danske Dagblades Forening*, Case C-5/08, 16 July 2009, ECLI:EU:C:2009:465 (*Infopaq I*).

[2] It further indicates that it may be more efficient for defendants in cases of online copyright infringement to rely on the so-called exceptions and limitations to copyright law, as incorporated within Art. 5 of the Information Society Directive (Directive 2001/29/EC) and the national laws that implemented it.

[3] *Levola Hengelo BV v Smilde Foods BV*, Case C-310/17, 13 November 2018, ECLI:EU:C:2018:899 (*Levola*).

[4] See indicatively *Nils Svensson and Others v Retriever Sverige AB*, Case C-466/12, 13 February 2014, ECLI:EU:C:2014:76 (*Svensson*); *BestWater International GmbH v Michael Mebes, Stefan Potsch*, Case C-348/13, 21 October 2014 (order of the Court), ECLI:EU:C:2014:2315 (*BestWater*); also see *Innoweb BV v Wegener ICT Media BV and Wegener Mediaventions BV*, Case C-202/12, 19 December 2013, ECLI:EU:C:2013:850 (*Innoweb*).

An important issue that has to be raised by reference to liability defeating claims which target the elements of copyright infringement is the distinction between copyright protection and defences. This is a distinction that becomes predominantly important by reference to scope limitations and can be viewed as the line between what falls within copyright protection and what does not. Much depends on judicial interpretation of the scope of exclusive rights, yet there are instances where normative considerations also come into play: this concerns, for instance, the copyright exception which allows activities of transient and incidental copying on the Internet to enhance the efficiency of networks.[5] Although not all claims made to defeat the elements of infringement will qualify as defences in a strict sense, they serve a defensive function on a practical level and can form the core of a defensive strategy.

Effectively, claims negating the elements of infringement will focus on one or more of the following bases: (a) copyright does not subsist in the allegedly infringed subject matter (Chapter 2); (b) copyright may subsist in the allegedly infringed work but authorial rights do not restrict the defendant from carrying out a particular activity by reference to the work (Chapter 3);[6] (c) the defendant's activity does not impact on acts restricted by copyright as it is not part of the reproduction right by virtue of the temporary copying exemption (Chapter 4); and (d) the defendant's activity has been allowed by the relevant rightsholder either expressly or implicitly through contract or conduct (Chapter 5).

---

[5] Information Society Directive (Directive 2001/29/EC), Art. 5(1); for a discussion see Chapter 4.
[6] In this regard, the abusive or excessive exercise of exclusive rights may also be regarded as a defensive claim incorporating a scope limitation, in that the allegations for copyright infringement exceed the statutory core of rights (Chapter 9).

2

Subsistence Negating Claims

One of the main defences against allegations for copyright infringement is that no infringement took place because copyright does not subsist in the subject matter at issue. This could be either because the subject matter is not a 'work' in the copyright sense, or, even where a work exists, it is not protected by copyright because it is not original or fixed in a tangible form. Digital technologies exacerbate controversy over copyright subsistence. For instance, does a copy of a public domain image qualify for a new copyright by virtue of its scanning and digital processing (for instance, through a raster graphics editor such as Photoshop)? Does a short sentence such as a tweet attract copyright and can strings of characters such as hashtags and hyperlinks be 'copyright works' in their own right? What about works created through artificial intelligence such as a search engine's automatic translations? Can they be protected in the absence of a human author? Or, what about cases where more than one human author is involved in the creation of a work through contributions of facts or pieces of information that are subject to constant modification, such as entries on Wikipedia? Can copyright subsist in such factual contributions and modifications?

The rationale of excluding subject matter from protection rests on the principle that mere ideas, facts, or commonplace and unoriginal elements should remain free for all to use with a view to ensuring a robust public domain. In this regard, requesting the negation of copyright subsistence can serve as a defence against allegations of infringement and in a broader sense it can help innovation and creativity through the re-use of subject matter that does not attract copyright protection. Subject to examination in this chapter will be the way in which a negation of copyright subsistence can form a defence against allegations of infringement by making specific references to new technological uses. Significant reference is made to the doctrinal interpretation of the concepts 'work' and 'originality' as developed by the Court of Justice of the European Union and the national courts of EU Member States, and the way in which these doctrines impact on the scope of permissible use.

Defences to Copyright Infringement. Stavroula Karapapa, Oxford University Press (2020). © Stavroula Karapapa.
DOI: 10.1093/oso/9780198795636.001.0001

Introduction

Subsistence negating claims focus on attacking one of the essential elements of copyright infringement. According to such claims, copyright does not subsist in the work that the copyright infringement pertains to. Such claims target either the quality of the work as subject matter eligible to attract copyright protection or the qualities that are necessary for such subject matter to be protected, namely originality and, in some jurisdictions, fixation. Defences targeting subsistence rely on such structural and interpretative claims, which tend to become more and more limited in the online context. The judicial interpretation of subsistence requirements in light of digitization and the Internet has been generous in the sense that restrictive approaches to protectable subject matter—available in some EU Member States—may no longer be viable and the construal of the originality requirement at the EU level seems to have a broader reach compared to certain pre-applicable national approaches. Subject to discussion in this chapter are liability-defeating claims targeting the subsistence of copyright in light of the emergent trend whereby copyright protection is likely to subsist on any kind of authorial output given that it is its author's own intellectual creation.

The concept of the work in copyright

In every copyright system, the work has a central role. As a matter of fact, the concept of the work is omnipresent and it features in statutory provisions of every legal system on a worldwide level. In the Information Society Directive[1] the term 'work' is repeated at least sixty-two times, and in the 179 sections of Part I of the UK Copyright, Designs, and Patents Act 1988 (CDPA), for instance, reference to the term is made no less than 746 times. Work is the 'thread' that brings together the various provisions of copyright law. The centrality of the concept of work is justified by the fact that the work is the subject matter of protection: rights subsist in a work and it is through the work that the rights conferred by copyright take effect. Unless a work in the copyright sense exists, legal action cannot flourish, allegations of infringement cannot be substantiated, and ownership over content cannot be established. In this light, the work is the means through which an author may exercise a series of statutorily recognized rights. A work is not only the shorthand for an authorial output or the umbrella term to cover the protectable subject matter, but has also been gradually elevated into the organizing principle of copyright laws

---

[1] Directive 2001/29/EC of the European Parliament and of the Council of 22 May 2001 on the Harmonisation of Certain Aspects of Copyright and Related Rights in the Information Society, OJ L 167, 22 June 2001, 10–19 (Information Society Directive).

on a worldwide basis, otherwise put, the 'basis on which the doctrinal edifice of modern copyright was built'.[2]

At the European level, the various Directives and national laws implementing them make reference either to the 'work' *in abstrato* or they specifically address the categories of protected subject matter. Remaining notoriously undefined,[3] the concept of work has subjected to various approaches across the European Union. As Jacob LJ observed in *Nova v Mazooma* in 2007,[4] this was (at least until recently) 'an aspect of [national] copyright law untouched by any EU harmonization'. The Directives and the national statutes which implement them do not provide a fully fledged definition of what the work is.[5] In this sense, copyright does not define the work, rather it instructs as to when a work is created and offers sufficient guidance on what is legally cognizable as work, i.e. on what is protected by copyright. Positive law mainly depicts the object of protection. The concept of work is therefore construed by a qualifying object and through the fulfilment of the requirements of copyright subsistence, namely originality and, under some national laws, fixation.[6]

In some EU Member States, it is at the court's discretion to determine what is protectable subject matter by interpreting the particular legal requirements, whereas in others there are only specific categories of subject matter that are eligible for protection. Different Member States follow different approaches on what qualifies as protectable subject matter and, in some instances, on what form the available protection can take. Some Member States, for example, do not offer protection to so-called entrepreneurial works under copyright, rather they do so through a system

---

[2] Brad Sherman, 'What is a Copyright Work?' (2010) 12(1) *Theoretical Inquiries in Law* 99, 102.

[3] Justin Hughes, 'Size Matters (or Should) in Copyright Law' (2005) 74 *Fordham Law Review* 575, 576 ('American copyright law is an enormous legal structure, full of defined terms, all built on one completely undefined term: the "work".')

[4] *Nova v Mazooma* [2007] EWCA Civ. 219; [2007] RPC 25 (UK).

[5] Of relevance in this context may be the US position as reflected in the statement of Marybeth Peters on a US Congress Hearing on the Family Movie Act of 2004, 'the [US] Copyright Act seems to have the functional equivalent of a partial definition of a work'. See Family Movie Act 2004—Hearing on H.R. 4586, 108th Congress, Statement of Marybeth Peters, Register of Copyrights before the Subcommittee on Courts, the Internet and Intellectual Property of the House Committee on the Judiciary, Washington, DC, 17 June 2004, 8, 12-13:

> Although one might expect the extensive list of definitions in §101 of the Copyright Act to include a definition of as fundamental a term as 'work,' no such definition is [sic] exists. However, §101 does tell us when a work is 'created':
> A work is 'created' when it is fixed in a copy or phonorecord for the first time where [sic]; where a work is prepared over a period of time, the portion of it that has been fixed at any particular time constitutes the work as of that time, and where the work has been prepared in different versions, each version constitutes a separate work.
> If a work is created when it is fixed in a copy or phonorecord for the first time, it is difficult to imagine that the work exists prior to that time. Thus, the Copyright Act seems to have the functional equivalent of a partial definition of a work; while it may not tell us everything that we need to know in order to recognize a 'work,' it does tell us that a work must be fixed in a copy or phonorecord. And if it is a work in progress, then at any point in time, the 'work' consists of that which has already been fixed.

[6] E.g. Cyprus, Ireland, Malta, and the United Kingdom.

of neighbouring rights which often afford a narrower scope of protection. At the same time, Member States follow different approaches towards protectable subject matter in their national laws, a result of the discretion that international copyright law allows. Article 2(1) of the Berne Convention[7] merely indicates that protection should be offered to 'literary and artistic works', but no further guidance is given to Contracting States. Hence, Member States may stipulate an exhaustive list of categories of protectable subject matter (a 'closed list') or adopt an 'open list' approach. Most EU Member States follow an 'open list' model, whereas a limited few afford protection to a 'closed list' of protectable works; these few include Cyprus, Ireland, and the United Kingdom.[8] In the United Kingdom, the CDPA defines a copyright work in a functional fashion, limiting its contours to a collective term that encompasses eight categories of protected subject matter.[9] Section 1(2) of the CDPA reads that ' "copyright work" means a work of any of those descriptions in which copyright subsists', namely original literary, dramatic, musical, or artistic works, sound recordings, films or broadcasts, and the typographical arrangement of published editions. Protection is afforded to these eight categories of protected subject matter only. Whereas the term 'work' is used as an umbrella term for the protected subject matter, the statute does not provide a unified idea as to what brings all those diverse descriptions of works together, nor does it explain the reason behind the insertion of new categories of works into statute, such as computer programs or databases. In the list of definitions outlined in section 178 the term 'work' is not defined.

---

[7] Berne Convention for the Protection of Literary and Artistic Works (as amended on September 28, 1979) (Berne Convention).

[8] Art. 17(2) of the Irish Copyright and Related Rights Act 2000 reads:

Copyright subsists, in accordance with this Act, in—

(a) original literary, dramatic, musical, or artistic works,
(b) sound recordings, films, broadcasts, or cable programmes,
(c) the typographical arrangement of published editions, and
(d) original databases.

Art. 3(1) of the Cypriot Copyright Act also offers a closed list of protected subject matter. It reads:

Subject to the provisions of this section, copyright shall subsist in the following works—

(a) scientific works;
(b) literary works;
(c) musical works;
(d) artistic works;
(e) cinematograph films;
(f) photographs;
(g) sound recordings;
(h) broadcasts.

See Copyright Laws 1976 to 1993 (Law No. 59 of 3 December 1976, as amended by Law No. 18(I), 1993), as last amended.

[9] Note that it was the 1988 Act that expanded the scope of the concept of work to all categories of protected subject matter. By contrast, the 1956 Copyright Act was distinguished between Part I 'works' (literary, dramatic, artistic, and musical) and Part II 'subject matter' (sound recordings, films, broadcasts, and typographical arrangements of printed editions).

The Court of Justice of the European Union addressed the gap in the unifying conditions of protectable subject matter, in particular with the *Levola* case,[10] effectively leading to the abolition of the categorization requirement available in some Member States; in this regard the closed systems of protectable subject matter may soon have to be subject to review.[11]

The requirement of a work

EU law requires Member States to ensure copyright protection for authorial works, namely works protected by virtue of Article 2 of the Berne Convention. The requirement to ensure protection for authorial works finds support in obligations of the European Union as a party to the Berne Convention,[12] the Agreement on Trade-Related Aspects of Intellectual Property Rights (TRIPs),[13] and the World Intellectual Property Organization Copyright Treaty (WCT).[14] According to Article 2 of the Berne Convention, contracting parties ought to recognize and protect copyright in the following 'protected works': literary or artistic works, including any literary, dramatic, musical, artistic, or other original expressive subject matter; dramatic, musical, cinematographic, artistic, informational works, such as maps; and 'every production in the literary, scientific, and artistic domain, whatever may be the mode or form of its expression'. Protection is also afforded to alterations and the collections of such works that fall under the scope of 'intellectual creation'. The Berne Convention expressly excludes 'news of the day [and] miscellaneous facts having the character of mere items of press information' because they do not demonstrate the authorial character required for the purposes of copyright protection.[15] The TRIPS Agreement and the WCT reinforce the Berne provisions by expanding protection to new subject matter, such as computer programs and compilations of data, and by requiring their respective contracting parties to comply with Articles 1 to 21 of the Berne Convention. Articles 9 and 10 of the TRIPS Agreement and Articles 1(4), 2, 4, and 5 of the WCT also exclude

[10] The broad construal of the concept of work at the EU level is challenged in light of cases such as *Levola Hengelo BV v Smilde Foods BV*, Case C-310/17, 13 November 2018, ECLI:EU:C:2018:899 (*Levola*). Following the Opinion of the Advocate General (ECLI:EU:C:2018:618), the Court of Justice did not afford copyright protection to the taste of food products.

[11] *Levola Hengelo BV v Smilde Foods BV*, Case C-310/17, 13 November 2018, ECLI:EU:C:2018:899 (*Levola*); see also in this regard Estelle Derclaye, 'Copyright does not Protect the Taste of Cheese' (2018) *The Conversation*; Caterina Sganga, 'Say Nay to a Tastier Copyright: Why the CJEU Should Deny Copyright Protection for Taste (and Smells)' (2019) 14(3) *Journal of Intellectual Property Law & Practice* 187.

[12] Berne Convention for the Protection of Literary and Artistic Works (as amended on 28 September 1979) (Berne Convention).

[13] Agreement on Trade-Related Aspects of Intellectual Property Rights (1994) (TRIPs).

[14] WIPO Copyright Treaty (WCT) (1996).

[15] Berne Convention, Art. 2(8); the extent to which the newly introduced press publishers' right under Art. 15 of the Digital Single Market Directive (Directive 2019/790) is questionable.

from copyright protection 'ideas, procedures, methods of operation, [and] mathematical concepts as such', but extend protection to computer programs as literary works and to 'compilations of data or other materials, in any form, which by reason of the selection or arrangement of their contents constitute *intellectual creations*'.[16]

The relevant EU provisions are included in Articles 2 to 4 of the Information Society Directive[17] and in certain other Directives.[18] The indication that protection is available to the author's own intellectual creation is clearly stated in three instances by reference to databases, computer programs, and photographs. Article 3(3) of the Database Directive[19] confers protection to databases as collections of independent works, data, and other materials 'which, by reason of the selection or arrangement of their contents, constitute the *author's own intellectual creation* ... be protected as such by copyright'; Article 1 of the Computer Programs Directive[20] requires Member States to protect by copyright computer programs as literary works insofar as they are original in the sense that they are their *author's own intellectual creation*; and Article 6 of the Term Directive[21] requires that protection should be ensured for photographs which are original in the sense that they are their *author's own intellectual creation*.

Even though the international standard of protection refers to 'intellectual creation' and addresses specific categories of works only, this standard has been refined into the requirement of the 'author's own intellectual creation' at the EU level, which—following its sporadic legislative references—was gradually judicially elevated into the governing standard applicable to every description of protected subject matter.

Protectable subject matter as a clear and precise expression

To be precise, the Court of Justice has recently upheld in *Levola*[22] that the subject matter protected by copyright has to be 'expressed in a manner which makes

---

[16] Emphasis added.

[17] Information Society Directive (Directive 2001/29/EC).

[18] Directive 96/9/EC of the European Parliament and of the Council of 11 March 1996 on the Legal Protection of Databases, OJ L 77, 27 March 1996, 20–28 (Database Directive); Directive 2009/24/EC of the European Parliament and of the Council of 23 April 2009 on the Legal Protection of Computer Programs, OJ L 111, 5 May 2009, 16–22 (Computer Programs Directive); Directive 2006/116/EC of the European Parliament and of the Council of 12 December 2006 on the Term of Protection of Copyright and Certain Related Rights, OJ L 372, 27 December 2006, 12–18 (Term Directive).

[19] Database Directive.

[20] Directive 2009/24/EC of the European Parliament and of the Council of 23 April 2009 on the Legal Protection of Computer Programs, OJ L 111, 5 May 2009, 16–22 (Computer Programs Directive).

[21] Directive 2006/116/EC of the European Parliament and of the Council of 12 December 2006 on the Term of Protection of Copyright and Certain Related Rights, OJ L 372, 27 December 2006, 12–18 (Term Directive).

[22] *Levola Hengelo BV v Smilde Foods BV*, Case C-310/17, 13 November 2018, ECLI:EU:C:2018:899 (*Levola*).

it identifiable with sufficient precision and objectivity, even though that expression is not necessarily in permanent form.'[23] The case concerned the taste of cheese and its capacity to attract copyright protection. As the Court of Justice remarked, it is important for both the authorities responsible for ensuring that the exclusive rights inherent in copyright are protected, and for individuals (in particular economic operators), to be able to identify, clearly and precisely, the subject matter so protected. At the same time, it is necessary to ensure that the concept of work remains resistant to subjectivity—given that this is detrimental to legal certainty—in the process of identifying the protected subject matter. In this regard, a work ought to be capable of being expressed in a precise and objective manner.[24] Such precision and objectivity cannot be assumed by reference to the taste of food products, unlike, for example, literary, pictorial, cinematographic, or musical works, and the reason is that identification relies on taste, sensations, and experiences, which are subjective and variable. In this light, the court concluded that the taste of a food product cannot be classified as a 'work'.[25]

The reasoning developed by the Court of Justice is a reminder of the construal of the concept of a 'sign' that is eligible for protection as a trade mark under European trade mark law. In *Sieckmann*, a case concerning the registration of a smell trade mark, the Court of Justice famously stated that 'a trade mark may consist of a sign which is not in itself capable of being perceived visually, provided that it can be represented graphically, particularly by means of images, lines, or characters, and that the representation is clear, precise, self-contained, easily accessible, intelligible, durable, and objective.'[26] Although in the context of trade mark law, *Sieckmann* signalled the end to the registration of certain so-called unconventional trade marks, such as smells and tastes, *Levola* is likely to have, at least *prima facie*, the opposite effect, namely it is expected to broaden the concept of work as protectable subject matter and, thereinafter, the breadth of copyright protection. Post-*Levola*, any precisely and objectively expressed subject matter that is its author's own intellectual creation can be subject to copyright protection. This has the effect of rendering the closed systems of protected subject matter out of date and in need of bringing into line with the *acquis communautaire*. By reference to defences in copyright, it is likely to narrow down the scope of defensive rules targeting the subject matter of copyright protection as, in principle, any clear and objective expression will now qualify for such protection.

---

[23] Ibid., [40].
[24] Ibid., [41].
[25] Ibid., [44].
[26] *Ralf Sieckmann v Deutsches Patent- und Markenamt*, Case C-273/00, 12 December 2002, ECLI:EU:C:2002:748, [55].

The importance of identifying the protectable subject matter

Examinations of copyright infringement start by clearly identifying the work or other subject matter in which copyright is alleged to subsist. This includes determining what the work is comprised of for the purposes of copyright. In this context, it is important to determine whether protection in a literary work, for instance, subsists merely in its expression or whether it also applies to the underlying plot, characters, and incidents, as this will determine its author's entitlement to protection, including the extent to which claims for infringement or joint ownership can flourish.[27] Even though protection is conceived expansively by reference to authorial works, and underlying ideas or visually significant elements can form part of protection, this is not the case for databases and computer programs. These latter categories of protected subject matter cannot benefit from protection of certain elements, e.g. the contents of a database, or the underlying ideas and principles of a computer program.[28] The result is that these aspects are excluded from copyright protection and thereinafter have the capacity to form successful copyright infringement claims.

Besides the issue of subsistence in non-literal elements of works, issues may also arise by reference to works that are too short in terms of length, works not qualifying as their author's own intellectual creation, or works lacking originality as a requirement of protection. These issues are examined below.

A work as the 'author's own intellectual creation'

The Information Society Directive does not determine the meaning and scope of the concept of a 'work'. It is accepted that in light of the need for a uniform application of EU law and the principle of equality, the concept of work ought to be given an autonomous and uniform interpretation throughout the European Union.[29] A work ought to be a clear and precise expression, and in order to attract protection two cumulative conditions must be satisfied: first, it is only something which is the expression of the author that may be classified as a 'work' within the meaning and the purposes of copyright protection,[30] and secondly, this subject matter should be original in the

---

[27] As Laddie QC observed in a famous UK case, however: 'if the copyright owner is entitled to redefine his copyright work so as to match the size of the alleged infringement, there would never be a requirement for substantiality.' See *Hyperion Records v Warner Music* (unreported case, 17 May 1991) 8 (Ch.) (UK).

[28] See in this regard Chapter 3.

[29] See *Levola Hengelo BV v Smilde Foods BV*, Case C-310/17, 13 November 2018, ECLI:EU:C:2018:899 (*Levola*), [33]; *Infopaq International A/S v Danske Dagblades Forening*, Case C-5/08, 16 July 2009, ECLI:EU:C:2009:465 (*Infopaq I*), [27] and [28]; *Deckmyn and Vrijheidsfonds*, Case C-201/13, 3 September 2014, ECLI:EU:C:2014:2132 (*Deckmyn*), [14] and [15].

[30] *Infopaq International A/S v Danske Dagblades Forening*, Case C-5/08, 16 July 2009, ECLI:EU:C:2009:465 (*Infopaq I*), [39]; *Football Association Premier League and Others*, Joint Cases C-403/08 and C-429/08, 4 October 2011, ECLI:EU:C:2011:631 (*FAPL*), [159].

sense that it is the author's own intellectual creation.[31] The Court of Justice has developed a broad, non-exhaustive approach towards protectable subject matter: what can attract protection under copyright is the 'author's own intellectual creation'.

The *Infopaq I* test

The leading approach in determining what amounts to the 'author's own intellectual creation' was developed in *Infopaq I*.[32] The copyright use at issue involved the storage and subsequent printing of eleven-word extracts from daily newspapers. The facts of the case are well known. Infopaq is a Danish company that delivers summaries of articles of daily newspapers. The selection of articles took place by means of a data capture process that relied on search criteria chosen by its customers. As part of this process, Infopaq scanned the publications and processed them by creating TIFF (Tagged Image File Format) files that were subsequently converted into text files and stored on its computers. A data capture process followed: the five words coming before and after the search word were captured, essentially creating an extract of eleven words. Among the questions referred to the Court of Justice from the Højesteret (the Danish Supreme Court) was whether the reproduction of such extracts might be considered as acts of reproduction within the meaning of Article 2 of the Information Society Directive. The court held that parts of a work are protected by copyright to the extent that they share the originality of the whole work by incorporating elements that are the expression of the intellectual creation of the author. A work is an expressive object resulting from its author's free creative choices and bearing the personal mark of the author. According to the court:

> copyright ... is liable to apply only in relation to a subject-matter which is original in the sense that it is its author's own intellectual creation.[33]

Certain isolated sentences of, or extracts from, newspaper articles may meet this condition and therefore benefit from the exclusive reproduction right. Although it would be for the national court to decide if that was the case with the eleven-word passages extracted by Infopaq,[34] the Court of Justice further stated that, because

---

[31] *Football Association Premier League and Others*, Joint Cases C-403/08 and C-429/08, 4 October 2011, ECLI:EU:C:2011:631 (*FAPL*), [97].

[32] *Infopaq International A/S v Danske Dagblades Forening*, Case C-5/08, 16 July 2009, ECLI:EU:C:2009:465 (*Infopaq I*).

[33] Ibid., [37].

[34] The Danish Supreme Court ruled on the matter in 2013 and held that eleven words are their author's own intellectual creation and hence works protected by copyright http://copyrightblog. kluweriplaw.com/2013/05/17/denmark-infopaq-case-finally-decided-after-eight-years/, accessed 11 November 2019.

the eleven-word extracts were being reproduced over multiple searches, said passages could cumulate and result in the reproduction of lengthy parts of the articles and, therefore, may indeed contain elements conveying the author's intellectual creation.[35]

The Court of Justice developed a *de minimis* rule by holding that individual words are not entitled to copyright because they 'are not as such an intellectual creation of the author who employs them'.[36] According to the Court of Justice, 'it is only through the choice, sequence, and combination of ... words that the author may express his creativity in an original manner and achieve a result which is an intellectual creation'.[37] Implicit in this finding is the affirmation that single words do not meet the first step of the *Infopaq I* test and an authorial work cannot subsist in them. This does not apply, however, to phrases that are capable of expressing an author's own intellectual creation and hence of attracting copyright protection.

In *Infopaq I*, the Court of Justice developed a test for identifying a protected work, consisting of two steps: an examination of whether the subject matter at issue can leave scope for free and creative choices on behalf of the author, and a determination of the extent to which the author exploited that scope towards the creation of a work. In other words, the test aims to establish whether the subject matter and the method of its creation are capable of attracting copyright protection. The concept of the author's own intellectual creation has thereinafter been elevated into both the definition of protectable subject matter and the test to determine whether the work is sufficiently original to attract protection.

The *Infopaq I* legacy

The requirement of the author's own intellectual creation has been discussed and further enriched in other cases that reached the Court of Justice. In *Football Association Premier League and Others* (*FAPL*), protection was denied to sporting events because they 'cannot be regarded as intellectual creations classifiable as works'[38] and are so constrained by the 'rules of the game' as to leave 'no room for creative freedom for the purposes of copyright'. It did subsist, however, in other kinds of creations, including graphic user interfaces,[39] football fixture

---

[35] *Infopaq International A/S v Danske Dagblades Forening*, Case C-5/08, 16 July 2009, ECLI:EU:C:2009:465 (*Infopaq I*), [50].

[36] Ibid., [45].

[37] Ibid.

[38] *Football Association Premier League and Others*, Joint Cases C-403/08 and C-429/08, 4 October 2011, ECLI:EU:C:2011:631 (*FAPL*).

[39] An interesting outcome was reached in *Bezpečnostní softwarová*, a case involving graphic user interfaces. The question at issue was whether such interfaces could be copyright protected. The Court of Justice held that an interface could be protected in its own right (and not as a computer program) as an original work if it was its 'author's own intellectual creation'. *Bezpečnostní softwarová asociace - Svaz*

lists,[40] programming languages, and the format of data files in computer programs.[41] These categories of works were held to be eligible for copyright protection insofar as they are their author's own intellectual creation.

The harmonization of the concept of work after *Infopaq I* had significant impact at three levels. First, it broadened the notion of protectable subject matter to what fits under the umbrella term the 'author's own intellectual creation'. Alongside the reasoning in *Levola*, this is likely to have an impact on those Member States that traditionally used different criteria to frame protectable subject matter, such as Cyprus, Ireland, and the United Kingdom.[42] The exhaustive approach followed in those Member States will arguably require rethinking and, in order to be brought into line with the author's own intellectual creation test, such national criteria may have to be reassessed. Second, *Infopaq I* affirmed that protection can subsist in an extract of eleven words. Although there is no minimum length requirement for copyright protection, this affirmation has significant impact with regards to online copyright infringement. The scope of defences premised on the argument that copyright does not subsist in a work and that therefore infringement did not take place is severely restricted. For instance, extremely short extracts can qualify for protection and thus the re-publication of headlines, tweets, or a couple of seconds of a musical or audiovisual work can, in principle, amount to infringement. This could also include titles and catchphrases which are traditionally excluded from protection in some Member States such as the United Kingdom. Third, the new condition of the author's own intellectual creation does not only affect the concept of work as protected subject matter, but also influences the conditions under which a work is protectable, i.e. the originality requirement and the notion of authorship. As will be seen below, the standard has been introduced alongside a new concept of originality, according to which a work is more likely to be found original when it results from its author's 'free and creative choices'. In this light, originality brings forward the concept of authorship and uniqueness of the authorial input. Member States that do not require creativity as part of the originality standard may have to reconsider their laws in light of this satellite requirement.

---

softwarové ochrany v Ministerstvo kultury, Case C-393/09, 22 December 2010, ECLI:EU:C:2010:816 (*BSA*), [46].

[40] *Football Dataco Ltd, Football Association Premier League Ltd, Football League Ltd, Scottish Premier League Ltd, Scottish Football League, PA Sport UK Ltd v Yahoo! UK Ltd, Stan James (Abingdon) Ltd, Stan James plc, Enetpulse ApS*, Case C-604/10, 1 March 2012, ECLI:EU:C:2012:115 (*Football Dataco*), [29]–[45].

[41] *SAS Institute Inc v World Programming Inc*, Case C-406/10, 2 May 2012, ECLI:EU:C:2012:259 (*SAS Institute*), [45].

[42] See in this regard Isabella Alexander, 'The Concept of Reproduction and the "Temporary and Transient" Exception' (2009) 68(3) *The Cambridge Law Journal* 520; Estelle Derclaye, 'Infopaq International A/S v. Danske Dagblades Forening (C-5/08): Wonderful or Worrisome? The Impact of the ECJ Ruling in Infopaq on UK Copyright Law' (2010) 32(5) *European Intellectual Property Review* 247; Jonathan Griffiths, 'Infopaq, BSA and the "Europeanisation" of United Kingdom Copyright Law' (2011) 16 *Media & Arts Law Review* 59.

Originality in an author's own intellectual creation: the test in steps

The requirement of an author's own intellectual creation is construed by a number of parameters as the doctrine of the Court of Justice indicates. The emphasis that the work ought to be the *author's* own reflects the emphasis on the personal stamp criterion developed in *Painer*. In this case, a photographic portrait was found to be capable of being an authorial work on the ground that its author can make 'free and creative choices in several ways and at various points in its production' in order to 'stamp the work created with his "personal touch"'.[43] The court held that the 'realistic image' of a photograph does not mean that the scope or depth of protection is limited. A photograph will attract copyright protection insofar as its author has consciously influenced the final visual output by leaving his personal touch on the photograph.

Works that do not bear such a personal stamp of their author cannot attract protection, hence claims of infringement in any of these works cannot be successfully substantiated. A number of computer-generated works would fall into this category, including search results, automated translations, CCTV recordings, computer-generated music, satellite images, or photographs created via automatically generated alterations on mobile applications.[44] Subsistence negating claims targeting such works are likely to have a successful outcome. The work also ought to be the author's *own* in that it should originate from the author and not be the product of copying. This aspect stresses a fact/information dichotomy, in that commonplace elements or factual information will be excluded from protection. The idea/expression dichotomy, discussed in detail in Chapter 3, is flagged in the requirement of an intellectual *creation* in the sense that protection will subsist in something that the author brings into existence.[45] This excludes mere thoughts or unexpressed ideas from protection. Single words or works of a rather short length (e.g. too short or too descriptive to bear the imprint of the author's personality) are also excluded. *Painer* also instructs that an important constituent of the test is the free and creative choices that the author made during the creative process: these would define the work as an *intellectual* creation. To some extent, these choices would indicate a degree of individuality in the work, what has been discussed as the test of 'individual character' required for the legal protection of designs. Article 6(2) of the Designs Regulation[46] requires a 'degree of the freedom of the designer'

---

[43] *Eva-Maria Painer v Standard VerlagsGmbH and Others*, Case C-145/10, 1 December 2011, ECLI:EU:C:2011:798 (*Painer*), [92].

[44] Scans like those which take place in mass digitization projects may also be included.

[45] See the definition of the term 'creation' in the Oxford English Dictionary.

[46] Council Regulation (EC) No. 6/2002 of 12 December 2001 on community designs (OJ EC No. L 3 of 5 January 2002), amended by Council Regulation No. 1891/2006 of 18 December 2006 amending Regulations (EC) No. 6/2002 and (EC) No. 40/94 to give effect to the accession of the European Community to the Geneva Act of the Hague Agreement concerning the international registration of industrial designs, OJ EC No. L 386, 29 December 2006, 1–24.

in order to assess a design's 'individual character'. The requirement for an *intellectual* creation incorporates the exclusion available for automatically generated works, but it is a broader concept since it also covers instances where the author exercises merely technical skill or adds functional qualities to the work. This means that mere snapshot photographs will be excluded from protection when not reflective of the creative choices of their author, and the same ought to apply to technical contributions of non-obvious authorial value, perhaps extending to works created through artificial intelligence.

The aforementioned aspects of the requirement of an author's own intellectual creation are cumulative. Establishing that one of these elements is missing can serve as a defence and could go against a finding of copyright infringement as subsistence of copyright cannot be successfully established. These elements have been developed in the rich case law of the Court of Justice and national courts across the European Union and are explored below.

Originality as personal touch

Drawing on the idea that the 'products of the intellect' constitute an expression of the author's person, it is often argued that the work may be seen as an 'expression' of 'the author's personality'.[47] Because works are an extension of the *persona* of the author, they deserve protection. These arguments are reflected in the way the object of protection is construed in several jurisdictions, mainly continental Europe, where copyright protection is premised on the belief that the relationship between the author and the work is what ought to be protected.[48] In Germany, for instance, copyright (*Urheberrecht*) does not protect the author nor the work as such; according to section 11 of the *Urheberrechtsgesetz* (Act on Copyright and Related Rights), copyright protects 'the author in his intellectual and personal relationship to the work and in his exploitation of the work'. By granting exclusive rights to the author, the author's right secures the *intellectual tie* that links the author to the work.[49]

Serving as proof of such a tie, a work receives protection insofar as it reflects the personality of its author. Even though such a standard of protection can be interpreted in various ways,[50] this requirement is in force in most civil law

---

[47] *Blackburn v ARC Ltd* [1998] Env LR 469. See also in this respect Maurizio Borghi and Stavroula Karapapa 'Non-Display Uses of Digital Works: Google Books and Beyond' (2011) 1(1) *Queen Mary Journal of Intellectual Property* 21, 35.

[48] With reference to the originality requirement and the personality theories see Abraham Drassinower, 'Sweat of the Brow, Creativity, and Authorship' (2003–4) 1 *University of Ottawa Law & Technology Journal* 105.

[49] This reference to the work differentiates the author's right from the general right of personality, while, owing to the reference to personality, the author's right is distinguished from the type of protection the law bestows on historical buildings and monuments. Haimo Schack, *Urheber- und Urheberverstragsrecht* (Tübingen: Mohr Siebeck, 2010, 5 Auflage) § 339.

[50] To Ginsburg, the reasoning followed in scenarios where authorship needs to be determined is peculiar: 'The courts appear to think it through as follows: "Were we to find authorship in this instance, then the consequence would be X, and, as X is an undesirable result, plaintiff cannot be an author".'

countries.[51] In continental Europe, courts regularly incant that a work is original and hence protected when it bears 'the imprint of its author's personality'.[52] Nonetheless, it is very rarely that courts hold content to this standard and most often they elucidate whether or not a work bears this imprint in a conclusionary fashion.[53] In Belgium, for instance, there is a long-standing judicial tradition under which the work to be protected should bear the 'stamp' of its author's personality,[54] even though more recent jurisprudence of the Belgian Supreme Court seems to have rejected the validity of this standard.[55] In Slovakia, to be eligible for copyright protection a work must be doctrinally the unique outcome of the author's creative intellect and an expression of their personality. On the basis of this doctrinal approach, the Court of Appeal of Bratislava found that a series of newspaper articles were not the 'results of creativity of unrepeatable and unique nature, which would reflect the author's personality', could not attract copyright protection, and hence their free use by the defendants was permissible.[56]

Consistent case law from France also echoes this position.[57] To cite some examples:

Archives as extensive as those of RATP (i.e. public transport in Paris and Île-de-France) material are, by definition, scattered. They are prepared by different persons under different conditions and on different dates. Thus, the selection of material which can be connected and arranged in such a way as to form a coherent audiovisual whole, rather than just a series of disconnected images, means the act of choosing from these materials suffices to characterize a work of intellectual

---

See Jane Ginsburg, 'The Concept of Authorship in Comparative Copyright Law' (2003) 52 *DePaul Law Review* 1063.

[51] Strowel, for example, argues that, 'in most European countries, starting with France ... it is understood that originality is the trace of personality that results from the effort of creation'. See Alain Strowel, *Droit d'Auteur et Copyright--Divergentes et Convergentes* (Paris: Librairie Générale de Droit et de Jurisprudente, 1993) 401.

[52] See e.g. RG 08/81955, Supreme Court (Cour de cassation, Chambre criminelle), 4 November 2008 (France).

[53] Jane Ginsburg, 'The Concept of Authorship in Comparative Copyright Law' (2003) 52 *DePaul Law Review* 1063.

[54] See e.g. Supreme Court, 26 January 2012, Nr. C.11.0108.N. 7–8 (Belgium).

[55] Supreme Court, 26 January 2012, Nr. C.11.0108.N. 7–8, 9 (Belgium):

In order to enjoy copyright protection a work does not therefore need to have an 'individual character'. Nor is it required that the work is influenced by the 'personality' of the individual (the author). In order to enjoy copyright protection, the work does not need to bear 'the stamp of the personality of the author'. To enjoy copyright protection, it is enough that the work is original in the sense that it is an intellectual creation of its author. Other or additional conditions may not apply.

[56] *Ecopress v Storin*, Appeals Court, 26 October 2011, 11Co/51/2010 (Slovakia).

[57] See e.g. *Bettina Rheims v M. Jakob Gautel et al*, Supreme Court (Cour de Cassation, Chambre Civile 1) 06-19.021, 13 November 2008 (France). For a comment on this case, see (2009) 40(4) IIC 485–6.

value which is a reflection of the author's personality and is therefore protected under the Act of 11 March 1957.[58]

The quality of the production of an audiovisual work presupposes the perfect command of the choice of the composition, the coordination between images and sound, i.e. a real contribution to the conception or the development of the work which bears the mark of the author's personality.[59]

The standard that holds that a work ought to reflect the author's personality has also influenced the EU construct of the originality requirement. Even though this requirement has only partially been subject to legislative harmonization,[60] it has been addressed by reference to all categories of protected subject matter in *Infopaq I*.[61] It was then *Painer*[62] and *Football Dataco*[63] that determined *how* the requirement of an author's intellectual creation ought to be understood.

In *Painer*,[64] the Court of Justice stressed that the work ought to be a reflection of the author's personality. Ruling on photographic works, and in particular on portrait photographs, the court found that an intellectual creation is an author's own if it reflects the author's personality. This occurs where the author, by making free and creative choices, stamps the work with their 'personal touch'.[65] To reach this point, the court cited as an authority Recital 17 of the Term Directive,[66] which reads:

A photographic work within the meaning of the Berne Convention is to be considered original if it is the author's own intellectual creation reflecting his personality, no other criteria such as merit or purpose being taken into account.

[58] *Sàrl Media and Others v Gerard Scher and Another*, Cour d'Appel (Court of Appeal), Paris, 12 December 1995 [1998] ECC 101, 106–7 (France).

[59] *Cadys Sosnowski v Didier Courtoux, Mazarine Pingeot, Gilbert Mitterand, Jean-Christophe Mitterand, Jean-Pierre Elkabbach, Société Nationale de Television France 2 Maison de France Television and Nil 2001*, Tribunal de Grande Instance de Paris (Third Chamber), RG: 01/16399, 16 September 2003, [2004] ECDR 311, 314 (France).

[60] Database Directive (Directive 96/9/EC), Art. 3 (databases which, 'by reason of the selection or arrangement of their contents, constitute the author's own intellectual creation' are protected by copyright)); Term Directive (Directive 93/98/EEC), Rec. 17 (which later became Recital 16 of Directive 2006/116/EC of the European Parliament and of the Council of 12 December 2006 on the term of protection of copyright and certain related rights, OJ L 372, 27 December 2006).

[61] *Infopaq International A/S v Danske Dagblades Forening*, Case C-5/08, 16 July 2009, ECLI:EU:C:2009:465 (*Infopaq I*).

[62] *Eva-Maria Painer v Standard VerlagsGmbH and Others*, Case C-145/10, 1 December 2011, ECLI:EU:C:2011:798 (*Painer*).

[63] *Football Dataco Ltd, Football Association Premier League Ltd, Football League Ltd, Scottish Premier League Ltd, Scottish Football League, PA Sport UK Ltd v Yahoo! UK Ltd, Stan James (Abingdon) Ltd, Stan James plc, Enetpulse ApS*, Case C-604/10, 1 March 2012, ECLI:EU:C:2012:115 (*Football Dataco*).

[64] *Eva-Maria Painer v Standard VerlagsGmbH and Others*, Case C-145/10, 1 December 2011, ECLI:EU:C:2011:798 (*Painer*).

[65] Ibid., [87]–[92]. See e.g. [92]: 'By making those various choices, the author of a portrait photograph can stamp the work created with his "personal touch".'

[66] Council Directive 93/98/EEC of 29 October 1993 harmonizing the term of protection of copyright and certain related rights, OJ L 290, 24 November 1993 (later Recital 16 of Directive 2006/116/EC).

Portrait photographs can attract copyright to the extent that this legal requirement is met.

The 'personal touch stamp' criterion has been repeated by the Court of Justice in *Football Dataco*,[67] where the court held that, with regards to databases, the

> criterion of originality is satisfied when, through the selection or arrangement of the data which it contains, its author expresses his creative ability in an original manner by making free and creative choices ... and thus stamps his 'personal touch'.[68]

Cases heard in national courts after the determination of the concept of originality at the EU level affirm that originality is likely to be established where the work is its author's own intellectual creation reflecting the author's creative choices. In France, for instance, the Supreme Court[69] found that lower courts should take into consideration all the choices that the author made in order to determine whether the work is original and hence copyright protected. Originality ought to be assessed as a whole by reference to all the different elements that make up the work, despite the fact that some of these may be common, simple, or already known.

In this light, creativity serves as a sorting tool: to attract protection a work needs to reflect the author's 'free and creative choices'. It does not have to be new or possess aesthetic quality or merit. The work should reflect the expression of its author's intellectual effort which can afford individual character to the work.[70] What is more, the work need not be novel and the requirement of statistical uniqueness, which has been used as a criterion for protection in some jurisdictions such as Switzerland, is not part of the originality threshold under the 'author's own intellectual creation' criterion. A work can even be a compilation using widely available data on condition that their selection, omission, and/or presentation are original.[71]

For literary works, the author's free and creative choices are reflected in the selection, sequence, and combination of words,[72] whereas for photographs

---

[67] *Football Dataco Ltd, Football Association Premier League Ltd, Football League Ltd, Scottish Premier League Ltd, Scottish Football League, PA Sport UK Ltd v Yahoo! UK Ltd, Stan James (Abingdon) Ltd, Stan James plc, Enetpulse ApS, Case C-604/10, 1 March 2012, ECLI:EU:C:2012:115 (Football Dataco).*

[68] Ibid., [38].

[69] 'Aïcha', Supreme Court (Cour de Cassation, Chambre Civile 1) 14-11944, 30 September 2015 (France).

[70] See e.g. *Desch. v Société anonyme Etablissements Lachaussée*, Supreme Court (Cour de Cassation), 27 April 1989 (Belgium) (where the Supreme Court found that the Belgian Copyright Act protects any literary, scientific, and artistic work that bears the imprint of its author's personality. To be protected, a photographic work should express the intellectual effort of its author, that gives the work its individual character); Supreme Court of Hungary (Magyar Köztársaság Legfelsőbb Bíróság), 1980 (Hungary) (where the Supreme Court found that every literary work that bears the mark of originality as a result of the intellectual activity of its creator benefits from copyright protection. The protection is irrespective of aesthetic judgments related to the work).

[71] Supreme Court, I CK 281/05, 25 January 2006, OSNC 2006, nr 11, poz. 1 (Poland).

[72] *Infopaq International A/S v Danske Dagblades Forening*, Case C-5/08, 16 July 2009, ECLI:EU:C:2009:465 (*Infopaq I*).

such choices are to do with the fixing of the background, lighting, framing, the choice of angle and atmosphere, and the use of techniques or computer software.[73] Photos which are the result of a purely mechanical and automatic process have been excluded from copyright protection[74] as the standard of protection requires creative engagement with the final output. Although this is arguably a low standard of protection, the Court of Justice has denied copyright subsistence to features of a work that are predetermined by technique or function and hence do not result from free and creative choices.[75] Challenging the originality or authorship of a work on the basis that a work is not its author's own intellectual creation can serve as a defence against allegations of infringement.

Originality and authorship

A defence targeting subsistence could emerge from the possibility that the plaintiff is not the author of the work that the alleged copyright infringement pertains to. Creativity is an important element through which the author reflects personal choices in the creation of the work. In various instances, the Court of Justice has held that the author, in order to develop his or her own intellectual creation, ought to have 'express[ed] his creativity in an original manner'.[76] This raises the threshold of protection: originality has to do with source and origin.[77] An intellectual creation should be, in the court's vernacular, the 'author's own'. Jurisprudence is rich with statements of this nature, especially in the common law tradition. For instance, in *Walter v Lane*—despite the low standard of authorship developed in this case that is probably no longer sustainable after *Infopaq* and *Painer*, Lord Davey held that 'it is a sound principle that a man shall not avail himself of another's skill, labour, and expense by copying the written product thereof'.[78] This standard, which precedes but can enlighten the 'author's own' test, is also well summarized in the opinion

---

[73] *Eva-Maria Painer v Standard VerlagsGmbH and Others*, Case C-145/10, 1 December 2011, ECLI:EU:C:2011:798 (*Painer*), [91].

[74] Court of Appeals Coimbra (Tribunal da Relação de Coimbra), 10 May 2011 (Portugal).

[75] *Bezpečnostní softwarová asociace - Svaz softwarové ochrany v Ministerstvo kultury*, Case C-393/09, 22 December 2010, ECLI:EU:C:2010:816 (*BSA*), [48]–[49]; *Football Association Premier League Ltd v QC Leisure* and *Karen Murphy v Media Protection Services Ltd*, Joined Cases C-403/08 and C-429/08, 4 October 2011, ECLI:EU:C:2011:631 (*FAPL*), [98]; *Football Dataco Ltd, Football Association Premier League Ltd, Football League Ltd, Scottish Premier League Ltd, Scottish Football League, PA Sport UK Ltd v Yahoo! UK Ltd, Stan James (Abingdon) Ltd, Stan James plc, Enetpulse ApS*, Case C-604/10, 1 March 2012, ECLI:EU:C:2012:115 (*Football Dataco*); *SAS Institute Inc v World Programming Ltd*, Case C-406/10, 2 May 2012, ECLI:EU:C:2012:259 (*SAS Institute*), [39].

[76] *Infopaq International A/S v Danske Dagblades Forening*, Case C-5/08, 16 July 2009, ECLI:EU:C:2009:465 (*Infopaq I*); *Bezpečnostní softwarová asociace - Svaz softwarové ochrany v Ministerstvo kultury*, Case C-393/09, 22 December 2010, ECLI:EU:C:2010:816 (*BSA*), [50].

[77] See indicatively *Ladbroke (Football) Limited v Williams Hill (Football) Limited* [1964] 1 WLR 273 (UK) (originality does not mean the work must be the expression of original or inventive thought, but rather that the work originates from the author).

[78] *Walter v Lane* [1900] AC 539, 552 (UK).

of the board given by Lord Atkinson in *MacMillan & Co Ltd v Cooper*,[79] which was concerned with copyright in textbooks which contain excerpts from existing works, with notes for students.[80] Lord Atkinson stated that

> it is the product of the labour, skill, and capital of one man which must not be appropriated by another, not the elements, the raw material, if one may use the expression, upon which the labour and skill and capital of the first have been expended.[81]

[79] *MacMillan & Co Ltd v Cooper* (1924) 40 TLR 186 (UK).

[80] In the United States too, natural rights arguments started featuring in statutory language very early in copyright history. This approach views the work as the product of the labour of a particular creator or producer. A person who labours on resources that are either unowned or 'held in common' has a natural property right to the fruits of their efforts. For instance, in the preambles of some acts the justification for copyright is outlined along these lines: 'there being no property more peculiarly a man's own than that which is procured by the labour of his mind.' See e.g. Mass. Act of Mar. 17, 1783, reprinted in U.S. Copyright Office, *Copyright Enactments of the United States, 1783-1906* (Washington: GPO, 1906, 2nd edn) 14–15. Similar arguments have also been raised in other contexts during the implementation of other acts: See e.g. Letter from D.P. Lewandowski, M.D., to Senator Alfred B. Kittredge, Chairman of the Senate Committee on Patents (5 June 1906), reprinted in U.S. Copyright Office, *Copyright Enactments of the United States, 1783-1906* (Washington: GPO, 1906, 2nd edn) 59 (complaining of 'piracy' by phonographic reproduction: 'I feel how dreadful it is in general to suffer and to be deprived of remuneration or the just and intelligent inventive brain work which a man produces by his genius.'). The US Supreme Court often uses a similar vocabulary. For example, Justice Reed ended his opinion in *Mazer v Stein* with the following statement: 'Sacrificial days devoted to … creative activities deserve rewards commensurate with the services rendered.' 347 US 201, 219 (1954) (US). In *Harper & Row*, the Court, again, acknowledged that 'the rights conferred by copyright are designed to assure contributors to the store of knowledge a fair return for their labors.' *Harper & Row*, 471 US 546–7 (US). Lower court opinions and appellate arguments often follow the same position (see in this regard Stewart E. Sterk, 'Rhetoric and Reality in Copyright Law' (1996) 94 *Michigan Law Review* 1197; Alfred C. Yen, 'Restoring the Natural Law: Copyright as Labor and Possession' (1990) 51 *Ohio State Law Journal* 517; Lloyd Weinreb, 'Copyright for Functional Expression' (1998) 111 *Harvard Law Review* 1149, 1211–14), and proponents of legislative extensions of copyright protection routinely argue that: 'the one who creates something of value is entitled to enjoy the fruits of his labor.' See Testimony of Elizabeth Janeway, Copyright Law Revision: Hearings on HR 4347, 5680, 6831, 6835 before Subcomm. No. 3 of the House Comm. on the Judiciary, 89th Cong., 1st Sess. (1965), reprinted in George S. Grossman, *Omnibus Copyright Revision Legislative History* (1976) 5 Hein 100. The work is 'what is worth copying' (as in Peterson J's famous quote in *University of London Press v University Tutorial Press* [1916] 2 Ch 601 (UK)), i.e. what is worth producing by saving one's own labour and intellectual effort. Albeit the sweat of the brow standard features in many instances in copyright history, it is no longer judicially recognized and supported in a pure form. See *Feist Publications, Inc v Rural Telephone Service Co.*, 499 U.S. 340 (1991) (US).
    Under this approach, a work is protected if this work is 'not copied', in the sense that it has been produced by spending *own* effort. It is commonly recognized that this approach is more inclined to allow the protection of works whose creation merely involves physical labour or investment, or in other words 'sweat of the brow'. As Drassinower puts it, the concern behind this standard, also referred to as the *effort and labour* standard, 'is not "authorship" in any special sense, but rather the "grievous injustice" involved in the misappropriation of another's effort'. In this light, this standard is 'part and parcel of a view of copyright as a remedy for the misappropriation of labour'. According to Drassinower, underlying this standard is a 'refusal to distinguish the labour of production from the labour of authorship' that 'goes hand in hand with a parallel insistence that the purpose of copyright is not to protect the specific labour of authorship—whatever that may mean—but rather the labour of production per se.' See Abraham Drassinower, 'Sweat of the Brow, Creativity, and Authorship: On Originality in Canadian Copyright Law' (2003–4) 1 *University of Ottawa Law & Technology Journal* 105.

[81] *MacMillan & Co Ltd v Cooper* (1924) 40 TLR 186, 188 (UK).

Originality, individuality, and uniqueness

The concept of statistical uniqueness was discussed in a number of cases in continental Europe before *Infopaq I*, where originality was not only found to mean that the work ought to bear the author's personal stamp,[82] it was also necessary for a work to be 'statistically unique', i.e. distinct in comparison to the existing array of works. This higher degree of originality could serve as a defensive rule in that not all works could meet the requirement of statistical uniqueness in order to attract copyright protection and enable their authors to bring in successful claims for copyright infringement. This is no longer the test, however, following the case law from the Court of Justice.

To some extent, the concept of statistical uniqueness was discussed alongside the requirement that the work must be the imprint of the author's personality. Although no longer the test in the European Union, it helps understand the requirement that the work ought to reflect the personality and personal choices of the author.In the *Bob Marley* case in Switzerland, the Supreme Court held that a work ought to be unique in that it should possess certain distinctive characteristics compared to existing protected works in order to receive protection. During a 1978 concert in Santa Barbara, a photographer took pictures of Bob Marley and in one of those photographs Bob Marley was depicted laterally, holding a microphone. The iconic black-and-white photograph was dominated by the artist's dreadlocks, which—following a fast movement of the head—whirled around his head. Under the 1992 Swiss Copyright Act, it sufficed for a work to be protected if it was 'statistically unique' and there was no requirement that the work should depict the author's personality or personal stamp. The Supreme Court found that even snapshot photographs are eligible for copyright protection if they are statistically unique and it is immaterial whether the photographer took the time and effort to arrange the photograph, choose the object, and decide the right time to press the button.[83] Under the 'author's own intellectual creation' test, however, it is precisely such considerations that would make the test. Even under a mechanical application of the 'author's own intellectual creation' test the outcome would have arguably been the same, although via different reasoning.[84]

This position was partially upheld and partially rejected in another Swiss case.[85] The case concerned a photograph depicting Mr Meili, a night watchman for a Swiss bank, holding two tomes containing the minutes of meetings of the board of

---

[82] See e.g. *Rudolph Jan Romme v Van Dale Lexicografie*, Supreme Court (Hoge Raad), NJ 1991/608, 4 January 1991 (Netherlands); '*Bob Marley*', Federal Supreme Court (Bundesgericht),130 III 168 (Switzerland).

[83] Federal Supreme Court (Bundesgericht), 5 September 2003 (Switzerland).

[84] Taking into account the interpretation of the requirement that the work ought to be the 'author's own intellectual creation' as developed in *Painer*, it is likely that the Court of Justice would have given emphasis to the various creative choices that the photographer had to make in order to produce the photograph at issue.

[85] '*Watchman Meili*', Federal Supreme Court (Bundesgericht), 19 April 2004 (Switzerland).

directors from the document shredding room of the bank. This event was widely reported by the media in connection with the debate about dormant accounts of Holocaust victims. The BBC used the photograph for its documentary *Nazi Gold* without permission. The Swiss Supreme Court found that copyright protection in a photograph is determined independently of the circumstances under which a picture was taken,[86] and that, at the same time, the uniqueness of the subject of a photograph does not automatically lead to copyright protection. A photograph may obtain its individual character from the choice or selection of its object, without this indicating that any photograph of a subject that is unique in the world—such as the last specimen of a bird species that is dying out—can attract copyright protection *ipso facto*. Rather, the subject must be chosen as an element of composition, which for its part lends the photograph its unique character. Upholding the *Bob Marley* decision, the court affirmed that a work does not necessarily need to bear the author's own personal stamp insofar as it exhibits statistical uniqueness. However, the fact that the photographer in the present case was 'at the right place at the right time' to take the picture, despite being a journalistic accomplishment, did not automatically result in copyright protection for the picture, as it did not demonstrate individual expression of thought. Hence, it was irrelevant that it took the plaintiff a long time to persuade Mr Meili to take part in the photo shoot and to pose in the manner he did. Similarly, it did not matter that the photographer had recognized the historic dimension of this case, which attracted worldwide attention, and that she had the idea to document the event by taking photographs. It is likely that the outcome reached in this case would have been different through the application of the 'author's own intellectual creation' test, especially as developed in *Painer*, as all the creative choices and efforts of the photographer would have counted towards a finding of originality in the work. Journalistic photographs, such as the one in the *Nazi Gold* case, would normally attract protection under the 'author's own intellectual creation' test.

It is unlikely that the Court of Justice, under the test of the 'author's own intellectual creation', especially in the particular way in which it was defined in *Painer*, by effectively focusing on the author's creative choices would have refused copyright in photographs such as the one in the *Bob Marley* or the *Nazi Gold* cases. However, because of the emphasis on the creativity and personal touch element, it is logical to assume that trivial or too obvious creations that do not reflect the author's creative choices shall not receive protection,[87] both because the works lack originality

---

[86] *'Bob Marley'*, Federal Supreme Court (Bundesgericht), 130 III 168 (Switzerland).

[87] This is in line with the traditional understanding of originality in most Member States. See e.g. *Express Newspapers plc v News (UK) Ltd* [1990] 1 WLR 1320 (UK) (skill and labour need not be directed to the creation of a mode of expression, but can be deduced from the choice of what should be included in the work). However, the approach of statistical uniqueness, which echoes to a large extent the position followed traditionally in some EU Member States, such as France and Greece, no longer seems to align with the jurisprudence of the Court of Justice that seems to have shifted the emphasis on the creative choices reflecting the authorial personal touch.

and because such a contribution would not be of an authorial nature. It is not likely that the images in the referred cases, e.g. in the *Bob Marley* case, would be considered trivial or obvious as this would negate the value resting in journalistic images depicting current events. This, however, would not be the case by reference to purely functional elements or those of a merely technical nature.

Technical contributions are insufficient

National case law—before and after *Infopaq I*—consistently indicates that input of a mere technical or functional nature is excluded from protection, making allowance for defensive claims which target the technical nature of a work. This could include automated translations or other subject matter created through algorithms. There are numerous cases where subsistence for works that are the result of technical contribution or where the contribution was not of the right kind, were refused protection and allegations of infringement could not be substantiated. Even though certain kinds of works such as computer programs may receive protection despite their functional purpose or technical outcome, elements of a work that are meant to serve a merely technical function cannot receive protection.

When deciding whether or not a contribution to a work is copyright protected or not, courts would distinguish creative activities from those of a merely technical or ancillary character. It is only creative activities that can attract copyright protection,[88] in a sense, aligning with the 'personal choices' discussion by the Court of Justice. Pre-*Infopaq I*, for instance, the District Court of Cologne[89] found that creating a virtual second life model based on photographs does not meet the requirements of copyright protection. Adapting photographs by correcting perspectives, modifying brightness, and selecting sections was considered to be a mere technical achievement. In this light, the work at issue could not meet the requirement of 'personal intellectual creation' featured in Article 2(2) of the German Copyright Act and by being excluded from protection, copyright infringement could not be established. Protection is, therefore, about original products of intellect, triggered by the unique personality of the author as reflected through the personal choices made in the creative process.

A specific instance of functional contributions is the case of typographical arrangements of printed editions. This latter kind of copyright work can attract copyright protection on its own in some jurisdictions,[90] with copyright resting in the layout and arrangement of text on a page.[91] Although copyright of a typographical

---

[88] *Miroslaw M. and Jacek S. v Zbigniew B.*, Supreme Court (Sąd Najwyższy), 5 July 2002 (Poland).

[89] 'Virtual Dome of Cologne', District Court Cologne (Landgericht Köln), 21 April 2008 (Germany).

[90] Expressly so in the United Kingdom (see s. 1(1)(c), Copyright, Designs and Patents Act 1988 (CDPA)); also in Ireland (see s. 17(2)(c), Copyright and Related Rights Act 2000).

[91] *Newspaper Licensing Agency v Marks and Spencer*, House of Lords, 12 July 2001, [2001] UKHL 38, [2002] RPC 4, [2001] ECDR 28, [2001] ECC 52, [2001] 3 All ER 977, [2003] 1 AC 551, (2001) 24(9) IPD 24055, [2001] 3 WLR 290, [2001] EMLR 43 (UK).

arrangement subsists in newspapers or other printed editions as a whole, when it comes to the taking of a part of a work, what matters is quality rather than quantity. The relevant quality is the literary originality of the work or, for an artistic work, the artistic originality that is determined by reference to the skill and labour involved in its creation. The same principles apply to typographical arrangements, the only difference being that the copying must be facsimile copying.

There are a wealth of cases from national courts which interpret the criterion of the author's own intellectual creation as developed in *Infopaq I*. In the Netherlands, the Supreme Court held that the famous children's toy, Rubik's Cube, could not benefit from copyright protection.[92] Litigation started when Mr Rubik brought a claim for infringement against Beckx Trading & Co BV, a company trading another toy, the Magic Cube. Affirming the position of the Arnhem Court of Appeal, the Supreme Court held that the Rubik's Cube was not protected by copyright on the basis that elements of a work that are meant to serve a mere technical function are excluded from protection. The same applies to elements that were implemented by the work merely because of particular technical requirements. In this light, the finding that copyright did not subsist in the work at issue brings to mind the exclusions applicable to shape trade marks that serve a technical function,[93] the rationale being to preserve a robust public domain. As with trade mark law, copyright seems reluctant to affirm protection to merely technical contributions and there is a need for a creative input for works to qualify for protection. In this regard, the exclusion of subject matter from protection on this ground can serve as a defence against allegations of infringement.

The criterion that the 'author's intellectual creation' does not include contributions of a mere technical or functional nature has also been upheld by other Member States too. In 2014, the Polish Supreme Court,[94] in a case concerning the design of grave lights, held that the creator's personality (his personal stamp), reflected in the work of authorship, differentiated the creation from other, similar intellectual creations and, in this light, the work resulted from an intellectual process which was neither the product of a mere technical nature nor the result of the implementation of planned functional requirements. Rather, the author had freedom to choose a specific concept and the resulting outcome differed from other creations.

Although mere technical contributions are not protected, a compilation of functional elements could, in principle, attract protection. In a case concerning a website, the French Supreme Court[95] quashed a judgment of the Court of Appeal

---

[92] *Rubik v Beckx Trading*, Supreme Court of the Netherlands, 19 September 2014, ECLI:NL:HR:2014:2737 (Netherlands); regarding the trade mark protection of the shape of the cube see *Simba Toys GmbH & Co. KG v EUIPO*, Case C-30/15 P, 10 November 2016, ECLI:EU:C:2016:849.

[93] *Koninklijke Philips Electronics NV v Remington Consumer Products Ltd*, Case C-299/99, 18 June 2002, ECLI:EU:C:2002:377.

[94] Supreme Court of Poland, V CSK 202/13, 6 March 2014 (Poland).

[95] Supreme Court (Cour de Cassation, Chambre civile 1) 12 May 2011, 10-17852 (France).

of Paris[96] which had ruled against the website's originality on the basis that its elements were either merely utilitarian or functional. The Court of Appeal had merely listed the elements of the website that did not 'exhibit a creative effort', that were 'not aesthetic', and not 'separable from their functional purpose'. In line with *Infopaq I*, the Supreme Court found that the Court of Appeal did not justify how the choice to put all of these elements together in combination lacked originality. The element of authorial choice was also paramount here and capable of affording copyright protection to the design of the website, effectively rejecting defensive claims based on the negation of subsistence requirements.

Originality in derivative works

One of the most profound instances in which the requirement for the author's 'personal choices' is exemplified is the case of derivative works. Before the launch of the 'author's own intellectual creation' test from the Court of Justice, national case law would stress the need for additional authorial input in the creation of the derivative work. Readers will remember the *Sawkins* case in the United Kingdom where copyright was found to subsist in modern performing editions of out-of-copyright works.[97] A number of pieces by Lalande, a seventeenth-century composer, which were previously effectively unplayable, had been adapted into modern notation by Dr Sawkins with minor editing additions. These were published in three performing editions and musicians could thereinafter use these editions in order to make a recording undertaken by Hyperion Records. Mummery LJ found that derivative works are 'original' if sufficient effort, skill, and time is expended in their creation and this would have to be 'in the limited sense that the author originated it by his efforts rather than slavishly copying it from the work produced by the efforts of another person.'[98] Mummery LJ held that

> the effort, skill, and time which ... Dr Sawkins spent in making the 3 performing editions were sufficient to satisfy the requirement that they should be 'original' works in the copyright sense. This is so even though (a) Dr Sawkins worked on the scores of existing musical works composed by another person (Lalande); (b) Lalande's works are out of copyright; and (c) Dr Sawkins had no intention of adding any new notes of music of his own.[99]

---

[96] Court of Appeal of Paris, 17 March 2010, Juris-Data No. 2010-010644 (France).

[97] *Hyperion Records Limited v Sawkins*, Court of Appeal (Civil Division), 19 May 2005, [2005] EWCA Civ 565, [2005] 1 WLR 3281, [2005] EMLR 688 (UK); for a comment, see Anthony Robinson, 'Hyperion Records and Dr Lionel Sawkins: It's Like That and That's the Way it is' (2005) 16(7) *Entertainment Law Review* 191.

[98] *Hyperion Records Limited v Sawkins*, Court of Appeal (Civil Division), 19 May 2005, [2005] EWCA Civ 565, [2005] 1 WLR 3281, [2005] EMLR 688, [31] (UK).

[99] Ibid., [36].

In this regard, a derivative work has the potential to be protected by copyright in its own right as a result of the originality it embodies, irrespective of its dependence on pre-existing content.

Another *Sawkins* case regarding the same kind of performing editions of music by Lalande was heard successfully in France at around the same time that the UK case was discussed;[100] following a different approach under a different law the French courts reached the same outcome, echoing the traditional position of French law with regards to derivative works. Under this approach, a traditional folk work can be protectable by copyright where a new song adds new elements to pre-existing subject matter.[101] The *Sawkins* cases are interesting because the intention of Dr Sawkins was to recreate the works of Lalande in the way that Lalande himself would have completed them, without inserting any creative input to demonstrate his own personality. Even this kind of creative labour, however, was deemed sufficient in order for the resulting works to attract independent copyright. The extent to which this standard would still be good law and compatible with the test of the author's own intellectual creation is uncertain.

It is very likely, however, that courts would have reached similar outcomes under different reasoning. A similar example of derivative work, where the creative freedom of the author is restrained by the very nature of the subject matter at hand, concerns portraits. When the *Painer* case was heard in Austria the Supreme Court held that the digital portrait was a work protected independently by copyright, despite its reliance on a pre-existing photographic portrait of the girl.[102] In reaching this conclusion, the Austrian Supreme Court acknowledged the defendant's limited creative freedom but held that the changes made were substantial and the relevant use qualified as a free use by virtue of Article 5(2) of the Copyright Act.

Adding new elements to a pre-existing work need not only be the reflection of creative input, but can also result from an innovative or transformative exercise, at least as was affirmed in Greece. This could, in principle, include automated translations or photographs that are the result of image manipulation software. In Greece, the collection of traditional music rhythms, created by the application of specially adjusted software and integrated in music cartridges, was found to be sufficiently original and thereinafter protected by copyright.[103] The finding of originality was independent of the fact that the music collection included very popular traditional music rhythms because the plaintiff made personal choices and expressed the traditional rhythm in a creative way. Originality was found to rest within the fact that, due to the specialized application of standard software, a virtual music orchestra,

---

[100] *Sawkins v Harmonia Mundi and Ors*, Nanterre Tribunal de Grande Instance, 19 January 2005 (France).

[101] Supreme Court (Cour de Cassation, Chambre civile 1) 1 July 1970, 68-14189 (France).

[102] 'Natascha K - identikit picture', Supreme Court (Oberster Gerichtshof), 8 July 2008, 4Ob102/08s (Austria).

[103] District Court Athens (Μονομελές Πρωτοδικείο Αθηνών), 30766/1996, ΔΕΕ 1997 (Greece).

formed by different musicians playing different musical instruments, could accompany the user of the synthesizer.

The element of individual creative addition as a condition for a finding of originality by reference to derivative works has also been upheld in Spain. The Spanish Supreme Court defined individuality as creativity in the sense that something original is added to the creation of a third party.[104] There ought to be some intrinsic features within a work, which—despite possible similarities—differentiate it from pre-existing works. This means that there is need for evidence of the existence of another work and that the 'new' work exhibits certain differences. The court denied copyright protection to the idea of a TV show as ideas, processes, systems, operational methods, concepts, principles, and discoveries are not by themselves protected by copyright. Copyright could only be claimed for the script of the TV show.

Although the Court of Justice has not been called to assess copyright subsistence in derivative works, it has to be assumed that the national tests that have been applied to such cases align with the rationale developed in *Painer*.[105] This can be seen as developing a line of defensive rules to the extent that additional creative input has been invested in the creation of a derivative work. Indicative in this regard is the recent ruling of the Court of Justice in *Pelham*,[106] which, although not directly addressing copyright subsistence in derivative works, affirmed that the reproduction right—as defined in Article 2 of the Information Society Directive—allows a phonogram producer to 'prevent another person from taking a sound sample, even if very short, of his or her phonogram for the purposes of including that sample in another phonogram, unless that sample is included in the phonogram in a modified form unrecognisable to the ear.' Such a use is carried out in the exercise of freedom of the arts and as such does not constitute 'reproduction' within the meaning of Article 2(c) of the Information Society Directive.[107] This indicates that once an extract is used in an altered form, the relevant use will not be part of authorial control and, hence, will not amount to infringement.

Defendants who are in a position to demonstrate that they have expended additional creative effort and made relevant choices of authorial nature in the creation of a derivative work will not only be acquitted from infringement, but may also possibly establish copyright protection in their own derivative subject matter. Even though, for certain works, both of these outcomes may be achieved, this cannot be necessarily argued by reference to all derivative works. For instance, translations created automatically through an algorithm[108] may be lawful and not in breach

---

[104] Supreme Court of Justice (Supremo Tribunal de Justiça) 29 April 2010 (Spain).

[105] *Eva-Maria Painer v Standard VerlagsGmbH and Others*, Case C-145/10, 1 December 2011, ECLI:EU:C:2011:798 (*Painer*).

[106] *Pelham GmbH, Moses Pelham, Martin Haas v Ralf Hütter, Florian Schneider-Esleben*, Case C-476/17, 29 July 2019, ECLI:EU:C:2019:624.

[107] Ibid., [31].

[108] E.g. Google's automated translation tool: <https://translate.google.com>.

of copyright, but they may not be in a position to attract copyright protection in their own right as contributions of a mere technical or functional nature.[109] The same ought to apply to automated image transformation tools and other algorithmically generated adaptations of works, but not to outputs created through tools such as raster graphic editors which require human input and creative choices and may, therefore, be eligible to attract independent copyright protection under the 'author's own intellectual creation' test.

Originality in works created through artificial intelligence and computer-generated works more broadly

Interesting questions arise in relation to works created through artificial intelligence. Such works are the result of numerous choices, often of a technical nature, but are these choices of an authorial kind and can non-human authorship arise? A notable example is the Next Rembrandt project,[110] whereby scientists were able to use artificial intelligence in order to create a brand new Rembrandt painting 347 years after the death of the painter. Would it be sufficient to confer the researchers involved in this project authorship over the painting for having mined data from Rembrandt's work and fed it into the relevant algorithms? Similarly, who is the author of Ray Kurzweil's Cybernetic Poet, a project following a similar logic to the Next Rembrandt initiative which used artificial intelligence to distil the style of various poets and produce its own original poem?[111] These questions reflect the controversy of authorship in artificial intelligence settings and raise broader questions on the interpretation of originality as the author's own intellectual creation and in terms of the duration of copyright protection for the life of the author, plus seventy years after their death.

The United Kingdom and Ireland are two of the few jurisdictions that took the decision to address the issue on the basis of express provisions. Computer-generated works are defined as works generated by computer in circumstances where the author of the work is not an individual. Section 9(3) of the UK CDPA and section 21(f) of the Irish Copyright Act[112] clearly state that by reference to computer generated works the author is the person who undertook the necessary arrangements for the creation of the work. In the United Kingdom, the term of protection for such works expires at the end of a period of fifty years from the end of the calendar year in which the work was made,[113] whereas in Ireland protection lasts for seventy years after the date on which the work was first lawfully made

---

[109] See, however, the Greek test of allowing protection to outputs of innovative or transformative nature as developed in District Court Athens (Μονομελές Πρωτοδικείο Αθηνών), 30766/1996, ΔΕΕ 1997 (Greece).

[110] <http://www.nextrembrandt.com>, accessed 11 November 2019.

[111] <http://www.kurzweilcyberart.com/poetry/rkcp_overview.php>, accessed 11 November 2019.

[112] Irish Copyright Act 2000.

[113] Copyright, Designs and Patents Act 1988 (CDPA), s. 12(7); see also in general by reference to the UK *Nova Production v Mazooma Games* [2006] EWHC 24 (Ch) (UK).

available to the public.[114] The United Kingdom clearly excludes moral rights protection on computer-generated works,[115] although Ireland does not seem to include a similarly express provision.

Whereas works created through artificial intelligence can be protected by copyright in Ireland and the United Kingdom, compatibility of these provisions with the EU *acquis* is dubious, especially in light of the 'author's own intellectual creation' test. According to EU copyright, the extent to which protection can be offered to such works is doubtful as it is not possible for these works to be a result of free and creative choices,[116] stamping the personal touch of the author[117] and not merely following rules and instructions.[118] It is likely that such works will not be able to attract copyright in their own right and, as a result, making further free use of such works shall not amount to infringement. Whereas the use of images and other copyright-protected subject matter as part of an artificial intelligence project may be permissible, depending on the context, the output of an artificial intelligence project as computer-generated work will not in itself attract copyright protection and will, therefore, allow free further use of that work. This is in line with the principle of fairness in the application of defensive rules, however, in that once one has made use or re-use of protected content in the process of offering a copy-reliant service, this party should not be allowed to restrict access to the materials they have themselves accessed through a permitted act, or to produce a copy-reliant service, possibly through the creation of new exclusive rights.[119]

---

[114] CDPA, s. 30.

[115] CDPA, ss 78 and 81.

[116] *Infopaq International A/S v Danske Dagblades Forening*, Case C-5/08, 16 July 2009, ECLI:EU:C:2009:465 (*Infopaq I*), [45]; *Bezpečnostní softwarová asociace - Svaz softwarové ochrany v Ministerstvo kultury*, Case C-393/09, 22 December 2010, ECLI:EU:C:2010:816 (*BSA*), [48]–[49]; *Football Dataco Ltd, Football Association Premier League Ltd, Football League Ltd, Scottish Premier League Ltd, Scottish Football League, PA Sport UK Ltd v Yahoo! UK Ltd, Stan James (Abingdon) Ltd, Stan James plc, Enetpulse ApS*, Case C-604/10, 1 March 2012, ECLI:EU:C:2012:115 (*Football Dataco*), [38].

[117] *Eva-Maria Painer v Standard VerlagsGmbH and Others*, Case C-145/10, 1 December 2011, ECLI:EU:C:2011:798 (*Painer*), [92]; *Football Dataco Ltd, Football Association Premier League Ltd, Football League Ltd, Scottish Premier League Ltd, Scottish Football League, PA Sport UK Ltd v Yahoo! UK Ltd, Stan James (Abingdon) Ltd, Stan James plc, Enetpulse ApS*, Case C-604/10, 1 March 2012, ECLI:EU:C:2012:115 (*Football Dataco*), [38].

[118] *Football Association Premier League Ltd v QC Leisure* and *Karen Murphy v Media Protection Services Ltd*, Joined Cases C-403/08 and C-429/08, 4 October 2011, ECLI:EU:C:2011:631 (*FAPL*), [98]; *Football Dataco Ltd, Football Association Premier League Ltd, Football League Ltd, Scottish Premier League Ltd, Scottish Football League, PA Sport UK Ltd v Yahoo! UK Ltd, Stan James (Abingdon) Ltd, Stan James plc, Enetpulse ApS*, Case C-604/10, 1 March 2012, ECLI:EU:C:2012:115 (*Football Dataco*), [39].

The argument could be made that the resulting work is the outcome of 'creative choices' made by the person who instructed the artificial intelligence algorithm. As a matter of fact, artificial intelligence systems do only what humans instruct them to do. See: James Grimmelmann, 'There's No Such Thing as a Computer-Authored Work – And It's a Good Thing, Too' (2016) 39 *Columbia Journal of Law & Arts* 403.

[119] Maurizio Borghi and Stavroula Karapapa, *Copyright and Mass Digitization: A Cross-Jurisdictional Perspective* (Oxford: Oxford University Press, 2013) 92 et seq.

Protection and minimum length

The assumption that copyright can, in principle, subsist in works irrespective of their length was affirmed in *Infopaq I*. This case upheld that even an eleven-word extract can attract protection, and protection can subsist in practically any portion of work insofar as this is the author's own intellectual creation. According to the Court of Justice in *Infopaq I*, 'it is only through the choice, sequence, and combination of ... words that the author may express his creativity in an original manner and achieve a result which is an intellectual creation'.[120] What the court instructs is that selective processes in the creation of a work are essential in establishing that it is its author's own intellectual creation. It is dubious whether single words can meet the *Infopaq I* test on the basis of this finding, even though a broader understanding of the *Infopaq I* requirement does not exclude this possibility. Single words can, in principle, be protected if they are sufficiently original, i.e. they are their author's own intellectual creation. However, they may not qualify as a work, however original they are (e.g. an invented word that is also protected as a trade mark). It is for this reason that there has been tremendous difficulty in finding originality for works of such a short length.

Before *Infopaq I*, a defensive rule could have succeeded in cases of subject matter of a short length. There is a well-established line of authority in various Member States which confirms the difficulty of granting protection to works of a short length. In the United Kingdom, for instance, factual information at the front of a diary was denied protection by being commonplace[121] and individual command names in a computer program were held incapable of attracting copyright protection as literary works.[122] In Estonia, a phrase was not found sufficiently original to attract protection, as it would pertain more closely to the world of ideas.[123] There have also been cases where song titles[124] or single words[125] were found not to be protectable. To a certain extent, this served as a defence in that the re-use of those short passages would not amount to infringement on the basis that copyright did not subsist in them in the first place. Such a kind of *de minimis* use is of particular

---

[120] *Infopaq International A/S v Danske Dagblades Forening*, Case C-5/08, 16 July 2009, ECLI:EU:C:2009:465 (*Infopaq I*), [45].

[121] *Cramp v Smythson* [1944] AC 329 (UK).

[122] *Navitaire Inc v EasyJet Airline Co.* [2005] ECDR 160 (UK).

[123] *Juliusz Machulski v RMF FM*, Court of Appeals Cracow (Sąd Apelacyjny Kraków), 5 March 2004 (Estonia); in Bulgaria, however, protection was held to subsist in general terms of a website, despite the fact that they consisted of well-known definitions due to the particular way in which they were arranged and selected. See Court of Appeal Sofia (Софийски Апелативен Съд), 18 May 2005 (Bulgaria); general terms have been found to be protectable subject matter in other Bulgarian cases too. See *O. v N.*, Sofia City Court (Софийски градски съд), 04 July 2003 (Bulgaria).

[124] *Francis Day v Twentieth Century Fox* [1940] AC 112 (Canada).

[125] *Exxon Corporation v Exxon Insurance Consultants* [1982] RPC 69 (UK); Supreme Court of 22 June 2010, IV CSK 359/09, OSNC 2011/2/16) (Poland); *S. SA and E. SA v A. SA*, Court of Justice of the Republic and Canton of Geneva, 21 February 1992, SMI 1993, 303 (Switzerland) (*Swatchissimo II*).

relevance in the online environment where a work can be used as a reference tool and use and re-use of very short passages or reduced versions of a work are frequent. Such uses, for instance, include posting thumbnails to enable fast navigation through search engine results or in the form of short extracts in media services. There may also be hyperlinked headings of news items that direct readers to the main news item, 'framed' images, GIFs, memes, or short video samples.[126] Even though there is no principle according to which words or short strings of words are excluded from protection, and *Infopaq I* seems to affirm that such subject matter can in principle attract protection, there have been numerous national cases prior to *Infopaq I* which have denied protection, thereby upholding an affirmative defence and freedom to use such short expressions. The extent to which this case law remains good law in the aftermath of *Infopaq I* is questionable; it does, however, develop insights into the function of defensive rules and the legal principles underpinning the copyright traditions of various EU Member States. Denial of copyright protection in these instances served as a defensive rule in that use and re-use of subject matter of a short length would be permitted. The extent to which the *de minimis* principle can still serve as a defence post-*Infopaq I* is questionable and the scope of the relevant defensive rule has been significantly narrowed. However, principles from national case law indicate that there may be some limited room for invoking a relevant defence.

Single words

Subsistence negating claims which target single words have often been successful. Indeed, affirming copyright protection in single words has been extremely rare, even in cases where such words were registered trade marks. Although trade mark registration could signify that there is a degree of statistical uniqueness of the word mark, through the mark's ability to serve a distinctive function, copyright protection will subsist on condition of originality, which does not necessarily coincide with trade mark registration requirements. When considering whether short forms of verbal expression are protected by copyright, the likelihood of lack of originality is high. It is often assumed in doctrine and jurisprudence that because of the lack of individual character single words cannot attract protection, regardless of the fact that the word may be unknown, have a fanciful version, or consist of a neologism.[127]

Consistent case law from various Member States confirms this point and has upheld defensive claims targeting copyright subsistence. In the United Kingdom,

---

[126] On sampling a two-second extract of a rhythm sequence, see *Pelham GmbH, Moses Pelham, Martin Haas v Ralf Hütter, Florian Schneider-Esleben*, Case C-476/17, 29 July 2019, ECLI:EU:C:2019:624.

[127] Regional Administrative Court of Warsaw, VI SA/Wa 152/04, 6 April 2005 (Poland).

the most notable case is *Exxon*,[128] where the court found that copyright cannot subsist in a name, invented or not. In Poland, the general rule is that single words cannot be recognized as an object capable of attracting copyright protection when they lack individual character.[129] Single words, not only drawn from everyday language, but also unknown words or neologisms, often fail to meet the threshold of copyright protection, unless there is evidence of independent value of creativity.[130] The use of the word as a trade mark does not exclude, but also does not guarantee, the possibility of copyright protection and there is a consistent line of authority to affirm this point. For example, in *Danjaq LLC v OHIM*[131] the court stated:

> The same sign may be protected as an original creative work by copyright and as an indicator of commercial origin by trade mark law. It is therefore a matter of different exclusive rights based on distinct qualities, that is to say the original nature of a creation, on the one hand, and the ability of a sign to distinguish the commercial origin of the goods and services, on the other (judgment of 21 October 2008 in Case T 73/06 *Cassegrain v OHIM (Shape of a bag)*, not published in the ECR, paragraph 32). Therefore, even if the title of a film can be protected pursuant to certain national laws as an artistic creation independent of the film itself, it cannot automatically enjoy the protection afforded to indicators of commercial origin, since only signs which develop characteristic trademark functions may enjoy that protection.[132]

This is to affirm that although there is no *de minimis* threshold of protection, single words (or titles) will have to meet the subsistence requirements of the various intellectual property rights for which protection is sought. Unless it can be demonstrated that a word (or title) is original in the copyright sense, it will not be capable of attracting copyright protection, hence any re-use of such subject matter without authorization will be permitted for the purposes of copyright protection.

Of particular interest in the context of words or phrases that serve as indicators of commercial origin and could, in principle, attract copyright protection, either on the literary element or artistic aspects of their representation, are cases of so-called keyword advertising. This kind of advertising involves the use of trade marks as 'adwords' and traders purchase a search engine keyword identical or similar to the claimant's mark so that when a user types the relevant word(s)

---

[128] *Exxon Corp v Exxon Insurance Consultants International Ltd* [1982] Ch. 119 (UK).
[129] 'Jogi', Supreme Court (Sąd Najwyższy), IV CSK 359/09, OSNC 2011/2/16, 22 June 2010 (Poland).
[130] 'Jogi', Supreme Court (Sąd Najwyższy), IV CSK 359/09, OSNC 2011/2/16, 22 June 2010 (Poland).
[131] *Danjaq LLC v OHIM and Mission Productions Film-Gesellschaft für, Fernseh-und Veranstaltungsproduktion mbH (Dr No)*, T-435/05, 30 June 2009, ECLI:EU:T:2009:226.
[132] Ibid., [26].

the featured sponsored link directs the user to results other than the claimant's business. The Court of Justice has held that service operators, such as Google, do not commit trade mark infringement by allowing competitors to select the proprietor's mark as an adword.[133] However, marketplace operators, such as eBay, that use Google's referencing service to acquire adwords which are then used to advertise its customer-sellers' products, commit trade mark infringement.[134] Although these rulings are mostly relevant in the context of trade mark law, copyright infringement may also be claimed if the word at issue qualifies for copyright protection.

Even where a word that qualifies for copyright protection is not protected as a trade mark, protection under alternative legal grounds, such as those incorporated in the common law tort of passing off in the United Kingdom, may be relevant. In such cases, defensive rules premised on the negation of copyright subsistence will be very difficult to establish. In a case brought before the UK High Court, for instance, US companies involved in the business of computer games were found to infringe copyright in the logo of a computer gaming magazine (*EDGE*), by using it on their letterhead, website, and games.[135] The logo was found to be sufficiently original as an artistic work to qualify for copyright protection 'of more than negligible or trivial effort or relevant skill', and there was insufficient evidence to uphold the defence of independent creation. The defendant's use amounted to copyright infringement, passing off, and breach of a trading agreement with the publisher of the magazine. The breaches were found to be deliberately calculated to generate confusion, which caused substantial damage to the claimant's reputation.

Although it is not possible to deduce a principle that single words cannot attract copyright protection on the basis of the requirement of an author's own intellectual creation, it can be said that words lacking a degree of individuality cannot qualify as works in the *Infopaq I* sense (and the national approaches that preceded *Infopaq I*).[136] To an extent, commonplace words would also fail to demonstrate that they are the author's *own* and hence not qualify as authorial outputs. Because copyright subsistence is more likely to be affirmed on the basis of *Levola* and *Infopaq I*, defensive claims which target subsistence in such subject matter may not have a broad scope of applicability.

---

[133] *Google France SARL and Google Inc. v Louis Vuitton Malletier SA* (C-236/08), *Google France SARL v Viaticum SA and Luteciel SARL* (C-237/08), and *Google France SARL v Centre national de recherche en relations humaines (CNRRH) SARL and Others* (C-238/08), 23 March 2010, ECLI:EU:C:2010:159.

[134] *L'Oréal SA and Others v eBay International AG and Others*, Case C-324/09, 12 July 2011, ECLI:EU:C:2011:474.

[135] *Future Publishing Ltd v Edge Interactive Media Inc*, [2011] EWHC 1489 (Ch), 13 June 2011 (UK).

[136] In the Internet context, it is not only single words which would be valuable signs that may find protection under trade mark laws but also 'hashtags' that may be reposted on a number of social networking websites.

Titles, headings, and short extracts—tweets, hashtags, and hyperlinks

Defences negating protection in titles and headlines have not been equally successful, although there is no consistent trend to be assumed from the available case law. Titles have been found to be protected[137] or not,[138] depending on the originality involved in their creation. Where the title was found to be original, its use and re-use had to be subject to authorial consent. The protection of titles as original literary works becomes important online, in cases which involve hyperlinked headlines in news aggregators or short extracts used to accompany search engine results. Although, as a general rule, such links are likely to be innocent, infringement may take place where the title is found to be sufficiently original to attract protection in its own right, independently from the article or news item to which it links.

In *Newspaper Licensing Agency v Meltwater Holding BV*,[139] the UK Court of Appeal found that copyright subsisted in a text extract of no more than 256 characters comprising the headline from an article, the first few words after the headline, and the context in which the keyword was found. Subject to examination were the activities of a media monitoring service, Meltwater, that functioned in a similar way to Infopaq. Taking into consideration *Infopaq I* and other cases, Proudman J held that, in determining the protectable elements of a work, it is originality that has become the test post-*Infopaq I*, instead of substantiality of the taking, a doctrinal principle of UK copyright law.[140] In this light, where the extract is an independent literary work that can attract copyright protection, communication of that content is itself an infringement.[141]

---

[137] Municipal Court of Budapest, Pf.II.20.171/1956 (Hungary), unpublished decision, commented in: Péter Gyertyánfy, *A Szerzői Jogi Törvény Magyarázata* (Budapest: Complex Publishing, 2006) 103, (the work title 'Csin-bumm cirkusz' is unique and is therefore protected by copyright); 'XEQMAT', Supreme Court of Justice (Supremo Tribunal de Justiça), 8 January 2009 (Portugal) (a title for math textbooks, 'XEQMAT', was found to be highly creative and use of the same title by textbooks in the same field would amount to infringement).

[138] Municipal Court of Budapest 6.P.20.595/92 (Hungary), unpublished decision; for a comment see: A Szerzői Jogi Szakértő Testület Szakvéleményeinek Gyűjteménye, 1990–1996, III. volume (Budapest: Eötvös József Publishing, 1998) 29 (Hungary) (translation of an English title is not unique and in this regard it cannot attract copyright. Translation into Hungarian lacked individuality and originality).

[139] *Newspaper Licensing Agency v Meltwater Holding BV* [2012] RPC 1 (UK) (reversed on a different point by the Supreme Court in *Public Relations Consultants Association Ltd v Newspaper Licensing Agency Ltd* [2013] RPC 469) (UK)).

[140] The notion of substantial taking has also been discussed recently at the EU level in *Pelham GmbH, Moses Pelham, Martin Haas v Ralf Hütter, Florian Schneider-Esleben*, Case C-476/17, 29 July 2019, ECLI:EU:C:2019:624, [40]–[55].

[141] Note that the case was later acquitted of infringement on the basis of the temporary copying exception; it was, however, a prima facie affirmation of infringement, indicating that a broader construal of originality, whereby 256 characters can attract copyright protection, can result to a more limited scope of defences based on the negation of the elements of the infringing action.

In another UK case, the *Infopaq I* principle was upheld with regards to broadcasts and in particular with reference to eight-second extracts from cricket games that could be uploaded to a website and various mobile applications by members of the public; these usually include highlights of the matches, such as action replays.[142] Arnold J noted that, in the light of *Infopaq I*, the interpretation of what amounts to 'substantial' taking in the case of literary and artistic works implies that the part of the work that has been taken is the author's intellectual creation. The same ought to apply to parts of broadcasts and first fixations of films. Protection subsists in the parts that reflect the rationale for protecting broadcasts and first fixations, i.e. the *investment* made by the broadcaster or producer. With regards to the question of whether eight seconds of a cricket game are considered to be a substantial part of the claimants' work, Arnold J held that

> quantitatively, 8 seconds is not a large proportion of a broadcast or film lasting two hours or more. Qualitatively, however, it is clear that most of the clips uploaded constituted highlights of the matches: wickets taken, appeals refused, centuries scored, and the like. Thus most of clips showed something of interest, and hence value. The majority of the clips also involved action replays of the kind discussed above. Thus each clip substantially exploited the Claimants' investment in producing the relevant broadcast and/or film. Accordingly ... each such clip constituted a substantial part of the relevant copyright work(s).[143]

By virtue of this understanding, defences which negate infringement on the basis of the length of the work at issue are difficult to establish, particularly when a short extract is significant in its own right. Cases that could be analogous to the eight-second clip could include parodic compilations of videos which are more and more common on online video channels. Most of these videos include highlights in that they have been purposively compiled to include a sequence of funny extracts of other videos. In order for such short extracts to be lawfully used, successful reliance on a supervening rule, such as a copyright exception or limitation, is required for the use to be lawful.

The Court of Justice in *Pelham*,[144] a case involving the sampling of a two-second extract of a rhythm sequence, did not enter into a discussion on copyright subsistence on the extract nor in an analysis of whether the short extract qualified as a substantial part of the original work. It did hold, however, that 'a phonogram which contains sound samples transferred from another phonogram does not constitute a "copy", within the meaning of [Article 9(1)(b) of the Rental and Lending

[142] *England And Wales Cricket Board Ltd & Anor v Tixdaq Ltd & Anor* [2016] EWHC 575 (Ch) (UK).
[143] Ibid., [99].
[144] *Pelham GmbH, Moses Pelham, Martin Haas v Ralf Hütter, Florian Schneider-Esleben*, Case C-476/17, 29 July 2019, ECLI:EU:C:2019:624.

Directive],[145] of that phonogram, since it does not reproduce all or a substantial part of that phonogram.'[146] It can be surmised on the basis of *Infopaq I,* that even such a short extract can qualify for copyright protection on condition that it is its author's own intellectual creation.

Advertisements and short commercial content

Defences negating copyright protection in short phrases are often unsuccessful, even where these are used in a marketing or commercial context. The reason is that such short phrases are likely to meet the originality threshold and attract copyright protection. An advertising tagline, 'IQ + ♥ = ...', was found to qualify for copyright protection in Slovakia[147] and using it beyond the scope of a contractual agreement with the relevant rightsholder would amount to copyright infringement. Similarly, in Poland an advertising slogan for an audiovisual work was found protectable by copyright on the basis of its original character.[148]

Despite the commerciality of the context, an unimaginative string of words will be refused protection. In Switzerland, for instance, a domain name (beam.to) was denied copyright protection.[149] Subject to examination in this case was whether the combination of the English word 'beam' with a country code top level domain (.to for Tonga) could attract copyright protection. The court denied that the domain name at issue was protectable subject matter: first, the second-level domain 'beam' was an existing English word, thus it was not newly created. In *Infopaq I* terms, we could say it was not the author's *own.* Second, the country code top level domain of Tonga, '.to', was not a new creation either. The court also denied that 'beam.to' was of individual character. Although single words or short sequences of words can exceptionally attract protection, the mere unimaginative combination of words cannot.

In cases where copyright protection was affirmed with regards to short phrases, such as part of the lyrics of popular songs, courts sought a high degree of originality and distinct individual character to affirm copyright protection. In a Czech case, three words taken from a popular song for the purposes of a billboard advertisement were found capable of attracting copyright protection and defensive rules

---

[145] Directive 2006/115/EC of the European Parliament and of the Council of 12 December 2006 on Rental Right and Lending Right and on Certain Rights Related to Copyright in the Field of Intellectual Property, OJ L 376, 27 December 2006, 28–35 (Rental and Lending Directive).

[146] *Pelham GmbH, Moses Pelham, Martin Haas v Ralf Hütter, Florian Schneider-Esleben*, Case C-476/17, 29 July 2019, ECLI:EU:C:2019:624, [55].

[147] Supreme Court of the Slovak Republic (Najvyšší súd Slovenskej republiky), 23 September 1997 (Slovakia).

[148] Supreme Court (Sąd Najwyższy), V CKN 750/00, 4 March 2002 (Poland).

[149] 'Beam.to', Chief Judge 2 Court District VIII Bern-Laupen (Gerichtspräsidentin 2 Gerichtskreis VIII Bern-Laupen), 2 June 2000 (Switzerland).

attacking copyright subsistence could not flourish.[150] The Supreme Court focused on the requirement that to be protected a work needs to exhibit unique character. This 'unique character' does not mean strict, absolute individuality, but there has to be something unique in the final output that will merit protection. This does not seem to adhere to the 'author's own intellectual creation' test, however, and it is questionable whether it remains good law. In Estonia, the Supreme Court found that a short phrase and a mnemonic scheme used to facilitate the learning of the Estonian language could attract copyright protection. According to the Supreme Court, the expression of a work might take any form or language and is original if it is the author's own intellectual creation.[151] In such cases, the burden of proof is with the person who contests the protection of a work or other subject matter by copyright.

Short pieces of text used in a commercial context have also been found to attract protection in line with the *Infopaq I* reasoning, limiting henceforth the possibility of claims negating subsistence in such short pieces of work. For instance, the Supreme Court of Spain held that short job advertisements published in newspapers could attract protection insofar as they meet the originality requirement.[152] Originality in this context was established on the basis that there was an offer of employment, which, with its social and economic significance, required an intellectual activity of some depth to make the offer attractive. Copying of the job advertisements without authorization was hence found to amount to infringement, no matter the short length of the extracts at issue. Although in earlier cases the Supreme Court had developed a reluctant doctrine towards the affirmation of originality, a generous definition was construed in the case at issue. This approach, which aligns with the 'author's own intellectual creation' test could be seen as an obstacle to the reposting of information online, e.g. by news aggregators or price comparison websites.

A similar approach has been followed in other Member States leaving room for the assumption that this is a consistent trend across Europe. In Italy, short extracts of advertisements on second hand cars were held to demonstrate originality by not being the expression of mere computation, but implying deep comparative research, careful elaboration, and critical synthesis, in line with the 'author's own intellectual creation' test. This meant that their use in a competitor's magazine was infringement of copyright pursuant to Article 101(2) of the Italian Copyright Law. Negation of copyright subsistence was not therefore upheld.[153] In the Netherlands too, the use of photographs and a full description of a house on the website of a sales agent were found to amount to infringement (and could also not benefit

---

[150] Supreme Court (Nejvyšší Soud), 30 April 2007 (Czech Republic).
[151] *Toom Õunapuu v AS Tea Kirjastus*, Supreme Court (Riigikohus), 8 December 2004 (Estonia).
[152] 'La Vanguardia', Supreme Court (*Tribunal Supremo*), 13 May 2002 (Spain).
[153] *Sanguinetti Editore v Rusconi Editore*, Tribunal of Milan, *AIDA*, 2001, 525, 9 October 2000 (Italy).

from the copyright exceptions on permitted quotations). According to the court, copying was considered lawful to a maximum of 194x145 pixels for photos and 155 characters for verbal descriptions.[154] Despite the seemingly arbitrary delineation of portion guidelines, mere referential use, subject to these indicative size limits, would have been permitted but this could not apply to verbatim copying. It would have been interesting to see to what extent use by other websites for direct or indirect (e.g. via ads) commercial activity would qualify as mere referential use or as a case of copying of the relevant images and advertisements.

As indicated above, short commercial advertisements were found to be protectable in a number of instances despite their short length and, to some extent, their factual character. This could create problems for news aggregators and crawling services that may rely on reposting such pieces of information on other websites. In such cases, a line of defence which denies subsistence is less likely to succeed and reliance on relevant copyright exceptions and limitations would be a preferable line of reasoning.

Conclusion

Claims targeted at negating infringing liability can be based on the negation of subsistence requirements. A defence attacking copyright subsistence may focus on either the fact that there is no qualifying object of protection in the first place or that the work does not meet the protection requirements, i.e. it is not the author's own intellectual creation. Defensive claims targeting subsistence seek judicial affirmation that a right *in rem* does not exist.[155] The 'author's own intellectual creation' standard, which was first applied to literary works in *Infopaq I* and later developed in a number of cases of the Court of Justice, aims to ensure that protection will be awarded to works that demonstrate their author's personal stamp and reflect the author's creative choices. Although the standard is not legislatively harmonized at the EU level, it has been subject to harmonization through case law and is now the leading test followed in EU Member States.

Because any subject matter can qualify for copyright protection, to the extent that it is capable of being expressed clearly and precisely post-*Levola* and insofar as it is its author's own intellectual creation, defendants will find it very difficult to centre their defensive claims on subsistence negation. Copyright protection is now the norm and the scope of relevant defensive claims has been significantly reduced. The 'author's own intellectual creation' test has limited the scope of defences negating infringing liability on the basis that copyright does not subsist

---

[154] *Stichting Baas in Eigen Huis v Plazacasa*, District Court Alkmaar (Rechtbank Alkmaar), 7 August 2007 (Netherlands).

[155] By contrast, claims attacking authorship seek to negate a right *in personam*.

in the claimant's work. This is particularly so in the case of works that would escape copyright protection prior to *Infopaq I*, notably works of a short length. Even though awarding copyright protection to single words is less likely after *Infopaq I*, that case, alongside *Levola*, has enlarged the concept of protectable subject matter. Any subject matter that is capable of precise and objective expression is in principle eligible for copyright protection, including short extracts. This has the effect that the breadth of subsistence negating claims will remain rather limited. These rulings, which have been repeated in national case law,[156] have an impact on the scope of defensive claims aiming to negate copyright subsistence. In this regard, the test of the 'author's own intellectual creation' raises the threshold of copyright protection across Europe and makes it more difficult to bring forward a defence based on the negation of copyright subsistence.

However, it has become clearer in the aftermath of *Infopaq I* and other case law of the Court of Justice that works that are either technical contributions or works of a merely functional nature will be less likely candidates for copyright subsistence. Allegations of copyright infringement of such works could be defeated on the basis of subsistence negating arguments. Such works could include works created through artificial intelligence or another algorithmic process that does not demonstrate creative input of authorial quality. In this regard, even though certain copy-reliant entities may benefit from the use of copyright-protected content on the basis that a certain use is permitted by copyright, they will not be in a position to generate exclusivity over the produce of their activity. This aligns aligning with the principle of fairness according to which benefits arising from a permissible use should not become exclusionary themselves. It shall only be when some additional creative effort has been expended in the creation of such works that a copyright claim on such derivative works can subsist.

Lack of copyright subsistence in an allegedly infringed work can form a defence against relevant allegations for infringement by attacking one of the main elements in which the claimant sues. Another liability-defeating claim can be found in the scope of authorial entitlement and, in particular, exclusive rights. This is examined in the next chapter.

---

[156] See e.g. in the *Tixdaq* case where eight seconds of a cricket match were found to qualify for copyright protection: *England And Wales Cricket Board Ltd & Anor v Tixdaq Ltd & Anor* [2016] EWHC 575 (Ch) (UK).

3

Scope Limitations

Copyright is not infringed in instances where the defendant's activity falls outside the scope of exclusive rights. This is likely to be the case when the factual background of an alleged infringement does not meet the statutory prerequisites of a restricted act, for instance, when taking from an original work has not been such to amount to an act reserved by copyright and hence falls beyond the scope of exclusive rights. As the Court of Justice affirmed in numerous cases, copyright protection is not absolute[1] and exclusive rights are subject to a variety of internal limits that can serve as the basis of defensive claims in a practical sense. For instance, the court has indicated that exclusive rights are subject to internal scope limitations, some of which are relevant in the context of new technological uses. Hyperlinks, for example, do not infringe copyright when they are not addressed to a 'new' public, namely an audience that the rightsholders did not have in mind while making the work available online.[2] Another example is the exhaustion principle according to which the first authorized sale of content exhausts the authorial entitlement to further distributions. This principle is available in the online context only in relation to the resale of software,[3] and this hinders innovative activity through the creation of electronic marketplaces for digital goods. Subject to examination in this chapter are the statutory and doctrinal limitations that inherently limit the scope of rights and remain outside the spectrum of proprietary entitlements.

---

[1] See e.g. *Scarlet Extended v SABAM*, Case C-70/10, 24 November 2011, ECLI:EU:C:2011:771 (*Scarlet*), [43]; *Belgische Vereniging van Auteurs, Componisten en Uitgevers CVBA (SABAM) v Netlog NV*, Case C-360/10, 16 February 2012, ECLI:EU:C:2012:85 (*Netlog*), [41]; *UPC Telekabel Wien GmbH v Constantin Film Verleih GmbH, Wega Filmproduktionsgesellschaft mbH*, Case C-314/12, 27 March 2014, ECLI:EU:C:2014:192, [61]; *Funke Medien NRW GmbH v Federal Republic of Germany*, C-469/17, 29 July 2019, ECLI:EU:C:2019:623 (*Funke Medien*), [72].

[2] *Nils Svensson and Others v Retriever Sverige AB*, Case C-466/12, 13 February 2014, ECLI:EU:C:2014:76 (*Svensson*); *BestWater International GmbH v Michael Mebes, Stefan Potsch*, Case C-348/13, 21 October 2014 (order of the court), ECLI:EU:C:2014:2315 (*BestWater*); also see *Innoweb BV v Wegener ICT Media BV and Wegener Mediaventions BV*, Case C-202/12, 19 December 2013, ECLI:EU:C:2013:850 (*Innoweb*). See in this regard, however, the opposing position of the European Parliament, Committee on Legal Affairs, Draft Report on the Implementation of Directive 2001/29/EC of the European Parliament and of the Council of 22 May 2001 on the Harmonisation of Certain Aspects of Copyright and Related Rights in the Information Society, 15 January 2015, 2014/2256(INI), point 15.

[3] *UsedSoft GmbH v Oracle International Corp*, Case C-128/11, 3 July 2012, ECLI:EU:C:2012:407 (*UsedSoft*).

Defences to Copyright Infringement. Stavroula Karapapa, Oxford University Press (2020). © Stavroula Karapapa.
DOI: 10.1093/oso/9780198795636.001.0001

Introduction

A defence commonly raised against allegations for copyright infringement is that the defendant's activity falls outside the scope of copyright protection because the exclusive rights enjoyed by authors and relevant rightsholders do not encompass the relevant conduct. If this is successfully claimed, infringement cannot be established. Such a defensive rule can be regarded as the inverse of rights, in that whatever is not part of the scope of protection remains (and ought to remain) free from proprietary claims. Unlike subsistence negating claims, the focus of relevant defensive arguments is that the conduct in question does not amount to an act reserved by copyright. For instance, with a subsistence negating claim, a defendant may argue that the claimant's intellectual product is not a work protected by copyright or that it does not meet the originality threshold. So, even though, for instance, the defendant copied the claimant's product, this is not a work subject to copyright and therefore the conduct in question does not amount to infringement. With a scope limitation, however, a defendant who, for instance, has independently created a work that is identical to, or shares strong similarities with, the claimant's can successfully claim that he or she did not engage in an act of reproduction.[4] The claimant's intellectual product is a work, but the defendant did not engage in an act of reproduction and hence did not touch on the claimant's exclusive rights.

Under EU copyright, exclusive rights are drafted in general terms. The most characteristic example is the reproduction right under Article 2 of the Information Society Directive[5] drafted to cover *every* act of copying irrespective of the duration of the copies produced, the portion of the work that has been copied, or the technology used. The generality in the formulation of exclusive rights, which is meant to be complemented through a broad understanding of their scope[6] in order to ensure a high level of protection and legal certainty across the European Union, means that copyright protection is the norm and any act that touches upon the acts reserved by copyright should—at least prima facie—amount to infringement. However, the Court of Justice has, on numerous occasions, held that exclusive rights are not absolute[7] and are (and should be)

---

[4] See e.g. *John Kaldor Fabricmaker v Lee Ann Fashions* [2014] EWHC 3779 (IPEC) (UK).

[5] Directive 2001/29/EC of the European Parliament and of the Council of 22 May 2001 on the Harmonisation of Certain Aspects of Copyright and Related Rights in the Information Society, OJ L 167, 22 June 2001, 10–19 (Information Society Directive).

[6] Information Society Directive (Directive 2001/29/EC), Recitals 9, 21, and 23.

[7] See e.g. *Scarlet Extended v SABAM*, Case C-70/10, 24 November 2011, ECLI:EU:C:2011:771 (*Scarlet*), [43]; *Belgische Vereniging van Auteurs, Componisten en Uitgevers CVBA (SABAM) v Netlog NV*, Case C-360/10, 16 February 2012, ECLI:EU:C:2012:85 (*Netlog*), [41]; *UPC Telekabel Wien GmbH v Constantin Film Verleih GmbH, Wega Filmproduktionsgesellschaft mbH*, Case C-314/12, 27 March 2014, ECLI:EU:C:2014:192, [61]; *Funke Medien NRW GmbH v Federal Republic of Germany*, C-469/17, 29 July 2019, ECLI:EU:C:2019:623 (*Funke Medien*), [72].

subject to internal limits. For instance, when addressing the purpose or the functions that a certain economic right means to serve the court sometimes refers to 'legitimate profit'[8] or to 'appropriate remuneration',[9] which means that rights are not absolute, but are subject to internal limitations. Indeed, there is an extended line of authority of the Court of Justice which affirms that when Member States transpose these provisions into national law they should ensure that a fair balance is achieved between the interests of copyright holders and related rights, on the one hand and, on the other, the protection of the interests and fundamental rights of users of protected objects, in particular their freedom of expression and information, as well as the general public interest. This reflects the various rights as incorporated into the Charter of Fundamental Rights of the European Union,[10] including the protection of intellectual property rights,[11] the right of third parties for the respect of their privacy, the protection of personal data and freedom of expression,[12] and the freedom of Internet service providers to conduct business.[13]

The scope of protection can be limited by effect of law or doctrine. Legal limitations include the very way in which exclusive rights, as the entitlements in which a claimant sues, are statutorily defined, whereas their appropriate scope has been subject to judicial interpretation and doctrine. These scope limitations are deliberated in this chapter and in Chapter 4, where subject to discussion is temporary copying; a special case in which a copyright exception can be better understood as a scope limitation to the reproduction right, rather than a mere defence against infringement. In particular, subject to discussion are instances where the statutory core of rights excludes certain activities, which can thereinafter be deemed as permissible uses.

---

[8] Corrigendum to Directive 2004/48/EC of the European Parliament and of the Council of 29 April 2004 on the Enforcement of Intellectual Property Rights (OJ L 157, 30 April 2004), OJ L 195, 2 June 2004, 16–25, Recital 2.

[9] Directive (EU) 2012/28 of the European Parliament and of the Council of 25 October 2012 on Certain Permitted Uses of Orphan Works Text with EEA relevance, OJ L 299, 27 October 2012, 5–12 (Orphan Works Directive), Recital 5; also, the framework of remunerated exceptions indicates that rights may be limited in certain instances to accommodate other legitimate interests and policy objectives.

[10] *Bonnier Audio AB v Perfect Communication Sweden AB*, Case C-461/10, 19 April 2012, ECLI:EU:C:2012:219 (*Bonnier*); *Belgische Vereniging van Auteurs, Componisten en Uitgevers CVBA (SABAM) v Netlog NV*, Case C-360/10, 16 February 2012, ECLI:EU:C:2012:85 (*Netlog*); *Scarlet Extended v SABAM*, Case C-70/10, 24 November 2011, ECLI:EU:C:2011:771 (*Scarlet*); *Productores de Música de Espana (Promusicae) v Telefónica de España SAU*, Case C-275/06, 29 January 2008, ECLI:EU:C:2008:54 (*Promusicae*).

[11] Charter of Fundamental Rights of the European Union (18 December 2000) 2000/C 364/01, OJ C 364, Art. 17(2), 1–22.

[12] Ibid., Arts 7, 8, and 11.

[13] Ibid., Art. 16.

Limitations by effect of law

Inherent limitations to exclusive rights that could serve as defensive rules against allegations of copyright infringement can be found in all exclusive rights. For the purposes of the present discussion, the focus shall be on those rights that are relevant in the context of digitization, the Internet, and the fourth industrial revolution, namely the reproduction right, the right of communicating or otherwise making works available to the public, and the adaptation right. Other rights that cover tangible copies of works, such as the distribution right or rights on rental and lending, are addressed as and where appropriate.

Reproduction right

Having been described as 'the core of copyright and related rights',[14] the reproduction right has been defined in Article 2 of the Information Society Directive.[15] The definition offered in Article 2 is very broad, effectively covering all instances of copying. The right also applies to all authorial works and to performance fixations, phonograms, first fixations of films and copies thereof, and broadcast fixations. The Recitals of the Directive indicate that the right is to be interpreted expansively in the interests of legal certainty within the Internal Market, with the view to ensuring that 'proper support for the dissemination of culture [is not] achieved by sacrificing strict protection of rights'.[16] Indeed, a very broad stipulation is offered under Article 2, reflecting Article 9(1) of the Berne Convention[17] and providing for 'the exclusive right to authorise or prohibit direct or indirect, temporary or permanent reproduction by any means and in any form, in whole or in part'. The reproduction right under Article 2 of the Information Society Directive is widely defined, offering protection to all categories of European rightsholders[18] and

---

[14] Green Paper on Copyright and Related Rights in the Information Society, COM (95) 382 final (19 July 1995).

[15] Also see the supplementary definitions offered in Arts 4(1)(a) and 5(1) of Directive 2009/24/EC of the European Parliament and of the Council of 23 April 2009 on the Legal Protection of Computer Programs, OJ L 111/16, 5 May 2009 (Computer Programs Directive) and Art. 5 of Directive 96/9/EC of the European Parliament and of the Council of 11 March 1996 on the legal protection of databases, OJ L 77, 27 March 1996 (Database Directive).

[16] Information Society Directive (Directive 2001/29/EC), Recitals 21 and 22.

[17] Berne Convention for the Protection of Literary and Artistic Works (hereinafter 'Berne Convention') (as amended on 28 September 1979).

[18] Art. 2 grants the reproduction right to authors and to the four categories of European neighbouring rightsholders, namely performers, phonogram producers, producers of the first fixation of films, and broadcasting organizations. For a detailed analysis, see Stefan Bechtold, 'Directive 2001/29/EC (Information Society Directive) of the European Parliament and of the Council of 22 May 2001 on the Harmonisation of Certain Aspects of Copyright and Related Rights in the Information Society' in Thomas Dreier and P. Bernt Hugenholtz (eds), *Concise European Copyright Law* (Alphen aan den Rijn: Kluwer Law International, 2006) 343, 361.

encompassing every act of reproduction, irrespective of the duration of the copies produced (permanent/temporary reproduction), the portion of the work that has been copied (in whole or in part), the technology or medium used (wire or wireless medium, digital/analogue reproduction), and the course of the reproduction process (direct/indirect reproduction).

The broad definition of the reproduction right is problematic in that it assumes that every act of copying amounts to infringement, insofar as it is not clearly permitted by one of the copyright exceptions and limitations available under Article 5 of the Information Society Directive. Effectively, to understand what falls within the scope of the reproduction right, the right has to be read with reference to the instances that have been either statutorily or doctrinally excluded from its scope, most of which are purpose-specific and rationale-based. Examples are the act of temporary copying within the meaning, and for the purposes, of Article 5(1) of the Directive, as well as other copyright exceptions and limitations, and their judicial interpretation. The broad definition of the right, alongside the guidance that it should be understood in a broad sense,[19] indicates that once copyright subsistence is affirmed, copyright protection is the norm and any exceptions to this rule are meant to play second fiddle. There is a plethora of such exceptions listed in various legal instruments, notably the Information Society Directive[20] and the Digital Single Market Directive,[21] indicating that more specificity in the legislative definition of the right could generate more certainty to end users of copyright protected content. In the online context in particular, not every copy made is one that qualifies as an actionable act of reproduction.[22] Examples include cached copies or use of works as reference tools, e.g. by way of thumbnail images. A more specific definition of the right would have been preferable to the extent that it would enrich legal certainty and also enhance fairness in the balance of rights and interests between the different categories of rightsholders and users of protected subject matter, which is one of the stated objectives of copyright protection in various Directives and cases.[23]

---

[19] Information Society Directive (Directive 2001/29/EC), Recital 21.

[20] Information Society Directive (Directive 2001/29/EC).

[21] Directive (EU) 2019/790 of the European Parliament and of the Council of 17 April 2019 on Copyright and Related Rights in the Digital Single Market and Amending Directives 96/9/EC and 2001/29/EC, PE/51/2019/REV/1, OJ L 130, 17 May 2019, 92–125 (Digital Single Market Directive).

[22] See broadly Jessica Litman, 'Fetishizing Copies' in Ruth L. Okediji (ed.), *Copyright Law in an Age of Limitations and Exceptions* (New York: Cambridge University Press, 2017) 107.

[23] Information Society Directive (Directive 2001/29/EC), Recital 31 (affirmed in various cases such as *Funke Medien NRW GmbH v Federal Republic of Germany*, C-469/17, 29 July 2019, ECLI:EU:C:2019:623, [32]; *Pelham GmbH, Moses Pelham, Martin Haas v Ralf Hütter, Florian Schneider-Esleben*, Case C-476/17, 29 July 2019, ECLI:EU:C:2019:624, [32]); Digital Single Market Directive (Directive 2019/790), Recitals 6, also 21, 61, 70, 75.

Copyright subsists in the work's authorial elements only

For the purposes of EU copyright protection, the reproduction right covers copying of any 'part' of a protected work. What constitutes such a 'part' has been at the core of a number of preliminary referrals to the Court of Justice. According to these rulings, elements of an authorial work will be part of the work for the purposes of copyright infringement if they manifest the intellectual creation of the author.[24] We have explored the concept of the 'author's own intellectual creation' in Chapter 2, as rooted in the concepts of originality and authorship and developed through the rich case law of the Court of Justice and national laws of the Member States.

In order for elements of a work to be protected they ought to be original in an authorial sense, representing their author's own intellectual creation. As flagged in the UK *Meltwater* case, the discussion on originality and the taking of a 'substantial part' of a protected work, as approached in the Anglo-Saxon legal tradition, have merged in light of the jurisprudence of the Court of Justice.[25] Even though the court has not expressly delineated what amounts to a 'part' of related rights subject matter, its reasoning indicates an expansive approach. Anything that qualifies as the 'author's own intellectual creation' can attract protection and its taking is likely to amount to an act of infringement. Albeit broadly framed, this interpretation draws a distinction between protected authorial elements of a work, the taking of which amounts to infringement, and non-protectable, non-authorial aspects, the taking of which is exempt from infringement. For uses concerning this second category of subject matter, a defensive claim can attack the elements of the work that are not subject to copyright protection by not being the author's own intellectual creation. By not being subject to protection, these elements will not be subject to proprietary entitlements or claims arising on the basis of the reproduction right. In the aftermath of *Infopaq I* and national case law implementing the *Infopaq I* principles,[26] the availability of this kind of defence has become more and more limited.

In *Pelham*[27] the Court of Justice affirmed that a two-second extract of a rhythm sequence featured in a phonogram containing sound samples fell within the phonogram producer's exclusive reproduction right. This means that the relevant copyright holder can prevent another person from taking a sound sample, even if very short, in order to include that sample in another phonogram. The only exception to this rule is when the sample is included in the phonogram in a modified form unrecognizable to the ear. This develops a defensive rule around creative engagement

---

[24] *Infopaq International A/S v Danske Dagblades Forening*, Case C-5/08, 16 July 2009, ECLI:EU:C:2009:465 (*Infopaq I*).

[25] Notably in cases such as *Infopaq I* and *Football Association Premier League and Others* (*FAPL*). See *Newspaper Licensing Agency v Meltwater Holding BV* [2012] RPC 1 (UK).

[26] See e.g. *England And Wales Cricket Board Ltd & Anor v Tixdaq Ltd & Anor* [2016] EWHC 575 (Ch) (UK).

[27] *Pelham GmbH, Moses Pelham, Martin Haas v Ralf Hütter, Florian Schneider-Esleben*, Case C-476/17, 29 July 2019, ECLI:EU:C:2019:624.

with a short extract of a work and its introduction into a new work to the extent that the portion taken has been subject to extensive creative modification.

A number of national cases have affirmed the link between originality and authorship to the protected part of an authorial work, notably from the United Kingdom, where the concept of infringement is linked to considerations of whether a 'substantial part' of a protected work has been taken. In a famous UK case, a photograph of a red Routemaster bus travelling across Westminster Bridge, with the Houses of Parliament and the bridge shown in greyscale, was found to infringe copyright in another, similar photograph, despite the differences in their making and in certain elements of their composition.[28] Upholding a long line of authority,[29] the court held that determining what a 'substantial part' is involves a qualitative rather than a quantitative examination in determining the protectable elements of the work. This involves an assessment of the elements of the work that have a visual significance. What is visually significant in artistic works is not the skill and labour that has been invested in their creation, i.e. the original authorial contribution, but the final output of this creative process. Even though the method of creating the two images in the case at issue differed (the claimant's picture was a photograph that was subsequently 'photoshopped', whereas the defendant's picture was the result of a collage), there was a substantial visual similarity between the works and infringement was established.

Effectively, the parts of a work that are protected are those that are their author's own intellectual creation and this has reached a high level of abstraction in the aftermath of *Infopaq I*. Defendants in cases where part of a work has been taken will more successfully rely on relevant copyright exceptions and limitations, unless they are able to demonstrate that the portion taken was very short to demonstrate the author's own intellectual creation and they applied modifications to the extent that the resulting work differs substantially from the original.

The idea/expression dichotomy and copyright protection for non-literal elements of a work

According to Article 9(2) of the Agreement on Trade-Related Aspects of Intellectual Property Rights (TRIPs), 'copyright protection shall extend to expressions and not to ideas, procedures, methods of operation, or mathematical concepts as such.' The idea/expression dichotomy does not find express mention in EU copyright law or case law, however. It is a matter for the various Member States to determine to what extent and under which protection copyright protection covers non-expressive or non-literal aspects of a work. In the UK case *Designers Guild Ltd v Russell Williams*

---

[28] *Temple Island Collections Ltd v New English Teas Ltd and Nicholas John Houghton* [2012] EWPCC 1 (UK).

[29] See, inter alia, *Designers Guild Ltd v Russell Williams (Textiles) Ltd* [2000] UKHL 58 (UK).

(Textiles) Ltd,[30] the House of Lords affirmed that the idea/expression dichotomy is not a separate principle outside examinations of copyright infringement. Lord Hoffmann held that copyright subsists in the literary, artistic, or other authorial aspects of a work to the extent that these meet the protection requirements. This indicates that the ideas included in a work, e.g. the characters or plot of a novel, are parts of what confers originality to the work and—in a sense—part of what copyright protects. An alternative conclusion, according to Lord Hoffmann, would support the false assumption that ideas can be distinguished from their expression.[31] The general rejection of an idea/expression dichotomy in copyright law in the *Designers Guild* case aligns with the EU policy objective to ensure a high level of copyright protection, as reflected in the Preamble of the Information Society Directive.[32] It also reflects the position adopted by other national courts that have affirmed that unauthorized reproduction of characters and aspects of a plot of a novel, or of TV formats, can amount to copyright infringement.[33] Chapter 2 has already discussed how the idea/expression dichotomy is reflected in the subsistence requirement of the author's own intellectual creation.

For certain categories of works, such as computer programs and databases, however, the recognition of the idea/expression dichotomy is necessary, particularly because of the availability of alternative forms of protection for the non-authorial aspects of such works. These include, for instance, patent protection with regard to technical aspects of computer programs and the *sui generis* database right for non-original databases.

Copyright protection for computer programs

The Computer Programs Directive offers protection to 'the expression in any form' of a computer program, marking a sharp contrast to its underlying ideas and principles which remain excluded from the scope of protection.[34] This exclusion applies to the programming language, functionality, and structure of the data file of a computer program, as affirmed in *SAS Institute Inc v World Programming Inc.*[35] Upholding the Opinion of Bot AG, the Court of Justice stated that 'to accept that the functionality of a computer program can be protected by copyright would amount to making it possible to monopolize ideas, to the detriment of technological progress and industrial development.'[36] Protection of non-authorial elements will either be afforded because they would be eligible for independent copyright protection or on the basis of another intellectual property right, such as a patent.

---

[30] *Designers Guild Ltd v Russell Williams (Textiles) Ltd* [2000] UKHL 58 (UK), point 6 per Lord Hoffmann.

[31] Ibid.

[32] Information Society Directive (Directive 2001/29/EC), Recital 4.

[33] See e.g. Court of Appeal of Warsaw, I ACa 1216/12, 16 April 2013 (Poland); 'Laras Tochter' (2000) 31 *IIC* 1050 (BGH) (Germany).

[34] Computer Programs Directive (Directive 2009/24/EC), Art. 1(2).

[35] *SAS Institute Inc. v World Programming Inc*, Case C-406/10, 2 May 2012, ECLI:EU:C:2012:259 (*SAS Institute*).

[36] Ibid., [40].

Database right and protection of facts and information

Databases too, may comprise both authorial and/or non-authorial elements. Copyright protection will subsist in the authorial aspects only, as follows from the definition of 'database' included in the Database Directive.[37] According to this definition, a database is the selection and arrangement of works, data, or other materials,[38] with copyright protection subsisting in those elements of a database that, by reason of their selection and arrangement, 'constitute the author's own intellectual creation'.[39] The contents of a database cannot attract copyright protection unless they are authorial works in their own right.

An interesting issue with regard to databases arises by reference to the protection of facts and information contained in a database, especially in those instances where information cannot be retrieved from another source. This is the issue of the so-called sole source database. Since discussions began on what the appropriate level of database protection should be, offering exclusive protection to information and raw data was regarded as unwelcome; there was a long standing consensus that such a protection should not prevent users from accessing and making use of information, facts, and 'raw' data, especially when these are available from a single source only.[40] The policy objective was to leave these pieces of information available for everyone to access and use and to offer a broader defensive rationale towards the preservation of a rigorous public domain. Despite scholarly concerns on the effect of the Directive on access to information,[41] it was thought that sufficient balancing elements were inserted in the law to overcome the risks associated with a possible 'lock-in' of information and raw data.[42]

---

[37] Database Directive (Directive 96/9/EC), Art. 1(2).

[38] Ibid.

[39] Ibid., Art. 3(2).

[40] As acknowledged in the Evaluation Report on the Database Directive, 'there is a long-standing principle that copyright should not be extended to cover basic information or "raw" data'. Commission of the European Communities, DG Internal Market and Services Working Paper. First Evaluation of Directive 96/9/EC on the Legal Protection of Databases, 12 December 2005, 23. The principle has been applied by the Court of Justice with reference to the *sui generis* right in *The British Horseracing Board Ltd v William Hill Organization Ltd*, Case C-203/02, 9 November 2004, ECLI:EU:C:2004:695.

[41] See e.g. William Cornish, 'European Community Directive on Database Protection' [1996] 21(1) *Columbia VLA J Law & the Arts* 1; Jerome H. Reichman and Pamela Samuelson, 'Intellectual Property Rights in Data' (1997) 50 *Vanderbilt Law Review* 51.

[42] See Common Position (EC) No. 20/95 adopted by the Council on 10 July 1995 on the Legal Protection of Databases, OJ No. C 288/14, s. 15.

The approach developed by the Court of Justice of the European Union in its early cases on subsistence of database right seemed to mitigate the risks of overprotection through the doctrinal affirmation that investment towards the 'creation' of data will not suffice to afford legal protection to databases. The doctrine has been developed in the 'database tetralogy' *The British Horseracing Board Ltd v William Hill Organization Ltd*, Case C-203/02, 9 November 2004, ECLI:EU:C:2004:695 (*British Horseracing*); *Fixtures Marketing Ltd v Organismos prognostikon agonon podosfairou AE (OPAP)*, Case C-444/02, 9 November 2014, ECLI:EU:C:2004:697 (*OPAP*); *Fixtures Marketing Ltd v Svenska Spel AB*, Case C-338/02, 9 November 2004, ECLI:EU:C:2004:696 (*Svenska Spel*); *Fixtures Marketing Ltd v Oy Veikkaus Ab*, Case C-46/02, 9 November 2004, ECLI:EU:C:2004:694 (*Oy Veikkaus*). See in general Maurizio Borghi and Stavroula Karapapa, 'Contractual Restrictions on Lawful Use of Information: Sole-Source Databases Protected by the Back Door?' (2015) 37(8) *European Intellectual Property Review* 505.

Because most sole source databases involve the creation of data, they would be excluded from protection, unless investment 'of the right kind' were also to be established.[43]

The issue of sole source databases can become meaningful in the context of price comparison websites that base their operation on the systematic extraction and re-utilization of raw data, such as flight details, hotel room availability, or product prices.[44] Other copy-reliant services routinely extract and re-utilize content from various databases and bring it together in the form of a new service, such as news aggregators or meta-search engines. In *Ryanair v PR Aviation*,[45] the Court of Justice was called upon to determine whether PR Aviation had a legitimate defence for extracting and re-utilizing Ryanair's database of flight data for the purposes of price comparison and to book flights upon payment of a commission. Even though the database was not protected by either copyright or the *sui generis* database right, this use was in breach of the terms and conditions set out on Ryanair's website, which included an express prohibition on unlicensed screen scraping and price comparison. However, PR Aviation contended that they had a defence under the 'lawful user exception' available in the Dutch Copyright Law and reflective of Article 15 of the Database Directive,[46] effectively stipulating that contractual restrictions to the available copyright exceptions and limitations would be null and void.

Even though the Directive mandates that contracts disallowing lawful users from carrying out certain permitted activities shall be null and void,[47] the Court of Justice in *Ryanair* interpreted the provision as applying only to databases covered by one of the two forms of protection available under the Directive. This means that makers of non-protected databases enjoy full freedom of contract, unlike makers of databases that happen to qualify for copyright or the *sui generis* right. It also indicates that protection could dangerously expand to raw data and information, despite the historical policy understanding that this is an unwelcome result. In this light, *Ryanair* reaches a paradoxical conclusion in that unprotected databases can benefit from stronger contractual protection than databases covered by copyright or the *sui generis* right.[48] The *Ryanair* judgment has significant impact on

---

[43] Estelle Derclaye 'The Court of Justice Interprets the Database Sui Generis Right for the First Time' [2005] *European Law Review* 420.

[44] See in this regard *Google Search (Shopping)*, Case AT.39740, Antitrust Procedure, Council Regulation (EC) 1/2003, Art. 7 Regulation (EC) 1/2003, C(2017) 4444 final, 27 June 2017.

[45] *Ryanair v PR Aviation*, Case C-30/14, 15 January 2015, ECLI:EU:C:2015:10; for a comment see Maurizio Borghi and Stavroula Karapapa, 'Contractual Restrictions on Lawful use of Information: Sole-Source Databases Protected by the Back Door?' (2015) 37(8) *European Intellectual Property Review* 505.

[46] Database Directive (Directive 96/9/EC).

[47] Database Directive (Directive 96/9/EC), Art. 15.

[48] Maurizio Borghi and Stavroula Karapapa, 'Contractual Restrictions on Lawful use of Information: Sole-Source Databases Protected by the Back Door?' (2015) 37(8) *European Intellectual Property Review* 505.

e-commerce and online services that routinely access databases from other web-sites in order to compare information, such as the price of goods and services.[49]

Independent creation defence

A defensive rule that is inherent within the reproduction right, despite its broad wording, is the so-called independent creation doctrine which has evolved or-ganically in national case law.[50] The doctrine of independent creation serves as a defence in cases where two works are very similar, or even identical, but there is no evidence of taking from either of the two authors. In such cases, infringe-ment cannot be established. Judicially developed at the national level, but not re-ceiving statutory support, the independent creation doctrine has not been subject to harmonization at the EU level, and there is no relevant case law from the Court of Justice. However, the doctrinally developed defensive rules applicable in the various Member States share common ground of application by requiring substan-tial similarity of the two works when compared to each other, but with no inference of copying. The burden to prove independence in the making of the work usually rests with the defendant.

The independent creation defence has an idiomatic legal nature. It rests on the ground that the defendant's work does not copy from the original, effectively denying that there was an act of copying in the first place.[51] It is in this regard that it is best viewed as a scope limitation. As a matter of fact, the defence instructs that copyright is not concerned with the 'novelty' of the work, but with the fact that the work is the product of a creative act of its author. In this respect, no right of 'pri-ority' subsists in authorial works, and a claim of infringement can, in principle, be dismissed even in the presence of objective similarity between the works. However, this rule does not apply consistently in all jurisdictions. In some countries, like the United Kingdom, courts require a 'causal connection' between the defendant's and the claimant's works. In other European countries, like Italy, the presence of objectively identical elements is non-rebuttable evidence of infringement. The ef-fectiveness of the defence rests on the strength of the evidence that negates causal connection.

---

[49] Some of these online services, often called price comparison operators or meta-search engines, do not infringe any intellectual property right, either because they are covered by the permissible uses or because the databases from which they crawl information are not protected by copyright or the *sui generis* right. See, however, *Innoweb BV v Wegener ICT Media BV and Wegener Mediaventions BV*, Case C-202/12, 19 December 2013, ECLI:EU:C:2013:850 (*Innoweb*) (a 'dedicated meta-search engine' that enables searches on third party websites infringes the *sui generis* right on the databases made avail-able on those websites by re-utilizing the whole or substantial part of those databases). For a thorough discussion see Martin Husovec, 'The End of (Meta) Search Engines in Europe?' (2014) Max Planck Institute for Innovation and Competition Research Paper, No. 14–15; Stephen Vousden 'Innoweb, Search Engines and Engineering Legitimacy in EU Law' [2014] *Intellectual Property Quarterly* 280.

[50] Including, for instance, Sweden and the United Kingdom.

[51] Perhaps the first case affirming the existence of the independent creation claim as a defence against allegations for infringement is *Roworth v Wilkes*, 1 Campbell 94, 98 (1807) (UK).

In the United Kingdom, the defence was upheld in a case where subject to examination were two very similar fabric designs.[52] What persuaded the court in this case was the defendant's evidence of the independence of the design. There was credibility in the argument that the designer created the fabric independently and the claimant's allegations of infringement were not sufficient for the court to reject the designer's evidence that she created the design independently, without influence from the claimant's fabric.

Similarly, the UK High Court affirmed the application of the independent creation doctrine in *Jumar Solutions*[53] where subject to consideration was infringement of copyright, breach of confidence, and breach of contract brought against a former employee due to the defendant's use of McKee Software, owned by the claimant. Mr John Baldwin QC accepted that a developer cannot slavishly copy works created for an employer on the basis that the works were themselves created from the developer's pre-existing materials. He did not, however, consider that the law of copyright prevents a developer from creating those or similar works again in circumstances where they flow naturally from pre-existing materials. If the law were otherwise, there would be a serious impediment on software developers with libraries of prototype code which they put together either for fun or to remain competitive in the market place. The claimant's argument for copyright infringement failed and, apart from the common code, there was insufficient similarity or evidence of derivation for the case to succeed; in respect of the similarities in the common code, the defendant's evidence of independent creation defeated the claim.[54]

The defence has not been successful in other cases, however, and this has mostly been the result of insufficient evidence to prove independence in the making of the defendant's work.[55] Independent creation could not be established in a case of two tableware designs where similarities were so striking as to create a prima facie inference of copying.[56] The UK High Court held that the stronger the case of copying that can be inferred from similarities, the more compelling the defendants' evidence of independent design must be to rebut that inference.

---

[52] *John Kaldor Fabricmaker v Lee Ann Fashions* [2014] EWHC 3779 (IPEC) (UK). In another UK case, the court refused to accept the defence of independent creation in a list of 'permanent memory absolute address (PM Abs address)' extracted from mobile phones for purposes of criminal investigation. This was despite the fact that defendant submitted evidence that 'the similarities identified [...] are "exactly what you would expect" if two parties independently attempted to ascertain PM Abs addresses for Nokia phones' (*Forensic Telecommunications Services Ltd v. Chief Constable of West Yorkshire* [2011] EWHC 2892 (Ch), [100]).

[53] *Jumar Solutions Limited v Derek McKee* [2016] EWHC 1361 (Ch) (UK).

[54] Ibid., [95]–[96].

[55] See e.g. *Bodo Sperlein v Sabichi*, High Court of England and Wales, Chancery Division [2015] EWHC 1242 (IPEC) (UK); *Temple Island Collections Ltd v New English Teas Ltd and Nicholas John Houghton* [2012] EWPCC 1 (UK); *Mei Fields Designs Ltd v Saffron Cards and Gifts Ltd*, Intellectual Property Enterprise Court [2018] EWHC 1332 (IPEC), [104] (UK).

[56] *Bodo Sperlein v Sabichi*, High Court of England and Wales, Chancery Division [2015] EWHC 1242 (IPEC) (UK).

To this effect, the defendants must: (a) point to designs available at the date of the alleged copying, other than the claimant's, which could be a plausible source of their design, and/or (b) establish that they did not have access to the claimant's design or copies thereof. If copying is established, the claimant must still show that his design was copied in substantial part. The defence could not be upheld in this particular case.

Evidence in determining whether the independent creation defence can be upheld may include preparatory work in the creation of the secondary work. Similarities of the two works ought to be assessed from the perspective of the average consumer of the category of works in question. This was held by the Belgian Court of Appeal which considered a claim for copyright infringement of two musical works and held that the evidence brought before the court, and in particular the preparatory materials in the creation of the secondary work, was not sufficient to establish a claim of independent creation.[57] Since it was not possible to establish such a claim, it was then essential to determine the auditory similarities between the two works. Such a comparison had to take place from the perspective of the average listener of music, rather than the technical analysis of musicologists. Looking at the facts at hand, the court concluded that there was strong inference of copying and hence copyright infringement.

In Sweden, the Supreme Court could not uphold the independent creation defence for two musical works that were substantially similar.[58] Prominent similarity between two works requires bringing proof of independent creation, with the burden of proof resting on the defendant. Determining this similarity takes place from the perspective of the average listener and should take into consideration the overall impression resulting from the comparison of the works at issue. In the present case, there were strong similarities between the two works. Where the two works are identical or almost identical, there is a strong presumption of copying. It is for the defendant to bring proof of independent creation which should demonstrate that the allegedly infringing work could have been created independently from the original work; this could not be established in the circumstances of the present case.

To be affirmed a defence which rests on a claim of independent creation should provide evidence that there was no access to the copyright protected work, or that there was no copying, and there is a reversed burden of proof in that it is the defendant who must establish the claim.

---

[57] 'Michael Jackson "You are not alone"', Court of Appeal, 8th ch. Brussels (Hof van Beroep, 8e kamer Brussel), 4 September 2007 (Belgium).

[58] 'Melody', Supreme Court (Högsta Domstolen), 11 April 2002, NJA 2002 s 178 (NJA 2002:23) (Sweden).

Right of communication to the public

Emanating from the relevant provisions of the World Intellectual Property Organization (WIPO) Copyright Treaty, Article 3 of the Information Society Directive lays down the communication right, according to which copyright holders should have

> the exclusive right to authorise or prohibit any communication to the public of their works, by wire or wireless means, including the making available to the public of their works in such a way that members of the public may access them from a place and at a time individually chosen by them.

The right has a broad scope of application and is meant to be understood in a broad sense[59] in order to ensure a high level of copyright protection. It is subject to a closed list of exceptions and limitations listed in Article 5(3) of the Information Society Directive and has been extensively discussed by the Court of Justice of the European Union, which has elaborated on the scope of the right and, importantly, on its internal limits.

The communication of a work usually involves copying.[60] The notorious overlap between the rights of communication and reproduction has been confirmed in the *Football Association Premier League and Others (FAPL)* case.[61] According to the Court of Justice, showing TV broadcasts in a public house involved two acts of reproduction: the creation of transient copies of the work within the decoder box and on the linked TV set, and the communication of works to the public. The temporary copying of fragments of a work in the memory of a device, as in the *FAPL* case, was found to qualify as an act of reproduction, but was exempt from infringement on the basis of Article 5(1) of the Information Society Directive, discussed in Chapter 4. As *FAPL* instructs,[62] such acts of copying merely facilitate the act of communicating the work and, in light of this, it is only communication that ought to be subject to authorial permission. Indeed, a key element of the court's reasoning was the sole purpose of the acts at issue was the facilitation of the reception of broadcasts which is not prohibited by UK or EU copyright law.

According to Recital 23 of the Information Society Directive, the communication right of Article 3 is construed broadly and include all broadcasts of a work by wire and wireless means, including communications over the air (terrestrial),

---

[59] Information Society Directive (Directive 2001/29/EC), Recital 23.

[60] EU Commission, Public Consultation on the Review of the EU Copyright Rules (2013), 11, available at < https://europa.eu/rapid/press-release_IP-13-1213_en.htm>, accessed 11 November 2019.

[61] *Football Association Premier League and Others*, Joint Cases C-403/08 and C-429/08, 4 October 2011, ECLI:EU:C:2011:631 (*FAPL*).

[62] *Football Association Premier League and Others*, Joint Cases C-403/08 and C-429/08, 4 October 2011, ECLI:EU:C:2011:631 (*FAPL*).

satellite, and cable broadcasting.[63] The broad definition of the right has been affirmed by the Court of Justice which has found that the right of communicating works to the public involves a number of activities, including the installation of TV sets in hotel rooms that would enable the cable retransmission of broadcasts[64] or the same via a TV antenna,[65] the showing of broadcasts in a public house,[66] the provision to a third party's subscribers to enable the receipt of encrypted TV broadcasts,[67] the streaming of TV broadcasts within the original broadcaster's catchment area,[68] hyperlinking,[69] and framing.[70] In all aforementioned instances the court found that an act of communication to the public was involved, and in this regard, authorial permission was required. This was because each activity involved the unauthorized transmission, or intervention for the transmission, of a work to an indeterminate and fairly large number of people (i.e. to a 'new public', as explained later in this chapter). In cases where such a portion of the public was not reached (namely when a new public was not involved), infringement of the communication right could not be established.[71] This flows from a newly elaborated doctrine of the 'new public' which determines the contours of the communication right. The doctrine is controversial and of profound interest because it could serve a defensive function against copyright infringement. It is examined as part of the doctrinal limits of the scope of protection later in this chapter and can, in some instances, be invoked to combat allegations of copyright infringement by denying that the re-communication at issue reached an audience beyond the one that the rightsholders had in mind when initially making the work available to the public.

---

[63] This recital reads:

This Directive should harmonise further the author's right of communication to the public. This right should be understood in a broad sense covering all communication to the public not present at the place where the communication originates. *This right should cover any such transmission or retransmission of a work to the public by wire or wireless means, including broadcasting.* This right should not cover any other acts. (Emphasis added.)

[64] *Sociedad General de Autores y Editores de España (SGAE) v Rafael Hoteles SA*, Case C-306/05, 7 December 2006, ECLI:EU:C:2006:764 (*Rafael Hoteles*).

[65] *Organismos Sillogikis Diacheirisis Dimiourgon Theatrikon kai Optikoakoustikon Ergon v Divani Acropolis Hotel and Rousim AE*, Case C-136/09, 18 March 2010, ECLI:EU:C:2010:151 (*Divani Acropolis*).

[66] *Football Association Premier League and Others*, Joint Cases C-403/08 and C-429/08, 4 October 2011, ECLI:EU:C:2011:631 (*FAPL*).

[67] *Airfield and Canal Digitaal v Sabam and Airfield NV v Agicoa Belgium BVBA*, Joined Cases C-431/09 and C-432/09, 13 October 2011, ECLI:EU:C:2011:648 (*Airfield*).

[68] *ITV Broadcasting Ltd v TV Catchup Ltd*, Case C-607/11, 7 March 2013, ECLI:EU:C:2013:147 (*ITV*).

[69] *Nils Svensson and Others v Retriever Sverige AB*, Case C-466/12, 13 February 2014, ECLI:EU:C:2014:76 (*Svensson*); also see *GS Media BV v Sanoma Media Netherlands BV, Playboy Enterprises International Inc., Britt Geertruida Dekker*, Case C-160/15, 8 September 2016, ECLI:EU:C:2016:644 (*GS Media*).

[70] *BestWater International GmbH v Michael Mebes, Stefan Potsch*, Case C-348/13, 21 October 2014 (order of the court), ECLI:EU:C:2014:2315 (*BestWater*).

[71] See e.g. *Società Consortile Fonografici (SCF) v Marco Del Corso*, Case C-135/10, 15 March 2012, ECLI:EU:C:2012:140 (*Del Corso*), [84]. See also to that effect *Mediakabel BV v Commissariaat voor de Media*, Case C-89/04, 5 June 2005, ECLI:EU:C:2005:348 (*Mediakabel*); *Nils Svensson and Others v Retriever Sverige AB*, Case C-466/12, 13 February 2014, ECLI:EU:C:2014:76 (*Svensson*).

As a general rule, the right of communication to the public is conceived broadly in that it should cover any transmission or retransmission of a protected work to members of the public. However, it is accepted that live performances are meant to be excluded with regards to all kinds of protected subject matter, but with the exception of databases. Indeed, the broad definition of the right of communicating works to the public was retained for databases only under the framework of EU copyright. According to Article 5(d) of the Database Directive, the author of a database has the right to 'carry out or authorize ... any communication, display or performance to the public.' With regards to other protected subject matter, however, the communication right covers only transmissions or retransmissions of the work to the public not present at the place where the communication originates.[72]

The Court of Justice upheld this position in *Circul Globus Bucureşti*,[73] a case involving the communication of musical works to the public in circus and cabaret shows. The court confirmed that such a communication of the works involved their live performance to a public that was in direct physical contact with the performers, i.e. the public was present at the place where the communication originated. This kind of communication was held to fall outside the scope of the communication right as defined in Article 3 of the Information Society Directive. Following *FAPL*, 'communication to the public' does not cover 'direct representation or performance'; this concept corresponds to that of 'public performance' which is protected by Article 11(1) of the Berne Convention and covers performances of works before a public that is in direct physical contact with the actor or performer. It is in this regard that Recital 23 refers to a public 'not present at the place where the communication originates'. According to the court, the right of communicating works to the public by virtue of Article 3 'does not cover any activity which does not involve a "transmission" or a "retransmission" of a work, such as live presentations or performances of a work'.[74] This can be read as an internal limitation to the communication right that effectively defines its scope.

<hr />

[72] Information Society Directive (Directive 2001/29/EC), Recital 23.

[73] *Circul Globus Bucureşti (Circ & Variete Globus Bucureşti) v Uniunea Compozitorilor şi Muzicologilor din România - Asociaţia pentru Drepturi de Autor* (UCMR - ADA), Case C-283/10, 24 November 2011, ECLI:EU:C:2011:772 (*Circul Globus*).

[74] Ibid., [40]. Note that Art. 3 applies to author's 'works' and not to other subject matter (e.g. performances, phonograms, films, and broadcasts). The latter is protected under Art. 3(2) (making available), but not under Art. 3(1) (communication to the public). This means broadcasters are protected against on-demand transmission of fixations of broadcasts ('making available'), but not against live streaming transmission of their broadcasts ('c2p'), thus it is not an infringement *of the broadcaster's right* to re-transmit broadcasts via Internet live streaming.

The key case is *C More Entertainment AB v Linus Sandberg*, C-279/13, 26 March 2015, ECLI:EU:C:2015:199. In this case, the Court held that:

   (a) 'making available' covers only on-demand transmission and cannot be interpreted as covering live transmission, and (b) Member States are free to extend the rights of broadcasters beyond those provided for by the Information Society and the Rental and Lending Directives.

Right of making available to the public

Article 3 of the Information Society Directive lays down the right to authorize or prohibit making a work available to the public 'in such a way that members of the public may access [it] from a place and at a time individually chosen by them.' This right expressly covers the act of making protected subject matter available online for download e.g. in peer-to-peer computer networks, including placing a hyper-link to a work hosted on a third party's website (as per *Svensson*)[75]. According to Recital 27 of the Information Society Directive, the mere provision of software or hardware facilities that enable such sharing of content are excluded from the scope of Article 3 and it is up to Member States to determine the conditions under which such a provision can give rise to secondary liability for copyright infringement by third parties such as Internet service providers.[76] In this context, the provisions of the e-Commerce Directive become relevant, including the safe harbours on caching and hosting content for the purpose of facilitating Internet transmissions.

The exhaustion principle

Exhaustion is a legal principle according to which, once a copy of a copyright work is distributed to the public by a sale or otherwise, the rightsholder's exclusive rights to control further distribution of that copy are exhausted and the purchaser is free to use or resell the work without further copyright restraints. The exhaustion principle applies to the distribution right only according to Article 4(2) of the Information Society Directive. In this sense, it is meant to cover tangible goods and not services. Unlike the distribution of hard copies of works, however, the electronic dissemination of copyright content is not 'exhausted' after the work has been first put on the market with the consent of the rightsholders. This flows from Article 3(3) of the Information Society Directive which reads that the reproduction, communication, and making available of rights 'shall not be exhausted by any act of communication to the public or making available to the public as set out in this Article.' In practice, this means that the rightsholders remain in control of every subsequent communication of works to the public.

There have been cases which discuss the possibility of copyright exhaustion for digital goods at worldwide level,[77] but the application of the exhaustion principle

---

This has the effect that the defence can work in Member States which have implemented the directives literally; but not in those that recognise a broad 'c2p' right to broadcasters (e.g. the United Kingdom or Sweden—the referring court in *C-More Entertainment*). The defence has practical interest as sport events do not attract copyright. Unless there are other copyrights in the broadcast (e.g. graphical works, musical works, etc.), the broadcast signal receives limited protection on the Internet in most Member States.

[75] *Nils Svensson and Others v Retriever Sverige AB*, Case C-466/12, 13 February 2014, ECLI:EU:C:2014:76 (*Svensson*).

[76] For an extensive discussion on the liability framework applicable to Internet service providers, see Chapter 9.

[77] See e.g. *Capitol Records LLC v ReDigi Inc.*, No. 12 Civ. 95 (RJS) (US).

by reference to EU copyright has been affirmed for computer programs only.[78] In *UsedSoft v Oracle*, the Court of Justice found that it is permissible to resell software licences even if the digital good has been downloaded directly from the Internet.[79] While the court affirmed that exhaustion can apply to electronic communication, it moved on to state that this is a *lex specialis* covering computer programs only, thus it does not apply to other categories of copyright content.[80] Recent cases from national courts have upheld the limited application of the court's ruling to software only.[81]

The exhaustion principle has traditionally been justified through the lens of property law in the sense that it marked the dividing line between two distinct yet colliding forms of property: the intellectual property rights on the 'intellectual creation' (work, invention, and brand) and the right of ownership over the embodiment thereof, i.e. the tangible medium (copy and product).[82] In copyright law the observation that the work is distinct from its physical embodiment made its way very early; it features in rulings of the mid eighteenth century, such as the UK case *Millar v Taylor*.[83] A normative explanation of exhaustion was originally developed in German scholarship, such as the work of Kohler,[84] and it also finds roots in the common law doctrine on the alienation of property.[85] Albeit conceptually implicit,

---

[78] *UsedSoft GmbH v Oracle International Corp*, Case C-128/11, 3 July 2012, ECLI:EU:C:2012:407 (*UsedSoft*).

[79] *UsedSoft GmbH v Oracle International Corp*, Case C-128/11, 3 July 2012, ECLI:EU:C:2012:407 (*UsedSoft*).

[80] *UsedSoft GmbH v Oracle International Corp*, Case C-128/11, 3 July 2012, ECLI:EU:C:2012:407 (*UsedSoft*); on the *lex specialis* nature of the Computer Programs Directive (Directive 2009/24/EC) see also *Nintendo Co. Ltd, Nintendo of America Inc., Nintendo of Europe GmbH v PC Box Srl, 9Net Srl*, Case C-355/12, 23 January 2014, ECLI:EU:C:2014:25 (*Nintendo*).

[81] See District Court Bielefeld (Landgericht Bielefeld), 4 O 191/11, 5 March 2013 (Germany); Court of Appeal of Hamm (Oberlandesgericht Hamm), 22 U 60/13, 15 May 2014 (Germany).

[82] Stavroula Karapapa, 'Reconstructing Copyright Exhaustion in the Online World' (2014) 4 *Intellectual Property Quarterly* 304.

[83] *Millar v Taylor* (1769) 4 Burrow 2303, at 2396–7 (UK):

> the copy thus abridged is equally a property in notion, and has no corporeal tangible substance. No disposition, no transfer of paper upon which the composition is written, marked, or impressed, (though it gives the power to print and publish,) can be construed a conveyance of the copy, without the author's express consent 'to print and publish;' much less, against his will. The property of the copy, thus narrowed, may equally go down from generation to generation, and possibly continue for ever; though neither the author nor his representatives should have any manuscript whatsoever of the work, original duplicate, or transcript.

[84] Josef Kohler, *Das Autorrecht: eine Zivilistische Abhandlung; zugleich ein Beitrag zur Lehre vom Eigenthum, vom Miteigenthum, vom Rechtsgeschäft und vom Individualrecht* (Jena: Fischer, 1880) 267.

[85] This was exemplified in *Dickens v Hawksley* [1935] Ch. 267, 274 (UK):

> The common law, therefore, had this conception with regard to rights of property in a literary work written, marked, or impressed or otherwise recorded upon some material thing namely, that the material thing might, as a subject of property, be separated from the literary work recorded on it and that the literary work might be regarded as an incorporeal subject of property and be owned separately from the material thing upon which it was recorded.

the central hypothesis behind the property justification for the exhaustion principle is the *tangibility* of the medium in which the intellectual creation has been incorporated. A hard copy can be distributed in hand-to-hand transactions, hence it can qualify as an object of property. It is not easy to assume this property rationale when it comes to electronic copies of works, however. This is not only because they lack tangibility, but also because they are usually licensed under terms and conditions that exclude any transfer of property.[86]

This point was affirmed in the *Allposters* case, where the Court of Justice found that exhaustion of the right of distribution under Article 4(2) of the Information Society Directive only applies to the tangible support of a work.[87] The case involved the unauthorized making and selling of altered versions of copyright protected artworks. In this case, the images were transferred on canvas first and were then sold on the Internet. The fact that there was an alteration, by means of the material used, was found to have a bearing in determining whether the distribution right had been exhausted, according to Cruz Villalón AG.[88] In line with the Opinion of the Advocate General, the court found that

the EU legislature, by using the terms 'tangible article' and 'that object', wished to give authors control over the initial marketing in the European Union of each tangible object incorporating their intellectual creation.

...

Accordingly, it should be found that exhaustion of the distribution right applies to the tangible object into which a protected work or its copy is incorporated if it has been placed onto the market with the copyright holder's consent.[89]

In a case with similar facts that reached the Canadian Supreme Court, transferring a work from paper to canvas was not held to amount to an infringement of the reproduction right on the basis that it did not involve the creation of new copies.[90] However, in *Allposters*, the focus was not on whether the act in question involved a reproduction or not, but whether the application of alterations of the medium of an authorized copy, giving the work a new form, allows the application

---

See also *Parfums Givenchy Inc. v C & C Beauty Sales Inc.*, 832 F. Supp. 1378, 1388–9 (C.D. Cal. 1993) (US); also see in this regard John M. Kernochan, 'The Distribution Right in the United States of America: Review and Reflections' (1989) 42 *Vanderbilt Law Review* 1407, 1412.

[86] Maurizio Borghi, Maria Lillà Montagnani, Mariateresa Maggiolino, and Massimiliano Nuccio, 'Determinants in the On-Line Distribution of Digital Content: an Exploratory Analysis' (2012) 3(2) *European Journal of Law and Technology* 1; also see in general Stavroula Karapapa, 'Reconstructing Copyright Exhaustion in the Online World' (2014) 4 *Intellectual Property Quarterly* 304.

[87] *Art & Allposters International BV v Stichting Pictoright*, Case C-419/13, 22 January 2015, ECLI:EU:C:2015:27 (*Allposters*).

[88] Opinion of AG Cruz Villalón in *Art & Allposters International BV v Stichting Pictoright*, Case C-419/13, 11 September 2014, ECLI:EU:C:2014:2214.

[89] Ibid., [37]–[40].

[90] See *Théberge v Galerie d'Art du Petit Champlain Inc.* [2002] 2 SCR 336, 2002 SCC 34 (Canada).

of the exhaustion principle. The court held that exhaustion cannot apply in situations where a reproduction of a protected work, after having been marketed in the European Union with the copyright holder's consent, has undergone an alteration of its medium, such as the transfer of that reproduction from a paper poster onto a canvas, and is placed on the market again in its new form.[91]

This judgment follows the rich body of preparatory work carried out before the adoption of the Information Society Directive, where it was systematically repeated that exhaustion applies to tangible copies only, without, however, addressing the issue of material alterations to the tangible copy circulated with the rightsholder's consent. The Follow-up to the Copyright Green Paper excluded the application of exhaustion from online communications of content: 'a large consensus exists that no exhaustion of rights occurs in respect of works and other subject matter exploited on-line, as this qualifies as a service.'[92] This restriction which results from the distinction between hard copies and content disseminated via online services, became more clear in the Proposal to the Information Society Directive,[93] which allowed exhaustion to the distribution of an 'object',[94] elsewhere referred to as 'tangible article', 'material copy', or 'material medium, namely an item of goods'.[95] Although statutory language would reflect early, and perhaps out-dated, models of online distribution, Recital 29 of the Information Society Directive expressly draws a line between material copies, the dissemination of which is subject to the exhaustion principle, and the delivery of content through services where dissemination is not exhausted and where any subsequent redistribution of those works is subject to the exclusive control of rightsholders.[96] It reads:

The question of exhaustion does not arise in the case of services and on-line services in particular. This also applies with regard to a material copy of a work or other subject-matter made by a user of such a service with the consent of the rightholder. Therefore, the same applies to rental and lending of the original and copies of works or other subject-matter which are services by nature. Unlike

---

[91] *Art & Allposters International BV v Stichting Pictoright*, Case C-419/13, 22 January 2015, ECLI:EU:C:2015:27 (*Allposters*), [49]; as explained by the Advocate General, in the present case exhaustion cannot apply because Art & Allposters meant to distribute a 'different object', through the alteration of the material support, and this ought to be taken into account.

[92] Follow-up to the Green Paper on Copyright and Related Rights in the Information Society of 20 November 1996, COM (96) 568 final, 2, 19, [4].

[93] Proposal for a European Parliament and Council Directive on the Harmonisation of Certain Aspects of Copyright and Related Rights in the Information Society, 98/C 108/03, COM (97) 628 final, OJ C 108, 7 April 1998, 6.

[94] Ibid., s. 4.2.

[95] Ibid., Recitals 18 and 19.

[96] This explains why the exhaustion doctrine does not apply to the rights of communicating and making works available to the public. See Information Society Directive (Directive 2001/29/EC), Art. 3(3). This position reflects consistent case law of the Court of Justice, e.g. *SA Compagnie Générale pour la diffusion de la télévision, Coditel SA v CinéVog Films SA and others*, Case C-62/79, 18 March 1980, ECLI:EU:C:1980:84 (*Coditel*).

CD-ROM or CD-I, where the intellectual property is incorporated in a material medium, namely an item of goods, every on-line service is in fact an act which should be subject to authorisation where the copyright or related right so provides.

The use of tangibility as the distinguishing factor of the nature of the transaction was based on an expansive interpretation of Article 6(1) of the WIPO Copyright Treaty (WCT) and Article 8 of the WIPO Performances and Phonograms Treaty that allegedly apply to tangible copies only. While allowing signatory countries the discretion to apply the principle of exhaustion 'after the first sale or other transfer of ownership of the original or a copy of the work with the authorization of the author',[97] the WIPO Treaties remain silent as to the application of the exhaustion rule in online transactions; it is only implicitly assumed that the question of exhaustion does not arise with regards to the online sale and delivery of content. Moving a step forward and exceeding the substantive minima, the Information Society Directive assimilated the copies distributed online to services with the effect that exhaustion does not apply.[98]

The fact that exhaustion does not apply to the right of communicating works to the public has an impact on the entitlement that consumers of electronic content get over that content. Effectively, they cannot resell this content to other parties since they often do not purchase an item of goods, but they access a service which they cannot claim to possess. This applies, for instance, to TV licences, electronic content available for download, or subscriptions to online streaming services. It also covers content that has been bought independently and not as part of a subscription in cases where access to the content is not autonomous—e.g. by having a lawfully downloaded copy on a computer's memory or portable media for an indefinite period of time—but depends on access through an online service. This is because consumers cannot exercise independent autonomous control over this content in a way that would amount to property rights over it. This inconsistent treatment of hard copies and online content becomes a source of legal uncertainty, as consumers arguably gain less entitlement over electronically disseminated content than over tangible copies of works, either analogue or digital.[99] It also demonstrates an imbalance in the protection of the freedom of movement of goods and of services within the European Union, in that a more stringent framework

---

[97] WIPO Copyright Treaty (WCT) 1996, Art. 6. See also WIPO Performances and Phonograms Treaty (WPPT) 1996, Art. 8.

[98] See André Lucas, 'International Exhaustion' in Lionel Bently, Uma Suthersanen, and Paul Torremans (eds), *Global Copyright Three Hundred Years Since the Statute of Anne, From 1709 to Cyberspace* (Cheltenham: Edward Edgar Publishing, 2010) 304, 309 et seq.; Pierre-Emmanuel Moyse, *Le Droit de Distribution: Analyse Historique et Comparative en Droit d'Auteur* (Cowansville, Québec: Les Editions Yvon Blais, 2007) 559–62.

[99] See in this regard Stavroula Karapapa, 'Reconstructing Copyright Exhaustion in the Online World' (2014) 4 *Intellectual Property Quarterly* 304.

governing the movement of services is in place in the context of the electronic dissemination of copyright protected content. In light of the principles and policy objectives underpinning the Content Portability Regulation[100] and the Geoblocking Regulation,[101] such an imbalanced approach does not merely limit user freedom, but it also impacts the objectives of the functioning of the European Union.

Exhaustion and computer programs

For software, however, online exhaustion does apply. In *UsedSoft v Oracle*,[102] the Court of Justice was asked to determine whether the distribution right applied only to 'tangible property' or whether it also applied to 'intangible copies', such as copies of computer programs.[103] The court found that intangible copies of software are also covered by the exhaustion principle. To reach this conclusion, it delved into an interpretation of Article 4(2) of the Computer Programs Directive in conjunction with Article 1(2) and Recital 7 of the Preamble. Article 4(2) refers to the 'sale ... of a copy of a program' and the protection afforded by the Directive is expanded through Article 1(2) to the expression 'in any form of a computer program', as also indicated in Recital 7.[104] The court stressed that the Computer Programs Directive is a *lex specialis* in relation to the broader framework of copyright protection outlined in the Information Society Directive,[105] without, however, offering an explanation as to how computer programs differ from other copyright works or whether the same outcome would be reached should the case be examined through the lens of the Information Society Directive.[106] The *UsedSoft* decision, however, waives the artificial premise of distribution on tangibility[107] and builds on a long

---

[100] Regulation (EU) 2017/1128 of the European Parliament and of the Council of 14 June 2017 on Cross-Border Portability of Online Content Services in the Internal Market, OJ L 168, 30 June 2017, 1–11.

[101] Regulation (EU) 2018/302 of the European Parliament and of the Council of 28 February 2018 on Addressing Unjustified Geo-Blocking and other forms of Discrimination based on Customers' Nationality, Place of Residence or Place of Establishment within the Internal Market and Amending Regulations (EC) No. 2006/2004 and (EU) 2017/2394 and Directive 2009/22/EC, OJ L 60I, 2 March 2018, 1–15.

[102] *UsedSoft GmbH v Oracle International Corp*, Case C-128/11, 3 July 2012, ECLI:EU:C:2012:407 (*UsedSoft*).

[103] Ibid., [53]–[61].

[104] Ibid., [55] and [57].

[105] Ibid., [56]. Also affirmed in District Court Bielefeld (Landgericht Bielefeld), 4 O 191/11, 5 March 2013 (Germany); Court of Appeal of Hamm (Oberlandesgericht Hamm), 22 U 60/13, 15 May 2014 (Germany).

[106] *UsedSoft GmbH v Oracle International Corp*, Case C-128/11, 3 July 2012, ECLI:EU:C:2012:407 (*UsedSoft*), [60]. In this light, the scope and impact of *UsedSoft* remains limited to the field of computer programs only, irrespective of whether these are disseminated in tangible form or not.

[107] Although this decision could be seen as a starting point for the need to revise legislation, two German decisions have affirmed the limited application of the *UsedSoft* ruling by upholding that the right of distribution is not subject to exhaustion when it comes to digital content other than software. See in this regard District Court Bielefeld (Landgericht Bielefeld), 4 O 191/11, 5 March 2013 (Germany); Court of Appeal of Hamm (Oberlandesgericht Hamm), 22 U 60/13, 15 May 2014 (Germany).

line of national authorities,[108] affirming that the exhaustion rule applies to the re-sale of computer programs.[109]

Exhaustion and e-books

The element of unrestricted autonomous control that was developed in *UsedSoft* cannot be justified by reference to other activities, such as the lending of e-books. In *VOB*,[110] the Court of Justice held *obiter* that exhaustion applies to 'the *physical* medium containing the work' (emphasis added),[111] confining the meaning of 'rental' under Article 2(1)(a) of the Rental and Lending Directive to tangible objects only[112] and effectively excluding the application of exhaustion by reference to e-lending.

The question of whether exhaustion covers the resale of e-books online has recently been addressed by the Court of Justice of the European Union following a referral from the Court of The Hague (Rechtbank Den Haag).[113] A website which

---

[108] '*Used' OEM-Software*, District Court Düsseldorf (Landgericht Düsseldorf), 26 November 2008, 12 O 431/08 (Germany) (where it was held that it is lawful to resell software separately from the hardware it was originally sold with, insofar as the first purchaser deleted the software from their own system, i.e. exhaustion could apply insofar as 'forward and delete' mechanisms are in place); *OEM-Vertrieb*, Federal Court of Justice (Bundesgerichtshof), 6 July 2000, I ZR 244/97 (Germany) (where the resale of software was found to be free, irrespective of restrictive licensing terms and conditions, when the software is put on the market by, or with the consent of, the rightsholders); District Court Hamburg (Landgericht Hamburg), 29 June 2008, 315 O 343/06 (Germany); *Gebrauchtsoftware*, Court of Appeal Hamburg (Hanseatisches Oberlandesgericht Hamburg), 7 February 2007 (Germany).
[109] Note that in *Ranks*, the Court of Justice held that back-up copying is limited to meet the needs of the person having the right to use that computer program and this does not include copying the program and offering it for resale. *Aleksandrs Ranks and Jurijs Vasiļevičs v Finanšu un ekonomisko noziegumu izmeklēšanas prokoratūra and Microsoft Corp.*, Case C-166/15, 12 October 2016, ECLI:EU:C:2016:762 (*Ranks*).
[110] *Vereniging Openbare Bibliotheken v Stichting Leenrecht*, Case C-174/15, 10 November 2016, ECLI:EU:C:2016:856 (*VOB*).
[111] Ibid., [59] (emphasis added).
[112] Ibid., [35]; Directive 2006/115/EC of the European Parliament and of the Council of 12 December 2006 on Rental Right and Lending Right and on Certain Rights Related to Copyright in the Field of Intellectual Property, OJ L 376, 27 December 2006, 28–35 (Rental and Lending Directive).
[113] See *Nederlands Uitgeversverbond and Groep Algemene Uitgevers v Tom Kabinet BV*, Case C-263/18 (*Tom Kabinet*). The questions are:

  1. Is Article 4(1) of the Copyright Directive to be construed as meaning that 'any form of distribution to the public by sale or otherwise of the original of their works or copies thereof' as referred to therein includes making available remotely by downloading, for use for an unlimited period, e-books (being digital copies of books protected by copyright) at a price by means of which the copyright holder receives remuneration equivalent to the economic value of the work belonging to him?
  2. If question 1 is to be answered in the affirmative, is the distribution right with regard to the original or copies of a work as referred to in Article 4(2) of the Copyright Directive exhausted in the Union, when the first sale or other transfer of that material, which includes making available remotely by downloading, for use for an unlimited period, e-books (being digital copies of books protected by copyright) at a price by means of which the copyright holder receives remuneration equivalent to the economic value of the work belonging to him, takes place in the Union through the rightholder or with his consent?

allows the resale of used e-books and takes measures to ensure that the illegal circulation of such books would be prevented was found lawful in three instances in the Netherlands[114] and the *UsedSoft* principles were held to apply.[115] However, the company hosting this website, Tom Kabinet, was held to be liable as an Internet service provider as they facilitated infringement by allowing the resale of illegal content. The Court of The Hague was unclear regarding the application of the exhaustion rule and referred the case to the Court of Justice.[116] The first two questions referred to the Court sought interpretative guidance on whether making e-books available remotely via a download, for use over an unlimited time and at a price which ensured that copyright holders receive appropriate remuneration, fell within the scope of the distribution right and was hence subject to the exhaustion rule. The questions strike at the heart of the legal classification of the sale of e-books either as a sale or a license and the impact of this classification on the application of exhaustion. Two critical considerations concern how computer programs (and their online sale) differ from e-books (and their online sale) and the possible functional equivalence between the distribution right and the communication right.[117] The last two questions of the referring court focus on acts of reproduction that inevitably take place in online transfers of e-books, seeking interpretative guidance on the legitimacy of the 'forward and delete' mechanisms, i.e. the transfer of e-books between successive acquirers of lawfully acquired copies in respect of which the distribution right has been exhausted. The prospects of a positive response to this examination are thin in light of *Allposters*.[118] What is more, the reasoning in *Redigi* about *new* and *additional* copies may be relevant in this case, as the reproduction right is likely impacted.[119]

3. Is Article 2 of the Copyright Directive to be construed as meaning that a transfer between successive acquirers of a lawfully acquired copy in respect of which the distribution right has been exhausted, constitutes consent to the acts of reproduction referred to therein, in so far as those acts of reproduction are necessary for the lawful use of that copy and, if so, which conditions apply?

4. Is Article 5 of the Copyright Directive to be construed as meaning that the copyright holder may no longer oppose the acts of reproduction necessary for a transfer between successive acquirers of the lawfully acquired copy in respect of which the distribution right has been exhausted and, if so, which conditions apply?

See also in this regard *NUV v Tom Kabinet*, Court of The Hague (Rechtbank Den Haag), 12 July 2017, ECLI:NL:RBDHA:2017:7543 (Netherlands); *NUV v Tom Kabinet*, Court of Appeal of Amsterdam, 20 January 2015, ECLI:NL:GHAMS:2015:66 (Netherlands).

---

[114] *NUV v Tom Kabinet*, Court of Appeal of Amsterdam, 20 January 2015, ECLI:NL:GHAMS:2015:66 (Netherlands).

[115] Ibid., [3.5.2], [3.5.3].

[116] *NUV v Tom Kabinet*, Court of Hague (Rechtbank Den Haag), 12 July 2017, ECLI:NL:RBDHA:2017:7543 (Netherlands).

[117] Stavroula Karapapa, 'Exhaustion of Rights on Digital Content under EU Copyright: Positive and Normative Perspectives' in Tanya Aplin (ed.), *Research Handbook on Intellectual Property and Digital Technologies* (Cheltenham: Edward Elgar, 2020), 481.

[118] *Art & Allposters International BV v Stichting Pictoright*, Case C-419/13, 22 January 2015, ECLI:EU:C:2015:27 (*Allposters*).

[119] *Capitol Records LLC v ReDigi Inc*, No. 12 Civ. 95 (RJS) (US), 6; Stavroula Karapapa, 'Exhaustion of Rights on Digital Content under EU Copyright: Positive and Normative Perspectives' in Tanya

Indeed, in his Opinion on the *Tom Kabinet* case, Szpunar AG identified three obstacles, from both a positivist and normative perspective, as to why digital exhaustion should not apply in reference to e-books. First, the Information Society Directive clearly intends to include downloading under the right of communication to the public, as numerous Recitals seem to indicate.[120] Secondly, the wording of various legislative instruments, including Article 4 of the Information Society Directive, have the effect that although distribution takes place by means of a transfer of ownership this cannot be claimed by reference to the right of communication to the public.[121] Finally, the resale of e-books inevitably involves acts of copying via downloading and acts of reproduction are not subject to the exhaustion rule[122] unless authorized by the rightsholders or permitted by the law. On the basis of these considerations, the Advocate General opined that the supply of e-books, by downloading for permanent use, is not covered by the distribution right, but it is covered by the right of communication to the public.

Following the Opinion of Szpunar AG, the Court of Justice[123] held that the supply of e-books, by downloading for permanent use, is covered by the right of communication to the public, in which case exhaustion is excluded under Article 3(3) of the Information Society Directive. In this light, a communication such as that effected by Tom Kabinet is made to a public that was not already taken into account by the copyright holders and, therefore, to a new public. This was because the making available of e-books is generally accompanied by a user licence which authorizes the user who has downloaded the relevant e-book only to read it from his or her own equipment. By excluding the application of the exhaustion rule in the context of the right of communication, the *Tom Kabinet* case offers definitive insights on the question of digital exhaustion, putting an end to the development of relevant defensive claims.

Adaptation right

Article 12 of the Berne Convention states that authors of literary or artistic works shall enjoy the exclusive right of authorizing adaptations, arrangements, and other

---

Aplin (ed.), *Research Handbook on Intellectual Property and Digital Technologies* (Cheltenham: Edward Elgar, 2020), 481.

[120] Information Society Directive (Directive 2001/29/EC), Recitals 24, 25, 28, and 29; also see Opinion of Advocate General Szpunar in *Nederlands Uitgeversverbond and Groep Algemene Uitgevers v Tom Kabinet BV*, Case C-263/18, 10 September 2019, ECLI:EU:C:2019:697, [36]–[42].
[121] Opinion of Advocate General Szpunar in *Nederlands Uitgeversverbond and Groep Algemene Uitgevers v Tom Kabinet BV*, Case C-263/18, 10 September 2019, ECLI:EU:C:2019:697, [44].
[122] Opinion of Advocate General Szpunar in *Nederlands Uitgeversverbond and Groep Algemene Uitgevers v Tom Kabinet BV*, Case C-263/18, 10 September 2019, ECLI:EU:C:2019:697, [45]–[48].
[123] *Nederlands Uitgeversverbond and Groep Algemene Uitgevers v Tom Kabinet BV*, Case C-263/18, 19 December 2019, ECLI:EU:C:2019:1111.

alterations of their works. Although not subject to EU harmonization, adaptation is understood as the transformation of a work into another form of expression that is not tantamount to a simple reproduction. That would include making a film out of a novel.

Unlike the reproduction right, the adaptation right has not been subject to full harmonization in the European Union. It has received only partial harmonization by reference to databases and to computer programs in Article 59(b) of the Database Directive and Article 4(1)(b) of the Computer Programs Directive respectively. It is, however, one of the rights that seems to have gained momentum on the Internet due to emergent technologies that modify content algorithmically. These technologies range from automatic translation tools to image modification techniques and can be the core business of various digital services. Significant differences remain in national laws as to whether adaptations are to be regarded as forms of reproduction, or whether they are subject to a separate right. France and the Netherlands, for instance, follow the former approach, whereas Germany and the United Kingdom follow the latter.

Although some insights may be drawn from the case law of the Court of Justice, uncertainty as to the scope of the adaptation right, and national divergence both on its scope and application, can prove impactful on the development of digital services that operate on the basis of acts of adaptation, especially when modifications or alterations are applied without the consent of the copyright holders. Discrepancies in national approaches may hinder innovation in that not all Member States equally encourage the development of services which rely on the adaptation of copyright-protected content.[124]

Doctrinal limits to rights

Exclusive rights are subject to certain doctrinal limitations that have evolved as part of the legislative definition and judicial interpretation of the scope of rights. These notably include (a) the nature of rights as acts of public address, in the sense that uses carried out in the private sphere are (usually) excluded from the scope of exclusive rights, and (b) the exploitative nature of rights, in that on certain (limited) occasions the non-commercial purpose of a given conduct may serve a defensive

---

[124] The Commission acknowledged this lack of harmonization in a leaked draft impact assessment on the modernization of EU copyright rules (available online at <http://statewatch.org/news/2014/apr/eu-com-copyright-ia-draft.pdf>, accessed 11 November 2019), where it states (at 99) that:

> Contrary to the reproduction right and the communication to the public/making available right, there is no express rule with respect to adaptations in the InfoSoc Directive (unlike the Software and in the Database Directive). However, the broad manner in which the reproduction right in Article 2 of that Directive is formulated and the CJEU's jurisprudence on the scope of the reproduction right notably in *Infopaq I* and *Eva-Marie Painer* seem to cover adaptations which give rise to a further reproduction within the meaning of Article 2.

function. With regard to the nature of exclusive rights as rights addressed to the public, the newly developed doctrinal concept of the 'new public' in the context of the right of communicating works to the public sets an internal limit to the scope of right by affirming that once an act of communication takes place to the same public that the rightsholders had in mind when making the initial communication of their works it does not amount to infringement. This overlap of the audience that has access to a work can serve a defensive function in that it does not impact on the normal exploitation of copyright works.

The 'public' as an inherent limitation to the scope of rights

Most rights in copyright law are addressed to the public, even indirectly. The Berne Convention, for instance, recognizes the rights of '*public* performance', of 'communication to the *public*', and of '*public* recitation'.[125] Articles 6(1) and 8 of the WCT provide for the right of making a work available to the *public*. Articles 10 and 14 of the WIPO Performances and Phonograms Treaty (WPPT) confer to performers and producers of phonograms, respectively, the right of making available their subject matter to the *public* and Article 15 of the same Treaty makes reference to the right of communicating the relevant subject matter to the *public*. In similar vein, the Information Society Directive provides a right of communicating works or, otherwise, making them available to the *public*[126] and a right of distribution to the *public*.[127]

The concept of the public remains elusive[128] and this is largely to do with the fact that its scope tends to shrink or expand depending on the right in question.[129] The meaning of the phrase 'to the public' in copyright law is not legislatively defined and, although numbers do not make the test, it is assumed that the public 'implies a fairly large number of persons.'[130] Because rights frame the scope of exclusivity and exploitation, judicial examination takes into account economic considerations

---

[125] Berne Convention, Arts 11, 11*bis*, 11*ter*, and 14. Also see TRIPs Agreement, Art. 11.

[126] Information Society Directive (Directive 2001/29/EC), Art. 3.

[127] Ibid., Art. 4.

[128] This is important beyond infringement. E.g. the subsistence of certain rights depends on publication (e.g. typographical arrangement of *published* editions in the UK), and the same applies to the exhaustion of the distribution right.

[129] ALAI, 'Report and Opinion on the Making Available and Communication to the Public in the Internet Environment: Focus on Linking Techniques on the Internet' (2014) 36(3) *European Intellectual Property Review* 149, 152.

[130] *Società Consortile Fonografici (SCF) v Marco Del Corso*, Case C-135/10, 15 March 2012, ECLI:EU:C:2012:140 (*Del Corso*), [84]. See also, to that effect, *Mediakabel BV v Commissariaat voor de Media*, Case C-89/04, 5 June 2005, ECLI:EU:C:2005:348 (*Mediakabel*), [30]; *Lagardère Active Broadcast v Société pour la perception de la rémunération équitable (SPRE) et al.*, Case C-192/04, 14 July 2005, ECLI:EU:C:2005:475 (*Lagardère*), [31]; *Sociedad General de Autores y Editores de España (SGAE) v Rafael Hoteles SA*, Case C-306/05, 7 December 2006, ECLI:EU:C:2006:764 (*Rafael Hoteles*), [37] and [38].

in determination of whether a particular use of copyright-protected works has reached the public. A line of recent rulings of the Court of Justice,[131] for instance, has indicated that with regard to the right of communicating works to the public, infringement will be established only when the audience reached through the subsequent (and unauthorized) communication of the work exceeds the public that the rightsholders had in mind when initially making the work available. This indicates that the impact of unauthorized conduct on exploitation is a key consideration and when no 'new public' is reached there cannot be infringement.

The copyright public is a legal fiction, largely shaped by qualitative criteria and economic considerations which flows from the nature of the various rights that are affected. Affirmative in this regard is the rich case law that was developed in English courts over a hundred years ago,[132] according to which an audience qualified as public where the relevant activity could whittle down the rightsholders' statutory monopoly. This 'monopoly' test[133] focuses on considerations regarding the exploitation of the works and was primarily developed with regard to public performances. In *Ernest Turner*,[134] the performance of music in a factory before 600 employees was held to be an infringement for the purposes of the Copyright Act.[135] Lord Greene opined that the 'statutory monopoly' granted under copyright law would be largely destroyed if such performances were to be permitted as rightsholders would likely consider this audience to form part of the public. In *Duck v Bates*,[136] however, the performance of a dramatic piece in a hospital room before 170 nurses, attendants, and other hospital workers, free of admission charge, was not to amount to infringement. This was because the hospital was not a place for public entertainment and such a performance would not, thereby, harm the rightsholder. A particular activity would reduce the value of the copyright 'monopoly' by depriving rightsholders of the public from whom they receive profit by selling their works. As indicated in the *Rangers* case, at a birthday party the 'use of a copyright work is not rebounding to the financial disadvantage of the owner of the copyright, since the selected audience is not employing the work under conditions in which they would normally pay for the privilege in one form or another.'[137] This marks a straight link between the copyright public and economic considerations inherent in the exploitative nature of performance rights. This historical understanding of exploitation, economic interests, and of reaching out to an audience in

---

[131] E.g. *Sociedad General de Autores y Editores de España (SGAE) v Rafael Hoteles SA*, Case C-306/05, 7 December 2006, ECLI:EU:C:2006:764 (*Rafael Hoteles*).

[132] See e.g. *Duck v Bates* (1883–84) L.R. 13 QBD 843 (UK).

[133] Stavroula Karapapa, *Private Copying* (London: Routledge, 2012) 68.

[134] *Ernest Turner Electrical Instruments v Performing Right Society* [1943] Ch. 167, 172–3 (UK); *Jennings v Stephens* [1936] Ch. 469 (UK); *Performing Rights Society v Rangers FC Supporters Club* [1974] SC 49 (UK).

[135] UK Copyright Act 1911, ss 1(2) and 2(3).

[136] *Duck v Bates* (1883–84) L.R. 13 QBD 843 (UK).

[137] *Performing Rights Society v Rangers FC Supporters Club* [1974] SC 49, 59 (UK).

a way that may affect copyright continues to inform discussions on whether a use is public or not. In the digital context, however, various aspects differ and this is not merely the ubiquitous nature of the Internet but also the very nature of digital content and the modes of electronic communication.

The doctrine of the 'new public' in the context of the communication right

In a line of recent decisions, the Court of Justice developed a reasoning similar to the 'monopoly test' of English courts when assessing if a use is public within the context of the communication right. This has given birth to the concept of the 'new public',[138] which is a doctrinal concept which stems from an extensive interpretation of the Berne Convention[139] with a view to assist in the interpretation of the scope of right. The 'new public' is an autonomous concept of EU copyright law; developed through the case law of the Court of Justice it serves as a doctrinal fine-tuning of the extremely broad scope of the communication right. A communication amounts to infringement whenever it is addressed to a 'new public', i.e. a public that was not taken into account by the rightsholders when authorizing the initial communication of the work. With its recent decisions, the Court of Justice doctrinally transformed the 'public', which features in the statutory language of Article 3 of the Information Society Directive, into a 'new public', which serves a central prerequisite for the application of the communication right.[140] When assessing infringement, it is no longer a new act of communication to the public that suffices; what matters is that this communication is addressed to a new public.[141] The concept of the 'new public' judicially frames the limits of the communication right towards a principle-based approach, centred on the very exploitative nature of the right.

Whereas an unauthorized communication on its own will likely amount to infringement if it ought to be subject to separate authorization, the finding that no

---

[138] See e.g. *Sociedad General de Autores y Editores de España (SGAE) v Rafael Hoteles SA*, Case C-306/05, 7 December 2006, ECLI:EU:C:2006:764 (*Rafael Hoteles*); *Società Consortile Fonografici (SCF) v Marco Del Corso*, Case C-135/10, 15 March 2012, ECLI:EU:C:2012:140 (*Del Corso*); *Teosto v A Taxi Driver* [2004] ECDR 3 (Finland).

[139] See Berne Convention, Art. 11*bis*(1)(i). Also see Emanuela Arezzo, 'Hyperlinks and Making Available Right in the European Union – what Future for the Internet after Svensson?' (2014) 45(5) *International Review of Intellectual Property and Competition Law* 524–55, 534; Association Littéraire et Artistique Internationale (ALAI), 'Opinion on the Criterion "New Public", Developed by the Court of Justice of the European Union (CJEU), Put in the Context of Making Available and Communication to the Public' (17 September 2014), available at http://www.alai.org/en/assets/files/resolutions/2014-opinion-new-public.pdf, accessed 11 November 2019.

[140] Stavroula Karapapa, 'The Requirement for a "New Public" in EU Copyright Law' (2017) 1 *European Law Review* 63.

[141] *Nils Svensson and Others v Retriever Sverige AB*, Case C-466/12, 13 February 2014, ECLI:EU:C:2014:76 (*Svensson*), [24].

new public was involved will serve as a defence. There will be no new public either because the communication in question does not need to be separately and individually authorized by the rightsholders, or the circle of recipients reached by an unauthorized activity has implicitly been licensed by the relevant rightsholders.

The 'new public' as an express requirement for infringement of the communication right

Although there were a few referrals in 2004 which concerned satellite broadcasting in the context of Directive 93/83/EEC, it was not until *Rafael Hoteles*[142] that the concept of the public started to gain momentum in the determination of infringement at the EU level. The case concerned the interpretation of the (then) newly introduced communication right under Article 3 of the Information Society Directive.[143] The referring court sought clarification as to what precisely 'the public' refers in the context of the right of communicating works to the public. Requesting insights as to whether installing TV sets in hotel rooms is included within the scope of this right, the questions expressly addressed the concept of the copyright public: does the fact that a hotel room is deemed to be a strictly domestic location mean that there is no communication to the public, and does the fact that successive viewers have access to the work mean that a communication effected through a television set inside a hotel bedroom be regarded as public?

On the basis of the principle that the right of 'communication to the public' must be interpreted broadly,[144] the court adopted a 'general approach',[145] taking into account customers who are present on the hotel premises instead of customers residing in hotel rooms and the fact that such customers tend to quickly succeed each other. This had the effect that 'a fairly large number of persons [were] involved'.[146] Qualitatively assessed, the public involved would become economically significant on the basis of their successive publicity. Despite the fact that hotel residents are usually a couple of individuals at a time, it was not the numbers that made the test, but the effect of the act in question on the exploitation of works, as in the English cases discussed earlier. Taken separately, the residents of hotel rooms are of limited economic significance, rather there is a cumulative effect when content is made

---

[142] *Sociedad General de Autores y Editores de España (SGAE) v Rafael Hoteles SA*, Case C-306/05, 7 December 2006, ECLI:EU:C:2006:764 (*Rafael Hoteles*).

[143] Before *Rafael Hoteles*, the Court of Justice discussed the communication right in two other cases, where it found that the term 'public' refers to an indeterminate number of potential television viewers. See *Mediakabel BV v Commissariaat voor de Media*, Case C-89/04, 5 June 2005, ECLI:EU:C:2005:348 (*Mediakabel*), [30]; *Lagardère Active Broadcast v Société pour la perception de la rémunération équitable (SPRE) et al.*, Case C-192/04, 14 July 2005, ECLI:EU:C:2005:475 (*Lagardère*), [31].

[144] Information Society Directive (Directive 2001/29/EC), Recital 23 (affirmed in *Sociedad General de Autores y Editores de España (SGAE) v Rafael Hoteles SA*, Case C-306/05, 7 December 2006, ECLI:EU:C:2006:764 (*Rafael Hoteles*), [36]).

[145] Ibid., [37].

[146] Ibid., [38]. Affirmed in *Mediakabel BV v Commissariaat voor de Media*, Case C-89/04, 5 June 2005, ECLI:EU:C:2005:348 (*Mediakabel*).

available to hotel clientele.[147] 'Thus, such a transmission is made to a public different from the public toward whom the original act of communication of the work is directed, that is, to a *new public*,' the court concluded.[148]

The court noted that, according to the Guide to the Berne Convention, an interpretative document drawn up by the WIPO in 1978, the public that the rightsholders have in mind when authorizing a broadcast comprises only 'direct users, that is, the owners of reception equipment who, either personally or within their own private or family circles, receive the programme'.[149] A reception that reaches a larger audience, i.e. a new section of the receiving public, amounts to an independent act through which the broadcast work is communicated to a new public. The absence of an intervention (the intervention itself created by the provision of television sets), would mean that hotel customers would not be able to enjoy the broadcast work.[150] Hence, what mattered in this case that the public was offered the *possibility* of accessing the work,[151] irrespective of whether they actually accessed the work or not. This places the emphasis on the 'enabling role' of the communication.[152]

Hotel clientele were also found to amount to a new public in other cases of the Court of Justice, such as the *Divani Acropolis* order[153] and *Phonographic Performance*.[154] In this latter case, the court stabilized its approach into three main criteria which form the test to assess infringement of the right of communication to the public. First, there is an act of communication and the hotel operator has a central role in the broadcasting of the protected subject matter. Second, a potentially broad, and a largely undetermined, number of people visit hotels and gain

---

[147] See e.g. Berne Convention, Art. 11*bis*(1)(ii). This Article defines the communication to the public right, and the court in both *Rafael Hoteles* and *FAPL* made a relevant mention.

[148] *Sociedad General de Autores y Editores de España (SGAE) v Rafael Hoteles SA*, Case C-306/05, 7 December 2006, ECLI:EU:C:2006:764 (*Rafael Hoteles*), [40]. Emphasis added. See contra *Svensson* (where the fact that a communication is initiated by an organization other than the original one did not by default mean that the communication was addressed to a new public). Regarding the word 'thus' in [40] of the *Rafael Hoteles* case, it has arguably been criticized as a *non sequitur*.

[149] *Sociedad General de Autores y Editores de España (SGAE) v Rafael Hoteles SA*, Case C-306/05, 7 December 2006, ECLI:EU:C:2006:764 (*Rafael Hoteles*), [40]. See in this regard the criticism expressed in Association Littéraire et Artistique Internationale (ALAI), 'Opinion on the Criterion "New Public", Developed by the Court of Justice of the European Union (CJEU), Put in the Context of Making Available and Communication to the Public' (17 September 2014), available at <http://www.alai.org/en/assets/files/resolutions/2014-opinion-new-public.pdf>, accessed 11 November 2019, 16 et seq. (stressing that the WIPO issued a newer version of the Guide in 2003, and, secondly, the old Guide considers retransmissions by loudspeakers).

[150] *Sociedad General de Autores y Editores de España (SGAE) v Rafael Hoteles SA*, Case C-306/05, 7 December 2006, ECLI:EU:C:2006:764 (*Rafael Hoteles*), [42].

[151] Ibid., [43]. Emphasis added.

[152] ALAI, 'Report and Opinion on the Making Available and Communication to the Public in the Internet Environment: Focus on Linking Techniques on the Internet' (2014) 36(3) *European Intellectual Property Review* 149, 152.

[153] *Organismos Sillogikis Diacheirisis Dimiourgon Theatrikon kai Optikoakoustikon Ergon v Divani Acropolis Hotel and Rousim AE*, Case C-136/09, 18 March 2010, ECLI:EU:C:2010:151 (*Divani Acropolis*).

[154] *Phonographic Performance (Ireland) Limited v Ireland and Attorney General*, Case C-162/10, 15 March 2012, ECLI:EU:C:2012:141.

access to these broadcasts. This means that there is a communication addressed to a new public. Finally, broadcasting has a lucrative purpose: hotel clients choose to access the broadcasts and pay to gain this access. On the basis of these conditions, the court found that there is communication for which an equitable remuneration should be provided to the relevant rightsholders.

Successive publicity by reference to electronic networks was discussed in the *Pirate Bay* case.[155] Reverting to established case law, the Court of Justice explained that the concept of the 'public' involves a certain *de minimis* threshold, excluding groups of persons that are too small or insignificant, but taking into consideration the cumulative effect of making the works available. In this regard, it is important to know how many persons can access the same work at the same time *and* also how many of them have access to it in succession.[156] On the basis of these principles, the Court of Justice held that the communication taking place in the *Pirate Bay* case covers, at the very least, all of the platform users who can access at any time, and simultaneously, the protected works which are shared through the platform. Where the communication is aimed at an indeterminate number of potential recipients and involves a large number of persons,[157] such as a communication which takes place through peer-to-peer networks, it is addressed to a 'public' within the meaning of Article 3(1) of the Information Society Directive. This seems to affirm that communications addressed to a small group of individuals will be exempt from infringement because the group does not qualify as a 'public', thus it serves a defensive function in relevant cases.

Although the 'new public' was first discussed in *Rafael Hoteles*, it was not until *FAPL* that it was raised into an express requirement for infringement.[158] When copyright holders authorize a broadcast of their works, they take into account solely the owners of TV sets who, either personally or within their own private or family circles, receive the signal and follow the broadcasts, hence any set of users outside this circle is likely to be a new public. The clientele of a public house were found to be an additional public and were not taken into account by the rightsholders when authorizing the broadcasting of their works.[159] It was immaterial that the relevant act of communication was of a profit-making nature[160] or generating financial profit for its owner.[161]

---

[155] *Stichting Brein v Ziggo BV, XS4ALL Internet BV*, Case C-610/15, 14 June 2017, ECLI:EU:C:2017:456 (*The Pirate Bay*).

[156] Ibid., [41]; also see *Stichting Brein*, C-527/15, 26 April 2017, ECLI:EU:C:2017:300, [44].

[157] *Stichting Brein v Ziggo BV, XS4ALL Internet BV*, Case C-610/15, 14 June 2017, ECLI:EU:C:2017:456 (*The Pirate Bay*), [42].

[158] *Football Association Premier League and Others*, Joint Cases C-403/08 and C-429/08, 4 October 2011, ECLI:EU:C:2011:631 (*FAPL*), [197]. For a comment, see Tanya Aplin, "'Reproduction" and "Communication to the Public": Rights in EU Copyright Law: FAPL v QC Leisure' (2011) 22(2) *King's Law Journal* 209.

[159] *FAPL*, [199].

[160] Ibid., [204]. Also see *Sociedad General de Autores y Editores de España (SGAE) v Rafael Hoteles SA*, Case C-306/05, 7 December 2006, ECLI:EU:C:2006:764 (*Rafael Hoteles*), [44].

[161] *Football Association Premier League and Others*, Joint Cases C-403/08 and C-429/08, 4 October 2011, ECLI:EU:C:2011:631 (*FAPL*), [205].

Just nine days after the *FAPL* case was issued, the requirement that there ought to be a 'new public' was expressly repeated and upheld in *Airfield v SABAM*, and a parallel action involving *Agicoa*.[162] The Court of Justice held that satellite platform operators may need to seek authorization before offering their customers access to broadcast channels because such access is a separate act of communication and the customers of the platform are likely to be a new public, i.e. a public wider than that targeted by the original broadcaster. There is no need to obtain authorization only in cases involving a limited intervention, such as the mere provision of physical facilities for enabling or making the communication.[163] The intervention in question was held to amount to an autonomous service, carried out with a profit-making purpose. This autonomous service did not merely enable access to the communication of a single broadcasting organization, but it brought together a number of channels from various organizations in a new audiovisual product, with the satellite package provider deciding upon the composition of the package thereby created. This had the effect that the satellite package provider expanded the circle of recipients of television programmes and was hence reaching out to a new public.[164]

Focusing on the online context, the court in *ITV*[165] ruled on the transmission of works included in a terrestrial broadcast and their being made available over the Internet. Because these two acts had to be subject to authorization individually and separately from the relevant rightsholders, there was no need to examine the requirement that there must be a new public.[166] The reason for the decision was that the mode of retransmission of the signal differed from that of the original communication and was hence a new act of communication, even though it was possibly reaching the same public. This indicates that the requirement that there must be a new public should be taken into consideration only where the retransmission is realized through the same technical means and is thereinafter subject to a single act of authorization. In this light, the *ITV* case raises doubts as to the viability of the 'new public' requirement as a determinant factor in decisions on infringement of the communication right.[167]

---

[162] *Airfield and Canal Digitaal v Sabam* and *Airfield NV v Agicoa Belgium BVBA*, Joined Cases C-431/09 and C-432/09, 13 October 2011, ECLI:EU:C:2011:648 (*Airfield*). Although this case is in line with *Rafael Hoteles* and *FAPL*, its implications are broader in the sense that it created the need for platform operators and also other program aggregators to review their licensing agreements with content suppliers and collecting societies.

[163] *Airfield and Canal Digitaal v Sabam* and *Airfield NV v Agicoa Belgium BVBA*, Joined Cases C-431/09 and C-432/09, 13 October 2011, ECLI:EU:C:2011:648 (*Airfield*), [74].

[164] Ibid., [81].

[165] *ITV Broadcasting Ltd v TV Catchup Ltd*, Case C-607/11, 7 March 2013, ECLI:EU:C:2013:147.

[166] *ITV Broadcasting Ltd v TV Catchup Ltd*, Case C-607/11, 7 March 2013, ECLI:EU:C:2013:147, [39].

[167] See in this regard Association Littéraire et Artistique Internationale (ALAI), 'Opinion on the Criterion "New Public", Developed by the Court of Justice of the European Union (CJEU), Put in the Context of Making Available and Communication to the Public' (17 September 2014),

Hyperlinks and the new public

Svensson[168]addressed the question as to whether hyperlinks constitute an act of communication to the public within the meaning of Article 3(1) of the Information Society Directive. Taking into account the broad construal that the communication right ought to ensure a high level of protection for copyright holders,[169] the court concluded, in just two paragraphs, that hyperlinking amounted to an act of communication.[170] Applying *Rafael Hoteles*, communication was equated to making works available 'to a public in such a way that the persons forming that public may access it, irrespective of whether they avail themselves of that opportunity'.[171] This had the effect that 'the provision of clickable links to protected works must be considered to be "making available" and, therefore, an "act of communication"'.[172] Perhaps this is the most problematic aspect in *Svensson* and one that is criticized by the EU Parliament itself in the so-called 'Reda' report.[173]

This preliminary conclusion reached in *Svensson* is unworkable for two main reasons. First, the facts in *Rafael Hoteles* differed substantially, hence reliance on the principle of analogy was not appropriate. Unlike the installation of TV sets in hotel rooms, hyperlinks do *not* amount to an act of communication as their function is to merely signpost an electronic address. This is not only well-established in academic literature,[174] but also in national case law.[175] Serving as 'location

available at <http://www.alai.org/en/assets/files/resolutions/2014-opinion-new-public.pdf>, accessed 11 November 2019, 19 et seq.

[168] *Nils Svensson and Others v Retriever Sverige AB*, Case C-466/12, 13 February 2014, ECLI:EU:C:2014:76 (*Svensson*), [26]–[28].

[169] Reference was made to, *Football Association Premier League and Others*, Joint Cases C-403/08 and C-429/08, 4 October 2011, ECLI:EU:C:2011:631 (*FAPL*), [193] and Recitals 4 and 9 of Directive 2001/29/EC. See *Nils Svensson and Others v Retriever Sverige AB*, Case C-466/12, 13 February 2014, ECLI:EU:C:2014:76 (*Svensson*), [19].

[170] *Nils Svensson and Others v Retriever Sverige AB*, Case C-466/12, 13 February 2014, ECLI:EU:C:2014:76 (*Svensson*), [19]–[20].

[171] Ibid., [19].

[172] Ibid., [20].

[173] European Parliament, Committee on Legal Affairs, Draft Report on the Implementation of Directive 2001/29/EC of the European Parliament and of the Council of 22 May 2001 on the Harmonisation of Certain Aspects of Copyright and Related Rights in the Information Society, 15 January 2015, 2014/2256(INI), point 15.

[174] See in this regard European Copyright Society, Opinion on the Reference to the CJEU in Case C-466/12 *Svensson*, 15 February 2013, [35] et seq.

[175] See *Handelsblatt Publishers Group v Paperboy*, [2005] ECDR 7 (Germany); *Napster.no* (2006) IIC 120 (27 January 2005), [44]–[47] (Norway); *Sociedad General de Autores y Editores (SGAE) v Jesús Guerra Calderón*, Case No. 67/10, Commercial Court No. 7 of Barcelona, 9 March 2010 (unreported) (Spain); Misdemeanous Court of Kilkis, 965/2010 (Greece); *Home A/S v Ofir A/S*, Maritime & Commercial Court (Sø-og Handelsretten), 1 February 2006, v-108-99 (Denmark); Bundesgerichtshof, 29 April 2010, I ZR 69/08, *aff'd* in I ZR 140/10 of 19 October 2011 (Germany); *Paramount Home Entertainment International Ltd, et al v British Sky Broadcasting Ltd* [2013] EWHC 3479 (Ch), [37] (UK); contra: *Reformation Publishing Co Ltd v Cruiseco Ltd*, Intellectual Property Enterprise Court, [2018] EWHC 2761 (Ch), 22 October 2018 (where the UK Intellectual Property Enterprise Court held that posting the video on a file-sharing platform did not amount to making the video available to anyone but sending a hyperlink to that site made its contents available to the recipient of the hyperlink).

tools',[176] hyperlinks merely redirect users to content made available by third parties,[177] they do not involve the *transmission* of content which is an important constituent of the scope of right, according to the new WIPO Guide.[178] Making the posting of hyperlinks which lead to freely available content subject to authorial consent would undermine the sound operation of the Internet which, as the Court of Justice itself has affirmed 'is of particular importance to freedom of expression and of information, enshrined in Article 11 of the Charter, as well as to the exchange of opinions and information in that network characterised by the availability of incalculable amounts of information.'[179] Secondly, *Svensson* equated the act of communication to an act of making works available and, in this regard, did not shed light on the seemingly distinct, yet oddly overlapping scope of the making available right.[180] By reference to the 'making available right', the new WIPO Guide indicates that 'what is relevant is the *first* making available of the work to the public',[181] however, hyperlinks cannot amount to such an act of first making available to the public as they presuppose that the content is already available via another electronic address; they merely redirect users to materials already posted online.

On the assumption that an act of communication takes place via hyperlinks, the court moved on to assess whether such a communication reaches a new public. According to the court in *Svensson*:

> the public targeted by the initial communication consisted of all potential visitors to the site concerned, since, given that access to the works on that site was not subject to any restrictive measures, all internet users could therefore have free access to them.[182]

---

[176] European Copyright Society, Opinion on the Reference to the CJEU in Case C-466/12 *Svensson*, 15 February 2013, [40].

[177] Ibid., [9] et seq., [35]–[40]. Embedded links through framing were found to amount to an act of communication: *BestWater International GmbH v Michael Mebes, Stefan Potsch*, Case C-348/13, 21 October 2014 (order of the court), ECLI:EU:C:2014:2315 (*BestWater*); also see *Innoweb BV v Wegener ICT Media BV and Wegener Mediaventions BV*, Case C-202/12, 19 December 2013, ECLI:EU:C:2013:850 (*Innoweb*).

[178] See e.g. *ITV Broadcasting Ltd v TV Catchup Ltd*, Case C-607/11, 7 March 2013, ECLI:EU:C:2013:147, [23].

[179] *Spiegel Online v Volker Beck*, Case C-516/17, 29 July 2019, ECLI:EU:C:2019:625 (*Spieleg Online*), [81]; *GS Media BV v Sanoma Media Netherlands BV, Playboy Enterprises International Inc., Britt Geertruida Dekker*, Case C-160/15, 8 September 2016, ECLI:EU:C:2016:644 (*GS Media*), [45]; *Land Nordrhein-Westfalen v Dirk Renckhoff*, Case C-161/17, 7 August 2018, ECLI:EU:C:2018:634, [40].

[180] Stavroula Karapapa, 'The Requirement for a "New Public" in EU Copyright Law' (2017) 1 *European Law Review* 63, [63, at 72].

[181] On the making available right see Mihály Ficsor, *Guide to the Copyright and Related Rights Treaties Administered by WIPO and Glossary of Copyright and Related Rights Terms* (Geneva: WIPO, 2003) 49: 'what is relevant is the *first* making available of the work to the public'; IFPI, 'The WIPO Treaties: 'Making Available' Right', March 2003, 1: 'Implementing legislation should cover the initial act of putting a work or phonogram on an interactive network, as well as any subsequent transmissions.'

[182] Ibid., [26].

This had the effect that the rightsholders were assumed to have offered free access to their protected subject matter to the public, understood to refer to 'all Internet users' because no access control protocols were put in place. Although implicit in this reasoning was the understanding that the relevant rightsholders retained full control to exercise their exclusive rights on condition that they had installed access mechanisms to indicate their wish to restrict the availability of their materials online, it has been argued that this controversial part of the decision introduces a 'waiver *erga omnes* (or at least, as to all members of the intended public)'[183] and in this regard has 'the unfounded and illegitimate effect of exhaustion of the communication to the public right or, rather, the scope of that right is *reduced* by the court from the outset.'[184]

As will be discussed in Chapter 5 the effect of the *Svensson* case is more akin to an affirmation of an implied license than to copyright exhaustion. Indeed, the Court of Justice itself seems to align with such reasoning in *GS Media*.[185] Referring to *Svensson* and *BestWater*,[186] the court held that

> as soon as and as long as that work is freely available on the website to which the hyperlink allows access, it must be considered that, where the copyright holders of that work have consented to such a communication, they have included all internet users as the public.[187]

This did not seem to apply to *GS Media*, however. Unlike *Svensson* and *BestWater*, the content was available without the consent of the rightsholders. GS Media published an article which included part of a photograph and ended with the words: 'And now the link with the pics you've been waiting for.' By clicking on this hyperlink, readers were directed to an Australian data storage website called Filefactory.com, where another hyperlink allowed them to download a file in .zip format which contained eleven files in .pdf format, each of which contained one of Sanoma's photographs. GS Media refused to remove the hyperlink in question (although the photographs were removed from the Filefactory.com website), despite Sanoma's demands, and they later published two further articles featuring new hyperlinks to photographs taken by Britt Dekker. Sanoma were successful in their

---

[183] Association Littéraire et Artistique Internationale (ALAI), 'Opinion on the Criterion "New Public", Developed by the Court of Justice of the European Union (CJEU), Put in the Context of Making Available and Communication to the Public' (17 September 2014), available at <http://www.alai.org/en/assets/files/resolutions/2014-opinion-new-public.pdf>, accessed 11 November 2019, 16.

[184] Ibid., 15–16.

[185] *GS Media BV v Sanoma Media Netherlands BV, Playboy Enterprises International Inc., Britt Geertruida Dekker*, Case C-160/15, 8 September 2016, ECLI:EU:C:2016:644 (*GS Media*).

[186] *Nils Svensson and Others v Retriever Sverige AB*, Case C-466/12, 13 February 2014, ECLI:EU:C:2014:76 (*Svensson*); *BestWater International GmbH v Michael Mebes, Stefan Potsch*, Case C-348/13, 21 October 2014 (order of the court), ECLI:EU:C:2014:2315 (*BestWater*).

[187] *GS Media BV v Sanoma Media Netherlands BV, Playboy Enterprises International Inc., Britt Geertruida Dekker*, Case C-160/15, 8 September 2016, ECLI:EU:C:2016:644 (*GS Media*), [42].

claims before the Amsterdam District Court and the Amsterdam Court of Appeal. Each court examined different aspects, but reached the same outcome. The District Court found that GS Media's activities had been unlawful because they encouraged website visitors to view photographs that were illegally posted on Filefactory.com. Without those hyperlinks, the photographs would not have been easy to find. The Court of Appeal held that GS Media had infringed copyright by posting part of one of the photographs on the relevant website but, at the same time, had not made the photographs available to the public through hyperlinks.

The Dutch Supreme Court stayed proceedings and referred a number of questions relating to the lawfulness of hyperlinks to the Court of Justice. According to the Court of Justice, central to the finding of infringement of the communication right was the profit-making nature of the activity, as a determinant factor in establishing if the website had knowledge of the infringing activity or not. As the court noted, it cannot be inferred either from *Svensson* or from *BestWater* that website posting of hyperlinks to protected works which have already been made freely available on another website, but without the consent of the copyright holders of those works, would be excluded, as a matter of principle, from the concept of 'communication to the public' within the meaning of Article 3(1) of the Information Society Directive. Rather, those decisions confirm the importance of such consent under that provision as the latter specifically provides that every act of communication of a work to the public is to be authorized by the copyright holder.[188]

Acknowledging that hyperlinks contribute to the sound operation of the Internet and exchange of information in that network, the court also noted the difficulty of individuals wishing to post such links to ascertain whether those links are protected or not, and whether authorial consent had been given, especially in light of the possibility that the status of consent may change at a later stage.[189] In order to determine whether a 'communication to the public' took place, it was, accordingly, necessary to take into account the fact that a person posting a hyperlink with no intention to pursue a profit does not know, and cannot reasonably know, that that work had been published on the Internet without the consent of the copyright holder. As the court noted, such a person does not, in principle, intervene with full knowledge of the consequences of his or her conduct in order to give customers access to a work illegally posted on the Internet.[190] By contrast, where evidence indicates that such a person knew or ought to have known that the hyperlink they posted provides access to a work illegally placed on the Internet, for example owing to the fact that they were notified thereof by the copyright holders, it is necessary to consider that the provision of that link constitutes a 'communication to the public'.

---

[188] *GS Media BV v Sanoma Media Netherlands BV, Playboy Enterprises International Inc., Britt Geertruida Dekker*, Case C-160/15, 8 September 2016, ECLI:EU:C:2016:644 (*GS Media*), [43].

[189] Ibid., [44]–[46].

[190] Ibid., [48].

This is important because, according to copyright principles, knowledge has never been a prerequisite for primary liability in Europe and in this regard the court bridged the conditions applicable to primary and secondary liability.

Most importantly, the court found in paragraph 51 of the judgment that:

> when the posting of hyperlinks is carried out for profit, it can be expected that the person who posted such a link carries out the necessary checks to ensure that the work concerned is not illegally published on the website to which those hyperlinks lead, so that it must be presumed that posting has occurred with the full knowledge of the protected nature of that work and the possible lack of consent to publication on the internet by the copyright holder. In such circumstances, and in so far as that rebuttable presumption is not rebutted, the act of posting a hyperlink to a work which was illegally placed on the internet constitutes a 'communication to the public' within the meaning of Article 3(1) of Directive 2001/29.

Interestingly, the court also stressed that if there is no new public there will be no communication to the public, where the works to which those hyperlinks allow access have been made freely available on another website with the consent of the rightsholder. The case is interesting, as well as controversial. For reasons explained in more detail below, the court focused on the profit-making nature of posting hyperlinks as a factor in establishing knowledge of the infringing nature of the activity, but not as a condition for the application of the communication right. This is odd given the doctrinal independence of the notion of primary infringement from the element of knowledge as, to a certain extent, the case appears to introduce conditions of secondary liability in cases of for-profit hyperlinking.

Reliance on the 'new public' requirement is based on a complicated logic that cannot result in legal certainty. As has been seen, this newly developed requirement depends on additional conditions being inserted in the test of infringement, e.g. the satellite requirement of the 'same technical means'.[191] This may lead to unpredictable outcomes, in that the indeterminate body of Internet users is in principle a far larger circle of recipients than residents of hotel bedrooms or a pub's clientele. Unlike what happens in the borderless web, the spatial element of an establishment delimits the use *ab initio*, no matter the fact that it is open to the general public. The test for infringement is, hence, not based on a simple rule that would match sensible user expectations and thus it becomes difficult to tell which communications amount to infringement and which do not.

---

[191] Association Littéraire et Artistique Internationale (ALAI), 'Opinion on the Criterion "New Public", Developed by the Court of Justice of the European Union (CJEU), Put in the Context of Making Available and Communication to the Public' (17 September 2014), 2, available at http://www.alai.org/en/assets/files/resolutions/2014-opinion-new-public.pdf, accessed 11 November 2019.

The complicated logic of the new public requirement could be overcome if reference was made to specific sets of users that do not fall under the public that the rightsholders had in mind when authorizing the initial communication.[192] Case law indicates that there are two kinds of audiences that do not fall under the authorial public. Firstly, there are private users, and secondly, there are those who have gained access to the content with express or implied authorization from the rightsholders. In both of these instances, economic considerations are paramount: private users are those to whom the rightsholders cannot have a reasonable expectation of licensing further copies of works and lawful users are those who have already bought or gained lawful access to the copies. Although bearing the same legal result, these kinds of users differ in one central aspect: lawful users are part of the public, but they have already received authorization, and private users do not need to receive authorization, as they are not part of the public in the first place.[193]

The owners of a copyright work, or those who have lawfully purchased access to it, are the public that the authors had in mind when authorizing a specific use. Lawful users are not only those who have actually purchased the protected works or those benefiting from a particular exception or limitation[194] but also those who have gained access to those works from the rightsholders or with their consent. Issuing the same copies of a protected work to these lawful owners or possessors cannot amount to infringement. This has been affirmed in the *FAPL* case where it was stressed that when authors authorize a broadcast of their works they take into account solely the owners of TV sets who, either personally or within their own private or family circles, receive the signal and follow the broadcasts. The same position has been upheld in the US jurisprudence, in cases such as *Aereo*,[195] where the question was whether a technologically complex service allowing its subscribers to watch television programmes over the Internet amounts to an act of public performance within the meaning of section 101 of the US Copyright Act. The Supreme Court found that Aereo communicated the same contemporaneously perceptible images and sounds to a large number of people who were unrelated and unknown to each other and stressed that the 'public' does not need to be situated together, spatially or temporally, hence Aereo transmitted a performance of the protected works to the public.

A private circle typically includes one's immediate family and close social acquaintances.[196] The problems with the private/public distinction lie in cases where

---

[192] Stavroula Karapapa, 'The Requirement for a "New Public" in EU Copyright Law' (2017) 1 *European Law Review* 63, [63, at 77 et seq].

[193] Stavroula Karapapa, 'The Requirement for a "New Public" in EU Copyright Law' (2017) 1 *European Law Review* 63, [63, at 77 et seq].

[194] See e.g. *Public Relations Consultants Association Ltd v Newspaper Licensing Agency Ltd and Others*, Case C-360/13, 5 June 2014, ECLI:EU:C:2014:1195, [59].

[195] *American Broadcasting Companies, Inc. et al, Petitioners v Aereo, Inc., FKA Bamboom Labs, Inc.*, 573 U.S. 431 (2014) 1 (US).

[196] Stavroula Karapapa, *Private Copying* (London: Routledge, 2012) 49, 52.

an audience qualifies neither as abstractly public nor as private.[197] Such a question was discussed in *Del Corso*,[198] and in particular whether a dentist who played background music in his practice broadcasted publicly protected subject matter without providing remuneration. The court stressed that there was an intentional communication through the deliberate intervention of the dentist and that the audience was not merely 'caught by chance' in listening to phonograms.[199] The number of individuals to which such a communication is addressed matters, but there is a certain *de minimis* threshold to be assumed, i.e. one which excludes from the concept 'groups of persons which are too small, or insignificant'.[200] They are also a 'very consistent group of persons and thus constitute a determinate circle of potential recipients',[201] therefore the fact that they succeed each other does not weigh heavily.[202] Finally, it was stressed that, unlike pubs and hotels, broadcasting phonograms in a dental practice does not impact its standing, nor the financial benefits, in that the dentist cannot expect a rise in the number of patients because of that broadcast alone, or charge a higher price for his service.[203] This latter point, along with the fact that *Del Corso* was a case on neighbouring rights,[204] marks the difference from the public involved in hotel rooms and public houses. The *Del Corso* case is a rather relevant precedent for cases where there is a communication *in* public that does not amount to a communication *to* the public and hence to infringement. The grounds for acquitting such a use from infringement rest on the lack of public character and profit-making purpose in the use.[205]

The 'new public' criterion has been affirmed in various instances in national courts.[206]

---

[197] See e.g. *American Broadcasting*, 573 U. S. 431 (2014), 14 (US). See also in this regard *Circul Globus Bucureşti (Circ & Variete Globus Bucureşti) v Uniunea Compozitorilor şi Muzicologilor din România - Asociaţia pentru Drepturi de Autor* (UCMR - ADA), Case C-283/10, 24 November 2011, ECLI:EU:C:2011:772 (*Circul Globus*), [40]–[41].

[198] *Società Consortile Fonografici (SCF) v Marco Del Corso*, Case C-135/10, 15 March 2012, ECLI:EU:C:2012:140 (*Del Corso*).

[199] Ibid., [93] and [94]. See also *Bezpečnostní softwarová asociace - Svaz softwarové ochrany v Ministerstvo kultury*, Case C-393/09, 22 December 2010, ECLI:EU:C:2010:816 (*BSA*).

[200] *Società Consortile Fonografici (SCF) v Marco Del Corso*, Case C-135/10, 15 March 2012, ECLI:EU:C:2012:140 (*Del Corso*), [86]. A dentist's clientele is not large or significant because the patients have appointments one at a time and because it is unlikely that they hear the same phonograms.

[201] Ibid., [95].

[202] Ibid., [96].

[203] Ibid., [97].

[204] Ibid., [74]–[77]; also *OSA—Ochranný svaz autorský pro práva k dílům hudebním o.s. v Léčebné lázně Mariánské Lázně a.s.*, Case C-351/12, 27 February 2014, ECLI:EU:C:2014:110, [35].

[205] This seems to be an enlarged version of the private copying defence, which features in Art. 5(2)(b) of the Information Society Directive, according to which reproductions made for private use and for a non-commercial purpose are exempt from infringement.

[206] *Estonian Authors Society v AS Viasat*, Tallinn Circuit Court, 28 February 2014, 2-11-17594 (Estonia) (where no new public was reached and hence there was no copyright infringement); '*Viasat*', Supreme Court of Estonia (Riigikohus), 29 May 2013, 3-2-1-50-13 (Estonia) (where it was held that authors have no right to claim royalties from satellite service providers if the broadcasting organization has already paid the royalties and no 'new public' has been created through satellite television services) contra: *Paramount Home Entertainment International Ltd v British Sky Broadcasting Ltd* [2013] EWHC 3479 (Ch), [33] (UK) (where the UK High Court found that hyperlinks to copies of films and television

Lack of commerciality

Although commerciality and profit-making purpose are not express constituents of rights, there are indications of such an assumption resulting from the way in which the Court of Justice discusses infringement of certain rights, such as the right of communication to the public, and also from the way in which exceptions and limitations are drafted in Article 5 of the Information Society Directive.

Various copyright exceptions and limitations listed in this Article exclude commercial uses from the scope of permissible activity, and the Directive attaches legal significance to whether a use is 'commercial' or 'non-commercial'[207] or to whether a user is a commercial or non-commercial entity.[208] These terms are rarely defined and the Directive offers no specific guidance on how to differentiate between commercial or non-commercial uses or users of copyright content. Even if there were a clear legal definition of what constitutes commerciality in a copyright use, however, the inverse definition would probably not adequately capture the concept of non-commerciality.[209] Some evidence in this regard can be found in national case law which examines different conditions to establish a commercial character in the use, and other conditions to determine non-commerciality; commercial uses are profit-making, whereas non-commercial uses are those where the defendant does not have a profit-making intention.[210] It is likely that website-hosted ads or bitcoin-sponsored activities will be included in the first category. Certain companies that are offered for free to users may gain profit in an indirect way, for instance, by collecting, processing, and possibly transferring to third parties, personal data or

---

programmes amounted to an act of communication to a new public); *ITV Broadcasting Ltd v TV Catchup Ltd* [2011] EWHC 1874 (Pat), [99] (UK) (where Floyd J held, 'I do not think that the fact that subscribers would be entitled to receive the broadcasts direct on their domestic televisions or computer screens means that the recipients of the TVC service are not a "new public". The Directive and the Act require only that the communication be to "the public", subject to the narrow limitations which I have discussed. If there is a communication to a new class of the public, then that is a clear indication that one is outside the exception. But to go further and hold that every communication to the originally contemplated class is exempted, goes much further than warranted by authority.'); *'The Reality II'*, Federal Court of Justice of Germany (Bundesgerichtshof), 9 July 2015, I ZR 46/12 [35] (Germany) (where the Federal Court of Justice held that if there is a notification from the copyright holder that consent to further communication of his or her protected subject matter is limited, the reposting of the content via framing shall amount to an act of communication to a new public); *'TV sets in hotel rooms'*, Court of Appeal of Lisbon, 27 December 2014, 163/14.8YHLSB.L1-6 (Portugal) (affirming that the clientele of a hotel is a new public for the purposes of showing videograms through the TV signal); *'Broadcasts in shops'*, Court of Appeal of Lisbon, 4 February 2016, 216-15.5YHLSB.L1-6 (Portugal) (where the transmission of sound recordings in a coffee shop was found to be performance to a new public).

[207] Information Society Directive (Directive 2001/29/EC), Arts 5(2)(c), 5(3)(a), 5(3)(b), and 5(3)(j).
[208] Information Society Directive (Directive 2001/29/EC), Recital 40.
[209] Note that in a recent study on the meaning of non-commerciality most respondents thought that if they had been given some definition of a commercial use, they would give non-commerciality the inverse definition. See Netpop Research, 'Defining "Non-Commercial": A Study on How the Internet Population Understands "Non-Commercial Use"', Creative Commons Corporation, September 2009, 50.
[210] See in general Stavroula Karapapa, *Private Copying* (London: Routledge, 2012) 79 et seq.

search habits of their users. Although this activity is not directly commercial, it may be found to serve an indirect commercial purpose.

At the same time, the discussion of certain rights, such as the communication right, from the Court of Justice includes, inter alia, a determination of the profit-making character of the activity as one of the parameters of its infringing nature.[211] This has been given weight in *GS Media* where the court held that in cases of for-profit hyperlinking, the person posting the hyperlinks can be expected to carry out the 'necessary checks to ensure that the work concerned is not illegally published on the website to which those hyperlinks lead, so that it must be presumed that that posting has occurred with the full knowledge of the protected nature of that work and the possible lack of consent to publication on the internet by the copyright holder.'[212] The case is interesting as it seems to condition the question of liability on two elements: knowledge and profit. Profit creates the presumption of knowledge, according to the court. In this sense, it is to be understood not as a condition of infringing liability, but as a ground for determining whether knowledge of infringing activity exists. The case is controversial as it leaves two questions open: one doctrinal and one purely legal. First, it implies that profit can have a bearing on infringing liability, even though no indication as to how profit is to be interpreted is offered. Second, it seems to merge the conditions applicable to primary and secondary liability. Although this strict distinction is not made in EU copyright and some of the national laws of EU Member States, the general principle of primary infringement is that it is not subject to a knowledge requirement. It can be argued, however, that by blurring the contours between primary and secondary liability of intermediaries, GS Media has heralded the approach taken by the Directive on Copyright in the Digital Single Market,[213] which develops a primary liability framework for online content-sharing providers.

Conclusion

Where the factual background of an alleged infringement does not meet the statutory prerequisites of an act restricted by copyright, a defendant may deny liability and invoke a defence which attacks the scope of right. Bringing forward claims regarding the scope of exclusive rights in order to deny infringement is a defensive mechanism that seems to become more and more limited, however, in light of the

---

[211] See, to that effect, *Football Association Premier League and Others*, Joint Cases C-403/08 and C-429/08, 4 October 2011, ECLI:EU:C:2011:631 (*FAPL*), [204]; *Società Consortile Fonografici (SCF) v Marco Del Corso*, Case C-135/10, 15 March 2012, ECLI:EU:C:2012:140 (*Del Corso*), [88]; *Phonographic Performance (Ireland) Limited v Ireland and Attorney General*, Case C-162/10, 15 March 2012, ECLI:EU:C:2012:141, [36].

[212] *GS Media BV v Sanoma Media Netherlands BV, Playboy Enterprises International Inc., Britt Geertruida Dekker*, Case C-160/15, 8 September 2016, ECLI:EU:C:2016:644 (*GS Media*), [51].

[213] Digital Single Market Directive (Directive (EU) 2019/790).

broad construal of rights under EU copyright. Indeed, the legislative definition of exclusive rights is characterized by a high degree of generality, which is complemented by the principle of understanding rights in a broad sense in order to ensure legal certainty and a high level of copyright protection. This has the effect that copyright protection is the norm and, although rights are not meant to be absolute but are indeed subject to internal limitations, these limits tend to become more and more narrow through judicial interpretation and policy choice.

The most important defences that could be developed in this context include the reproduction of a work in part or the rule of independent creation. It has been shown that, progressively, judicial trends at the EU level have been marked with an expansion of what amounts to a substantial part, the taking of which amounts to infringing liability. This has notably been the result of *Infopaq*, but other cases have also developed similar conclusions, such as *Pelham* where the Court of Justice held that a copyright holder has the authority to control the taking of an extract, however short, of their protected subject matter, unless the part taken has been modified to an extent that makes it unrecognizable. Interestingly, when alterations are applied to a two-second extract of a protected phonogram that is sampled within another phonogram they do not result in an actionable act of reproduction within the meaning of Article 2 of the Information Society Directive. This could be seen as developing a defensive rule for certain kinds of creative engagement with pre-existing works or other subject matter, such as phonogram sampling.[214] However, material alterations of copies of artistic works that have been marketed within the European Union with the consent of the relevant rightsholders, such as the transfer of an authorized copy from a paper poster onto a canvas, and placing the work on the market in its new form, is not subject to the exhaustion of the distribution right within the meaning of Article 3 of the Information Society Directive and hence amounts to infringement. The exhaustion rule lays down an important scope limitation to the distribution right, but it does not cover the right of communicating works and otherwise making them available to the public, with the exception of computer programs in the aftermath of *UsedSoft*.

On a doctrinal level, exclusive rights are subject to inherent limitations that have evolved as part of the legislative definition and judicial interpretation of the scope of rights, notably (a) the nature of rights as acts of public address, and (b) the exploitative nature of rights, which may in limited instances exclude non-commercial activities from the scope of rights and serve a defensive function. The newly developed doctrine of the 'new public', namely an audience that the rightsholders did not

---

[214] Although such extracts would not qualify as actionable copies, the exact same extracts, as modified, would not benefit under the quotation exception for purposes of criticism and review, which is available in Art. 5(3)(d) of the Information Society Directive (Directive 2001/29/EC); because there would be absence of infringement in such a case, there would be no need to revert to the supervening rule outlined in the quotation exception.

have in mind when making the work available online,[215] can function, on certain occasions, as a defence against allegations of infringement of the communication right. What the judicially developed doctrine of the 'new public' does is to further our understanding of the communication right by developing a new doctrinal interpretation of its appropriate scope.[216] It restricts and expands the scope of online copyright infringement at the same time, and in this light it fundamentally changes the scope of the right, serving as a doctrinal filter in assessing infringement.[217]

In terms of statutory limitations applicable to the scope of rights, the temporary copying exception available under Article 5(1) of the Information Society Directive could be viewed as such a limitation instead of a supervening defence against allegations of infringement. Temporary copying is subject to discussion in the next chapter.

---

[215] *Nils Svensson and Others v Retriever Sverige AB*, Case C-466/12, 13 February 2014, ECLI:EU:C:2014:76 (*Svensson*); *BestWater International GmbH v Michael Mebes, Stefan Potsch*, Case C-348/13, 21 October 2014 (order of the court), ECLI:EU:C:2014:2315 (*BestWater*); also see *Innoweb BV v Wegener ICT Media BV and Wegener Mediaventions BV*, Case C-202/12, 19 December 2013, ECLI:EU:C:2013:850 (*Innoweb*). See in this regard, however, the opposing position of the European Parliament, Committee on Legal Affairs, Draft Report on the Implementation of Directive 2001/29/EC of the European Parliament and of the Council of 22 May 2001 on the Harmonisation of Certain Aspects of Copyright and Related Rights in the Information Society, 15 January 2015, 2014/2256(INI), point 15.

[216] Stavroula Karapapa, 'The Requirement for a "New Public" in EU Copyright Law' (2017) 1 *European Law Review* 63.

[217] Ibid.

4

Transient Uses and Temporary Copying

This chapter discusses defences that exempt certain activities from infringement on the basis of their transient or incidental character. These tend to be of paramount importance in cases of electronic communications and, more specifically, on the Internet as a result of the very nature and function of online networks. The exception available for temporary copying, for instance, which features in Article 5(1) of the Information Society Directive, has specifically been drafted with a view to covering online activities, such as caching and browsing, that enhance the efficiency of the Internet. Subject to discussion is the temporary copying exception in its broader contextual framework, including the relevant statutory provisions and case law, such as *Infopaq I* and *II*, *Football Association Premier League and Others* (*FAPL*), *Meltwater*, and *Filmspeler* decisions.[1] It is argued that although Article 5(1) of the Information Society Directive[2] takes, organically, the form of a copyright exception, the relevant provision should be better understood to be setting a scope limitation on the reproduction right and an exemption from copyright infringement.

Introduction

The duration of an act of reproduction became important with the advancement of digital technologies. Indeed, before the emergence of electronic means of communication and computer programs, there was no express mention of the duration of copies on statutes. In the United Kingdom, for instance, it was considered that the law was construed broadly enough to cover storage of the work in digital form by

---

[1] *Infopaq International A/S v Danske Dagblades Forening*, Case C-5/08, 16 July 2009, ECLI:EU:C:2009:465 (*Infopaq I*); *Infopaq International A/S v Danske Dagblades Forening*, Case C-302/10, 17 January 2012, ECLI:EU:C:2012:16 (*Infopaq II*); *Public Relations Consultants Association Ltd v Newspaper Licensing Agency Ltd* [2013] UKSC 18, [2013] 2 All E.R. 852 (UK); *Public Relations Consultants Association Ltd v Newspaper Licensing Agency Ltd and Others*, Case C-360/13, 5 June 2014, ECLI:EU:C:2014:1195.

[2] Directive 2001/29/EC of the European Parliament and of the Council of 22 May 2001 on the Harmonisation of Certain Aspects of Copyright and Related Rights in the Information Society, OJ L 167, 22 June 2001, 10–19 (Information Society Directive).

Defences to Copyright Infringement. Stavroula Karapapa, Oxford University Press (2020). © Stavroula Karapapa. DOI: 10.1093/oso/9780198795636.001.0001

including copying 'in any material form'.[3] Short-lived copying, such as writing on a blackboard, would be mentioned only peripherally in court decisions and would be exempt from infringement on the basis of a *de minimis* rule.[4] It was digital technology that unveiled the importance of temporary acts of copying, such as those involved in running a computer program using RAM memory or in the ordinary use of the Internet.

With the spectacular growth of web content by more than a million pages every day, caching is one of the essential functions that enable the proper functioning of the Internet.[5] Access providers automatically cache copies of webpages in order to easily feed them to requests for identical documents from various end users, with a view to retaining efficiency in dealing with end user requests and to reduce congestion on popular websites. Streaming is also becoming more and more popular, with a growing number of websites offering relevant services. Such activities have spurred the growth of a wide range of online services. They have become controversial in the context of copyright, however, in light of the overly broad scope of the reproduction right discussed in Chapter 3, and the corresponding provision of Article 5(1) of the Information Society Directive which allows acts of temporary copying to be carried out without authorial permission. Even though browsing and caching are likely to be covered by Article 5(1),[6] other emergently popular activities, such as streaming,[7] buffering, or search-engine indexing,[8] may also be exempt from infringement.

The rationale of the temporary copying exception

The definition of the reproduction right of Article 2 of the Information Society Directive, which covers both permanent and temporary reproductions, is wide enough to potentially encompass copying of content from a website in the memory or on the screen of a computer as part of Internet browsing. Unlike the 1996 World Intellectual Property Organization (WIPO) Copyright Treaty,[9] which remains neutral, the Information Society Directive contains specific language regarding the scope of the reproduction right in the digital environment. Despite the fact that

---

[3] See Copyright Act 1966, s. 3(5)(a); Copyright, Designs and Patents Act (CDPA) 1988, s. 17(2).

[4] Kevin Garnett, Gillian Davies, and Gwilym Harbottle (eds), *Copinger and Scone James on Copyright* (London: Sweet and Maxwell, 2009, 15th edn) 9–16.

[5] On a detailed analysis of caching see P. Bernt Hugenholtz, 'Caching and Copyright: the Right of Temporary Copying' (2000) 22(10) *European Intellectual Property Review* 482.

[6] Ibid., 487–9.

[7] See in general Maurizio Borghi, 'Chasing Copyright Infringement in the Streaming Landscape' (2011) 42(3) *International Review of Intellectual Property and Competition Law* 1.

[8] Ben Allgrove and Paul Ganley, 'Search Engines, Data Aggregators and UK Copyright Law: A Proposal' (2007) 29(6) *European Intellectual Property Review* 227, 233.

[9] WIPO Copyright Treaty (hereinafter 'WCT') (1996); WIPO Performances and Phonograms Treaty (hereinafter 'WPPT') (1996).

various proposals were set forth during the Diplomatic Conference that resulted in the WIPO Copyright Treaty (WCT), a compromise Agreed Statement accompanying Article 1(4) of the WCT was eventually adopted:

> The reproduction right, as set out in Article 9 of the Berne Convention, and the exceptions permitted there-under, fully apply in the digital environment, in particular to the use of works in digital form. It is understood that the storage of a protected work in digital form in an electronic medium constitutes a reproduction within the meaning of Article 9 of the Berne Convention.

Indeed, the Explanatory Memorandum to the Information Society Directive reflects a distinction between temporary and permanent copies, created as part of digitization and the Internet.[10] As indicated in the Explanatory Memorandum:

> the second element (temporary/permanent) is intended to clarify the fact that in the network environment very different types of reproduction might occur which all constitute acts of reproductions within the meaning of this provision. The result of a reproduction may be a tangible permanent copy, like a book, but it may just as well be a non-visible temporary copy of the work in the working memory of a computer. Both temporary and permanent copies are covered by the definition of an act of reproduction.[11]

In this context, Article 5(1) of the Information Society Directive on temporary copying was introduced with a view to excluding acts of transient copying, and other related activities, such as caching, from infringement. The purpose of this exception, which is the only mandatory exception included in the Information Society Directive, was to '*exclude from the scope of the reproduction right* certain acts of reproduction which are dictated by technology, but which have no separate economic significance of their own' (emphasis added).[12] The exception of Article 5(1) reads that:

> Temporary acts of reproduction referred to in Article 2, which are transient or incidental, which are an integral and essential part of a technological process and whose sole purpose is to enable:
> (a)   a transmission in a network between third parties by an intermediary, or
> (b)   a lawful

---

[10] Proposal for a European Parliament and Council Directive on the Harmonisation of Certain Aspects of Copyright and Related Rights in the Information Society, Brussels, 10 December 1997, COM (97) 62, OJ C 108, 7 April 1998, 6, Explanatory Memorandum, 30.

[11] Proposal for a European Parliament and Council Directive on the Harmonisation of Certain Aspects of Copyright and Related Rights in the Information Society, Brussels, 10 December 1997, COM (97) 62, OJ C 108, 7 April 1998, 6.

[12] Ibid., Art. 5(3) (emphasis added).

use of a work or other subject-matter to be made, and which have no independent economic significance, shall be exempted from the reproduction right provided for in Article 2.[13]

The conditions of Article 5(1) are cumulative and lack of compliance with either one means that an activity cannot benefit from the exemption. Some guidance as to the scope of the various conditions is offered in the Recitals to the Information Society Directive and relevant case law from the Court of Justice of the European Union.

Most of the cases where Article 5(1) has been invoked concern acts of reproduction with the sole purpose of enabling a lawful use of the work or other subject matter that was subject to copying. In all these cases,[14] two essential considerations played key roles, namely to identify both the lawful use and the technological process of which the act of reproduction was an integral part. According to the Court of Justice, the exemption for temporary copying under Article 5(1) has to be subject to strict interpretation with a view to enhance legal certainty, to ensure the development of new technologies, and to safeguard 'a fair balance between the rights and interests of rights holders and of users of protected works who wish to avail themselves of those technologies'.[15]

Recital 33 indicates that 'the acts of reproduction concerned should have no separate economic value on their own', and that the exception should

include acts which enable browsing as well as acts of caching to take place, including those which enable transmission systems to function efficiently, provided that the intermediary does not modify the information and does not interfere with the lawful use of technology, widely recognised and used by industry, to obtain data on the use of the information.

---

[13] Note that the English version of the Information Society Directive, as published in the Official Journal, contained a typographical mistake; it allowed acts 'which are transient or incidental [and] an integral and essential part of a technological process'. This was later corrected to 'which are transient or incidental, which are an integral and essential part of a technological process'. See in this regard Corrigendum to Directive 2001/29/EC of the European Parliament and of the Council of 22 May 2001 on the Harmonisation of Certain Aspects of Copyright and Related Rights in the Information Society (OJ L 167 of 22 June 2001), OJ L No. 6, 10 January 2002, 70.

[14] *Infopaq International A/S v Danske Dagblades Forening*, Case C-5/08, 16 July 2009, ECLI:EU:C:2009:465 (*Infopaq I*); *Infopaq International A/S v Danske Dagblades Forening*, Case C-302/10, 17 January 2012, ECLI:EU:C:2012:16 (*Infopaq II*); *Football Association Premier League and Others*, Joint Cases C-403/08 and C-429/08, 4 October 2011, ECLI:EU:C:2011:631 (*FAPL*); *Public Relations Consultants Association Ltd v Newspaper Licensing Agency Ltd* [2013] UKSC 18, [2013] 2 All E.R. 852 (UK); *Public Relations Consultants Association Ltd v Newspaper Licensing Agency Ltd and Others*, Case C-360/13, 5 June 2014, ECLI:EU:C:2014:1195 (*Meltwater*).

[15] *Public Relations Consultants Association Ltd v Newspaper Licensing Agency Ltd* [2013] UKSC 18, [2013] 2 All E.R. 852 (UK); also *Football Association Premier League and Others*, Joint Cases C-403/08 and C-429/08, 4 October 2011, ECLI:EU:C:2011:631 (*FAPL*).

As indicated in this Recital, one of the purposes of the exception is to exclude from the scope of the reproduction right, and thereinafter from infringement, acts of routine copying which take place on behalf of Internet intermediaries. Such a risk would be the unintended effect of the overly broad scope of the reproduction right of Article 2, which prima facie includes temporary copying under its ambit. In this context, the temporary copying exception of Article 5(1) can be viewed as a scope interpretation or complimentary definition of the reproduction right of Article 2, instead of an exception or limitation with a supervening force, even though technically and structurally it is listed as such.[16] Further support to this reading of Article 5(1) can be seen by the very fact that this provision lays down the only mandatory exception under the Directive, whereas all other exceptions and limitations are left to the discretion of Member States to introduce or not into their national laws.[17] A further reason has to do with the very justification of the exception, which is premised on a public policy rationale, namely the enhancement of the efficiency of online networks and communications by enabling certain transient or incidental acts of copying that have no economic significance of their own.

Because temporary copying is in principle included within the broadly defined reproduction right, copyright holders have the right to authorize or prohibit acts of temporary copying, unless these fall within the purposes of Article 5(1) of the Directive. This exception has the effect of absolving a defendant from liability in situations that would otherwise amount to infringement, namely in situations to which the reproduction right would otherwise apply. If we were to say that the claimant's right is an exclusive right to reproduce the work permanently or temporarily *for purposes other than* making transient or incidental copies that are an integral and essential part of a technological process and whose sole purpose is to enable network transmissions and lawful uses of works or other subject matter of no independent economic significance, then the defendant would not have to rely on an exception. Formulating the reproduction right in such a way would have lowered the level of generality in which the right is drafted.

In this context, Article 5(1) can be regarded as outlining a denial to the elements of infringement in certain cases by offering a definition of the scope of the overly broad reproduction right instead of laying down a rationale-based justification for an allegedly infringing conduct.

[16] Contra: Michel M. Walter and Silke von Lewinski, *European Copyright Law: A Commentary* (Oxford: Oxford University Press, 2010) 11.5.14.

[17] See Maurizio Borghi, 'Chasing Copyright Infringement in the Streaming Landscape' (2011) 42(3) *International Review of Intellectual Property and Competition Law* 1, 18.

Early case law on temporary copying

Before the Court of Justice started hearing the first cases on the interpretation of the various elements of Article 5(1) of the Information Society Directive, national courts had already been called to examine cases invoking the relevant defences available under the respective national laws. These interpretations are important to the extent that they indicate consistency in the understanding of the various parameters of the conditions necessary for the temporary copying exception to be established.

In 2008, the District Court of Paris found that Wizzgo, a website offering a digital video recording service, cannot benefit from the private copying and the temporary copying exceptions.[18] After subscribing to the service, Wizzgo users could set up their hard disk drive with specific software, create a personalized account, and select the program they want to record.. The recording would start at the request of the user; on its creation from the online service it was encrypted and then made available to the requester. The recording started at the request of the user and upon its creation from the online service it was encrypted and made available to the user requesting it. The court rejected Wizzgo's argument that there were two distinct copies, a temporary one made by Wizzgo and covered by the temporary copying exception, and a permanent one made by users for their private use and covered by the private copying exception. To the court there was only one copy, the one made by Wizzgo on behalf of the user. The fact that the copy was encrypted was immaterial to the finding that the copy was temporary in nature. In this light, according to the court, the user's decrypted copy was not different from the copy made by Wizzgo. Since the user could permanently store the decrypted copy, the copy made by Wizzgo could not be temporary. What is more, the copy had an economic significance because it had the force to attract clientele, despite the fact that the service was offered at no financial cost to the user. This could be seen as a way of starting a business by becoming known to customers and eventually making a profit through its users' data and the advertising space available on the website. The private copying exception was not applicable either.

In a UK case on Internet live streaming retransmission of TV broadcasts and films,[19] the High Court ruled that the retransmission of broadcasts and films through live streaming amounted to an act of communication to the public. In particular, the live retransmission via streaming qualified as authorization of reproduction of a substantial part of the films—but not of the broadcasts—in buffers and computer screens. However, the court found that reproductions of broadcasts and

---

[18] 'WIZZGO', District Court Paris (Tribunal de Grande Instance Paris), 25 November 2008 (France).
[19] ITV Broadcasting Ltd v TV Catchup Ltd, High Court of England and Wales (Patents Court), 18 July 2011 (UK).

films in the buffers were non-infringing as they were covered by the exception for acts of temporary copying included in section 28A of the Copyright, Designs, and Patents Act (CDPA), corresponding to Article 5(1). Referring to *Infopaq*, Floyd J raised doubts as to whether the reproduction at issue had independent economic significance. He observed that the reproduction in buffers of parts of broadcasts and films did not have independent economic significance, unlike the reproduction of parts of films (but not of broadcasts) on the screens of users, which may actually have such an independent economic significance. Although the case was referred to the Court of Justice,[20] the issue of independent economic significance under Article 5(1) of the Information Society Directive was not subject to examination.

An online service that enables the on-demand receipt and recording of TV programmes was found to infringe German copyright law and the law on unfair competition.[21] Confirming in principle the first instance judgment, the Court of Appeal found that the defendant's service infringed the plaintiff's reproduction right. According to the court, the plaintiff's reproduction right was infringed[22] and the provision concerning temporary acts of reproduction could not apply.[23] An important constituent of the relevant provision was that copying had to lack independent significance and that the copies made had to be generated automatically within, and as an integral part of, technical processes, e.g. caching. The defendant's business model, on the contrary, would prove that the reproduction was, in this case, of self-contained commercial relevance. The Court did not apply other defences, such as the private copying exception, but found that the defendant was liable for unfair competition,[24] ruling that the parties would at least act in 'substitutive competition', since users might have been using the defendant's service rather than watching the plaintiff's broadcast (which could reduce the plaintiff's viewer ratings).

The requirements of Article 5(1) of the Information Society Directive under the interpretative guidance of the Court of Justice

Article 5(1) of the Information Society Directive lays down five cumulative conditions, each one of which should be read and satisfied in light of the others:[25]

---

[20] *ITV Broadcasting Ltd v TV Catchup Ltd*, Case C-607/11, 7 March 2013, ECLI:EU:C:2013:147.

[21] 'Virtual Personal Videorecorder', Court of Appeal Dresden (Oberlandesgericht Dresden), 28 November 2006 (Germany).

[22] German Copyright Act (GCA), Art. 87(1), No. 2.

[23] GCA, Art. 44a.

[24] German Act Against Unfair Competition, Arts 3, 4, No. 11.

[25] The UK Supreme Court in *Meltwater* offered interesting insight as to the application of the conditions of Art. 5(1). To Lord Sumption:

(a) copying ought to be transient or incidental; (b) it should be an integral and essential part of a technological process; (c) the sole purpose of such a process should be to enable either a transmission in a network between third parties by an intermediary or a lawful use; and (d) such an activity should have no independent economic significance. The Court of Justice has been called to shed light on the requirements of Article 5(1) on five occasions: *Infopaq I*[26] and *Infopaq II*,[27] *FAPL*,[28] *Meltwater*,[29] and *Filmspeler*.[30]

1. Temporary copies: transient or incidental

For the exception of Article 5(1) to apply, copies must be temporary.[31] In particular, such copies should be 'transient or incidental' and 'an integral and essential part of a technological process'.

There is a key distinction between transient and incidental copies. Transient copies are those that are ephemeral and very short in terms of duration of life. According to *Infopaq I*,[32] an act can be held to be 'transient'

> only if its duration is limited to what is necessary for the proper completion of the technological process of which it forms an integral and essential part, being understood that that process must be automated so that it deletes that act automatically, without human intervention, once its function of enabling the completion of such a process has come to an end.[33]

notwithstanding that the five conditions are laid out in five separate sub-paragraphs, they are not free-standing requirements. They are overlapping and repetitive, and each of them colours the meaning of the others. They have to be read together so as to achieve the combined purpose of all of them. This is, as the case-law demonstrates, what the Court of Justice has always done.

See *Public Relations Consultants Association Ltd v Newspaper Licensing Agency Ltd* [2013] UKSC 18, [2013] 2 All E.R. 852 (UK), [11].

[26] *Infopaq International A/S v Danske Dagblades Forening*, Case C-5/08, 16 July 2009, ECLI:EU:C:2009:465 (*Infopaq I*).

[27] *Infopaq International A/S v Danske Dagblades Forening*, Case C-302/10, 17 January 2012, ECLI:EU:C:2012:16 (*Infopaq II*).

[28] *Football Association Premier League and Others*, Joint Cases C-403/08 and C-429/08, 4 October 2011, ECLI:EU:C:2011:631 (*FAPL*).

[29] *Public Relations Consultants Association Ltd v Newspaper Licensing Agency Ltd and Others*, Case C-360/13, 5 June 2014, ECLI:EU:C:2014:1195 (*Meltwater*).

[30] *Stichting Brein v Jack Frederik Wullems*, Case C-527/15, 26 April 2017, ECLI:EU:C:2017:300 (*Filmspeler*).

[31] On the respective requirement of US Copyright law, see Aaron Perzanowski, 'Fixing RAM Copies' (2010) 104(3) *Northwestern University Law Review* 1067.

[32] *Infopaq International A/S v Danske Dagblades Forening*, Case C-5/08, 16 July 2009, ECLI:EU:C:2009:465 (*Infopaq I*).

[33] *Infopaq International A/S v Danske Dagblades Forening*, Case C-5/08, 16 July 2009, ECLI:EU:C:2009:465 (*Infopaq I*), [64].

We have already examined, to a certain extent, the facts in *Infopaq I* and *Infopaq II*,[34] both of which originated from proceedings in the Netherlands and involved a media monitoring service that identified and summarized articles from Danish newspapers.[35] The service operated through a so-called 'data capture process' which included copying at various levels. It involved: scanning the pages of articles and generating a TIFF (Tagged Image File Format) file for each page; translating the TIFF files into text files by transferring them to an Optical Character Recognition (OCR) server; searching the files for key words that the subscribers fed to the service; generating for each, search data with details of the article and an eleven-word extract from the article including the search word; deleting TIFF and text files with the exception of the extracts; and printing a cover sheet with the resulting data and emailing them to the relevant subscriber. The Supreme Court of Denmark (Højesteret) stayed proceedings and sought clarification as to whether this procedure required the consent of the rightsholders. According to the Court of Justice, the service involved various acts of reproduction, with the last one (namely printing and emailing the resulting data to Infopaq subscribers) not benefiting from the exception of Article 5(1).[36] The reason for this was that it involved the creation of a material record that could only be destroyed by means of discretionary human intervention. This meant that the copy was permanent instead of temporary or transient, and hence the conditions of Article 5(1) could not be met. As a result, the Infopaq service could not be offered without the authorization of those holding the copyright on the monitored articles. The case is important as it developed the meaning of what an act of transient or incidental copying is for the purposes of Article 5(1), introducing the implied condition of human intervention in the test.

According to the definition of transient copying developed in *Infopaq*, the assessment of the transient character of the reproduction should take place by reference to the proper completion of the technological process. In particular: (a) storage and deletion of copyright content ought to be automatic and irrespective of the user's decision to initiate or terminate the relevant technological process (i.e. there should be a lack of discretionary human intervention), and (b) the duration of the copy should be limited to what is necessary for the completion of the relevant technological process.[37] The Court of Justice has not offered guidance on how to determine how long a copy should last to qualify as transient.

---

[34] *Infopaq International A/S v Danske Dagblades Forening*, Case C-302/10, 17 January 2012, ECLI:EU:C:2012:16 (*Infopaq II*).

[35] In Chapter 2.

[36] *Infopaq International A/S v Danske Dagblades Forening*, Case C-5/08, 16 July 2009, ECLI:EU:C:2009:465 (*Infopaq I*).

[37] *Infopaq International A/S v Danske Dagblades Forening*, Case C-5/08, 16 July 2009, ECLI:EU:C:2009:465 (*Infopaq I*), [62], [64].

'Incidental' copies are those where the reproduction lasts longer than for 'transient' copies, but they still remain temporary.[38] The relation between transient and incidental copies was revealed in *Meltwater*.[39] In this case, which originates from UK proceedings, the Newspaper Licensing Agency (NLA) Ltd sought a declaration that Public Relations Consultants Association Ltd, a professional association representing UK public relations providers, required a licence or consent from the NLA in order to lawfully receive and/or use the Meltwater News Service. Unlike *Infopaq*, the result data was made available to its subscribers on the service provider's website instead of being delivered to them by email. Besides this factual difference, the question addressed to the court differed in that it did not focus on whether the service provider itself needed the permission of the relevant rightsholders to offer the service, but on whether the individual subscribers themselves needed such permission. The High Court of Justice and the Court of Appeal of England and Wales decided that such copies cannot be covered by the temporary copying exception.[40] The Supreme Court, however, disagreed, holding that the creation of transient copies of the result data in the memory and on the screen of the subscribers' computers merely enabled the works to be viewed. This is not an act restricted by copyright. Even if the works at issue could be saved indefinitely in the cache memory of a computer, such copying remained transient and temporary in nature to the extent that there was no need for human intervention for the deletion of the files. In the words of Lord Sumption, 'it is not enough that forensic ingenuity can devise a method of extending to some extent the life of copies which are by their nature temporary.'[41] On the distinction between 'transient' and 'incidental' copies, Lord Sumption held:

> If, as I consider, the copies made in the internet cache or on screen are 'transient', it is strictly speaking unnecessary to consider whether they are also 'incidental'. But I think it clear that they are. The software puts a webpage on screen and into the cache for the purpose of enabling a lawful use of the copyright material, i.e.

---

[38] Note that a subtle contradiction arises with regard to incidental copying to the extent that it also ought to be an integral and essential—rather than merely incidental—part of a technological process. See in this regard Michel M. Walter and Silke von Lewinski, *European Copyright Law: A Commentary* (Oxford: Oxford University Press, 2010) 11.5.16.

[39] *Public Relations Consultants Association Ltd v Newspaper Licensing Agency Ltd and Others,* Case C-360/13, 5 June 2014, ECLI:EU:C:2014:1195 (*Meltwater*); for a discussion on the *Meltwater* case, see Luke McDonagh, 'Headlines and Hyperlinks: UK Copyright Law Post-Infopaq - Newspaper Licensing Agency Ltd and Others v Meltwater Holding BV and Other Companies' (2011) 1(2) *Queen Mary Journal of Intellectual Property Law* 184.

[40] For a comment on the Court of Appeal decision see Iona Harding, 'Is NLA v Meltwater the End of Browsing?' (2012) 7(7) *Journal of Intellectual Property Law and Practice* 525.

[41] *Public Relations Consultants Association Ltd v Newspaper Licensing Agency Ltd* [2013] UKSC 18, [2013] 2 All E.R. 852 (UK), [32].

viewing it. The creation of the copies is wholly incidental to the technological process involved.[42]

In this light, transient copies are those that have a very short lifespan and incidental copies are those that have no particular significance from a copyright perspective.[43] Examples of transient copies with a very short lifetime are those created through browsing, copies made in web routers, or in computer RAM memory. Copies created in proxy servers or caches usually last longer but are incidental reproductions and—to the extent they qualify as such—they will benefit from the exception of Article 5(1).

In particular, according to Lord Sumption, the relevant requirements in *Infopaq I* were that: (a) the storage and deletion of copyright material should be automatic and not dependent on 'discretionary human intervention', and (b) the duration of the copy should only be 'necessary for the completion of the technological processes in question'. According to his Lordship, the object of the restriction to 'transient' and 'temporary' copies was to ensure that the exception does not extend to cover downloading or other forms of copying, which are as permanent as an end user chooses to make them. Unlike Proudman J, who considered that the end users' objective is the making of the copy,[44] Lord Sumption found that the end user does not set out to make a copy of the webpage. Unless they choose to download or print it, the objective is merely to view the content, with the temporary retention of on-screen or cache copies being the incidental consequence of the use of a computer. The Supreme Court concluded that if mere viewing of copyright content—without downloading or printing it—would be infringement, this would be an 'unacceptable result' in that individuals who browse the Internet would unintentionally incur civil liability, at least in principle, which

> would make infringers of many millions of ordinary users of the internet across the EU who use browsers and search engines for private as well as commercial purposes.[45]

Responding to a referral from the UK Supreme Court, the Court of Justice agreed with the Supreme Court's decision and reasoning. The Court of Justice held that an

---

[42] *Public Relations Consultants Association Ltd v Newspaper Licensing Agency Ltd* [2013] UKSC 18, [2013] 2 All E.R. 852 (UK).

[43] See in this regard Stefan Bechtold, 'Directive 2001/29/EC (Information Society Directive) of the European Parliament and of the Council of 22 May 2001 on the Harmonisation of Certain Aspects of Copyright and Related Rights in the Information Society' in Thomas Dreier and P. Bernt Hugenholtz (eds), *Concise European Copyright Law* (Alphen aan den Rijn: Kluwer Law International, 2006) 343, 371.

[44] *Newspaper Licensing Agency Ltd et al v Meltwater Holding BV et al*, [2010] EWHC 3099 (Ch) (UK).

[45] *Public Relations Consultants Association Ltd v Newspaper Licensing Agency Ltd* [2013] UKSC 18, [2013] 2 All E.R. 852 (UK), [36].

act should be held to be 'transient' where its duration is limited to what is necessary for a technological process to work properly. Such a process must be automated, i.e. it should not involve human intervention in the deletion of the copies. In this light, the Court of Justice concluded that an act of copying does not lose its transient character just because the deletion of the copy is automated and does not involve the discretionary interference of an end user. In this sense, the court elaborated on the absence of human intervention as a parameter in establishing the permissible character of the use at issue. What is more, an act of copying can be seen as 'incidental' where it neither exists independently of, nor has a purpose independent of, the technological process of which it forms part. Copying is likely to be incidental with regard to the main act of exploitation of the work,[46] to the extent that the reproduction remains 'temporary'. In this light, Lord Sumption's reasoning is echoed. This interpretation of what an 'incidental copy' is may prove useful to legitimate non-'transient' copies that are essential parts of a technological process in making works available.

Agreeing with the stance of the UK Supreme Court in *Meltwater*,[47] the court held that since on-screen copies were deleted when the Internet user moved away from the website, and since cached copies were automatically replaced with other content after a given time, such copies were temporary in nature. It was immaterial that the on-screen copies remained in existence for as long as the Internet user kept the browser open and stayed on a particular website because, during that period, the technological process used for viewing that website remained active. In this light, the duration of life of these on-screen copies was limited to what was necessary for the proper functioning of the technological process used for viewing a website and, therefore, such copies could be considered to be 'transient'. Since it was the technological process that determined the purpose for which those copies were created, and used in a way that the cached copies neither existed independently of, nor had a purpose independent of, the technological process at issue, they had to be regarded as 'incidental'. It was therefore concluded that on-screen and cached copies meet the first three conditions set out in Article 5(1).

2. Integral and essential part of a technological process

The exception of Article 5(1) of the Information Society Directive applies to copies made as an integral and necessary part of a 'technological process' and—in particular—as part of the digital processing of data. To this end, making copies is a

---

[46] Jean-Paul Triaille, 'La Question des Copies "Cache" et la Responsabilité des Intermédiaires: Copiepresse c. Google, Field v. Google' in A. Strowel and Jean–Paul Triaille (eds), *Google et les Nouveaux Services en Ligne* (Bruxelles: Larcier, 2008) 257.

[47] *Public Relations Consultants Association Ltd v Newspaper Licensing Agency Ltd and Others*, Case C-360/13, 5 June 2014, ECLI:EU:C:2014:1195 (*Meltwater*).

'necessary' part of such a technological process, insofar as it enables it to function 'correctly and efficiently'.[48] Copying that takes place in proxy servers and Internet routers does not primarily aim to reproduce copyright works, but to solve network management and performance issues. Such technical necessities justify the permissibility of temporary copying that is essential in addressing them. Limiting the scope of the permitted use of such copying, that is technically predetermined, is in line with the three-step test of Article 5(5) of the Information Society Directive.[49]

As discussed in Chapter 2, in *Infopaq I* the Court of Justice held that the taking of eleven words could amount to copyright infringement if the copied elements constitute the expression of the intellectual creation of their author, which was a matter for the national courts to decide. In consideration of the exemption of Article 5(1), the court defined 'transient or incidental' copying to cover activities that are limited in duration to what is necessary in order to complete the relevant technological process and then deleted automatically—without the need for human intervention—at the moment that their function in this technological process is complete.[50] It also found that

> legal certainty for rightholders further requires that the storage and deletion of the reproduction *not be dependent on discretionary human intervention*, particularly by the user of protected works. There is no guarantee that in such cases the person concerned will actually delete the reproduction created or, in any event, that he will delete it once its existence is no longer justified by its function of enabling the completion of a technological process.[51]

Even though Article 5(1) and the Recitals of the Information Society Directive make no express reference to the criterion of human intervention, the Court of Justice based its reasoning on a reference to Recital 33, according to which acts that enable browsing and caching, including acts that enable transmission systems to function efficiently, are, by definition, created and deleted automatically, and without human intervention.[52]

In *Infopaq I*, Article 5(1) was found to apply to some, but not all, parts of the data capture process on the basis of the criterion of discretionary human intervention.

---

[48] *Infopaq International A/S v Danske Dagblades Forening*, Case C-302/10, 17 January 2012, ECLI:EU:C:2012:16 (*Infopaq II*), [30], [37].

[49] Stefan Bechtold, 'Directive 2001/29/EC (Information Society Directive) of the European Parliament and of the Council of 22 May 2001 on the Harmonisation of Certain Aspects of Copyright and Related Rights in the Information Society' in Thomas Dreier and P. Bernt Hugenholtz (eds), *Concise European Copyright Law* (Alphen aan den Rijn: Kluwer Law International, 2006) 343, 372.

[50] *Infopaq International A/S v Danske Dagblades Forening*, Case C-5/08, 16 July 2009, ECLI:EU:C:2009:465 (*Infopaq I*). The requirement that the use ought not to have independent economic significance was also defined to mean that the act should not generate any economic advantage beyond what is derived from the transmission or lawful use at issue.

[51] *Infopaq International A/S v Danske Dagblades Forening*, Case C-5/08, 16 July 2009, ECLI:EU:C:2009:465 (*Infopaq I*), [62] (emphasis added).

[52] The Court of Justice held that:

The final part of the Infopaq process in particular was not considered to be 'transient' as the print-outs were destroyed following such a discretionary human intervention. Whereas in *Infopaq I* the focus was centred around the absence of human intervention in the technological process (most notably the absence of manual activation of the technological process), in *Infopaq II* the Court of Justice decided it was irrelevant that the technological process was activated by the manual insertion of newspaper articles into a scanner with the view to achieving a temporary copy (the so-called TIFF file) and its termination by an act of temporary copying, resulting in the creation of an eleven-word extract. In the absence of the acts of temporary copying involved during the data capture process, the technological process in question could not function correctly and efficiently. This had the consequence that the acts of temporary copying are an integral and essential part of a technological process, even if they did involve human intervention.

Based on the *Infopaq I* decision, Proudman J held in *Meltwater*, when the case was heard at the UK High Court,[53] that the storage and deletion of the copy should not be dependent on human intervention and must be automated. At the same time, she held that cache and screen copies are excluded because the storage of such copies and the duration of their storage are within the discretion of the end users, given that the making of the copies and their deletion is within end user control. According to Proudman J, the temporary copies exception

is solely concerned with incidental and intermediate copying so that any copy which is 'consumption of the work', whether temporary or not, requires the permission of the copyright holder.[54]

Proudman J found that the defence could not be upheld simply because a person had been browsing due to the fact that the initial step was to demonstrate that making the copy was lawful. The copy was not part of the technological process when generated by the user's own volition and making the copy had an independent economic significance as it was the very product for which end users were paying Meltwater.

When the case was discussed at the Court of Justice of the European Union,[55] the court repeated its common position that acts of reproduction should be carried

an act can be held to be 'transient'... only if its duration is limited to what is necessary for the proper completion of the technological process in question, it being understood that that process must be automated so that it deletes that act automatically, without human intervention, once its function of enabling the completion of such a process has come to an end. See *Infopaq International A/S v Danske Dagblades Forening*, Case C-5/08, 16 July 2009, ECLI:EU:C:2009:465 (*Infopaq I*), [64].

[53] *Newspaper Licensing Agency Ltd et al v Meltwater Holding BV et al*, [2010] EWHC 3099 (Ch) (UK).
[54] *Newspaper Licensing Agency Ltd et al v Meltwater Holding BV et al*, [2010] EWHC 3099 (Ch) (UK), [109].
[55] *Public Relations Consultants Association Ltd v Newspaper Licensing Agency Ltd and Others*, Case C-360/13, 5 June 2014, ECLI:EU:C:2014:1195 (*Meltwater*).

out entirely in the context of a technological process and that the completion of those acts is necessary for the correct and efficient function of the technological process. According to the court, on-screen and cached copies are created and deleted entirely in the context of a technological process used for viewing websites. As the court stressed, because Article 5(1) does not specify at which stage of the technological process temporary copying should take place, it is assumed that such copying can either initiate or terminate the technological process. What is more, case law does not exclude the possibility that human intervention may be involved in the technological process. For instance, the process may be activated or completed manually. This slightly relaxes the criterion of the absence of human intervention and enlarges the scope of the temporary copying defence to the extent, however, that all relevant conditions for its application are cumulatively met.

Despite the principle of strict interpretation of copyright exceptions and limitations, this understanding may allow some flexibility in the understanding of the condition of absence of human intervention. On-screen and cached copies were found to be an integral part of the technological process in *Meltwater* and this ruling has allowed a degree of freedom towards the establishment of relevant online services. In the absence of caching, the process of viewing content online would be significantly less efficient. This would not only hinder essential functions of the Internet, but also the development of services and technologies that cache content in order to enable browsing on the Internet.

3. Enabling transmission of content by an intermediary

The exception of Article 5(1) of the Information Society Directive covers copies made with a view to enable the transmission of copyright content through intermediaries in a network. Examples include Internet routers that direct copyright works from a sender to a recipient or www proxy servers, the sole purpose of which is to facilitate the transmission of content over a network. Article 5(1) may also apply to other communication networks, such as wireless or telephone networks.

A key principle is included in Recital 33 of the Preamble to the Directive, according to which an intermediary should not modify the information transmitted, nor interfere with the lawful use of technology. Article 8(3) of the Information Society Directive ensures that rightsholders can apply for an injunction against intermediaries whose services are used by third parties with a view to infringe copyright, and further rules governing the liability of service providers are outlined in Articles 12–14 of the e-Commerce Directive[56] and Article 17 of the Directive on

---

[56] Directive 2000/31/EC of the European Parliament and of the Council of 8 June 2000 on Certain Legal Aspects of Information Society Services, in Particular Electronic Commerce, in the Internal Market, OJ L 178, 17 July 2000, 1–16 (e-Commerce Directive); discussed in detail in Chapter 9.

Copyright in the Digital Single Market.[57] It would only be if Article 5(1) does not apply and infringement is established that these provisions would take effect in order to determine intermediary liability.

A definition of what entities qualify as intermediaries within the context of this provision has been offered in *LSG v Tele2 Telecommunication*.[58] LSG, a collecting society in Austria which enforces the rights of recorded music producers to their sound recordings and the rights of recording artists in respect of the exploitation of those recordings in Austria, applied for an order requiring an Internet service provider, Tele2, to disclose the names and addresses of persons to whom it had provided an Internet access service and whose IP addresses, together with the day and time of the connection, were known. The Austrian Supreme Court (Oberster Gerichtshof) referred two questions to the Court of Justice, the first of which was as follows:

> Is the term 'intermediary' in Article 5(1)(a) and Article 8(3) of Directive [2001/29] to be interpreted as including an access provider who merely provides a user with access to the network by allocating him a dynamic IP address but does not himself provide him with any services such as email, FTP, or file-sharing services and does not exercise any control, whether *de iure* or *de facto*, over the services which the user makes use of?

Tele2 argued that it was not an intermediary, claiming inter alia that intermediaries must be in a position to bring copyright infringements to an end. Internet access providers, by contrast, to the extent that they exercise no control, either de iure or de facto, over the services accessed by the user, cannot bring such infringements to an end and hence are not 'intermediaries' within the meaning of the Information Society Directive. The Court of Justice rejected this argument on the basis that providers merely offer Internet access to users without, however, providing other services such as email, FTP, or file-sharing services or exercising any control, whether de iure or de facto, over the services of which users make use.[59] The broad understanding of entities qualifying as intermediaries aligns with policy objectives towards the establishment of more stringent mechanisms of liability for service providers, such as the primary liability framework outlined in Article 17 of the Directive on Copyright in the Digital Single Market. Under such a broad definition, any party that facilitates or enables the process of making

---

[57] Directive (EU) 2019/790 of the European Parliament and of the Council of 17 April 2019 on Copyright and Related Rights in the Digital Single Market and Amending Directives 96/9/EC and 2001/29/EC, OJ L 130, 17 May 2019, 92–125 (Digital Single Market Directive).

[58] *LSG-Gesellschaft zur Wahrnehmung von Leistungsschutzrechten GmbH v Tele2 Telecommunication GmbH*, C-557/07, 19 February 2009, ECLI:EU:C:2009:107; see also relevant discussion in Chapter 9.

[59] *LSG-Gesellschaft zur Wahrnehmung von Leistungsschutzrechten GmbH v Tele2 Telecommunication GmbH*, C-557/07, 19 February 2009, ECLI:EU:C:2009:107, [46]; also see [43]–[45].

copies of copyright-protected content online, including online content-sharing service providers as per Article 17, or information society service providers as per the e-Commerce Directive, will be deemed to qualify as an intermediary. The broader definition of entities that qualify as intermediaries will have the effect that a special legal framework, and corresponding set of defensive rules, becomes available.

4. Lawful uses

The exception of Article 5(1) is not limited to copies made with a view to enabling the transmission of copyright content through intermediaries in a network; it also covers copies made for the sole purpose of enabling lawful uses, such as Internet browsing.[60]

Recital 33 of the Information Society Directive indicates a use should be considered lawful if it is authorized by the rightsholder or not restricted by law.[61] A lawful use may consist of an intended use that is authorized, permitted by an exception or limitation, or one that is not restricted by the applicable legislation. The Directive hence adopts a broad interpretation of the notion of lawful use.[62] A use can be either implicitly or expressly authorized by the rightsholder. Implied authorial consent, which is discussed in Chapter 5, could include transient copies made in the process of browsing in cases where the rightsholders themselves have uploaded materials online without applying access restriction protocols.[63] A use is not restricted by law if it is permitted by an exception or limitation available under national law (essentially mirroring the provisions available in Articles 5(2) and 5(3) of the Information Society Directive and the copyright exceptions which feature in the Digital Single Market Directive, which shall soon be transposed into the national laws of Member States), and/or it is not prohibited by the applicable national legislation. For instance, web browsing may be covered by the private copying exception available under Article 5(2)(b) of the Information Society Directive and Article 5(1) may cover transient or incidental copying involved in this process, to the extent that such copying has no independent economic significance.

A use of the material is lawful, even when it has not been authorized by the rightholders, if it is consistent with EU legislation on the reproduction right,

---

[60] *Infopaq International A/S v Danske Dagblades Forening*, Case C-5/08, 16 July 2009, ECLI:EU:C:2009:465 (*Infopaq I*), [63]; *Infopaq International A/S v Danske Dagblades Forening*, Case C-302/10, 17 January 2012, ECLI:EU:C:2012:16 (*Infopaq II*), [49].

[61] See in this regard, WCT (1996); WPPT (1996).

[62] Tatiana-Eleni Synodinou, 'The Lawful User and a Balancing of Interests in European Copyright Law' (2010) 41(7) *International Review of Intellectual Property and Competition Law* 819, 827.

[63] See in this regard *Nils Svensson and Others v Retriever Sverige AB*, Case C-466/12, 13 February 2014, [26] (*Svensson*).

including Article 5(1) itself.[64] This was first developed in *FAPL*, where the Court of Justice found that the mere viewing of broadcasts in private circles was not an act restricted by EU or UK legislation and was, therefore, lawful.[65] In particular, the mere reception of the broadcasts in itself did not reveal an act restricted by the relevant legislation and had to be considered lawful in the case of broadcasts from a Member State when brought about by means of a foreign decoding device. *FAPL* involved the broadcast of Premier League football matches. Football Association Premier League (FAPL) owned the copyright in those works and had authorized the works' TV broadcast by a single licensee in each EU Member State. For instance, the licensee in Greece was NetMed Hellas, whereas in the United Kingdom it was BSkyB. BSkyB charged its subscribers a higher fee to offer access to the broadcasts. A publican, Mrs Karen Murphy, and other UK publicans and restaurateurs, imported cheaper foreign decoding devices from other states, including Greece, and showed the broadcasts to their customers in restaurants and pubs in the United Kingdom. Having been charged and convicted of criminal offences concerning the dishonest receipt of broadcasts, they appealed to the High Court of Justice arguing that Article 54 of the Treaty on the Functioning of the European Union prevented FAPL from restricting their access to broadcasts transmitted in other parts of the European Union; and that the Information Society Directive permitted them to show the broadcasts in their pubs and restaurants without clearing permissions from the relevant copyright holders. The Court of Justice, where the case was referred, agreed with the first of these arguments. With regards to the second issue, however, concerning the broadcasts of football matches in a pub without the permission of the relevant copyright holders, the Court of Justice held that showing the broadcasts involved two acts of reproduction within the meaning of Article 2 of the Information Society Directive. These were the creation of transient copies of the works within the decoder box and on the TV screen, and also involved the communication of the works to the public within the meaning of Article 3 of the Information Society Directive. By reference to acts of copying, the exception of Article 5(1) on temporary copying was found to apply and, therefore, there was no infringement of the reproduction right. The court concluded that the sole purpose of the acts of reproduction was to enable a 'lawful use' of the works within the meaning of Article 5(1)(b) of the Information Society Directive.

---

[64] *Football Association Premier League and Others*, Joint Cases C-403/08 and C-429/08, 4 October 2011, ECLI:EU:C:2011:631 (*FAPL*), [168]–[173]; *Infopaq International A/S v Danske Dagblades Forening*, Case C-302/10, 17 January 2012, ECLI:EU:C:2012:16 (*Infopaq II*), [42].

[65] *Football Association Premier League and Others*, Joint Cases C-403/08 and C-429/08, 4 October 2011, ECLI:EU:C:2011:631 (*FAPL*), [167]–[172]; the reasoning of the Court of Justice in *FAPL* raises concerns as to the extent that the sole purpose of reproducing the works in the course of showing the broadcasts in restaurants and pubs was to enable the reception of those broadcasts, which was a lawful act. The concern rests with the lack of clarity in the distinction between acts of reproduction (by turning the TV on) and acts of communication to the public (by enabling the reception of broadcasts through adjustments to the screen and the volume).

In *Infopaq II* the Court of Justice also found that the technological process was only intended to enable a more efficient drafting of summaries of newspaper articles. Neither European Union nor Danish legislation restricted this act under copyright and it was therefore lawful, despite the fact that it was not authorized by the relevant copyright holders. The court did not require that the intended use be an integral part of the technological process; it was sufficient that there was no indication that the technical process was used for another purpose.

The meaning of lawful use was further exemplified in *Stichting Brein v Jack Frederik Wullems*,[66] where the Court of Justice, considering both *FAPL* and *Infopaq II*, held that the ephemeral acts of reproduction in question were not carried out in the context of lawful use. The Dutch District Court (Rechtbank Midden-Nederland) brought proceedings to the Court of Justice regarding two questions on the temporary copying exception. In this case, Stichting Brein, the Dutch anti-piracy organization, sued Wullems for copyright infringement before the Dutch District Court, claiming that through the sale of the Filmspeler player, Wullems was carrying out an unauthorized 'communication to the public' in breach of Dutch copyright law. Filmspeler is a player for connecting a source of image and/or sound signals to a TV screen. Wullems, inter alia, installed add-ons containing hyperlinks which, if clicked, would redirect users to streaming websites, subject to third party control, on which protected content could be enjoyed free of charge, with or without the authorization of the relevant rightsholders. In his Opinion,[67] Manuel Campos Sánchez-Bordona AG found that

> lawfulness, in objective terms, depends ... on the authorisation of the right holder or his licensee. Excusable ignorance or reasonable lack of knowledge, on the part of the end user, of the fact that no such authorisation exists could, undoubtedly, exempt the user from liability, but it does not exclude—I repeat, in strictly objective terms—the unlawfulness of the 'use' referred to in Article 5(1) of Directive 2001/29.[68]

In this light, according to the Advocate General, since there was no authorization from the relevant rightsholders, streaming by end users would not be consistent

---

[66] In particular, the questions 3 and 4 were the following:

(3)   Should Article 5 of Directive 2001/29 be interpreted as meaning that there is no 'lawful use' within the meaning of Art. 5(1)(b) of that directive if a temporary reproduction is made by an end user during the streaming of a copyright-protected work from a third-party website where that copyright-protected work is offered without the authorisation of the right holder(s)?

(4)   If the answer to the third question is in the negative, is the making of a temporary reproduction by an end user during the streaming of a copyright-protected work from a website where that copyright-protected work is offered without the authorisation of the right holder(s) then contrary to the 'three-step test' referred to in Art. 5(5) of Directive 2001/29?

[67] Opinion of Advocate General Campos Sánchez-Bordona in *Stichting Brein v Jack Frederik Wullems, acting under the name of Filmspeler*, Case C-527/15, 8 December 2016, ECLI:EU:C:2016:938.

[68] Ibid., [71].

with 'lawful use' for the purposes of Article 5(1)(b) of the Information Society Directive.[69]

This understanding was upheld in the decision of the Court of Justice,[70] which held that acts of temporary copying on a multimedia player of a protected work obtained by streaming from a third party website offering unauthorized access to that work, does not satisfy the conditions set out in Article 5(1). As the Court stressed, these conditions are cumulative; they should be interpreted strictly[71] and be compliant with Article 5(5) of the Directive outlining the three-step test. The court clarified that lawful use is either authorized by the rightsholder or not restricted by the applicable legislation, further to Recital 33.[72] In *Filmspeler*, the use was not authorized by the relevant copyright holders, hence it was necessary to assess whether the aim of the acts in question was to enable a use of the works that was not restricted by the applicable legislation, in light of the three-step test.[73] Unlike *FAPL* and *Infopaq II*, the main attraction of the service in *Filmspeler* would be the installation of add-ons 'deliberately and in full knowledge of the circumstances' that the purchaser would be accessing a free and unauthorized offer of copyright-protected works.[74] Since the main attraction of the multimedia player for potential purchasers was the pre-installation of add-ons, it was deliberately, and in full knowledge of the circumstances, that the purchaser of such a player accessed a free and unauthorized offer of protected works.[75] What is more, temporary acts of reproduction such as those in *Filmspeler* adversely affected the normal exploitation of protected works and caused unreasonable prejudice to the legitimate interests of the rightsholder because, as the Advocate General also noted,[76] such practice would usually result in a diminution of lawful transactions related to the protected works which would cause unreasonable prejudice to copyright holders. The acts in question did not therefore satisfy the conditions set out in Article 5(1) and (5) of the Information Society Directive and the defence on temporary copying could not be upheld.

It follows that the assessment of lawful use has to take into consideration the three-step test of Article 5(5) and ensure that any acts of temporary copying should

---

[69] Ibid., [72].

[70] *Stichting Brein v Jack Frederik Wullems*, Case C-527/15, 26 April 2017, ECLI:EU:C:2017:300 (*Filmspeler*).

[71] Ibid., [61]–[62]; *Infopaq International A/S v Danske Dagblades Forening*, Case C-5/08, 16 July 2009, ECLI:EU:C:2009:465 (*Infopaq I*), [55]; *Infopaq International A/S v Danske Dagblades Forening*, Case C-302/10, 17 January 2012, ECLI:EU:C:2012:16 (*Infopaq II*), [26].

[72] See also *Football Association Premier League and Others*, C-403/08 and C-429/08, EU:C:2011:631 (*FAPL*), [168]; *Infopaq International A/S v Danske Dagblades Forening*, Case C-302/10, 17 January 2012, ECLI:EU:C:2012:16 (*Infopaq II*), [42].

[73] *Stichting Brein v Jack Frederik Wullems*, Case C-527/15, 26 April 2017, ECLI:EU:C:2017:300 (*Filmspeler*), [66].

[74] Ibid., [69].

[75] Ibid., [69].

[76] See Opinion of the Advocate General Campos Sánchez-Bordona, *Stichting Brein v Jack Frederik Wullems*, Case C-527/15, 8 December 2016, ECLI:EU:C:2016:938, [78]–[79].

not have an adverse effect on the normal exploitation of the original work or come into conflict with the legitimate interests of copyright holders. The three-step test, in this sense, becomes the standard for determining lawfulness, where there is no express authorization from the relevant rightholders.

5. No independent economic significance

According to consistent case law of the Court of Justice of the European Union, the making of the temporary copy must have no 'independent economic significance'. This does not mean that the temporary copy should have no commercial value, but that it must have no *independent* commercial value, namely no value additional to that which is derived from the mere act of digitally browsing or viewing the material.[77] Recital 33 of the Directive uses the words 'no separate economic value of their own'. Both formulations are indicative of the legislative intention to exclude activities that have no economic relevance and subsist for technical reasons only. This requirement reflects the need to satisfy the conditions of the three-step test of Article 5(5) of the Information Society Directive, in that the normal economic exploitation of works should not be affected.

In *FAPL*,[78] the Court of Justice held that the relevant acts of reproduction enabled access to the protected works and, because the works had economic value, such access inevitably had economic significance. The court, however, also stressed that for the exemption of Article 5(1) to be meaningful the economic significance ought to be independent in that it should go 'beyond the economic advantage derived from mere reception of a broadcast containing protected works'.[79] Temporary copies made in the memory of a decoder and on a television screen were an inseparable part of the technical process as they were performed without influence, or even awareness, on behalf of the viewers. This meant that such copies were not capable of generating an additional economic advantage than that derived from mere reception of the broadcasts at issue. For example, if a publican's use of the unauthorized decoding card was not merely for the reception of the broadcasts on TV screens, but was also carried out with a view to stream the broadcasts to other premises beyond a restaurant or a pub, that could be seen as an independent economic advantage.

The policy emphasis was different when the *FAPL* case was heard by the Court of Justice of the European Union, focusing on the purpose of Article 5(1) towards

---

[77] *Football Association Premier League and Others*, Joined Cases C-403/08 and C-429/08, 4 October 2011, ECLI:EU:C:2011:631 (*FAPL*), [175]; *Infopaq International A/S v Danske Dagblades Forening*, Case C-302/10, 17 January 2012, ECLI:EU:C:2012:16 (*Infopaq II*), [50].

[78] *Football Association Premier League and Others*, Joined Cases C-403/08 and C-429/08, 4 October 2011, ECLI:EU:C:2011:631 (*FAPL*).

[79] *Football Association Premier League and Others*, Joined Cases C-403/08 and C-429/08, 4 October 2011, ECLI:EU:C:2011:631 (*FAPL*), [175].

the enhancement of access to new technologies in line with Recital 31 of the Information Society Directive. According to the court:

> If the acts at issue were not considered to comply with the conditions set by Article 5(1) [of the Information Society Directive], all television viewers using modern sets which, in order to work, need those acts of reproduction to be carried out would be prevented from receiving broadcasts containing broadcast works, in the absence of an authorisation from copyright holders. That would impede, and even paralyse, the actual spread and contribution of new technologies, in disregard of the will of the European Union legislature as expressed in recital 31 in the preamble to [the Information Society Directive].[80]

In *Infopaq II*, temporary copies were found to have economic significance because those acts, including caching and browsing, which are meant to enable the achievement of efficiency gains in the context of such use, consequently lead to increased profits or a reduction in production costs. However, those acts were found not to have independent economic significance in that the economic advantage derived from their implementation was neither distinct nor separable from the economic advantage derived from the lawful use of the work concerned. Neither did it generate an additional economic advantage beyond that derived from the use of the protected work.[81] In order for an act of independent economic significance to be established, there should be an advantage derived from an act of temporary copying that is distinct and separable; this can be established, for instance, where the party making the temporary copies is likely to make a profit owing to the economic exploitation of the temporary copies themselves or where temporary copying leads to a modification of a work.[82]

What ought to be stressed by reference to the *Infopaq* acts of temporary copying (and those of *Meltwater*), however, is that although the Court of Justice found they were devoid of economic significance, those reproductions were the very product for which subscribers were paying. The UK High Court of Justice had made a relevant observation in *Meltwater*, where it noted that

> any copy which is 'consumption of the work', whether temporary or not, requires the permission of the copyright holder ... [M]aking the copy does have an independent economic significance as the copy is the very product for which the End Users are paying Meltwater.

---

[80] *Football Association Premier League and Others*, Joined Cases C-403/08 and C-429/08, 4 October 2011, ECLI:EU:C:2011:631 (*FAPL*), [179].

[81] See *Infopaq International A/S v Danske Dagblades Forening*, Case C-302/10, 17 January 2012, ECLI:EU:C:2012:16 (*Infopaq II*), [49]–[50].

[82] *Infopaq International A/S v Danske Dagblades Forening*, Case C-302/10, 17 January 2012, ECLI:EU:C:2012:16 (*Infopaq II*), [52], [54].

The exception cannot have been intended to legitimize all copies made in the course of browsing or users would be permitted to watch pirated films and listen to pirated music. The kind of circumstance where the defence may be available is where the purpose of the copying is to enable efficient transmission in a network between third parties by an intermediary, typically an internet service provider.[83]

Perhaps for policy reasons, the justifications outlined by the UK Supreme Court, and the Court of Justice decisions in *Meltwater*, differ, despite the fact that both courts seem to have reached the same conclusion. According to Lord Sumption, it would be preferable for rightsholders to seek a single, higher licensing fee from Meltwater than many small licensing fees from end users. A finding of infringement was thought to 'make infringers of many millions of ordinary users of the internet across the EU'.[84]

Temporary copying and the three-step test

To the extent that the conditions of Article 5(1) of the Information Society Directive are met, no additional restrictions can be derived from the three-step test of Article 5(5).[85] Following the stipulation of Article 9(2) of the Berne Convention,[86] Article 5(5) of the Information Society Directive provides that exceptions and limitations included in the Directive

shall only be applied in certain special cases which do not conflict with a normal exploitation of the work or other subject matter and do not unreasonably prejudice the legitimate interests of the rightholder.

The wording of Article 5(5) is problematic and raises a number of questions.[87] The three-step test was first introduced by the Berne Convention in its 1967 revision,[88] providing in its Article 9(2) a 'catch-all' limitation for all applicable exceptions to the reproduction right. Before making its way into Article 5(5) of the Information Society Directive,[89] the test was repeated several times in international law, such as in

---

[83] *Newspaper Licensing Agency Ltd et al v Meltwater Holding BV et al*, [2010] EWHC 3099 (Ch) (UK), [109]–[110].

[84] *Public Relations Consultants Association Ltd v Newspaper Licensing Agency Ltd* [2013] UKSC 18, [2013] 2 All E.R. 852 (UK), [36].

[85] See indicatively: *Infopaq International A/S v Danske Dagblades Forening*, Case C-5/08, 16 July 2009, ECLI:EU:C:2009:465 (*Infopaq I*), at [58]; for a comment, see Isabella Alexander, 'The Concept of Reproduction and the "Temporary and Transient" Exception' (2009) 68(3) *Cambridge Law Journal* 520.

[86] Berne Convention for the Protection of Literary and Artistic Works (hereinafter 'Berne Convention') (as amended on 28 September 1979).

[87] See in general Jonathan Griffiths, 'The "Three-Step Test" in European Copyright Law - Problems and Solutions' (2009) 4 *Intellectual Property Quarterly* 428.

[88] Berne Convention, Art. 9(2).

[89] For an analysis and comment on Art. 5(5), see e.g. Jenoram Cohen, 'The Place of the User in Copyright Law' (2005) 74 *Fordham Law Review* 347, 364.

Article 13 of the 1994 Agreement on Trade-Related Aspects of Intellectual Property Rights and in Article 10 of the WCT, as a criterion for evaluating the permissibility of *all* applicable national exceptions and limitations.[90] As formulated under the relevant international instruments, the three-step test is meant to serve as a standard for legislative use only. Article 5(5), however, represents a shift in this approach. It stipulates that copyright exceptions and limitations 'shall only be applied' when the conditions of the test are met. This means that, under the Information Society Directive (and also the Digital Single Market Directive),[91] the test is aimed directly at the application of copyright exceptions and limitations and not only at their introduction into national law. Recital 44 of the Copyright Directive specifies that

> such exceptions and limitations may not be applied in a way that prejudices legitimate interests of the rightholder or which conflicts with the normal exploitation of his work or other subject matter.

The three-step test has, therefore, evolved from a criterion that has to be considered at the legislative stage to a test that has to be applied by the judiciary.[92] Von Lewinski and Reinbothe argue that it is the European Court of Justice and not national courts that should control the interpretation and implementation of copyright limitations,[93] even though national courts have been using the test as yet another condition for the application of exceptions and limitations.[94] Koelman is sceptical as to the application of the test by national judges[95] and Geiger anticipates the issue of a Court of Justice of the EU ruling determining who the true addressee of the test is.[96] Unlike the fair use test in the United States,[97] which is set as a standard to be applied by courts, the three-step test does not give judges sufficient latitude for consideration of interests other than those of the rightsholders, even though copyright limitations are essential for the preservation of the interests of end users and, therefore, for maintaining an area of user freedom.[98] This is because the three-step

---

[90] For an analysis, see Mihály Ficsor, *The Law of Copyright and the Internet: the 1996 WIPO Treaties, their Interpretation and Implementation* (Oxford: Oxford University Press, 2002) 521.

[91] Digital Single Market Directive (Directive 2019/790), Art. 7(2).

[92] See broadly Richard Arnold and Eleonora Rosati, 'Are National Courts the Addressees of the InfoSoc Three-Step Test?' (2005) 10(10) *Journal of Intellectual Property Law & Practice* 741; Stavroula Karapapa, *Private Copying* (London: Routledge, 2012) 99 et seq.

[93] Silke von Lewinski and Jörg Reinbothe, 'The WIPO Treaties 1996: Ready to Come into Force' (2002) 24(4) *European Intellectual Property Review* 199, 204.

[94] Examples include *Google v Copiepresse*, Brussels District Court, 13 February 2007 (2007) 1–2 A&M 107 (Belgium); *Google Inc. v Copiepresse et al.*, Brussels Court of Appeal (9th Chamber), 5 May 2011 (Belgium); Federal Supreme Court, 11 July 2002 [2002] GRUR 963 (Germany); Federal Court of 26 June 2007, 4c.73/2007/len (Switzerland).

[95] Kamiel Koelman, 'Fixing the Three-Step Test' (2006) 28(8) *European Intellectual Property Review* 407.

[96] Christophe Geiger, 'From Berne to National Law, via the Copyright Directive: The Dangerous Mutations of the Three-Step Test' (2007) 29(12) *European Intellectual Property Review* 486, 488; P. Bernt Hugenholtz et al., *The Recasting of Copyright and Related Rights for the Knowledge Economy* (Amsterdam: IvIR, 2006) 71.

[97] Section 107 of title 17 of the US Code.

[98] Stavroula Karapapa, *Private Copying* (London: Routledge, 2012) 99 et seq.

test is inherently an economic prejudice test which measures the effect that a use may have on the normal exploitation of works and its potential prejudice over the rightsholder's interests; in this regard, in every interpretation that this test may receive, the impact of an activity on the rightsholders' interests is decisive.[99]

Early discussions on the application of the three-step test of Article 5(5) raised concerns as to the particular wording of this provision which seemed to indicate that it would be necessary for an activity to meet the conditions of an exception or limitation and a second set of conditions set by the three-step test.[100] Indeed, this would raise significant problems as to the viability and scope of application of exceptions and limitations.

In *Infopaq I*, the Court of Justice held that if acts of reproduction fulfil all the conditions of Article 5(1), it must be held that they do not conflict with the normal exploitation of the work or unreasonably prejudice the legitimate interests of the rights owner.[101] This can be seen as an implicit affirmation that the three-step test should not be applied as an additional set of conditions to determine the applicability of copyright exceptions and limitations. Similar was the position taken in the *FAPL* case, where the Court of Justice held that although Mrs Murphy and her pub clientele were viewing copyright-protected content, such viewing could benefit from the exemption of Article 5(1), hence it satisfied Article 5(5).[102] This indicates that national laws which have introduced the three-step test as a condition for the judicial affirmation of the applicability of a defence may have to be subject to review as the test would thereinafter have to be applied twice—once at the legislative and later at the judicial stage—unjustifiably restricting the applicability of said defences.

Conclusion

The temporary copying defence incorporated in Article 5(1) of the Information Society Directive and the national laws by which it is implemented, specify that certain activities are exempt from infringement on the basis of their transient or incidental character. The purpose of exempting such activities from infringement is that they lack the economic significance that permanent acts of reproduction have, while at the same time they enable the efficient function of online communications on the Internet. These tend to be of paramount importance in cases of electronic communications and, more specifically, on the Internet as a result of the very nature and function

---

[99] Ibid.

[100] See e.g. Michael Hart, 'The Legality of Internet Browsing in the Digital Age' (2014) 36(10) *European Intellectual Property Review* 630, 631–2.

[101] *Infopaq International A/S v Danske Dagblades Forening*, Case C-5/08, 16 July 2009, ECLI:EU:C:2009:465 (*Infopaq I*), at [58]; for a comment, see Isabella Alexander, 'The Concept of Reproduction and the "Temporary and Transient" Exception' (2009) 68(3) *Cambridge Law Journal* 520.

[102] *Football Association Premier League and Others*, Joined Cases C-403/08 and C-429/08, 4 October 2011, ECLI:EU:C:2011:631 (*FAPL*), [181].

of online networks. Examples of activities which can be covered by the exemption include copies created in the RAM memory of computers; caching in local memory of proxy servers, computer systems or Internet routers;[103] browsing of web content; and streaming of digital content. Various online services and new business models rely on such kinds of copying and five key cases—*Infopaq I* and *II, FAPL, Meltwater,* and *Filmspeler*—have shed light on the scope of the exception available under Article 5(1) of the Information Society Directive and its conditions of application.

Even though Article 5(1) is organically listed in the set of exceptions and limitations enumerated under the Information Society Directive, it is argued that the temporary copying exception should also (and perhaps primarily) be understood as offering definitional boundaries to the broad scope of the reproduction right (and hence outlining a denial to the elements of infringement in certain cases) instead of putting forward a supervening defence in the form of a justification for an alleged wrongdoing. This is for three reasons. First, the historical principles and interpretative guidance on the function of this exception within the copyright system indicate that the temporary copying exception means to frame the limits of the reproduction right, define its scope more clearly, and lower the level of generality in which the right is drafted. Second, the defence is compulsory for Member States to implement and, as a matter of fact, it is the only compulsory exception included within the Information Society Directive. This means that the public policy objective that the exception means to serve was placed at the top of the harmonization agenda at the time that the Directive was introduced. Third, the Court of Justice has affirmed that Article 5(1) is a derogation from the general rule established by that Directive that the copyright holder must authorize any reproduction of his or her protected work and hence the conditions which underlie the temporary copying exception ought to be subject to strict interpretation.[104] In this regard, the temporary copying exception can be understood as serving both as a scope limitation to an exclusive right and as an exemption from infringement.[105] In light of such considerations, it is argued that the temporary copying exception can be understood as setting a scope limitation to the reproduction right and an exemption from copyright infringement.[106]

---

[103] Report to the Council, the European Parliament and the Economic and Social Committee on the Application of Directive 2001/29/EC on the Harmonisation of Certain Aspects of Copyright and Related Rights in the Information Society, 30 November 2007, SEC(2007) 1556, 2.1.

[104] *Infopaq International A/S v Danske Dagblades Forening*, Case C-5/08, 16 July 2009, ECLI:EU:C:2009:465 (*Infopaq I*), [56] and [57]; *Football Association Premier League and Others*, Joined Cases C-403/08 and C-429/08, 4 October 2011, ECLI:EU:C:2011:631 (*FAPL*), [162]; *Public Relations Consultants Association Ltd v Newspaper Licensing Agency Ltd and Others*, Case C-360/13, 5 June 2014, ECLI:EU:C:2014:1195 (*Meltwater*), [23].

[105] See in this regard the decision of the UK Supreme Court: *Public Relations Consultants Association Limited (Appellant) v The Newspaper Licensing Agency Limited and others (Respondents)* [2013] UKSC 18, [36].

[106] Ibid.

5

Implicitly Authorized Uses

Another way in which a defendant can combat allegations of copyright infringement by the denial of one of the elements in which the plaintiff sues is to argue that the copyright holder authorized the activity at issue, either expressly or implicitly. Exclusive rights under copyright have a common constituent: they represent activities that the copyright holder can authorize or prohibit. Authorization is at the heart of copyright, and permission from the copyright holders is necessary to avoid liability for infringement. There are instances where the consent of the copyright holder to authorize a particular activity will be express and will not raise interpretative difficulties. It is possible, however, for such consent to be found to be implied, upon judicial examination. The doctrine of implied consent has not received harmonization at EU level, but it can be found in national laws either as a matter of interpreting a contractual relationship or a conduct that gives the impression that a particular activity is permitted. With regard to contracts, written agreements, such as assignments, licenses, or waivers of rights, may include implied contractual terms. In this context, the implied license doctrine is viewed as a ramification of contract law, applicable in contractual or quasi-contractual relations in order to identify the intent of the parties. Implied authorization to carry out certain activities, however, may also be assumed in cases where the parties do not have an agreement, or even prior communication, but the conduct of copyright holders gives the impression that a particular activity is permitted. This understanding of implied consent can be traced to German jurisprudence and, in particular, to a body of recent cases that have affirmed the existence of implied authorization where copyright holders did not take affirmative steps to signify their refusal to consent to a specific activity, e.g. by way of an express licensing term or through their conduct. An example of such an instance is where copyright holders have not enacted access control mechanisms in their online content or website. Many scholars have discussed the potential of the implied license doctrine to solve contemporary conflicts.[1] The judicially created doctrine of 'implied consent' is crucial

---

[1] Orit Afori, 'Implied License: An Emerging New Standard in Copyright Law' (2008) 25 *Santa Clara Computer and High Technology Law Journal* 275; Raghu Seshadri, 'Bridging the Digital Divide: How the Implied License Doctrine Could Narrow the Copynorm-Copyright Gap' (2007) *II UCLA Journal of Law and Technology* 1; John S. Sieman, 'Using the Implied License To Inject Common Sense into Digital Copyright' (2007) 85 *North Carolina Law Review* 885.

Defences to Copyright Infringement. Stavroula Karapapa, Oxford University Press (2020). © Stavroula Karapapa. DOI: 10.1093/oso/9780198795636.001.0001

to the functioning of essential Internet facilities such as search engines, which often base their business model on the aggregation of crawling content which they make available free of charge to their users without seeking permission from the copyright holders. This chapter discusses the scope of this doctrine, which has been mainly developed in Germany,[2] its applicability to other Internet services, and its potential in serving as a defensive rule. It also discusses how *Svensson*[3] can be read as to introduce an implied consent defence into EU copyright and the impact of this case on interpretation of the intention of copyright holders when they upload materials to the Internet, but fail to enact access control protocols.

Introduction

Authorization is at the heart of copyright and any activity touching upon exclusive rights will be permitted where the rightsholders have given their permission. According to Recital 30 of the Information Society Directive, exclusive rights 'may be transferred, assigned, or subject to the granting of contractual licenses, without prejudice to the relevant national legislation on copyright and related rights.' Even though express contractual arrangements would raise very few possibilities of uncertainty, problems may arise either because of unclear contractual terms, because a license has not been concluded, or because a term may have been implied. Since copyright contract law has not been subject to harmonization, it is up to the national laws to determine the concept of implied license with regard to assignments and waivers.[4]

Although of minor significance when it was first developed, the implied license doctrine became more relevant with digitization and the Internet due to the common perception that Internet users have wider access to content and that rightsholders are expected to be familiar with the particularities of the electronic environment when they upload their materials freely online.[5] A number of

---

[2] See e.g. 'Vorschaubilder I', Supreme Court (Bundesgerichtshof), 29 April 2010, I ZR 69/08, 14–15 (Germany), available in German at <http://www.bundesgerichtshof.de>, accessed 11 November 2019; 'Vorschaubilder II', Supreme Court (Bundesgerichtshof), 19 October 2011, I ZR 140/10 (Germany); Court of Appeal of Jena (Oberlandesgericht Jena), 2 U 319/07, 27 February 2008, *Kommunikation und Recht* 2008, 301 (Germany).

[3] *Nils Svensson and Others v Retriever Sverige AB*, Case C-466/12, 13 February 2014, ECLI:EU:C:2014:76 (*Svensson*).

[4] Taina Pihlajarinne, 'Setting the Limits for the Implied License in Copyright and Linking Discourse – the European Perspective' (2012) 43(6) *International Review of Intellectual Property and Competition Law* 700, 706.

[5] Taina Pihlajarinne, 'Setting the Limits for the Implied License in Copyright and Linking Discourse – the European Perspective' (2012) 43(6) *International Review of Intellectual Property and Competition Law* 700, 701.

Internet-related features, such as thumbnails or web links, involve use of works for which authorization from the rightsholders is often not sought. Search engines or news aggregators base their business model on the routine extraction and re-use of content that is openly available online, without seeking the permission of the copyright holders. Even though there is no express legislative provision on the matter, there is a growing body of national case law that relies upon legal principles, such as the doctrine of implied consent, to exempt such activities from infringement.[6] Reflecting the need for fairness and equity, these doctrinal legal principles may acquit infringement activities that cannot safely be covered by any copyright exception and limitation, but which are rooted in the doctrine of implied license or consent. Implied license is often seen as declaration of intent,[7] and a particular activity may be deemed lawful where rightsholders have created the impression that third parties acting in good faith are implicitly authorized to carry out an activity that would otherwise amount to infringement.

Different legal systems have developed similar yet distinct approaches to implied licenses. In Anglo-American copyright, an activity will be considered as implicitly licensed if it falls within the scope of the initial authorization or is inherent within the ownership of a product.[8] By contrast, the German approach is broader as it also covers instances where the rightsholders failed to take positive steps to ensure that an activity remains prohibited.[9] This indicates that copyright holders are bound by certain positive obligations to remain proactive towards the protection of their content instead of standing back and waiting for infringement to take place. For instance, in cases involving content made available online by the relevant rightsholders which is crawled by search engines without authorization, German courts found that rightsholders had given their implied consent for these works to be made available in online searches. This was either because they had not applied technical measures to prevent crawling, i.e. the systematic browsing and copying

---

[6] See e.g. 'Vorschaubilder I', Supreme Court (Bundesgerichtshof), 29 April 2010, I ZR 69/08, 14–15 (Germany), available in German at <http://www.bundesgerichtshof.de>, accessed 11 November 2019; 'Vorschaubilder II', Supreme Court (Bundesgerichtshof), 19 October 2011, I ZR 140/10 (Germany); Court of Appeal of Jena (Oberlandesgericht Jena), 2 U 319/07, 27 February 2008, *Kommunikation und Recht* 2008, 301 (Germany).

[7] Alexandre Cruquenaire, 'Electronic Agents as Search Engines: Copyright-Related Aspects' (2001) 9 *International Journal of Law and Information Technology* 327, 334 et seq.

[8] See in this regard *British Leyland Motor Corp. v Armstrong Patents Co.* [1986] AC 577, 625 (UK), where Lord Bridge observed:

> It seems to me that when one is considering machinery which is not the subject of any patent protection, it is unnecessary and may be misleading to introduce the concept of an implied licence. The owner of a car must be entitled to do whatever is necessary to keep it in running order and to effect whatever repairs may be necessary in the most economical way possible. To derive this entitlement from an implied licence granted by the original manufacturer seems to me quite artificial. It is a right inherent in the ownership of the car itself.

[9] It can be said that the Anglo-American approach is to interpret the possibility of an implied license positively, i.e. as broadening the scope of initial authorization, whereas the German approach is based on a negative construal, i.e. what has not been prohibited will be included within the scope of the license.

of web pages for the purpose of indexing and searching,[10] or because they had optimized their websites to attract more users.[11] The common denominator in both
legal traditions is that the defence is essentially construed around the claim that
the defendant carried out a particular activity under the impression that copyright
holders were in agreement. Hence, such claims attack an allegation of copyright
infringement at its heart by arguing that the relevant party has authorized the use.
Effectively, the defence does not excuse infringement but, if successful, affirms that
infringement never took place.

The implied authorization defence, particularly consent that is implied through
conduct, has gained significance and become increasingly relevant in EU copyright after its affirmation in *Svensson*.[12] In this case, the Court of Justice brought
forward an implied consent rationale according to which, when rightsholders
place their works online with no access control mechanisms, the retransmission
of the content via hyperlinks does not amount to copyright infringement. This is
not to say that copyright holders do not remain in control over their right of communicating works or otherwise making them available to the public; it does, however, add weight to conduct which implies that certain activities are permitted. As
defensive rules which govern implied consent have not been harmonized at the
EU level, subject to examination below are the two leading approaches towards
implied consent, focusing on the way in which such a consent may be assumed,
namely either by conduct or by contract. The way in which these approaches have
been developed through case law and legal principles, and instances in which they
may serve a defensive function, are also subject to discussion with a view to assessing the potential, if any, of implied authorization being included to the breadth
of copyright defences.

Consent implied by conduct

Permission to carry out certain activities with regard to copyright-protected works
or other subject matter may be implied on the basis of an interpretation of the conduct of copyright holders. The centrality of conduct in this assessment and its importance in ascertaining the consent of the copyright holders has been affirmed

---

[10] 'Vorschaubilder II', Supreme Court (Bundesgerichtshof), 19 October 2011, I ZR 140/10
(Germany); Alain Strowel and Vicky Hanley, 'Secondary Liability for Copyright Infringement with re-
gard to Hyperlinks' in Alain Strowel (ed.), *Peer-to-Peer File Sharing and Secondary Liability in Copyright
Law* (Cheltenham: Edward Elgar, 2008) 88.

[11] Court of Appeal of Jena (Oberlandesgericht Jena), 2 U 319/07, 27 February 2008, *Kommunikation
und Recht* 2008, 301 (Germany); also see '*Sommer unseres Lebens*', Supreme Court (Bundesgerichtshof),
12 May 2010, I ZR 121/08 (Germany); '*Halzband*', Supreme Court (Bundesgerichtshof), 11 March
2009, I ZR 114/06 (Germany).

[12] *Nils Svensson and Others v Retriever Sverige AB*, Case C-466/12, 13 February 2014,
ECLI:EU:C:2014:76 (*Svensson*).

primarily in German jurisprudence and also underpins the Court of Justice's reasoning in *Svensson*. Many of the cases where consent by conduct was implied are relevant in an online context, indicating that implied consent may be of increasing relevance on the Internet.

German jurisprudence is rich in cases where consent by conduct was implied. The German Federal Supreme Court, in *Vorschaubilder I*,[13] developed a doctrine of implied consent to acquit Google of infringing liability for the reproduction and making available to the public of 'thumbnail' images. In the case at issue, the copyright holder had made the works available online without enacting any technical mechanism to block the automated indexing and displaying of online content by search engines. In this sense, the copyright holder was held to have implicitly consented to the use of the works on the image search service.[14] Even though the court did not infer an implicit contractual license for indexing content on the Internet,[15] it did hold that Google's use of the pictures was not unlawful and thereby affirmed the application of implied consent as a defence in cases of allegations of copyright infringement on the Internet.

The position of the Supreme Court was upheld in *Vorschaubilder II*.[16] The claimant in this case had not assigned any exploitation rights to his photographs to third parties, but had allowed other users to publish the photographs on the Internet. The German Supreme Court observed that it is 'commonly known' that search engines do not distinguish between images that have been uploaded by authorized or unauthorized sources. The court rejected the plaintiff's argument that implied consent could not justify indexing of content on behalf of a search engine in cases where thumbnails were generated from unauthorized third parties. Although this activity amounted to an act of making content available to the public according to Article 19a of the German Copyright Act, effectively requiring the

---

[13] 'Vorschaubilder I', Supreme Court (Bundesgerichtshof), 29 April 2010, I ZR 69/08, 14–15 (Germany), available in German at <http://www.bundesgerichtshof.de>, accessed 11 November 2019. For a comment on this case, see Matthias Leistner, 'The German Federal Supreme Court's Judgment on Google's Image Search—A Topical Example of the "Limitations" of the European Approach to Exceptions and Limitations' (2011) 42(4) *International Review of Intellectual Property and Competition Law* 417.

The decision follows the judgments of the regional and appellate courts. See District Court of Erfurt, 15 March 2007, No. 3 O 1108/05 (Germany) (where the court assumed that there was implied consent in a case of thumbnails and stressed their potential benefits to the interests of the copyright holder on the basis of the ease in locating their works on the Internet); Thuringian Higher Regional Court, 27 February 2008, No. 2 U 319/07, MMR 2009 (Germany) (where the Court was not convinced that the implicit consent defence applies but used, however, a variation of this defence. Since the plaintiff was engaged in search engine optimization, they had attracted crawlers and were, hence, estopped from raising claims against search engines, despite the fact that—as the Court acknowledged—uploading a work on a website does not imply that the copyright owner agrees to *all* search engine uses).

[14] 'Vorschaubilder I', Supreme Court (Bundesgerichtshof), 29 April 2010, I ZR 69/08, 14–15 (Germany) 15–19.

[15] Ibid.

[16] 'Vorschaubilder II', Supreme Court (Bundesgerichtshof), 19 October 2011, I ZR 140/10 (Germany).

copyright holder's consent, in cases where the protected material was made available online without measures being taken to ensure that search engine indexing would be excluded (e.g. by means of a robots.txt entry or equivalent), the consent of the copyright holders would be implied. Hence, it was assumed that the claimant had given his implied consent, despite the fact that the content was uploaded by third parties. In this regard, the Court elaborated on its reasoning in *Vorschaubilder I*,[17] by holding that the implied consent doctrine could also apply in cases where the various images were published by third parties, without the consent of the copyright holder. According to the court, search engines operate on the basis of automated systems that do not have the capacity to differentiate between legally or illegally generated images. In this light, the consent that the copyright holders impliedly gave to third parties extended to indexing of their content and, because technological protection measures had not been applied, search engine providers would reasonably interpret this conduct as though the rightsholders did not object to the use of their images by search engines.[18]

This judicial trend, which appears to introduce a degree of flexibility to the understanding of what amounts to permissible use in the online context, has also been affirmed in another case concerning the lawfulness of thumbnail images. The Court of Appeal of Jena, in Germany, dismissed a claim for injunctive relief to stop the unauthorized display of thumbnails of photographs in an Internet search service, despite the fact that the act at issue was found to amount to infringement.[19] The thumbnails in this case were found to be adaptations within the meaning of Article 23 of the German Copyright Act, meaning that their exploitation had to be authorized by the relevant rightsholders. There was no defence available in the form of copyright exceptions and limitations; the court ran through a number of possible available defences to conclude that none of them would be applicable in the case at issue. However, the court found that the claimant's argument for injunctive relief would be abusive by virtue of Article 242 of the Civil Code; the reason for this was that she had optimized her website to attract search engines. This indicates the relevance of the general prohibition on the abusive exercise of copyright, discussed in more detail in Chapter 9, in understanding the extent to which copyright holders have authorized a given activity or not on the basis of both their conduct and breadth of proprietary entitlement. At the same time, the claimant had not modified the metadata of her website to block indexing in search results, indicating that the copyright holder's conduct implied that the relevant activities were not prohibited. The ruling, which is in line with other case law from

---

[17] 'Vorschaubilder I', Supreme Court (Bundesgerichtshof), 29 April 2010, I ZR 69/08, 14–15 (Germany), available in German at <http://www.bundesgerichtshof.de>, accessed 11 November 2019.

[18] According to the Court, the copyright owner was free to pursue third parties who published the images on the Internet without authorization.

[19] Court of Appeal of Jena (Oberlandesgericht Jena), 2 U 319/07, 27 February 2008, *Kommunikation und Recht* 2008, 301 (Germany).

Germany, indicates that copyright holders ought to take some positive steps to indicate their desire to prohibit the unauthorized re-use of their content, otherwise a defensive claim centred around the doctrine of implied consent may be invoked.

On the very same day that the *Vorschaubilder I* case[20] was issued, the German Supreme Court issued yet another case with implied consent as a defensive rule; however, this particular case set limits on the way in which the doctrine is applied.[21] The case concerned a motor vehicle accident investigator who, after a car accident, had been hired by a car owner to take professional images of the damage and deliver expert opinion on the accident. The defendant, an insurance company, received the photographs in order to process the car owner's claim, but later the company posted the images on an online platform in order to resell the car. The Supreme Court held that the photographs in question were subject to protection under the neighbouring right, outlined in Article 72 of the German Copyright Act, and that the defendant's use included an act of making the images available within the meaning of Article 19a of the German Copyright Act. The claimant had agreed to offer his services to the car owner, but not to the defendant insurance company. It was standard practice for accident investigators to send the images of damaged vehicles directly to the insurance company, no matter the fact that it was the vehicle's owners who appointed them. This could not signify—express or implied—consent to any kind of re-use of the images. Taking into consideration this contextual parameter, the court stressed that implied consent can be assumed only where this is necessary in order to fulfil the contract and in the present case this included the fulfilment of the claimant's obligations towards the car owner in order to process a claim with the insurance company. This limit on implied consent can be read parallel to the way in which consent has been developed in other areas of law, e.g. the concept of specific consent used in data protection.[22] In this regard, the principle of necessity can be a useful tool in determining the limits of the implied consent doctrine.

In the United Kingdom too, there are numerous judicial affirmations that consent may be implied as a result of conduct, i.e. without the parties having a contractual relationship. The test that is followed in order to ascertain whether consent is implied is objective.[23] Payment and acceptance of royalties in view

---

[20] 'Vorschaubilder I', Supreme Court (Bundesgerichtshof), 29 April 2010, I ZR 69/08, 14–15 (Germany), available in German at <http://www.bundesgerichtshof.de>, accessed 11 November 2019.

[21] 'Residual Value Platform', Supreme Court (Bundesgerichtshof), 29 April 2010, I ZR 69/08 (Germany).

[22] Art. 29 Data Protection Working Party, 'Guidelines on Consent under Regulation 2016/679', 17/EN WP259, 28 November 2017; also see the earlier position of Art. 29 Data Protection Working Party, 'Opinion 15/2011 on the Definition of Consent', 01197/11/EN WP187, 13 July 2011; on theoretical aspects and empirical data on the way in which consent was approached before the enactment of the General Data Protection Regulation of 2018, see Maurizio Borghi, Federico Ferretti, and Stavroula Karapapa, 'Online Processing Consent under EU Law: A Theoretical Framework and Empirical Evidence from the UK' (2013) 21 *International Journal of Law and Information Technology* 1.

[23] *Redwood Music Ltd v Chappell & Co. Ltd* [1982] RPC 109 (UK).

of the exploitation of a work, for example, could be considered proof of the recipient's consent to the acts of the party paying.[24] Other examples include the production of an advertisement by a marketing agency which was held to include a licence to use the advertisement for as long as the client wished.[25] Depending on the context and the relevant circumstances, general website terms that may attract copyright protection due to their original selection and arrangement are assumed to imply that their use is permitted by the public at large, unless protective measures are taken.[26] The reason for this is that such terms are usually designated to a large number of individuals since they are published on websites. In this regard, the UK approach tends to bear similarities with the German one, to the extent that the interpretation of conduct of a particular copyright holder is concerned.

The aforementioned case law indicates that the implied consent doctrine becomes relevant in the online context, and there have been a number of judicial affirmations of the doctrine in cases which involve the unauthorized extraction of content under conditions indicating that copyright holders were in accord with third parties making use of their protected content. Beyond national courts, the Court of Justice also developed a doctrinal approach to affirm the applicability of the implied license doctrine online.

Svensson and implied licensing

We have already seen that in *Svensson*,[27] the question was whether hyperlinks constitute an act of communication to the public within the meaning of Article 3(1) of the Information Society Directive. In this case, the Court of Justice held that the retransmission of the same works as those covered by the initial communication must be addressed to a new public in order to amount to infringement.[28] In *Svensson*:

> the public targeted by the initial communication consisted of all potential visitors to the site concerned, since, given that access to the works on that site was not subject to any restrictive measures, all internet users could therefore have free access to them.[29]

---

[24] Ibid.; *Redwood Music Ltd v Francis Day & Hunter Ltd* [1978] RPC 429 (UK).
[25] *Drabble (Harold) Ltd v The Hycolite Manufacturing Co.* (1928) 44 TLR 264 (UK).
[26] Court of Appeal Sofia (Софийски Апелативен Съд), 18 May 2005 (Bulgaria).
[27] *Nils Svensson and Others v Retriever Sverige AB*, Case C-466/12, 13 February 2014, ECLI:EU:C:2014:76 (*Svensson*), [26]–[28].
[28] Ibid., [24].
[29] Ibid., [26].

This meant that the rightsholders—by their failure to apply access restriction protocols—were assumed to have offered free access of the content to this public, comprised of 'all Internet users'. It has been argued that the way in which the court applied the new public condition in *Svensson* introduced a 'waiver *erga omnes* (or at least, as to all members of the intended public)'[30] that has

> the unfounded and illegitimate effect of exhaustion of the communication to the public right or, rather, the scope of that right is *reduced* by the court from the outset.[31]

In Chapter 3 it was seen that exhaustion is the legal principle according to which the rightsholders' control over any further distribution, sale, hire, or loan of copies of works that have been placed on the market within the European Economic Area on their behalf or with their consent, e.g. by way of distribution to the public,[32] is 'exhausted'.[33] The Information Society Directive excludes its application to electronic communications, even though the World Intellectual Property Organization (WIPO) Treaties—which the Directive implements—do not expressly exclude this option.[34] This has the important implication that the scope of the communication right, which in any case ought to be interpreted broadly under the Information Society Directive,[35] offers a very wide authorial entitlement subject to the limitations expressly listed in Article 5(3). This has become a source of controversy, not only because it creates a schism in the modalities of issuing hard and electronic copies to the public but also because it does not make allowance for the creation of second-hand markets for digital goods, such as those which are legally possible

---

[30] Association Littéraire et Artistique Internationale (ALAI), 'Opinion on the Criterion "New Public", Developed by the Court of Justice of the European Union (CJEU), Put in the Context of Making Available and Communication to the Public' (17 September 2014), available at <http://www.alai.org/en/assets/files/resolutions/2014-opinion-new-public.pdf>, accessed 11 November 2019, 16.

[31] Association Littéraire et Artistique Internationale (ALAI), 'Opinion on the Criterion "New Public", Developed by the Court of Justice of the European Union (CJEU), Put in the Context of Making Available and Communication to the Public' (17 September 2014), available at <http://www.alai.org/en/assets/files/resolutions/2014-opinion-new-public.pdf>, accessed 11 November 2019, 15–16. Also see in this respect Mihály J. Ficsor, '*Svensson*: Honest Attempt at Establishing Due Balance Concerning the Use of Hyperlinks – Spoiled by the Erroneous "New Public" Theory', 2015, available online at <http://www.copyrightseesaw.net>, accessed 11 November 2019, at 1.2.3.

[32] See e.g. *Musik-Vertrieb Membran GmbH and K-tel International v GEMA - Gesellschaft für Musikalische Aufführungs- und Mechanische Vervielfältigungsrechte*, Joined Cases 55/80 and 57/80, 20 January 1981, ECLI:EU:C:1981:10 (*Musik-Vertrieb Membran*); also see *Deutsche Grammophon and Musik-Vertrieb Membran and K-tel International*, Case C-78/70, 8 June 1971, ECLI:EU:C:1971:59 (*Deutsche Grammophon*).

[33] Information Society Directive (Directive 2001/29/EC), Art. 4(2); *Laserdisken ApS v Kulturministeriet*, Case C-479/04, 12 September 2006, ECLI:EU:C:2006:549, [21]. The American counterpart of copyright exhaustion is the 'first-sale' doctrine. Copyright Act of 1976, 17 USC s. 109.

[34] Information Society Directive (Directive 2001/29/EC), Art. 3(3). The signatory countries are left with the discretion to apply the principle of exhaustion 'after the first sale or other transfer of ownership of the original or a copy of the work with the authorization of the author'. WIPO Copyright Treaty (WCT) 1996, Art. 6. See also WIPO Performances and Phonograms Treaty (WPPT) 1996, Art. 8.

[35] Information Society Directive (Directive 2001/29/EC), Recital 23.

with regards to tangible copies.[36] Although the *UsedSoft* decision[37] gave rise to the expectation that exhaustion may also apply in the online context, by affirming that the resale of used software online is legal, it was meant to be *lex specialis*, applicable only to software and not to digital content in general. Two recent decisions from the German Courts affirmed this, by refusing to accept the applicability of this principle with regards to categories of content not included in the Computer Programs Directive;[38] a very restrictive position also taken in the *Allposters* case.[39]

Although bearing a similar effect, *Svensson* does not introduce exhaustion.[40] This case echoes an implied licence rationale without expressly stating so. *Svensson* seems to affirm that rightsholders cannot have a viable claim of infringement unless they have taken active steps, such as the application of access restriction protocols, to limit the circle of potential recipients of a communication. This does not cover the act of communication as such, rather it covers its intended recipients at a certain point in time.[41] It is not a 'waiver *erga omnes*', as has been argued in literature,[42] and the reason is that rightsholders may decide, at any point in time, to apply access control protocols and restrict the availability of their works with the effect that any audience beyond the public who has lawful access to the work is a new public. *Svensson* outlines a rationale similar to that upheld in German jurisprudence.

---

[36] See Stavroula Karapapa, 'Reconstructing Copyright Exhaustion in the Online World' (2014) 4 *Intellectual Property Quarterly* 304; Stavroula Karapapa, 'Exhaustion of Rights on Digital Content under EU Copyright: Positive and Normative Perspectives' in Tanya Aplin (ed.), *Research Handbook on Intellectual Property and Digital Technologies* (Cheltenham: Edward Elgar, 2019) [481].

[37] *UsedSoft GmbH v Oracle International Corp*, Case C-128/11, 3 July 2012, ECLI:EU:C:2012:407 (*UsedSoft*). See David Naylor and Emily Parris, 'After ReDigi: Contrasting the EU and US Approaches to the Re-Sale of Second-Hand Digital Objects' (2013) 35(8) *European Intellectual Property Review* 487; Tatiana-Eleni Synodinou, 'The Principle of Technological Neutrality in European Copyright Law: Myth or Reality?' (2012) 34(9) *European Intellectual Property Review* 618; Franziska Schulze, 'Resale of Digital Content such as Music, Films or eBooks under European Law' (2014) 36(1) *European Intellectual Property Review* 9.

[38] Landgericht Bielefeld, 4 O 191/11, 5 March 2013 (Germany); Oberlandesgericht Hamm, 22 U 60/13, 15 May 2014 (Germany).

[39] See *Art & Allposters International BV v Stichting Pictoright*, Case C-419/13, 22 January 2015, ECLI:EU:C:2015:27 (*Allposters*); also see Opinion of Cruz Villalón AG in *Art & Allposters International BV v Stichting Pictoright*, Case C-419/13, 11 September 2014, ECLI:EU:C:2014:2214.

[40] See contra Association Littéraire et Artistique Internationale (ALAI), 'Opinion on the Criterion "New Public", Developed by the Court of Justice of the European Union (CJEU), Put in the Context of Making Available and Communication to the Public' (17 September 2014), available at <http://www.alai.org/en/assets/files/resolutions/2014-opinion-new-public.pdf>, accessed 11 November 2019; Jan Rosén, 'Chapter 12: How Much Communication to the Public is "Communication to the Public"?' in Irini A. Stamatoudi (ed.), *New Developments in EU and International Copyright Law* (Alphen aan den Rijn: Kluwer Law International, 2016—Information Law Series, Volume 35) 331.

[41] Since hyperlinking will be unlawful if the rightholders apply restrictive measures *ex post*, it remains to be seen what the implications on this ruling will be. Will this introduce, for instance, an indefinite obligation to 'monitor' hyperlinking by cross-referring to the original source? Emanuela Arezzo, 'Hyperlinks and Making Available Right in the European Union – What Future for the Internet after Svensson?' (2014) 45(5) *International Review of Intellectual Property and Competition Law* 524, 543–8.

[42] Association Littéraire et Artistique Internationale (ALAI), 'Opinion on the Criterion "New Public", Developed by the Court of Justice of the European Union (CJEU), Put in the Context of Making Available and Communication to the Public' (17 September 2014), available at <http://www.alai.org/en/assets/files/resolutions/2014-opinion-new-public.pdf>, accessed 11 November 2019, 16.

A copyright holder's failure to take active steps in technologically restricting access is assumed to imply that the work was meant to be publicly accessible.

As the court noted in *GS Media*,[43] it cannot be inferred, either from *Svensson* or from *BestWater*[44] that posting, on a website, hyperlinks to protected works which have already been made freely available on another website, albeit without the consent of the copyright holders of those works, would be excluded from the concept of 'communication to the public' within the meaning of Article 3(1) of the Information Society Directive. Rather, those decisions confirm the importance of such a consent, as Article 3(1) specifically provides that every act of communication of a work to the public is to be authorized by the copyright holder.[45]

Implied consent, although only partially affirmed in *Svensson* and not subject to harmonization across Europe, does not only result from a party's conduct, but may also result as part of the interpretation of a particular agreement, oral or written.

Consent implied in copyright contracts

Difficulties may arise where permission to carry on with a particular activity is either wholly implied or only partly explicit, arising either in the context of a contract or less formally. The important questions that need to be decided are generally: who are the beneficiaries of the licence?[46] What is the extent of the permitted use? And what is the licence's duration? Implied licenses need to be construed carefully in all cases,[47] and it is the defendant who carries the burden of proof as it is the defendant who raises the issue of license as a defence.[48]

Where the parties are in a contractual relationship, the question of whether there is an implied licence depends on an objective assessment; would someone construing the contract objectively reasonably understand that the parties intended there to be a licence? Should this be answered in the affirmative, the license that will be implied has to be the minimum necessary in order to give effect to the original intention of the parties,[49] although it is possible for implied licenses to be exclusive.[50]

---

[43] *GS Media BV v Sanoma Media Netherlands BV, Playboy Enterprises International Inc., Britt Geertruida Dekker*, Case C-160/15, 8 September 2016, ECLI:EU:C:2016:644 (*GS Media*).

[44] *BestWater International GmbH v Michael Mebes, Stefan Potsch*, Case C-348/13, 21 October 2014 (order of the court), ECLI:EU:C:2014:2315 (*BestWater*).

[45] *GS Media BV v Sanoma Media Netherlands BV, Playboy Enterprises International Inc., Britt Geertruida Dekker*, Case C-160/15, 8 September 2016, ECLI:EU:C:2016:644 (*GS Media*), [43].

[46] Some licenses may extend to the world at large. See *Plix Products Ltd v Frank M. Winstone (Merchants)* [1986] FSR 63 (UK).

[47] See e.g. *Booth v Edward Lloyd Ltd* (1909) 26 TLR 549 (UK).

[48] See e.g. *Noah v Shuba* [1991] FSR 14 (UK).

[49] *Ray v Classic FM plc* [1998] FSR 622 (UK); *Stovin-Bradford v Volpoint Ltd* [1971] Ch. 1007 (UK).

[50] See *Coward v Phaestos Ltd* [2013] EWHC 1292, [248]–[249] (UK).

Matters differ with regards to informal licenses. The test is objective and takes into consideration the purposes for which a reasonable person would consider they could use the work. Where a work is supplied in the knowledge that it will be used for a specific purpose, the licence may be limited to that purpose only.[51] In cases where the purpose is left vague or remains undetermined, the license may not include the immediate purposes that the parties had in mind.[52]

Ambiguous contracts are often interpreted in favour of the author or relevant rightsholder. In a recent case heard at the Patents Court of England and Wales, Judge Birss QC (as he then was) found that a health authority (SHA) had an implied licence with regards to certain copied materials and could exploit its exclusive rights to the new material as it saw fit.[53] The training materials were prepared by the claimant to be used by the health authority in the process of teaching communication skills to medical personnel working in the field of cancer care and research. A written agreement with the health authority allocated all intellectual property rights arising from the performance of services to the health authority. The materials that were copied, however, were subject to the claimant's copyright ('established works'). Interestingly, Judge Birss QC (as he then was) held that the copyright did indeed belong to the claimant, but that the defendant had not infringed it, finding that there was an implied licence to use these parts. In order not to fetter SHA's rights, the implied licence had to be irrevocable, royalty-free, and assignable, so that when SHA granted a licence under their own copyright, a sublicence of the claimant's copyright had to accompany it. This meant that the health authority was free to exploit the SHA works in any possible manner, regardless of whether, by doing so, they could compete with the claimant in the provision of training courses. Equally, the claimant was free to exploit the established works as he saw fit, since the agreement did not operate to assign any of the claimant's copyright to those works.

An interesting case in Sweden on the extent of an implied license concerned the use of a photograph on the packaging of a product (a CD cover) intended for resale to consumers. The Supreme Court found that even though according to general principles of contract law unclear licenses are to be interpreted in favour of the author, in this case the license should be understood to include the right of the producer of the goods and downstream distributors to use the package in normal promotional activities.[54] The court outlined the general principles of interpreting copyright contracts, including the so-called 'principle of specification', according to which ambiguous contracts have to be interpreted in favour of the author. Based on these principles and legal provisions, the license would cover

---

[51] See *Trumpet Software Pty Ltd v Ozemail Pty Ltd* (1996) 34 IPR 481, 500 (UK).
[52] See e.g. *Brighton v Jones* [2004] EWHC (Ch) 1157, [76] (UK).
[53] *Wilkinson v London SHA* [2012] All ER (D) 165 (Nov) (UK).
[54] '*CD cover*', Supreme Court (Högsta Domstolen), 23 November 2010 (Sweden).

only what was expressly agreed between the author and the user, meaning that in the present case there was a prima facie infringement of the reproduction right as the photograph was copied in marketing materials with no express permission. However, the court moved on to stress that in cases where the rightsholder assigns the right to use the work in relation to the packaging of a product that is intended to enter the retail market, it is assumed that the license includes the advertisement of the product. A generally accepted method of marketing products to consumers is to reproduce an image of the product or its packaging in an advertisement. Copyright holders have a limited interest in controlling who carries out such marketing and middlemen are often used in this process. Unless the licensing agreement clearly excludes marketing, it is assumed in such cases that the license implies that the packaging of a product will be used for marketing purposes. This would not mean that the copyright holder's entitlement is exhausted, but that the rights are transferred to subsequent acquirers of the product. In this light, the Supreme Court affirmed an implied license of the right to market the product featuring the copyright-protected photograph.[55]

Although a restrictive interpretation of the contract is the norm, terms which make allowance for certain activities may be implied to the extent that this aligns with market practices.

Implied licenses and moral rights

In some jurisdictions, a waiver of moral rights must be made explicitly and cannot be based on implicit consent. This was held in a German case concerning an injunction, according to which the claimant, an amateur photographer, argued that his right to be recognized as the author had been violated.[56] One of his photos was uploaded and offered for download on a German-based website (Pixelio.de) containing royalty-free stock images. There was a clause in the general terms and conditions of the website, according to which

> the User shall be obliged to name PIXELIO and the Author (with his/her photographer's name as stipulated during the upload of the Image from PIXELIO), in such a way as is usual for the corresponding utilization and—to the extent that this is technically possible—close to the Image itself or at the end of the page, in the following form: '© Photographer's name / PIXELIO'.

---

[55] Although the Supreme Court reached the same outcome as the Court of Appeal, it followed a different rationale. The Court of Appeal preferred to take the view that the marketing of the product was an exhibition of the goods (i.e. the CD cover featuring the photograph), instead of an exhibition of the copyright work (i.e. the photograph). See 'CD cover', Svea Court of Appeal Stockholm (Svea Hovrätt Stockholm), 19 December 2008 (Sweden).

[56] 'Pixelio', Court of Appeal of Dusseldorf, LG Köln 14 O 427/13, 30 January 2014 (Germany).

On the main website, where the photo was listed, and under the direct URL featuring the full resolution of the photograph, the indication of the source was missing. The court considered moral rights and concluded that a waiver of moral rights must be expressly made and cannot be based on implicit consent.

In another German case, it was found that an agreement cannot imply a change in the name of the author of a computer program.[57] According to Articles 13 and 69a(4) of the German Copyright Act, software developers have the right to have their authorship recognized. However broad its scope, a license to exercise exclusive rights over the software cannot imply a waiver to the paternity right of the author.

Beyond attribution, the integrity right may be affected. Some relevant cases have been heard in the United Kingdom. Case law indicates that it is an infringement to make substantial alterations to a signed article submitted for publication without the author's consent.[58] However, limited consent to make alterations to such an article may be implied where alterations involve reducing the article in length to fit the available space.[59]

Implied licenses and new technologies

An issue that often arises in the context of licenses and assignments is whether a grant made before the emergence of a new technology also covers the exploitation of that technology. The question is whether the license should extend to the new technology and if the license is drafted broadly enough to cover it. Usually, this is a matter of the construction of the license and, in written agreements, it may include expressions that are indicative of intention, such as 'by all means whether known or unknown'. Implied licenses cannot extend beyond activities that were in the contemplation of the parties at the time, and this has to be assessed objectively. It is up to the party claiming the license to establish the basis for its extension to what otherwise would amount to infringement.

In a case concerning the use of photographs in a newspaper following a license by conduct, the UK Court of Appeal found that the license did not extend to making these photographs more widely available to the public as part of the newspaper's online archive.[60] According to the court:

> there are many reported cases in which the issue arose as to whether a written
> licence extended to subsequent forms of technology. That has depended on

---

[57] 'Right of recognition of authorship of software developers', Court of Appeal Hamm (Oberlandesgericht Hamm), 4 U 14/07, 7 August 2007 (Germany).

[58] Joseph v National Magazine Co Ltd [1959] Ch. 14 (UK), approved in Frisby v British Broadcasting Corp [1967] Ch. 932 (UK).

[59] Ibid.

[60] MGN Ltd v Grisbrook [2010] EWCA Civ 1399, [2011] ECDR 4 (UK).

the form of words used and has not, for the most part, been limited to the technology which the parties contemplated at the time they entered into the relevant licence ... In those cases the modern jurisprudence on the interpretation of written agreements ... may need to be re-examined. But this appeal does not concern a written contract. The implication is not to be made into a written contract from the words used in their context but into a contract by conduct 'from the manner and for the purpose in which and for which it was contemplated between the parties that it would be used at the time' the contract was made.[61]

The court stressed that the operation of the websites extended to a global area, having greater coverage compared to that achieved through hard copies of the newspapers. The websites enabled a member of the public to read a newspaper before deciding whether they wanted a hard copy and also enabled the production of hard copies of the newspapers by the public in excess of anything the publisher could have produced. The court further observed that

newspapers are essentially ephemeral and generally retain no long-lasting status: the parties would have intended that they would be treated as daily papers are generally treated, i.e. read and replaced with the following day's edition. To incorporate the pictures into the websites was to provide a permanent and marketable record easily available world-wide which could well reduce the value of the further use of the photographs. This was not just a question of degree but of kind.[62]

This case law becomes relevant where a new technology creates a new market or a new mode of experiencing works. A new market is not just a new mode of exploitation, but also a new public and in this regard the construal of a license containing implied terms should be made with caution as it could have a negative impact on the normal exploitation of copyright works and, thereinafter, the royalties of the copyright holder, effectively being in conflict with the three-step test.[63]

Implied licenses and related doctrines

Implied licenses share similarities with other doctrines, such as estoppel and copyright exhaustion, although they essentially differ in some key aspects.

---

[61] Ibid., [31].
[62] Ibid., [38].
[63] Information Society Directive (Directive 2001/29/EC), Art. 5(5).

Unlike the implied license doctrine, the exhaustion principle functions as a formal statutory limitation on the scope of the copyright holder's rights.[64] It does not bestow the lawful owner of a copy of a copyright work a license to use the work in ways that remain within the copyright entitlement. It is also limited in that it covers only the distribution right. Delineating two distinct forms of property, exhaustion allows certain use privileges on the work that are transferred with the title to a lawfully owned copy of the work. The lawful owner of the copy does not need a license to benefit from those privileges because the authorized transfer of the copy has exhausted the rightsholder's entitlement over that exact same copy.

The doctrine of implied license is related to that of equitable estoppel. Although there is overlap between the two doctrines, they differ in that implied license is not an equitable doctrine, rather it is a legal one.[65] Implied license attempts to identify situations where the copyright owner would be considered as having licensed an activity without an express grant. Estoppel, on the contrary, attempts to identify situations where equity ought to intervene to prevent owners from engaging in opportunistic conduct due to someone's lack of understanding that a license was not concluded.[66] This may involve the deliberate fostering of the defendant's lack of understanding through activities that are meant to induce justified reliance. This reliance interest is considered to disqualify the copyright holder from pursuing an infringement action. Where a copyright owner allows another party to assume that no objection will be made by reference to the exploitation of the work, the copyright owner may be estopped from claiming that no consent was given or that consent has been revoked. In such a case, the ordinary principles of estoppel, available under national law, will take effect.[67]

In the UK case *Fisher v Brooker*,[68] the claimant had contributed to a musical composition but left the band soon afterwards without making a claim to the copyright. The defendant continued to exploit the composition for almost forty years. The claimant argued that such an exploitation was the result of an implied licence, which he purported to revoke. At first instance,[69] it was held that the claimant's contribution entitled him to a 40 per cent share. For the most part, the House of Lords upheld the judgment.[70] Giving the leading judgment, Lord Neuberger rejected the argument that the claimant impliedly assigned his interest in the musical copyright and the claimant's delay in bringing proceedings did not prevent him from making such a claim. In this light, declarations of joint authorship and joint

---

[64] See Chapter 3.

[65] Christopher M. Newman, 'What Exactly are you Implying? The Elusive Nature of the Implied Copyright License' (2014) 32(3) *Cardozo Arts and Entertainment Law* 501.

[66] Ibid.

[67] See e.g. *Godfrey v Lees* [1995] EMLR 307 (UK); *Ibcos Computers Ltd v Mercantile Highlands Finance Ltd* [1994] FSR 275 (UK); and *Brighton v Jones* [2004] EWHC 1157 (Ch) (UK).

[68] *Fisher v Brooker* [2009] UKHL 41, [2009] 1 WLR 1764, [2009] FSR 25 (UK).

[69] [2006] EWHC 3239 (Ch) (UK).

[70] *Fisher v Brooker* [2009] UKHL 41, [2009] 1 WLR 1764, [2009] FSR 25 (UK).

ownership were granted, together with a declaration that the implied licence had been revoked. Defences of laches, acquiescence, and estoppel were rejected. The claim could not be undermined merely because of the passage of time and for this to happen laches would need to be established. The defendants had not demonstrated any acts during the course of the delay period which had resulted in a 'balance of justice' which would justify the refusal of the relief to which the claimant would otherwise be entitled.[71] They could not show any prejudice resulting from the delay and, even if they could, the benefit they had obtained from the delay would outweigh any such prejudice. Even though a defence of proprietary estoppel can be made, no affirmation will take place if the relevant representations are expressly stipulated to be subject to contract. A defence of proprietary estoppel could be made on this ground by reference to copyright in eight songs by The Beatles that were infringed through their inclusion in a documentary of a recording of The Beatles' first concert performance in the United States.[72]

In another UK case, the contributor of a violin part to a song that later became a success was found to be a joint author of that song.[73] The court drew a distinction between two periods of the song's success, before and after its gaining popularity in 1993. During the first period of the song's marketing presence, the claimant had knowingly permitted the band to assume that he would not seek a share of the royalties. With regards to this period, it would be unconscionable to change his position after the passage of all these years. However, with regards to the period after 1993, the new success of the song differed and the claimant was entitled to seek his share of it. It was not unconscionable for him to revoke the licence in 1993. In cases of estoppel it is also essential to demonstrate detriment. In the present case, the defendant argued that, owing to the claimant's failure to assert his rights, he did not have the opportunity to delete the violin contribution from the recording; he also claimed that the assertion of rights at this stage would be harmful to his reputation as a songwriter. Both claims were rejected.

Conclusion

A defence against allegations for infringement includes claims according to which the copyright holder had authorized a particular activity and the defendant was under the impression that they had permission to carry on with the said activity. Authorization may not always be straightforward as there may not be an express agreement indicating that an activity is permitted. Problems may arise when a

---

[71] Ibid., [71].
[72] *Sony/ATV Music Publishing LLC v WPMC Ltd*, High Court of England and Wales, Chancery Division, HC-2012-000143, 1 July 2015 (UK).
[73] *Beckingham v Hodgens* [2002] EWHC 2143 (UK).

particular activity is subject to unclear contractual terms or because no license has been concluded. Copyright contract law has not been harmonized at the EU level. Courts may have to imply a license, subject to the general principles available under the relevant national contract laws. Consent may also be inferred through conduct. The doctrine of implied consent seems to have gained momentum in the online context and it has been used a number of times by reference to hyperlinks or thumbnail images, mostly in Germany. Recently, the Court of Justice brought forward an implied consent rationale in *Svensson*, according to which, when rightsholders post their works online with no access control mechanisms in place, the retransmission of the content via hyperlinks does not amount to copyright infringement. However, in a limited capacity, the doctrine of implied license can be used as a defence in cases where the rightholders have implied through their conduct that a particular activity is allowed to take place without their authorization. This can be crucial to the functioning of essential Internet facilities such as search engines, which index content that is seemingly freely available online. This is even more so when website operators use optimization tools in order to make their content more easily visible to search engines.

The way in which the implied consent doctrine has evolved indicates that some similarities may exist with copyright exhaustion and estoppel but these doctrinal principles remain conceptually distinct. The way in which German jurisprudence has developed the concept of implied consent shares a number of similarities with equitable estoppel in that a specific activity may be exempt from infringement when the rightsholder has not taken affirmative steps to signify their refusal to consent, e.g. via an express licensing term or through their conduct.

***

Denials of the element of copyright infringement, for instance, negate claims in which the claimant sues by targeting subsistence, scope, or authorization to carry out the allegedly infringing act. The recognition of such instances does not undercut any of the broad objectives of copyright because the defendant has done nothing the legislature has defined as offensive. There is no harm done to the copyright holders and hence nothing to condemn. In this regard, negations of the elements of infringement are not supervening claims, rather they are affirmations of the absence of infringement. In successful claims which deny liability for infringement, the defendants' conduct does not exemplify the harm that liability seeks to prevent and condemn. A potential issue is that because the minimum requirements of infringement—as defined in the relevant statutory provisions—are met, the defendant's acquittal of infringement may have an impact on the definition of infringement by undercutting the general prohibition of a particular conduct. It seems more likely, however, that such an acquittal will be viewed as a refinement of the definition of infringement, instead of having spillover effects that could have an impact on other defendants.

PART B

RATIONALE-BASED DEFENCES TO INFRINGEMENT

Introduction to Part B

Defensive rules that bring forward a justification or an explanation as to why a particular activity ought to be exempt from infringement are premised on the protection of fundamental human rights, the promotion of public policy objectives, or compliance with general legal principles. Often they take the shape of so-called exceptions and limitations to copyright and represent express legislative affirmations that an activity is exempt from infringement to the extent that the relevant statutory conditions are met. This kind of defence may come in the form of an open system, such as the broadly framed United States 'fair use' doctrine,[1] or a closed regime of exceptions and limitations, such as those listed under the Information Society and Digital Single Market Directives.[2] Where exclusive rights are drafted in specific terms, exceptions and limitations to these rights are broadly construed. For instance, the narrow definition of economic rights in the United States is balanced against fair use, i.e. an open defence that remains sufficiently flexible for the judiciary to include every activity which meets the four-factor test.[3] By contrast, as we

---

[1] As codified in s. 107 of title 17 of the US Code.

[2] Directive 2001/29/EC of the European Parliament and of the Council of 22 May 2001 on the Harmonisation of Certain Aspects of Copyright and Related Rights in the Information Society, OJ L 167, 22 June 2001, 10–19 (Information Society Directive); Directive (EU) 2019/790 of the European Parliament and of the Council of 17 April 2019 on Copyright and Related Rights in the Digital Single Market and Amending Directives 96/9/EC and 2001/29/EC, OJ L 130, 17 May 2019, 92–125 (Digital Single Market Directive); Directive 96/9/EC of the European Parliament and of the Council of 11 March 1996 on the Legal Protection of Databases, OJ L 77, 27 March 1996, 20–8 (Database Directive); Directive 2009/24/EC of the European Parliament and of the Council of 23 April 2009 on the Legal Protection of Computer Programs, OJ L 111, 5 May 2009, 16–22 (Computer Programs Directive).

In essence, the distinction between open and closed systems of exceptions is a distinction between flexibility and certainty. See Séverine Dusollier, Yves Poullet and Mireille Buydens, 'Copyright and Access to Information in the Digital Environment' (2000) XXXIV(4) *Copyright Bulletin* 4, 9–10; Séverine Dusollier, 'Exceptions and Technological Measures in the European Copyright Directive of 2001: An Empty Promise' (2003) 34(1) *International Review of Intellectual Property and Competition Law* 62–4; Jaap H. Spoor, 'General Aspects of Exceptions and Limitations: General Report' in Libby Baulch, Michael Green, and Mary Wyburn (eds), *Les Frontières du Droit d'Auteur: ses Limites et Exceptions* (Cambridge: Ed. Australian Copyright Council, 1999) 27.

[3] S. 107 of title 17 of the US Code. This section reads:

In determining whether the use made of a work in any particular case is a fair use the factors to be considered shall include:

1. the purpose and character of the use, including whether such use is of a commercial nature or is for nonprofit educational purposes;
2. the nature of the copyrighted work;
3. the amount and substantiality of the portion used in relation to the copyrighted work as a whole; and
4. the effect of the use upon the potential market for or value of the copyrighted work.

Also see in this regard Alain Strowel, *Droit d'Auteur et Copyright: Divergences et Convergences* (Paris: Bruylant and L.G.D.J., 1993) 173.

have already seen, EU copyright law defines exclusive rights broadly and then sets exceptions that are strictly defined and narrow in scope.[4] This high degree of generality[5] in drafting exclusive rights is demonstrated by the following example: while the reproduction right of Article 2 of the Information Society Directive encompasses a wide range of acts of exploitation, the exceptions and limitations applicable to this right apply to a series of specifically worded and exhaustively enumerated cases. In this light, whereas exclusive rights are construed broadly to ensure a high degree of harmonization, limitations are subject to strict interpretation and cannot be applied by way of analogy,[6] as the Court of Justice has stressed.[7]

The way in which rights, and exceptions and limitations to rights, are drafted in EU copyright law impacts their legal status and function within the copyright system. Exceptions and limitations are not necessarily proper exceptions to rights but can arguably be considered, in some cases, to be limitations which attack the generality of the definition of the right and as equally constitutive of the core of protection. At the same time, they are more likely to be considered as liability-defeating claims which function as derogations from the general rule that the exclusive rights delineate, instead of fully fledged user rights. In most instances where an exception or limitation can be raised as a defence, its successful admission by the court will follow an initial affirmation of an infringement claim. This is primarily due to the high degree of generality in which exclusive rights are drafted, which has the effect that copyright protection is the norm. In this light, copyright exceptions and limitations are supervening rules: there will be a prima facie infringement, but an activity will be exempt from infringement because the conditions of an exception or limitation apply. In this sense, this kind of defence can be viewed as offering a set of legislatively accepted *justifications* for infringement.

Exceptions and limitations are often premised on a fundamental rights rationale or a public policy objective. In either case, there is a rational defensibility of the acts in question and, given that the conditions of the relevant copyright exceptions and limitations are met, there will be a decision for the defendant, even though the elements of copyright infringement are established. There is a difference, however. Activities that are permitted on the basis of fundamental human rights rationale

---

[4] Alain Strowel, *Droit d'Auteur et Copyright: Divergences et Convergences* (Paris: Bruylant and L.G.D.J., 1993) 144.

[5] See to this effect Frederick Schauer, 'Exceptions' (1991) 58 *University of Chicago Law Review* 871.

[6] André Lucas and Henri-Jacques Lucas, *Traité de la Propriété Littéraire et Artistique* (Paris: Litec, 2004, 3rd edn,) 253. The restrictive interpretation of copyright limitations implies that copyright holders' rights have priority over these limitations. See Robert Burrell and Allison Coleman, *Copyright Exceptions: The Digital Impact* (Cambridge: Cambridge University Press, 2005) 181. A strict interpretation of fair-dealing exceptions in the United Kingdom was made in *Hyde Park v Yelland* [2001] Ch. 143 (UK); *Ashdown v Telegraph Group* [2001] Ch. 685 (UK).

[7] See e.g. *Infopaq International*, Case C-5/08, 16 July 2009, ECLI:EU:C:2009:465, [56] and [57]; *Football Association Premier League and Others*, Joined Cases C-403/08 and C-429/08, 4 October 2011, ECLI:EU:C:2011:631, [162]; *Public Relations Consultants Association Ltd v Newspaper Licensing Agency Ltd and Others*, Case C-360/13, 5 June 2014, ECLI:EU:C:2014:1195, [23].

relieve the defendant of liability on the basis that he or she acted reasonably and hence bring forward justifications for infringement. In such cases, the defendant seeks to avoid liability not by denying the elements of alleged infringement, but by going around the claimant's allegations. In practice, the defendant's argument would be that, even though infringement took place, there should be no liability because a particular statutory rule or legal principle makes allowance for a particular conduct. The defendant would hence invoke an explanation for his or her conduct according to which the use is permitted, permissible, or non-infringing.

There are various terms used in order to refer to this new kind of defence, including copyright 'limitations', 'exceptions', 'exemptions',[8] or 'restrictions'. Each of these terms raises different connotations,[9] although they are often used interchangeably.[10] Guibault argues that while the term 'exception' is widely accepted and used in many international instruments,[11] the term 'limitation' has the merit of being more neutral: it can be understood as permitting certain activities that would otherwise infringe copyright.[12] What is more, the term 'limitation' reflects more appropriately the concept of the 'limits' that determine the legal nature of legally guaranteed freedoms. These 'limits' are tools which determine the scope of exclusive rights, they are not 'exceptions' to a rule.[13] Elsewhere in the literature, limitations are deemed to cover remunerated defences, such as private copying or reprography, in the sense that these uses set limits to the rights, but do not offer true derogations from the general rules that rights delineate.

Exceptions and limitations to infringement are rules that are external to the claimant's action in that they do not mean to attack any of the elements of infringement, but instead bring forward a justification for an allegedly infringing

---

[8] There are some 'full exemptions' from the scope of the exclusive rights of the rightsholders, such as the temporary copying exception of Art. 5(1) of the Information Society Directive (Directive 2001/29/EC). In this case, the exclusive rights are withdrawn without any compensation being paid to rightsholders. In this respect, see Lucie Guibault, *Copyright Limitations and Contracts: An Analysis of the Contractual Overridability of Limitations on Copyright* (The Hague/London/Boston, MA: Kluwer Law International, 2002) 20–2; also see Pascale Chapdelaine, *Copyright User Rights: Contracts and the Erosion of Property* (Oxford: Oxford University Press, 2017).

[9] Jaap H. Spoor, 'General Aspects of Exceptions and Limitations: General Report' in Libby Baulch, Michael Green, and Mary Wyburn (eds), *Les Frontières du Droit d'Auteur: ses Limites et Exceptions* (Cambridge: Ed. Australian Copyright Council, 1999) 27, 29.

[10] On the legal nature of exceptions and limitations, see Lucie Guibault, *Copyright Limitations and Contracts: An Analysis of the Contractual Overridability of Limitations on Copyright* (The Hague/London/Boston, MA: Kluwer Law International, 2002) 21–110; Pierre Sirinelli, 'Exceptions et Limites aux Droit d'Auteur et Droits Voisins' Atelier sur la mise en œuvre du Traité de l'OMPI sur le droit d'auteur, *Les Frontières du droit d'auteur: ses limites et exceptions*, Geneve, 6–7 décembre 1999, 3.

[11] Berne Convention for the Protection of Literary and Artistic Works (as amended on 28 September 1979), Art. 9; World Intellectual Property Organization (WIPO) Copyright Treaty (1996), Art. 10; WIPO Performances and Phonograms Treaty (1996), Art. 16; Agreement on Trade-Related Aspects of Intellectual Property Rights (1994), Art. 13; Information Society Directive (Directive 2001/29/EC), Art. 5.

[12] Lucie Guibault, *Copyright Limitations and Contracts: An Analysis of the Contractual Overridability of Limitations on Copyright* (The Hague/London/Boston, MA: Kluwer Law International, 2002) 16.

[13] See Christophe Geiger, 'De la Nature Juridique des Limites au Droit d'Auteur' (2004) 13 *Propriétés Intellectuelles* 882.

conduct. The justifications that can be brought forward are exhaustively enumerated in legislation, although in a few instances they may be traced in general
legal principles, such as good faith or the prohibition of the abusive exercise of
rights.[14] By reference to their legal basis, statutory defences can be broadly classified into two categories. First, there may be liability-defeating rules that rely on
grounds that are external to copyright law, such as unfair competition principles
or the provisions of the e-Commerce Directive,[15] namely provisions belonging
to a different legal order. They are external defences and general legal principles,
in that legal orders other than copyright law may acquit a particular activity of
infringement, without this being primarily a matter addressed within copyright
law. Second, they may rely on fundamental values and freedoms that, although
rooted in human rights protection or other external public policy goals, have been
internalized within copyright law by means of express statutory provision;[16] these
include defences which reflect a public policy objective or a fundamental human
rights rationale. Such 'fundamentally free' exceptions and limitations may promote new authorship, foster public access to information, or enhance the furtherance of social and cultural objectives.

'Fundamentally free' uses

Recital 31 of the Information Society Directive stresses that 'a fair balance of rights
and interests between the different categories of rightsholders, as well as between the
different categories of rightholders and users of protected subject matter, must be safeguarded.'[17] Such a fair balance includes interests and rights, including those which derive from the EU Charter of Fundamental Rights[18] and the European Convention of

---

[14] In this context also see the concept of *ius usus innocui*, a Roman legal principle according to which
the use that does not harm one, and benefits another, is fair. This doctrinal principle has been used in Spain
to exempt search engines from infringement. See Supreme Court, Civil Chamber, Sentencia n 172/2012, 3
April 2012 (Spain).

[15] Directive 2000/31/EC of the European Parliament and of the Council of 8 June 2000 on Certain
Legal Aspects of Information Society Services, in Particular Electronic Commerce, in the Internal
Market, OJ L 178, 17 July 2000, 1–16 (e-Commerce Directive).

[16] For a discussion on the internal or external encounter of copyright and human rights see Abraham
Drassinower, 'Exceptions Properly-So-Called' in Ysolde Gendreau and Abraham Drassinower (eds), *Langues
et Droit d'Auteur / Language and Copyright* (Montreal: Carswell and Brussels: Bruylant, 2009) 205, 223.

[17] Affirmed in various cases such as *Funke Medien NRW GmbH v Federal Republic of Germany*, C-469/17,
29 July 2019, ECLI:EU:C:2019:623 (*Funke Medien*), [32]; *Pelham GmbH, Moses Pelham, Martin Haas v Ralf
Hütter, Florian Schneider-Esleben*, Case C-476/17, 29 July 2019, ECLI:EU:C:2019:624 (*Pelham*), [32]); see,
for example, *Productores de Música de España v Telefónica de España SAU*, Case C-275/06, 29 January 2008,
ECLI:EU:C:2008:54 (*Promusicae*), [68]–[70]; *Scarlet Extended SA v Société Belge des Auteurs, Compositeurs
et Éditeurs SCRL (SABAM)*, Case C-70/10, 24 November 2011, ECLI:EU:C:2011:771 (*Scarlet*), [49]; *UPC
Telekabel Wien GmbH v Constantin Film Verleih GmbH and Wega Filmproduktionsgesellschaft mbH*,
Case C-314/12, 27 March 2014, ECLI:EU:C:2014:192, [46]–[47]; *McFadden v Sony Music Entertainment
Germany GmbH*, Case C-484/14, 15 September 2016, ECLI:EU:C:2016:689 [83]–[89]; also see Digital
Single Market Directive (Directive 2019/790), Recitals 6, 21, 61, 70, 75.

[18] Charter of Fundamental Rights of the European Union (18 December 2000) 2000/C 364/01, OJ C 364, 1.

Human Rights.[19] EU copyright law ought to be interpreted and applied in a manner which ensures fundamental rights are protected. The impact of the Charter of Fundamental Rights in the realm of copyright has increasingly attracted protection by national courts, the Court of Justice, and the European Court of Human Rights.[20]

A number of copyright exceptions and limitations reflect the need to protect freedom of expression and freedom of the media.[21] In recognition of a possible conflict between copyright and the aforementioned fundamental freedoms, there is an exception for reproductions by the press and communication of published articles on current topics,[22] uses of works in connection with the reporting of current events,[23] quotations made for purposes such as criticism or review of a published work,[24] and uses for the purpose of caricature, parody, and pastiche.[25] The purpose of these exceptions and limitations is to promote a number of related policy objectives, such as ongoing authorship and readership, and the need to enhance user access to information. Other permissible uses mean to preserve user independence and enhance access and participation of persons with disabilities.[26] They are referred to in this book as speech entitlements.

---

[19] European Convention on Human Rights (1950).

[20] See, for example, *Productores de Música de España v Telefónica de España SAU*, Case C-275/06, 29 January 2008, ECLI:EU:C:2008:54(*Promusicae*); (*Scarlet Extended SA v Société Belge des Auteurs, Compositeurs et Éditeurs SCRL (SABAM)*, Case C-70/10, 24 November 2011, ECLI:EU:C:2011:771 (*Scarlet*); (*UPC Telekabel Wien GmbH v Constantin Film Verleih GmbH and Wega Filmproduktionsgesellschaft mbH*, Case C-314/12, 27 March 2014, ECLI:EU:C:2014:192; *Eva-Maria Painer v Standard VerlagsGmbH and Others*, Case C-145/10, 1 December 2011, ECLI:EU:C:2011:798 (*Painer*); *Johan Deckmyn and Another v Helena Vandersteen and Others*, Case C-201/13, 3 September 2014, ECLI:EU:C:2014:2132 (*Deckmyn*); *GS Media BV v Sanoma Media Netherlands BV, Playboy Enterprises International Inc., Britt Geertruida Dekker*, Case C-160/15, 8 September 2016, ECLI:EU:C:2016:644 (*GS Media*); *Ashby Donald and others v France*, Appl. nr. 36769/08, ECHR (Fifth Section), 10 January 2013; *Fredrik Neij and Peter Sunde Kolmisoppi (The Pirate Bay) v Sweden*, Appl. nr. 40397/12, ECHR (Fifth Section) 19 February 2013; for a comment see P. Bernt Hugenholtz, 'Flexible Copyright: Can the EU Author's Rights Accommodate Fair Use' in Ruth L. Okediji (ed.), *Copyright Law in an Age of Limitations and Exceptions* (New York: Cambridge University Press, 2017) 275, 287 et seq.

[21] Charter of Fundamental Rights of the European Union, Art. 11.

    1. Everyone has the right to freedom of expression. This right shall include freedom to hold opinions and to receive and impart information and ideas without interference by public authority and regardless of frontiers.

    2. The freedom and pluralism of the media shall be respected.

[22] Information Society Directive (Directive 2001/29/EC), Art. 5(3)(c).

[23] Ibid.

[24] Information Society Directive (Directive 2001/29/EC), Art. 5(3)(d).

[25] Information Society Directive (Directive 2001/29/EC), Art. 5(3)(k).

[26] See Art. 26 of the EU Charter, which reads, 'The Union recognises and respects the right of persons with disabilities to benefit from measures designed to ensure their independence, social and occupational integration and participation in the life of the community'. Also see Art. 21(1) of the Charter on non-discrimination: 'Any discrimination based on any ground such as sex, race, colour, ethnic or social origin, genetic features, language, religion or belief, political or any other opinion, membership of a national minority, property, birth, disability, age or sexual orientation shall be prohibited.'

Directive (EU) 2017/1564 of the European Parliament and of the Council of 13 September 2017 on Certain Permitted Uses of Certain Works and Other Subject Matter Protected by Copyright and Related Rights for the Benefit of Persons who are Blind, Visually Impaired or Otherwise Print-Disabled and Amending Directive 2001/29/EC on the Harmonisation of Certain Aspects of Copyright and Related Rights in the Information Society, OJ L 242, 20 September 2017, 6–13 (Directive on Permitted Uses for Disabled

Other copyright exceptions and limitations also reflect the need to protect fundamental freedoms, even if their justificatory basis is not fully grounded on such freedoms and there are important public policy objectives which underpin their permissible scope. An example is the private copying limitation included in Article 5(2)(b) of the Information Society Directive, which aims, inter alia, to preserve respect for user privacy and autonomy. This is only a partial justification, however, and other reasons for the necessity of this exception have been put forward, including economic justifications on market failure, the need to preserve user autonomy and, to an extent, the exhaustion principle.[27]

Certain exceptions are premised on the freedom of the arts and sciences, protected by Article 13 of the EU Charter, according to which: 'The arts and scientific research shall be free of constraint. Academic freedom shall be respected.' These include specific non-commercial acts of reproduction by publicly accessible libraries, educational establishments or museums, or by archives,[28] and certain uses for the purpose of illustration for non-commercial teaching or scientific research.[29] They also cover uses for the purpose of research or private study to individual members of the public under specific conditions.[30] This latter set of permissible uses is not available to any member of the public at large, but to individuals who meet certain qualification criteria, such as students and researchers. There are also exceptions reflecting the need to protect freedom of thought, conscience, and religion, as safeguarded under Article 10 of the EU Charter,[31] including uses during religious celebrations or official celebrations organized by a public authority.[32]

The variety of the justificatory grounds for the available copyright exceptions and limitations, alongside the specificity and certainty that ought to characterize such defensive rules in accordance with the three-step test,[33] has resulted in an

---

Individuals); Regulation (EU) 2017/1563 of the European Parliament and of the Council of 13 September 2017 on the Cross-Border Exchange Between the Union and Third Countries of Accessible Format Copies of Certain Works and Other Subject Matter Protected by Copyright and Related Rights for the Benefit of Persons who are Blind, Visually Impaired or Otherwise Print-Disabled, OJ L 242, 20 September 2017, 1–5.

[27] Stavroula Karapapa, *Private Copying* (London: Routledge, 2012) 15 et seq.

[28] Information Society Directive (Directive 2001/29/EC), Art. 5(2)(c).

[29] Information Society Directive (Directive 2001/29/EC), Art. 5(3)(a); Digital Single Market Directive (Directive (EU) 2019/790), Art. 5.

[30] Information Society Directive (Directive 2001/29/EC), Art. 5(3)(n).

[31] This Article reads:

1. Everyone has the right to freedom of thought, conscience and religion. This right includes freedom to change religion or belief and freedom, either alone or in community with others and in public or in private, to manifest religion or belief, in worship, teaching, practice and observance.
2. The right to conscientious objection is recognised, in accordance with the national laws governing the exercise of this right.

[32] Information Society Directive (Directive 2001/29/EC), Art. 5(3)(g).

[33] Information Society Directive (Directive 2001/29/EC), Art. 5(5); also applicable to the copyright exceptions and limitations of the Directive on Copyright in the Digital Single Market (Directive (EU) 2019/790) by virtue of Art. 7(2) of that Directive.

extremely long list of defensive rules. These can be found in various Directives, and in an unparalleled level of case-specificity. This does not only result in a fragmented approach, whereby permitted uses can only flourish at the limited boundaries of each of the copyright exceptions and limitations, but also a rather complex legal framework which has to be read by cross-references to various legal instruments, notably Directives, in order to ascertain the contours of permissibility.

Because EU copyright exceptions and limitations are numerous and divergent as to their beneficiaries, conditions of application, and underpinning justificatory grounds, they resist strict classification. For the purposes of the present analysis, however, they are divided on the basis of their intrinsic characteristics, the objectives they mean to pursue, and the kind of justification that is brought forward to explain why an allegedly infringing use should be permitted. To this end, four main categories of rationale-based defensive rules are identified: defences justified on the basis of freedom of speech and press, which for the purposes of the present analysis are referred to as speech entitlements (Chapter 6); public policy privileges, namely defensive rules that are designed in the pursuit of public policy objectives (Chapter 7); copyright exceptions that are subject to the requirement that the copyright holders shall be fairly remunerated (Chapter 8); and defensive rules whose roots are found in external legal disciplines, such as competition law or e-commerce provisions, or principles, such as the prohibition of the abusive exercise of rights (Chapter 9).

6

Speech Entitlements

A number of copyright exceptions and limitations aim to promote the production of new copyright works and new authorship, and the protection of the
public interest in gaining access to information and knowledge embodied in
copyright-protected works. Most of these exceptions are premised on a fundamental human rights justification, such as freedom of speech or freedom of the
press, or the right to access protected works without discrimination on grounds
of disability. These include, for instance, reproduction by the press for the reporting of current events, quotations for criticism or review, and uses for the
purpose of caricature, parody, or pastiche. They also include exceptions and limitations available to persons who are blind, visually impaired, or otherwise print-
disabled.[1] Although these exceptions and limitations are express manifestations
of fundamental human rights, their scope remains relatively narrow and their
legal nature and status against contractual overridability is not settled. Indeed,
the permissibility of the relevant activities is subject to a number of internal limitations that may not work well in light of modern uses of materials in the online
context. These include purpose limitations, such as the requirement that some
uses ought to be non-commercial, scope limits (e.g. the doctrinal requirement
that parodies have to be an expression of humour and mockery to be lawful),[2] or
restrictive principles that are inherent within copyright, like attribution to the
source of the original work.

---

[1] Directive (EU) 2017/1564 of the European Parliament and of the Council of 13 September 2017 on
Certain Permitted Uses of Certain Works and Other Subject Matter Protected by Copyright and Related
Rights for the Benefit of Persons who are Blind, Visually Impaired or Otherwise Print-Disabled and
Amending Directive 2001/29/EC on the Harmonisation of Certain Aspects of Copyright and Related
Rights in the Information Society, OJ L 242, 20 September 2017, 6–13 (Directive on Permitted Uses for
Disabled Individuals).

[2] *Johan Deckmyn and Another v Helena Vandersteen and Others*, Case C-201/13, 3 September 2014,
ECLI:EU:C:2014:2132 (*Deckmyn*); contra: European Parliament, Committee on Legal Affairs, Draft
Report on the Implementation of Directive 2001/29/EC of the European Parliament and of the Council
of 22 May 2001 on the Harmonisation of Certain Aspects of Copyright and Related Rights in the
Information Society, 15 January 2015, 2014/2256(INI), point 17.

Defences to Copyright Infringement. Stavroula Karapapa, Oxford University Press (2020). © Stavroula Karapapa.
DOI: 10.1093/oso/9780198795636.001.0001

Introduction

Speech entitlements refer to defences that are meant to enhance freedom of speech and expression by pursuing two distinct, yet possibly overlapping, objectives: the promotion of authorship and readership, and the protection of the public interest in gaining access to information and knowledge in copyright-protected works. The first category includes: copyright exceptions and limitations for the purposes of parody, caricature, or pastiche;[3] uses permitted for the reporting of current events and those carried out by the press;[4] quotations for purposes such as criticism and review;[5] and research and private study.[6,7] The second category includes uses of political speeches and public lectures[8] and uses which ensure that copyright-protected works are made available in accessible formats to persons who are blind, visually impaired, or otherwise print-disabled.[9]

An important aspect of speech entitlements is that they aim to strike a fair balance between the interest of the holders of copyright and related rights in the protection of their intellectual property rights guaranteed by Article 17(2) of the EU Charter of Fundamental Rights[10] and, on the other hand, the protection of the interests and fundamental rights of users of protected subject matter.[11] In this regard, they represent the manifestation of a legislative balancing of rights: proprietary interests arising through copyright and the need to protect fundamental rights, which are enshrined at three levels: the national constitutional level, the European Convention of Human Rights, and the EU Charter. With particular

---

[3] Information Society Directive (Directive 2001/29/EC), Art. 5(3)(k).

[4] Information Society Directive (Directive 2001/29/EC), Art. 5(3)(c).

[5] Information Society Directive (Directive 2001/29/EC), Art. 5(3)(d).

[6] Information Society Directive (Directive 2001/29/EC), Art. 5(3)(n).

[7] The United Kingdom was the first EU Member State to introduce an exception on data analytics and this is organically included as a sub-category of fair dealing for research purposes. See Copyright, Designs and Patents Act 1988 (CPDA), s. 29A (introduced by Copyright and Rights in Performances (Research, Education, Libraries and Archives) Regulations 2014). The Commission and the Parliament consider introducing a text mining and data analytics exception in the revised Information Society Directive. See European Commission, Proposal for a Directive of the European Parliament and of the Council on Copyright in the Digital Single Market, Brussels, 14 September 2016, COM (2016) 593 final, 2016/0280 (COD), Art. 3 https://ec.europa.eu/transparency/regdoc/rep/1/2016/EN/1-2016-593-EN-F1-1.PDF, accessed 11 November 2019.

[8] Information Society Directive (Directive 2001/29/EC), Art. 5(3)(f).

[9] Directive on Permitted Uses for Disabled Individuals (Directive 2017/1564).

[10] Charter of Fundamental Rights of the European Union (18 December 2000) 2000/C 364/01, OJ C 364, 1.

[11] Information Society Directive (Directive 2001/29/EC), Recital 31 (affirmed in various cases such as *Funke Medien NRW GmbH v Federal Republic of Germany*, C-469/17, 29 July 2019, ECLI:EU:C:2019:623 (*Funke Medien*), [32]; *Pelham GmbH, Moses Pelham, Martin Haas v Ralf Hütter, Florian Schneider-Esleben*, Case C-476/17, 29 July 2019, ECLI:EU:C:2019:624 (*Pelham*), [32]); Digital Single Market Directive (Directive 2019/790), Recitals 6, also 21, 61, 70, 75; an interesting discussion of the interplay between freedom of artistic expression and copyright in cases of creative appropriation is offered in Christophe Geiger, '"Fair Use" through Fundamental Rights in Europe: When Freedom of Artistic Expression allows Creative Appropriations and Opens up Statutory Copyright Limitations' (2018) Center for International Intellectual Property Studies (CEIPI) Research Paper No. 2018-09.

regard to users' freedom of expression and information enshrined in Article 11 of the Charter, in *Spiegel Online*[12] and *Funke Medien*,[13] the Court of Justice clarified that these freedoms are not capable of justifying, beyond the exceptions or limitations provided in the Information Society Directive (and, in particular, the exception permitting the reporting of current events), a derogation from the author's exclusive rights of reproduction and of communication to the public as stipulated in that Directive.[14] This is not only because of the exhaustive nature of copyright exceptions and limitations, at which level the relationship between copyright and fundamental rights was settled, but also because of the principle of consistent application of copyright exceptions and limitations in the various Member States with a view to enhance legal certainty and the proper functioning of the Internal Market. In this sense, speech entitlements represent a particular set of defensive rules in copyright law in that they do not merely offer defensive grounds for particular activities carried out in relation to copyright-protected works, but they also regulate the possible conflict of proprietary entitlements which arise due to copyright and fundamental freedoms.

Importantly, speech entitlements are rules that align with the function of copyright as an instrument of communication, and which promote its objectives. Such an understanding of copyright's purpose emanates from the work of Immanuel Kant, who dealt directly with the issue of authors' rights.[15] Considering works as crystallizations of their authors' communications, Kant theorized on authors' rights as speech instead of property.[16] Many academics have elaborated on Kant's work on authorship as an act of speech,[17] developing insights on copyright as a right in speech instead of a proprietary claim.[18] Implicit in this view is the understanding that permitted uses as user rights can only make sense when authors are regarded as speakers and works of authorship as acts of communication.[19]

---

[12]   *Spiegel Online v Volker Beck*, Case C-516/17, 29 July 2019, ECLI:EU:C:2019:625 (*Spiegel Online*).

[13]   *Funke Medien NRW GmbH v Federal Republic of Germany*, Case C-469/17, 29 July 2019, ECLI:EU:C:2019:623 (*Funke Medien*).

[14]   *Spiegel Online v Volker Beck*, Case C-516/17, 29 July 2019, ECLI:EU:C:2019:625 (*Spiegel Online*), [49]; *Funke Medien NRW GmbH v Federal Republic of Germany*, Case C-469/17, 29 July 2019, ECLI:EU:C:2019:623 (*Funke Medien*), [64].

[15]   See in this regard Immanuel Kant, 'On the Wrongfulness of Unauthorized Publication of Books' (1785) in Mary J. Gregor (ed.), *Immanuel Kant: Practical Philosophy* (Cambridge: Cambridge University Press, 1998) 29; Immanuel Kant, 'The Metaphysics of Morals' (1797) in Mary J. Gregor (ed.), *Immanuel Kant: Practical Philosophy* (Cambridge: Cambridge University Press, 1998) 353.

[16]   Anne Barron, 'Kant, Copyright and Communicative Freedom' (2012) 31 *Law and Philosophy* 1, 4.

[17]   See e.g. Abraham Drassinower, 'Authorship as Public Address: on the Specificity of Copyright vis-à-vis Patent and Trade-Mark' (2008) 1 *Michigan State Law Review* 1999; Abraham Drassinower, 'From Distribution to Dialogue: Remarks on the Concept of Balance in Copyright Law' (2009) 34(4) *Journal of Corporation Law* 991; Maurizio Borghi, 'Copyright and Truth' (2011) 12(1) *Theoretical Inquires in Law* 1; Anne Barron, 'Kant, Copyright and Communicative Freedom' (2012) 31 *Law and Philosophy* 1; Leslie Kim Treiger-Bar-Am, 'Kant on Copyright: Rights of Transformative Authorship' (2008) *Cardozo Arts and Entertainment Law Journal* 1059.

[18]   Abraham Drassinower, *What's Wrong with Copying?* (Cambridge, MA: Harvard University Press, 2015).

[19]   Abraham Drassinower, 'Subject Matter, Scope and User Rights in Copyright Law' (2015) 67 *Studies in Law, Politics and Society Special Issue: Thinking and Rethinking Intellectual Property* 59.

Should such an understanding be accepted as a principle-based view on the theoretical justification underpinning copyright protection, activities that enable such a dialogue between authors and users and, at a broader level, the promotion of authorship and readership are integral to the very function of copyright, essential for its purpose and necessary for the achievement of a balanced copyright framework. Speech entitlements, in particular, share a mutual theoretical underpinning with copyright. On this basis, a normative claim can be made that the same theoretical principles on which authorship is rewarded via copyright protection ought to form the basis for further creativity and innovation that depend on pre-existing works, notably so through the set of permitted uses here called speech entitlements. This becomes more relevant in the online context where new, interactive means of using and re-using copyright works emerge and thereby offer unprecedented opportunities for growth in the creative and business sector.

Speech entitlements can be read as offering definitional boundaries to the broad scope of exclusive rights to which they set limits. Indeed, some of these defensive rules, such as the copyright exceptions for news reporting, parody, criticism and review, and research and private study, are part and parcel of what copyright is about as an act of speech and communication between authors and users. In this regard, if we were to say that the claimant's right is an exclusive right to reproduce the work permanently or temporarily *for purposes other than* the making of quotations for purposes such as criticism and review, for instance, then the defendant would not have to rely on an exception. Formulating exclusive rights in such a way would have lowered the level of generality in which rights are drafted and have offered more certainty on the scope of copyright protection. Even though speech entitlements serve as important limits to the scope of exclusive rights, the way in which they are legislatively formulated means they do not serve as instruments to deny elements of infringement. Instead, they set forth justifications for why a certain activity took place, borrowing their normative fiat from the need to protect the exercise of fundamental rights of copyright users.

Speech entitlements as defensive rules that are drafted with the view to protect fundamental freedoms, notably speech, authorship, and access to information, and to regulate the possible conflict of proprietary copyright interests and these freedoms, are examined below with a view to determine the extent to which they can accommodate emergent technological activities and business models. In particular, subject to discussion are the copyright exceptions covering parody, caricature, and pastiche; reproductions made by the press and reporting of current events; quotations, criticism, and review; research and private study; uses which enable access to disabled individuals; and copyright exceptions which govern the dissemination of political speeches.

Parody, caricature, and pastiche

Article 5(3)(k) of the Information Society Directive allows Member States to offer an exception to the reproduction right and/or the rights of communication and making available to the public, for the purposes of caricature, parody, and pastiche.[20] Parody, caricature, and pastiche are permitted under a broad stipulation that is inflated by the use of the grammatical conjunction 'or' as an indicator of non-exhaustiveness. The Directive does not further define these terms, however insights can be drawn from the decision of the Court of Justice in *Deckmyn*.[21] In this case, examined in detail below, the court confirmed that the concept of parody must be regarded as an autonomous concept of EU law, having two essential characteristics: (i) it must evoke an existing work whilst being noticeably different from it; and (ii) it must constitute an expression of humour or mockery. These are considered to be the doctrinal limits to the scope of the exception.

Parody as freedom of speech

Parody represents a central instance of the collision between intellectual property and human rights. Being an expression of the fundamental right of freedom of speech,[22] parody reflects the right to voice one's opinion publicly without fear of censorship or punishment. Echoing the language of the Universal Declaration of Human Rights, Article 10 of the European Declaration of Human Rights provides that:

> Everyone has the right to freedom of expression. This right shall include freedom to hold opinions and to receive and impart information and ideas without interference by public authority and regardless of frontiers. This article shall not prevent States from requiring the licensing of broadcasting, television or cinema enterprises.

---

[20] Ricketson has expressed concerns on whether this exception abides by the EU's international obligations under the Berne Convention and other international instruments. According to Ricketson:

> The only exception in Article 5 that may give rise to obvious problems is ... use for the purpose of "caricature, parody or pastiche." This does not fall within any of the specific exceptions recognized under Berne, although it is conceivable that such an exception could arise under Article 9(2) in relation to reproductions and might likewise be justified as a minor reservation with respect to performing and broadcasting rights. It will be necessary for this to be so, however, for the purposes of both TRIPS and WCT compliance, as both these treaties do not envisage that members can create new exceptions or limitations that fall outside what is allowed by Berne (see above).

See Sam Ricketson, World Intellectual Property Organization (WIPO) Study on Limitations and Exceptions of Copyright and Related Rights in the Digital Environment, SCCR/9/7, WIPO, 5 April 2003, 72.

[21] *Johan Deckmyn and Another v Helena Vandersteen and Others,* Case C-201/13, 3 September 2014, ECLI:EU:C:2014:2132 (*Deckmyn*).

[22] European Convention on Human Rights (1950), Art. 10.

The right to freedom of speech, however, is not absolute and it is commonly subject to limitations, such as libel, slander, intellectual property infringement, revelation of information that is classified, or otherwise.[23]

Parody exceptions, like the one which features in Article 5(3)(k) of the Information Society Directive, and the national laws that implemented it, although rooted in the fundamental right of freedom of speech, do not introduce a user right to make parodies. The defence for purposes of parody, caricature, or pastiche is not enforceable in the courts and does not give copyright users an entitlement to sue in instances where their freedom to parodic use is contractually or technologically restricted. However, it does give users the privilege to carry out parodies, caricatures, and pastiches to the extent that copyright and human rights law permit. Copyright law, in particular, permits an activity that would otherwise amount to copyright infringement if taking place without the authorization of the relevant rightholders.

The problems with parody

Originating from the Greek word παρῳδία, the word parody derives from *para* (meaning alongside, beside, or near) and *odê* (song). Implicit in the etymology of the word is a comparison between the parody and its original source. Even though mocking criticism or comic review may be perceived as parody, this is not an essential etymological constituent, and some scholars argue that the element of ridicule as a defining attribute of parody has trivialized it.[24] In the work of Hutcheon, for instance, parody is defined as 'imitation characterized by ironic inversion, not always at the expense of the parodied text',[25] reflecting 'the intersection of creation and re-creation, of invention and critique'.[26]

Parody raises a number of difficulties for copyright as it is the product of imitation and appropriation of a pre-existing work in order to critique it, often—but

---

[23] The second paragraph of Art. 10 reads:

> The exercise of these freedoms, since it carries with it duties and responsibilities, may be subject to such formalities, conditions, restrictions or penalties as are prescribed by law and are necessary in a democratic society, in the interests of national security, territorial integrity or public safety, for the prevention of disorder or crime, for the protection of health or morals, for the protection of the reputation or the rights of others, for preventing the disclosure of information received in confidence, or for maintaining the authority and impartiality of the judiciary.

Similar is the definition offered to Art. 11 of the Charter of Fundamental Rights of the European Union.

[24] Linda Hutcheon, *A Theory of Parody: The Teachings of Twentieth-Century Art Forms* (Urbana: University of Illinois Press, 1985). For a different perspective, however, see the work of Mark Rose who defines parody as the 'comic refunctioning of preformed linguistic or artistic material'. See Mark Rose, *Parody: Ancient, Modern and Post-Modern* (Cambridge: Cambridge University Press, 1993) 52.

[25] Linda Hutcheon, *A Theory of Parody: The Teachings of Twentieth-Century Art Forms* (Urbana: University of Illinois Press, 1985) 6.

[26] Ibid., 2.

not always—in a comic way. A parody will inevitably need to reproduce, as much as possible, the pre-existing work, especially its most distinctive features, because its success depends on its ability to recall the parodied work in the audience's mind, essentially ensuring that the critical point of the parody is understood. Since it touches upon the reproduction right, a parody will amount to the liability of its maker in cases that fall beyond what is expressly permitted by law. The relevant exemption included in Article 5(3)(k) of the Information Society Directive introduces a supervening rule that offers a justification of the conduct with a view to regulating instances of conflict between copyright and freedom of speech. The end result of such a conflict of rights, namely a permissible parody, caricature, or pastiche, may receive copyright protection in its own right to the extent that it meets the originality requirement. This is an issue that increases controversy with regard to this permitted use, as the author of a parody, caricature, or pastiche may have independent copyright claims on a work that sufficiently copies a pre-existing work to produce humour or mockery. Indeed, where the parodic version demonstrates the exercise of additional creative activity by being the author's own intellectual creation, it can attract independent copyright protection. This becomes even more complicated when there is no 'author' of a parody, caricature, or pastiche, but rather these uses can be carried out algorithmically in a mobile app, through artificial intelligence tools, or any kind of image transformation tool, on demand, by a user of this service.[27] Can such a use amount to parody, caricature, or pastiche within the meaning of the relevant copyright exception?

Parody and *Deckmyn*

The Court of Justice of the European Union offered indicative guidance on the meaning and scope of parody in *Johan Deckmyn and Another v Helena Vandersteen and Others*.[28] The referring court, the Brussels Court of Appeal, sought clarification on the concept of parody and its essential characteristics in order for it to be exempt from infringement. The proceedings involved calendars that Mr Deckmyn, a Belgian politician, distributed to the public at an event hosted by his far-right political party, Vlaams Belang. The calendars included an image adapted from the cover of a comic book from Mr Vandersteen's 'Suske en Wiske' ('Spike and Suzy') series, in which the mayor of Ghent was depicted as one of the comic book characters, strewing gold coins to immigrants. The Court of Justice found that, in order to meet the harmonization objectives, the concept of parody must be regarded as an

---

[27] See e.g. image transformation tools that are operated via algorithms, such as the Zao app on face transformations, which raises additional privacy concerns: Agence France-Presse in Shanghai, 'Chinese Deepfake App Zao Sparks Privacy Row after Going Viral' *The Guardian* (2 September 2019).

[28] *Johan Deckmyn and Another v Helena Vandersteen and Others,* Case C-201/13, 3 September 2014, ECLI:EU:C:2014:2132 (*Deckmyn*).

autonomous concept of EU law and should be interpreted uniformly throughout the European Union.

Following the Advocate General's opinion,[29] the Court of Justice clarified that a permissible parody should display an original character of its own, rather than displaying noticeable differences from the original parody's work; reasonably be attributed to a person other than the author of the original work; and relate to or mention the source of the original work itself. The court found that a parody has two essential characteristics. First, it should evoke an existing work while being noticeably different from it and, second, it ought to constitute an expression of humour or mockery. The Court of Justice also stated that the copyright holder has a legitimate interest in ensuring that their work is not associated with the message conveyed by the parody if that message is discriminatory pursuant to the principle of non-discrimination based on race, colour, and ethnic origin.[30]

The issue that parody should evoke a pre-existing work, while bearing some noticeable differences from it, results from the very nature of parody and has been affirmed in a number of parody cases heard at a worldwide level.[31] The best-known example comes from the United States and *Campbell v Acuff-Rose Music*,[32] perhaps the most famous and influential case on the topic. Subject to examination in this case was whether the parody of Roy Orbison's song 'Pretty Woman' by 2 Live Crew was fair use. According to the Supreme Court:

> Even if 2 Live Crew's copying of the original's first line of lyrics and characteristic opening bass riff may be said to go to the original's 'heart', that heart is what most readily conjures up the song for parody, and it is the heart at which parody takes aim. Moreover, 2 Live Crew thereafter departed markedly from the Orbison lyrics and produced otherwise distinctive music[33]

In this particular case, the transformative element of the parodic use, as reflected in Judge Leval's interpretation of the first fair use factor[34]—which includes an examination of the purpose and character of the use—was so profound as to overcome

---

[29] AG Opinion in *Johan Deckmyn and Another v Helena Vandersteen and Others*, Case C-201/13, 22 May 2014, ECLI:EU:C:2014:458.

[30] As specifically defined in Council Directive 2000/43/EC (also confirmed by Art. 21(1) of the Charter of Fundamental Rights of the European Union). See Council Directive 2000/43/EC of 29 June 2000 Implementing the Principle of Equal Treatment between Persons Irrespective of Racial or Ethnic Origin, OJ L 180, 19 July 2000, 22–6.

[31] See, however, *Allen v Redshaw*, Patent Court London, CC 12 P2645, 15 May 2013 (UK). In this case, that was issued a few months before *Deckmyn* and before the parody exception was introduced into UK law, the court found that there is no defence of parody in cases where a substantial part of the claimant's work has been copied, with the motives of the respondent being immaterial in this examination.

[32] *Campbell v Acuff-Rose Music Inc.*, 510 US 569 (1994) (US); for a comment on *Campbell*, see Edward Samuels, 'Campbell v. Acuff Rose: Bringing Fair Use into Focus?' [1994] *Media Law & Policy* 4.

[33] *Campbell v Acuff-Rose Music Inc.*, 510 US 569, 570 (1994) (US).

[34] Pierre Leval, 'Toward a Fair Use Standard' (1990) 103 *Harvard Law Review* 1105.

factors that usually weigh against a finding of fairness. Such factors included the commercial nature of the use in question or that the work used was 'expressive' in nature.

Although the EU test is clearly not premised on the transformative character of the use and the element of commerciality in a parody has not been addressed in *Deckmyn*, it has been subject to discussion in national courts that found there is no room for permissible parody in a commercial context. This restrictive approach was upheld by the Austrian Supreme Court in a case involving the photograph of a politician with a child alongside a satirical text for the purpose of the politician's self-promotion in a magazine.[35] Engaging in a long discussion on the specific use of the child's photograph and the issue of consent for this use, the Supreme Court also explored the commerciality of the activity in question, which was aimed at self-promotion, rather than making political satire. When weighing the interests of the parties in the context of parody and satire, it is decisive, the court stressed, to identify whether the emphasis is on the parodic aspect or on commercial motives. In the present case, the parody defence could not be established because the event during which the claimant was photographed was not dealt with satirically, and the focus lay on the commercial aims of self-advertisement. This is a far more restrictive approach than the one adopted in the United States where the scope of the available defence is broader and covers commercial uses.

However, it should be kept in mind that the aforementioned case of the Austrian Supreme Court precedes *Deckmyn* and the issue of commerciality in a parodic use has not been addressed at the European level. It has to be assumed, however, that because Article 5(3)(k) of the Information Society Directive adopts a broad wording and does not clearly exclude commercial uses, as it does in every other instance where certain activities are permitted on the basis of their non-commerciality, commercial uses are to be kept within the scope of the relevant copyright exception. Such an interpretation would allow for the commercial use of parodies and, in this light, enable the creation of second-hand markets and the development of innovative image transformation services, such as mobile applications and relevant software. This could be in line with the approach adopted in *Deckmyn*, which arguably appears to deviate from the principle of strict interpretation of copyright exceptions and limitations, adopting a broad understanding of permissible parody.[36]

The necessity for an apparent departure of the parody from the pre-existing work has been addressed in various cases, even in jurisdictions where parody was not expressly a permitted use under copyright law. In particular, a relevant case was brought to the UK High Court years before the parody exception was introduced

---

[35] Supreme Court (Oberster Gerichtshof), 15 December 2010 (Austria).

[36] Christophe Geiger, Jonathan Griffiths, Martin Senftleben, et al., 'Limitations and Exceptions as Key Elements of the Legal Framework for Copyright in the European Union – Opinion of the European Copyright Society on the Judgment of the CJEU in Case C-201/13 *Deckmyn*' (2015) 46(1) *International Review of Intellectual Property and Competition Law* 46.

into the Copyright, Designs and Patents Act (CDPA).[37] The case involved a number of articles that Associated Newspapers were publishing under the title 'Alan Clark's Secret Election Diaries' as parodies of the well-known diaries of Mr Alan Clark, who was a member of parliament and an author. Mr Clark brought proceedings for false attribution and passing off. In their defence, Associated Newspapers pointed out that the aim of the pieces was parody and the joke would not work unless the articles were obviously exaggerated. However, Lightman J took the view that the contradiction in this case was not sufficiently clear and the evidence showed that a substantial number of members of the public were deceived. Therefore, Lightman J found the defendant was in breach of section 84 of the CDPA on false attribution. The learned judge also stressed that his judgment should not be seen as a bar to parodies and that the defendant could carry on publishing parodies of the 'Diaries' insofar as there was no attribution of authorship to the claimant and there was a clear indication of who the author was.

Drawing a distinctive line between the original work and a parody thereof is in line with case law from other EU jurisdictions, such as France and Germany, only the focus in these areas is not authorship and paternity, rather it is the very nature of the derivative work and the original contribution embedded within it that distinguishes it from the original. Pre-harmonization case law in Germany seemed to require an internal distance between the original work and its parody for the parody to be permitted and protected in its own right. According to Article 24 of the German Copyright Act, it is more likely for parody to be permitted where the new work is autonomous compared to the existing work upon which it is based. There ought to be an internal distance between the two works for parody to be permitted, with the attributes of the original work 'fading from the spotlight'.[38] By reference to parodies, an autonomous derivative work can be created when the representative creative attributes of the pre-existing work are subsumed in comparison to the individual creative aspects of the new work. This aligns with the position that the Advocate General and the Court of Justice expressed in *Deckmyn*,[39] whereby a parody should exhibit an original character that departs from the original work with some noticeable differences. Similarly, in France, the Court of Appeal of Paris stressed that a parody should not result in the likelihood of confusion; the key elements of the parodied work should be distinctively identified.[40]

---

[37] *Clark v Associated Newspapers*, High Court (Chancery Division), 21 January 1998 (UK); for a comment see Richard Harrison, 'Pastiched-Off' (1998) 9(5) *Entertainment Law Review* 181; Clive D. Thorne, 'The Alan Clark Case – What it is; What it is Not' (1998) 20(5) *European Intellectual Property Review* 194; note that the parody exception was introduced into UK law in 2014 via 30A of the CDPA.

[38] 'Asterix', Federal Court of Justice (Bundesgerichtshof), 11 March 1993 (Germany).

[39] Opinion of the Advocate General Cruz Vilallón in *Johan Deckmyn and Another v Helena Vandersteen and Others*, Case C-201/13, 22 May 2014, ECLI:EU:C:2014:458, [57]–[58].

[40] *Societe Sebdo Jacques Faizant v Editions Enoch* (Unreported - France); see comment by Elisabeth Logeais, 'France: Copyright - Parody as a Defence to Copyright Infringement' (1993) 4(6) *Entertainment Law Review* E110.

The EU approach to parody after *Deckmyn* also requires that the parody becomes the expression of humour and mockery. The Court of Justice appears to affirm that a humorous effect is a prerequisite for legal permissibility, rather than an attribute which is frequently—but not always—met in parodic works. This has implications on the way in which the conflict between copyright and freedom of speech—as encapsulated by reference to parody—is addressed. Requiring that parodies should be funny to be permitted could be read as imposing a limit to the parody exception and more broadly on freedom of speech, in that it is only funny speech that can be permitted under the parody exception. The latter is a particular form of freedom of speech and aims to address the collision of copyright and fundamental rights. The requirement that a parody ought to be the expression of humour or mockery to be permitted generates a circular logic: parodies as manifestations of freedom of speech are permissible under copyright law and prevail in a possible conflict of rights, but at the same time copyright requires that these parodies are an expression of humour or mockery and in this regard limits the parody exception and, by effect, the exercise of the fundamental right on which it is premised.

The requirement for parody to be a 'humorous metamorphosis' finds its roots in national case law before *Deckmyn* was issued. A special issue of the French weekly magazine *Le Point* which honoured Yves Montand, who passed away around that time, featured a drawing of Montand's silhouette over the words of a famous song ('Les Feuilles Mortes') performed by Yves Montand. The plaintiff, Société Sebdo, who owned the copyright in the text of the song authored by Jacques Prévert, sued the cartoonist and the magazine for damages, arguing that the text was an unauthorized adaptation of the original work.[41] In this case, the parody was distinct from the original work, there was an indication of such a distinction through the use of the words 'after Prévert', and, in addition, the meaning of the text was adapted into a humoristic tribute to the memory of Yves Montand. This is just an example of national case law where the humorous effect of a parody supported its permissibility under copyright law.[42]

The requirement for humour and mockery significantly limits the application of the exception in the online context. It is an open question how the requirement that a parody is the expression of humour and mockery can be met by reference to online services and tools which enable image transformations. It is likely that the algorithmic editing of images through filters or photo effects will not meet this condition. Other copyright exceptions and limitations under EU copyright, such as criticism or review, tend to be purpose-specific and limited in scope, and also may not cover the aforementioned services.

---

[41] *Societe Sebdo Jacques Faizant v Editions Enoch* (Unreported - France).
[42] See indicatively Laetitia Lagarde and Carolyn Ang, 'Parody in the UK and France: defined by humour?' *Practical Law* (24 March 2016).

The object of parody

An interesting aspect of *Deckmyn* has to do with the object of the parody; in *Deckmyn*, this was not the original work as such, rather the object was the mayor of Ghent and his political activity. This raises an important theoretical aspect on the permissibility of parodies and the applicability of the relevant defensive claims, which has been discussed in the literature as the distinction between target and weapon parodies.

Broadly put, there are two kinds of parodies, the distinction between which depends on the object of the parody. Where the focus is a copyright-protected work, its style or form, or its author, the result is a so-called target parody. A parody, however, may address other issues, cultural, social, or political, or it could question contemporary ideas and values. In such cases, often called weapon parodies, the original (usually a well-known) work becomes a vehicle, or—otherwise put—a weapon used in order to mock or criticize other issues of broader relevance. As Michael Spence observes:

> the conflict between free speech and intellectual property is far more difficult to resolve in the situation exemplified by weapon parody than it is in the situation exemplified by target parody.[43]

The distinction between target and weapon parodies was expressly articulated in *Campbell v Acuff-Rose Music*,[44] examined earlier. In this case, the US Supreme Court noted there is a risk that the creator of a target parody might draw on the text simply to 'get attention or to avoid the drudgery in working up something fresh.'[45] The Supreme Court further clarified that a permissible parody in the United States must make use of, and target, a specific copyright work for the fair use doctrine to apply.[46]

This distinction between content and target parodies was not discussed in *Deckmyn*, a case which arguably involved a target parody. Certain scholars have expressed concerns regarding the broad definition of parody adopted in this case as a parodist can use any work to mock something entirely unrelated.[47] At the centre of the criticism is that this could result in unfair exploitation of another author's work without adding sufficiently significant creative input. Unless the Court of Justice

---

[43] Michael Spence, 'Intellectual Property and the Problem of Parody' (1998) 114 *Law Quarterly Review* 594, 613; also see in this regard Richard A. Posner, 'When is Parody Fair Use?' (1992) 21 *Journal of Legal Studies* 67.

[44] *Campbell v Acuff-Rose Music Inc.*, 510 US 569 (1994) (US).

[45] 510 US 569, 580 (1994) (US).

[46] 510 US 569, 592 (1994) (US).

[47] Jonathan Griffiths, 'Fair Dealing after Deckmyn - The United Kingdom's Defence for Caricature, Parody or Pastiche' in Megan Richardson and Sam Ricketson (eds), *Research Handbook on Intellectual Property in Media and Entertainment* (Cheltenham: Edward Elgar, 2017) 64.

refines the *Deckmyn* doctrine in a new referral, however, the scope of the defence remains broad enough to cover any kind of parody to the extent that it is an expression of humour and mockery.

An interesting case indicating the importance of the distinction between target and weapon parodies was heard in Germany in the aftermath of *Deckmyn*. The case before the German Federal Court of Justice concerned a photograph of an actress that was altered in such a way that she appeared to be overweight.[48] This was part of a competition asking participants to make celebrities 'look fat' by modifying their photographs. The photographer argued that the photograph had been distorted. Article 24 of the German Copyright Act provides that a number of activities including parodies are free uses. The literature considers this to be an inherent limitation of copyright rather than an exception to rights. Giving up its traditional stance that a parody has to constitute an original, protectable work, and the requirement that the parody must comment on the original work itself, the court embraced the broader definition of parody in *Deckmyn* and found that the parody at issue fulfilled the conditions of the EU jurisprudence: it was noticeably different, while still evoking the original work, and was also mocking the portrayal of celebrities in the media. However, the court also stressed that the parodist's free speech argument would have been stronger had the parody targeted the work itself, instead of a broader theme, i.e. the contemporary portrayal of women in the media. In terms of possible infringements of other rights of third parties outside copyright law, the court highlighted the importance of free speech to social life, indicating that the balance of conflicting interests should not be confused with political correctness. The case is interesting as it is the first post-*Deckmyn* affirmation of the broad scope of parodies that do not have to cover the work or its author as such, but which may address broader issues. However, before a new referral to the Court of Justice is made to address this issue, Member States have the discretion to adopt their own approach according to their national legal traditions.

The impact of *Deckmyn*

Deckmyn may have an impact on the parody exceptions available under the national laws of the various Member Stares as 'parody' has been held to be an autonomous concept of EU law, hence national judges will have to follow the test developed by the Court of Justice. The condition according to which a parody has to be an expression of humour or mockery to be permitted will have a limiting effect on the number of parodies that can be lawfully produced; it may also have an impact on the development of modern services of image manipulation, such as

---

[48]   Federal Supreme Court (Bundesgerichtshof), I ZR 9/15, 18 July 2016 (Germany).

mobile phone applications and other relevant software. *Deckmyn* is also important because it departs, marginally, from the doctrine of strict interpretation of exceptions and limitations when the protection of fundamental rights is involved. This has been welcomed by scholarship as a positive development in that, among other things, it supports a purposive interpretation of copyright exceptions as and when appropriate.[49]

Reproductions by the press, and reporting of current events

On the basis of Articles 10(1) and 10bis of the Berne Convention, and similarly Article 10(1)(b) of the Rental Right Directive,[50] Article 5(3)(c) of the Information Society Directive permits Member States to introduce two exceptions in their national laws, which reflect the need to protect the exercise of freedom of speech and the freedom of the media, enshrined in Article 11 of the EU Charter of Fundamental Rights.[51] In a number of cases the Court of Justice has indicated that the purpose of the press, in a democratic society governed by the rule of law, justifies it in informing the public without restrictions other than those that are strictly necessary.[52]

In terms of scope and application, the first exception of Article 5(3)(c) includes reproductions by the press and acts of communication or making available to the public published articles or broadcast works, or other subject matter on current economic, political, or religious topics, provided that such use is not expressly reserved and that the source of the work or subject matter used, including the author's name, is indicated. The second exception covers uses of works and subject matter in connection with the reporting of current events, to the extent justified by the informatory purpose and provided that the source of the work or other subject matter used is indicated, unless this is deemed to be impossible. In addition to the two internal requirements of source acknowledgement and proportionality, the main restriction on the scope of these defences rests on the need for published articles or broadcast works to be on 'current economic, political, or religious topics',

---

[49] Christophe Geiger, Jonathan Griffiths, Martin Senftleben, et al., 'Limitations and Exceptions as Key Elements of the Legal Framework for Copyright in the European Union – Opinion of the European Copyright Society on the Judgment of the CJEU in Case C-201/13 *Deckmyn*' (2015) 46(1) *International Review of Intellectual Property and Competition Law* 46.

[50] Directive 2006/115/EC of the European Parliament and of the Council of 12 December 2006 on Rental Right and Lending Right and on Certain Rights Related to Copyright in the Field of Intellectual Property, OJ L 376, 27 December 2006, 28–35 (Rental and Lending Directive).

[51] Charter of Fundamental Rights of the European Union.

[52] *Eva-Maria Painer v Standard VerlagsGmbH and Others*, Case C-145/10, 1 December 2011, ECLI:EU:C:2011:798 (*Painer*), [113]; *Spiegel Online v Volker Beck*, Case C-516/17, 29 July 2019, ECLI:EU:C:2019:625 (*Spiegel Online*), [72].

or for 'the reporting of current events' respectively.[53] The justificatory basis for each defence is to facilitate the dissemination of information on current events with a view to serve the public interest. As in the Berne Convention, these topics are not offered as examples, rather they are listed in an exclusionary fashion in that other topics are not covered by Article 5(3)(c).[54]

The Court of Justice was recently called upon to offer interpretative guidance on the exception covering the reporting of current events in *Spiegel Online*.[55] The case concerned a contentious article written by Mr Beck, a German politician. The piece was published in a book in 1988 after having been modified by the publisher without the author's consent. When the manuscript of the article was discovered and presented to Mr Beck in 2013, he made the manuscript available to various newspaper editors for the purposes of proving that it had been altered, but did not consent to the publication of the manuscript. He also published the two versions of the manuscript on his own website. When Spiegel Online published an article where it contended that the essential statement had not been altered, contrary to Mr Beck's claim, and made the original versions of both manuscripts available to its readers for download through hyperlinks, Mr Beck took the view that making the texts available amounted to copyright infringement and started proceedings before the German Courts. The case reached the Federal Court of Justice (Bundesgerichtshof), which stayed proceedings and sought preliminary guidance on the scope of the exceptions relating to the reporting of current events and to quotations.

With regard to the exception covering the reporting of current events, the court held that, although merely announcing that a current event has occurred does not amount to reporting it, the usual meaning of the word 'reporting' does not require the user to analyse such an event in detail.[56] In addition, 'a current event is an event that, at the time at which it is reported, is of informatory interest to the public.'[57] In the online context, in particular, it is necessary that information on a current event is diffused rapidly and, as the Court noted, this is difficult to reconcile with a requirement for the author's prior consent as this could make it excessively difficult to offer timely information to the public, or may prevent it altogether.[58] What is more, requiring users to seek the authorization of the rightsholder where reasonably possible would mean disregarding the need for the exception or limitation on the reporting of current events, if the conditions for its application are satisfied.

---

[53] '*Elektronischer Pressespiegel*', German Federal Supreme Court (Bundesgerichtshof), 2002 GRUR 963, 11 July 2002 (Germany); for a comment see Silke von Lewinski, 'News from Germany' (2005) 206 *RIDA* 261.

[54] Michel M. Walter and Silke Von Lewinski, *European Copyright Law: A Commentary* (Oxford: Oxford University Press, 2010) 11.5.65.

[55] *Spiegel Online v Volker Beck*, Case C-516/17, 29 July 2019, ECLI:EU:C:2019:625 (*Spiegel Online*).

[56] Ibid., [66].

[57] Ibid., [67].

[58] Ibid., [71].

Importantly, the court noted that the exception on reporting of current events should be understood as precluding corresponding national exceptions that restrict the application of the defence where it is not reasonably possible for a user to gain permission to use a protected work.

With regard to whether the exception applies to electronic press clippings, it has to be assumed that it does. The reason is that the exception is organically incorporated within Article 5(3) of the Information Society Directive which lays down exceptions applicable to both the rights of reproduction and communication. It is up to the national laws to decide the particulars of the applicability of the defences, but EU copyright allows for the exception to cover acts of electronic communication. German case law indicates that acts of communication can be covered. In a case that followed the implementation of the Information Society Directive in Germany,[59] the Supreme Court held that a limitation covering digital in-house press-clipping services is in compliance with Article 5(3)(c). The question was whether the exemptions that were available under Article 49 of the German Copyright Act could apply by analogy in the online context and, in particular, whether the rules available for press reviews printed on paper could also cover electronic press reviews. The court held they did, but did not enter into a discussion on whether such reproductions should only be made 'by the press'. The court stressed that events ought to be current in the sense that they should still have an informatory value and interest to the public,[60] as was later also affirmed in *Spiegel Online*.[61]

With respect to reporting current events in particular, just because the event being reported is not recent in time does not matter where the issues raised have contemporary relevance at the time that the news reporting takes place. The concept of a 'current event' has received liberal interpretations in national case law,[62] including not only recent occurrences,[63] but also incidents that have a real interest to the public, even past events, to the extent that they retain a legitimate public interest. There is a wealth of national precedents affirming this principle, even though the Court of Justice has not been called to address the issue. In the United Kingdom, *Ashdown* is a leading authority in developing the interpretative standards for the exceptions of news reporting, and criticism and review.[64] In this case,

---

[59] '*Elektronischer Pressespiegel*', German Federal Supreme Court (Bundesgerichtshof), 2002 GRUR 963, 11 July 2002 (Germany).

[60] *Hyde Park v Yelland* [2001] Ch. 143 (UK).

[61] *Spiegel Online v Volker Beck*, Case C-516/17, 29 July 2019, ECLI:EU:C:2019:625 (*Spiegel Online*), [67].

[62] See e.g. *Pro Sieben v Carlton* [1999] FSR 610, 620 (UK); *Ashdown v Telegraph Group* [2002] Ch 149, 172 (UK); '*Elektronischer Pressespiegel*', German Federal Supreme Court (Bundesgerichtshof), 2002 GRUR 963, 11 July 2002 (Germany).

[63] See e.g. *Pro Sieben v Carlton* [1998] FSR 43, 54 (UK) (where it was argued that the exception is limited to events less than twenty-four hours old but the interpretation was rejected).

[64] *Ashdown v Telegraph Group Ltd* [2001] EWCA Civ 1142; [2002] Ch. 149 (UK); Michael D. Birnhack, 'Acknowledging the Conflict between Copyright Law and Freedom of Expression under the Human Rights Act' (2003) 14(2) *Entertainment Law Review* 24–34; Jonathan Griffiths, 'Copyright Law after Ashdown - Time to Deal Fairly with the Public' (2002) 3 *Intellectual Property Quarterly* 240;

the expression 'reporting current events' was interpreted liberally,[65] i.e. in a democratic society, a meeting between a prime minister and the leader of the opposition party to discuss cooperation is likely to be of public interest, even if it took place two years before being reported in the news.[66] The rationale for this defence is that the reporting of current events should not be hindered by the need to clear licenses or authorial consent.[67]

With regard to what qualifies as reporting that can be exempted from infringement, the *Tixdax* case in the United Kingdom has offered some interpretive insight.[68] In this case, uploading short clips of cricket match broadcasts on a website without the authorization of the relevant rightsholders could not be considered as fair dealing for the purposes of reporting current events in accordance with section 30(2) of the CDPA. Even though Arnold J found that a contemporaneous sporting event is a current event within the meaning of the defence, the term 'reporting' depended on the basis of the context, thus it was capable of bearing a broad or narrow meaning. According to Arnold J, the exception ought to be given a 'living' interpretation, i.e. one that takes into account recent developments in technology and the media. Because, in the present case, users made comments on the clips they uploaded they did not create a report and hence, the use of the claimants' works was not for the purpose of reporting current events. As Arnold J remarked in paragraph 129 of the judgment:

> The clips were not used in order to inform the audience about a current event, but presented for consumption because of their intrinsic interest and value.

Even if there would have been an affirmation that the purpose was to report current events, the dealing at issue could not be considered fair as the defendant's

---

Phillip Johnson, 'The Public Interest: Is it Still a Defence to Copyright Infringement?' (2005) 16(1) *Entertainment Law Review* 1; Alexandra Sims, 'The Public Interest Defence in Copyright Law: Myth or Reality?' (2006) 28(6) *European Intellectual Property Review* 335.

[65] In Australia, the words 'criticism' and 'review' have both been given their dictionary definitions. *De Garis v Neville Jeffress Pidler Pty Ltd* (1990) 18 IPR 292, 299.

[66] In the UK, the House of Lords could not find fair dealing for reporting of current events because the subject matter of the cuttings could not be said to fall within the category of 'current events', and it was also not fair. See *Newspaper Licensing Agency v Marks and Spencer*, House of Lords, 12 July 2001 (UK).

[67] See in this regard and by reference to Art. 10*bis*(2) of the Berne Convention: Sam Ricketson and Jane Ginsburg, *International Copyright and Neighbouring Rights* (Oxford: Oxford University Press, 2006, 2nd edn) 13.54–5; Silke von Lewinski, *International Copyright Law and Policy* (Oxford: Oxford University Press, 2008) 5.161–2. What is more, according to the Advocate General's Opinion in *Infopaq*, the exception on reporting of current events does not exclude the—at least indirectly—commercial objective of providing information on current events. See Opinion of Advocate General Trstenjak, *Infopaq International A/S v Danske Dagblades Forening*, Case C-5/08, 12 February 2009, ECLI:EU:C:2009:89, [135].

[68] *England and Wales Cricket Board Ltd & Anor v Tixdaq Ltd & Anor*, High Court of England and Wales, Chancery Division, HC-2015-002993, 18 March 2016 (UK).

activities were commercially damaging to the claimants, i.e. they were in conflict with a normal exploitation of their works as they were based on the extraction of a portion of protected materials that could not be justified by any informatory purpose. This may be relevant, more broadly, with regard to electronic services that require input from users, such as social media or electronic platforms, the operation of which is premised on the addition of content from users and other forms of user-generated input.

Quotations, criticism, and review

An exception that is part and parcel of copyright concerns the entitlement to reproduce another's copyright-protected work for purposes of review and criticism. Article 5(3)(d) of the Information Society Directive stipulates that:

> Member States may provide for exceptions or limitations to the rights provided for in Articles 2 and 3 … quotations for purposes such as criticism or review, provided that they relate to a work or other subject-matter which has already been lawfully made available to the public, that, unless this turns out to be impossible, the source, including the author's name, is indicated, and that their use is in accordance with fair practice, and to the extent required by the specific purpose.

To rely on this defence, a defendant ought to demonstrate that the use is for purposes *such as* criticism or review, that the work has been previously made available to the public, that the use is made in accordance with fair practices to the extent required by the specific purpose, and that the use is accompanied by sufficient acknowledgement. As the words 'such as' indicate, the terms criticism and review are used for illustrative purposes to indicate some kind of use that could fall under the exception. However, the combination of these words also indicates that the permissible use has to involve some critical engagement in that merely reproducing the work would not be covered by Article 5(3)(d). This enhances specificity of the exception in line with the three-step test.[69]

Interpretative standards

Three issues need to be discussed with regard to the exception on criticism and review: firstly, what the concept of 'quotation' is, that can fall under the permissible scope of the exception; secondly, what should be the object of criticism and

---

[69] Information Society Directive (Directive 2001/29/EC), Art. 5(5).

review for the exception to apply; and, finally, what is the purpose specificity of the exception? These issues have been addressed in case law from national courts and, recently, three rulings of the Court of Justice, all issued on the same day, that shed light on the quotation exception and, in particular, on what qualifies as a 'quotation' and what can lawfully fall under its scope.

In *Funke Medien*,[70] the court stated that Article 5(3)(d) of the Information Society Directive merely sets out an illustrative list of permissible quotation, as is clear from the use of the words 'for purposes such as criticism or review'.[71] Although discussed in reference to the degree of discretion that Member States have in implementing the provisions of the Information Society Directive, this case affirmed that criticism and review are indicative examples of purposes for which permissible quotations are made. This enlarges the scope of permissible quotations, the meaning of which was discussed in *Pelham*[72] and *Spiegel Online*.[73]

In *Pelham*,[74] the court was called to offer interpretative guidance on the scope of the quotation exception and also to clarify whether limiting copyright beyond the admitted catalogue of limitations laid out in the Information Society Directive is compatible with EU law. One of the questions on which the referring court sought guidance on was whether Article 5(3)(d) of the Information Society Directive must be interpreted as meaning that the concept of 'quotations' extends to a situation in which it is not possible to identify the work concerned by the quotation in question. The case involved two-second phonogram extracts for sampling purposes. The court stressed that in order for the exception on quotations for criticism and review to apply 'the use in question must be made "in accordance with fair practice, and to the extent required by the specific purpose", so that the use at issue for the purposes of quotation must not be extended beyond the confines of what is necessary to achieve the informatory purpose of that particular quotation'.[75] Because the term 'quotation' is not defined, its meaning and scope had to be determined on the basis of its usual meaning in everyday language, while taking into account the contextual parameters of the legislative framework of which it is part.[76] Such usual meaning of the term 'quotation' includes 'the use, by a user other than the copyright holder, of a work or, more generally, of an extract from a work for the purposes of illustrating an assertion, of defending an opinion, or of allowing an

---

[70] *Funke Medien NRW GmbH v Federal Republic of Germany*, C-469/17, 29 July 2019, ECLI:EU:C:2019:623 (*Funke Medien*).

[71] *Funke Medien NRW GmbH v Federal Republic of Germany*, C-469/17, 29 July 2019, ECLI:EU:C:2019:623 (*Funke Medien*), [43].

[72] *Pelham GmbH, Moses Pelham, Martin Haas v Ralf Hütter, Florian Schneider-Esleben*, Case C-476/17, 29 July 2019, ECLI:EU:C:2019:624 (*Pelham*).

[73] *Spiegel Online v Volker Beck*, Case C-516/17, 29 July 2019, ECLI:EU:C:2019:625 (*Spiegel Online*).

[74] *Pelham GmbH, Moses Pelham, Martin Haas v Ralf Hütter, Florian Schneider-Esleben*, Case C-476/17, 29 July 2019, ECLI:EU:C:2019:624 (*Pelham*).

[75] *Pelham GmbH, Moses Pelham, Martin Haas v Ralf Hütter, Florian Schneider-Esleben*, Case C-476/17, 29 July 2019, ECLI:EU:C:2019:624 (*Pelham*), [69].

[76] Ibid., [70].

intellectual comparison between that work and the assertions of that user, since the user of a protected work wishing to rely on the quotation exception must therefore have the intention of entering into "dialogue" with that work.[77] Such a dialogue cannot be possible when the extract is no longer identifiable and hence cannot be covered under the meaning of the concept of 'quotation' and the applicability of the relevant defensive rule. *Pelham* instructs that permissible quotations are not those where the dialectic of the new work with the pre-existing work is interrupted.

In *Spiegel Online*,[78] the court held that the concept of 'quotations', referred to in Article 5(3)(d) of the Information Society Directive, covers references made through hyperlinks to files that can be downloaded independently online. In particular, the court held that it is not necessary that the quoted work be inextricably integrated, by way of insertions or reproductions in footnotes, into the subject matter in which it is cited. On the contrary, such quotations may also be made by including a hyperlink to the quoted work. To reach this conclusion, the court relied on the usual meaning of the term 'quotation' and the Opinion of the Advocate General,[79] according to whom the application of the exception for quotations necessitates the establishment of a direct and close link between the quoted work and the defendant's own reflections, thereby allowing for an intellectual comparison to be made with the work of another, because Article 5(3)(d) states that a quotation must inter alia be intended to enable criticism or review. It also follows that the use of the quoted work must be secondary in relation to the assertions of that user since the quotation of a protected work cannot (under Article 5(5) of Directive 2001/29) be so extensive as to conflict with a normal exploitation of the work or another subject matter or prejudice unreasonably the legitimate interests of the rightsholder. The court noted that the use in question must be made in accordance with fair practice, to the extent required by the specific purpose, i.e. the use of the work should not be extended beyond the confines of what is necessary to achieve the informatory purpose of that particular quotation, and only if the quotation relates to a work which has already been lawfully made available to the public. Although it is up to the national court to decide whether the content published by the politician on his website was lawfully made available to the online portal on which hyperlinks to it were placed, the case is important as it clarifies aspects of the exception. Importantly, it affirms a wide scope on what qualifies as permissible quotation, despite the fact that there are numerous conditions that need to be met for the quotation to apply.

---

[77] Ibid., [71] (affirming the position of the Advocate General); also see *Spiegel Online v Volker Beck*, Case C-516/17, 29 July 2019, ECLI:EU:C:2019:625 (*Spiegel Online*), [77]–[78].

[78] *Spiegel Online v Volker Beck*, Case C-516/17, 29 July 2019, ECLI:EU:C:2019:625 (*Spiegel Online*).

[79] Opinion of Advocate General Szpunar in *Spiegel Online v Volker Beck*, Case C-516/17, 10 January 2019, ECLI:EU:C:2019:16, [43]; for a comment see Jonathan Griffiths, 'European Union copyright law and the Charter of Fundamental Rights—Advocate General Szpunar's Opinions in (C-469/17) *Funke Medien*, (C-476/17) *Pelham GmbH* and (C-516/17) *Spiegel Online*' (2019) 20(1) *ERA Forum* 35.

In the context of identifying the purpose of the use of the works and the appropriate scope of exceptions allowing quotations, the Norwegian Supreme Court[80] emphasized that, to be exempt from infringement, such copying should not extend beyond the purpose of making a quotation.[81] This case concerned the unauthorized TV broadcasting of short extracts (ten and two seconds respectively) from a film featuring the contribution of actress Gørild Mauseth. The defendant TV company invoked the quotation exception available under section 22 of the Norwegian Copyright Act and freedom of speech as the legal basis underpinning the quotation exception. The Supreme Court held that both extracts were covered by section 42 of the Copyright Act that offers protection to performer's rights and that the quotation exception could not apply as the quotations—especially the shorter one that included a nudity scene—had not induced further debate or discussion, as is the purpose of the quotation exception. In Norway too, it seems that the purpose of the defence ought to be objectively assessed.

National case law on the exception covering quotations for the purposes of criticism and review indicates that an aspect worth considering is the degree to which the allegedly infringing use competes with the exploitation of the original work. This takes into account the three-step test featured in Article 5(5) of the Information Society Directive, and in particular the need to ensure that an activity does not conflict with a normal exploitation of the work. Another important factor to be taken into consideration is whether the work has been published or not. This is an express requirement under the relevant articles of the Information Society Directive. It is also important to consider the extent and substantiality of the amount of the original work that was taken.

An interesting issue that was raised by the UK Court of Appeal when discussing the *Ashdown* case was the object of criticism and review.[82] In *Ashdown*, the use was not found to amount to fair dealing since the criticism or review was not directed at the minutes, but at the actions of the prime minister and Ashdown. This bears a resemblance to the rationale which distinguishes between target and weapon parodies.[83] More recent cases, however, have adopted a broader approach to the appropriate scope of permissible criticism and review under which criticism does not need to relate to the work at issue but can relate to another work, or other unrelated issues.[84]

In another UK case which discussed the defence allowing quotations for the purposes of criticism and review, it was established that the test to determine

---

[80] '*Mauseth-case*', Supreme Court of Norway, HR-2010-527A, Rt 2010, s. 399, March 2010 (Norway).
[81] Ibid., [45].
[82] *Ashdown v Telegraph Group*, Court of Appeal (Civil Division), 18 July 2001 (UK).
[83] See discussion at page 176.
[84] *Fraser-Woodward Limited v BBC* [2005] EWHC 472 (UK); *Pro Sieben Media AG v Carlton UK Television Ltd* [1999] 1 W.L.R. 605, [1999] F.S.R. 610, CA (UK).

whether the use amounts to fair dealing is objective.[85] The case concerned a current affairs programme which copied an extract from a TV show on a woman pregnant with octuplets. The court observed that the phrase 'for the purpose of' does not mean that a subjective test should be used in order to assess whether a use is for the purpose of criticism and review; the intentions and motives of the user are not irrelevant, they should be taken into consideration in an assessment of whether a dealing is 'fair' and not in relation to its purpose. A liberal approach should be taken in order to assess the appropriate scope of 'criticism or review'. It is a standard approach of the courts to construe the composite phrases 'for the purpose of non-commercial research' and 'for the purpose of private study', instead of each single word. In this case, the use of the extract was found to be fair dealing because it was very short, it did not include any words spoken by Ms Allwood, and it did not compete unfairly with the claimant's programme. The original work was also sufficiently acknowledged. The requirement that the purpose of the defence is to be construed objectively aligns with the principle of strict interpretation of exceptions that has been developed by the Court of Justice.[86]

Quotations

An interesting transposition of Article 5(3)(d) of the Information Society Directive recently took place in the United Kingdom. It introduced a specific exception on quotations to supplement the fair dealing provision for criticism and review. According to the new section 30(1ZA) of the CDPA:

> Copyright in a work is not infringed by the use of a quotation from the work (whether for criticism or review or otherwise) provided that—
> (a) the work has been made available to the public,
> (b) the use of the quotation is fair dealing with the work,
> (c) the extent of the quotation is no more than is required by the specific purpose for which it is used, and
> (d) the quotation is accompanied by a sufficient acknowledgement (unless this would be impossible for reasons of practicality or otherwise).

---

[85] *Pro Sieben Media A.G. v Carlton U.K. Television and Another*, Court of Appeal (Civil Division), 17 December 1998 (UK); for a comment see David Bradshaw, 'Copyright, Fair Dealing and the Mandy Allwood Case: the Court of Appeal Gets the Max out of a Multiple Pregnancy Opportunity' (1999) 19(5) *Entertainment Law Review* 125; Mark Haftke, 'Pro Sieben Media AG v Carlton UK Television Ltd [1999] 1 WLR 605 (CA)' (1999) 10(4) *Entertainment Law Review* 118; Jeremy Phillips, 'Fair Stealing and the Teddy Bears' Picnic' (1999) 10(3) *Entertainment Law Review* 57.

[86] See in this regard *Infopaq International A/S v Danske Dagblades Forening*, Case C-5/08, 16 July 2009, ECLI:EU:C:2009:465 (*Infopaq I*), [56]; *Infopaq International A/S v Danske Dagblades Forening*, Case C-302/10, 17 January 2012, ECLI:EU:C:2012:16 (*Infopaq II*), [26]; *Stichting Brein v Jack Frederik Wullems*, Case C-527/15, 26 April 2017, ECLI:EU:C:2017:300 (*Filmspeler*), [61]–[62].

This new section is interesting as it was drafted in fairly broad terms to the extent that some scholars argue that it introduces a fair use style defence in the United Kingdom.[87] Indeed the exception does not require that the activity should be for the purposes of criticism or review but allows quotations to be permitted more broadly. At the same time, the exception is meant to be imperative against contractual restriction in that any contractual term purporting to prevent or restrict the doing of the permitted activity would be unenforceable.[88]

Such a defensive rule with a broader scope is not available under EU copyright, despite some discussion at the policy and legislative level prior to the introduction of the Directive on Copyright in the Digital Single Market. In particular, the EU Parliament's proposal on a Directive on Copyright in the Digital Single Market aspired to include such a general exception allowing quotations beyond the purposes of criticism, review, and parody. In particular, Recital 21a of the Parliament's proposal[89] acknowledged that technological developments have given rise to information society services which enable their users to upload content and make it available in diverse forms and for various purposes. These include the illustration of ideas, criticism, parody, or pastiche by use of short extracts of pre-existing protected works or other subject matter, that may have been altered, combined, or otherwise transformed. However, despite some overlap with existing copyright exceptions and limitations, not all content that is uploaded or made available by Internet users (that reasonably includes extracts of protected works or other subject matter) is covered by Article 5 of the Information Society Directive. Recital 21b of the Parliament's proposal acknowledged that a situation of this type creates legal uncertainty for both users and rightsholders and thus required the introduction of a new specific exception to permit the legitimate uses of extracts of content uploaded or made available by users. The exception, which did not make its way into the final version of the Directive, was envisaged to cover the short and proportionate use of a quotation or of an extract of a protected work or other subject matter for a legitimate purpose by Internet users, subject to the framework of conditions outlined in the three-step test. Criteria to establish fairness of the use would include the degree of originality of the content concerned, the length of the quotation or extract, the professional nature of the content, and the degree of economic harm to the claimant. The beneficiaries of the exception would be Internet users, but not information society service providers, so that the scope of their obligations

---

[87] Lionel Bently and Tanya Aplin, 'Whatever Became of Global Mandatory Fair Use? A Case Study in Dysfunctional Pluralism' in Suzy Frankel (ed.), *Is Intellectual Property Pluralism Functional?* (Cheltenham: Edward Elgar, 2018) 8.

[88] CDPA 1988, s. 30(4).

[89] European Parliament, Copyright in the Digital Single Market, Amendments adopted by the European Parliament on 12 September 2018 on the proposal for a Directive of the European Parliament and of the Council on copyright in the Digital Single Market (COM (2016)0593 – C8-0383/2016 – 2016/0280(COD))1.

under the then Article 13 (now Article 17) of the Digital Single Market Directive would not be reduced.[90]

A quotation exception would have made a breakthrough in the ordinary use of the Internet by end users and could have introduced a limited US-style fair use defence into EU copyright.[91] Importantly, the exception would have offered a balanced approach towards the expansive construal of protected subject matter in the aftermath of *Infopaq*.[92] However welcome this exception would have been in enhancing the freedom to use fair extracts in line with the communicative function of copyright and within a framework of proportionality and fairness, an agreement was not reached at the legislative level and the exception was hence excluded from the final version of the Directive. Use of extracts such as those that would have been covered by the exception should it have passed into law, are now to be permitted only on the basis of other available exceptions under EU copyright which allow quotations that are made in the pursuit of specified purposes.

Research and private study

Article 5(3)(n) of the Information Society Directive stipulates that

> Member States may provide for exceptions or limitations to the (reproduction and communication rights) in the following cases: … use by communication or making available, for the purpose of research or private study, to individual members of the public by dedicated terminals on the premises of establishments

---

[90] European Parliament, Copyright in the Digital Single Market, Amendments adopted by the European Parliament on 12 September 2018 on the Proposal for a Directive of the European Parliament and of the Council on Copyright in the Digital Single Market (COM (2016)0593 – C8-0383/2016 – 2016/0280(COD))1, Recital 21c.

[91] Indicative in this regard was the use of criteria that would determine fairness and the degree of prejudice that rightsholders face owing to the re-use of short extracts. These criteria seemed to mirror, to a certain extent, the four fair use factors. 17 US Code, s. 107:

> Notwithstanding the provisions of sections 106 and 106A, the fair use of a copyrighted work, including such use by reproduction in copies or phonorecords or by any other means specified by that section, for purposes such as criticism, comment, news reporting, teaching (including multiple copies for classroom use), scholarship, or research, is not an infringement of copyright. In determining whether the use made of a work in any particular case is a fair use the factors to be considered shall include—
> (1) the purpose and character of the use, including whether such use is of a commercial nature or is for nonprofit educational purposes;
> (2) the nature of the copyrighted work;
> (3) the amount and substantiality of the portion used in relation to the copyrighted work as a whole; and
> (4) the effect of the use upon the potential market for or value of the copyrighted work.

The fact that a work is unpublished shall not itself bar a finding of fair use if such finding is made upon consideration of all the above factors.

[92] *Infopaq International A/S v Danske Dagblades Forening*, Case C-5/08, 16 July 2009, ECLI:EU:C:2009:465 (*Infopaq I*).

(such as publicly accessible libraries, educational establishments or museums, or by archives, which are not for direct or indirect economic or commercial advantage) of works and other subject-matter not subject to purchase or licensing terms which are contained in their collections.

The provision refers to two different kinds of activities: research and private study. Research includes work that is done by an individual and often has a public character in that it may include published outputs. This could take place for the benefit of an organization or for the promotion of knowledge in general. On the contrary, private study is made for the individual's own benefit and can be part of the pursuit of a formal qualification. The distinction between research and private study is important because for non-commercial research to be permitted it should also include sufficient acknowledgement. Non-commercial research means research that is not made for profit, either directly or indirectly.

Determining permissibility

The exception on research and private study came under the scrutiny of the Court of Justice in *TU Darmstadt*.[93] TU Darmstadt is a regional academic library that installed electronic reading points which allowed the public to consult works contained in its collection. Part of this collection was a book published by Ulmer, a scientific publishing house. Although Ulmer offered the library the opportunity to purchase and use its textbooks in 2009, the library did not take up this offer and digitized the book at issue to make it available to users on its electronic reading points. Users of the reading points could print the work onto paper or store it on a USB stick, and thus take it out of the library. Ulmer brought an action against the library for copyright infringement. Following partial victory before the Frankfurt District Court, both parties appealed before the Federal Supreme Court, which decided to stay the proceedings and refer three questions to the Court of Justice for a preliminary ruling. The Court of Justice was asked to rule on whether a work is 'subject to purchase or licensing terms', within the meaning of Article 5(3)(n), where the rightsholder offers to conclude agreements with the establishments referred to in that provision for the use of that work on appropriate terms; whether Article 5(3)(n) should be interpreted to mean that it entitles Member States to confer on establishments referred to in that provision the right to digitize the works contained in their collections, if that is necessary in order to make those works available on terminals; and on whether the rights which the Member States

---

[93] *Technische Universität Darmstadt v Eugen Ulmer KG*, Case C-117/13, 11 September 2014, ECLI:EU:C:2014:2196 (*Technische Universität Darmstadt*).

lay down pursuant to Article 5(3)(n) may go as far as to enable users of the terminals to print onto paper or store on a USB stick the works made available on those terminals.

The court interpreted the first question as relating to whether a work is subject to 'purchase or licensing terms' within the meaning of Article 5(3)(n) and held that

> a comparison of the language versions of Article 5(3)(n) ... —which use the words 'terms', 'conditions', 'Regelung' and 'condiciones', respectively—shows that, in that provision, the EU legislature used the concepts 'terms' or 'provisions', which refer to contractual terms actually agreed as opposed to mere contractual offers.[94]

Therefore, the court held that the concept of 'purchase or licensing terms' must be understood as requiring that the rightsholder and an establishment, such as a publicly accessible library, have concluded a licensing agreement in respect of the work in question, which sets out the conditions under which the establishment may use the work.

With regard to the second question, the court held that the act of digitization at issue must be considered an 'act of communication' for the purposes of Article 3(1) because what matters is the possibility that the public may access the work, irrespective of whether they avail themselves of that opportunity.[95] In particular, it stressed that the activity in question has to be considered to be 'making [that work] available' and, therefore, an 'act of communication' for the purposes of Article 3(1) of the Information Society Directive.[96] This was because the relevant activity would allow the offering of access to a 'public', namely all of the individual members of the public who use the dedicated terminals installed on its premises for the purpose of research or private study.[97]

The court reiterated that the limitation of Article 5(3)(n) permits only certain acts of communication to the public and this does not include acts such as the

---

[94] Ibid., [26].

[95] Ibid., [41].

[96] Ibid., [42].

[97] What is more, by virtue of Art. 5(2)(c) of the Information Society Directive (Directive 2001/29/EC), establishments such as publicly accessible libraries are recognized as having an ancillary right to digitize works in order to secure the meaningfulness and effectiveness of the right of communication of works that they enjoy, provided that 'specific acts of reproduction' are involved. The scope of the ancillary right of digitization has to be determined through the lens of the three-step test of Art. 5(5), under which the limitation should only be made available in certain special cases that do not prejudice the normal exploitation of the work or other protected objects or cause unjustified harm to the legitimate interests of the rightsholder. In *Technische Universität Darmstadt*, the applicable national legislation took due account of the conditions provided for in Art. 5(5) since it limited the number of hard copies of each work made available to users, and the making available of the work in digital format through dedicated terminals gave rise to a duty to make payment of adequate remuneration. Therefore, the Court of Justice held that Member States are not precluded from granting publicly accessible libraries the right to digitize the works contained in their collections, if such copying is necessary for the purpose of making those works available to users by means of dedicated terminals within those establishments.

printing of a work onto paper or its storage on a USB stick. Such activities amount to acts of reproduction which, however, cannot be permitted under an ancillary right stemming from Articles 5(2)(c) and 5(3)(n), as they are: (a) not necessary for the purpose of making the work available to users of that work via dedicated terminals and (b) carried out by the users of the dedicated terminals rather than the establishment. Thus, the Court of Justice held that Article 5(3)(n) must be interpreted to mean that it does not extend to acts such as the printing of works onto paper or their storage on a USB stick carried out by users from dedicated terminals installed in publicly accessible libraries. However, such acts may be authorized under national legislation transposing the exceptions or limitations provided for in Article 5(2)(a) or (b), provided that relevant conditions, under national laws, are met. Typical conditions that national courts examine to determine the permissibility of a particular use include the amount and substantiality of the portion taken; the purpose and character of the use; and whether the work is published or unpublished.[98] As with other copyright exceptions and limitations, the amount copied matters as it can determine whether the use has a financial impact on the copyright holder.

What matters is that the portion taken is not excessive, rather that it is proportionate to the requirements of research and study. This issue was discussed in *Universities UK Ltd v Copyright Licensing Agency Ltd.*,[99] where it was held that

> a student who takes a photocopy for the purposes of his course of a relevant article, or a relevant short passage from a book is likely to do so in circumstances which amount to fair dealing. At the other extreme, if he were to take a photocopy of a whole textbook, we think that his dealing would not be fair, even if done for the purposes of private study.[100]

Such a proportionality requirement aligns with the three-step test and ensures that the scope of the exceptions remains appropriate.

It is assumed that the copyright exception can only be invoked at a personal level as a defence against allegations of infringement by researchers and students

---

[98] Some general guidance on how fairness in a use is assessed has been offered in *Forensic Telecommunications Services Ltd v Chief Constable of West Yorkshire*:

> Relevant factors to be taken into account in judging whether the dealing was fair have been identified in various cases. None is determinative and the weight to be attached to them will vary from case to case. In particular, the various factors will carry different weight according to the type of dealing. Cases of fair dealing for purposes of criticism, review and the reporting of current events usually raise more difficult problems than cases of non-commercial research and private study.

Forensic Telecommunications Services Ltd v Chief Constable of West Yorkshire [2011] EWHC 2892 (Ch), [111].

[99] *Universities UK Ltd v Copyright Licensing Agency Ltd* [2002] EMLR 35.

[100] Ibid., [34].

only, or by people making copies on their behalf. This could include, for instance, librarians who make a copy of a protected work under the exception, to the extent that they are satisfied that the person requesting the copy requires it for research or private study, and insofar as that person is given a single copy of the same material of no more than a reasonable proportion of the copied work. The exception does not cover making multiple copies for third parties and lecturers/teachers cannot rely on the exception to supply copies of the same journal article to all the students in their class.[101]

Exceptions for disabled individuals

Even though there is a network of international law provisions ensuring that everyone shall enjoy the right to equal participation in cultural life without discrimination,[102] the relationship between human rights, intellectual property, and disability was first addressed at the international level in Article 30 of the International Convention on the Rights of Disabled Persons.[103] According to this Article:

> States Parties shall take all appropriate steps, in accordance with international law, to ensure that laws protecting intellectual property rights do not constitute an unreasonable or discriminatory barrier to access by persons with disabilities to cultural materials.[104]

---

[101] This was affirmed in a UK case which found that

> materials provided by the staff for distribution to a number of students at more or less the same time would not in general amount to fair dealing ... If a lecturer were to instruct every member of his class to make copies of the same material, we consider that this too would not be fair dealing. But the mere distribution of a reading list, without any instructions to copy, is not in our view an infringement of copyright at all.

Ibid., [35].

[102] See e.g. Art. 15(1)(a) of the International Covenant on Economic, Social and Cultural Rights (ICESCR):

> The States Parties to the present Covenant recognize the right of everyone: (a) To take part in cultural life.

See also Art. 5(e)(vi) of the Committee on the Elimination of Racial Discrimination (CERD):

> In compliance with the fundamental obligations laid down in article 2 of this Convention, States Parties undertake to ... guarantee the right of everyone, without distinction as to race, colour, or national or ethnic origin, to equality before the law, notably in the enjoyment of the following rights ... (e) Economic, social and cultural rights, in particular: (vi) The right to equal participation in cultural activities.

[103] For a commentary see Stavroula Karapapa, 'Article 30(3) of the International Convention on the Rights of Disabled Persons' in Ilias Bantekas, Michael Stein, and Dimitrios Anastasiou (eds), *Commentary on the International Convention on the Rights of Disabled Persons* (Oxford: Oxford University Press, 2018) 888.

[104] Art. 30 stresses the importance of 'accessibility to the physical, social, economic and cultural environment, to health and education and to information and communication, in enabling persons with

The Article aims to ensure that intellectual property rights will not prevent access for disabled individuals to cultural goods. Indeed, of all the books that are published each year it is only a very small percentage of materials are published in accessible formats. According to the World Blind Union, it is only between 1 and 7 per cent of the millions of books that are published each year are available to the 285 million persons in the world who are blind, partially sighted, or otherwise print-disabled.[105]

The rights of disabled individuals to have access to copyright materials is also addressed at the international level in the Marrakesh Treaty to Facilitate Access to Published Works for Persons Who Are Blind, Visually Impaired, or Otherwise Print Disabled. Signed under the auspices of the World Intellectual Property Organization in (WIPO) 2013, this Treaty aims 'to create a set of mandatory limitations and exceptions for the benefit of the blind, visually impaired, and otherwise print-disabled (VIPs)'.[106] In line with the protection afforded to human rights at the international level,[107] the Marrakesh Treaty embraces the principles of non-discrimination, accessibility, equal opportunity, and effective participation in society, while also recognizing the importance of protecting copyright as a reward for creation. It lays down the minimum standard of mandatory copyright exceptions for blind, visually impaired, and print-disabled individuals, notably creating exceptions to make works available in accessible formats (e.g. Braille or DAISY navigation).

In 2013, when the Marrakesh Treaty was just being signed, exceptions for the benefit of disabled individuals had gained momentum at the international level. This was through the landmark *Google Books* case.[108] Google's unauthorized scanning of millions of copyright-protected materials, the creation of a search functionality, and the display of snippets from those works to the public were held to be non-infringing fair uses. As Judge Chin of the US District Court for the Southern District of New York observed—inter alia—in his opinion, Google Books expands access to books since

traditionally underserved populations will benefit as they gain knowledge of and access to far more books. Google Books provides print-disabled individuals with

disabilities to fully enjoy all human rights and fundamental freedoms'. International Convention on the Rights of Disabled Persons (CRPD), preamble, para V.

[105] See World Blind Union (WBU) Press Release, June 2013, available at <http://www.worldblindunion.org/English/news/Pages/JUne-17-Press-Release-for-WIPO-Book-Treaty.aspx>, accessed 11 November 2019.
[106] See WIPO website <http://www.wipo.int/treaties/en/ip/marrakesh/>, accessed 11 November 2019.
[107] E.g. Universal Declaration of Human Rights (UDHR) and the Convention on the Rights of Persons with Disabilities (CRDP).
[108] See *The Author's Guild et al v Google Inc*, 05 Civ. 8136 (DC), 2013 WL 6017130, at 11 (S.D.N.Y. 14 November 2013) (US).

the potential to search for books and read them in a format that is compatible with text enlargement software, text-to-speech screen access software, and Braille devices. Digitization facilitates the conversion of books to audio and tactile formats, increasing access for individuals with disabilities.[109]

This finding of fair use was affirmed on October 2015,[110] when the Second Circuit upheld that the Google Books project provides a public service without infringing intellectual property law. The US Supreme Court declined to review the case,[111] leaving the lower court's decision standing.

The *HathiTrust* case[112] also affirmed fair use of copyright materials for the benefit of the print-disabled. Print disability was there defined as

any disability that prevents a person from effectively reading printed material. Blindness is one example, but print disabilities also include those that prevent a person from physically holding a book or turning pages.[113]

Judge Chin, ruling on the same day that he ruled for the *Google Books* case, held that access to materials scanned by the Google Books project, and making them available to affiliate libraries of the HathiTrust project, was fair use.[114] In this regard, both Google Books and HathiTrust were acquitted from infringement as the services they operated were found to serve the interests of disabled individuals.

Exceptions for the disabled under EU copyright

At the European level, provision for the rights of disabled individuals to accessible formats is made in the Directive on certain permitted uses of certain works and other subject matter protected by copyright and related rights for the benefit of persons who are blind, visually impaired, or otherwise print-disabled.[115] The

---

[109] See *The Author's Guild et al v Google Inc*, 05 Civ. 8136 (DC), 2013 WL 6017130, at 11 (S.D.N.Y. 14 November 2013) (US); *The Authors Guild et al v Google Inc*, 13-4829-cv (2d Cir. 16 October 2015) (US).
[110] *The Author's Guild et al v Google Inc*, 05 Civ. 8136 (DC), 2013 WL 6017130, at 11 (S.D.N.Y. 14 November 2013) at 11 (US).
[111] *The Authors Guild et al v Google Inc*, 13-4829-cv (2d Cir. 16 October 2015) (US).
[112] *The Authors Guild v HathiTrust*, 902 F.Supp.2d 445 (S.D.N.Y. 10 October 2012), aff'd in part in *The Authors Guild v HathiTrust* (2d Cir. 10 June 2014) (US).
[113] *The Authors Guild v HathiTrust* (2d Cir. 10 June 2014) 7–8 (US).
[114] See *The Author's Guild et al v HathiTrust et al*, 11 CV 6351 (HB), at 21 (S.D.N.Y. 14 November 2013) 21. Also see 42 U.S.C. s. 12101(7) (US).
[115] Directive (EU) 2017/1564 of the European Parliament and of the Council of 13 September 2017 on Certain Permitted Uses of Certain Works and Other Subject Matter Protected by Copyright and Related Rights for the Benefit of Persons who are Blind, Visually Impaired or Otherwise Print-Disabled and amending Directive 2001/29/EC on the Harmonisation of Certain Aspects of Copyright and Related Rights in the Information Society, OJ L 242, 20 September 2017, 6–13 (Directive on Permitted Uses for Disabled Individuals).

Directive implements the Marrakesh Treaty within the European Union and introduces a framework of permitted uses for the benefit of disabled individuals. It is complemented by a Regulation[116] which enhances the cross-border exchange of accessible format copies of protected materials between the European Union and third countries and it stresses the need to ensure the availability of accessible formats.[117] The latter are defined as copies of a work or other subject matter taking on an alternative manner or form that gives a beneficiary access to protected content, including allowing such a person to have access as feasibly and comfortably as a person without any impairments or disabilities of the beneficiary.[118] The Directive requires that Member States shall ensure that an authorized entity established in their territory may make an accessible format copy of a work or other subject matter to which it has lawful access, or to communicate, make available, distribute, or lend an accessible format copy to a beneficiary person or other authorized entity on a non-profit basis for a beneficiary person or other authorized entity established in any Member State. Member States shall also ensure that a beneficiary person or an authorized entity established in their territory may obtain or may have access to an accessible format copy from an authorized entity established in any Member State.[119]

The Directive also amended Article 5(3)(b) of the Information Society Directive on copyright exceptions for the benefit of disabled individuals. This Article now reads:

> Member states may provide for exceptions or limitations to the rights provided for in articles 2 and 3 in the following cases: (b) uses, for the benefit of people with a disability, which are directly related to the disability and of a non-commercial nature, to the extent required by the specific disability, without prejudice to the obligations of Member States under Directive (EU) 2017/1564 of the European Parliament and of the Council.

Neither Directive offers a definition of the term 'disability'. The ordinary meaning of the term includes physical or mental unfitness to carry out certain acts that result in total incapacity, but it also covers activities of substantiate impairment. This includes visual impairment that could necessitate copying a work in Braille or making an audio recording to enhance accessibility of the content. The Directive on permitted uses for those who are blind, visually impaired, or otherwise

---

[116] Regulation (EU) 2017/1563 of the European Parliament and of the Council of 13 September 2017 on the Cross-Border Exchange Between the Union and Third Countries of Accessible Format Copies of Certain Works and Other Subject Matter Protected by Copyright and Related Rights for the Benefit of Persons who are Blind, Visually Impaired or Otherwise Print-Disabled, OJ L 242, 20 September 2017, 1–5, Art. 2.

[117] Directive on Permitted Uses for Disabled Individuals (Directive 2017/1564) , Art. 3(1).

[118] Ibid., Art. 2(3).

[119] Ibid., Art. 4.

print-disabled offers an exhaustive definition of the beneficiary persons. This includes, according to Article 2(2):[120]

> a person who:
> (a) is blind;
> (b) has a visual impairment which cannot be improved so as to give the person visual function substantially equivalent to that of a person who has no such impairment, and who is, as a result, unable to read printed works to substantially the same degree as a person without such an impairment;
> (c) has a perceptual or reading disability and is, as a result, unable to read printed works to substantially the same degree as a person without such disability; or
> (d) is otherwise unable, due to a physical disability, to hold or manipulate a book or to focus or move their eyes to the extent that would be normally acceptable for reading.

According to Article 5(3)(b) of the Information Society Directive the uses ought to be directly related to the disability in that a copy in Braille, for instance, should make the work accessible to a visually impaired individual. What is more, the use is only permitted to the extent that a specific disability requires. This, when an accessible format is already available on the market the exception will not cover further copying. This differs, however, if such an accessible copy is an abridged version. In this case, copying of the whole work in an accessible format is justified and hence is covered by the exception. Where the full content is not available in an accessible format, copying for the benefit of people with disability will be justified. The exception covers only copying that is justified and proportionate to enhancing the accessibility of copyright-protected content to disabled individuals.

It is immaterial who makes the copy, what matters is that the copy is made for the benefit of the disabled individual, meaning that third party copying is allowed. However, the use should be of a non-commercial nature. It is unclear to what extent this internal limitation of Article 5(3)(b) hinders the efficacy of the provision. This is because publishers of Braille editions are not covered by the exception if they pursue a commercial advantage, and—to date—Braille editions are very expensive as the market tends to be concentrated.[121]

Despite its underlying human rights rationale, Article 5(3)(b) is merely optional for Member States to implement, even after its revision through the

---

[120] See also Regulation (EU) 2017/1563 of the European Parliament and of the Council of 13 September 2017 on the Cross-Border Exchange Between the Union and Third Countries of Accessible Format Copies of Certain Works and Other Subject Matter Protected by Copyright and Related Rights for the Benefit of Persons who are Blind, Visually Impaired or Otherwise Print-Disabled, OJ L 242, 20 September 2017, 1–5, Art. 2.

[121] Michel M. Walter and Silke Von Lewinski, *European Copyright Law: A Commentary* (Oxford: Oxford University Press, 2010) 11.5.52.

Directive for the benefit of disabled individuals. Most EU Member States, however, have incorporated in their national laws the international law provisions which reflect the need to preserve the right of disabled individuals to access copyright-protected materials. Examples include the UK copyright law which specifically addresses disability. The Copyright (Visually Impaired Persons) Act 2002 (CVIPA 2002)[122] allows making accessible copies of a literary, dramatic, musical, or artistic work by, or for, visually impaired persons without the consent of the copyright owner.[123] The provision, which is the result of joint lobbying from the publishing industry, the National Library for the Blind (NLB), and the Royal National Institute of Blind People (RNIB), does not only concern instances of visual impairment, but also covers persons who are unable to hold a book.[124]

There is nothing to exclude the application of Article 5(3)(b) in the online environment where particular accessible formats are also available. These include, for instance, large print, videos with captions and/or audio description, easy read, and Makaton. Especially in light of the *Google Books* and *HathiTrust* cases, it is ever more important to ensure that disabled individuals shall have unfettered access to copyright materials online.

Exceptions for political speeches

Article 5(3)(f) of the Information Society Directive permits Member States to introduce exceptions and limitations to the reproduction right and the right of communicating works to the public for

> use of political speeches as well as extracts of public lectures or similar works or are subject-matter to the extent justified by the informatory purpose and provided that the source, including the author's name, is indicated, except where this turns out to be impossible.

This Article finds its origin in Article 2bis(1) of the Berne Convention, which allows the exclusion from copyright protection, in whole or in part, of political speeches and speeches delivered in the course of legal proceedings. Article 2bis(2) of the Convention leaves it to the contracting parties

---

[122] In force since 31 October 2003.

[123] Subject to limitations: see CDPA 1988, ss 81–3.

[124] S. 31F(9): 'Visually impaired person' means a person- (a) who is blind; (b) who has an impairment of visual function which cannot be improved, by the use of corrective lenses, to a level that would normally be acceptable for reading without a special level or kind of light; (c) who is unable, through physical disability, to hold or manipulate a book; or (d) who is unable, through physical disability, to focus or move his eyes to the extent that would normally be acceptable for reading.

to determine the conditions under which lectures, addresses and other works of the same nature which are delivered in public may be reproduced by the press, broadcast, communicated to the public by wire and made the subject of public communication ... when such use is justified by the informatory purpose.

The aim of Article 5(3)(f) is to facilitate the free and unimpeded dissemination of political speeches and public lectures to the extent that this is justified by the informatory purpose—which is likely concerned with issues relevant to the participation of individuals in political life. Although there is no case from the Court of Justice regarding the meaning of political speeches and public lectures, the Article ought to be read liberally for its efficacy to be ensured. Political speeches in this context should not only cover speeches delivered by politicians, but also speeches which cover topics of a political nature. They also need not be delivered in public, unlike public lectures. Public lectures may cover, in principle, any topic insofar as they have been delivered in public. Similar works could include, as per the Berne Convention, 'addresses and other works of the same nature' to the extent that these are also delivered in public.[125] These may only relate to literary works that can be spoken, given the requirement for an informatory purpose.[126] Other subject matter may only be related to such speeches, e.g. recordings thereof.[127]

Sufficient acknowledgement

An important element of the copyright exceptions available for news reporting, reproductions by the press, quotations for purposes such as criticism and review, research and private study, and use of political speeches and public lectures, is the requirement that the source, including the author's name, is sufficiently acknowledged. For all aforementioned copyright exceptions and limitations, with the exception of reproductions by the press,[128] the Information Society Directive indicates that acknowledgment of the work may take the form of identification of its title, or some other description of it.[129] The author does not need to be identified by their proper name,[130] and use of a pseudonym by which an author is known to the public will be sufficient. Alternative forms of identification can suffice. These could include, for example, the television transmission of a company logo where

---

[125] Sam Ricketson and Jane C. Ginsburg, *International Copyright and Neighbouring Rights: The Berne Convention and Beyond* (Oxford: Oxford University Press, 2006, 2nd edn) 13.56–13.58.
[126] Michel M. Walter and Silke Von Lewinski, *European Copyright Law: A Commentary* (Oxford: Oxford University Press, 2010) 11.5.61.
[127] Ibid.
[128] Information Society Directive (Directive 2001/29/EC), Art. 5(3)(c)(a).
[129] See e.g. indicative guidance offered in CDPA 1988, s. 178.
[130] See e.g. *Pro Sieben Media AG v Carlton UK Television Ltd* [1999] 1 WLR 605, [1999] FSR 610 (UK); *Newspaper Licensing Agency Ltd v Marks and Spencer plc* [1999] RPC 536 (CA) (UK).

the author of the programme is accustomed to using this logo as identification. Mere reference in a newspaper article to the fact that a story originates with another newspaper would not be sufficient, however. This could be relevant to the reporting of news items via online platforms or aggregators where such acknowledgement may be absent.

With regard to the exception on reporting current events, the Court of Justice clarified, in *Spiegel Online*,[131] that there are instances where it is not possible to name the source. Especially on the Internet, the reporting of current events requires the rapid diffusion of information which may not be easily reconciled with the requirement to clear authorial permission. The court affirmed that the exception to the reporting of current events should be understood as precluding corresponding national exceptions that restrict the application of the defence where it is not reasonably possible for a user to clear permission to use a protected work.

Speech entitlements and contractual overridability

Although speech entitlements align with the function of copyright as an instrument of communication in the Kantian sense and are part and parcel of the protection that copyright accords, they are not user rights that can be enforced before courts and, in addition, they are not laid down as imperative against possible contractual override.

In principle, rightsholders and users are free to negotiate the terms of a licensing agreement so as to best suit their respective needs and to ensure the most efficient exploitation of copyright content.[132] Due to the high costs involved in securing individual licensing agreements, especially in the context of mass-market transactions, negotiating different licensing terms with potential users has been gradually replaced by unilateral contractual practices. Many websites contain standard terms and conditions of use that involve licensing of rights on a per-transaction, per-use or other basis. In some cases, these terms and conditions may require users to waive 'rights' that they otherwise enjoy under copyright, or prohibit activities permissible by law.

The relationship between copyright limitations and their contractual overridability is not yet set and remains controversial.[133] Unlike the Digital Single Market Directive, which expressly mandates that certain copyright exceptions and

---

[131] *Spiegel Online v Volker Beck*, Case C-516/17, 29 July 2019, ECLI:EU:C:2019:625 (*Spiegel Online*).

[132] On the technological and contractual overridability of copyright exceptions, see Patricia Akester, 'The New Challenges of Striking the Right Balance between Copyright Protection and Access to Knowledge, Information and Culture' (2010) 32(8) *European Intellectual Property Review* 372.

[133] Séverine Dusollier, Yves Poullet and Mireille Buydens, 'Copyright and Access to Information in the Digital Environment' (2000) XXXIV(4) *Copyright Bulletin* 4, 12; James Griffin, 'The Interface Between Copyright and Contract: Suggestions for the Future' (2011) 2(1) *European Journal of Law and Technology*, available at <http://ejlt.org/article/view/23/110>, accessed 11 November 2019.

limitations shall be imperative against contractual restrictions,[134] the Information Society Directive does not clarify the relationship between copyright exceptions and contract, moreover it does not set exceptions and limitations as mandatory against potential contractual restriction. Equally silent are most of the national laws throughout Europe. The only exceptions are Belgium, Ireland, Portugal, and the United Kingdom. In particular, the Belgian Copyright Act recognizes that all copyright exceptions and limitations are mandatory against contractual restriction.[135] Similarly, in Portugal, any contractual provision that eliminates or impedes the normal exercise of copyright limitations is null and void.[136] In the United Kingdom, some of the newly introduced copyright exceptions are meant to be imperative against contractual clauses,[137] arguably this indicates that the remaining permitted uses can be foreclosed by contract. However, there is no indication as to what determines which exceptions are mandatory against possible contractual override and which are not, resulting in a degree of legal uncertainty.

For many commentators, certain exceptions should be declared mandatory against contractual restriction. These mainly include exceptions safeguarding fundamental freedoms,[138] and this could impact their status against contractual overridability. According to Derclaye and Favale, 'such exceptions cannot be limited unless we question the principles from which they derive, and this is not possible in a democratic society.'[139] Accordingly, users cannot be forced to contract out of their fundamental freedoms as contracts cannot override such norms.[140] The same has been argued by reference to exceptions reflecting the general public interest.[141] Copyright exceptions based on regulatory practices, such as the facilitation of trade or the promotion of competition, and those that are mere

---

[134] Digital Single Market Directive (Directive 2019/790), Art. 7(1).

[135] Art. 23bis of the Belgian Copyright Act of 30 June 1994, inserted by an Act of 31 August 1998 implementing the Database Directive into national law. The mandatory status of Belgian copyright limitations was maintained in the Act of 22 May 2005 (M.B., 27 May 2005, 24997). See Marie-Christine Janssens, 'Implementation of the 2001 Copyright Directive in Belgium' (2006) 37 *International Review of Intellectual Property and Competition Law* 50.

[136] Lucie Guibault, et al. 'Study on the Implementation and Effect in Member States' Laws of Directive 2001/29/EC on the Harmonisation of Certain Aspects of Copyright and Related Rights in the Information Society' (2007) Report to the European Commission 160–1.

[137] These are documents supplied under s. 42A(6) of the CDPA, copying for the disabled (s. 31F(8)), text and data mining (s. 29A(5)), and illustration for instruction under s. 32(3).

[138] Mireille Buydens and Séverine Dusollier, 'Les Exceptions au Droit d'Auteur dans l'Environnement Numérique: Evolutions Dangereuses' (2001) *Communication – Commerce Electronique* 13–14.

[139] Estelle Derclaye and Marcella Favale, 'Copyright and Contract Law: Regulating User Contracts: The State of the Art and a Research Agenda' (2010) 18(1) *Journal of Intellectual Property Law* 65, 70; Martin Kretschmer et al., 'The Relationship between Copyright and Contract Law' (2010) 4 *Strategic Advisory Board for Intellectual Property Policy* 85.

[140] Neil Weinstock Netanel, 'Copyright and the First Amendment: What *Eldred* Misses – and Portends' in Jonathan Griffiths and Uma Suthersanen (eds), *Copyright and Free Speech: Comparative and International Analyses* (Oxford: Oxford University Press, 2005) 129, 143.

[141] Mireille Buydens and Séverine Dusollier, 'Les Exceptions au Droit d'Auteur dans l'Environnement Numérique: Evolutions Dangereuses' (2001) *Communication – Commerce Electronique* 14; Thomas Vinje, 'Copyright Imperilled' (1999) 21 *European Intellectual Property Review* 192, 193.

responses to market failure, are considered to have a less strong legal basis. This is not absolute in reference to the first category and the de-compilation exception for computer programs illustrates this point. This exception has been made mandatory in Europe[142] because free competition is in the public interest.[143] Market failure exceptions are considered to be less strong in the digital environment where rightsholders have the technical tools to monitor and control each and every single use of their works. Defences premised on a market failure justification are more likely to start losing weight and be contractually overridden due to the new enforcement possibilities. These include, for instance, copyright exceptions concerning the incidental inclusion of subject matter in other material, freedom of panorama,[144] or the making of ephemeral recordings by broadcasting organizations. Making clear distinctions is not entirely possible, mainly because some of the available copyright exceptions and limitations do not have a single justificatory basis. For instance, exceptions that may be seen as correcting market failures, such as the private copying limitation, also entail a privacy rationale. That said, there cannot be a uniform answer as to the legal status of all copyright exceptions against contract.

Unlike other copyright defences, however, speech entitlements engender academic consensus as to their solid legal nature and the need to be declared imperative against contractual restriction. One of the reasons for this is that these defences are meant to promote ongoing authorship and readership and to offer individuals access to information as a form of speech, thereby having a profound ability to promote innovation. Recital 4 of the Information Society Directive acknowledges that copyright itself plays an important role in fostering innovation. Even though the common assumption is that copyright promotes innovation through the rights it extends to creators, it is submitted that innovation can be enhanced by the promotion and encouragement of ongoing authorial activity that may take place on the basis of uses permitted by copyright. Speech entitlements promote innovation-driven competition in that promotion of this kind of defence has an important effect on competition by acting as a balance on the price charged by the copyright holders and also on contractual restrictions or technological protection measures used along with a work.[145] Innovation-driven competition results from the appearance of innovative products as encouraged by law. The European Commission has

---

[142] Directive 2009/24/EC of the European Parliament and of the Council of 23 April 2009 on the Legal Protection of Computer Programs, OJ L 111, 5 May 2009, 16–22 (Computer Programs Directive).

[143] Mireille Buydens and Séverine Dusollier, 'Les Exceptions au Droit d'Auteur Dans l'Environnement Numérique: Evolutions Dangereuses' (2001) *Communication – Commerce Electronique* 13–14.

[144] See e.g. German Copyright Act, Art. 59; UK CDPA, s. 62; Greek Law 2121/93, Art. 26.

[145] For an analysis of the effects of innovation-driven competition on copyright law see Thomas Heide, 'Copyright, Contract and the Legal Protection of Technological Measures – Not "the Old Fashioned Way": Providing a Rationale to the "Copyright Exceptions Interface"' (2003) 50 *Journal of the Copyright Society of the USA* 315.

expressly embraced the economic effect of intellectual property rights on innovation in its Evaluation Report on the Technology Transfer Regulation.[146]

Speech entitlements serve as a balancing act between the protection of author's rights and the public interest. For this balance to be meaningful, copyright should ensure remuneration to authors while making allowance for certain activities that will enable further creativity, innovation, and the development of new services and business models. The viability of this objective is inextricably premised on a circular logic: the same theoretical principles on which authorship is rewarded via copyright protection ought to form the basis for further creativity and innovation that depends on pre-existing works. This premise, which—although straightforward— often escapes attention,[147] becomes more relevant in the online context where new, interactive means of using and re-using copyright works emerge, thereby offering unprecedented opportunities for growth in the creative and business sector. It is for this reason that contractual terms restricting speech entitlements should be null and void and a clarification of this point at the EU level would be desirable.

Conclusion

Speech entitlements are defences that mean to enhance ongoing authorship and access to information as manifestations of a balancing act in the possible collision between copyright and fundamental freedoms. Defendants in cases of allegedly infringing conduct that bring about justifications underpinned by a fundamental human rights cannot forward defensive claims rooted directly in the relevant fundamental rights, rather they should rely on one of the available copyright exceptions and limitations embodying a so-called speech entitlement.[148] Possible conflicts of interests between proprietary copyright interests and fundamental freedoms are deemed to have been addressed at the legislative stage, and thereby clarify the extent to which the relevant defensive rules can apply.

---

[146] In this document, the Commission states that:

innovation in new products and new technologies are the ultimate source of substantial and major

See Commission Evaluation Report on the Technology Transfer Block Exemption Regulation 240/96, (2002) [190], available at <https://ec.europa.eu/transparency/regdoc/rep/1/2016/EN/1-2016-593-EN-F1-1.PDF>, accessed 11 November 2019.

[147] Art. 6(4) of the Information Society Directive (Directive 2001/29/EC), for instance, creates uncertainty in this regard as a distinction is made between two sets of exceptions: for some exceptions Member States ought to ensure that their beneficiaries shall be able to exercise them and for others there is no such obligation.

[148] *Funke Medien NRW GmbH v Federal Republic of Germany*, C-469/17, 29 July 2019, ECLI:EU:C:2019:623 (*Funke Medien*); *Spiegel Online v Volker Beck*, Case C-516/17, 29 July 2019, ECLI:EU:C:2019:625 (*Spiegel Online*); *Pelham GmbH, Moses Pelham, Martin Haas v Ralf Hütter, Florian Schneider-Esleben*, Case C-476/17, 29 July 2019, ECLI:EU:C:2019:624 (*Pelham*).

Despite their importance and vitality within the copyright system, these permitted uses are very narrow in scope. Indeed, they are subject to a number of internal limitations that may not work well in light of modern uses of materials in the online context. Such limitations include purpose or scope restrictions,[149] or emanate from inherent copyright principles, such as attribution to the source. The jurisprudence of the Court of Justice has been enlightening with regard to certain exceptions, such as parody,[150] quotation,[151] and research and private study,[152] and adopted a relatively flexible interpretation of certain criteria of permissibility or definitional standards.[153]

Although speech entitlements are express manifestations of fundamental human rights and vital for the promotion of creativity and accessibility, their legal nature and status against contractual overridability is not settled. Speech entitlements manifest defensive rules that align with the function of copyright as an instrument of communication and promote its objectives towards the development of new authorship and access to knowledge. A principle-based view would require looking at these defensive rules as mandatory against contractual or technological restriction, the reason being that these entitlements do not only ensure protection of fundamental freedoms, but they also rest on a mutual justificatory basis as copyright law itself. Normatively, copyright should not stop what it itself is all about. If we are to regard copyright as a right in speech, accommodating speech entitlements as entitlements that are compulsory against contractual override may enable not only a balanced approach but also the fulfilment of policy objectives that EU copyright aspires to promote. Declaring speech entitlements as mandatory against contractual restrictions is essential in order to ensure the objectives of innovation, creativity, investment, and production of new content, with a view to avoiding fragmentation of the Internal Market.

---

[149] *Johan Deckmyn and Another v Helena Vandersteen and Others*, Case C-201/13, 3 September 2014, ECLI:EU:C:2014:2132 (*Deckmyn*); contra: European Parliament, Committee on Legal Affairs, Draft Report on the Implementation of Directive 2001/29/EC of the European Parliament and of the Council of 22 May 2001 on the Harmonisation of Certain Aspects of Copyright and Related Rights in the Information Society, 15 January 2015, 2014/2256(INI), point 17.

[150] *Johan Deckmyn and Another v Helena Vandersteen and Others*, Case C-201/13, 3 September 2014, ECLI:EU:C:2014:2132 (*Deckmyn*).

[151] *Pelham GmbH, Moses Pelham, Martin Haas v Ralf Hütter, Florian Schneider-Esleben*, Case C-476/17, 29 July 2019, ECLI:EU:C:2019:624 (*Pelham*).

[152] *Technische Universität Darmstadt v Eugen Ulmer KG*, Case C-117/13, 11 September 2014, ECLI:EU:C:2014:2196 (*Technische Universität Darmstadt*).

[153] See e.g. the way in which the requirement that the source ought to be acknowledged has been interpreted in *Spiegel Online v Volker Beck*, Case C-516/17, 29 July 2019, ECLI:EU:C:2019:625 (*Spiegel Online*).

7

Public Policy Privileges

A substantial body of defences is primarily available to institutional users, such as educational establishments, libraries, and archives. In light of the advent of the Internet and mass digitization, the availability of defences has been enlarged through a set of legislative instruments, such as the Orphan Works Directive[1] and the Directive on Copyright in the Digital Single Market.[2] Public policy privileges are meant to make allowances for modern methods of teaching provision, such as online courses, distance learning, and cross-border education programmes, as well as exempt from infringement new methods of carrying out research, such as text mining and data analytics, and enable the extraction of value from the plethora of works that are currently out of print. Although the policy reason behind the expansion of available defences has been the promotion of growth in the educational and cultural sector, there is a strong public interest underpinning the very presence of these exceptions in the statute. This has to do with the promotion of a rigorous public domain, whereby certain works shall be made more accessible for users to use and re-use. Subject to examination in this chapter is the breadth of these permissible activities and their ability to accommodate modern online services, including also the defences available for uses made by public administration.

Introduction

Certain exceptions and limitations manifest the need to protect the public interest, as reflected in the policy objectives of advancing innovation, research, culture, or education. These so-called public policy privileges exist in recognition of the fact that the objectives of copyright law are subordinate to other interests and concerns. They serve as a balancing act between copyright law and broader public policy objectives. For instance, they aim to enable particular functions of institutional users,

---

[1] Directive (EU) 2012/28 of the European Parliament and of the Council of 25 October 2012 on Certain Permitted Uses of Orphan Works (Orphan Works Directive), OJ L 299/5, 27 October 2012.

[2] Directive (EU) 2019/790 of the European Parliament and of the Council of 17 April 2019 on Copyright and Related Rights in the Digital Single Market and amending Directives 96/9/EC and 2001/29/EC (Digital Single Market Directive), OJ L 130, 17 May 2019, 92–125.

Defences to Copyright Infringement. Stavroula Karapapa, Oxford University Press (2020). © Stavroula Karapapa.
DOI: 10.1093/oso/9780198795636.001.0001

such as library copying for preservation purposes or copying materials for educational purposes. By being sufficiently specific as to which uses are permitted, they allow third parties to make use of copyright-protected content—without authorial permission or license—whilst offering sufficient incentives to authors to create. Hence, a balancing act is one between the private interests of the copyright holders towards the enjoyment of the economic benefits arising from exclusive rights, and the public interest in having access to and making use of copyright-protected works.[3]

Unlike speech entitlements, which rest at the core of fundamental rights, public policy privileges may, or may not, have a fundamental human rights underpinning. When they do, these privileges are set to *enable* the exercise of fundamental rights and to an extent they make allowances for neighbouring activities stemming from the exercise of speech entitlements. Activities permitted due to the availability of a public policy privilege, however, do not overlap with the exercise of fundamental rights. For instance, educational exceptions and library privileges are set to enable the exercise of the right to education or the right to access information, and effectively the exercise of certain speech entitlements such as the exception for research and private study. To this end, it can be seen that public privileges and speech entitlements may have a partially overlapping or at least a neighbouring scope of application in that both types of defence may be raised in parallel. At the same time, public policy is a normative vision of values and goals, defined by the legislature, to be pursued prospectively, whereas fundamental rights refer to rights and freedoms considered essential to the functioning of a democratic society.

When advancing a public policy defence, the defendant does not attempt to offer an explanation as to why they committed an infringement. There is a rational defensibility of such conduct. The defendant does not have to justify the use on the basis of the public policy, social, and/or cultural goals that the use means to serve. It is sufficient that the use in question serves such goals (and is carried out within the framework of a particular exception or limitation). Relevant activities include exceptions and limitations available for the purposes of teaching and scientific research, specific activities—most notably preservation—carried out by libraries and archives, and other publicly accessible institutions. In all aforementioned cases, copyright plays second fiddle to more pressing concerns, which primarily include public policy objectives.

Modern technologies have expanded the means through which certain uses reflect that a public policy rationale can be carried out. This includes new methods of offering educational services, including distance learning and cross-border

---

[3] See in general Pamela Samuelson, 'Justifications for Copyright Limitations and Exceptions' in Ruth L. Okediji (ed.), *Copyright Law in an Age of Limitations and Exceptions* (New York: Cambridge University Press, 2017) 12; Anne Lepage, 'Overview of Exceptions and Limitations to Copyright in the Digital Environment', *E-Copyright Bulletin*, UNESCO, January–March (2003).

educational programmes, and online courses in general. It also includes new technological tools in order to preserve cultural heritage, such as those used in mass digitization initiatives that have the potential to extract value from various sources of content, including works that are orphaned or out-of-commerce. This is partly due to the fact that most legislative drafting at the level of public policy exceptions does not take place at a time that is contemporaneous to the advancement of a new copy-reliant technology, but occurs years after its emergence; in this regard there are times that copyright law may either be unable to accommodate a modern use of protected content or is not in a position to anticipate it.

Subject to discussion in this chapter are public policy privileges, their scope and legal nature, initiatives towards the expansion of the availability of the relevant defences, and possible overlap with other defensive rules, notably speech entitlements. In particular, subject to discussion are exceptions allowing: educational uses, including teaching, scientific research, and text mining and data analytics; library privileges, including document delivery services and privileges which enable cultural preservation; exceptions on orphan works and out of print works; and exceptions available for the purposes of public security.

Teaching, scientific research, and educational uses

Article 5(3)(a) of the Information Society Directive allows Member States to permit certain uses of a work or subject matter

> for the sole purpose of illustration for teaching or scientific research, as long as the source, including the author's name, is indicated, unless this turns out to be impossible and to the extent justified by the non-commercial purpose to be achieved.[4]

Exceptions for education and scientific research have a theoretical justification in the need to protect fundamental human rights. The Universal Declaration of Human Rights sets out the right 'freely to participate in the cultural life of the community, to enjoy the arts, and to share in scientific advancement and its benefits'.[5] A similar stipulation features in the International Covenant on Economic, Social, and Cultural Rights.[6] In both instruments, the right to education is laid down as a human right.[7] It is in this context that lawmakers have to approach the delicate

---

[4] The Article was revised via Art. 24(2)(b) of the Directive on Copyright in the Digital Single Market (Directive 2019/790) to indicate that it shall have no prejudice to the exceptions and limitations provided for in the Digital Single Market Directive.

[5] Universal Declaration of Human Rights (2015), Art. 27(1).

[6] International Covenant on Economic, Social and Cultural Rights (1966), Art. 15.

[7] Universal Declaration of Human Rights, Art. 26; International Covenant on Economic, Social and Cultural Rights, Art. 13.

balance between the interests of copyright holders to receive compensation for their creations and the public interest in having access to educational and scientific materials for the purposes of teaching, learning, research, and science. When encountering copyright law, the aforementioned fundamental rights are preserved through the exceptions which allow research and private study (Article 5(3)(n) of the Information Society Directive), discussed in Chapter 6. However, these exceptions are not fully inclusive of the set of activities that ought to be permitted in order to enable the exercise of the right to education and a list of further exceptions is made available.

The public interest in setting exceptions to enable education and scientific research has been recognized since the early discussions on the Berne Convention. As Numa Droz, President of the first Diplomatic Conference for the Berne Convention in 1884, observed at the time:

> Limitations on absolute protection are dictated, rightly in my opinion, by the public interest. The ever-growing need for mass instruction could never be met if there were no reservation of certain reproduction facilities, which at the same time should not degenerate into abuses.[8]

Striking a fair balance of rights and interests at the stage of introducing exceptions for educational and research purposes requires appreciation of the various interests of the parties involved; this poses additional challenges in light of emergent technologies and societal changes. As Dietz stressed in regard to exceptions and limitations for education and research, the question is political and it is difficult to draw a line between exclusive rights, remuneration rights, and free uses from a theoretical perspective.[9]

The international context

The 1886 text of the Berne Convention included a specific provision for exceptions in the context of education, which is now reflected in Article 10(2) of the Convention:

> It shall be a matter for legislation in the countries of the Union, and for special agreements existing or to be concluded between them, to permit the utilization,

---

[8] Numa Droz, quoted in Herman Cohen Jehoram, 'Some Principles of Exceptions to Copyright' in Peter Ganea, Christopher Heath, and Gerhard Schricker (eds), *Urheberrecht Gestern – Heute – Morgen (Writings in Honour of Adolf Dietz)* (Munich: Verlag C.H. Beck, 2001) 381, 382.

[9] Adolf Dietz, 'Private Study and Research; Disabilities; Education; Libraries and Archives' in Libby Baulch, Michael Green, and Mary Wyburn (eds), *ALAI Study Days – The Boundaries of Copyright: Its Proper Limitations and Exceptions* (Sydney: Australian Copyright Council, 1999) 95, 96.

to the publications, broadcasts, or sound or visual recordings for teaching, provided such utilization is compatible with fair practice.

What is more, the Appendix to the Berne Convention includes a system of granting compulsory licences for the translation of works for purposes of balancing copyright protection against the need to protect education and research within a human rights discourse.

Since 1886, however, when the Berne Convention was signed, the societal and technological context in which educational exceptions were drafted has evolved. Education as a societal value is vigorously protected and—in light of digitization and the Internet—access to information becomes essential. What is more, online methods of teaching provision, such as distance learning courses, and purely technological methods of research, such as text and data mining, signify the evolution of practices in teaching and research since the drafting of early copyright statutes.

Educational uses under EU copyright

Unlike other copyright exceptions, the copyright exception for education and research is multifaceted and it was very difficult—if at all possible—to include all activities likely to fall under its scope in one single provision. This is particularly true in light of modern forms of teaching delivery, e.g. via online platforms, through distance learning, and cross-border educational programmes. Whereas at the time that the Berne Convention was drafted it was possible to have just one exception for education covering the use of extracts in publications destined for educational or scientific purposes,[10] nowadays the framework for educational and scientific exceptions has become increasingly elaborate. Indeed, the purposes of education and research are reflected and embodied in various copyright exceptions. EU copyright includes a network of provisions that cover educational uses. These include various provisions within the Information Society Directive, such as illustration for teaching (Article 5(3)(a)), research and private study (Article 5(3)(n)), copying for private use (Article 5(2)(b)), reprographic copying (Article 5(2)(a)), and provisions related to uses available to educational establishments and libraries, including e.g. university libraries (Article 5(2)(c)). There are also the newly introduced exceptions on cross-border teaching activities, laid down in the Directive on Copyright in the Digital Single Market (Article 5). We have already discussed the exception on research and private study as a speech entitlement (Article 5(3)(n) of the Information Society Directive) in Chapter 6 . The exercise of this entitlement

---

[10] Berne Convention for the Protection of Literary and Artistic Works (hereinafter 'Berne Convention') (as amended on 28 September 1979), Art. 10(2).

is surrounded by a framework of neighbouring provisions that complement its scope, enable its applicability, and are set to ensure the broader contextualization of the exercise of both fundamental freedoms and related public policy objectives.[11]

One of the central exceptions to cover educational uses under EU copyright, included in Article 5(3)(a) of the Information Society Directive, concerns illustration for teaching purposes (and scientific research, discussed later in this chapter). This exception follows the model of Article 10 of the Berne Convention and Article 15(1)(d) of the Rome Convention.[12] The exception has a considerably narrow scope, even though distance learning seems to be acknowledged as part of the concept of teaching in Recital 42 of the Directive. It is premised on two conditions, namely that the source shall be acknowledged and that the use is non-commercial. The latter condition is an important limitation to the scope of the exceptions included in Article 5(3)(a). This limitation increases the complexity of the relevant exceptions as it raises the question of what qualifies as non-commercial teaching (and scientific research). Indeed, many teaching—and research—related activities are not entirely free and take place in exchange for some form of remuneration, often conditional on the availability of licenses. This means that if a strict interpretation of non-commerciality is accepted, including both direct and indirect commercial purposes, the exceptions of Article 5(3)(a) will remain too limited to have a meaningful scope. It would be plausible to exclude from their scope directly and obviously commercial activities, such as training courses for professionals and in-house research for the creation of new products, the latter often taking place in research and development departments of corporate entities. It is unclear whether research funded by a public body or other third party should also be covered by the exception, but the applicability of the exception would arguably be defeated if such copying was meant to be excluded from the scope of permissibility.

The exception has been subject to discussion in light of its appropriate scope for the needs of the twenty-first century where new methods of teaching provision, such as distance learning courses, are available. Indeed, discussion on the appropriate scope of copyright exceptions in the recent reform of EU copyright that took place in the context of the Digital Single Market Directive is intertwined with a theoretical framework that supports the protection of human rights. In particular, the 2015 Draft Report on the implementation of the Information Society

---

[11] Besides the educational exceptions listed in the aforementioned Directives, a variety of provisions enabling educational uses are also available in the various Member States. In the United Kingdom, for example, until recently fair dealing did not cover education as such but did apply to relevant objectives, such as research or private study, criticism or review. The UK provisions on fair dealing have been recently expanded to include educational purposes (although the interpretation of fair dealing may impact on their scope). See The Copyright and Rights in Performances (Research, Education, Libraries, and Archives) Regulations 2014, 2014 No. 1372, Regulation 4 (amending the Copyright, Designs and Patents Act (CDPA) 1988).

[12] Rome Convention for the Protection of Performers, Producers of Phonograms and Broadcasting Organizations (1961).

Directive[13] brings forward the protection of the right to education that features in the European Charter of Fundamental Rights and calls

> for a broad exception for research and education purposes, which should cover not only educational establishments but any kind of educational or research activity, including non-formal education.[14]

The need to modernize copyright in the area of education and research is also reflected in the resolution from the European Parliament which calls for an exception for research and education purposes,[15] and a European Commission Communication announcing further legislative work on exceptions related to education and research.[16] These policy initiatives have resulted in the recommendation to introduce new exceptions for the educational sector that are reflective of novel methods of providing educational services and feature in Article 5 of the Directive on Copyright in the Digital Single Market,[17] discussed later in this chapter.

Illustration for teaching

In line with the international framework, the exception for the purposes of teaching illustration under Article 5(3)(a) of the Information Society Directive permits proportionate uses accompanied by an acknowledgement of the work or subject matter used. It also includes uses of works and other protected subject matter in both face-to-face and distance learning. According to Recital 42 of the Directive:

> When applying the exception or limitation for non-commercial educational and scientific research purposes, including distance learning, the non-commercial nature of the activity in question should be determined by that activity as such.

---

[13] Committee on Legal Affairs, Report on the Implementation of Directive 2001/29/EC of the European Parliament and of the Council of 22 May 2001 on the Harmonisation of Certain Aspects of Copyright and Related Rights in the Information Society (2014/2256(INI)), 24 June 2015.

[14] Committee on Legal Affairs, Draft Report on the Implementation of Directive 2001/29/EC of the European Parliament and of the Council of 22 May 2001 on the Harmonisation of Certain Aspects of Copyright and Related Rights in the Information Society (2014/2256(INI)), 15 January 2015, 6, point 19.

[15] European Parliament, Resolution of 9 July 2015 on the Implementation of Directive 2001/29/EC of the European Parliament and of the Council of 22 May 2001 on the Harmonisation of Certain Aspects of Copyright and Related Rights in the Information Society (2014/2256(INI)), P8_TA-PROV(2015)0273, paragraph 50.

[16] European Commission, Communication from the Commission to the European Parliament, the Council, the European Economic and Social Committee and the Committee of the Regions, Towards a Modern, more European Copyright Framework, 9 December 2015, COM (2015) 626 final.

[17] European Parliament, Copyright in the Digital Single Market, Amendments adopted by the European Parliament on 12 September 2018 on the Proposal for a Directive of the European Parliament and of the Council on Copyright in the Digital Single Market (COM (2016)0593 – C8-0383/2016 – 2016/0280(COD))1.

The organizational structure and the means of funding of the establishment concerned are not the decisive factors in this respect.

It seems that the exception is broad enough to include acts carried out by and on behalf of teachers and students at all levels of education to the extent that these acts are connected to clarifying points made in the delivery or in the examination of formal educational courses. Examples include the reproduction, communication, or distribution of protected materials to students as part of a lecture, or as teaching materials, or a discussion which exemplifies aspects of the teaching curriculum. The direct link between the educational purpose of the use and the copying and communication of the work to a specified portion of the public, i.e. a student cohort, is a useful sorting tool when determining which uses fall under the scope of the exception and which should not. This criterion is in line with the principle of strict interpretation of exceptions, whilst ensuring that exceptions shall be construed on the basis of the purpose that they mean to serve.

However, the exception is so broad as to cover online teaching provision and cross-border uses of copyright works for educational purposes. This is an issue that has been addressed by the Directive on Copyright in the Digital Single Market.

Online teaching and cross-border educational services

As the Directive on Copyright in the Digital Single Market acknowledges in Recitals 3 and 5, the emergence of modern technologies has affected the educational sector, enabling cross-border uses, online teaching provision, and new modes of copyright use. Indeed, digital technologies in the fields of research and education, and also in the context of preservation of cultural heritage, enable new types of use that were not addressed by EU copyright before the launch of the Directive on Copyright in the Digital Single Market. The increasing importance and relevance of online educational and research activities in the digital environment was addressed in Article 5 of the Directive on Copyright in the Digital Single Market, which expressly addresses instances of distance learning courses. Section 1 of the Article reads that

> Member States shall provide for an exception or limitation to the rights provided for in Article 5(a), (b), (d), and (e) and Article 7(1) of Directive 96/9/EC, Articles 2 and 3 of Directive 2001/29/EC, Article 4(1) of Directive 2009/24/EC, and Article 15(1) of this Directive in order to allow the digital use of works and other subject matter for the sole purpose of illustration for teaching, to the extent justified by the non-commercial purpose to be achieved, on condition that such use:
> (a) takes place under the responsibility of an educational establishment, on its premises or at other venues, or through a secure electronic environment

accessible only by the educational establishment's pupils or students and teaching staff; and

(b) is accompanied by the indication of the source, including the author's name, unless this turns out to be impossible.

The beneficiaries of the aforementioned exception are expected to be all educational establishments offering primary, secondary, vocational, and higher education to the extent that they pursue their educational activity for a non-commercial purpose. Cultural heritage institutions pursuing an educational objective and involved in teaching activities can also be deemed as educational establishments for the purposes of Article 5(1), and thus benefit from the exception.[18] All aforementioned institutions shall benefit from the exception to the extent that their teaching and learning activities are carried out in a 'secure electronic environment'. Such an environment is defined by Recital 22 of the Directive as a

> digital teaching and learning environments access to which is limited to an educational establishment's teaching staff and to pupils or students enrolled in a study programme, in particular through appropriate authentication procedures including password-based authentication.

Another condition of the exception allowing the use of works and other subject matter in digital and cross-border teaching activities—which aspires to enlarge the scope of other available exceptions for educational purposes—is that it covers non-commercial teaching only. This means that its application would be limited to rather specific instances of online teaching, such as MOOC courses or compulsory online training carried out within educational establishments. It would not cover, however, other cases of online delivery of educational courses, such as distance learning programmes offered by various higher education institutions that charge tuition fees. Recital 20 of the Directive clarifies that the organizational structure and the means of funding of an educational establishment should not be the decisive factors in determining whether the activity is non-commercial in nature.[19] In light of the principle of strict interpretation of copyright exceptions and limitations, it is not clear how this Recital contributes to the concept of commercial or non-commercial use. Should the exception be understood as covering non-commercial use only in a strict sense, the scope of the defence becomes unrealistically narrow, excluding, for instance, indirect commercial advantage (such as the increased goodwill or reputation to an establishment offering a free course), which

---

[18] Digital Single Market Directive (Directive 2019/790), Recital 20.

[19] Identical guidance is offered in Recital 42 of the Information Society Directive (Directive 2001/29/EC) in explaining the scope of non-commerciality in the context of the teaching and scientific research exceptions of Art. 5(3)(b).

would arguably have a significant impact on the exception and severely limit its scope to the extent of rendering it meaningless. This is particularly so in light of the fact that the exception may also be subject to an obligation to pay rightsholders fair compensation.[20] Member States are indeed given the option to set in place mechanisms of fair compensation for the harm that rightsholders suffer as a result of the use of the works in the context of the proposed copyright exception. This is likely to enlarge the so-called levy systems already available in most EU Member States in the context of other exceptions, such as private copying.[21]

Non-commerciality is just one limitation to the scope of the exception for illustration for teaching purposes. A further limitation is offered in Section 2 of Article 5, according to which Member States may exclude specific types of works or other subject matter to the extent that adequate licenses authorizing the activities permitted under the exception are easily available in the market, giving prominence to the availability of licensing mechanisms. Such works and relevant subject matter include material that is primarily intended for the educational market or sheet music. For purposes of clarity, Section 3 explains that in the context of online teaching, the use of works and other subject matter through secure electronic environments shall be deemed to occur solely in the Member State where the educational establishment is established.

Recital 21 indicates that the exception covers digital uses of works and other subject matter to support, enrich, or complement teaching and includes related learning activities. It shall be granted as long as the work or other subject matter used indicates the source, including the authors' name, unless that turns out to be impossible for reasons of practicability. Another condition for the permissibility of the exception is its purpose specificity and the necessity principle in that the relevant activities should be aimed at teaching and learning activities carried out under the responsibility of educational establishments and should be limited to what is necessary for the purpose of such activities.[22] Recitals 23 and 24 of the Directive outline the conditions under which Member States will be able to provide systems which ensure that rightsholders shall be fairly remunerated for the activities falling under the exception and the conditions under which they will be able to decide to subject the exception, in full or in part, to the availability of adequate licenses.

Albeit considerably narrow in terms of applicable scope, the exception allowing uses of works and other subject matter in digital and cross-border teaching activities is a first step towards recognition of the need to address emergent trends in the educational sector and the delivery of online courses. Importantly, the exception is mandatory against contractual override by virtue of Article 7(1) and, in addition,

---

[20] Digital Single Market Directive (Directive 2019/790), Art. 5(4).
[21] However, established rules of EU copyright indicate that if harm is minimal, no fair compensation is due to the rightholders.
[22] Digital Single Market Directive (Directive 2019/790), Recital 21.

Member States ought to take appropriate measures to ensure that rightsholders make available to the beneficiary of the cross-border teaching exception the *means* of benefiting from it, to the extent necessary for the purposes of benefiting from the exception and on condition that the beneficiary has legal access to the protected work or subject matter concerned.[23] This has the effect that any contractual restrictions on the scope of the exception shall be unenforceable.

Scientific research

As with the exception concerning illustration for teaching purposes, there is no case law from the Court of Justice on the meaning of scientific research under Article 5(3)(a) of the Information Society Directive. The exception is subject to the same conditions as the exception on teaching available under this Article, namely that the source should be acknowledged and the use should be carried out for non-commercial purposes.

There is a likely overlap with the exception on research and private study available under Article 5(3)(n) of the Information Society Directive, discussed in Chapter 6. In understanding what is covered by scientific research in this context, a reasonable possibility that aligns with the usual meaning of the term 'research' is that the exception covers proportionate uses of works or other subject matter for the purposes of undertaking a systematic investigation into a particular topic with a view to test a hypothesis or reach a conclusion.

A liberal and broad interpretation was adopted in Canada, where the Supreme Court found in *SOCAN v Bell Canada*[24] that making available online previews of musical works, with a view to enable Internet users to decide whether to buy the full copy amounted to fair dealing with the works for the purposes of research. The court gave the term 'research' a broad meaning in that it did not require the publication of research outputs. According to the court, the fair dealing exception 'must not be interpreted restrictively and "research" must be given a large and liberal interpretation'.[25] Interestingly, the court stressed that the purpose of 'research' should be evaluated from the perspective of the consumer as the ultimate user, not the online service provider. This would likely not be the case in the European Union, however, where the purpose of copyright law is to ensure a high level of protection for authors in respect of their works,[26] and where exceptions are subject to strict interpretation. In particular, concerning the interpretation of exceptions

---

[23] According to Art. 7(2) of the Directive on Copyright in the Digital Single Market, (Directive 2019/790), Art. 6(4) of the Information Society Directive (Directive 2001/29/EC) applies to the text mining exception of Art. 3.

[24] *SOCAN v Bell Canada* (2012) SCC 36 (Canada).

[25] Ibid., [51].

[26] Information Society Directive (Directive 2001/29/EC), Recitals 4 and 9.

and limitations to copyright, it is not clear whether this should take place from the perspective of copyright users in general or, specifically, from the viewpoint of the defendant. EU case law indicates that the perspective taken into consideration is that of the beneficiary of an exception, which is often the defendant in relevant proceedings.

Scientific research in the digital context may be carried out through text and data mining techniques, although it is not likely that the Information Society Directive made allowance for this kind of research. Such techniques include text and image analysis, information extraction, automatic translation, and indexing and search.[27] Because copying is involved, activities of electronic processing of copyright works become legally relevant and significant from the perspective of copyright law.[28] These kinds of uses have been directly addressed in the Directive on Copyright in the Digital Single Market. In the context of the permissibility of these kinds of copyright uses as part of scientific research, the Directive defines scientific research as covering both the natural sciences and the human sciences.

Text and data mining

Until recently, there was no copyright exception to cover reproductions made for the purposes of text mining and data analytics at the EU level. It was the United Kingdom that first introduced such an exception after a long-lasting review of its copyright system,[29] followed by Ireland,[30] and France.[31] Discussions at the national[32] and the EU level reflected both the need and the policy desire to introduce a copyright exception for text mining and data analytics. Indeed, the Directive

---

[27] For a critical discussion see Pamela Samuelson, 'Google Book Search and the Future of Books in Cyberspace' (2009) 94 *Minnesota Law Review* 1308, 1353–4.

[28] Maurizio Borghi and Stavroula Karapapa, *Copyright and Mass Digitization: A Cross-Jurisdictional Perspective* (Oxford: Oxford University Press, 2013) 45 et seq.

[29] See s. 29A of the CDPA 1988 (introduced by Copyright and Rights in Performances (Research, Education, Libraries and Archives) Regulations 2014); Ian Hargreaves, Digital Opportunity: A Review of Intellectual Property and Growth, An Independent Report (May 2011).

[30] Copyright and Other Intellectual Property Law Provisions Act 2019, No. 19 of 2019, available at <https://data.oireachtas.ie/ie/oireachtas/act/2019/19/eng/enacted/a1919.pdf>, accessed 11 November 2019, Art. 14 requesting the inclusion of Art. 53A in the Copyright Act; Copyright and Other Intellectual Property Law Provisions Bill 2018 as passed by Dáil Éireann, No. 31b of 2018, Art. 13.

[31] Law for a Digital Republic (Loi pour une république numérique) 2016.

[32] See e.g. the Irish Copyright and Other Intellectual Property Law Provisions Act 2019, No. 19 of 2019, available at <https://data.oireachtas.ie/ie/oireachtas/act/2019/19/eng/enacted/a1919.pdf>, accessed 11 November 2019, Art. 14:

> 53A. (1) Subject to subsection (3), the making of a copy of a work by a person who has lawful access to the work does not infringe copyright in the work where the copy is—
>
> (a) made in order that the person may carry out a computational analysis of anything in the work for the sole purpose of research for a non-commercial purpose, and
> (b) accompanied by a sufficient acknowledgement.

on Copyright in the Digital Single Market exempts text and data mining from infringement. Article 2(2) of the Directive defines 'text and data mining' as:

> any automated analytical technique aimed at analysing text and data in digital form in order to generate information which includes but is not limited to patterns, trends, and correlations

As explained in Recital 8 of the Directive, text and data mining enables 'the processing of large amounts of information with a view to gaining new knowledge and discovering new trends possible'. Indeed, this kind of scientific research can result in the development of knowledge that is not readily available in the works being mined—at least not readily available by human reading, e.g. it can unveil an association between a drug and a side effect, which may not be expressly stated in any of the mined works. To an extent, text mining and data analytics can be understood as an activity that electronically substitutes human reading.[33] These technologies consist of the electronic analysis of large amounts of information, including copyright works, allowing researchers to discover patterns, trends, and other useful information that usual 'human' reading cannot detect.

Text mining and data analytics have gained momentum in the era of mass digitization.[34] As acknowledged in Recital 8 of the Digital Single Market Directive, '[whilst] text and data mining technologies are prevalent across the digital economy ... there is widespread acknowledgment that text and data mining can, in particular, benefit the research community and, in so doing, support innovation'. During discussions concerning the introduction of a data analytics exception in

(2) A copy made under subsection (1) of a work which was, at the time when the copy was made, available without a restriction as to its access does not infringe copyright, and whether or not that work continues to be so available after that time.

(3) Where a copy of a work has been made under subsection (1) by a person, the copyright in the work is infringed where the copy—

    (a) is transferred to any other person, except where the transfer is authorised by the copyright owner, or

    (b) is used for any purpose other than the purpose referred to in subsection (1)(a).

(4) Without prejudice to section 374, nothing in Part VII shall be construed as operating to prevent a person from undertaking an act permitted by this section.

(5) Without prejudice to the generality of section 52(1), where the publication of the results of a computational analysis referred to in subsection (1)(a) of a copy of a work includes the reproduction of extracts from the work, such inclusion shall constitute inclusion in an incidental manner referred to in section 52(1) if the extracts are not more than are reasonably necessary to explain, or to assist in explaining, the results of the analysis.

Note that the Bill also includes relevant provisions with regard to performances to be inserted as ss 225A to 225D.

[33] Maurizio Borghi and Stavroula Karapapa, *Copyright and Mass Digitization: A Cross-Jurisdictional Perspective* (Oxford: Oxford University Press, 2013) 51 et seq.

[34] Maurizio Borghi and Stavroula Karapapa, *Copyright and Mass Digitization: A Cross-Jurisdictional Perspective* (Oxford: Oxford University Press, 2013) 45 et seq.; Irini Stamatoudi, 'Text and Data Mining' in Irini Stamatoudi (ed.), *New Developments in EU and International Copyright Law* (Alphen aan den Rijn: Kluwer Law International, 2016) 251.

the United Kingdom, the benefits of the activity to the fields of life sciences and pharmaceutical research were at the top of the agenda, even though there are other fields that can benefit from this kind of research, such as the humanities. At the EU level too, the exception on text and data mining is meant to broadly cover 'innovation and scientific research', the latter being defined to cover 'both the natural sciences and the human sciences'.[35]

The main legal problem that arises by reference to text mining and data analytics is that despite the prevalent role of these technologies in the digital economy, the widespread acknowledgement of their benefits to research and innovation, and relevance in artificial intelligence, there is legal uncertainty on the extent to which these activities can be lawfully carried out without authorization. As acknowledged in Recital 8 of the Directive, research organizations, including universities and research institutions, were until recently confronted with legal uncertainty as to the extent to which they could perform text and data mining of protected content without seeking authorization for each and every copyright-protected work. The reason is that these technologies may involve acts protected by copyright and may also touch upon the protection offered by the *sui generis* database right, meaning that authorization from the copyright holders is necessary unless research is carried out in relation to mere facts or data that are not protected by copyright. As discussed in Chapter 3, the purpose of copyright has never been to restrict the use of the ideas, facts, and information underlying a work. This copyright principle is reiterated in the Directive on Copyright in the Digital Single Market and has also been firmly acknowledged in *Meltwater*, a UK case concerning Internet browsing. In this case, the Supreme Court found that

> Broadly speaking, it is an infringement to make or distribute copies or adaptations of a protected work. Merely viewing or reading it is not an infringement.[36]

However, text and data mining often operates on the basis of copying large volumes of copyright-protected works and, in this light where it is not expressly permitted by the law, it amounts to infringement unless expressly authorized. Indeed, the bigger the volume of works, the more effective data analysis will be. Seeking individual licenses from various publishers may not be feasible, or may be time consuming and cost prohibitive. This would go against the goals of enhancing research, innovation, and access to information, and also the production of new knowledge based on pre-existing works. The exception means to address the legal

---

[35] Digital Single Market Directive (Directive 2019/790), Recital 12.
[36] *Public Relations Consultants Association Ltd v The Newspaper Licensing Agency Ltd* [2013] UKSC 18 (UK).

uncertainty that research organizations may face and challenges in clearing individual licenses for large volumes of content, which may be extremely difficult and prohibitively costly.

The EU exception for text and data mining

The Directive on Copyright in the Digital Single Market aspires to lay down a modernized system of exceptions and limitations, whereby researchers will benefit from a clearer legal framework on the use of innovative text and data mining research tools. It therefore includes two exceptions on text and data mining, both of which are compulsory for Member States to implement and are included in Articles 3 and 4 of the Directive.

Article 3 of the Directive, entitled 'Text and data mining for the purposes of scientific research' reads

1. Member States shall provide for an exception to the rights provided for in Article 5(a) and Article 7(1) of Directive 96/9/EC, Article 2 of Directive 2001/29/EC, and Article 15(1) of this Directive for reproductions and extractions made by research organisations and cultural heritage institutions in order to carry out, for the purposes of scientific research, text and data mining of works or other subject matter to which they have lawful access.

2. Copies of works or other subject matter made in compliance with paragraph 1 shall be stored with an appropriate level of security and may be retained for the purposes of scientific research, including for the verification of research results.

3. Rightholders shall be allowed to apply measures to ensure the security and integrity of the networks and databases where the works or other subject matter are hosted. Such measures shall not go beyond what is necessary to achieve that objective.

4. Member States shall encourage rightholders, research organisations, and cultural heritage institutions to define commonly agreed best practices concerning the application of the obligation and of the measures referred to in paragraphs 2 and 3 respectively.

The text and data mining exception for purposes of scientific research allows the reproduction and extraction of copyright-protected works from the databases of research organizations and cultural heritage institutions without a requirement to clear the permission of the relevant rightsholders or an obligation to pay any form of compensation. The EU text mining exception applies to acts of reproduction covered by the Information Society Directive and the Database Directive. The wording of the exception may be indicative of the desire to set limits on the scope of the reproduction rights provided for in these Directives. In this sense, the exception could be read as going beyond the introduction of a supervening rule and may be viewed as scope limitation and an organic limit to exclusive rights.

Supportive of this claim is the fact that the exception is expressly laid down as compulsory against any contractual restrictions, but rightsholders are allowed to apply measures to ensure the security and integrity of the networks where the works or other subject matter are hosted. Database owners often condition access to a database on the acceptance of terms and conditions that restrict the use of certain activities, such as text and data analysis. It would be interesting to see how this will be reconciled with the jurisprudence of the Court of Justice in *Ryanair*, examined earlier.[37] As we have seen, in this case the Court of Justice held that when a database does not receive protection by copyright or the 'database right', its owner can freely determine the contractual conditions of the use of the database:

> If the author of a database decides to authorise the use of its database or a copy thereof, he has the option ... to regulate that use by an agreement concluded with a lawful user which sets out ... the 'purposes and the way' of using that database or a copy thereof.[38]

It is expressly stated that measures ensuring the security and integrity of the networks where the works or other subject matter are hosted ought to abide by the proportionality principle in that they should not go beyond what is necessary to achieve the objective of network security. Moving a step forward, the Directive on Copyright in the Digital Single Market imposes an obligation on Member States to encourage rightholders and research organizations to define commonly agreed best practices concerning the application of technological measures enhancing the security of networks. An interesting aspect of the exception is the fact that it is not conditional upon the non-commercial nature of the activities involved, unlike its UK counterpart, discussed later in this Chapter. A justification for this may be that UK provision was formulated at the borders of what the then EU legislative norms enabled, and the discussions before the launch of the UK exceptions centred on how to ensure its compatibility with EU copyright.

An aspect that the exception does not address (and is equally not dealt with by the text mining exception of Article 4) is the possible access restriction to databases by way of technological measures impeding access to a database and disabling extraction of its contents. In such cases, researchers engaged in text and data mining may not only need to gain access to the contents, but may additionally need technical support in order to engage in computational analysis.

Interestingly, harm in the context of the text and data mining exception, because of the nature and scope of the exception (which is limited to entities carrying

---

[37] *Ryanair Ltd v PR Aviation BV*, Case C-30/14, 15 January 2015, ECLI:EU:C:2015:10 (*Ryanair*).
[38] Ibid., [43].

out scientific research), is deemed to be minimal and hence does not justify the introduction of a requirement to recompense copyright holders.[39] The exception is limited in scope in that the beneficiaries of the exception should have lawful access to the data. Recital 14 of the Directive explains that lawful access in this context means access based on an open access policy or through contractual arrangements between rightsholders and research organizations or cultural heritage institutions. This includes subscriptions or other lawful means of accessing content and it is also expected to cover access to content that is freely available online.

The beneficiaries of the exception include universities and other research organizations, as well as cultural heritage institutions. It is expected that public libraries and not-for-profit public establishments such as public hospitals will also benefit from the exception. Recital 11 of the Directive specifies that research organizations should also benefit from the exception when their research activities are carried out within the framework of public-private partnerships. It is there explained that 'while research organisations and cultural heritage institutions should continue to be the beneficiaries of that exception, they should also be able to rely on their private partners for carrying out text and data mining, including by using their technological tools'.

Importantly, the exception is mandatory against contractual override by virtue of Article 7(1) and, in addition, Member States ought to take appropriate measures to ensure that rightsholders make available to the beneficiary of the text mining exceptions the means of benefiting from those exceptions, to the extent necessary for the purposes of benefiting from those exceptions, and on condition that the beneficiary has legal access to the protected work or subject matter concerned.[40] This strengthens the applicability of the relevant defensive rule in that it is not within the discretion of the copyright holders to reduce its scope through contractual means.

Article 4, entitled exception or limitation for text and data mining, introduces an exception with a seemingly broader scope. It reads:

1. Member States shall provide for an exception or limitation to the rights provided for in Article 5(a) and Article 7(1) of Directive 96/9/EC, Article 2 of Directive 2001/29/EC, Article 4(1)(a) and (b) of Directive 2009/24/EC, and Article 15(1) of this Directive for reproductions and extractions of lawfully accessible works and other subject matter for the purposes of text and data mining.

2. Reproductions and extractions made pursuant to paragraph 1 may be retained for as long as is necessary for the purposes of text and data mining.

---

[39]   Information Society Directive (Directive 2001/29/EC), Recital 17.

[40]   According to Art. 7(2) of the Directive on Copyright in the Digital Single Market (Directive 2019/790), Art. 6(4) of the Information Society Directive (Directive 2001/29/EC) applies to the text mining exception of Art. 3.

3. The exception or limitation provided for in paragraph 1 shall apply on condition that the use of works and other subject matter referred to in that paragraph has not been expressly reserved by their rightholders in an appropriate manner, such as machine-readable means in the case of content made publicly available online.

4. This Article shall not affect the application of Article 3 of this Directive.

This exception too is mandatory for Member States to implement, unlike draft versions preceding it,[41] but is broader in scope when compared to its sister exception provided for in Article 3. First, its scope is not limited to the purposes of scientific research indicating that it can, in principle, cover any kind of text and data mining, even on a commercial scale. Second, in addition to the rights of reproduction and extraction as envisaged in the relevant provisions of the Information Society Directive and the Database Directive (that are also covered by Article 3), it also covers the reproduction right as available in the Computer Programs Directive, including both the temporary or permanent reproduction of computer programs and the translation, adaptation, arrangement, and any other alteration of a computer program, and the reproduction of the results thereof. Finally, the exception of Article 4 is made available to any entity, i.e. is not limited to specified institutional beneficiaries. Private institutions, such as corporate entities, may also benefit from the exception as its aim is to encourage innovation in the private sector.[42]

However, despite its seemingly broader scope compared to the text and data mining exception of Article 3, the exception relies on an 'opt-out' mechanism. According to Article 3(3), rightsholders may be exempted from the application of the exception on condition that they have opted-out in an 'appropriate manner' from the activities that the exception permits. This is a rather uncommon stipulation for a defensive rule and is to be found nowhere in EU copyright: a mandatory exception is left to the discretion of copyright holders to determine whether to implement it in national law or not. To some extent, this wording resembles the

---

[41] See e.g. EU Parliament, Proposal for a Directive of the European Parliament and of the Council on Copyright in the Digital Single Market (SWD(2016) 301) (SWD(2016) 302), COM (2016) 593 final, 2016/0280 (COD), Brussels, 14 September 2016, Art. 3a. This Article reads as follows:

1. Without prejudice to Article 3 of this Directive, Member States may provide for an exception or a limitation to the rights provided for in Article 2 of Directive 2001/29/EC, Articles 5(a) and 7(1) of Directive 96/9/EC and Article 11(1) of this Directive for reproductions and extractions of lawfully accessible works and other subject-matter that form a part of the process of text and data mining, provided that the use of works and other subject matter referred to therein has not been expressly reserved by their rightholders, including by machine readable means.

2. Reproductions and extractions made pursuant to paragraph 1 shall not be used for purposes other than text and data mining.

3. Member States may continue to provide text and data mining exceptions in accordance with point (a) of Article 5 (3) of Directive 2001/29/EC.

[42] Information Society Directive (Directive 2001/29/EC), Recital 18.

assertion requirement of the paternity right as it features in UK copyright law,[43] but in the context of the text mining exception of Article 4 it is likely that the application of the exception will be rendered largely ineffective, especially by reference to large databases of copyright-protected content.

An interesting question that emerges by reference to both of the text and data mining exceptions, but particularly the one embodied in Article 4, concerns the extent to which beneficiaries of the exceptions can disable other parties from mining outputs produced on the basis of the exception(s), particularly by making use of Article 4(3). A principle-based view would be that copyright exceptions allowing the generation of new content should have a viral effect in the sense that those who benefited from an exception should enable the exercise of the same exception by reference to the content they produced. This would be in line with principles of property law and concepts of ownership according to which the privatization of public access is not permitted.

The EU text and data mining exceptions clearly demonstrate the policy desire to enable research and innovation both in the public but also in the private sector. Their efficacy is to be tested in practice, particularly so by reference to the exception of Article 4, the exercise of which is left at the discretion of copyright holders. However, it is expected that the fact that the exceptions cover commercial research will be a positive development that may enable the policy objectives that the exceptions mean to serve and conform with the purpose of copyright protection as a facilitator of the generation of new knowledge.

Examples of defensive rules allowing the text and data mining of copyright-protected works that preceded the Directive are offered notably from three EU jurisdictions: the United Kingdom, Ireland, and France. Because all three of these national examples predate the Directive, they introduced 'hesitant' defences in that they permit only non-commercial text mining and set limitations on the set of beneficiaries that can invoke the relevant exceptions. In light of the new EU text mining exceptions, it is likely that the national laws will have to be revised, and possibly be expanded, to reflect more appropriately the dicta of the Directive. The national provisions, however, offer an indicative outline of the historical trend towards the launch of the EU text mining exceptions and the ways in which the overly broad scope of the reproduction right in the Information Society and Database Directives served as a norm for the national enlargement of the breadth of permissible uses.

The UK data analytics exception
The UK exception on data analytics was introduced in the 2014 copyright reform and was bound by the then-norms of EU copyright, having a correspondingly

---

[43] Copyright, Designs and Patents Act (CDPA) 1988, s. 78.

narrow scope. It is a pioneering provision, however, as it was the first exception (at least within the European Union)[44] to make allowance for text and data mining. Section 29A of the Copyright, Designs and Patents Act (CDPA) provides an exception that allows researchers to make copies of works 'for text and data analysis'. Where a user has lawful access to a work, they can make a copy of it with the view to carrying out a computational analysis of anything recorded in the work. An interesting aspect of the UK provision is that the activities that the defence covers cannot be ruled out by contract and any contractual terms purporting to restrict or prohibit acts permitted under the exception are unenforceable. In particular, Section 29A reads

(1) The making of a copy of a work by a person who has lawful access to the work does not infringe copyright in the work provided that—
   (a) the copy is made in order that a person who has lawful access to the work may carry out a computational analysis of anything recorded in the work for the sole purpose of research for a non-commercial purpose, and
   (b) the copy is accompanied by a sufficient acknowledgement (unless this would be impossible for reasons of practicality or otherwise).
(2) Where a copy of a work has been made under this section, copyright in the work is infringed if—
   (a) the copy is transferred to any other person, except where the transfer is authorised by the copyright owner, or
   (b) the copy is used for any purpose other than that mentioned in subsection (1)(a), except where the use is authorised by the copyright owner.
(3) If a copy made under this section is subsequently dealt with—
   (a) it is to be treated as an infringing copy for the purposes of that dealing, and
   (b) if that dealing infringes copyright, it is to be treated as an infringing copy for all subsequent purposes.
(4) In subsection (3) 'dealt with' means sold or let for hire, or offered or exposed for sale or hire.
(5) To the extent that a term of a contract purports to prevent or restrict the making of a copy which, by virtue of this section, would not infringe copyright, that term is unenforceable.

As acknowledged in Hargreaves' *Review of Intellectual Property and Growth* of May 2011,[45] which recommended the introduction of an exception allowing text and data mining into UK law, 'that these new uses happen to fall within the scope of

---

[44] See e.g. Japan Copyright Act, Art. 47(7) (permitting reproduction 'for the purpose of information analysis by using a computer').

[45] Ian Hargreaves, *Digital Opportunity: A Review of Intellectual Property and Growth, An Independent Report* (May 2011).

copyright Regulation is essentially a side effect of how copyright has been defined, rather than being directly relevant to what copyright is supposed to protect'.[46]

The United Kingdom has limited the scope of the defence in numerous ways, including the requirement that the source ought to be acknowledged, unless this turns out to be practically impossible. In order for the exception to apply, the computational analysis must be for the purpose of non-commercial research and the copy should be accompanied by sufficient acknowledgment (unless this is practically impossible). These are significant limitations to the scope of the exception and this has been partly attributed to the then-copyright framework at the EU level, which at the time did not make allowance for text mining, but was also subject to limitations emerging from the broad scope of the reproduction right of copyright materials and databases. This would prove problematic in cases where the non-commercial nature of the activity could not be clearly ascertained, such as research carried out in educational establishments receiving funding from a public body.

The instances where the defence is meant to apply are limited to acts of copying required by *human* researchers to carry out research, instead of automated extraction and use of large volumes of text and information. Fairness in the context of fair dealing shall be difficult to establish in cases of wholesale copying of materials for purposes of automated processing and large volume computational analysis.[47] This is so despite the UK Government's acknowledgement of the added value of computational research[48] and of the fact that the larger the volume of information, the better the research results shall be.

The UK exception on text and data analysis has been laid down as mandatory against contractual and technological restrictions imposed by copyright holders and, according to paragraph 5 of section 29A, 'to the extent that a term of a contract purports to prevent or restrict the making of a copy which, by virtue of this section, would not infringe copyright, that term is unenforceable'.

The Irish data analytics exception
Following the UK example and the broader impetus for an EU-wide exception on text and data analysis, the Irish government introduced a relevant exception into

---

[46] Ibid., 47.

[47] See e.g. *Hubbart v Vosper* [1972] 2 QB 84 (UK); *Zamacois v Douville & Marchande* [1943] 2 DLR 257 (Canada).

[48] See in this regard HM Government, Modernising Copyright: A Modern, Robust and flexible Framework, Government response to consultation on copyright exceptions and clarifying copyright law, December 2012, at 37:

> The copying involved in text and data analytics is a necessary part of a technological process, and is unlikely to substitute for the work in question (such as a journal article). It is therefore unlikely that permitting mining for research will of itself negatively affect the market for or value of copyright works. Indeed, it may be that removing restrictions from analytic technologies would increase the value of articles to researchers.

Irish law in 2019.[49] According to the exception, the acts permitted shall include non-commercial text and data analysis, which would be in line with the research exception included in Article 5(3)(a) of the Information Society Directive. The beneficiaries of the Irish exception are not specified; in this sense, the exception is not limited to 'research organizations' or institutional entities such as educational establishments and cultural heritage institutions conducting scientific research.[50] These aspects are likely to be subject to revision upon implementation of the Directive on Copyright in the Digital Single Market.

In terms of contractual overridability, the exception is expected to be mandatory, subject to the general rule under Irish copyright that 'where an act which would otherwise infringe any of the rights conferred by this Act is permitted under this Act it is irrelevant whether or not there exists any term or condition in an agreement which purports to prohibit or restrict that act.'[51] Ireland is one of the few jurisdictions in the European Union containing such a broad stipulation regarding the mandatory status of copyright exceptions and limitations.[52] In reference to technological restrictions, section 374, which was also subject to reform, stipulates that in cases where a technological protection measure disables a permitted use, the beneficiary may request the owner or licensee of rights in a protected work to provide an effective means of carrying out that permitted act. What is more, where the beneficiary is entitled to access the protected work or subject matter concerned, the copyright holder or licensee should make available the means of benefiting from the permitted act, save where other copies of such work have been made available to the public on reasonable and agreed contractual terms by, or with the authority of, the copyright holder, in a form which does not prevent or unreasonably restrict the beneficiary from undertaking the permitted act.[53]

The French data mining exception

As in Ireland and the United Kingdom, France introduced a text and data mining exception for the purposes of non-commercial public research in October 2016 through the Law for a Digital Republic (Loi pour une république numérique).[54]

---

[49] Irish proposal for the introduction of a text and data analytics exception included in Copyright and Other Intellectual Property Law Provisions Bill 2018 as passed by Dáil Éireann, No. 31b of 2018, Art. 13.

[50] In addition, the Irish exception stipulates, in its third paragraph, that the copy made should not be transferred to a third party unless the copyright holders have given consent for such a transfer and that the copy should not be used for purposes other than non-commercial research. Interestingly, the proposed exception clarifies that where the publication of the results of a computational analysis includes the reproduction of extracts from a protected work, such inclusion shall constitute inclusion in an incidental manner if the extracts are not more than are reasonably necessary to explain, or to assist in explaining, the results of the analysis.

[51] Irish Copyright and Related Rights Act, 2000, s. 2(10).

[52] Other Member States with relevant provisions are Belgium and Portugal.

[53] Copyright and Other Intellectual Property Law Provisions Bill 2018 as passed by Dáil Éireann, No. 31b of 2018, at 27.

[54] The text of the Act is available at <http://www.assemblee-nationale.fr/14/amendements/3399/AN/180.asp>, accessed 11 November 2019.

According to Article L. 122-5, 10° of the Intellectual Property Code,[55] rightsholders cannot prohibit 'copies or digital reproductions made from a lawful source for text and data mining for the purposes of public research, excluding any commercial purpose'. The detailed parameters on the application of the provision are outlined in a separate decree but the exception is limited in scope as it does not merely cover lawful access but refers to lawful source, and the beneficiaries are limited in that the exception applies for the purposes of public research only. As with the Irish exception discussed earlier, it is likely that the French exception on text and data mining will be revised (and enlarged in scope) upon implementation of the Directive on Copyright in the Digital Single Market.

All national initiatives, legislatively drafted on the margins of EU copyright norms, demonstrate the desire to enlarge the scope of available defences so that they correspond to modern trends in scientific research. With the enlarged scope of the EU text and data mining exceptions it is likely that the aforementioned jurisdictions will revise, and possibly enlarge the scope of, their relevant exceptions.

Library privileges

Another set of exceptions with an underlying public policy rationale are the so-called library privileges. Exceptions for libraries find their roots in the UK Copyright Act of 1956; they were subsequently adopted on a worldwide basis and extended, in some cases, to other establishments, such as museums and archives.[56] There is a public policy objective underlying the need to introduce specific provisions which enable certain uses carried out by libraries and archives, including the overarching aims of facilitating education and scholarship, creating new knowledge, preserving cultural heritage, and enabling participation in cultural life.[57]

Whereas the Berne Convention and the Agreement on Trade-Related Aspects of Intellectual Property Rights do not include exceptions or limitations specifically covering libraries and archives, there are various relevant provisions in the World Intellectual Property Organization (WIPO) Copyright Treaty. In the Agreed Statement concerning Article 1(4), the reproduction right and the exceptions permitted thereunder fully apply in the digital environment, including the

---

[55] There is also a separate provision with corresponding scope, Art. L. 342-3°, which applies by reference to the *sui generis* database right.

[56] On the national provisions concerning libraries and archives see Kenneth D. Crews, 'Study on Copyright Limitations and Exceptions for Libraries and Archives: Updated and Revised' (Geneva: WIPO, 2015). On the exceptions available for museums, see Jean-François Canat and Lucie Guibault, 'Study on Copyright Limitations and Exceptions for Museums' (Geneva: WIPO, 2015), available at <http://www.wipo.int/edocs/mdocs/copyright/en/sccr_30/sccr_30_2.pdf>, accessed 11 November 2019.

[57] See, e.g. Farida Shaheed, 'Report of the Special Rapporteur in the Field of Cultural Rights: Copyright Policy and the Right to Science and Culture', United Nations Human Rights Council Document A/HRS/28/57, 24 December 2014.

use of works in digital form. Practically, this means that any copyright exception or limitation for analogue uses of libraries and archives that is available in a contracting state should also apply in the digital context. Although this is an important safeguard, various activities of libraries and archives which take place online, particularly in the context of mass digitization projects, cannot be sufficiently covered by the systems of exceptions and limitations available under EU copyright and national laws. Indeed, national regimes remain largely diverse. According to a WIPO study on exceptions and limitations for libraries and archives,[58] about one in six country members of WIPO do not have relevant exceptions,[59] another one in six has a general exception available, more than half country members of WIPO have exceptions to cover research and study,[60] and copying for preservation purposes,[61] and just a handful of countries have exceptions which allow interlibrary loans.[62]

Possibly because of this diversity, the issue of exceptions and limitations to copyright infringement for certain uses of works carried out by libraries and archives is justifiably one of the items on the agenda of the Standing Committee on Copyright and Related Rights (SCCR) of the WIPO. Whereas some states urge for the negotiation of an international instrument on exceptions for libraries and archives, no consensus has yet been reached. With the limited scope of Article 345 of the Treaty on the Functioning of the European Union (TFEU)[63] and the legislative norms arising from EU copyright, the European Union opposed the adoption of a binding international agreement and suggested instead the adoption of measures of exchange of best practices among states.

At the EU level, there is a bundle of initiatives carried out in the context of delivering content to consumers, and preserving it through libraries and archives. Following a meeting in Lund in 2001 where the principles of digitization initiatives were discussed,[64] the Commission carried out extensive work in the area of exceptions and limitations for libraries and archives. These include the launch of the 'Europeana', the online portal to Europe's cultural collections,[65] and the introduction of the ARROW database of rights information.[66] At the policy level, the Commission put forward the so-called 'Minerva IPR guidelines' for

---

[58] Kenneth D. Crews, 'Study on Copyright Limitations and Exceptions for Libraries and Archives: Updated and Revised' (Geneva: WIPO, 2008), revised in 2014, updated and revised in 2015.

[59] 32 countries out of 188.

[60] 98 countries out of 188.

[61] 99 out of 188.

[62] 9 out of 188.

[63] Treaty on the Functioning of the European Union (TFEU) [2012] OJ C 326/1.

[64] See Nadine Klass and Hajo Rupp, 'EUROPEANA, ARROW and Orphan Works: Bringing Europe's Cultural Heritage Online' in Irini Stamatoudi (ed.), *EU Copyright Law: A Commentary* (Cheltenham: Edward Elgar, 2014) 946.

[65] See <https://www.europeana.eu/portal/en>; Jonathan Purday, 'Intellectual Property Issues and Europeana, Europe's Digital Library, Museum and Archive' (2010) 10(3) *Legal Information Management* 174.

[66] <www.arrow-net.eu>.

librarians,[67] published a 'Recommendation on the digitization and online accessibility of cultural material and digital preservation',[68] introduced a Directive aimed at the harmonization of treatment on orphan works across Europe,[69] undertook initiatives regarding the use of out of print works, such as a 'Memorandum of Understanding',[70] and introduced two relevant copyright exceptions via the Digital Single Market Directive.[71]

Library privileges in EU copyright

Under the Information Society Directive, Member States are given the option to incorporate library privileges into their national copyright laws. In particular, Article 5(2)(c) allows Member States to lay down exceptions and limitations to the reproduction right with regard to 'specific acts of reproduction made by publicly accessible libraries, educational establishments, or museums, or by archives, which are not for direct or indirect economic commercial advantage'. The Directive on Copyright in the Digital Single Market specifies in Article 24(2)(a) that the exception should not prejudice the exceptions and limitations provided for in the Digital Single Market Directive.

Article 5(2)(c) of the Information Society Directive extends the benefit of the exception to various institutions, i.e. not only libraries and archives, but also educational establishments and museums. It is not clear whether educational establishments and museums should also be publicly accessible.[72] According to Walter and Lewinski, the syntax of the English version, and other versions in different languages, implies that it is only libraries, educational establishments, and museums that have to be publicly accessible, whereas archives do not, as indicated by the separation of these latter set of institutions by the repetition of the word 'by'.[73] The Directive does not specify how broadly the concept of the public should be defined, but—to the extent that any member of a given public has equal opportunities to access the institution—the latter shall be deemed to be publicly accessible.[74] Whereas

---

[67] <http://www.minervaeurope.org/IPR/IPR_guide.html>.

[68] <http://ec.europa.eu/digital-agenda/>.

[69] Orphan Works Directive (Directive 2012/28/EU).

[70] Memorandum of Understanding (MoU) on Key Principles on the Digitization and Making Available of Out-of-Commerce Works (2011) available at <https://ec.europa.eu/commission/presscorner/detail/en/MEMO_11_619>, accessed 11 November 2019; also see Uma Suthersanen and Maria Mercedes Frabboni, 'The Orphan Works Directive' in Irini Stamatoudi and Paul Torremans (eds), *EU Copyright Law: A Commentary* (Cheltenham: Edward Elgar, 2014) 653.

[71] Digital Single Market Directive (Directive 2019/790), Arts 6 and 8.

[72] Michel M. Walter and Silke Von Lewinski, *European Copyright Law: A Commentary* (Oxford: Oxford University Press, 2010) 11.5.36.

[73] Michel M. Walter and Silke Von Lewinski, *European Copyright Law: A Commentary* (Oxford: Oxford University Press, 2010) 11.5.36. Also see Information Society Directive (Directive 2001/29/EC), Recital 40.

[74] Michel M. Walter and Silke Von Lewinski, *European Copyright Law: A Commentary* (Oxford: Oxford University Press, 2010) 11.5.36.

Article 5(2)(c) covers the reproduction right only, Article 5(4) allows for an extension of this and other exceptions to the distribution right to the extent that the three-step test permits.[75]

The Information Society Directive does not offer guidance on the attributes that the relevant institutions should possess in order to benefit from the exception. It is accepted in the literature that libraries and archives are arguably different in nature.[76] Although libraries are primarily concerned with commercially published content—focusing on aggregating, organizing, and enabling access to knowledge—archives are centres of documentation that most often include unique records which are rarely aimed at commercial exploitation.

Article 5(2)(c) permits Member States to make allowances for 'specific acts' of reproduction. This reflects the wording of the three-step test, i.e. that exceptions ought to apply to certain special cases. In this light, permitted acts of reproduction should be precisely defined and strictly available in certain special cases. This is also affirmed by Recital 40 of the Directive which expressly states that 'such an exception or limitation should not cover uses made in the context of online delivery of protected works or other subject matter.' The Recital also promotes contractual arrangements 'which, without creating imbalances, favour such establishments and the disseminative purposes they serve.' Such purposes may vary, spanning from archival and preservation purposes, but not other activities, such as indexing and scanning. This has the effect that big digitization projects cannot find a refuge in Article 5(2)(c).

Article 5(2)(c) covers only activities that are not meant for direct or indirect commercial advantage. This excludes activities that are carried out for profit or under the payment of a fee that exceeds administration costs. Indirect commercial advantage could be, for instance, the goodwill or publicity that the library attracts.[77] It is immaterial whether the institution is publicly funded or not; private institutions may also be covered by the exception to the extent that they are publicly accessible and do not aim to achieve a direct or indirect commercial advantage.

The internal limitations of the exception, i.e. the extent to which the use is permissible, aim to ensure compliance with the three-step test incorporated in Article 5(5) of the Information Society Directive. However, the scope of permitted use is subject to limitations and, as such, it fails to embrace the dynamic of modern uses

---

[75] WIPO, 'Study on Copyright and Limitations and Exceptions For Libraries and Archives, Standing Committee on Copyright and Related Rights', SCRR/29/3 (Geneva: WIPO, 2008) 24; also see Kenneth D. Crews, 'Study on Copyright Limitations and Exceptions for Libraries and Archives: Updated and Revised', SCCR/30/3 (Geneva: WIPO, 2015).

[76] Martin Kretschmer et al., 'The European Commission's Public Consultation on the Review of EU Copyright Rules: a Response by the CREATe Centre' (2014) 36(9) *European Intellectual Property Review* 547, 549.

[77] Michel M. Walter and Silke Von Lewinski, *European Copyright Law: A Commentary* (Oxford: Oxford University Press, 2010) 11.5.38.

of copyright materials in the online context. One such case is that of document delivery services.

Document delivery services

Online document delivery and offers of access to materials within dedicated terminals is a controversial issue in the digital context, justifiably so. We have discussed some of the relevant debates with regard to the exceptions allowing research and private study in Chapter 6. However, there is another aspect that ought to be addressed, namely the legitimacy of library privileges in the context of online document delivery services. Scanning copies of works for preservation and offering such copies to e-library users are different activities that enable the fulfilment of different goals. The legitimacy of document delivery services is an issue that became the subject of intense debate across Europe, both at the judicial and the legislative level, raising questions of lawful use in the context of institutional users, such as libraries and archives, and thereinafter private users making use of their services.

Germany is one of the Member States where the issue of document delivery services has been heavily debated. This was particularly so during the discussion for the implementation of the Information Society Directive, which required the introduction of the so-called 'second basket' of legislative provisions. Controversy started a few years before the implementation of the Directive. In 1999, the Federal Court of Justice (Bundesgerichtshof) found that a public library that photocopies and distributes copyright-protected articles by mail or facsimile upon individual user request does not infringe the copyright of the publisher if the user benefits from the private copying exception, available under paragraph 53(2)(4)(a) of the German Copyright Act.[78] This copyright exception was found to cover document delivery services to the extent that libraries pay adequate compensation to the responsible collecting society.

Although primarily addressing the private copying exception, the case developed insights regarding the legitimacy of document delivery services. The case involved a non-gratuitous document delivery service, called 'subito', which was offered and operated by a public library in Hanover. Upon user requests, the library copied and sent single articles contained in magazines or books to users by post or facsimile. The library also provided an online catalogue that included a list of available publications. An association representing the interests of publishers and booksellers in Germany, the 'Boersenverein des deutschen Buchhandels e.V', claimed copyright infringement of materials included in its catalogue and sought injunctive relief and compensation for damages. Although the District Court dismissed the claim, the Court of Appeal held that the distribution of materials to

---

[78] 'Kopienversanddienst', Federal Court of Justice (Bundesgerichtshof), 25 February 1999 (Germany).

the users by mail or facsimile was an essential part of a document delivery service and covered by the exception on reproductions for private purposes available under paragraph 53(2)(4)(a) of the German Copyright Act. This established a legal basis for document delivery services, holding that they serve the public interest by making available materials of scientific and educational nature to the public.

The Federal Court of Justice upheld the decision of the Court of Appeal, finding that copying of articles would be legitimate. Paragraph 53(2)(4) of the German Copyright Act allows making copies of copyright-protected works for private use, irrespective of whether the copies are made by the user themselves or by a third party on behalf of the user. In the context of document delivery services, third party copying merely offers technical assistance. The delivery of the articles to the user was not in breach of the publishers' distribution right, available under Article 17 of the German Copyright Act, because such an act of dissemination would be an essential part of the document delivery service and therefore covered by the exception for private use. However, in order to meet the conditions of the three-step test,[79] the Federal Court held that such a document delivery service had to be subject to an equitable remuneration payable to the authors.[80] The introduction of such a claim to equitable remuneration was meant to balance the conflicting interests of authors and publishers to financial compensation and the interests of society in general towards access to information; in essence, the Federal Court restricted the scope of the reproduction and distribution rights, on the grounds of a specific public policy, by introducing a remuneration claim, which had the benefit of ensuring easy and affordable access to the document delivery service, whilst at the same time offering rightsholders adequate compensation.

German jurisprudence traditionally followed the principle of strict interpretation of copyright exceptions and limitations. According to this approach, which aligns with the interpretative standards of the Court of Justice, it is up to the legislator—and not the courts—to adapt the scope of exceptions and limitations in cases where this is affected by changes in technology, society, or the economy. In this case, however, the Federal Court expressly stated that copyright exceptions and limitations can be subject to a broader interpretation and application depending on the context. Although the jurisprudential contribution of the case is very important, its impact was not as high as anticipated because more efficient and faster dissemination technologies, such as email, emerged around that time and shifted attention to emergent technological advances.

It is no surprise that the publisher's association brought another case against the 'subito' delivery service with allegations of infringement by electronic delivery

---

[79] Berne Convention, Art. 9(2); Agreement on Trade-Related Aspects of Intellectual Property Rights (1994), Art. 13.

[80] The claim to equitable remuneration is rooted in Arts 27(3), 49(1), and 54h(1) of the German Copyright Act.

of materials. In the first instance, the District Court of Munich found that such delivery methods where comparable to the analogue distribution model and on this basis dismissed the claim.[81] In 2009, the Court of Appeal of Frankfurt (Oberlandesgericht Frankfurt am Main) held[82] that public libraries are allowed to digitize published works and make the copies available on dedicated terminals located in their premises. It also found, however, that they are not entitled to allow users to copy the articles. The plaintiff, an academic publishing house, brought a case against a university library, which owned copies of a book published by the plaintiff. The library had digitized the book at issue with a view to making it available on dedicated reading terminals within library premises. Even though the files could not be modified by the use of common word processing software, they could be viewed on screen, printed, and/or stored on USB sticks by library users for the purposes of private use. There was a copyright notice at every terminal indicating that users could not make copies for third parties and—although initially there was no login procedure—such a system was later put in place. Unlike the District Court, which rejected the claims, the Court of Appeal accepted the appeal in part. Article 52b of the German Copyright Act was held to permit document delivery services to the extent that e-books were used for non-commercial purposes within library premises. This applied irrespective of the fact that the copyright holder may have offered the possibility of concluding an individual licensing agreement. Such an interpretation, according to the court, was in line with the Information Society Directive on which Article 52b is premised. However, the court accepted the appeal with regard to copying of the digitized book by end users and stressed that Article 52b permits libraries to display book files to be read only at the terminals within the library premises.

There was, however, no jurisprudential consensus in Germany on the legitimacy of document delivery services and—although some courts developed a purposive approach—others followed strict interpretation standards, finding that document delivery services are in breach of copyright. For instance, in 2007 the Munich Court of Appeal found that a public library offering a document delivery service infringed the reproduction right by enabling users to order single articles contained in periodicals and books against the payment of a fee to receive, in return, a digitized copy by email or via an access-restricted file transfer protocol server.[83] In another case,[84] the Dresden Court of Appeal held that an online personal video recording service that enabled users to receive and record TV programmes on-demand was

---

[81] 'Subito', District Court Munich (Landgericht Munchen), 15 December 2005, 7 O 11479/04 (Germany).

[82] 'Digital use in public institutions', Court of Appeal Frankfurt/Main (Oberlandesgericht Frankfurt am Main), 24 November 2009 (Germany).

[83] See Börsenverein des Deutschen Buchnandels et al., Court of Appeal Munich (Oberlandesgericht), 10 February 2007, 29 U I638/06 (Germany).

[84] Court of Appeal of Dresden (Oberlandesgericht, Dresden), 28 November 2006, 14 U 1071/06 (Germany).

in breach of the plaintiff's reproduction right, despite the fact that the service was provided for free. What is more, users could not benefit from the private copying exception available under Article 53 of the German Copyright Act.

The legitimacy of document delivery services has also been debated in Switzerland. In 2014, the Commercial Court of the Canton of Zurich held that the document delivery service of ETH Zurich was not covered by the exception for private use under Article 19 of the Copyright Act.[85] This service consisted of individual articles being scanned on-demand and sent to users via email. Because each journal article was a work on its own and was therefore payable individually, the service was in direct competition with the publishers' services and therefore contrary to Article 19(3) of the Copyright Act. Copying an entire journal article was a reproduction of a whole work and as such prohibited. However, this did not mean that private users were not entitled to make themselves entire copies at the library by use of photocopying machines or scanners. Although this point is controversial, it falls within the scope of permitted private use of Article 19(1) of the Copyright Act since the main mission of the library, namely enabling the public's right to information, was not endangered. This is because private users had free access to its premises and visiting the library to make copies of works was considered to be reasonable conduct.

The ETH Zurich library filed an appeal to the Federal Supreme Court, which reversed the decision of the Commercial Court.[86] The Supreme Court held that the library can rely on the exception on private use of Article 19 with regard to its document delivery service. Even though copying an entire work outside the private sphere is not permitted as a matter of law, a user that benefits from the private use exception of Article 19 can also have copies made by libraries and sent by email. The Supreme Court held that such a delivery service is not in direct competition with the publishers' services because the library does not offer access to an entire online database, rather it merely scans individual articles upon the request of users. The Supreme Court's decision was important as it clarified the scope of the exception for private use and confirmed the legitimacy of document delivery services. It was also forward-looking as it allowed the development of online libraries within the contours of existing law.

Document delivery after *TU Darmstadt*

As examined in Chapter 6, the European Court of Justice found inter alia in *TU Darmstadt*[87] that where it is necessary for the purpose of making a work available

---

[85] '*Library ETH Zurich*', Commercial Court of the Canton of Zurich, HG110271-O, 7 April 2014 (Switzerland).

[86] '*ETH document delivery service*', Federal Supreme Court of Switzerland, 1st Civil Law Chamber, 4A_295/2014, 28 November 2014 (Switzerland).

[87] *Technische Universität Darmstadt v Eugen Ulmer KG*, Case C-117/13, 11 September 2014, ECLI:EU:C:2014:2196 (*Technische Universität Darmstadt*).

to the public, Member States can grant publicly accessible libraries the right to digitize works in their collections through dedicated terminals. However, this is not meant to cover acts carried out by users, including printing onto paper or storing such works on a USB stick.

In *Technische Universität Darmstadt v Eugen Ulmer KG*,[88] the Court of Justice held that Article 5(3)(n) of the Information Society Directive did not foreclose the possibility that Member States grant libraries the right to digitize works included in their collections and to make them available at dedicated terminals if necessary. However, this Article did not cover printed copies of works or storing them on USB sticks, even though this could be covered under the reprography and private copying exceptions available respectively under Article 5(2)(a) and (b) of the Information Society Directive. The ruling is an important precedent as it allows the establishment of e-libraries within the relevant provisions of EU copyright. To a large extent, it echoes national case law (mostly German cases) which deals with document delivery services, and adopts a proportionate approach reflected in Recital 31 of the Information Society Directive, according to which 'a fair balance of rights and interests between the different categories of rightholders, as well as between the different categories of rightholders and users of protected subject matter must be safeguarded.'

Indeed, the Court of Justice makes use of the important legal principle of proportionality when discussing judicial remedies in copyright. This principle is enshrined in Article 5 of the TFEU[89] and mandated by Article 3(2) of the Enforcement Directive.[90] Fischman Afori[91] offers Barak's definition of proportionality as one that requires 'proper purpose, rational connection, necessary means, and a proper relation between the benefit gained by realizing the proper purpose and the harm caused to the constitutional right, the last component also being known as "balancing".'[92] According to Fischman Afori, proportionality can be used as 'a means of allaying and moderating the growing constitutional tensions within copyright law'. In this light, and in conjunction with Recital 31 of the Information Society

---

[88] Ibid.

[89] Consolidated version of the Treaty on the Functioning of the European Union (TFEU), OJ C 326, 26 October 2012, 47–390.

[90] Art. 3(2) of the Enforcement Directive (Directive 2004/48/EC of the European Parliament and of the Council of 29 April 2004 on the Enforcement of Intellectual Property Rights (OJ L 195/16, 2 June 2004)) reads:

> Those measures, procedures and remedies shall also be effective, proportionate and dissuasive and shall be applied in such a manner as to avoid the creation of barriers to legitimate trade and to provide for safeguards against their abuse.

See Directive 2004/48/EC of the European Parliament and of the Council of 29 April 2004 on the enforcement of intellectual property rights.

[91] Orit Fischman Afori, 'Proportionality: A New Mega Standard in European Copyright Law' (2014) 45(8) *International Review of Intellectual Property and Competition Law* 889.

[92] Orit Fischman Afori, 'Proportionality: A New Mega Standard in European Copyright Law' (2014) 45(8) *International Review of Intellectual Property and Competition Law* 889, 896.

Directive, which was invoked in *TU Darmstadt*, it could serve as a principle for the interpretation of the closed list of exceptions available in the Directive.[93] A purposive approach to copyright exceptions within the framework of proportionality could enhance the quest for flexibilities in EU copyright and could boost the evolution of mass digitization initiatives.

Related to the exceptions available for libraries and archives—yet distinct as an issue—is the use of so-called orphan materials available in such institutions.

Cultural preservation privileges

The Directive on Copyright in the Digital Single Market aspires to extend the exceptions that are available to libraries, archives, and cultural institutions with a view to establishing a special mandatory exception for the purpose of preserving cultural heritage. Article 6 of the Directive reads

> Member States shall provide for an exception to the rights provided for in Article 5(a) and Article 7(1) of Directive 96/9/EC, Article 2 of Directive 2001/29/EC, Article 4(1)(a) of Directive 2009/24/EC, and Article 15(1) of this Directive, in order to allow cultural heritage institutions to make copies of any works or other subject matter that are permanently in their collections, in any format or medium, for purposes of preservation of such works or other subject matter and to the extent necessary for such preservation.

The provision aims to address challenges in the preservation of cultural heritage materials[94] and to harmonize the divergent approaches in Member States which are expected to hamper cross-border cooperation, leading to inefficient use of resources and effectively having a negative impact on the preservation of cultural heritage.[95] In light of these objectives, Member States have to set in place a mandatory exception that will allow the making of copies for preservation purposes 'by the appropriate preservation tool, means, or technology, in any format or medium, in the required number, at any point in the life of a work or other subject matter, and to the extent required for preservation purposes'.[96] The beneficiaries of the exception are cultural heritage institutions, namely publicly accessible libraries or museums, archives, or film or audio heritage institutions, as per Article 2(3). A requirement for the application of the exception is its purpose specificity and also the

---

[93] Alison Firth and Beverley Pereira, 'Exceptions for Libraries and Archives' in Irini Stamatoudi (ed.), *New Developments in EU and International Copyright Law* (Alphen aan den Rijn: Kluwer Law International, 2016) 2, 19–20.

[94] Digital Single Market Directive (Directive 2019/790), Recital 25.

[95] Ibid., Recital 26.

[96] Ibid., Recital 27.

condition that the copies made for preservation purposes are permanently owned by the relevant institutions; this may be either the result of owing or permanently holding the relevant works or other subject matter but not having temporary access to materials via a third party server.[97]

The exception is important in enhancing value in Europe's cultural heritage and ensuring that efficient preservation initiatives are put in place. However, a particularly noteworthy aspect of the exception that featured in earlier drafts, but which was removed from the final proposal, was that it did not allow the creation of new copyright for a faithful copy of a public domain work made for public preservation purposes.[98] This aimed to (a) ensure that copyright on works that have fallen into the public domain shall not be unjustifiably extended, (b) avoid monopolizing access to works which are no longer subject to copyright, and (c) prevent the creation of digital monopolies over cultural materials.[99]

An interesting aspect of the exception is that by virtue of Article 7(1) it is laid down as mandatory against contractual override and, in addition, Member States ought to take appropriate measures to ensure that rightsholders make available to the beneficiary of the cultural preservation privilege the means of benefiting from that exception, to the extent necessary for the purposes of benefiting from the exception, and on condition that the beneficiary has legal access to the protected work or subject matter concerned.[100]

Two distinct, yet related, issues arise in the context of cultural preservation: legal issues related to orphan and out-of-commerce works. Both have been addressed at the legislative level fairly recently via the Orphan Works Directive[101] and the Digital Single Market Directive.[102]

Exceptions for orphan works

With digitization and the Internet has come growing consensus on the need to enhance access to European digital content.[103] This has not been easy to accomplish, however, due to copyright norms. One of the most prominent legal issues in this context has been the issue of orphan works, which challenges digital cultural

---

[97] Ibid., Recitals 28 and 29.

[98] Ibid., Art. 5(1)(a).

[99] Maurizio Borghi and Stavroula Karapapa, *Copyright and Mass Digitization: A Cross Jurisdictional Approach* (Oxford: Oxford University Press, 2013) 92 et seq.

[100] According to Art. 7(2) of the Digital Single Market Directive (Directive 2019/790), Art. 6(4) of the Information Society Directive (Directive 2001/29/EC) applies to the text mining exception of Art. 3.

[101] Directive (EU) 2012/28 of the European Parliament and of the Council of 25 October 2012 on Certain Permitted Uses of Orphan Works (Orphan Works Directive), OJ L 299/5, 27 October 2012.

[102] Digital Single Market Directive (Directive 2019/790).

[103] See Council of the European Union and Commission of the European Communities, Action plan: eEurope 2002 – An Information Society for All, for the Feira European Council, 19–20 June 2000.

heritage organizations.[104] Even though such organizations own physical copies of copyright-protected materials, they need to gain authorization in order to make such content available online. Because it is impossible to locate the rightsholders and clear licenses for the digitization of orphan works, cultural institutions would either have to make use of the works and face the risk of legal liability or refrain from using the works altogether, thus leaving thus a great part of cultural heritage unexplored. This has an impact on access to and preservation of cultural heritage. In effect, the issue of orphan works is one that affects society as a whole.[105]

The Google Books project in 2004,[106] a project which aspired to create a comprehensive digital library, motivated a number of initiatives in Europe in the pursuit of addressing the so-called orphan works problem. Following an unsuccessful attempt to adopt a soft law approach to the matter, the Commission eventually adopted a Directive to specifically address this issue, the so-called Orphan Works Directive.[107] Other relevant initiatives include the Memorandum of Understanding on Key Principles on the Digitization and Making Available of Out-of-Commerce Works in 2011,[108] and more recently the proposal for a Directive on Copyright in the Digital Single Market.[109] Although the Orphan Works Directive was expected to enhance legal certainty in the Internal Market,[110] it is arguably not the most efficient mechanism to deal with the orphan works problem for reasons that are

---

[104] Even though data are not available, orphan works do represent a significant part of the collections of cultural organizations in Europe. See Commission Staff Working Paper, Impact Assessment on the Cross-Border Online Access to Orphan Works accompanying the document Proposal for a Directive of the European Parliament and of the Council on certain permitted uses of orphan works, SEC(2011) 615 final, 11–12; see also Katharina de la Durantaye, 'Orphan Works: A Comparative and International Perspective' in Daniel J. Gervais (ed.), *International Intellectual Property: A Handbook of Contemporary Research* (Cheltenham: Edward Elgar, 2015) 190, 191, fn 4.

[105] Green Paper; Copyright in the Knowledge Economy, COM (2008) 466, 8. For an extensive account of the underlying legal and practical problems, see Stef van Gompel, 'Unlocking the Potential of Pre-Existing Content: How to Address the Issue of Orphan Works in Europe?' (2007) 38(6) *International Review of Intellectual Property and Competition Law* 669.

[106] Maurizio Borghi and Stavroula Karapapa, *Copyright and Mass Digitization: A Cross-Jurisdictional Approach* (Oxford: Oxford University Press, 2013) 11.

[107] Directive (EU) 2012/28 of the European Parliament and of the Council of 25 October 2012 on Certain Permitted Uses of Orphan Works, OJ /L 299/5, 27 October 2012. For a more detailed analysis, see Uma Suthersanen and Maria Mercedes Frabboni, 'The Orphan Works Directive' in Irini Stamatoudi and Paul Torremans (eds), *EU Copyright Law: A Commentary* (Cheltenham: Edward Elgar, 2014) 653; Marie-Christine Janssens and Rán Tryggvadóttir, 'Facilitating Access to Orphan and Out-of-Commerce Works to Make Europe's Cultural Resources Available to the Broader Public' in Irini Stamatoudi (ed.), *Copyright and the Digital Agenda for Europe: Current Challenges for the Future* (Athens: Sakkoulas Publications, 2015) 27; Eleonora Rosati, 'The Orphan Works Directive, or Throwing a Stone and Hiding the Hand (2013) 8 *Journal of Intellectual Property Law & Practice* 303.

[108] Memorandum of Understanding on Key Principles on the Digitization and Making Available of Out-of-Commerce Works, 20 September 2011.

[109] Proposal for a Directive of the European Parliament and of the Council on copyright in the Digital Single Market, Brussels, 14 September 2016, COM (2016) 593 final, 2016/0280 (COD), available at <https://ec.europa.eu/transparency/regdoc/rep/1/2016/EN/1-2016-593-EN-F1-1.PDF>, accessed 11 November 2019.

[110] Directive (EU) 2012/28 of the European Parliament and of the Council of 25 October 2012 on Certain Permitted Uses of Orphan Works, OJ /L 299/5, 27 October 2012, Recitals 3, 9, and 25.

explained below. One of the most important issues is that the relevant activities are subject to numerous internal limitations that shrink the scope of lawful uses by reference to orphan works.

Orphan works under EU copyright

The 2012 Orphan Works Directive[111] was specifically introduced with a view to facilitating large-scale digitization of materials available in public institutional collections and—through the creation of European digital libraries—to enhance access to Europe's cultural heritage and promote the free movement of knowledge within the European Union. In particular, its objective was to facilitate certain uses of orphan works that belong to the collections of cultural heritage organizations. The Orphan Works Directive supplements the exceptions and limitations available under the Information Society Directive for certain—but not all—categories of work and other subject matter that qualify as orphan works. It requires Member States to permit qualifying public institutions to carry out specific uses of orphan works and other subject matter available in their collections with a view to pursuing their public interest mission.[112] As is shown below, however, the uses permitted under the Directive are subject to numerous internal limitations that render the scope of the Directive too narrow to efficiently deal with the digital challenge.

Orphan work status
For the Orphan Works Directive to apply it should first be established whether the work or other subject matter qualifies as an orphan work. In order for a work to qualify as orphan, it should be impossible for any of the rightholders of that work or phonogram to be identified or, even if one or more of them is identified, it should be impossible to locate any of them, despite a diligent search having been carried out and recorded in accordance with the provisions of the Directive.[113]

Not all works can meet the conditions necessary to attract an orphan work status. The first eligibility criterion is that works and other subject matter should belong to the collections or archives of publicly accessible institutions. The second condition is that the Directive covers only works that have been first published or broadcast in a Member State. [114] This excludes works that have been first published

---

[111] Directive (EU) 2012/28 of the European Parliament and of the Council of 25 October 2012 on Certain Permitted Uses of Orphan Works.

[112] Directive (EU) 2012/28 of the European Parliament and of the Council of 25 October 2012 on Certain Permitted Uses of Orphan Works, OJ /L 299/5, 27 October 2012, Art. 1; even though the Directive refers to works, it also seems to cover related rights too: see Art. 1(2), and Recitals 3 and 4(3).

[113] Directive (EU) 2012/28 of the European Parliament and of the Council of 25 October 2012 on Certain Permitted Uses of Orphan Works, OJ /L 299/5, 27 October 2012, Art. 2(1).

[114] Directive (EU) 2012/28 of the European Parliament and of the Council of 25 October 2012 on Certain Permitted Uses of Orphan Works, OJ /L 299/5, 27 October 2012, Art. 1(2).

or broadcast elsewhere in the world.[115] Specific mention is made to unpublished works. If a beneficiary organization holds works that have never been published or broadcast in its collection, these may also be covered by the protection available under the Directive if they have been made publicly accessible subject to the rightsholders' authorization and to the extent that it is reasonable to assume that rightsholders would not oppose the uses that the Directive permits.[116] A third condition is that the Directive applies to certain categories of works only. These are enumerated in Articles 1(2) and (4). According to these Articles, the provisions of the Directive apply to: writings, such as books, journals, newspapers, and magazines; phonograms; cinematographic and other audiovisual works; and works that are incorporated in, or constitute an integral part of, any of the three major aforementioned categories of work. Once the orphan work status is established in one Member State, the work should be considered an orphan in all other Member States. This is the so-called principle of mutual recognition that responds to the challenges raised by the territorial nature of copyright and aims to enable cross-border uses of works and phonograms.[117]

Within the meaning of Article 1, the Orphan Works Directive covers only certain types of institutions—not individuals—insofar as they are established in a Member State.[118] These are listed exhaustively and include publicly accessible libraries, archives,[119] educational establishments, museums, public service broadcasting organizations, and film or audio heritage institutions. Some of these beneficiary institutions are also covered by the exception available for libraries and archives under Article 5(3)(c) of the Information Society Directive, so the overlapping scope of both exceptions allows a greater breadth of permissible use.

---

[115] See Directive (EU) 2012/28 of the European Parliament and of the Council of 25 October 2012 on Certain Permitted Uses of Orphan Works, OJ /L 299/5, 27 October 2012, Recital 12. There is no guidance offered in cases where identifying the place of first publication or broadcast is not possible.

[116] Directive (EU) 2012/28 of the European Parliament and of the Council of 25 October 2012 on Certain Permitted Uses of Orphan Works (Orphan Works Directive), OJ L 299/5, 27 October 2012, Art. 1(3). Uma Suthersanen and Maria Mercedes Frabboni, 'The Orphan Works Directive' in Irini Stamatoudi and Paul Torremans (eds), *EU Copyright Law: A Commentary* (Cheltenham: Edward Elgar, 2014) 653, 661–2; Jean-Paul Triaille et al., Study on the Application of Directive 2001/29/EC on Copyright and Related Rights in the Information Society (2013) 253–4, 398.

[117] Directive (EU) 2012/28 of the European Parliament and of the Council of 25 October 2012 on Certain Permitted Uses of Orphan Works, OJ /L 299/5, 27 October 2012, Art. 4 and Recital 23.

[118] Directive (EU) 2012/28 of the European Parliament and of the Council of 25 October 2012 on Certain Permitted Uses of Orphan Works, OJ /L 299/5, 27 October 2012, Art. 1(1).

[119] Presumably archives need not be publicly accessible; see Stefan Bechtold, 'Directive 2001/29/EC (Information Society Directive) of the European Parliament and of the Council of 22 May 2001 on the Harmonisation of Certain Aspects of Copyright and Related Rights in the Information Society' in Thomas Dreier and P. Bernt Hugenholtz (eds), *Concise European Copyright Law* (Alphen aan den Rijn: Kluwer Law International, 2006) 343, 376.

Diligent search

The beneficiary institutions are primarily responsible for carrying out the diligent search before confining an orphan works status to a work. Other organizations, however, may also be commissioned to carry out the search.[120]

There is no precise definition of 'diligent search' offered in the Orphan Works Directive. The latter makes reference to threshold conditions that need to be met. In particular, the search should be carried out in a diligent way, in good faith with regard to each individual work, and it should take place before the use is made. For the diligence requirements to be met, the beneficiary institutions should consult a minimum number of resources, as identified in the Annex to the Directive. As Article 3 indicates, Member States may supplement the list.

An important feature of the Directive that arguably increases faster and lower-cost diligent searches is the principle of 'one' search. This is meant to ensure that costly and time consuming duplication of search efforts shall be avoided. Relevant searches should take place in the Member State of the first publication or first broadcast only.[121] With regard to cinematographic or audiovisual works, the search should take place in the country where the producer has their headquarters or habitual residence, unless there is evidence of relevant information in sources available in other countries. In that case, these additional sources should be consulted.[122] It is not clear whether the term 'countries' refers to EU Member States only or not, but in case it is not, and there is currently no guidance on this matter, it arguably covers a broader area than the European Union and this enhances the efficiency of the diligent search mechanism.

In order to verify that the search was diligent, the beneficiary institutions ought to record and maintain the results of the search,[123] and to transmit those records to a competent national authority, including information on the uses of orphan works, contact details, and information on possible changes of the orphan work status.[124] Although the Directive does not specify the responsibilities of such a national authority,[125] leaving the determination to Member States, it is likely to

---

[120] Directive (EU) 2012/28 of the European Parliament and of the Council of 25 October 2012 on Certain Permitted Uses of Orphan Works, OJ /L 299/5, 27 October 2012, Recital 13.

[121] In the case of unpublished or not broadcast works, the search is to be carried out where the beneficiary institution is established, cf Directive (EU) 2012/28 of the European Parliament and of the Council of 25 October 2012 on Certain Permitted Uses of Orphan Works, OJ /L 299/5, 27 October 2012, Art. 3(3).

[122] Directive (EU) 2012/28 of the European Parliament and of the Council of 25 October 2012 on Certain Permitted Uses of Orphan Works, OJ /L 299/5, 27 October 2012, Art. 3(4).

[123] Directive (EU) 2012/28 of the European Parliament and of the Council of 25 October 2012 on Certain Permitted Uses of Orphan Works, OJ /L 299/5, 27 October 2012, Art. 3(5) and Recitals 15 and 19.

[124] Directive (EU) 2012/28 of the European Parliament and of the Council of 25 October 2012 on Certain Permitted Uses of Orphan Works, OJ /L 299/5, 27 October 2012, Art. 3(5).

[125] Art. 2(2)(k) of Regulation (EU) No. 386/2012 of the European Parliament and of the Council of 19 April 2012, L 129/1, 16 May 2012, requires EUIPO (formerly OHIM) to work with national authorities with a view to develop an online network.

impact on their role by including transmission of the relevant records to the single publicly accessible online database managed by the European Union Intellectual Property Office (EUIPO, formerly the Office for Harmonization in the Internal Market (OHIM)).[126]

Permitted uses

Uses of orphan works under the Orphan Works Directive are facilitated by a mandatory exception or limitation.[127] By virtue of Article 6, permitted uses include the making of a work available to the public[128] and acts of copying for the purposes of digitization, making available, indexing, cataloguing, preservation, or restoration.[129] To a certain extent, there is an overlap between this exception and the one available in Article 5(2)(c) of the Information Society Directive concerning specific permitted uses carried out by publicly accessible libraries and archives. Indeed, the word 'specific', which features in Article 5(2)(c) of the Information Society Directive, can be seen as excluding the realization of mass digitization initiatives of works included in the collections of beneficiary institutions.[130] Unlike Article 5(2)(c) of the Information Society Directive, however, the exception available under the Orphan Works Directive is mandatory for Member States to implement and specifies the purposes for which copying is permitted.

According to Articles 1(1) and 6(2) of the Orphan Works Directive, only uses which serve the public interest mission of the beneficiary institutions are allowed.[131] Although the list is not exhaustive, some indication is offered in Recital 20, which refers to activities such as 'the preservation of, the restoration of, and the provision of cultural and educational access to, their collections, including their digital collections'. The Directive does not specify what a public interest mission is, even though this seems to be a central parameter of the applicability of the Directive. This is surprising given that at the time the Directive was introduced EU

---

[126] <https://oami.europa.eu/orphanworks/>.

[127] Directive (EU) 2012/28 of the European Parliament and of the Council of 25 October 2012 on Certain Permitted Uses of Orphan Works, OJ /L 299/5, 27 October 2012, Art. 6(1). Recital 20 of the Directive states that the exception ought to be added to the list of exceptions and limitations available under Art. 5 of the Information Society Directive.

[128] Information Society Directive (Directive 2001/29/EC), Art. 3.

[129] Directive (EU) 2012/28 of the European Parliament and of the Council of 25 October 2012 on Certain Permitted Uses of Orphan Works, OJ /L 299/5, 27 October 2012, Art. 6(2). There are uses which fall outside the scope of the Directive, such as distribution, performance, and public display of the work. See in this regard Katharina de la Durantaye, 'Finding a Home for Orphans: Google Book Search and Orphan Works Law in the United States and Europe' (2011) 21(2) *Fordham Intellectual Property, Media & Entertainment Law Journal* 229.

[130] See in this regard *Technische Universität Darmstadt v Eugen Ulmer KG*, Case C-117/13, 11 September 2014, ECLI:EU:C:2014:2196 (*Technische Universität Darmstadt*), [38]; Jean-Paul Triaille et al., Study on the Application of Directive 2001/29/EC on Copyright and Related Rights in the Information Society (2013) 253–4, 280–1.

[131] Directive (EU) 2012/28 of the European Parliament and of the Council of 25 October 2012 on Certain Permitted Uses of Orphan Works, OJ /L 299/5, 27 October 2012, Arts 1(1) and 6(2).

lawmakers were familiar with the challenges posed by the *Google Books* case[132] and other mass digitization initiatives.

The implementation and drawbacks of the Orphan Works Directive

Even though most Member States have opted for a literal implementation of the provisions of the Directive into their national laws, certain differences in national transpositions were inevitable due to the considerable flexibility that the Directive adopts by reference to various issues. These include the criteria of diligent search,[133] compensation, and end of orphan work status. For instance, with regard to the diligent search criterion, various Member States have merely specified the mandatory list of sources that need be consulted,[134] but diversity remains as to which institution shall serve as a competent national authority.[135] As an example of the diverse approaches initiated by Member States, public institutions in Austria ought to stop using an orphan work once they become aware of the location and identity of the rightsholder, whereas in Finland for instance, the orphan work status stops as soon as a relevant notice has been placed in the EUIPO database. Differences also exist with regard to the conditions of compensation, which is meant to expire after ten years in Austria but not in Finland, where such a limitation is not available.[136] Such divergences, which tend to be widespread across Europe, may have an impact on the award of orphan work status and the effectiveness of the objectives pursued by the Directive.

Mainly because the diligent search mechanism is based on individual searches of works, which are costly and time consuming, the Orphan Works Directive does not offer the most appropriate solution for cases of mass use of orphan works and other subject matter. At the same time, its scope is limited to specific institutions, namely publicly accessible organizations; specific uses, i.e. uses that are made in connection with the public interest mission of the beneficiary organizations, excluding commercial uses; and specific categories of works. Indeed, one of the

---

[132] *Authors Guild, Inc. v Google Inc.*, No. 13-4829-cv (2d Cir. Oct. 16, 2015) (US).

[133] Maurizio Borghi, Kris Erickson and Marcella Favale, 'With Enough Eyeballs All Searches are Diligent: Mobilizing the Crowd in Copyright Clearance for Mass Digitization' (2016) 16(1) *Journal of Intellectual Property* 135.

[134] Directive (EU) 2012/28 of the European Parliament and of the Council of 25 October 2012 on Certain Permitted Uses of Orphan Works, OJ /L 299/5, 27 October 2012, Art. 3(2); see also ACE Survey on the Implementation of the Orphan Works Directive (January 2015), available at <http://project-forward.eu/2015/04/03/ace-survey-on-the-implementation-of-the-orphan-works-directive/>, accessed 11 November 2019.

[135] Directive (EU) 2012/28 of the European Parliament and of the Council of 25 October 2012 on Certain Permitted Uses of Orphan Works, OJ /L 299/5, 27 October 2012, Art. 3(5).

[136] For Austria, see s. 56e(6) Urheberrechtsgesetz, as amended in 2014 (öBGBl. I Nr. 11/2015); for Finland, see Art. 8 of the Act 764/2013 on the Use of Orphan Works.

problematic aspects of the Directive, and one that generates legal uncertainty, is that it does not cover all works and other subject matter. There are important exclusions from the scope of available protection, such as standalone photographs and other images. These works, however, are at the heart of the problem of orphan works,[137] particularly because it is usually not possible to name the author of every copy. What is more, the Directive does not cover audiovisual works and phonograms produced by public service broadcasting organizations after 31 December 2002,[138] and foreign works, i.e. those published outside the European Economic Area.[139] Legal uncertainty can also be demonstrated by the fact that the EUIPO database was not as successful as anticipated. In the first six months following the implementation of the Directive, only 100 works were registered. However, it is expected that the database may play an important role in the future, when it truly becomes an authoritative one-stop search for orphan works.[140]

Albeit limited in its scope, the Orphan Works Directive marks significant progress in the protection of cultural heritage that remains unused due to copyright norms, thereby putting the public interest in the access to these materials at the forefront. The Directive did not address the issue of out-of-commerce works and, although this emerged at around the same time as the orphan works problem and received sporadic legislative response at the national level, it was not until the Digital Single Market Directive that it was regulated within the context of EU copyright.

Out-of-commerce works

Other works and subject matter that may remain unused due to copyright restrictions are the so-called out-of-commerce works. According to Article 8(5) of the Directive on Copyright in the Digital Single Market:

> A work or other subject matter shall be deemed to be out-of-commerce when it can be presumed in good faith that the whole work or other subject matter is not available to the public through customary channels of commerce, after a reasonable effort has been made to determine whether it is available to the public.

---

[137] Commission Staff Working Paper, Impact Assessment on the Cross-Border Online Access to Orphan Works, accompanying the document Proposal for a Directive of the European Parliament and of the Council on Certain Permitted Uses of Orphan Works, SEC(2011) 615 final, 24 May 2011, 11.

[138] Directive (EU) 2012/28 of the European Parliament and of the Council of 25 October 2012 on Certain Permitted Uses of Orphan Works, OJ /L 299/5, 27 October 2012, Art. 1(2)(c).

[139] Recital 12 indicates that this is due to 'reasons of international comity'.

[140] Specifically, there were only fifty-two audiovisual and cinematographic works, forty-nine literary works, and between one and two titles in other categories that were declared to be orphan. Data from the Framework for an EU-Wide Audiovisual Orphan Works Registry, available at <http://project-forward.eu/2015/04/03/52-orphan-films-registered-in-ohim/>, accessed 11 November 2019.

There is a large volume of such works and there is a growing number of cultural institutions seeking to digitize them with the view to making cultural heritage available online.[141] Whereas some orphan works also qualify as out-of-commerce works, not all out-of-commerce works are also orphan. Out-of-commerce works differ from orphan works in that they are either commercially unavailable or have stopped being commercially exploited.[142] This could be due to authorial reasons (such as the moral right of withdrawal in France)[143] or publishing strategies (such as an updated edition of a book or a remastered version of a sound recording).[144] As the Commission and the Parliament acknowledged in Recital 22 of the respective proposals for a Directive on Copyright in the Digital Single Market, clearing a license may also be difficult 'due, for example, to the age of the works or other subject matter, their limited commercial value, or the fact that they were never intended for commercial use' or have never been in commerce.[145] Making sure that the use of out-of-commerce works shall be facilitated was at the top of the EU reform agenda. The legislative action initiated via the Directive on Copyright in the Digital Single Market is discussed in detailed below.

As with orphan works, out-of-commerce works are an important constituent of our cultural heritage that remains unused due to difficulties in clearing a license with the relevant rightsholders. Cultural institutions are engaged in the preservation of their collections for the benefit of future generations. However, because copying is involved in the process of preserving cultural collections, host institutions may face liability unless the use is authorized by rightsholders or permitted by law. The unavailability of defensive rules which expressly permit copying in this context hinders the development of initiatives engaged in the digitization and possible exhibition of such works on the Internet.

---

[141] Katharina de la Durantaye, 'Orphan Works: A Comparative and International Perspective' in Daniel J. Gervais (ed.), *International Intellectual Property: A Handbook of Contemporary Research* (Cheltenham: Edward Elgar, 2015) 190, 212.

[142] See in this regard US Copyright Office, Report on Orphan Works: A Report of the Register of Copyrights (January 2006) 34; i2010: Digital Libraries High Level Expert Group – Copyright Subgroup: Final Report on Digital Preservation, Orphan and Out-of-Print Works, 4 June 2008, s. 6.1; Maurizio Borghi and Stavroula Karapapa, *Copyright and Mass Digitization: A Cross-Jurisdictional Perspective* (Oxford, Oxford University Press, 2013) 88.

[143] Intellectual Property Code (Code de la Propriété Intellectuelle), Art. L121-4 (France).

[144] Maurizio Borghi and Stavroula Karapapa, *Copyright and Mass Digitization: A Cross-Jurisdictional Approach* (Oxford: Oxford University Press, 2013) 89; Maria Lillà Montagnani and Maurizio Borghi, 'Positive Copyright and Open Content Licences: How to Make a Marriage Work by Empowering Authors to Disseminate Their Creations' (2007) 12 *International Journal of Communications Law and Policy* 244.

[145] EU Parliament, Proposal for a Directive of the European Parliament and of the Council on Copyright in the Digital Single Market (SWD(2016) 301) (SWD(2016) 302), COM (2016) 593 final, 2016/0280 (COD), Brussels, 14 September 2016; European Commission, Proposal for a Directive of the European Parliament and of the Council on Copyright in the Digital Single Market, Brussels, 14 September 2016 COM (2016) 593 final, 2016/0280 (COD), Art. 13, available at <https://ec.europa.eu/transparency/regdoc/rep/1/2016/EN/1-2016-593-EN-F1-1.PDF>, accessed 11 November 2019.

EU copyright law has very recently addressed the issue of out-of-commerce works through the Directive on Copyright in the Digital Single Market, even though the Commission has undertaken a number of initiatives since 2011. For instance, before the launch of the Digital Single Market Directive, the Commission encouraged a stakeholder dialogue[146] that led to the signing of a Memorandum of Understanding on Key Principles on the Digitization and Making Available of Out-of-Commerce Works on 20 September 2011.[147] The Memorandum aimed to encourage voluntary agreements in the context of collective licensing for those uses carried out by non-commercial publicly accessible institutions of out-of-commerce books and journals, contained in their collections and first published in the country of the licensing agreement. Out-of-commerce works are there defined as those that 'in all versions and manifestations [are] no longer commercially available in customary channels of commerce'.[148] However, whether a work is commercially available shall ultimately be determined in the country of first publication.[149] The Memorandum has no binding effect on its signatories, and—even though specific rules on the use of out-of-commerce works have recently been introduced via the Directive on Copyright in the Digital Single Market—the Memorandum has influenced legislation in some EU Member States.

National legislative initiatives

Following the 2011 Memorandum, some—but not all—Member States included relevant provisions in their national laws.

In the Nordic countries, i.e. Sweden, Norway, Denmark, Finland, and Iceland, legal provisions with the capacity to regulate the use and possible exploitation of out-of-commerce works have been applied since the 1960's.[150] This system instantaneously covers all authors of a relevant subject matter, even those who are not members of a collecting society, and a collecting society concludes a collective agreement with users. Rightholders can claim individual remuneration from the

---

[146] Commission Recommendation of 24 August 2006 on the Digitization and Online Accessibility of Cultural Material and Digital Preservation, OJ L 236/28, Art. 6(b).

[147] Memorandum of Understanding on Key Principles on the Digitization and Making Available of Out-of-Commerce Works of 20 September 2011.

[148] Ibid., at 2.

[149] Memorandum of Understanding on Key Principles on the Digitization and Making Available of Out-of-Commerce Works of 20 September 2011: see under the sub-heading 'Definition' and Principle 1(2).

[150] For a detailed discussion on extended collective licensing see Stef Van Gompel, 'Unlocking the Potential of Pre-existing Content: How to Address the Issue of Orphan Works in Europe?' (2007) 38(6) *International Review of Intellectual Property and Competition Law* 669, 687–9; Tarja Koskinen-Olsson, 'Collective Management in the Nordic Countries' in Daniel Gervais (ed.), *Collective Management of Copyright and Related Rights* (Alphen aan den Rijn: Kluwer Law International, 2006) 257; Gunnar Karnell, 'Extended Collective License Clauses and Agreements in Nordic Copyright Law' (1985–6) 10 *Columbia-VLA Journal of Law & the Arts* 73.

collecting society and can also individually prohibit the use of their works under the collective license. It is only when rightholders express an opposition to their works being included in the scheme by opting out that the collecting society will not manage their rights on a collective basis. Although this scheme efficiently covers mass uses of works because it is not premised on individual clearance of rights, offering—according to some commentators[151]—offering an arguably viable solution to the problems associated with orphan and out-of-commerce works, the Nordic model has also attracted criticism for imposing conditions both on the exercise and enjoyment of exclusive rights under copyright and depriving rightsholders of the power to negotiate royalties.[152]

In Germany, based on the principles of the 2011 Memorandum, the digitization and making available of out-of-commerce works was made possible with an amendment to the Copyright Administration Act.[153] The aim of the new legislation that came into force on 1 January 2014 was to implement the Orphan Works Directive and to introduce a collective management system for out-of-commerce works. Works that are in the collection of a publicly accessible institution, and that have been published before 1 January 1966, can be entered into the registry for out-of-commerce works which is maintained by the German Patent and Trademark Office.[154] It is then presumed that the relevant collecting management organization can conclude licensing agreements for non-commercial uses of those works with third parties, including acts of reproduction and making the works available to the public,[155] unless the rightsholders have objected to the entry of their works into the registry within a six-week period.[156] Rightsholders are also given the opportunity to express their opposition to their work being included in the registry at any time.[157]

---

[151] See e.g. see Johan Axhamn and Lucie Guibault, 'Cross-border Extended Collective Licensing: a Solution to Online Dissemination of Europe's Cultural Heritage?' (2012) Amsterdam Law School Research Paper No. 2012-22, available at <https://ssrn.com/abstract=2001347>, accessed 11 November 2019.

[152] See in this regard Bernard Lang, 'Orphan Works and the Google Book Settlement: An International Perspective' in J Grimmelmann (ed.), *D is for Digitize* (2010) 55 *New York Law School Law Review* 111, 118–19; Silke Von Lewinski, 'Mandatory Collective Administration of Exclusive Rights – A Case Study on its Compatibility with International and EC Copyright Law', *e-Copyright Bulletin* (January-March 2007), UNESCO.

[153] Act of 1 October 2013, 'zur Nutzung verwaister und vergriffener Werke und einer weiteren Änderung des Urheberrechtsgesetzes' (BGBl. I 2013, s. 3728 (Nr. 59)), amending das Urheberrechtswahrnehmungsgesetz vom 9 September 1965. Also see Elisabeth Niggemann, 'National Libraries and Copyright in the Digital Age - the German Situation for Orphan Works and Out-of-Print Works' (2012) 23 *Alexandria: The Journal of National and International Library and Information Issues* 125.

[154] Act of 1 October 2013, 'zur Nutzung verwaister und vergriffener Werke und einer weiteren Änderung des Urheberrechtsgesetzes' (BGBl. I 2013, s. 13(d)(4)).

[155] Ibid., s. 13(d)(1)–(3).

[156] Ibid., s. 13d(1)(5).

[157] Ibid., s. 13(d)(2).

One of the first initiatives in Europe to address the issue of out-of-commerce works is the French Act on the Digital Exploitation of Unavailable Books of the 20th Century. According to the French Act, a book is considered to be commercially unavailable if it was published in France before 1 January 2001, is no longer disseminated by a publisher, and is no longer published in either print or digital form.[158] Article L.134-2 of the French Act introduces a registry of out-of-commerce books, developed and managed by the French National Library. This is meant to be a freely accessible online public database and already contains a list of thousands of unavailable books.[159] When a book is registered in this database for more than six months, the right to authorize its reproduction and electronic dissemination is exercised by a collecting management organization. A work registered in the database of the National Library can be digitized and made available on a non-exclusive basis for a period of five years that can be subject to renewal. Copyright holders are entitled to compensation for such a use. After the six months of registration lapses, the rights of reproduction and making the work available are administered by the relevant collecting society that can also grant free-of-charge licenses to libraries under specific conditions. These conditions are the lack of commercial or economic advantage to the institutional user and the fact that their rightsholder cannot be traced within a ten-year period from the date of the first authorization to exploit. Rightsholders can at any time terminate this gratuitous authorization if they so decide.

The 2012 Act was challenged before the French Constitutional Court soon after its introduction with a 'priority issue of constitutionality'.[160] The question was whether Articles L 134-1 to L 134-9 of the French Intellectual Property Code (Article 1 of Act No. 2012-287 of 1 March 2012 on the Digital Exploitation of Unavailable Books of the 20th Century) were in compliance with constitutionally protected rights and freedoms. In particular, the claim was that the collective management system established in these Articles is in breach of the right to property guaranteed by Articles 2 and 17 of the Declaration of Human and Civic Rights of 1789.[161] The Constitutional Court found that the 2012 Act is in compliance with the French Constitution. The right to property may be subject to limitations to the extent that these are justified for reasons of public interest and insofar as they do not exceed this objective. The 2012 Act was held to serve the public interest as it means to ensure preservation of, and access to, unavailable books that were

---

[158] Act No. 2012-287 relating to the Digital Exploitation of Unavailable Books of the 20th Century, 1 March 2012, Art. L.134-1 IPC.

[159] Available at <https://relire.bnf.fr/registre-gestion-collective>, accessed 11 November 2019.

[160] French Act No. 2012-287 relating to the Digital Exploitation of Unavailable Books of the 20th Century, 1 March 2012.

[161] According to Art. 17,

Since the right to Property is inviolable and sacred, no one may be deprived thereof, unless public necessity, legally ascertained, obviously requires it, and just and prior indemnity has been paid.

published before 1 January 2001, but which are not yet in the public domain. What is more, the system of collective management established by the Act was held not to be in conflict with the constitutional right to property as the relevant provisions only concern books that are not currently exploited, ensure fair distribution of royalties to the right holders, and do not violate the authors' right to paternity and disclosure of their works.

Soulier and Doke and its impact on national initiatives

Even though, in 2014, the French Constitutional Court found in favour of the constitutional compliance of the collective management system introduced by the 2012 Act on the Digital Exploitation of Unavailable Books of the 20th Century, the European Court of Justice—affirming the position of the Advocate General[162]— found that the Act was in violation of the exclusive rights of copyright holders as established by the Information Society Directive. This was in Soulier and Doke,[163] where the Court of Justice was called to assess the compatibility of the 2012 Act with the Information Society Directive, following a referral for a preliminary ruling from the French Conseil d'État (Council of State). In particular, the French Constitutional Court sought clarification as to whether Articles 2 and 5 of the Information Society Directive preclude national legislation (such as the 2012 Act), which gives approved collecting societies the right to authorize the reproduction and the representation in digital form of 'out-of-print books', while allowing the authors of those books, or their successors in title, to oppose or put an end to that practice, subject to specific conditions laid down in the Act.

Clarifying that the case did not involve copyright exceptions and limitations as available under Article 5 of the Information Society Directive, the Court of Justice stressed at the outset that the protection available under Articles 2(a) and 3(1) of the Directive ought to be given a broad interpretation. In line with the Berne Convention, this does not only involve the enjoyment of those rights, but also extends to their exercise.[164] As the court noted, such exclusive rights are preventive in nature in that their legitimate exercise depends on prior authorization from the relevant rightsholders and any use of a work by an unauthorized third party must be regarded as infringing copyright in that work, unless permitted under the copyright exceptions and limitations available in Article 5.[165] Although neither Article

[162] Opinion of Advocate General Wathelet in Marc Soulier and Sara Doke v Premier Ministre and Ministre de la Culture et de la Communication, Case C-301/15, 7 July 2016, ECLI:EU:C:2016:536.
[163] Marc Soulier and Sara Doke v Premier Ministre and Ministre de la Culture et de la Communication, Case C-301/15, 16 November 2016, ECLI:EU:C:2016:878.
[164] Marc Soulier and Sara Doke v Premier Ministre and Ministre de la Culture et de la Communication, Case C-301/15, 16 November 2016, ECLI:EU:C:2016:878, [31].
[165] Marc Soulier and Sara Doke v Premier Ministre and Ministre de la Culture et de la Communication, Case C-301/15, 16 November 2016, ECLI:EU:C:2016:878, [33] and [34].

2(a) nor Article 3(1) specify the way in which prior authorial consent must be expressed, they do not require that such a consent be given explicitly. As the court noted, these provisions also allow that consent is expressed implicitly, giving the example of the right of communicating works to the public in the online environment under the concept of the 'new public' as elaborated in *Svensson*.[166] In light, however, of the objective of increased protection as underlined in Recital 9 of the Directive, implied consent can only be admitted in strictly defined circumstances in order not to deprive of effect the very principle of authorial consent. Indeed, authors should be informed of future use of their work by third parties and the means at their disposal to prohibit it if they so wish; should this not be the case, it would be de facto impossible for authors to adopt any position regarding such a use.[167]

The 2012 French Act did not appear to offer a mechanism to ensure that authors are actually informed and it is not therefore inconceivable that some authors, by not being aware of future uses of their works, cannot adopt a position on such a use. As the court stressed, 'a mere lack of opposition on their part cannot be regarded as the expression of their implicit consent to that use'.[168] This is an important statement regarding the legitimacy of opt-out mechanisms, in general, and is likely to put into question various national systems premised on such a mechanism.

However, *Soulier and Doke* is not meant to set an absolute ban on the future of national initiatives pursuing a public interest objective, such as the digital exploitation of out-of-commerce works.[169] Article 2(a) and Article 3(1) of the Information Society Directive was hence interpreted as

> precluding national legislation, such as that at issue in the main proceedings, that gives an approved collecting society the right to authorise the reproduction and communication to the public in digital form of 'out-of-print' books, namely, books published in France before 1 January 2001 which are no longer commercially distributed by a publisher and are not currently published in print or in digital form, while allowing the authors of those books, or their successors in title, to oppose or put an end to that practice, on the conditions that that legislation lays down.[170]

---

[166] *Marc Soulier and Sara Doke v Premier Ministre and Ministre de la Culture et de la Communication*, Case C-301/15, 16 November 2016, ECLI:EU:C:2016:878, [35].

[167] *Marc Soulier and Sara Doke v Premier Ministre and Ministre de la Culture et de la Communication*, Case C-301/15, 16 November 2016, ECLI:EU:C:2016:878, [37]–[40].

[168] *Marc Soulier and Sara Doke v Premier Ministre and Ministre de la Culture et de la Communication*, Case C-301/15, 16 November 2016, ECLI:EU:C:2016:878, [43].

[169] *Marc Soulier and Sara Doke v Premier Ministre and Ministre de la Culture et de la Communication*, Case C-301/15, 16 November 2016, ECLI:EU:C:2016:878, [45]: 'However, the pursuit of that objective and of that interest cannot justify a derogation not provided for by the EU legislature to the protection that authors are ensured by that directive.'

[170] *Marc Soulier and Sara Doke v Premier Ministre and Ministre de la Culture et de la Communication*, Case C-301/15, 16 November 2016, ECLI:EU:C:2016:878, [53].

It follows that the 2012 French Act on out-of-commerce books was in breach of the exclusive right of authors as established by the Information Society Directive. Although in the early days following the *Soulier and Doke* ruling the latter was viewed as having the potential to undermine extended collective licensing systems across Europe (including the Nordic model and the UK licensing scheme), the European Union has in the meantime offered a specific exception covering the use of out-of-commerce works through the Directive on Copyright in the Digital Single Market.

The EU exception on out-of-commerce works

The Directive on Copyright in the Digital Single Market introduced a mechanism under which certain institutions, such as libraries, archives, and museums across Europe, will be entitled, and permitted as a matter of law, to carry out specific uses of such works with a view to enhancing access to Europe's cultural heritage. In light of digital technologies that enable new ways of preserving cultural heritage and, at the same time, create new challenges, the Directive on Copyright responds to the need to adapt the current legal framework by offering a mandatory exception to the reproduction right for such acts of preservation. Despite some national initiatives, discussed earlier, EU copyright law did not address the issue of out-of-commerce works until recently.

Article 8 of the Directive on Copyright in the Digital Single Market offers a mandatory exception concerning the use of out-of-commerce works, that reads as follows:

1. Member States shall provide that a collective management organization, in accordance with its mandates from rightholders, may conclude a non-exclusive licence for non-commercial purposes with a cultural heritage institution for the reproduction, distribution, communication to the public, or making available to the public of out-of-commerce works or other subject matter that are permanently in the collection of the institution, irrespective of whether all rightholders covered by the licence have mandated the collective management organisation, on condition that:

   (a) the collective management organisation is, on the basis of its mandates, sufficiently representative of rightholders in the relevant type of works or other subject matter and of the rights that are the subject of the licence; and

   (b) all rightholders are guaranteed equal treatment in relation to the terms of the licence.

2. Member States shall provide for an exception or limitation to the rights provided for in Article 5(a), (b), (d), and (e) and Article 7(1) of Directive 96/9/EC,

Articles 2 and 3 of Directive 2001/29/EC, Article 4(1) of Directive 2009/24/EC, and Article 15(1) of this Directive, in order to allow cultural heritage institutions to make available, for non-commercial purposes, out-of-commerce works or other subject matter that are permanently in their collections, on condition that:

(a) the name of the author or any other identifiable rightholder is indicated, unless this turns out to be impossible; and

(b) such works or other subject matter are made available on non-commercial websites.

3. Member States shall provide that the exception or limitation provided for in paragraph 2 only applies to types of works or other subject matter for which no collective management organisation that fulfils the condition set out in point (a) of paragraph 1 exists.

4. Member States shall provide that all rightholders may, at any time, easily and effectively, exclude their works or other subject matter from the licensing mechanism set out in paragraph 1 or from the application of the exception or limitation provided for in paragraph 2, either in general or in specific cases, including after the conclusion of a licence or after the beginning of the use concerned.

Article 8(1) seems to introduce systems of collective licensing by reference to out-of-commerce works. In particular, Member States should give a collective management organization the authority, in accordance with its mandate from rightsholders, to conclude a non-exclusive licence for non-commercial purposes with cultural heritage institutions for the reproduction, distribution, communication to the public, or making available to the public of out-of-commerce content that is permanently in the collection of the institution. This should apply irrespective of whether all rightsholders have mandated the collective management organization, insofar as the collecting organization is sufficiently representative of rightholders. What is more, the principle of equal treatment of all rightsholders shall be guaranteed. This collective license scheme for out-of-commerce works allows Member States a degree of flexibility in determining the specific parameters of the scheme, in accordance with their legal traditions, practices, and circumstances. Indicative in this regard is Recital 33 of the Digital Single Market Directive, which offers a detailed outline of various collective management mechanisms, leaving Member States the flexibility to choose the most appropriate one. These include extended collective licensing, legal mandates, or legal presumptions of representation facilitating the licensing of out-of-commerce works. As this Recital effectively allows Member States the flexibility to carry on with collective licensing schemes they had put in place to deal with out-of-commerce works,[171] this

---

[171] Also see in this regard EU Parliament, Proposal for a Directive of the European Parliament and of the Council on Copyright in the Digital Single Market (SWD(2016) 301) (SWD(2016) 302), COM (2016) 593 final, 2016/0280 (COD), Brussels, 14 September 2016, Recital 22a.

is seemingly in contrast with the outcome that the Court of Justice reached in *Soulier and Doke*.[172]

Article 8(2) outlines an exception or limitation enabling the use of out-of-commerce works. It requires Member States to provide for an exception or limitation to the rights provided for in Article 5(a), (b), (d), and (e) and Article 7(1) of Directive 96/9/EC, Articles 2 and 3 of Directive 2001/29/EC, Article 4(1) of Directive 2009/24/EC, and Article 15(1) of this Directive, in order to allow cultural heritage institutions to make available, for non-commercial purposes, out-of-commerce content that is permanently in their collections. The exception is subject to a number of conditions. These include that the source ought to be attributed, unless this turns out to be impossible, and that the content should be made available on non-commercial websites. Importantly, by virtue of Article 8(3) the exception will only be applicable to types of works or other subject matter for which there exists no collective management organization, as envisaged in the first paragraph of Article 8. This means that collective management should be the norm and, should such a mechanism not be set in place, the exception or limitation of Article 8(2) should take effect. As with the cultural preservation exception of Article 6, the beneficiaries of the exception are cultural heritage institutions, namely publicly accessible libraries or museums, archives, or film or audio heritage institutions, as per Article 2(3).

An important limitation to the scope of the collective licensing scheme and the mandatory exception on the use of out-of-commerce works is laid down in Article 8(4). This outlines an opt-out mechanism, effectively offering rightsholders the opportunity under national law to exclude their works or other subject matter from the licensing mechanism, at any time, easily and effectively. Recital 35 clarifies that where a rightsholder excludes the application of the collective management schemes or the relevant copyright exceptions or limitations to one or more works or other subject matter, any ongoing uses are terminated within a reasonable period. Where such uses take place under a collective licence, the collective management organization should cease to issue licences covering the uses concerned upon receiving notification. Should rightsholders express their wish to be excluded, this should not affect their claims to remuneration for the actual use of their protected content under the licence.

Specific provisions are in place with regard to cross-border uses of out-of-commerce works. These are laid down in Article 9, which reads that

1. Member States shall ensure that licences granted in accordance with Article 8 may allow the use of out-of-commerce works or other subject matter by cultural heritage institutions in any Member State.

---

[172] *Marc Soulier and Sara Doke v Premier Ministre and Ministre de la Culture et de la Communication*, Case C-301/15, 16 November 2016, ECLI:EU:C:2016:878.

2. The uses of works and other subject matter under the exception or limitation provided for in Article 8(2) shall be deemed to occur solely in the Member State where the cultural heritage institution undertaking that use is established.

The mechanism envisaged by the Directive departs from *Soulier and Doke* in that it allows the continuation of national schemes, including extended collective licensing mechanisms, and is also based on an opt-out logic that is not entirely in line with the reasoning developed in *Soulier and Doke*.

Works of visual art in the public domain

In the context of exceptions available to cultural heritage institutions for purposes of preservation, and in the context of the mass digitization of out-of-commerce works, but also more broadly, Article 14 of the Directive on Copyright in the Digital Single Market becomes highly relevant. This Article introduces an exception that is mandatory for Member States to implement regarding reproductions of works of visual art and clarifies that

> Member States shall provide that, when the term of protection of a work of visual art has expired, any material resulting from an act of reproduction of that work is not subject to copyright or related rights, unless the material resulting from that act of reproduction is original in the sense that it is the author's own intellectual creation.

The exception was introduced in the Digital Single Market Directive at a late stage in the legislative process. As explained in Recital 53, when the term of protection of a work expires this work enters into the public domain and is no longer subject to the rights that Union copyright law provides. The circulation of faithful reproductions of works of visual art in the public domain contributes to access to, and promotion of, culture, as well as access to cultural heritage. However, such reproductions may still receive protection in the digital context in a way that is inconsistent with the expiry of the term of protection and there are divergent approaches in the various Member States on the protection that such reproductions receive. In the context of mass digitization projects and cultural heritage preservation initiatives, copying of public domain images is a usual practice. This may include not only photographs in the collections of archives but could also include images featured in other materials that are subject to digitization. Article 14 therefore standardizes the protection afforded to works of visual art and clarifies that certain reproductions of such works, once they fall in the public domain, should not attract protection by copyright or related rights. Recital 58 further indicates that this should not prevent cultural heritage institutions from selling reproductions, such as postcards.

In the Parliament's proposal for a Directive on Copyright in the Digital Single Market, a relevant provision was included as part of the exception on the preservation of cultural heritage. Although more specific in terms of its context, it had a broader scope in that the then-proposed exception was not meant to allow the creation of new copyright on faithful copies of a public domain work which is made for public preservation purposes.[173] The reason was to ensure that copyright on works that have fallen in the public domain would not be unjustifiably extended and also to prevent the creation of digital monopolies on cultural materials that are no longer subject to copyright protection.[174] This internal limit to the cultural preservation exception was not retained in the final version of the Directive, but the provision of Article 14 was introduced in order to ensure that the digitization of public domain images shall not be subject to exploitation, unless it can qualify as an author's own intellectual creation.

It is unclear what the true purpose of this provision is as it does not seem to offer anything beyond clarity in the context of the use of works of visual art and a broader perspective on the concept of the originality requirement under EU law. In fact, the Term Directive seems to offer protection both to original photographs, which are protected by copyright, and sub-original photographs, which may receive protection under related rights. To this effect, Article 6 of the Term Directive reads:

> Photographs which are original in the sense that they are the author's own intellectual creation shall be protected in accordance with Article 1. No other criteria shall be applied to determine their eligibility for protection. Member States may provide for the protection of other photographs.

Although the protection afforded to original photographs seems to remain unaffected, it is likely that Member States offering related rights protection to sub-original photographs will have to revise their national laws. Such protection is, for instance, available in Germany and there is recent case law addressing the protection of digitized copies of public domain images[175] concerning, in particular, copies of paintings held by a group of German museums that were uploaded to Wikimedia Commons. Copyright in the paintings had expired by virtue of Article 64 of the German Copyright Act. The Federal Court of Justice held that Article 72 of the German Copyright Act, which offers protection to sub-original photographs

---

[173] EU Parliament, Proposal for a Directive of the European Parliament and of the Council on Copyright in the Digital Single Market (SWD(2016) 301) (SWD(2016) 302), COM (2016) 593 final, 2016/0280 (COD), Brussels, 14 September 2016, Art. 5(1)(a).

[174] Maurizio Borghi and Stavroula Karapapa, *Copyright and Mass Digitization: A Cross-Jurisdictional Approach* (Oxford: Oxford University Press, 2013) 92 et seq.

[175] *Reiss-Engelhorn Museen*, Federal Court of Justice (Bundesgerichtshof), 20 December 2018, I ZR 104/17 (Germany).

under a neighbouring right, applied even in cases involving mere copying of a painting as this requires a significant amount of effort.[176] The court moved on to affirm that the protection of Article 72 applies to photographs of paintings that are no longer protected by copyright.[177] The protection afforded to sub-original photographs will have to be made unavailable in the aftermath of Article 14.

Exceptions for purposes of public security

Among exceptions that are set in place with a view to serving a public interest objective is the one available in Article 5(2)(e) of the Information Society Directive. This provision aspires to permit uses that impact on the reproduction right and the right of communicating works to the public 'for the purposes of public security or to ensure the proper performance or reporting of administrative, parliamentary, or judicial proceedings'.

The purpose of the exception is to safeguard the integrity of the legal order, including state institutions, but also the life, property, and freedom of individual citizens. In this light, the concept of public security has to be understood in the broadest sense. An interesting aspect of this copyright exception is that the use in question does not have to be *justified* on the basis of a public security purpose; it should only *serve* such purpose.[178] This is an important element which demonstrates that public policy defences exist in recognition of the fact that the objectives of copyright law must on occasion play second fiddle to other interests or concerns, without the defendant having to explain why they carried out a particular use that would otherwise lead to copyright infringement.

A similar exception is also provided in Article 6(2)(c) of the Database Directive.[179] There, however, 'proper performance or reporting' is not mentioned. The permitted use should ensure proper performance or reporting of administrative, parliamentary, or judicial proceedings, meaning that uses which are not essential in achieving this purpose should not benefit from the copyright exception. The exception has a narrower scope by reference to protected databases. Unlike Article 6(2)(c) of the Database Directive, however, which introduces a *lex specialis*, Article 5(2)(e) of the Information Society Directive has a broader ambit, covering in principle any category of work.

With the introduction of the text mining exception, discussed earlier in this chapter, the scope of uses permitted for the purposes of public security and for

---

[176] Ibid., [26].

[177] Ibid., [30].

[178] Michel M. Walter and Silke Von Lewinski, *European Copyright Law: A Commentary* (Oxford: Oxford University Press, 2010) 9.6.34.

[179] Digital Single Market Directive (Directive 2019/790); Directive 96/9/EC of the European Parliament and of the Council of 11 March 1996 on the Legal Protection of Databases, OJ L 77, 27 March 1996, 20–8 (Database Directive).

the proper performance of administrative, parliamentary, or judicial proceedings, will likely be significantly broadened. In the context of biology and medicine, text mining through natural language processing techniques could be used for a wide corpora of scientific literature and official documents of medical authorities in order 'to automatically generate and rank hypothesis that a scientist can test in a laboratory'.[180] As researchers from the National Centre for Text Mining at Manchester explain, text mining 'goes far beyond its cousin, information retrieval', by providing the 'means to rapidly drill down to individual facts, rather than, like information retrieval, providing many documents to wade through'.[181] Text and data mining may also prove useful in the context of matters of public security and, in this regard, the two relevant defensive rules may possibly overlap, expanding the scope of activities permitted in this context and the breadth of a relevant defensive rule.

Public policy privileges and contractual overridability

Unlike speech entitlements, which derive from the very principles on which copyright protection subsists, policy objectives reside in a variety of prerogatives, some of which may have an indirect fundamental rights rationale. As with their underpinning, the focus of the various defensive rules, which notably take the form of copyright exceptions and limitations, remains largely diverse and it is not possible to develop a simple rule regarding their power against contractual or technological override. It comes as no surprise that the various exceptions and limitations that help promote public policy objectives do not come under a one-size-fits-all rule and some of them are compulsory against contractual override whereas others are not.[182] The question of contractual override and the corresponding status of a copyright exception or limitation becomes a matter of policy decision and balancing the importance of meeting a particular policy objective. Although for various copyright exceptions and limitations there is lack of certainty as to whether they are compulsory against their technological restriction or contractual override, the Directive on Copyright in the Digital Single Market has specified that some of the defensive rules available in it shall render their possible contractual restriction unenforceable. These are the text mining exception of Article 3, the cross-border teaching exception of Article 5, and the cultural preservation exception of Article 6.[183] In addition, the Directive on Copyright in the Digital Single Market cross refers to Article 6(4) of the Information Society Directive and specifies that Member States should take appropriate measures to ensure that rightholders make available to beneficiaries of

---

[180] 'Text Mining and IP', Submission to the Independent Review of Intellectual Property and Growth (Hargreaves Review) from the National Centre for Text Mining, University of Manchester, May 2001, 2.
[181] Ibid., 2–3.
[182] See e.g. Digital Single Market Directive (Directive 2019/790).
[183] Digital Single Market Directive (Directive 2019/790), Art. 7.

exceptions the means of benefiting from them.[184] This is meant to apply to both of the text mining exceptions and, in addition, the cross-border teaching and cultural preservation exceptions. This has the effect that the aforementioned exceptions are designed to have a stronger legal grounding compared to other exceptions and limitations included in this Directive, but also other legislative instruments at the EU level, where the interplay between copyright exceptions and contract is not expressly addressed, with the (rather limited) exception of Article 6(4) of the Information Society Directive.

Where the matter of contractual override is not expressly addressed, it has to be assumed that licensing agreements may be used to restrict the scope and/or availability of certain copyright exceptions and limitations. This raises the normative question on whether this is a practice that *should* be allowed or not. Although for speech entitlements it is argued that there are principle-based reasons why the relevant copyright exceptions and limitations should not be subject to contractual override or licensing limitations, this cannot be equally argued by reference to the public policy privileges discussed in this chapter, unless this was decided at the legislative level. The reason for this is that the balance of rights and interests is decided at the policy level. Even in this case, however, excessive or overreaching copyright claims that are also governed with relevant contractual arrangements may be regulated under the general legal principle that prohibits the abusive exercise of rights, which is available in many EU Member States and discussed in Chapter 9.

A problematic aspect of declaring some, but not all, copyright exceptions and limitations mandatory against their contractual or technological restriction at the legislative level is the fact that those exceptions and limitations that do not receive the protective shelter of being declared mandatory may be overridden, without offering sufficient relief to beneficiaries to claim the benefit of the exception.

Conclusion

A network of copyright exceptions and limitations under EU copyright make allowances for certain uses of protected works without authorization from the rightsholders, with a view to enable the fulfilment of public policy objectives. Because of the diversity of these objectives, the relevant exceptions and limitations are largely diverse in terms of their beneficiaries, conditions of application, and conceptual underpinning. The most recent legislative attempts to promote public policy via copyright exceptions and limitations are defensive rules that were introduced with a view to enabling and enhancing the advancement of online teaching and

---

[184] According to Art. 7(2) of the Directive on Copyright in the Digital Single Market (Directive 2019/790), Art. 6(4) of the Information Society Directive (Directive 2001/29/EC) applies to the text mining exception of Art. 3.

mass digitization initiatives. Indeed, in light of the Internet and (mass) digitization, the scope of available defences has been enlarged through a set of legislative instruments, such as the Orphan Works Directive[185] and the Directive on Copyright in the Digital Single Market.[186] There are also related national initiatives addressing the impact of digitization initiatives on copyright, such as the German Law on out-of-commerce works and the Nordic system of extended collective licenses. In their diversity, the relevant exceptions that are premised on public policy grounds are meant to make allowances for modern methods of teaching provision, such as on-line courses and distance learning programmes, to allow the creation of online collections of materials in dedicated terminals, and to extract value from the plethora of works that have become orphan or are currently out-of-commerce. Although the policy reason behind this scope expansion has been the promotion of growth in the educational and cultural sector, there is a strong public interest underpinning the very presence of these exceptions in the statute, the reason being that they allow certain freedoms in the dissemination of information and knowledge.

Unlike other copyright exceptions and limitations, certain public policy privileges have the merit of having been declared imperative against contractual override. This is a recent novelty of EU copyright, which through the Digital Single Market Directive stipulates that any contractual provision contrary to the exceptions on text and data mining,[187] cross-border teaching,[188] and cultural preservation[189] shall be unenforceable.[190] This strengthens the relevant copyright exceptions against possible contractual override. However, it is not clear why the relevant defensive rules have been chosen or what the determinant factor is, although in jurisdictions where a mixed approach towards contractual override is taken, such as the United Kingdom, the defensive rules that are imperative against contract broadly coincide. This leaves numerous other public policy privileges at the contractual discretion of parties and their exercise and resulting benefit is rather thin, given that the Internet allows individualized licensing, often under unilateral terms and conditions. Interestingly, defendants advancing public policy defences do not need to offer an explanation as to why they committed infringement as a conduct serving the public interest is rationally defensible. However, they would need to demonstrate that the use at issue serves such goals and meets the conditions specifically set by law.

---

[185] Directive (EU) 2012/28 of the European Parliament and of the Council of 25 October 2012 on Certain Permitted Uses of Orphan Works, OJ /L 299/5, 27 October 2012.

[186] Digital Single Market Directive (Directive 2019/790).

[187] Digital Single Market Directive (Directive 2019/790) , Art. 3.

[188] Ibid., Art. 5.

[189] Ibid., Art. 6.

[190] Ibid., Art. 7(1).

8

Remunerated Exceptions

Under European Union copyright, certain permitted uses are subject to the requirement that the rightsholders shall be fairly compensated. These 'permitted-but-paid'[1] uses include private copying, reprography, and the reproduction of broadcasts that are made by social institutions pursuing non-commercial purposes.[2] A number of questions arise with regard to the concept of fair compensation as a condition for the application of said exceptions, some of which have been discussed in the Court of Justice.[3] Still, uncertainty remains regarding the way in which the requirement of fair compensation has been implemented by the various Member States, the notoriously vague and variably interpreted concept of harm on which fair compensation is premised, and the impact of compensation on the legal nature of uses. This has an impact on how the relevant remunerated exceptions are understood in terms of their legal nature: are they statutory licenses, legitimate entitlements of the rightsholders to compensation, or fully fledged rights of the users who have actually paid for their entitlement to a specific permitted use? Answers to questions like this one are becoming more pressing in the online context, where the concept of harm could take unprecedented dimensions, especially with regard to private copying.

---

[1] See in this regard Jane C. Ginsburg, 'Fair Use for Free, or Permitted-but-Paid?' (2014) 29 *Berkeley Technology Law Journal* 1383.

[2] They also include exceptions on cross-border teaching activities, available under Art. 5 of the Digital Single Market Directive, but it is at the discretion of Member States to decide whether or not to lay the relevant exception as a remunerated exception or not. See Directive (EU) 2019/790 of the European Parliament and of the Council of 17 April 2019 on Copyright and Related Rights in the Digital Single Market and amending Directives 96/9/EC and 2001/29/EC (Digital Single Market Directive), OJ L 130, 17 May 2019, 92–125.

[3] *Padawan SL v Sociedad General de Autores y Editores de España (SGAE)*, Case C-467/08, 21 October 2010, ECLI:EU:C:2010:620 (*Padawan*); *Stichting de Thuiskopie v Opus Supplies Deutschland GmbH and Others*, Case C-462/09, 16 June 2011, ECLI:EU:C:2011:397 (*Opus*); *Martin Luksan v Petrus van der Let*, Case C-277/10, 9 February 2012, ECLI:EU:C:2012:65 (*Luksan*); *Verwertungsgesellschaft Wort (VG Wort) v Kyocera and Others and Canon Deutschland GmbH and Fujitsu Technology Solutions GmbH and Hewlett-Packard GmbH v Verwertungsgesellschaft Wort*, Cases C-457/11, C-458/11, C-459/11, C-460/11, 27 June 2013, ECLI:EU:C:2013:426 (*VG Wort*); *Amazon.com International Sales Inc. and Others v Austro-Mechana Gesellschaft zur Wahrnehmung mechanisch-musikalischer Urheberrechte Gesellschaft mbH*, Case C-521/11, 11 July 2013, ECLI:EU:C:2013:515 (*Amazon*); *Copydan Båndkopi v Nokia Danmark A/S*, Case C-463/12, 5 March 2015, ECLI:EU:C:2015:144 (*Copydan*); *Hewlett-Packard Belgium SPRL v Reprobel SCRL*, Case C-572/13, 12 November 2015, ECLI:EU:C:2015:750 (*Reprobel*).

Defences to Copyright Infringement. Stavroula Karapapa, Oxford University Press (2020). © Stavroula Karapapa.
DOI: 10.1093/oso/9780198795636.001.0001

Introduction

Even though most copyright exceptions and limitations are not subject to the requirement to pay remuneration to copyright holders, there are a few copyright exceptions that are available on such a condition. This is an intrinsic feature of the relevant defensive rules and an important constituent of their legal nature. The leading view is that this latter set of exceptions does not amount to the creation of enforceable user rights, despite the fact that it may be claimed that users have paid for the activity.[4] The reason is that authors can still exercise control over the relevant uses of their works; even though the scope of rights is limited, authors are entitled to remuneration. Remunerated exceptions are deemed to be an intermediary form of permitted use; they can be seen less as exceptions to rights and more as detailed articulations of exclusive rights.[5] In practice, they are said to be a form of legal licence, whereby rightsholders are statutorily prevented from prohibiting certain activities and because their full proprietary claim is limited they are entitled to receive compensation.[6] With regard to uses having these qualities and essential characteristics—i.e. remuneration but not full control—Calabresi and Melamed explain that property is construed under a liability, instead of a property rule.[7] Even though limited when compared to the control resulting from exclusive rights, uses are assumed to be part of the proprietary entitlement of authors.[8] Under EU copyright, the most noteworthy remunerated exceptions are private copying, reprography, the reproduction of broadcasts that are made by social institutions pursuing non-commercial purposes,[9] permitted uses on orphan works,[10] and uses which take place in the context of cross-border teaching activities,[11] although in the latter exception fair compensation is optional for Member States to implement.

---

[4] See indicatively *Studio Canal et al v S. Penguin and Union Federale des Consommateurs Que Choisir*, Cour de Cassation, 19 June 2008, No 07-142777 (France).

[5] Ysolde Gendreau, 'Chapter 2: Exceptions for Education and Research' in Irini A. Stamatoudi (ed.), *New Developments in EU and International Copyright Law* (Alphen aan den Rijn: Kluwer Law International, 2016) 56, 70.

[6] See in general Jörg Reinbothe, 'Chapter 11: Private Copy Levies' in Irini A. Stamatoudi (ed.), *New Developments in EU and International Copyright Law* (Alphen aan den Rijn: Kluwer Law International, 2016) 298.

[7] Guido Calabresi and A. Douglas Melamed, 'Property Rules, Liability Rules, and Inalienability: One View of the Cathedral' (1972) 85(6) *Harvard Law Review* 1089.

[8] Ibid.

[9] Directive 2001/29/EC of the European Parliament and of the Council of 22 May 2001 on the Harmonisation of Certain Aspects of Copyright and Related Rights in the Information Society, OJ L 167, 22 June 2001, 10–19 (Information Society Directive), Arts 5(2)(a), 5(2)(b), and 5(2)(e).

[10] Directive (EU) 2012/28 of the European Parliament and of the Council of 25 October 2012 on Certain Permitted Uses of Orphan Works Text with EEA relevance, OJ L 299, 27 October 2012, 5–12 (Orphan Works Directive), Art. 6.

[11] Directive (EU) 2019/790 of the European Parliament and of the Council of 17 April 2019 on Copyright and Related Rights in the Digital Single Market and Amending Directives 96/9/EC and 2001/29/EC, OJ L 130, 17 May 2019, 92–125 (Digital Single Market Directive), Art. 5.

Remunerated exceptions are deemed to find their root in Article 9(2) of the Berne Convention which lays down the three-step test. Meaning to serve as a balancing act, the test aims to ensure that economic prejudice caused as a result of copyright exceptions and limitations should remain within a reasonable level. The test reads:

> It shall be a matter for legislation in the countries of the Union to permit the reproduction of such works in certain special cases, provided that such reproduction does not conflict with a normal exploitation of the work and does not unreasonably prejudice the legitimate interests of the author.

The test has been formulated as a result of the historical desire to avoid unreasonable prejudice towards the legitimate interests of the rightsholders that has the potential to cause intolerable loss of income, actual or potential. Although the Berne Convention and also the treaties that thereinafter repeated—and expanded on the scope and beneficiaries of[12]—the three-step test, including the Agreement on Trade-Related Aspects of Intellectual Property Rights (TRIPs) and the World Intellectual Property Organization (WIPO) Treaties,[13] do not refer to an obligation of users to pay remuneration, historically it has been accepted that making certain activities permissible under copyright would not come into conflict with the authors' legitimate interests and the normal exploitation of the work if authors were fairly compensated or (as elsewhere[14] referred to) equitably remunerated for actual or possible harm that can arise in this context. An important consideration was the understanding that harm of authorial interests was becoming greater with the emergence of equipment and methods that make home copying easier and cheaper.

Uncertainty remains as to the way in which the requirement of fair compensation has been implemented by the various Member States, the notoriously vague and variably-interpreted concept of harm on which fair compensation is premised, and the impact of compensation on the legal nature of uses. A recent expansion of the beneficiaries of fair compensation via the Directive on Copyright in the Digital

---

[12] Stavroula Karapapa, *Private Copying* (London: Routledge, 2012) 99 et seq.

[13] Agreement on Trade-Related Aspects of Intellectual Property Rights (TRIPs) (1994), Art. 13; WIPO Copyright Treaty (WCT) (1996), Art. 10; Information Society Directive (Directive 2001/29/EC), Art. 5(5): 'The exceptions and limitations ... shall only be applied in certain special cases which do not conflict with a normal exploitation of the work or other subject matter and do not unreasonably prejudice the legitimate interests of the rightholder'.

[14] Directive 2006/115/EC of the European Parliament and of the Council of 12 December 2006 on Rental Right and Lending Right and on Certain Rights Related to Copyright in the Field of Intellectual Property (Rental and Lending Directive), OJ L 376, 27 December 2006, 28–35, Arts 5(1) and 8(2); Council Directive 93/83/EEC of 27 September 1993 on the Coordination of Certain Rules Concerning Copyright and Rights Related to Copyright Applicable to Satellite Broadcasting and Cable Retransmission (Satellite Broadcasting and Cable Retransmission Directive), OJ L 248, 6 October 1993, 15–21, Art. 4(1).

Single Market[15] who are no longer merely the authors of the works that are used on the basis of a relevant copyright exception but also the publishers, challenges the boundaries of remunerated exceptions, erodes their scope, and comes into conflict with established case law of the Court of Justice.[16]

In the context of national divergence and also the EU approach towards fair compensation, it is not clear what the function of remunerated permitted uses is; are they statutory licenses, legitimate entitlements of the rightsholders to compensation, or fully fledged rights of the users who have actually paid for their entitlement to a specific permitted use? Answers to questions like this are becoming more pressing in the online world, where the concept of harm could take unprecedented dimensions, especially in the context of private copying and in light of modern technologies that challenge the traditional scope of exceptions, such as 3D printing. Determining the nature of said exceptions, however, is important in understanding the breadth of user freedom and the underlying opportunities in developing markets and services which rely on the benefit of permissible copyright use.

The remunerated exceptions under EU copyright

The Information Society Directive lays down three remunerated exceptions in Article 5(2). These include private copying, reprography, and the reproduction of broadcasts that are made by social institutions pursuing non-commercial purposes. According to this Article:

> Member States may provide for exceptions or limitations to the reproduction right provided for in Article 2 in the following cases:
> (a) in respect of reproductions on paper or any similar medium, effected by the use of any kind of photographic technique or by some other process having similar effects, with the exception of sheet music, provided that the rightholders receive fair compensation;
> (b) in respect of reproductions on any medium made by a natural person for private use and for ends that are neither directly nor indirectly commercial, on condition that the rightholders receive fair compensation which takes account of the application or non-application of technological measures referred to in Article 6 to the work or subject-matter concerned;
>
> ...

---

[15] Digital Single Market Directive (Directive (EU) 2019/790), Art. 16.

[16] *Hewlett-Packard Belgium SPRL v Reprobel SCRL*, Case C-572/13, 12 November 2015, ECLI:EU:C:2015:750, [49] (*Reprobel*).

(e) in respect of reproductions of broadcasts made by social institutions pursuing non-commercial purposes, such as hospitals or prisons, on condition that the rightholders receive fair compensation.

All aforementioned exceptions are optional for Member States to implement but the great majority have included relevant exceptions in their respective national statutes.

The aforementioned acts that are exempt from infringement on a remunerated basis are seemingly unrelated. Reprography and private copying are general exceptions in the sense that their beneficiaries are not specified and any member of the public may, in principle, claim the benefit of the exceptions. With regard to private copying, the only qualifying criterion is that the beneficiary ought to be a natural person, effectively excluding legal entities from successfully relying on a private copying defence. The exception of Article 5(2)(e), however, is rather specific with regard to its beneficiaries, which can only be social institutions pursuing non-commercial purposes. The examples of hospitals or prisons are merely indicative but, although not exhaustive, the list of eligible beneficiaries remains limited by the social and non-commercial objective that the institutional users ought to pursue.[17]

In terms of substantive scope, copying of broadcasts by social institutions is far more narrow compared to reprographic and private copying that apply with respect to every category of protected subject matter, broadcasts included. It is only sheet music that is expressly excluded from the scope of the reprography exception and there are 'portion' conditions available under national laws, indicating the amount of reprographic copying that can be carried out with regard to various categories of works.

In addition to the aforementioned remunerated exceptions listed in the Information Society Directive, there is also the recently introduced exception for cross-border teaching activities under Article 5 of the Directive on Copyright in the Digital Single Market. This exception too may be subject to the requirement of fair compensation, but it is left to the discretion of Member States to introduce it on a remunerated basis or not. The exception could, in principle, qualify as a remunerated exception, but is not classified as such for two reasons. First, fair compensation is only an optional requirement, and second, the exception is underpinned by the same, strong public policy ground as the educational exceptions preceding it. It is for this reason that it is discussed in Chapter 7.

The common denominator of the aforementioned exceptions is the fact that the rightsholders ought to be fairly remunerated. The concept of fair compensation was first introduced into EU copyright via the Information Society Directive with the purpose of recompensing for the harm that rightsholders suffer as a result

---

[17] The same applies to the remunerated exceptions on permitted uses of orphan works and cross-border teaching activities, which are enjoyed by specified institutional users.

of specific permitted uses. This is explained in Recital 35 of the Preamble of the Directive, which reads:

> In certain cases of exceptions or limitations, rightholders should receive fair compensation to compensate them adequately for the use made of their protected works or other subject matter. When determining the form, detailed arrangements and possible level of such fair compensation, account should be taken of the particular circumstances of each case. When evaluating these circumstances, a valuable criterion would be the possible harm to the rightholders resulting from the act in question. In cases where rightholders have already received payment in some other form, for instance as part of a licence fee, no specific or separate payment may be due. The level of fair compensation should take full account of the degree of use of technological protection measures referred to in this Directive. In certain situations where the prejudice to the rightholder would be minimal, no obligation for payment may arise.

This Recital indicates that harm is a central criterion in determining the form, detailed arrangements, and level of fair compensation. It is certainly not the sole criterion, even though in the absence of any harm, or when such a prejudice is minimal, there is no requirement to impose fair compensation on users. It is unclear what kind of harm qualifies as minimal in this context. It is likely that there can never be minimal harm when digital private copying is concerned. An example of a failed attempt to substantiate minimal harm that would not give rise to fair remuneration owing to acts of private copying comes from the United Kingdom and its 2014 copyright reform. The United Kingdom introduced a private copying exception on very narrow terms and with no accompanying obligation to pay fair compensation; it had its exception quashed under judicial review as the evidence taken into consideration did not exemplify how harm was minimal to allow exclusion of the obligation to fairly remunerate the copyright holders.[18]

What is more, double payments to the rightsholders are to be avoided, however difficult it may be to ensure this. For instance, because the most usual form that fair compensation takes across Europe has been the so-called copyright levies that are applied to blank media and copying equipment,[19] it is likely that users may end up paying more than once for making copies for their private use or photocopies in general (or even for not making copies of protected content at all). The issue is not expressly addressed at the EU level, with the exception of some general

---

[18] *BASCA v Secretary of State for Business and Innovation* [2015] EWHC 1723 (UK); *R (British Academy of Songwriters, Composers and Authors and Others) v Secretary of State for Business, Innovation and Skills* [2015] EWHC 2041 (Admin) (UK).

[19] In Norway, however, instead of a levy system there is a mechanism of state subsidies.

recommendations included in the Report of the EU High Level Mediator.[20] This Report urges a higher degree of harmonization on the concept of fair compensation, which at the moment is subject to discrepancies and variations among Member States. There has been no guidance in the Information Society Directive on how fair compensation may take place in a uniform manner and Recital 38 encourages Member States' discretion. It specifies that:

> Member States should be allowed to provide for an exception or limitation to the reproduction right for certain types of reproduction of audio, visual, and audiovisual material for private use, accompanied by fair compensation. This may include the introduction or continuation of remuneration schemes to compensate for the prejudice to rightholders. Although differences between those remuneration schemes affect the functioning of the internal market, those differences, with respect to analogue private reproduction, should not have a significant impact on the development of the information society. Digital private copying is likely to be more widespread and have a greater economic impact. Due account should therefore be taken on the differences between digital and analogue private copying and a distinction should be made in certain respects between them.

Despite the discrepancies in the application and detailed parameters of fair compensation schemes, especially towards the development of the information society, the great majority of Member States have introduced into their national laws an obligation to compensate authors .

Reprographic copying

Article 5(2)(a) of the Information Society Directive outlines an exception that is optional for Member States to implement, covering reproductions on paper or any similar medium. Most countries across Europe have provisions to the effect that this kind of copying shall be permitted within the framework of the national legal provisions.

Photocopying and the historical emergence of the exception

The emergence of the photocopier has been a breakthrough into *how* copying can be carried out, *who* can make photocopies—which no longer remains a privilege of

---

[20] António Vitorino, Recommendations Resulting from the Mediation on Private Copying and Reprography Levies, Brussels, 31 January 2013, available at https://ec.europa.eu/commission/presscorner/detail/en/IP_13_80 , accessed 11 November 2019.

large corporate entities—and the *amount* of copying carried out.[21] Those changes have not only become a source of complaints from copyright holders, but also created uncertainty for various institutional users, such as libraries and information centres. This uncertainty became the impetus for change and the Director General of the United Nations Educational, Scientific, and Cultural Organization declared that reprographic copying of copyright-protected content had to be addressed at the international level.[22] Although discussions lasted over twenty years, no consensus was reached and it was decided that it should be up to national laws to address the issue.[23] This left a degree of discretion to national legislators who had already started introducing legislative provisions to address the phenomenon. In the European Union the issue was addressed through the Information Society Directive, although variations still exist in the respective national exceptions of Member States. Some countries lay down a stand-alone limitation on reprographic copying,[24] whereas others include it within a broader private copying exception.[25] Variety exists as to the scope, subject matter, and possible involvement of third parties in the copying exercise. In all Member States the exception applies to literary works, whereas it may also cover artistic works,[26] news articles,[27] and illustrations from books in other states.[28]

Excluded subject matter

The exception outlined in Article 5(2)(a) of the Information Society Directive covers all descriptions of copyright-protected subject matter with the exception of sheet music. The express exclusion of sheet music is meant to limit its permissible scope and to introduce a special regime for this category of protected subject matter. As explained in *Reprobel*, this kind of copying cannot benefit from the exception and, hence, should not be taken into consideration when calculating the

---

[21] Leanne Wiseman, 'Chapter 8: Making Copies: Photocopying and Copyright' in Brad Sherman and Leanne Wiseman (eds), *Copyright and the Challenge of the New* (Alphen aan den Rijn: Kluwer Law International 2012) 198.

[22] Intergovernmental Copyright Committee, Photoduplication of Copyrighted Materials by or for Libraries, Documentation Centres and Scientific Institutions, Sixth Session - Madrid - September 1961, IGC/VI/8, WS/0761.96, 28 July 1961, Item No. 7.1.

[23] See summary by Gerhard Dahlmanns, 'Reprography and Copyright' (1974) 2 *International Journal of Law Libraries* 55.

[24] Belgium, Cyprus, Estonia, Hungary, Italy, Latvia, Malta, the Netherlands, Portugal, Slovakia, and Slovenia.

[25] See e.g. in Austria: Federal Law on Copyright in Literary and Artistic Works and Related Rights (Copyright Law 1936, as amended up to Federal Law published in the Federal Law Gazette I No. 105/2018 (BGBl.I No. 105/2018)), s. 42a.

[26] Austria, Cyprus, the Czech Republic, Germany, and Latvia.

[27] Austria and Germany.

[28] Belgium and Lithuania.

amount of fair compensation.[29] The vast majority of Member States have excluded notations from the reprographic exception.[30]

Scope

There is a technologically neutral approach in determining what qualifies as a reproduction by reprography since Article 5(2)(a) of the Information Society Directive refers to copies that are made by the use of any kind of photographic technique or by some other process having similar effects. It is understood that this broad definition does not merely include photocopying but also other forms of copying, including microfilm, microfiche, facsimile, scanning etc. It is an open question as to what extent the exception covers copying carried out in the context of emergent technologies, such as 3D printing. As the Court of Justice explained in *VG Wort*,[31] 'in order to be similar to paper as a medium for reproduction, a substrate must be capable of bearing a physical presentation capable of perception by human senses.'[32] This broadens the permissible scope of the exception in that it is not only photocopying that is permitted. This is further exemplified in *VG Wort*, which offers an interpretation of what is meant by 'some other process having similar effects' to mean 'any other means allowing for a similar result to that obtained by a photographic technique to be achieved, that is to say the analogue representation of a protected work or other subject matter'. In principle, this could be read as covering 3D printing technologies and other forms of copying beyond photocopying.

This broader understanding of the kind of copying that is eligible for the benefit of the exception included in Article 5(2)(a) has an impact on the requirement that rightsholders receive fair compensation. Where a particular device or piece of equipment is used for copying that can qualify under the relevant exception, it may then be subject to an additional payment to reflect the amount of fair compensation that is due. In a 2007 case of the German Federal Court of Justice,[33] the court was called upon to assess whether printers are devices 'destined to make photocopies or similar reproductions' within the meaning of Article 54A of the German Copyright Act. Overturning the decisions of the Court of First Instance and the

---

[29] This was clarified in *Hewlett-Packard Belgium SPRL v Reprobel SCRL*, Case C-572/13, 12 November 2015, ECLI:EU:C:2015:750 (*Reprobel*).

[30] Lithuania and Poland are the only exceptions. See Guido Westcamp, 'The Implementation of Directive 2001/29/EC in the Member States, Part II' (February 2007) Queen Mary Intellectual Property Research Institute, Centre for Commercial Law Studies, 14.

[31] *Verwertungsgesellschaft Wort (VG Wort) v Kyocera and Others and Canon Deutschland GmbH and Fujitsu Technology Solutions GmbH and Hewlett-Packard GmbH v Verwertungsgesellschaft Wort*, Cases C-457/11, C-458/11, C-459/11, C-460/11, 27 June 2013, ECLI:EU:C:2013:426 (*VG Wort*).

[32] Ibid., [67].

[33] 'Levies for printers', Federal Court of Justice (Bundesgerichtshof), 6 December 2007 (Germany).

Appeals Court, the Federal Supreme Court found that Article 54A of the German Copyright Act applied only to devices that are designed for reprography and for acts of analogue reproduction only, such as facsimile copying or copying made by use of a scanner and a printer. The court stressed that copying that takes place by use of a computer and a printer is only carried out for the making of digital copies and cannot, by analogy, be covered by the exception on reprography. It has to be understood that in the aftermath of *VG Wort* this restrictive approach is not in line with the broader definition of copying under Article 5(2)(a) adopted by the Court of Justice.

Uses and purposes covered

With regard to reprographic copying, Article 5(2)(a) of the Information Society Directive does not list any specific purposes which should be permitted. This seemingly broad scope is limited in those Member States that have introduced an exception for reprographic copying as part of their private copying exceptions,[34] in the sense that any photocopying should be made in the context of private non-commercial use. This creates an obligation for third party copying services to inquire as to the purpose of relevant copying and to ensure its private and non-commercial nature in order to carry it out lawfully.

Beneficiaries and third party copying

The exception does not specify who its beneficiaries are and it is understood that any member of the public can qualify for its benefit, including natural persons, legal entities, and other institutional users, such as libraries and educational establishments. National approaches vary regarding the beneficiaries of the exception, with some Member States allowing reprographic copying in public institutions as a copyright limitation for the benefit of a natural person, while in other Member States it is the public establishment as such that is deemed to be the beneficiary.[35]

Third party copying is not expressly regulated and it is a matter of national law to determine whether third parties may also benefit from the exception. Different approaches are followed in the various Member States. Italy excludes third party copying, whereas Austria, the Czech Republic, and Germany allow copying made upon request of a beneficiary.

Uncertainty on the matter has been partially addressed in *Reprobel*,[36] where the Court of Justice clarified that for the purposes of understanding fair compensation within the meaning of the reprography exception it is essential to distinguish

---

[34] E.g. Austria.

[35] Austria and Slovakia allow legal entities to benefit from the exception on reprographic copying, whereas in Italy, Greece, and Slovenia they are explicitly excluded and the exception covers natural persons only.

[36] *Hewlett-Packard Belgium SPRL v Reprobel SCRL*, Case C-572/13, 12 November 2015, ECLI:EU:C:2015:750 (*Reprobel*).

whether *any* user carries out the relevant activity or whether such an activity is carried out by a natural person for purposes of their own private use and for purposes that are not commercial. This is because the harm that rightsholders suffer differs depending on the use in question.

Copying from lawful sources

In *Reprobel*,[37] the Court of Justice created an implied condition that the exception should cover only copies made from lawfully acquired originals.[38] This is a prerequisite of the private copying exception according to *ACI Adam*[39] and, because there has to be consistency in the application of the private copying and reprography exceptions, the reprography exception cannot be deemed to cover copies made from unlawful sources. Determining what amounts to a lawful source is a matter of national law and copies borrowed from libraries may be eligible under some national laws but not under others.[40] Although seemingly broad, the reprography exception is subject to a number of conditions that narrow its scope of application.

Private copying

Article 5(2)(b) of the Information Society Directive allows Member States to introduce exceptions in respect of reproductions on any medium made by a natural person for private use and for ends that are neither directly nor indirectly commercial, on condition that the rightsholders receive fair compensation which takes account of the application, or non-application, of technological measures on the work or subject matter concerned. The exception typically includes back-up copying, format and time shifting, passing copies to family and close friends, and downloading materials for private use.

Even though this copyright exception was optional for Member States to implement, the vast majority of Member States do have a provision allowing private copying in their national laws. The exception emerged from, and is a compilation of, the various national exceptions that used to be available across Europe before the introduction of the Directive. Most Member States decided to keep their national laws as intact as possible during the implementation process. The United Kingdom was one of the few Member States not to have a relevant exception for many years and, soon after its statutory introduction following the Hargreaves

---

[37] *Hewlett-Packard Belgium SPRL v Reprobel SCRL*, Case C-572/13, 12 November 2015, ECLI:EU:C:2015:750 (*Reprobel*).

[38] Ibid., [64].

[39] *ACI Adam BV and Others v Stichting de Thuiskopie and Stichting Onderhandelingen Thuiskopie vergoeding*, Case C-435/12, 10 April 2014, ECLI:EU:C:2014:254 (*ACI Adam*).

[40] See e.g. the UK short-lived exception on private copying.

Report,[41] it was quashed upon judicial review.[42] In Ireland too, despite some policy discussions in 2014 concerning the introduction of a private copying exception,[43] the 2019 revision of Irish Copyright law does not make allowance for this activity.[44]

Private copying is the copyright exception that has attracted the highest number of referrals for interpretative guidance from the Court of Justice of the European Union.[45] Even though there are variations in terms of the scope of national exceptions, most of the cases referred to the court concern the interpretation of the fair compensation requirement and its parameters of application, although there have also been some cases addressing substantial issues. Insights on the normative scope of the exception can be drawn with regard to cases from national courts that have elaborated on the private copying exception on a number of occasions.

Private use

Article 5(2)(b) of the Information Society Directive allows copying for the private use of natural persons. Private use involves both the personal enjoyment of a work and activities that could, in principle, touch upon copyright, including making back-up copies or uploading videos to social media. The first kind of use has always remained free as the most welcome outcome of the production of copyright works. It is the latter kind of private use, namely that including activities that could have an impact on restricted acts which is more controversial as it involves activities that initially fall within the ambit of exclusive rights. Indeed, the development of private copying exceptions or statutory references to private use did not emerge

---

[41] Ian Hargreaves, *Digital Opportunity: A Review of Intellectual Property and Growth, An Independent Report* (May 2011).

[42] *BASCA v Secretary of State for Business and Innovation* [2015] EWHC 1723 (UK); *R (British Academy of Songwriters, Composers and Authors and Others) v Secretary of State for Business, Innovation and Skills* [2015] EWHC 2041 (Admin) (UK).

[43] Copyright Review Committee 2013 for the Department of Jobs, Enterprise, and Innovation, 'Modernising Copyright', Dublin 2013, available at <https://dbei.gov.ie/en/Publications/Publication-files/CRC-Report.pdf>, accessed 11 November 2019.

[44] Copyright and Other Intellectual Property Law Provisions Act 2019, No. 19 of 2019, available at <https://data.oireachtas.ie/ie/oireachtas/act/2019/19/eng/enacted/a1919.pdf>, accessed 11 November 2019; also see earlier draft: Copyright and Other Intellectual Property Law Provisions Bill 2018, available at <https://data.oireachtas.ie/ie/oireachtas/bill/2018/31/eng/initiated/b3118d.pdf>.

[45] *Padawan SL v Sociedad General de Autores y Editores de España (SGAE)*, Case C-467/08, 21 October 2010, ECLI:EU:C:2010:620 (*Padawan*); *Stichting de Thuiskopie v Opus Supplies Deutschland GmbH and Others*, Case C-462/09, 16 June 2011, ECLI:EU:C:2011:397 (*Opus*); *Martin Luksan v Petrus van der Let*, Case C-277/10, 9 February 2012, ECLI:EU:C:2012:65 (*Luksan*); *Verwertungsgesellschaft Wort (VG Wort) v Kyocera and Others and Canon Deutschland GmbH and Fujitsu Technology Solutions GmbH and Hewlett-Packard GmbH v Verwertungsgesellschaft Wort*, Cases C-457/11, C-458/11, C-459/11, C-460/11, 27 June 2013, ECLI:EU:C:2013:426 (*VG Wort*); *Amazon.com International Sales Inc. and Others v Austro-Mechana Gesellschaft zur Wahrnehmung mechanisch-musikalischer Urheberrechte Gesellschaft mbH*, Case C-521/11, 11 July 2013, ECLI:EU:C:2013:515 (*Amazon*); *Copydan Båndkopi v Nokia Danmark A/S*, Case C-463/12, 5 March 2015, ECLI:EU:C:2015:144 (*Copydan*); *Hewlett-Packard Belgium SPRL v Reprobel SCRL*, Case C-572/13, 12 November 2015, ECLI:EU:C:2015:750 (*Reprobel*).

before the evolution of home copying technologies. Provisions regarding private use were not available in the eighteenth and nineteenth centuries and there is no relevant mention in the original text of the Berne Convention of 1886. Some of the early inclusions of private use in statutes were the German Copyright Act of 1901 and the Dutch Act of 1912. They both involved copying for private use or study and excluded further dissemination of the work from the benefit of the exception. With the emergence of home copying technologies, exceptions on private copying gradually became more widespread across Europe. The 1967 Study Group for the Berne Convention noted that private use was one of the most frequent justifications for permitted use included in continental European copyright.[46]

It has later become a matter of national law and judicial interpretation to determine which uses qualify as private. Whereas in some jurisdictions a private use is one carried out among family, friends, and social acquaintances,[47] other Member States follow a narrower approach, offering the benefit of the exceptions to natural persons for their strictly personal use.[48] Despite the number of referrals before the Court of Justice, this is an issue that has not been determined at the EU level and remains within the discretion of national legislators.

Non-commercial purposes

Article 5(2)(b) of the Information Society Directive expressly stipulates that permissible private copying should be carried out for non-commercial purposes, either directly or indirectly. This means that the use should not be made in the context of trade or with the view to making a profit from the copies made.[49] A good number of EU Member States do not expressly state that private copying should be carried out for non-commercial purposes to be permitted.[50] Even though courts clearly look for both trade and profit elements in order to determine whether a use is directly commercial, they would mostly focus on the intent of the copier, including the number of the copies made, in order to assess whether the activity

[46] See Records of the Intellectual Property Conference of Stockholm (Geneva: WIPO 1967) Vol. 1, 112.

[47] A group of four colleagues in Belgium was deemed to be a private circle (unreported); in France it was held that the exception does not only cover strictly personal use but can extend to friends and family. See *Studio Canal et al v S. Penguin and Union Federale des Consommateurs Que Choisir*, Paris Court of Appeal, 4 April 2007 (France); by contrast, an Internet user who was lending copies of CD-ROMs (some were downloaded from peer-to-peer networks and some borrowed from friends) to friends could not benefit from the private copying exception. See *Ministère Public, BSS, FNDF, Twentieth Century Fox et al v Aurélien D.*, Court of Appeal of Aix-en-Provence, Arrêt 5ème Ch. No. 2007/501, 5 September 2007 (France).

[48] See e.g. Art. 28B of the Copyright and Rights in Performances (Personal Copies for Private Use) Regulations 2014.

[49] Stavroula Karapapa, *Private Copying* (London: Routledge, 2012) 79 et seq.

[50] See Austria, Belgium, Cyprus, France, Germany, Greece, Ireland, Liechtenstein, Poland, Portugal, Switzerland.

was indirectly commercial.[51] National case law indicates that companies that offer services which enable copying for profit infringe copyright and cannot benefit from available defences, even where third party copying is legislatively permitted. Placing advertisements on a website was found to amount to commercial use, despite the fact that there was no direct financial advantage.[52] Similarly, intention to profit from making content available for sharing online has also been found to amount to commercial use.[53] Indirect commerciality has been affirmed in national cases involving the performance of background music in a pizzeria[54] and in a taxi.[55] This is also the case with regard to companies serving a clearly differentiated primary function, e.g. restaurants or shops, which are engaged in commercial activities while playing background music.[56]

Lawfulness of the source copy

Even though the Information Society Directive remains silent, various Member States, including, among others, Italy and Spain,[57] have introduced a statutory requirement that permissible private copying can only take place from a lawfully purchased original. This normative requirement takes different shape in the various Member States that decided to introduce it into national law. In Spain, for instance, the criterion took the form of lawful access, which has been interpreted to mean that the users have legally purchased their Internet subscription,[58]

---

[51] *EGEDA et al. v F.T.D.M.L.L.*, Provincial Court of Murcia (Audiencia Provincial de Murcia), 16 September 2009, 215/2009 (Spain) (www.elitedivx.com), accessed 11 November 2019; contra: *Columbia TriStar, EGEDA, PROMUSICAE v Sharemula.com*, Provincial Court of Madrid (Audiencia Provincial de Madrid), 11 September 2008, Auto 582/08 (Spain).

[52] See e.g. *Sony Music Entertainment (UK) Limited and Others v Easyinternetcafé Limited* [2003] EWHC 62 (Ch) (UK).

[53] *'Finreactor I'*, Supreme Court (Korkein oikeus), 30 June 2010 (Finland); *'Finreactor II'*, Supreme Court (Korkein oikeus), 30 June 2010 (Finland).

[54] *Esittävien Taiteilijoiden Ja Äänitteiden Tuottajien Tekijänoikeusyhdistys Gramex Ry v Pizzeria Papegoya Oy*, Case No. 2862, The Supreme Court of Helsinki, 29 October 2002, [2003] ECDR 9 (Finland).

[55] *Teosto v A Taxi Driver* [2004] ECDR 16 (Finland).

[56] *Esittävien Taiteilijoiden Ja Äänitteiden Tuottajien Tekijänoikeusyhdistys Gramex Ry v Pizzeria Papegoya Oy*, Case No. 2862, The Supreme Court of Helsinki, 29 October 2002 [2003] ECDR 9 (Finland); *Teosto v A Taxi Driver* [2004] ECDR 16 (Finland).

[57] Art. 71*sexties*(4) of the Italian Law for the Protection of Copyright and Neighbouring Rights, Law No. 633 of 22 April 1941, as last amended by Legislative Decree No. 68 of 9 April 2003, as last amended 2004 (Italy); Art. 25(5)(3) of the Spanish Copyright Act (Law on Intellectual Property, Regularizing, Clarifying and Harmonizing the Applicable Statutory Provisions) approved by Royal Legislative Decree No. 1/1996 of 12 April 1996, and amended up to Royal Decree-Law No. 2/2019 of 1 March 2019 (Spain). Express reference to the lawful source requirement is also made in other Member States, such as Finland and Latvia; it used to apply until repealed in Germany: Art. 53(1) of the German Copyright Act of 9 September 1965 (Federal Law Gazette I, 1273), as last amended by Art. 1 of the Act of 1 September 2017 (Federal Law Gazette I, 3346) (Germany).

[58] *Sociedad General de Autores y Editores (SGAE) v Jesus Guerra Calderon*, Case 67/10, Commercial Court No. 7 of Barcelona, 9 March 2010 (Spain).

whereas a broader test is used in Germany according to which the source copy should not be 'manifestly illegal'.[59] At the judicial level, the validity of this criterion and its normative value have been subject to scrutiny but the relevant rulings have been largely diverse regarding both their outcomes and interpretative guidance. Whereas Dutch courts, for instance, have rejected the validity of the requirement that the source copy should be lawful,[60] the French version of this requirement does not expressly feature in a particular legal provision but is, however, an implied condition, with a number of cases having upheld its validity.[61]

Uncertainty regarding the validity of the lawfulness of the source requirement has been waived by the interpretative guidance that the Court of Justice offered in *ACI Adam*,[62] affirming that legitimate private copying can only take place from a lawfully acquired original. This was meant to flow from the three-step test incorporated in Article 5(5) of the Information Society Directive and the general objective of Article 5(2)(b), which aspires to ensure a fair balance between the competing interests of rightsholders and users, and the need to respect the legal traditions of the various Member States, while also protecting the proper functioning of the Internal Market.

At around the same time that the *ACI Adam* case was decided, there were heated discussions on how the lawful source requirement would be implemented into the UK private copying exception, which was at that time under consideration following the Hargreaves Report.[63] Because the aspiration of UK legislators was to introduce a private copying exception that would correspond to legitimate user expectations and, at the same time, remain unremunerated in order to avoid the launch of a remuneration scheme there was a strong desire to minimise harm arising due to private copying.[64] To this end, law and policy makers were examining the possibility of introducing sufficient substantive norms, e.g. that the use would be for the strictly personal use of individuals, that third party copying would be excluded, and that the source copy would have to be lawful. By reference to this latter condition, there was a very detailed explanation of what qualifies as a lawful source

---

[59] Stavroula Karapapa, *Private Copying* (London: Routledge, 2012) 110.

[60] *Stichting Bescherming Rechten Entertainment Industrie Nederland (BREIN) v Techno Design 'Internet Programming' BV, Haarlem District Court*, 12 May 2004 (Netherlands); aff'd in *Stichting Bescherming Rechten Entertainment Industrie Nederland (BREIN) v Techno Design 'Internet Programming' BV* [2006] E.C.D.R. 21 at [4.6] (Netherlands).

[61] See e.g. *Syndicat de l'industrie de matériels audiovisuels electroniques*, Supreme Administrative Court (Conseil d'Etat), No. 298779, 11 July 2008 (France); *Procureur de la Republique SCPP and SPPF v Madame A.*, Tribunal de Grande Instance de Rennes, Correctional Judgment, 30 November 2006, 7 (France); CA Versailles, 9th Division, 16 March 2007, July–August 2007, Comm. Com. Électr. 30 (France); *Le Ministere Public v Ludovic L*, TGI Saint-Quentin, 10 January 2006, 7 (France).

[62] *ACI Adam BV and Others v Stichting de Thuiskopie and Stichting Onderhandelingen Thuiskopie vergoeding*, Case C-435/12, 10 April 2014, ECLI:EU:C:2014:254 (*ACI Adam*).

[63] Ian Hargreaves, *Digital Opportunity: A Review of Intellectual Property and Growth, An Independent Report* (May 2011).

[64] See in general Stavroula Karapapa, 'A Copyright Exception for Private Copying in the United Kingdom' (2013) 35(3) *European Intellectual Property Review* 129.

copy in what later became the (rather short-lived) UK private copying exception. The text of that provision, included in (quashed) Article 28B of the Copyright and Rights in Performances (Personal Copies for Private Use) Regulations 2014, used to read as follows:

(1) The making of a copy of a work, other than a computer program, by an individual does not infringe copyright in the work provided that the copy—
    (a) is a copy of—
        (i)   the individual's own copy of the work, or
        (ii) a personal copy of the work made by the individual,
    (b) is made for the individual's private use, and
    (c) is made for ends which are neither directly nor indirectly commercial.
(2) In this section 'the individual's own copy' is a copy which—
    (a) has been lawfully acquired by the individual on a permanent basis,
    (b) is not an infringing copy, and
    (c) has not been made under any provision of this chapter which permits the making of a copy without infringing copyright.
(3) In this section a 'personal copy' means a copy made under this section.
(4) For the purposes of subsection (2)(a), a copy 'lawfully acquired on a permanent basis'—
    (a) includes a copy which has been purchased, obtained by way of a gift, or acquired by means of a download resulting from a purchase or a gift (other than a download of a kind mentioned in paragraph (b)); and
    (b) does not include a copy which has been borrowed, rented, broadcast or streamed, or a copy which has been obtained by means of a download enabling no more than temporary access to the copy.

   ....

This formulation is the result of lengthy discussions and delegations and the tension is reflected in the relevant impact assessments. In the 2011 impact assessment, it was not clear whether copies had to be lawfully purchased or owned, with ownership covering a broader set of entitlements. The 2012 impact assessment introduced a lawful source requirement, which was further clarified in the final text of Article 18A. This Article stipulated that copies could be made from works that had been lawfully acquired on a permanent basis. In the indicative examples offered, lawful acquisition covered copies that were purchased or obtained by way of a gift—either as hard copies or as copies downloaded from the Internet. Lawful acquisition could not include other kinds of lawfully possessed materials, such as copies of works borrowed from libraries or accessed through streaming ownership, which are meant to refer to time-restricted ways of possession. The narrow delimitation of what qualified as a lawfully acquired original was meant to limit the scope of the exception and correspondingly the extent of harm that would arise from the activities in question. Despite this attempt, harm resulting from private copying was not found to be minimal, nor to give rise to an obligation to fairly recompense copyright holders. Hence, the relevant exception was quashed under judicial review.

The beneficiaries: natural persons, corporate entities, and third party copying

The private copying exception of Article 5(2)(b) of the Information Society Directive clearly stipulates that the beneficiaries of the exception should be natural persons. This excludes corporate entities and other legal bodies from claiming the benefit of the exception. Situations in which legal uncertainty can emerge include third party copying, i.e. copies made for natural persons on behalf of a corporate entity or possibly even a social or cultural institution, e.g. a library. These are, however, the cases on the basis of which online content delivery methods might emerge, e.g. new business models or electronic services that could enhance easier and faster access to knowledge.

In order to rely on Article 5(2)(b), it is settled case law of the Court of Justice that it is not necessary that the natural persons concerned possess reproduction equipment, devices, or media; they may also use copying services provided by a third party, which is the factual precondition for those natural persons to obtain private copies.[65] However, as affirmed in *VCAST*, Article 5(2)(b) has to be interpreted as precluding national legislation that permits commercial undertakings providing private individuals with cloud services for the remote recording of private copies of works protected by copyright, by means of a computer system, by actively involving itself in the recording, without the rightsholder's consent.[66]

Because there was no clear formulation on this issue under the Information Society Directive, and no interpretative guidance from the court for many years, Member States used a variety of approaches towards third party copying. Some Member States expressly prohibited this kind of copying by excluding it from the benefit of the private copying exception—at least with regard to certain categories of copyright-protected works[67]—whereas other States allowed third party copying

---

[65] *Padawan SL v Sociedad General de Autores y Editores de España (SGAE)*, Case C-467/08, 21 October 2010, ECLI:EU:C:2010:620 (*Padawan*), [48].

[66] *VCAST Limited v RTI SpA*, Case C-265/16, 29 November 2017, ECLI:EU:C:2017:913 (*VCAST*).

[67] Third party copying is expressly prohibited only in Hungary. See Art. 35(3) of the Copyright Act (Act LXXVI of 1999 on Copyright) 15 March 2014–28 October 2014 (Hungary). Italy does not allow third party copying only by reference to certain categories of works, such as sound and video recordings, by virtue of Art. 71*sexties*(2) of the Italian Law on the Protection of Copyright and Neighbouring Rights, Law No. 633 of 22 April 1941, as last amended by Legislative Decree No. 68 of 9 April 2003, as last amended 2004 (Italy). Similar limitations are available under Art. 12 of the Swedish Act on Copyright in Literary and Artistic Works, Swedish Statute Book, SFS, 1960:729, as amended up to 1 April 2011 (Sweden); Art. 12 of the Finnish Copyright Act, Act No. 404/1961 of 8 July 1961, as amended up to Act

under certain conditions which often have to do with the type of protected subject matter that was subject to copying.[68]

Third party copying has been the subject of discussion in national case law. In the United Kingdom, the issue was addressed in *Sony v Easyinternetcafé*,[69] a case heard in the High Court about ten years before the private copying exception entered into the Copyright, Designs and Patents Act (CDPA). In this case, it was held that a café which offered a CD burning service for a £5 fee was in breach of the time-shifting exception of section 70 of the CDPA because the use in question could neither qualify as 'private and domestic' nor as a non-commercial practice. The exception could apply if copying took place outside a commercial context. French cases dealing with services which burn content onto digital carriers on-demand have reached similarly restrictive results.[70] A service that allowed its clients to download television programmes for free could benefit neither from the temporary copying exception, nor from the private copying exception with regard to copies made by their customers.[71] The argument that there were two separate copies, each one falling under one of the aforementioned exceptions, was rejected and the court held that third party copying could not benefit from the private copying exception.

The restrictive approach towards third party copying could be problematic in terms of the development of new business models of content delivery. In the online environment, third party copying becomes relevant in the context of document delivery services, which we have already discussed by reference to the exceptions on private study and library privileges.[72] We have seen that there has been a lengthy discussion on the matter in Germany during the implementation of the Information Society Directive, which focused on whether public libraries can make copies on behalf of their users for their private use.[73] The issue of document

---

No. 972/2016 of 18 November 2016 (Finland); for an overview and detailed discussion see Stavroula Karapapa, *Private Copying* (London: Routledge, 2012) 50, 53 et seq.

[68] Examples include the Czech Republic, Finland, Liechtenstein, and Switzerland.

[69] *Sony Music Entertainment (UK) Limited and Others v Easyinternetcafé Limited* [2003] EWHC 62 (Ch) (UK).

[70] Grenoble Court of Appeal, 18 January 2001 (France).

[71] *Wizzgo.com v Metropole Television SA (M6)*, High Court of Paris (*Tribunal de Grande Instance*), Unreported, 25 November 2008 (France); similarly by reference to the reprography exception see *Rannou-Graphie*, Cassation Civile 1er, 7 March 1984, JCP, 1985 II 21351 (France).

[72] See Chapter 7.

[73] The outcome of these discussions was to permit this kind of copying on condition that it would be made on a non-commercial basis, for private use of the library users, and covering hard—not digital—copies only. The online delivery of digital copies was addressed in 1999 when the German Federal Supreme Court ruled that a well-developed system of communicating information and knowledge was important for a modern nation like Germany. See Federal Supreme Court (*Bundesgerichtshof*), Case I ZR 118/96, 25 February 1999 [2000] ECC 237 (*Kopienversanddienst*) (Germany). Art. 53(2)(4) (a) of the German Copyright Act offered the basis for an argument in favour of the legitimacy of online delivery services as it permitted copying materials for personal scientific purposes, including the electronic communication of such copies on condition that the rightholders were fairly remunerated. Since 1999 when this case was decided, however, German Courts have either upheld or rejected this

delivery services was settled at the EU level in *Technische Universität Darmstadt,*[74] where the Court of Justice examined the extent to which Article 5(2)(b) allowed the use of dedicated terminals under Article 5(3)(n) Information Society Directive so that copyright-protected materials could be printed or stored on USB sticks. As the court noted, where an establishment, e.g. a publicly accessible library, provides access to a work contained in its collection to members of the public who use its dedicated terminals for the purpose of research or private study, that use qualifies as an 'act of communication' for the purposes of Article 3(1) of the Information Society Directive.[75] By reference to the copies made on USB sticks or printed as hard copies, even though these acts cannot qualify for the benefit of Article 5(3)(n), they could be subject to the authorization of the national laws of Member States insofar as the conditions of the private copying exception of Article 5(2)(b) are fulfilled.[76]

Private copying of software and databases

Article 5(2) of the Computer Programs Directive[77] expressly allows back-up copying, specifying that it 'may not be prevented by contract in so far as it is neces-sary for that use.' In this regard, this provision does two things. First, it outlines the mandatory nature of the exception against possible contractual restriction. Recital 16 indicates that any such contractual terms and conditions shall be 'null and void'. Second, the exception is subject to a purposive limitation in the sense that no fur-ther copies beyond back-up copies can be lawfully made. This was discussed in *Ranks,*[78] where the Court of Justice held that back up copying was limited to merely meeting the needs of the person having the right to use that computer program but did not include copying the program to resell it to a third party.

The Database Directive[79] allows two exceptions for private use: one with re-gard to copyright and one with regard to the database right. These are outlined in

judicial stance. See e.g. Court of Appeal of Hamburg (*Hanseatisches Oberlandesgericht, Hamburg*), 9 September 2005, 6 U 90/05 (Germany); contra *Börsenverein des Deutschen Buchnandels et al.*, Court of Appeal Munich (*Oberlandesgericht*), 10 February 2007, 29 U I638/06; Court of Appeal of Dresden (*Oberlandesgericht*), 28 November 2006, 14 U 1071/06 (Germany).

[74] *Technische Universität Darmstadt v Eugen Ulmer KG*, Case C-117/13, 11 September 2014, ECLI:EU:C:2014:2196 (*Technische Universität Darmstadt*).
[75] Ibid., [42].
[76] Ibid., [19] and [57].
[77] Directive 2009/24/EC of the European Parliament and of the Council of 23 April 2009 on the Legal Protection of Computer Programs (repealing and replacing Directive 91/250/EEC), OJ L 111, 5 May 2009, 16–22 (Computer Programs Directive).
[78] *Aleksandrs Ranks and Jurijs Vasiļevičs v Finanšu un Ekonomisko Noziegumu Izmeklēšanas Prokoratūra and Microsoft Corp.*, Case C-166/15, 12 October 2016, ECLI:EU:C:2016:762 (*Ranks*).
[79] Directive 96/9/EC of the European Parliament and of the Council of 11 March 1996 on the Legal Protection of Databases, OJ L 77, 27 March 1996, 20–8 (Database Directive).

Articles 6(2)(a) and 9(a) respectively. They allow copying or extracting contents of a protected database for private purposes. It is accepted that the scope of these exceptions is considerably narrower than those available for copyright works under Article 5(2)(b) of the Information Society Directive. Recital 35 draws 'a distinction ... between exceptions for private use and exceptions for reproduction for private purposes, which concerns provisions under national legislation of some Member States on levies on blank media or recording equipment'.

Reproductions of broadcasts made by social institutions

Article 5(2)(e) of the Information Society Directive allows for reproductions of broadcasts made by social institutions. This copyright exception has a seemingly narrow scope and a very specific set of beneficiaries. There are no Recitals in the Information Society Directive explaining the rationale behind the exception beyond obvious reasons of public policy and there is only one case from the Court of Justice that touches peripherally upon it. In *OSA*,[80] the Court of Justice held that Article 3(1) of the Information Society Directive (right of communication to the public) does not preclude national legislation that excludes the right of authors to authorize or prohibit the communication of their works by a business, such as a spa establishment, through the intentional distribution of a signal by means of television or radio sets in the bedrooms of the establishment's patients. According to the court, Article 5(2)(e) is not such as to affect that interpretation.

Because of the optional character of this Article, the exception has not been introduced in all Member States,[81] and it was very few that transposed it into their national laws, including Belgium, Cyprus, Italy, Malta, and Portugal. Similar provisions can also be found in Denmark, Finland, Germany, Hungary, Ireland, and Norway[82] but the Danish and Finnish versions of the exception are not subject to a requirement of fair compensation.[83]

Fair compensation as the basis of remunerated exceptions

The requirement that the aforementioned exceptions ought to be fairly compensated is justified on a variety of grounds. At a practical level, enforcing exclusive

---

[80]   *Ochranný Svaz Autorský pro Práva k Dílům Hudebním o.s. (OSA) v Léčebné lázně Mariánské Lázně a.s.*, Case C-351/12, 27 February 2014, ECLI:EU:C:2014:110 (*OSA*).

[81]   Austria, the Czech Republic, Estonia, France, Greece, Latvia, Lithuania, Luxembourg, the Netherlands, Poland, Slovakia, Slovenia, Spain, Sweden, and the United Kingdom.

[82]   Norway has an extended collective licensing system regarding uses covered by the exception.

[83]   Guido Westcamp, 'The Implementation of Directive 2001/29/EC in the Member States, Part II', Queen Mary Intellectual Property Research Institute, Centre for Commercial Law Studies, February 2007, 28.

rights or licensing the use of works to individual users was extremely difficult, perhaps impossible, in the analogue environment. Where it would be feasible, it could go against fundamental rights, such as the right to privacy, and negatively affect the reputation of the rightsholders; identifying individual infringers would encroach upon their privacy, as protected under Article 8(2) of the European Convention on Human Rights, and at the same time it could have a negative reputational impact on rightsholders who decided to enforce their rights. This practical necessity established a historical understanding that it is market failure that justifies levy schemes,[84] an argument that started to lose part of its strength in light of digitization and the Internet, where individual licensing of works has become feasible.

Beyond market failure and high transaction costs, however, the partial replacement of the proprietary claim with an entitlement to remuneration was justified on the basis that technology impacted on the amount that can be copied and who can make the copies, resulting in a greater degree of public access to copyright-protected materials. This was not only the result of a certain expectation of autonomy in the use of copyright-protected content,[85] but was also due to the desire not to interfere with user privacy and to leave certain kinds of use of, and access to, works unhindered.

Because Member States enjoy discretion in the calculation and detailed arrangements of fair compensation on the basis of Recital 35 of the Information Society Directive, there are discrepancies at the national level regarding the application of fair compensation. Despite these discrepancies, the Court of Justice has moved towards the harmonization of what has been affirmed to be an autonomous concept of EU law. Fair compensation was held to be an autonomous concept in *Padawan*, a case concerning private copying levies, where the court held that, even though it is up to Member States to introduce exceptions in their national laws, any exception reflecting Article 5(2)(b) has to be implemented in a uniform and harmonized manner.[86]

The EU history of remunerated exceptions

Remunerated exceptions are a product of German copyright jurisprudence. Compensation schemes, also called copyright levies in continental Europe, were first introduced in Germany in the mid-1960s. There were two landmark decisions of the German Federal Supreme Court that gave birth to the concept of compensation for the harm that certain permitted uses may cause. In *Personalausweise*,[87]

---

[84] Stavroula Karapapa, *Private Copying* (London: Routledge, 2012) 25–6.

[85] Stavroula Karapapa, *Private Copying* (London: Routledge, 2012) 27.

[86] For a commentary, see Stavroula Karapapa, 'Padawan v SGAE: A Right to Private Copy?' (2011) 33(4) *European Intellectual Property Review* 252.

[87] 'Personalausweise', German Federal Supreme Court (Bundesgerichtshof), *GRUR* 02/1965, 104 (Germany).

the Federal Court was called upon to assess whether the producers and suppliers of recording equipment were liable for contributory copyright infringement for acts of private copying carried out by their customers that were becoming increasingly popular. GEMA, the German collecting society that brought proceedings, sought for producers and suppliers to be ordered to disclose the purchasers' identity in order to thereinafter sue them for primary infringement. Following the outcome of an earlier case,[88] the Federal Supreme Court held that even though the defendants had not been engaged in copying themselves, they were still liable for enabling infringement to be carried out by their customers. Disclosing the identities of their customers, however, would come into conflict with the right of inviolability of the home[89] and hence with the privacy of the individuals involved. The court therefore recommended that the importation and sale of recording equipment should be subject to remuneration and such an obligation was introduced into German law the year after.[90]

German jurisprudence subsequently developed the understanding that to achieve a balance between copyright and certain permitted uses which touch upon fundamental freedoms, alternative monetary compensation is required whereby the act in question remains reserved by copyright, but the relevant exclusive rights cannot be enforced by the relevant rightsholders. It was on this premise that the German Copyright Act of 1965 included a specific provision allowing home copying by end users for private and non-commercial purposes on condition, however, that the rightsholders would receive compensation for the acts in question. Authorization from the rightsholders that would otherwise be required for the acts in question was replaced by a claim for compensation. Although it would be the users who made the payment, such a payment would be levied directly from the producers and importers of recording equipment and media. The relevant amount, according to the 1965 Act, would be calculated in the final retail price of the equipment and media. Although levies were initially introduced on the sale of recording equipment, about twenty years later their application was expanded to blank media through the 1985 Copyright Act.[91] The rationale for this expansion was the exponential growth of media and equipment enabling home copying to an extent that exceeded the dimension of the phenomenon back in 1965.

The German approach to the emergence of new technologies enabling copying, including home copying, was a catalyst of change for the relevant legislations across Europe, resulting in the introduction of remuneration schemes in various

---

[88] *Gema v Grundig*, 1 ZR 8/54, 17 BGHZ 266, [1955] *GRUR* 492 (Germany).

[89] Basic Law of the Federal Republic of Germany (*Grundgesetz*), 23 May 1949, last amended on 20 December 1993, Art. 13(1): 'The home is inviolable'.

[90] German Copyright Act (*Urheberrechtsgesetz*) 1965, Art. 53.

[91] The same year a statutory levy was also introduced with respect to photocopying, following *Kopierläden*, BGH, 9 June 1983, *GRUR* 1984/1, 54; see also Jörg Reinbothe, 'Chapter 11: Private Copy Levies' in Irini A. Stamatoudi (ed.), *New Developments in EU and International Copyright Law* (Alphen aan den Rijn: Kluwer Law International, 2016) 298, 300.

EU Member States.[92] Remuneration schemes were also launched with regard to the reprography exception in most Member States.[93] Because the concept of fair compensation was not subject to harmonization before 2001 when the Information Society Directive was introduced, the national approaches used were very diverse and there were differences as to the object,[94] the rates, and the method of calculation of levies, even with regard to identical recording equipment and blank media.[95] Even after the launch of the Directive, variations regarding remuneration schemes remain, the reason being that the amount, application, and specific parameters of compensation is left at the discretion of Member States.[96] An interesting aspect of the variety of national approaches, which results in differences in the end price of the relevant products, is the divergence on the levies applicable to multifunctional devices, an issue that will be examined below, particularly in reference to private copying.[97] A key constituent of the concept of fair compensation in the vast majority of Member States, however, is the concept of harm.

Fair compensation and harm

Unlike the German statutory license scheme that triggered the application of levies across Europe, the EU construal of fair compensation under the Information Society Directive relies on the concept of harm. The concept of harm has been put at the centre of fair compensation. Even though Recital 35 of the Directive indicates that it is a valuable criterion in determining the level of fair compensation— which could be interpreted to mean that harm is just one condition that ought to

---

[92] Excluding Cyprus, Ireland, Luxembourg, Malta, and the United Kingdom. In Norway, a system of state subsidies is available.

[93] For a comprehensive outline on fair compensation schemes with regard to the reprography exception see Lucie Guibault, 'The Reprography Levies Across the European Union', IvIR, University of Amsterdam (March 2003) available at <https://www.ivir.nl/publicaties/download/reprography_levies.pdf>, accessed 11 November 2019.

[94] In some Member States, levies apply to both equipment and media, whereas this is not so in other Member States. Levies on blank media such as CDs and DVDs apply in all Member States with a remuneration scheme. There is also diversity regarding the media that are subject to a levy. Austria, the Czech Republic, France, Hungary, and Poland apply levies to memory cards. Hard discs and memory cards are also subject to a levy in Switzerland ('*Remuneration for digital devices*', Federal Supreme Court (Bundesgericht), 19 June 2007, 2A.53/2006, 2A.338/2006 (Switzerland)).

[95] For a comparative analysis on the private copying levies see Willem Wanrooij, 'Remuneration Systems for Private Copying in Europe' in Péter Báldy, *Creators' Rights in the Information Society* (Budapest: KJK-Kersov legal and business publishers (with the assistance of the Hungarian Patent office), 2003) 371.

[96] Information Society Directive (Directive 2001/29/EC), Recital 38.

[97] For a detailed outline of the different rates that apply in EU Member States, see Martin Kretschmer, 'Private Copying and Fair Compensation – Study II: Empirical Effects on Copyright Levy Schemes', A Report for the UK Intellectual Property Office, 2011, available at <www.cippm.org.uk/ publications/comparative-study-of-copyright-levies-in-europe.html>, accessed 11 November 2019.

be examined[98]—the Court of Justice in *Padawan* stressed that it is the essential constituent of fair compensation. In this case, it was held that

> fair compensation must necessarily be calculated on the basis of the criterion of the harm caused to authors of protected works by the introduction of the private copying exception.[99]

As we will see later in this chapter, the compensatory nature of the obligation to pay the rightsholders has an impact on the legal nature of remunerated exceptions. Although they could arguably be said to qualify as user rights for activities that the users have paid to carry out, the compensatory nature of this payment means to recompense rightsholders for the limitation of their exclusive rights through a statutory license. Fair compensation does not only mean recompense for the actual and potential harm that the rightsholders suffer due to the said exceptions but also an offer of restitution for the replacement of exclusive rights with a statutory licensing mechanism that enables the public to benefit from certain uses of protected materials that would otherwise require authorial permission.

However central, the concept of harm is not defined and there is no uniform method for its calculation. Harm can be seen as loss of income or a lost licensing opportunity.[100] Economists often equate harm to loss of sales, even though they acknowledge the difficulty in measuring this with precision. In the context of private copying, Besen and Kirby outline the parameters that ought to be examined in order to assess the impact of the activity, such as assumptions on the substitutability between copies and originals and on their cost.[101] Various factors come into this consideration including the number of end users who would have been willing to pay the price of the original, but who prefer to make a copy for free.[102]

---

[98] Jörg Reinbothe, 'Chapter 11: Private Copy Levies' in Irini A. Stamatoudi (ed.), *New Developments in EU and International Copyright Law* (Alphen aan den Rijn: Kluwer Law International, 2016) 298, 317.

[99] *Padawan SL v Sociedad General de Autores y Editores de España (SGAE)*, Case C-467/08, 21 October 2010, ECLI:EU:C:2010:620 (*Padawan*), [42], [50]; *Stichting de Thuiskopie v Opus Supplies Deutschland GmbH and Others*, Case C-462/09, 16 June 2011, ECLI:EU:C:2011:397 (*Opus*), [24]; *Martin Luksan v Petrus van der Let*, Case C-277/10, 9 February 2012, ECLI:EU:C:2012:65 (*Luksan*); *Verwertungsgesellschaft Wort (VG Wort) v Kyocera and Others and Canon Deutschland GmbH and Fujitsu Technology Solutions GmbH and Hewlett-Packard GmbH v Verwertungsgesellschaft Wort*, Cases C-457/11, C-458/11, C-459/11, C-460/11, 27 June 2013, ECLI:EU:C:2013:426 (*VG Wort*), [31]; *Copydan Båndkopi v Nokia Danmark A/S*, Case C-463/12, 5 March 2015, ECLI:EU:C:2015:144 (*Copydan*), [21]–[22]; *Hewlett-Packard Belgium SPRL v Reprobel SCRL*, Case C-572/13, 12 November 2015, ECLI:EU:C:2015:750 (*Reprobel*), [36]; High Court [2015] EWHC 1723 (Admin), Case No. CO/5444/2014, [199] et seq. (UK); António Vitorino, Recommendations Resulting from the Mediation on Private Copying and Reprography Levies, Brussels, 31 January 2013, available at <http://ec.europa.eu/internal_market/copyright/docs/levy_reform/130131_levies-vitorino-recommendations_en.pdf>, accessed 11 November 2019.

[100] Stavroula Karapapa, 'A Copyright Exception for Private Copying in the United Kingdom' (2013) 35(3) *European Intellectual Property Review* 129, 131.

[101] Stanley Besen and Sheila Nataraj Kirby, 'Private Copying, Appropriability, and Optimal Copying Royalties' (1989) 32 *Journal of Law and Economics* 255, 270.

[102] Stanley Besen and Sheila Nataraj Kirby, 'Private Copying, Appropriability, and Optimal Copying Royalties' (1989) 32 *Journal of Law and Economics* 255, 255–80.

Any calculation of the extent of harm caused by permitted uses would ultimately depend on the way in which harm is defined,[103] however, even with a definition, it would be extremely difficult to get a clear picture of quantitative data on each and every copy made in the context of a permitted use and the impact on authorial rights thereinafter. Although national collecting societies use survey evidence from samples of the population as a method of calculating harm, the Commission has rejected the validity of such evidence.[104] During the recent UK copyright reform, the concept of harm was one of the key issues discussed in the context of the private copying exception, however, the relevant impact assessments do not seem to offer precise economic data estimating the extent of the phenomenon and exemplifying the way in which the rights and interests of copyright holders are prejudiced.[105] Such data is difficult to collect and may not offer an accurate estimate of the extent of the harm caused due to private copying.

Most of the analysis on the concept of harm is based on estimates which depend on qualitative data, such as ways in which the breadth of the exception—and harm thereinafter—can be narrowed down. Even on a qualitative, more theoretical level, however, understanding the extent of harm proves difficult for the very reason that the relevant activities are permitted, often for important public policy reasons, and it is hence not clear whether harm has even occurred as—at the stage of designing policy and launching legislation—public policy prevailed over the private exploitation of works. At the legislative stage, by virtue of the standards set in the three-step test—exceptions are subject to important internal limitations to ensure that harm will remain at a tolerated level. There are further arguments which challenge the concept of harm in the context of statutorily outlined permitted uses. These include the fact that not everyone making a private copy or a photocopy would have valued the original enough to purchase it.[106] But, even for those who have lawfully acquired their own copies of works and photocopied them or made copies for private use, it would not be unjustifiable for rightholders to expect to sell multiple copies of works to those individuals, even where these copies were not made for strictly personal use, but made and used by a closed circle of recipients, such as the nuclear family circle. This cannot be assumed to result in a loss of sales and there

---

[103] Stavroula Karapapa, 'A Copyright Exception for Private Copying in the United Kingdom' (2013) 35(3) *European Intellectual Property Review* 129, 131.

[104] To the Commission, this method cannot reliably assess either the proportion or the scale of copying: European Commission, Stakeholder Consultation on Copyright Levies in a Converging World (June 2006) 7, available at <http://ec.europa.eu/internal_market/copyright/docs/levy_reform/stakeholder_consultation_en.pdf>, accessed 11 November 2019.

[105] Intellectual Property Office, Impact Assessment BIS1055, Copyright Exception for Private Copying (2011); Intellectual Property Office, Impact Assessment BIS1055, Copyright Exception for Private Copying, Final (2012), available at <http://www.ipo.gov.uk/consult-ia-bis1055.pdf>, accessed 11 November 2019.

[106] Stavroula Karapapa, 'A Copyright Exception for Private Copying in the United Kingdom' (2013) 35(3) *European Intellectual Property Review* 129, 132.

are instances where harm is considered to be minimal and, hence, do not invoke the need to introduce fair compensation schemes.

Such an obligation does not arise only in cases where harm is considered to be minimal.

Minimal harm, no fair compensation?

The only instances in which fair compensation for permitted activities is not due is when harm is minimal, as affirmed in Recital 35 of the Information Society Directive. This results from the understanding that the broader the scope of an exception the greater the harm will be. It is assumed that harm arising from permitted activities is minimal when the scope of permitted use is narrowed down, e.g. by way of statutorily introducing internal limits to what the exception permits. In the private copying exception, for instance, this could include the requirement that the use is permitted for the strictly personal consumption of individuals, that the use ought to be non-commercial, and/or that the copy should be made from a lawfully acquired original.

However, this assumption has been challenged in light of the recently quashed private copying exception in the United Kingdom. Discussions on the introduction of a private copying exception into the United Kingdom[107] reflected the desire to keep the scope of the exception minimal—yet realistic—and to retain, therefore, the exception unremunerated. To this end, the scope of the exception was drafted in very narrow terms compared to other national exceptions and was subject to three key limitations. These had to do with the restriction of permissibility of the personal use of the individual making the copy, the scope of permitted activities, and the condition that the source copy had to be lawfully acquired, not merely lawfully possessed. Importantly, it was claimed that the permitted acts of personal copying were already 'priced-into' the sales price of the relevant content, with the result that any remaining harm that the rightsholders suffered would be as minimal as to not invoke the need to recompense them. Despite these efforts, the exception could not pass judicial scrutiny and nine months after its introduction it was quashed under legislative review.[108] The main ground for quashing the exception was that even though the government correctly interpreted the law, the evidence it relied on was not adequate to justify its conclusion that the exception caused minimal harm. In particular, what would amount to *de minimis* harm was not defined. The result was that the decision to introduce the exception into UK

---

[107] See Copyright and Rights in Performances (Personal Copies for Private Use) Regulations 2014, Art. 28B.

[108] *BASCA v Secretary of State for Business and Innovation* [2015] EWHC 1723 (UK).

law was therefore unlawful. In a follow-up judgment,[109] just a month later, Green J quashed the Regulations that introduced the private copying exception with prospective effect. The UK Intellectual Property Office states on its website that the government does not intend to take further action to reintroduce the exception.[110]

In the aftermath of the decisions that quashed the private copying exception in the United Kingdom, it is very difficult to see what could qualify as *de minimis* harm in this context or how an exception could be construed to maintain harm at a minimum level.[111] This effectively means that the private copying exception needs to be remunerated and instances where harm is minimal—if any—would be extremely rare. It is easier to see how this requirement may be met with regard to the exception of Article 5(2)(b) which has a narrower scope of application than private copying, but even there digital copying may be deemed harmful. At the same time, while the threshold of minimum harm is difficult to establish, it is important in the context of a balanced approach to ensure that harm shall not be construed as broadly as to extend fair compensation to double payments—which is clearly precluded in the Preamble of the Directive—or to apply it with regard to multifunctional devices without taking into account that they may not be used solely to copy copyright-protected materials.

Multifunctional devices

Levies have been gradually applied to all forms of technology devices and media that have some memory capacity, including smartphones, personal computers, and tablets. The reason is that these kinds of devices, although serving a distinct primary function, tend to replace devices or equipment that used to be more popular in the context of copying materials in the past, such as CDs, DVDs, and VHS.[112] This becomes problematic in that these devices are not destined to copy protected content—at least not primarily—although they entail such a function. In cases where a levy is applied to multifunctional devices with some memory capacity, users are obliged to pay for the mere possibility of making copies of protected materials and their ability to rely on statutory exceptions. To date, mobile phones are subject to a levy in numerous jurisdictions,[113] irrespective of the fact that there

---

[109] *R (British Academy of Songwriters, Composers and Authors and Others) v Secretary of State for Business, Innovation and Skills* [2015] EWHC 2041 (Admin) (UK).

[110] See <https://www.gov.uk/government/news/quashing-of-private-copying-exception>, accessed 11 November 2019.

[111] The French Supreme Court held that the private copying exception cannot exist without an accompanying requirement to fair remuneration and the absence of a decision on the imposition of levies from the relevant committee or the annulment of such a decision have the effect that courts ought to determine the amount of remuneration due. See *Sony v Copie France*, Supreme Court (Cour de Cassation), Commercial Law Chamber, 17 March 2016, 15-10895 (France).

[112] See in this regard '*Blank tape levy III*', Tallinn Circuit Court, 31 October 2017, 3-13-366 (Estonia).

[113] Indicatively, in the Czech Republic, Italy, France, and Spain, where a levy on mobile phones applies. Courts have affirmed the validity of such levies in some instances. The French Cour d'Etat

may be individuals who do not use their phones to copy and store protected materials. The same applies to personal computers and CD recorders, which are subject to levies in some jurisdictions,[114] although not in others.[115]

Merely because they entail the possibility of copying, multifunctional devices may not be used with a view to copy protected materials and may have an independent primary function, e.g. smart phones, or may be capable of performing significant non-infringing uses, which could form a defence against allegations of infringement in the United States.[116] This has also been upheld to an extent by national courts in Europe. The Austrian Supreme Court has held that multifunctional devices, such as personal computers, should not be subject to a levy because of the possibility that other materials, besides copyright-protected content, may be copied and stored.[117] MP3 players could not qualify for this exemption, however, as they were said to ordinarily involve copying of protected materials.[118] A more nuanced stance was taken by the Belgian Constitutional Court which criticized the indiscriminate application of fair compensation to devices and recording equipment, but held that levies are justifiable to the extent that no viable alternative exists.[119]

The issue reached the Court of Justice twice. In *Padawan*,[120] the court held that fair compensation should be confined to equipment and services that are deemed to be used for private copying; the levy should not apply indiscriminately to equipment or services not meant for this particular use, even though it is not necessary to show that the equipment or services were indeed used to make private copies. In *Copydan*,[121] the court addressed multifunctional devices directly, holding that the multifunctionality of the relevant medium, or the ancillary nature of its copying function, *may* be treated at the national level as affecting the amount of fair compensation, especially in cases where a Member State has exercised its discretion to limit the obligation to pay fair compensation regarding uses causing minimal

confirmed the validity of a 2012 decision to adopt new tariffs on portable media players, external hard drives, smartphones, and tablet computers. 'Apple Distribution International', Council of State, 19 November 2014, 358734 (France); also see in this respect 'Groupe Canal Plus et al.', Council of State, 19 November 2014, 366322, (France); a similar decision was reached by reference to mobile phones in Sweden. 'The Music Mobile', Supreme Court of Sweden, 29 December 2017, T 3973-15 (Sweden).

[114] See e.g. Higher Regional Court of Stuttgart (Oberlandesgericht Stuttgart), 4 September 2001, 4 U 142/01 (Germany); Federal Constitutional Court (Bundesverfassungsgericht), 30 August 2010, 1 BVR 1631/08 (Germany); Federal Court of Justice (Bundesgerichtshof), 5 July 2001, I ZR 335/98 (Germany); a 2 per cent levy on smart devices and computers was introduced in Greece on 15 May 2018.
[115] See e.g. Austria and Belgium.
[116] *Sony Corp. of America v Universal City Studios, Inc.*, 464 U.S. 417 (1984) (US).
[117] See 'GERICOM', Supreme Court (Oberster Gerichtshof), 12 July 2005, 4 Ob 115/05y (Austria).
[118] Ibid.
[119] Grondwettelijik Hof/Cour Constitutionnelle, 6 November 2008 (Belgium).
[120] *Padawan SL v Sociedad General de Autores y Editores de España (SGAE)*, Case C-467/08, 21 October 2010, ECLI:EU:C:2010:620 (*Padawan*).
[121] *Copydan Båndkopi v Nokia Danmark A/S*, Case C-463/12, 5 March 2015, ECLI:EU:C:2015:144 (*Copydan*).

harm. In such cases, the court held, if all users of a medium rarely use its copying function in practice, the making available of that function may produce minimal prejudice to the rightsholder and thereby prevent the obligation to pay fair compensation from arising under domestic law.

This interpretative guidance regarding the fairness of compensatory measures is particularly useful in establishing a framework that takes into account the interests of the copyright holders, but also the interests of the public in benefiting from exceptions with no disproportionate burdens. Such a balancing exercise is not just reflected in the policy objectives that the Directive means to serve,[122] but is also supported by the principles upon which the three-step test was developed. A healthy copyright system is one that promotes creativity and incentives for innovation and, in so doing, offers protection to copyright holders without disproportionately impacting on public and private interests in accessing works and protected subject matter. Emergent technologies may have the potential to identify materials that have been subject to copying and calculate how much has been copied in order to successfully ensure that double payments are avoided.

The compensatory nature of fair compensation in the context of remunerated exceptions has to be discussed in light of other forms of monetary payment that are used in EU copyright and may result in higher payment to the rightsholders. Because fair compensation sets a minimum standard, Member States have the discretion to set in place mechanisms resulting in higher payments to the copyright holders.

Fair compensation and equitable remuneration

Fair compensation is a new construct of EU copyright and before the launch of the Information Society Directive reference was made to other forms of monetary payments, notably equitable remuneration, which were not centred on the concept of harm and were likely to result in higher payments.

Equitable remuneration is used in Articles 5(1) and 8(2) of the Rental and Lending Directive[123] and in Article 4(1) of the Satellite and Cable Directive.[124] As with fair compensation, equitable remuneration is yet another construct of German jurisprudence. Equitable remuneration should be distinguished from fair compensation as it is not equally dependent on the concept of harm and, as a result, does not mean to recompense for the availability of a copyright exception.

---

[122] See e.g. Information Society Directive (Directive 2001/29/EC), Recital 31.
[123] Rental and Lending Right Directive (Directive 2006/115/EC).
[124] Satellite Broadcasting and Cable Retransmission Directive (Directive 83/93/EEC); note that the concept of royalty is used by reference to the artists' resale right.

Interpreting the concept of equitable remuneration under Article 5(1) of the Rental and Lending Directive,[125] the Court of Justice has ruled that this provision was

> designed to establish recompense for authors and mentions 'harm' as a criterion, but, at the same time, points at the need to assess the amount 'in the light of the value of the use of the protected work in trade' and to provide authors with 'adequate income'.[126]

Further guidance on the concept of equitable remuneration by reference to Article 8(2) of the Rental and Lending Directive[127] was given in *SENA*,[128] where the Court of Justice found that the entitlement to equitable remuneration is an autonomous concept of EU law, one has to be viewed as enabling a proper balance between the interests of performing artists and producers in obtaining remuneration for the broadcast of a particular phonogram, and the interests of third parties in being able to broadcast the phonogram on reasonable terms. The EU Commission too has stressed that harm does not have to be evaluated in order for equitable remuneration to be due.[129] Because equitable remuneration is linked to the concepts of equity and fairness, instead of harm, it is expected to result in higher payments.[130]

Fair compensation was historically seen as a compromise solution; von Lewinski remarks that diversity of legal options in EU copyright—fair compensation, equitable remuneration, or royalty by reference to the author's resale right—may be due to the fact that the higher level of equitable remuneration may have not been possible in all instances.[131] Indeed, with regard to the private copying exception of Article 5(2)(b), the EU Parliament Rapporteur of the Directive in First Reading, Roberto Barzanti, proposed the introduction of a form of monetary compensation for both analogue and digital private copying as minimum justice to the

---

[125] This Article reads: 'where an author or performer has transferred or assigned his rental right concerning a phonogram or an original or copy of a film to a phonogram or film producer, that author or performer shall retain the right to obtain an equitable remuneration for the rental'.

[126] *Vereniging van Educatieve en Wetenschappelijke Auteurs (VEWA) v Belgische Staat*, Case C-271/10, 30 June 2011, ECLI:EU:C:2011:442 (*VEWA*), [29], [32], [34].

[127] It reads: 'Member States shall provide a right in order to ensure that a single equitable remuneration is paid by the user, if a phonogram published for commercial purposes, or a reproduction of such phonogram, is used for broadcasting by wireless means or for any communication to the public, and to ensure that this remuneration is shared between the relevant performers and phonogram producers. Member States may, in the absence of agreement between the performers and phonogram producers, lay down the conditions as to the sharing of this remuneration between them'.

[128] *Stichting ter Exploitatie van Naburige Rechten (SENA) v Nederlandse Omroep Stichting (NOS)*, Case C-245/00, 6 February 2003, ECLI:EU:C:2003:68 (*SENA*), [36].

[129] Martin Kretschmer, 'Private Copying and Fair Compensation – Study II: Empirical Effects on Copyright Levy Schemes', A Report for the UK Intellectual Property Office, 2011, available at <www.cippm.org.uk/ publications/comparative-study-of-copyright-levies-in-europe.html>, accessed 11 November 2019.

[130] P. B. Hugenholtz, L. Guibault, S. van Geffen, *The Future of Levies in a Digital Environment* (Amsterdam: Institute for Information Law (IViR), 2003).

[131] Michel M. Walter and Silke Von Lewinski, *European Copyright Law: A Commentary* (Oxford: Oxford University Press, 2010)6.5.10.

rightsholders for these kinds of permitted uses.[132] There was no consensus about introducing equitable remuneration but at the same time there had to be a solution that would not call into question the existing levy schemes. Delegations resulted in the introduction of the concept of 'equo compenso', translated into English as fair compensation,[133] that would offer authors basic justice for the restriction of their rights in light of copyright exceptions and rough justice for end users, especially with regard to levies, which are applied on blank equipment and recording media, irrespective of whether they will be used to copy third party content, or not.

In this light, although relying on harm, fair compensation is also based on fundamental principles of justice in that the rightholders should receive an appropriate share of the economic exploitation of the works or other subject matter, even in cases where the exclusive rights have to be limited in the context of the statutorily permitted use.[134] The history of the delegations for the Information Society Directive indicates that fair compensation should be seen within the broader objective of the Directive to enhance the smooth functioning of the Internal Market,[135] achieve a high level of protection,[136] provide rightholders with an appropriate reward for the use of their works through satisfactory returns, and strike a fair balance of all rights and interests at stake.[137] Unlike an equitable remuneration, however, fair compensation means to offer a basic minimum level of payment, implying minimum harmonization[138] in the sense that Member States may go beyond this standard—even offering equitable remuneration—to the extent that this does not impact on the smooth functioning of the Internal Market.[139] Although the Information Society Directive does not expressly address this issue, certain Recitals in the Preamble can be read to that effect.[140] Recital 38 refers to the 'introduction or a continuation of remuneration schemes' and Recital 39 generically refers to 'remuneration schemes'. The Court of Justice has also confirmed that

---

[132] Report of 28 January 1999 on the Proposal for a European Parliament and Council Directive on the Harmonisation of Certain Aspects of Copyright and Related Rights in the Information Society, COM (97)0628 - C4-0079/98 - 97/0359(COD).

[133] Jörg Reinbothe, 'Chapter 11: Private Copy Levies' in Irini A. Stamatoudi (ed.), New Developments in EU and International Copyright Law (Alphen aan den Rijn: Kluwer Law International, 2016) 298, 314.

[134] Jörg Reinbothe, 'Chapter 11: Private Copy Levies' in Irini A. Stamatoudi (ed.), New Developments in EU and International Copyright Law (Alphen aan den Rijn: Kluwer Law International, 2016) 298, 315.

[135] Information Society Directive (Directive 2001/29/EC), Recital 7.

[136] Information Society Directive (Directive 2001/29/EC), Recitals 4 and 9.

[137] Information Society Directive (Directive 2001/29/EC), Recitals 10 and 31.

[138] This is to be surmised from the optional character of most copyright exceptions, with the temporary copying exception of Art. 5(1) excluded.

[139] See in this regard ACI Adam BV and Others v Stichting de Thuiskopie and Stichting Onderhandelingen Thuiskopie vergoeding, Case C-435/12, 10 April 2014, ECLI:EU:C:2014:254 (ACI Adam), [34]; Amazon.com International Sales Inc. and Others v Austro-Mechana Gesellschaft zur Wahrnehmung mechanisch-musikalischer Urheberrechte Gesellschaft mbH, Case C-521/11, 11 July 2013, ECLI:EU:C:2013:515 (Amazon), [20]; Copydan Båndkopi v Nokia Danmark A/S, Case C-463/12, 5 March 2015, ECLI:EU:C:2015:144 (Copydan), [20]; Directive 2001/29/EC, Recitals 7, 31, 32, 36.

[140] Jörg Reinbothe, 'Chapter 11: Private Copy Levies' in Irini A. Stamatoudi (ed.), New Developments in EU and International Copyright Law (Alphen aan den Rijn: Kluwer Law International, 2016) 298, 318.

Member States have a right to maintain levy schemes to the extent that these are deemed appropriate in achieving a balance of rights and interests.[141]

As Reinbothe observes, there are no indications that the concept of fair compensation had to replace the levy schemes that were already available in the various Member States or that Member States were prevented from going beyond the lower standard of fair compensation by introducing, for instance, equitable remuneration in certain cases,[142] on condition that the three-step test would be satisfied. The requirement of fair compensation was designed as a minimum obligation in order to accommodate Member States that did not have private copying remuneration schemes in place at the time of the introduction of the Directive and who were not ready to make substantial revisions in their national law to introduce them. In this sense, fair compensation can be seen as a compromise solution, laying down a minimum standard, which differs from—but does not replace—levies as a form of monetary compensation.[143] Fair compensation and equitable remuneration may coexist in the European Union, and both have to comply with the remunerated exceptions, the three-step test, and the related court rulings.[144]

Another concept with which fair compensation in the context of remunerated exceptions ought to be contrasted is fair compensation in the context of the permitted exceptions for orphan works. The reason for this is that, even though the principle remains similar, fair compensation in the orphan works context is used as a backstop provision. We have already discussed the permitted uses of orphan works in Chapter 7, as copyright exceptions that have been introduced for important public policy objectives. Article 6(5) of the Orphan Works Directive imposes a condition of fair compensation in the case that relevant rightsholders come forward and put an end to the orphan work status of their works.[145] Even though the introduction of the requirement to recompense reappearing rightsholders is compulsory for Member States to introduce, the obligation to pay fair compensation emerges only in cases where a rightsholder comes forward. This means that, even though the Directive uses the concept of fair compensation, this should be distinguished from the fair compensation that is due for the aforementioned

---

[141] *Padawan SL v Sociedad General de Autores y Editores de España (SGAE)*, Case C-467/08, 21 October 2010, ECLI:EU:C:2010:620 (*Padawan*), [46]; *Stichting de Thuiskopie v Opus Supplies Deutschland GmbH and Others*, Case C-462/09, 16 June 2011, ECLI:EU:C:2011:397 (*Opus*), [28]; *Amazon.com International Sales Inc. and Others v Austro-Mechana Gesellschaft zur Wahrnehmung mechanisch-musikalischer Urheberrechte Gesellschaft mbH*, Case C-521/11, 11 July 2013, ECLI:EU:C:2013:515 (*Amazon*), [24], [31] et seq.; *Copydan Båndkopi v Nokia Danmark A/S*, Case C-463/12, 5 March 2015, ECLI:EU:C:2015:144 (*Copydan*) [23].

[142] Jörg Reinbothe, 'Chapter 11: Private Copy Levies' in Irini A. Stamatoudi (ed.), *New Developments in EU and International Copyright Law* (Alphen aan den Rijn: Kluwer Law International, 2016) 298, 318.

[143] Ibid., 327.

[144] Ibid., 321.

[145] It reads: 'Member States shall provide that a fair compensation is due to rightholders that put an end to the orphan work status of their works or other protected subject matter for the use that has been made by the organisations referred to in Article 1(1) of such works and other protected subject matter in accordance with paragraph 1 of this Article'.

remunerated exceptions. The reason for this is that, in the context of orphan works, fair compensation does not introduce a general obligation to subject these permitted uses to a payment, rather it merely serves as a backstop provision to ensure that reappearing rightsholders shall be compensated for the use that has been made—or is about to be made—of their works. Member States retain full autonomy to determine the conditions of such a payment.[146]

Harmonization of remuneration schemes via case law

Despite the discrepancies between remuneration schemes at the national level, the Court of Justice has elaborated on the concept of fair compensation on a number of occasions, leading to harmonization via case law on certain aspects of fair compensation. This includes certain modalities on the collection of fair compensation, the determination of who is responsible to pay,[147] who is eligible to receive compensation, and what types of media and equipment can be subject to a compensatory payment.[148]

In *Padawan*,[149] the court developed general principles on the application of private copying levies, clearly linking the concept of fair compensation to harm and explaining that fair compensation does not need to be paid directly by the users of works or other subject matter but by third parties supplying equipment or offering services enabling copying of protected content. Those third parties may then pass

[146] Nordic countries have an extended collective licensing mechanism for the use of orphan works. See indicatively the discussion in Chapter 7. In the United Kingdom, Art. 7 of the Copyright and Rights in Performances (Certain Permitted Uses of Orphan Works) Regulations 2014, outlines the framework that applies to copyright holders that have not been identified or located in relation to a relevant work. When such a rightsholder comes forward, an institution that uses or has used the orphan work must, within a reasonable period, provide the rightsholder with fair compensation, together with information on how the fair compensation has been calculated. In case an agreement on the amount of compensation cannot be reached, either party may apply to the Copyright Tribunal to determine the amount due.

[147] *Padawan SL v Sociedad General de Autores y Editores de España (SGAE)*, Case C-467/08, 21 October 2010, ECLI:EU:C:2010:620 (*Padawan*), [46]; *Stichting de Thuiskopie v Opus Supplies Deutschland GmbH and Others*, Case C-462/09, 16 June 2011, ECLI:EU:C:2011:397 (*Opus*), [27] et seq.; *Verwertungsgesellschaft Wort (VG Wort) v Kyocera and Others and Canon Deutschland GmbH and Fujitsu Technology Solutions GmbH and Hewlett-Packard GmbH v Verwertungsgesellschaft Wort*, Cases C-457/11, C-458/11, C-459/11, C-460/11, 27 June 2013, ECLI:EU:C:2013:426 (*VG Wort*), [76]; *Amazon.com International Sales Inc. and Others v Austro-Mechana Gesellschaft zur Wahrnehmung Mechanisch-Musikalischer Urheberrechte Gesellschaft mbH*, Case C-521/11, 11 July 2013, ECLI:EU:C:2013:515 (*Amazon*), [24]; *Copydan Båndkopi v Nokia Danmark A/S*, Case C-463/12, 5 March 2015, ECLI:EU:C:2015:144 (*Copydan*), [23].

[148] *Padawan SL v Sociedad General de Autores y Editores de España (SGAE)*, Case C-467/08, 21 October 2010, ECLI:EU:C:2010:620 (*Padawan*), [52] et seq.; *Amazon.com International Sales Inc. and Others v Austro-Mechana Gesellschaft zur Wahrnehmung Mechanisch-Musikalischer Urheberrechte Gesellschaft mbH*, Case C-521/11, 11 July 2013, ECLI:EU:C:2013:515 (*Amazon*), [28]; *Copydan Båndkopi v Nokia Danmark A/S*, Case C-463/12, 5 March 2015, ECLI:EU:C:2015:144, [26] et seq.

[149] *Padawan SL v Sociedad General de Autores y Editores de España (SGAE)*, Case C-467/08, 21 October 2010, ECLI:EU:C:2010:620 (*Padawan*); for a comment see Stavroula Karapapa, 'Padawan v SGAE: a right to private copy?' (2011) 33(4) *European Intellectual Property Review* 244.

on the cost to the users by charging more for the equipment or services that enable copying. Confirming *Padawan, Stichting de Thuiskopie*[150] upheld that Member States have broad discretion in deciding who should discharge the obligation to pay fair compensation and clarified that the obligation of a Member State to ensure fair compensation for the purposes of the relevant domestic private copying exception also arises where those responsible for paying the compensation are established outside the borders of that Member State. In *Amazon*,[151] this discretion was found to apply with regard to 'the form, detailed arrangements, and possible level of such compensation'. It extends to enable a state to pay such compensation, or part of it, indirectly to its beneficiaries, including social and cultural institutions established for those beneficiaries. The discretion of Member States to decide who should pay compensation was also considered in *Copydan*,[152] where the Court of Justice found that equipment and media that enabled private copying could be subject to a levy and this did not only apply to natural persons but also to business customers to the extent that those paying the levy were aware that the equipment would be sold on by those customers.[153]

Private copying levies cannot apply to copies that are not permitted under the relevant copyright exception, and are also not permitted to apply to acts beyond such a permitted use. This is to ensure that activities that would amount to infringement are not accommodated under the statutory license terms that remunerated exception seems to outline. *ACI Adam*[154] clarified that fair compensation ought to make a distinction between permissible private copying of lawfully acquired materials and copying from unlawful sources. What is more, fair compensation ought to cover activities which fall under the exception and not unrelated uses, according to *MiBAC*.[155]

Regarding the beneficiaries of fair compensation, *Reprobel*[156] clarified that the reprography and private copying exceptions included in Articles 5(2)(a) and 5(2)(b) of the Information Society Directive preclude national legislation that

[150] *Stichting de Thuiskopie v Opus Supplies Deutschland GmbH and Others*, Case C-462/09, 16 June 2011, ECLI:EU:C:2011:397 (*Opus*).

[151] *Amazon.com International Sales Inc. and Others v Austro-Mechana Gesellschaft zur Wahrnehmung mechanisch-musikalischer Urheberrechte Gesellschaft mbH*, Case C-521/11, 11 July 2013, ECLI:EU:C:2013:515 (*Amazon*).

[152] *Copydan Båndkopi v Nokia Danmark A/S*, Case C-463/12, 5 March 2015, ECLI:EU:C:2015:144 (*Copydan*).

[153] *EGEDA* established that the Spanish fair compensation scheme that was financing fair compensation through the State budget was in conflict with the Information Society Directive as it did not guarantee that the cost of fair compensation would be ultimately borne by the end users making private copies. See *Entidad de Gestión de Derechos de los Productores Audiovisuales (EGEDA) and Others v Administración del Estado and Others*, Case C-470/14, 9 June 2016, ECLI:EU:C:2016:418 (EGEDA).

[154] *ACI Adam BV and Others v Stichting de Thuiskopie and Stichting Onderhandelingen Thuiskopie vergoeding*, Case C-435/12, 10 April 2014, ECLI:EU:C:2014:254 (*ACI Adam*).

[155] *Microsoft Mobile Sales International Oy and Others v Ministero per i Beni e le Attività Culturali (MiBAC) and Others*, Case C-110/15, 22 September 2016, ECLI:EU:C:2016:717 (*MiBAC*).

[156] *Hewlett-Packard Belgium SPRL v Reprobel SCRL*, Case C-572/13, 12 November 2015, ECLI:EU:C:2015:750 (*Reprobel*).

authorizes a Member State to allocate a part of the fair compensation payable to rightsholders to the publishers of works created by authors.[157] Besides publishers, this also seems to apply with regard to film producers too. *Luksan*[158] stressed that the principal director of a cinematographic work, in his capacity as author of that work, must be entitled directly and originally to the right to fair compensation provided for in Article 5(2)(b), which outlines the private copying exception; however, Member States cannot lay down a presumption of transfer of the entitlement to fair compensation vesting in the principal director of a cinematographic work in favour of the producer of that work. *Reprobel* and *Luksan* effectively outline a framework whereby it is authors alone who are entitled to fair compensation but this entitlement does not extend to related rightsholders, such as publishers and film producers.

The aforementioned cases of the Court of Justice, and in particular *Reprobel*, seem to have been rendered ineffective in light of the recent revision of the EU copyright rules via the Directive on Copyright in the Digital Single Market. Indeed, Article 16 of this Directive, entitled 'Claims to fair compensation', appears to be in conflict with the dictum in *Reprobel*. It reads:

> Member States may provide that where an author has transferred or licensed a right to a publisher, such a transfer or licence constitutes a sufficient legal basis for the publisher to be entitled to a share of the compensation for the use of the work made under an exception or limitation to the transferred or licensed right.

This is an optional expansion of the beneficiaries of fair compensation schemes, which is left at the discretion of Member States to decide. As acknowledged in Recital 30 of the Directive, although publishers often operate on the basis of the transfer of authors' rights through contractual arrangements or statutory provisions and make an investment towards the exploitation of the works, they may be deprived of revenues where works are used under remunerated exceptions. The Directive aspires to improve legal certainty arising from the divergent approaches used in various Member States and allows the continuation of existing national schemes where fair compensation is shared between authors and publishers. As Recital 30 indicates, this is particularly important for Member States that had such compensation-sharing mechanisms before 12 November 2015, although in other Member States compensation is not shared, rather it is due solely to authors in accordance with national cultural policies. Clearly, 12 November 2015 is the date when *Reprobel* was issued and Article 16 renders the ruling of this case ineffective.

---

[157] See, however, the newly enacted right for press publishers in Art. 15 of the Digital Single Market Directive (Directive 2019/790).

[158] *Martin Luksan v Petrus van der Let*, Case C-277/10, 9 February 2012, ECLI:EU:C:2012:65 (*Luksan*).

Article 16 does not aspire to introduce a compensation-sharing mechanism in Member States where such a mechanism is not in place but will allow the continuation of relevant schemes by reversing the effect of *Reprobel* and empowering publishers, including press publishers who receive special protection and a new right under Article 15 of the Digital Single Market Directive.

Even though it is accepted that the aforementioned rulings on fair compensation apply both to fair compensation and equitable remuneration, certain cases expressly address fair compensation, as such, and as a result do not have broader application to schemes that have been introduced on the basis of equitable remuneration principles.[159]

Remunerated exceptions, the parallel application of technological protection measures, and contractual override

Article 6(4) of the Information Society Directive outlines the conditions upon which the application of technological protection measures may affect the exercise of certain copyright exceptions, including those that are subject to a requirement of fair compensation. It reads:

> Notwithstanding the legal protection provided for in paragraph 1, in the absence of voluntary measures taken by rightholders, including agreements between rightholders and other parties concerned, Member States shall take appropriate measures to ensure that rightholders make available to the beneficiary of an exception or limitation provided for in national law in accordance with Article 5(2)(a) ... [and] ... (2)(e) ... the means of benefiting from that exception or limitation, to the extent necessary to benefit from that exception or limitation and where that beneficiary has legal access to the protected work or subject matter concerned.
>
> A Member State may also take such measures in respect of a beneficiary of an exception or limitation provided for in accordance with Article 5(2)(b), unless reproduction for private use has already been made possible by rightholders to the extent necessary to benefit from the exception or limitation concerned and in accordance with the provisions of Article 5(2)(b) and (5), without preventing rightholders from adopting adequate measures regarding the number of reproductions in accordance with these provisions.

---

[159] Jörg Reinbothe, 'Chapter 11: Private Copy Levies' in Irini A. Stamatoudi (ed.), *New Developments in EU and International Copyright Law* (Alphen aan den Rijn: Kluwer Law International, 2016) 298, 320; compare in this regard *Martin Luksan v Petrus van der Let*, Case C-277/10, 9 February 2012, ECLI:EU:C:2012:65 (*Luksan*), [99], [107] et seq. and *Hewlett-Packard Belgium SPRL v Reprobel SCRL*, Case C-572/13, 12 November 2015, ECLI:EU:C:2015:750 (*Reprobel*), [44] et seq.

Unlike the optional character of the provision that relates to private copying, the reprography exception, and the exception covering reproductions of broadcasts by social institutions, is compulsory for Member States to implement.[160] In this latter case, Member States have to take measures to ensure that the benefit of these exceptions shall not be restricted by the application of technological protection measures. This means that these exceptions are laid down as imperative against possible attempts to technologically restrict their exercise. The optional nature of Article 6(4)(2) has been the result of divergence, with some Member States, such as Greece and Lithuania, having put in place mediation procedures and others, such as Germany and Spain, having launched a court procedure. There are also Member States that have refrained from setting in place a relevant mechanism.[161]

The distinction in the way the aforementioned exceptions are dealt with may be understood as connoting preference towards private ordering mechanisms in the context of digital private copying.[162] Another issue worth noting is that Article 5(2)(b) expressly indicates that fair compensation must take into account the application of any technical protection measures within the meaning of Article 6 of the Information Society Directive. In *VG Wort*,[163] one of the questions that the German Federal Supreme Court referred to the Court of Justice was whether the possibility of applying technological measures renders inapplicable the condition relating to fair compensation within the meaning of the private copying exception. As the court stressed, it is the Member States and not the rightsholders who establish the private copying exception and authorize such a use of copyright-protected materials.[164] Because technological measures are voluntary, even where the possibility of applying such measures exists, the fact that rightsholders decided not to use them does not deprive them of fair compensation.[165] However, Member States have discretion to make the actual level of compensation owed to rightsholders dependent on the application of such technological measures, so that rightsholders are encouraged to make use of them and thereby voluntarily contribute to the proper application of the private copying exception.[166]

---

[160] Stavroula Karapapa, *Private Copying* (London: Routledge, 2012) 147–50.

[161] Austria, Bulgaria, the Czech Republic, Poland, Romania, and Slovakia.

[162] Mihály Ficsor, *The Law of Copyright and the Internet: the 1996 WIPO Treaties, their Interpretation and Implementation* (Oxford: Oxford University Press, 2002) s. 11.29, 560–1; this may also be the reason why, in the context of the exception on cross-border teaching activities under the Digital Single Market Directive (Directive 2019/790), the question of fair compensation is left at the discretion of Member States.

[163] *Verwertungsgesellschaft Wort (VG Wort) v Kyocera and Others and Canon Deutschland GmbH and Fujitsu Technology Solutions GmbH and Hewlett-Packard GmbH v Verwertungsgesellschaft Wort*, Cases C-457/11, C-458/11, C-459/11, C-460/11, 27 June 2013, ECLI:EU:C:2013:426 (*VG Wort*).

[164] *Verwertungsgesellschaft Wort (VG Wort) v Kyocera and Others and Canon Deutschland GmbH and Fujitsu Technology Solutions GmbH and Hewlett-Packard GmbH v Verwertungsgesellschaft Wort*, Cases C-457/11, C-458/11, C-459/11, C-460/11, 27 June 2013, ECLI:EU:C:2013:426 (*VG Wort*), [52].

[165] Ibid., [57].

[166] Ibid., [58].

Although the reprography exception and the exception available to social institutions on the copying of broadcasts seem to have a stronger basis in that they are compulsory against technological override, unlike private copying, their legal nature is not entirely distinct from the private copying exception. This is because all exceptions are subject to the common requirement of fair remuneration. This requirement has an impact on the legal nature of the relevant exceptions; are they statutory licenses, legitimate entitlements of the rightsholders to compensation, or fully fledged rights of the users who have actually paid for their entitlement to a specific permitted use?

The legal nature of remunerated exceptions

Remunerated exceptions can be viewed as an interim form of permitted use in that they replace exclusive rights with a license in exchange for making a use freely available to the public. They represent a balancing act between authorial entitlements and public policy, serving as an intermediary form of permitted use that better clarifies the scope of exclusive rights.[167] In order to achieve such a balance, exceptions have a relatively broad scope and are subject to a corresponding entitlement to remuneration. Such a remunerated exception may be viewed as a particular way to exploit the works.[168] When permitting a particular activity as desirable for policy reasons, limiting exclusive rights may result in replacing these rights with an entitlement to equitable remuneration or fair compensation. This means that there is still authorial control over a particular use, but such control is limited compared to the power that is embedded in an exclusive right to authorize or prohibit a specific activity. As with all copyright exceptions and limitations, the copyright holders' right to authorize or prohibit certain activities is narrowed. However, in the case of remunerated exceptions, it is replaced by an entitlement to receive a monetary compensation. In this sense, it is said that remunerated exceptions take the form of statutorily imposed licenses. They impose legal restrictions on rightsholders who can no longer prohibit certain activities, but who are compensated for the actual or potential harm they may suffer.

Despite the fact that compensation may give the impression that users have acquired a license to carry out a particular activity and hence have a 'right' to carry out activities falling under the scope of a given exception, jurisprudence has established that no such right exists under the national laws of EU Member States. There

---

[167] Ysolde Gendreau, 'Chapter 2: Exceptions for Education and Research' in Irini A. Stamatoudi (ed.), *New Developments in EU and International Copyright Law* (Alphen aan den Rijn: Kluwer Law International, 2016) 56, 70.

[168] See interpretative guidance offered in *Syndicat de l'Industrie de Matériels Audiovisuels Electroniques*, Supreme Administrative Court (Conseil d'Etat), No. 298779, 11 July 2008 (France).

have indeed been a number of cases that have affirmed such a finding, originating from Belgium and France and primarily focusing on private copying.

In the Belgian *Test Achats* case,[169] it was held that a remunerated exception, private copying, was not a user right that could be enforced before the courts. A consumer group brought proceedings against a record company claiming that the application of technological protection measures on music CDs deprived consumers of their ability to make private copies. As is the case with very few Member States in Europe,[170] Belgium lays down a mandatory private copying exception in that copyright holders cannot restrict its exercise by means of contractual terms and conditions. Hence, the plaintiffs claimed that because the exception had a mandatory nature and because payment of a levy had taken place, consumers had a positive right to carry out the particular activity and bring proceedings in the case of its exercise being restricted. Both of these arguments were rejected, however, and the Brussels Court held that private copying was a statutory immunity against prosecution, instead of a positive right that could be enforceable against its abuse.

A similar conclusion was reached in France, in the *Mulholland Drive* case,[171] where the Supreme Court found that the private copying limitation is a statutory limitation, rather than a user right and, in this sense, could not be invoked against rightholders in cases where the users' ability to make copies for private use was technologically restricted. The payment of the levy was immaterial and had no bearing on the legal nature of the exception. Partly affirming the position of the High Court that there was no user right to make private copies, the Court of Appeals and the Supreme Court elaborated on this point and held that even though the exception was just a statutory limitation to exclusive rights and not a user right, its exercise was not left at the discretion of copyright holders in the sense that restricting the availability of the exception through technological protection measures was not allowed. In this sense, it was judicially confirmed that the exercise of the copyright exception prevails over the application of technological protection measures, irrespectively of the payment of a levy.

Similar to the *Mulholland Drive* case, the French Supreme Court[172] was called to assess a case involving the application of technological protection measures on

---

[169] *L'ASBL Association Belge des Consomateurs Test Achats v La SA EMI Recorded Music Belgium et al.*, Tribunal of First Instance of Brussels, 2004/46/A, 27 April 2004 (Belgium); *L'ASBL Association Belge des Consomateurs Test Achats v La SA EMI Recorded Music Belgium et al.*, Brussels Court of Appeal, 9 September 2005, Case 2004/AR/1649 (Belgium); Natalie Helberger, 'It's not a Right, Silly! The Private Copying Exception in Practice', *INDICARE Monitor*, 7 October 2004.

[170] E.g. Ireland, Malta, Portugal, the United Kingdom.

[171] *Studio Canal et al v S. Penguin and Union Federale des Consommateurs Que Choisir*, Cour de Cassation, 19 June 2008, No 07-142777 (France); *Studio Canal et al v S. Penguin and Union Federale des Consommateurs Que Choisir*, Paris Court of Appeal, 4 April 2007, *Gaz. Pal.* 18 July 2007 No. 199, 23 (France); *Studio Canal et al v S. Penguin and Union Federale des Consommateurs Que Choisir*, Cour de Cassation, 1st civil section, 28 February 2006, Case No. 549, Bull. 2006 I No. 126, 115 ('*Mulholland Drive*') (France).

[172] Supreme Court (Cour de Cassation), No. 07-18778, 27 November 2008 ('*Phil Collins*') (France).

a CD which restricted consumers' ability to make private copies. Affirming the decision of the Paris Court of Appeal,[173] the Supreme Court held in *Phil Collins* that private copying is not a right but a legal exception to the exclusive right to authorize or prohibit the reproduction of works. In this sense, it could only be used as a defence, not as a positive right to start legal action to stop rightsholders applying technological protection measures, irrespective of the fact that consumers had paid a private copying levy. The indication on the CD cover that 'this CD is protected against copying' was sufficient indication of compliance with consumer law and, in particular, Article L.111-1 of the Consumer Code. In this regard, the Court of Appeal agreed with the Paris District Court[174] on the legal nature of the exception but disagreed with its stance that the application of technological measures should respect the exercise of the exception.

Even though a levy is payable to compensate for the possibility that copyright holders suffer harm owing to private copying, it cannot be claimed that users have a broader entitlement to benefit from a remunerated exception than they would in other exceptions. This is because it is generally understood that in remunerated exceptions rightsholders retain some form of control over their works, which may not be as strong as the control resulting from exclusive rights, but still justifies an entitlement to fair compensation. Unlike copyright exceptions that are premised on fundamental freedoms, remunerated exceptions are often underpinned by strong policy reasons as well as a market failure justification. Theory accepts that exceptions based on fundamental freedoms should qualify as user rights, even though there has been no judicial affirmation to this effect so far.[175] This is partly because it was until recently assumed[176] that they can be invoked in parallel with the right on which they are premised, e.g. freedom of press or freedom of speech. The argument is less strong with regard to remunerated exceptions in the sense that payment of the levy indicates a degree of authorial control, rather than a solid basis for user entitlements.

Of the remunerated exceptions under EU copyright, it is only the private copying exception that finds partial justification on fundamental rights; the right to privacy under Article 8 of the European Convention on Human Rights and Article 7 of the Charter of Fundamental Rights of the European Union. As we have already seen earlier in this chapter, enforcement of copyright in the context of private copying would involve invasion of the private sphere or requests to

---

[173] *Fnac Paris v UFC Que Choisir et autres*, Court of Appeal Paris (Cour d'appel Paris), 20 June 2007 ('*Phil Collins*') (France).

[174] *Mr. X and UFC Que Choisir v Warner Music France and FNAC Paris*, Paris District Court, 10 January 2006 ('*Phil Collins*') (France).

[175] With the exception of *CCH Canadian Ltd v Law Society of Upper Canada*, 2004 SCC 14 (CCH); also see Estelle Derclaye and Marcella Favale, 'Copyright and contract law: Regulating user contracts: The state of the art and a research agenda' (2010) 18(1) *Journal of Intellectual Property Law* 65, 70.

[176] Not, however, in the aftermath of *Funke Medien NRW GmbH v Federal Republic of Germany*, C-469/17, 29 July 2019, ECLI:EU:C:2019:623 (*Funke Medien*), [64].

Internet service providers to disclose the identities of users allegedly involved in infringements. That would amount to a breach of privacy (or to a violation of data protection laws). The privacy right, however, is subject to limitations according to its second paragraph and these limitations include the rights of others. To this end, the fundamental right to privacy may not offer a solid justificatory rationale. Importantly, such a rationale takes effect *ex ante*, namely after an alleged infringement has taken place.

Besides the German cases which developed the privacy justification for private copying, the Court of Justice has also addressed the issue of the disclosure of user identities. In *Promusicae*,[177] it held that EU law does not require—but neither does it prohibit—Member States from laying down an obligation to communicate personal data in order to ensure effective protection of copyright in the context of civil proceedings. In *Scarlet*,[178] the court held that the filtering of user behaviour on the Internet may contravene fundamental rights, notably the right for protection of personal data and the freedom to receive or impart information, both of which receive protection through Articles 8 and 11 of the Charter of Fundamental Rights of the European Union respectively. In light of the General Data Protection Regulation,[179] it is likely that the privacy justification for the private copying exception will become more powerful, despite the fact that this is a theoretical justification that emerges *ex ante*, namely at the stage of enforcing copyright.[180] Indeed, the fundamental right justification of private copying is relevant not at the time that the particular activity took place, as is the case for instances with fundamentally free exceptions, such as parody or news reporting, but at the stage of enforcing copyright. In this regard, the fundamental right rationale for private copying can be seen as a justification against the enforcement of copyright instead of a defensive ground for carrying out the activity in the first place.

Conclusion

Although copyright holders cannot restrict the exercise of remunerated exceptions with the application of technological protection measures,[181] and despite the fact

---

[177] *Productores de Música de España (Promusicae) v Telefónica de España SAU*, Case C-275/06, 29 January 2008, ECLI:EU:C:2008:54 (*Promusicae*).

[178] *Scarlet Extended SA v Société belge des auteurs, compositeurs et éditeurs SCRL (SABAM)*, Case C-70/10, 24 November 2011, ECLI:EU:C:2011:771 (*Scarlet*), [50].

[179] Regulation (EU) 2016/679 of the European Parliament and of the Council of 27 April 2016 on the Protection of Natural Persons with Regard to the Processing of Personal Data and on the Free Movement of such Data, and Repealing Directive 95/46/EC (General Data Protection Regulation), OJ L 119, 4 May 2016, 1–88.

[180] Stavroula Karapapa, *Private Copying* (London: Routledge, 2012) 19–25.

[181] Art. 5(2)(b) indicates that the intersection between the payment of fair compensation and technological protection measures should be taken into consideration; Art. 6(4)(a) requires Member States to have appropriate mechanisms in place to ensure that the exercise of the exceptions on reprography and

that these exceptions are subject to the condition that copyright holders should be fairly compensated, remunerated exceptions cannot qualify as user rights that end users can invoke before the courts in cases where their benefit from an exception has been technologically or—possibly—contractually restricted. They may only benefit from the national mechanisms that have been set in place by virtue of Article 6(4) of the Information Society Directive that aim to ensure that the exercise of the exceptions shall not be hindered; however, this is available only for the reprography exception and that which covers the reproduction of broadcasts by social institutions—and to a lesser extent by reference to private copying.

Determining the appropriate scope of remunerated exceptions in the online environment is important as it influences the development of online services and the enhancement of modern, innovative uses of copyright works. We have already seen that third party copying is not settled and this impacts on the scope of the reprography and private copying exceptions. Diversity in the understanding of third party copying in the various Member States does not create a level playing field and could be seen as an impediment to the development of electronic commerce and the fulfilment of the objectives that aid the functioning of the Internal Market. The approach adopted in certain Member States, such as Germany, that permits third parties to copy content on behalf of a beneficiary, subject to the conditions of the reprography or the private copying exception, allows sufficient room for the development of electronic services, new methods of content delivery, and the availability of access to a broader set of materials with a view to enhancing knowledge and creativity.

It has been affirmed in a number of national cases that the role of remunerated exceptions is to serve as defences against allegations of infringement, no matter the fact that they are activities for which users pay fair compensation (in some Member States the payment of higher amounts of private copying levies is available). They do, however, represent user entitlements to carry out certain activities on the basis of a statutory license. In this sense, remunerated exceptions become a manifestation of the dual nature of authorial entitlements, namely exclusivity and remuneration, whereby exclusive rights are limited in light of specific public policy reasons but are replaced by a requirement for remuneration. In an era where exceptions are deemed more and more beneficial towards the achievement of various policy objectives, introducing further remunerated exceptions may enable the permissibility of a broader set of uses, particularly in instances where the use and re-use of copyright-protected materials takes place on a large scale, as it does with search engines and news aggregators. In this context, it would be opportune to consider rendering certain uses permissible on condition that payment of fair compensation is due.

reproduction of broadcasts by social institutions shall not be hindered; Member States enjoy discretion on whether to introduce relevant mechanisms by reference to the private copying exception.

9

External Defences

Some defences are available on grounds that are extraneous to copyright and are based either on other bodies of law, such as competition law or e-commerce protection, or on general legal principles. These include, for instance, defences available to Internet service providers for infringements carried out by their users, including defences for hosting, caching, and 'mere conduit'. Others are available on grounds of competition law, such as refusal to license, or abuse of dominant position, which could have a legal basis of application—inter alia—in certain mass digital activities of online services. Other available defences fall under general legal principles that can be invoked in cases where copyright exceptions do not cover an activity for which there is a principle-based justification for the particular conduct. Such a justification could be the public interest or the doctrine of the 'abuse of right'. There are also a number of uses that can be permitted on grounds of benign infringement on the basis of the 'innocuous use' doctrine.[1]

Unlike other defences to copyright, these defensive rules represent instances where copyright may be subject to limitations as a result of its encounter with other legal orders. Such instances have either not been institutionalized within copyright law, such as speech entitlements or public policy privileges, or may have been partially included within it while offering principle-based explanations for acts of copyright infringement on the basis of legal grounds found in other areas of law or broader legal principles. These defences are an essential component to the understanding of the scope of permissible copyright use on the Internet as they can be extremely relevant in cases which involve online services and business models, such as hosting services, and online content use more broadly.

Introduction

A special category of liability-defeating rules in copyright includes grounds external to copyright that have the power to exempt a particular activity

---

[1] Supreme Court, Civil Chamber, 3 April 2012, Sentencia n 172/2012 (Spain).

Defences to Copyright Infringement. Stavroula Karapapa, Oxford University Press (2020). © Stavroula Karapapa.
DOI: 10.1093/oso/9780198795636.001.0001

involving the use and re-use of copyright-protected works from infringement. In these cases, even though infringement takes place, liability of the defendant cannot be established as a matter of claims based on legal rules that are extraneous to copyright law. In their majority,[2] these rules are supervening in that they offer a justification for an act of infringement that has taken place and their basis is located in other legal disciplines. These include competition law or e-commerce protection, or general legal principles that either offer protection to the defendant's activity or do not tolerate the behaviour of the claimant. These are instances where copyright encounters other judicial orders, but where the emergent conflict between rights is not capable of integration into the copyright system. For instance, the general prohibition of the abusive exercise of rights, which features in various civil law codes across the European Union and has been sporadically addressed by the Court of Justice, may serve a defensive function against allegations of copyright infringement but has not been legislatively or judicially addressed as a matter of copyright law.

In this sense, the protection of the defendant on such extraneous grounds may be justified because the general public interest has to prevail in its conflict with private rights arising as a matter of copyright law, or because other legal orders, such as the protection of e-commerce, list special grounds on which the encounter of copyright and e-commerce protection has to be regulated. What is more, in unregulated or under-regulated instances where copyright-protected materials are used, i.e. cases that are not clearly subject to either an exclusive right or a copyright exception, it is likely that the general prohibition of abusive exercise of rights will apply. Such a prohibition is available under certain national laws[3] and dictates that excessive or disproportionate claims on behalf of copyright holders aiming to block third parties from using copyright-protected works are not allowed. In this light, the maximum threshold of copyright protection is balanced against this general legal principle that serves as a balancing act between private rights and public access, including the use and re-use of copyright-protected materials. In some Member States,[4] as we shall see below, there is a general legal principle prohibiting the abusive exercise of rights, which is less frequently incorporated in copyright statutes but is, to some extent,

---

[2] The doctrine of abuse of right could also be read as an external limitation to the scope of rights, attacking the rightsholder's entitlement to bring forward an excessive claim. However, it does not qualify *stricto sensu* as a limitation of a right because there is no right as such over the objects or the uses they apply to.

[3] E.g. France. See indicatively Supreme Court, 1st Civil Division, 14 May 1991, 89-21.701, 151 RIDA 1992, 273 (France); Supreme Court, Commercial Division, 26 November 2003, 00-22.605, Bulletin 2003 IV, No. 178, 195(France).

[4] Ibid.

reflected in competition law principles, such as the refusal to license the use of copyright-protected content.

Below, we examine three of the most notable external legal defences, as claims that protect the defendant's activity on grounds external to copyright. In the first instance, subject to discussion shall be the defensive rules applicable to Internet service providers, included primarily in the e-Commerce Directive.[5] Although for many years the liability of Internet service providers was dealt with as a form of secondary liability, the Directive on Copyright in the Digital Single Market[6] recently launched a system of primary liability of online content-sharing service providers. This has significantly narrowed the breadth of defensive rules for online content-sharing service providers, who may no longer qualify for the benefit of the e-Commerce Directive safe harbours. Second, subject to discussion shall be the principle of the public interest, which is available in certain Member States such as the United Kingdom and Italy, and can serve as a balancing act in decisions which concern the conflict between proprietary claims and the general good. The availability and ambit of this legal principle is becoming more and more limited as a result of the broader legal framework governing the EU copyright, including its likely conflict with the three-step test as an international and EU-wide norm. Finally, subject to discussion shall be the principle of the prohibition of the abusive exercise of rights, which has only received partial harmonization at the EU level and remains a matter of national law. The principle is often used to address claims that result from the excessive or abusive exercise of authorial entitlement[7] and may either stem from a general legal rule or relate to the rules of competition law and policy.

Safe harbours for Internet intermediaries

Emergent business models and innovative electronic services rely on intermediaries that enable access, use, and participation on the Internet. Because a growing number of online services rely on the use and re-use of copyright works, the defences that are available to Internet intermediaries have gained increased significance. Internet service provider liability may arise under the provisions available for secondary or indirect infringement.

---

[5] Directive 2000/31/EC of the European Parliament and of the Council of 8 June 2000 on Certain Legal Aspects of Information Society Services, in Particular Electronic Commerce, in the Internal Market (e-Commerce Directive), OJ L 178, 17 July 2000, 1–16.

[6] Directive (EU) 2019/790 of the European Parliament and of the Council of 17 April 2019 on Copyright and Related Rights in the Digital Single Market and amending Directives 96/9/EC and 2001/29/EC, OJ L 130, 17 May 2019, 92–125 (Digital Single Market Directive).

[7] Note that other external defences may also be in place in some Member States, but they are not exhaustively mentioned here because of their limited, sporadic, or local applicability. These include, for instance, provisions of consumer law that could be relevant with regard to the use of copyright materials.

The agreed statement concerning Article 8 of the World Intellectual Property Organization (WIPO) Copyright Treaty of 1996 indicates that Internet service provider liability may arise under the provisions available for secondary or indirect infringement:

> It is understood that the mere provision of physical facilities for enabling or making a communication does not in itself amount to communication within the meaning of this Treaty or the Berne Convention.

This effectively means that the international *minima* dictate that mere intermediation in electronic communications is not a matter to be dealt with under the rules of primary liability.

Until recently, and in particular before the launch of the Directive on Copyright in the Digital Single Market, the approach taken in the European Union was to deal with intermediary liability as a matter of secondary or indirect liability. This was primarily so because information society service providers would merely offer the technical means and physical facilities to enable their users to thereinafter upload content and possibly carry out acts of primary infringement. Targeting identifiable (and more lucrative) targets, such as Internet service providers, instead of individual end users, however, was adopted as a preferable approach in cases concerning allegations of copyright infringement. Even though secondary liability has not been subject to harmonization at the EU level, it was partially harmonized with regard to what concerns the liability of information society service providers. The e-Commerce Directive[8] is the key instrument which lays down the regulatory framework on Internet service provider liability, having harmonized the protection available to electronic commerce in the Internal Market and having enhanced legal certainty for Internet users and stakeholders.[9] An interesting aspect of the liability framework outlined in the e-Commerce Directive is that it negatively defines what amounts to liability. Its focus is placed on the available exemptions from infringement, rather than to outline the particular parameters of intermediary liability, which in some Member States is developed in line with national tort law traditions. In cases where information society service providers engage in a specific set of services that qualify under one of the immunities listed in Articles 12–15 of the Directive, such as the offer of hosting services, and to the extent that such intermediaries comply with the series of legal requirements laid down in each and every exception, they will escape liability.

---

[8]   e-Commerce Directive (Directive 2000/31/EC).
[9]   Patrick Van Eecke and Barbara Ooms, 'ISP Liability and the E-Commerce Directive: A Growing Trend Toward Greater Responsibility for ISPs' (2007) 11 *Journal of Internet Law* 3.

Recent times have faced a rise in blocking injunctions[10] and the award of damages,[11] and discussions at the policy and legislative level have centred on an approach that would enhance the responsibility of information society intermediaries towards the users of their services.[12] Article 17 of the Directive on Copyright in the Digital Single Market (formerly referred to as Article 13 of the proposal for a Directive on Copyright in the Digital Single Market) was one of the most contentious provisions of the Directive and the source of fierce criticism since its very inception.[13] Criticism attacked the proposed definition of online content-sharing service providers and the compatibility of the then-Article 13 with the *acquis communautaire*, notably Article 15 of the e-Commerce Directive and Articles 8 and 22 of the General Data Protection Regulation.[14] Indeed, the proposal for the Directive on Copyright in the Digital Single Market rested on the policy objective to enhance the responsibility of Internet service providers towards their users through the use of filtering activities in order to oversee activities taking place on their platforms; this would arguably be in breach of the monitoring immunity offered in Article 15 of the e-Commerce Directive and also may have an impact on the protection of their users personal data.

The framework of liability that was launched via the Directive on Copyright in the Digital Single Market, however, went a step further. Instead of relying on the approach of secondary liability that traditionally applies to online service providers, the Directive introduced a system of primary liability for online content-sharing service providers. Article 17(1) of the Directive reads that

> Member States shall provide that an online content-sharing service provider performs an act of communication to the public or an act of making available to the

---

[10] See e.g. *Twentieth Century Fox and Others v British Telecommunications plc* [2011] EWHC 1981 (Ch) (UK); *Cartier International and Others v BSkyB and Others* [2014] EWHC 3354 (Ch) (UK); for an overview of the legal framework governing blocking injunctions in Europe see Christina Angelopoulos, 'Are Blocking Injunctions against ISPs Allowed in Europe? Copyright Enforcement in the Post-Telekabel EU Legal Landscape' (2014) 10 *Journal of Intellectual Property Law & Practice* 812; also see in general Martin Husovec, *Injunctions against Intermediaries in the European Union: Accountable but not Liable* (Cambridge: Cambridge University Press, 2017).

[11] *D.M. v APP, Microsoft, Sacem and Others*, Paris Court of Appeal, Pol 5, Ch 13, 7 June 2017 (France); First Instance Criminal Court of Paris, 2 April 2015 (France) (where damages of thirteen million euros and a prison sentence of one year were awarded for secondary liability of copyright infringement).

[12] See e.g. EU Parliament, Proposal for a Directive of the European Parliament and of the Council on Copyright in the Digital Single Market (SWD(2016) 301) (SWD(2016) 302), COM (2016) 593 final, 2016/0280 (COD), Brussels, 14 September 2016.

[13] See European Commission, Proposal for a Directive of the European Parliament and of the Council on Copyright in the Digital Single Market, Brussels, 14 September 2016, COM (2016) 593 final, 2016/0280 (COD), Art. 13, available at https://ec.europa.eu/transparency/regdoc/rep/1/2016/EN/1-2016-593-EN-F1-1.PDF, accessed 11 November 2019.

[14] Regulation (EU) 2016/679 of the European Parliament and of the Council of 27 April 2016 on the Protection of Natural Persons with Regard to the Processing of Personal Data and on the Free Movement of such Data, and Repealing Directive 95/46/EC (General Data Protection Regulation), OJ L 119, 4 May 2016, 1–88.

public for the purposes of this Directive when it gives the public access to copyright protected works or other protected subject matter uploaded by its users.

An online content-sharing service provider shall therefore obtain an authorisation from the rightholders referred to in Article 3(1) and (2) of Directive 2001/29/EC, for instance by concluding a licensing agreement, in order to communicate to the public or make available to the public works or other subject matter.

As identified in the Preamble to the Directive:

although (online content-sharing service providers) enable diversity and ease of access to content, they also generate challenges when copyright protected content is uploaded without prior authorisation from rightholders. Legal uncertainty exists as to whether the providers of such services engage in copyright-relevant acts, and need to obtain authorisation from rightholders for content uploaded by their users who do not hold the relevant rights in the uploaded content, without prejudice to the application of exceptions and limitations provided for in Union law.

Under this newly enacted framework of primary liability of online content-sharing service providers, which was adopted at the eleventh hour and departed significantly from earlier drafts of the Directive, such providers should obtain authorization, including via a licensing agreement, from the relevant rightsholders in order to lawfully perform acts of communication to the public or make available to the public by giving the public access to copyright-protected content.[15] In the preliminary discussions concerning intermediary liability, the position adopted by both the Parliament and the Commission[16] reflected the approach on secondary liability with some extended duties of care; it was not until the final version of the Digital Single Market Directive that primary liability was introduced.

To some extent, it can be argued that *GS Media*,[17] discussed in Chapter 3, heralded this outcome by blurring the contours of primary and secondary liability. It was not until the final version of the Directive, however, that such an approach was taken and in all the drafts that preceded the Directive there was nothing to indicate a departure from the secondary liability approach, even though the proposal was

---

[15]   Digital Single Market Directive (Directive 2019/790), Art. 17(2).

[16]   EU Parliament, Proposal for a Directive of the European Parliament and of the Council on Copyright in the Digital Single Market (SWD(2016) 301) (SWD(2016) 302), COM (2016) 593 final, 2016/0280 (COD), Brussels, 14 September 2016; European Commission, Proposal for a Directive of the European Parliament and of the Council on Copyright in the Digital Single Market, Brussels, 14 September 2016, COM (2016) 593 final, 2016/0280 (COD), available at <https://ec.europa.eu/transparency/regdoc/rep/1/2016/EN/1-2016-593-EN-F1-1.PDF>, accessed 11 November 2019.

[17]   *GS Media BV v Sanoma Media Netherlands BV, Playboy Enterprises International Inc., Britt Geertruida Dekker*, Case C-160/15, 8 September 2016, ECLI:EU:C:2016:644 (*GS Media*).

for a stricter framework of accountability with enhanced duties of care.[18] What the Directive on Copyright in the Digital Single Market did was impose a system of primary liability for a specific set of Internet service providers, the so-called online content-sharing providers, who are now subject to a dual framework of liability, namely the provisions outlined in the Directive on Copyright in the Digital Single Market and also the relevant provisions of the e-Commerce Directive. Unlike the e-Commerce Directive, which outlines a net of defensive rules for information society service providers (commonly referred to as safe harbours) and which was effectively defining liability in a negative fashion by indicating exemptions from liability, the Directive on Copyright in the Digital Single Market primarily focuses on laying down a positive framework of liability and clarifies when an online content-sharing service provider may be found liable for acts of communication to the public.

Who is an information society service provider and who is an online content-sharing provider?

At the outset it is worth drawing a line between the concepts of information society service providers, as beneficiaries of the exceptions in the e-Commerce Directive, and online content-sharing service providers, as per the Directive on Copyright in the Digital Single Market.

The e-Commerce Directive offers a broad definition of 'information society services' as 'any service normally provided for remuneration, at a distance, by means of electronic equipment for the processing (including digital compression) and storage of data, and at the individual request of a recipient of a service.'[19] An almost identical definition is found in the Directive on Information Society Services,[20] which is also accepted by the Directive on Copyright in the Digital Single Market.[21] The e-Commerce Directive specifies that service provider means 'any natural or legal person providing an information society service'.[22] Information society services cover a wide range of economic activities, including the sale of goods online, the transmission of information through electronic networks, the hosting of

---

[18] See e.g. EU Parliament, Proposal for a Directive of the European Parliament and of the Council on Copyright in the Digital Single Market (SWD(2016) 301) (SWD(2016) 302), COM (2016) 593 final, 2016/0280 (COD), Brussels, 14 September 2016; European Commission, Proposal for a Directive of the European Parliament and of the Council on Copyright in the Digital Single Market, Brussels, 14 September 2016, COM (2016) 593 final, 2016/0280 (COD), Art. 13, available at <https://ec.europa.eu/transparency/regdoc/rep/1/2016/EN/1-2016-593-EN-F1-1.PDF>, accessed 11 November 2019.

[19] e-Commerce Directive (Directive 2000/31/EC), Recitals 17–18.

[20] Directive (EU) 2015/1535 of the European Parliament and of the Council of 9 September 2015 Laying down a Procedure for the Provision of Information in the Field of Technical Regulations and of Rules on Information Society Services, OJ L 241, 17 September 2015, 1–15.

[21] Digital Single Market Directive (Directive 2019/790), Art. 2(5).

[22] e-Commerce Directive (Directive 2000/31/EC), Art. 2(b).

information provided by users, and the point-to-point transmission of content, such as video on demand and email communications.

There are service providers that do not meet these requirements and hence cannot benefit from the immunities listed in the e-Commerce Directive. These are services that are not provided at a distance, services that are not offered through electronic means, and services that do not take effect at the individual request of a recipient. To give some examples, telephony services which are not offered electronically, and TV or radio broadcasting (which is not on-demand), are not deemed to qualify as Internet service providers and cannot benefit from the safe harbours listed in Articles 12–15 of the e-Commerce Directive. It is currently unclear whether voice-over IP services, made available via software, terminated on a public switched telephone network to a fixed or mobile number, are regarded as an electronic communications services.[23]

Although it is a requirement that the service should be offered for remuneration in order to qualify for the safe harbours of the e-Commerce Directive, it is immaterial whether the user pays for service directly. The provider may receive remuneration from other sources and this could include generating income by advertisements posted on a website, as the Court of Justice has established.[24] Where the performance of a service is provided, free of charge, for the purpose of advertising the goods sold and services provided by that service provider, it is immaterial that the cost of that activity is incorporated into the price of those goods or services.[25] Services that are offered either without directly payable remuneration or free of charge are included in the definition of an Internet service provider, to the extent that they are provided as part of an economic activity.[26] This includes services that are merely ancillary to the operator's business, including the operation of an open wireless network. As far as electronic commerce is concerned, the Court of Justice has also held that an access provider, one which merely permits Internet access without proposing other services or exercising a review, provides a service which is capable of being used by a third party to infringe intellectual property rights and must be classified as an 'intermediary'.[27]

---

[23] *Skype Communications Sàrl v Institut Belge des Services Postaux et des Télécommunications (IBPT)*, Case C-142/18, OJ C 161, 7 May 2018, 39–40 (Request for a preliminary ruling from the Cour d'appel de Bruxelles (Belgium) 23 February 2018).

[24] *Sotiris Papasavvas v O Fileleftheros Dimosia Etairia Ltd, Takis Kounnafi, Giorgos Sertis*, Case C-291/13, 11 September 2014, ECLI:EU:C:2014:2209 (*Papasavvas*).

[25] *Bond van Adverteerders and Others v The Netherlands State*, Case C-352/85, 26 April 1988, ECLI:EU:C:1988:196 (*Bond van Adverteerders*) [16]; *Christelle Deliège v Ligue Francophone de Judo et Disciplines Associées ASBL, Ligue Belge de Judo ASBL, Union Européenne de Judo and François Pacquée*, Cases C-51/96 and C-191/97, 11 April 2000, ECLI:EU:C:2000:199 (*Deliège*), [56].

[26] *Tobias Mc Fadden v Sony Music Entertainment Germany GmbH*, Case C-484/14, 15 September 2016, ECLI:EU:C:2016:689 (*Mc Fadden*), [41]–[43].

[27] *LSG-Gesellschaft zur Wahrnehmung von Leistungsschutzrechten GmbH v Tele2 Telecommunication GmbH*, Case C-557/07, 19 February 2009 (order), ECLI:EU:C:2009:107, [43]; *UPC Telekabel Wien GmbH v Constantin Film Verleih GmbH and Wega Filmproduktionsgesellschaft mbH*, Case C-314/12, 27 March 2014, ECLI:EU:C:2014:192, [32].

The Directive on Copyright in the Digital Single Market adopts a similar definition of information society services as that included in the e-Commerce Directive[28] and moves on to offer a definition of 'online content-sharing service providers'. These are defined in Article 2(6) of the Directive to mean

a provider of an information society service of which the main or one of the main purposes is to store and give the public access to a large amount of copyright-protected works or other protected subject matter uploaded by its users, which it organises and promotes for profit-making purposes.

Implicit in this definition is the understanding that online content-sharing service providers are a subcategory of information society service providers that focus their modus operandi on storage of, and provision of public access to, copyright-protected content by their users. It is a requirement that such an organization and the promotion of its content is carried out on a commercial, profit-making basis and that the service engages in storage and communication of protected content. The Directive expressly excludes certain content providers from the definition of an online content-sharing provider. The second paragraph of Article 2(6) includes an indicative list of excluded parties, which are thereinafter not subject to the primary liability framework outlined in the Directive:

Providers of services, such as not-for-profit online encyclopedias, not-for-profit educational and scientific repositories, open source software-developing-and-sharing platforms, providers of electronic communications services as defined in Directive (EU) 2018/1972, online marketplaces, business-to-business cloud services, and cloud services that allow users to upload content for their own use, are not 'online content-sharing service providers' within the meaning of this Directive.[29]

At the same time, the Court of Justice refused to accept that an intermediation service, such as *Uber*, qualifies as an information society service provider. In particular, a service which aims to connect through a smartphone application, and for remuneration of non-professional drivers using their own vehicle with persons who wish to make urban journeys, has to be regarded as being inherently linked to a transport service and, accordingly, it must be classified as 'a service in the field of transport' within the meaning of Art. 58(1) Treaty on the Functioning of the European Union (TFEU). This had the consequence that such a service has to be excluded from the scope of—inter alia—the e-Commerce Directive and the framework of protection it offers. See *Asociación Profesional Élite Taxi v Uber Systems Spain SL*, Case C-434/15, 20 December 2017, ECLI:EU:C:2017:981 (*Uber*).

[28] e-Commerce Directive (Directive 2000/31/EC), Art. 2(5).
[29] The definition of an online content-sharing provider as finally adopted has the merit of being more clear than that available in earlier drafts. See indicatively Report on the Proposal for a Directive of the European Parliament and of the Council on Copyright in the Digital Single Market (COM (2016)0593 - C8-0383/2016 - 2016/0280(COD)), Committee on Legal Affairs Rapporteur: Axel Voss, A8-0245/2018, PE601.094v02-00, 29 June 2018; also see EU Parliament, Proposal for a Directive of the European Parliament and of the Council on Copyright in the Digital Single Market (SWD(2016) 301) (SWD(2016) 302), COM (2016) 593 final, 2016/0280 (COD), Brussels, 14 September 2016, Art. 2(1)(4b), where 'online content-sharing service provider' is defined as:

The list is not exhaustive, as the words 'such as' indicate, and Recital 62 of the Directive indicates that services excluded are those having 'a main purpose other than that of enabling users to upload and share a large amount of copyright-protected content with the purpose of obtaining profit from that activity.'

Although the Directive on Copyright in the Digital Single Market does not affect the system of liability outlined (negatively) in the e-Commerce Directive, and is merely meant to complement it,[30] there is an indication that online content-sharing providers shall be subject to two regimes of liability: primary liability for possible infringements of the right of communicating or otherwise making works available to the public by their users under the provisions of the Directive on Copyright in the Digital Single Market (and for the purposes of this Directive), and secondary liability for activities falling within the e-Commerce Directive which are subject to a set of defensive rules. This dual regime of liability for online content-sharing providers is implicit in Article 17(3) and Recital 65 of the Directive on Copyright in the Digital Single Market. Article 17(3) reads:

When an online content-sharing service provider performs an act of communication to the public or an act of making available to the public under the conditions laid down in this Directive, the limitation of liability established in Article 14(1) of Directive 2000/31/EC shall not apply to the situations covered by this Article.

The first subparagraph of this paragraph shall not affect the possible application of Article 14(1) of Directive 2000/31/EC to those service providers for purposes falling outside the scope of this Directive.

Article 14(1) of the e-Commerce Directive exempts from liability information society service providers that store information at the request of a recipient of the service, on condition that the provider does not have actual knowledge of illegal activity or information, or, upon obtaining such knowledge or awareness, the provider acts expeditiously to remove or to disable access to the information. The so-called 'hosting' exemption is not available for online content-sharing service

a provider of an information society service one of the main purposes of which is to store and give access to the public to a significant amount of copyright-protected works or other protected subject matter uploaded by its users, which the service optimises and promotes for profit-making purposes. Microenterprises and small-sized enterprises within the meaning of Title I of the Annex to Commission Recommendation 2003/361/EC and services acting in a non-commercial purpose capacity such as online encyclopaedia, and providers of online services where the content is uploaded with the authorisation of all right holders concerned, such as educational or scientific repositories, shall not be considered online content-sharing service providers within the meaning of this Directive. Providers of cloud services for individual use which do not provide direct access to the public, open source software developing platforms, and online market places whose main activity is online retail of physical goods, should not be considered online content sharing service providers within the meaning of this Directive.

[30] Digital Single Market Directive (Directive (EU) 2019/790), Art. 1(2) and Recital 4.

providers. However, according to the Directive on Copyright in the Digital Single Market, the unavailability of the hosting exemption for online content-sharing service providers should not affect the application of Article 14(1) of the e-Commerce Directive for purposes falling outside the scope of the Digital Single Market Directive, indicating the parallel application of both systems of intermediary liability and corresponding immunity regimes. Besides the unavailability of the hosting defence of the e-Commerce Directive for online content-sharing service providers, the defences available to intermediaries under Articles 12–15 of the e-Commerce Directive are considered to be available, in principle. What is more, Article 17 of the Digital Single Market Directive does not affect legitimate uses of copyright-protected works and lawful content that is covered by copyright exceptions or limitations, such that quotation, criticism, review, use for the purpose of caricature, parody or pastiche, should not be blocked or removed.[31]

Defences available to Internet intermediaries

The immunities available to information society service providers, including online content-sharing service providers, cover hosting, caching, and mere conduit and, in addition, there is no general obligation to monitor the content that is stored and transmitted within their platforms and networks.[32] The specific scope of immunities available to Internet service providers has been elaborated in numerous instances by the Court of Justice.[33] The rationale of the available defences is to ensure the uninterrupted flow of information and to develop structures that will enhance e-commerce within the Internal Market. For instance, there is no general obligation to monitor content that is stored and transmitted via electronic networks to ensure that transaction costs remain reasonable and that there are no breaches on freedom of expression. The list is merely indicative and Member States

---

[31] Digital Single Market Directive (Directive (EU) 2019/790), Art. 17(7).

[32] For an overview of the regulatory framework in Europe see Christina Angelopoulos, *European Intermediary Liability in Copyright* (Kluwer Law International: Information Law Series, 2016); Jaani Riordan, *The Liability of Internet Intermediaries* (Oxford: Oxford University Press, 2016); Martin Husovec, *Injunctions against Intermediaries in the European Union: Accountable but not Liable* (Cambridge: Cambridge University Press, 2017).

[33] See: *Scarlet Extended SA v Société belge des auteurs, compositeurs et éditeurs SCRL (SABAM)*, Case C-70/10, 24 November 2011, ECLI:EU:C:2011:771 (*Scarlet*); *Belgische Vereniging van Auteurs, Componisten en Uitgevers CVBA (SABAM) v Netlog NV*, Case C-360/10, 16 February 2012, ECLI:EU:C:2012:85 (*Netlog*); *Google France SARL and Google Inc. v Louis Vuitton Malletier SA*, Case C-236/08, *Google France SARL v Viaticum SA and Luteciel SARL*, Case C-237/08, and *Google France SARL v Centre National de Recherche en Relations Humaines (CNRRH) SARL and Others*, Case C-238/08, 23 March 2010, ECLI:EU:C:2010:159 (*Google France*); *L'Oréal SA and Others v eBay International AG and Others*, Case C-324/09, 12 July, 2011, ECLI:EU:C:2011:474 (*eBay*); also see with regard to the harmonization of Internet service provider liability in Europe Christina Angelopoulos, 'Beyond the Safe Harbours: Harmonising Substantive Intermediary Liability for Copyright Infringement in Europe' (2013) 3 *Intellectual Property Quarterly* 253.

enjoy the discretion of adding to it. For instance, Sweden has statutorily introduced an immunity regarding streaming services,[34] and Croatia an exemption for acts of linking.[35] Linking is also expressly addressed in Austria, Portugal, and Spain, which have each laid down provisions regarding hyperlinks and search engines.[36]

Mere conduit

An exemption for providers acting as mere conduits is offered in Article 12 of the e-Commerce Directive. Mere conduits play a passive role by merely transmitting information for content providers. Recital 43 indicates that a service provider can benefit from the exemption, together with the caching exemption of Article 13 (examined below), when it is in no way involved with the information transmitted, including any modifications of that information. However, it is understood that manipulations of a mere technical nature are not included as they do not alter the integrity of the information contained in the transmission.

Article 12 outlines two types of 'mere conduit' activities. Firstly, it covers the transmission of the information in a communication network by its user and, secondly, the provision of Internet access that includes the automatic, intermediate, and transient storage of the transmitted information, provided that these activities are meant to enable the transmission and that once the information is transmitted it will no longer be stored.

According to the exception of Article 12, liability will not arise where the provider:

(a) does not initiate the transmission;
(b) does not select the receiver of the transmission; and
(c) does not select or modify the information contained in the transmission.

All these conditions are indicative of the passive role of providers that qualify for immunity. It is also explained that the exemption includes the automatic, intermediate, and transient storage of the information transmitted to the extent that this takes place for the sole purpose of carrying out the transmission in the communication network and that the information is not stored for any period longer than what is reasonably necessary for the transmission. The most recent study on intermediary liability, prepared for the Commission, indicates that there have been

---

[34] e-Commerce Law (2002:562), Art. 17 (Sweden).
[35] e-Commerce Act (173/03, 67/08, 36/09, 130/11), Art. 19 (Croatia).
[36] Report from the Commission to the European Parliament, the Council and the European Economic and Social Committee, First Report on the application of Directive 2000/31/EC of the European Parliament and of the Council of 8 June 2000 on Certain Legal Aspects of Information Society Services, in particular Electronic Commerce, in the Internal Market, COM (2003) 702 final, Brussels, 21 November 2003.

'few problems concerning the application and interpretation of the liability privileges regulated in article 12.'[37]

Caching

Article 13 of the e-Commerce Directive outlines an exception for caching, i.e. instances where information is transmitted in a communications network upon request and is stored for a short period of time in order for the same information to be retransmitted more efficiently. The activity is meant to enhance the efficiency of networks, resulting in faster browsing. It covers the automatic, intermediate, and temporary storage of data on local servers and is meant to avoid overloading the network with repetitive requests for popular material. In such cases, the provider transmits information in a communications network at the request of a recipient and stores that information for a shorter period of time in order to retransmit the same information more efficiently.

According to Article 13, there are numerous conditions on which the hosting immunity is premised, namely that

(a) the provider does not modify the information;

(b) the provider complies with conditions on access to the information;

(c) the provider complies with rules regarding the updating of the information, specified in a manner widely recognised and used by industry;

(d) the provider does not interfere with the lawful use of technology, widely recognised and used by industry, to obtain data on the use of the information; and

(e) the provider acts expeditiously to remove or to disable access to the information it has stored upon obtaining actual knowledge of the fact that the information at the initial source of the transmission has been removed from the network, or access to it has been disabled, or that a court or an administrative authority has ordered such removal or disablement.

The most important conditions are that Internet service providers should not modify the information and that they should update it regularly to abide by industry standards. This defensive rule overlaps, to a certain extent, with the temporary copying exception of Article 5(1) of the Information Society Directive.[38]

Hosting under the e-Commerce Directive

Article 14 of the e-Commerce Directive addresses the liability of information society service providers that offer hosting services. These include the storage of

---

[37] Thibault Verbiest et al., 'Study on the Liability of Internet Intermediaries', Markt/2006/09/E, Service Contract ETD/2006/IM/E2/69, 12 November 2007, 12, available at <http://ec.europa.eu/internal_market/e-commerce/directive_en.htm#consultation>, accessed 11 November 2019.

[38] See relevant discussion in Chapter 4.

information that recipients of the service provide; users generate the content and the providers store it and make it accessible to the public. Even though providers do not need to approve the content before it is uploaded to their servers, they do have the ability to remove it retroactively, often upon request.[39]

This resulted in a unique construal of the liability regime in that information society service providers are excluded from liability regarding third party content only until they gain knowledge that illegal content has been uploaded to their servers. Article 14 urges Member States to ensure that service providers are not liable for the information stored at the request of a recipient of the service, on condition that:

(a) the provider does not have actual knowledge of illegal activity or information and, as regards claims for damages, is not aware of facts or circumstances from which the illegal activity or information is apparent; or

(b) the provider, upon obtaining such knowledge or awareness, acts expeditiously to remove or to disable access to the information.

This has been the most controversial and contentious provision within the e-Commerce Directive, not only in light of relevant case law, but also due to the fact that the Directive on Copyright in the Digital Single Market renders it inapplicable with regard to online content-sharing service providers.

In *Google France v Louis Vuitton*[40] and *L'Oréal v eBay*,[41] the Court of Justice interpreted the meaning of the hosting exception, effectively defining limits on the liability of Internet service providers. The court held that, even if it were established that a user had been engaged in infringing activity, the service provider would be exempt from liability if their conduct had been automatic, passive, and merely technical. By contrast, where the service provider had control over the illegal information, a basis for liability could be established.[42] Such an active role can be ascertained in cases where the service provider has optimized or promoted the presentation of counterfeit goods and hence offers assistance towards infringement.[43] This is particularly the case where the service provider has gained

[39] Broder Kleinschimdt, 'An International Comparison of ISP's Liabilities for Unlawful Third Party Content' (2010) 18(4) *International Journal of Law and Information Technology* 332, 345.

[40] *Google France SARL and Google Inc. v Louis Vuitton Malletier SA*, Case C-236/08, *Google France SARL v Viaticum SA and Luteciel SARL*, Case C-237/08, and *Google France SARL v Centre National de Recherche en Relations Humaines (CNRRH) SARL and Others*, Case C-238/08, 23 March 2010, ECLI:EU:C:2010:159 (*Google France*).

[41] *L'Oréal SA and Others v eBay International AG and Others*, Case C-324/09, 12 July, 2011, ECLI:EU:C:2011:474 (*eBay*).

[42] *Google France SARL and Google Inc. v Louis Vuitton Malletier SA*, Case C-236/08, *Google France SARL v Viaticum SA and Luteciel SARL*, Case C-237/08, and *Google France SARL v Centre National de Recherche en Relations Humaines (CNRRH) SARL and Others*, Case C-238/08, 23 March 2010, ECLI:EU:C:2010:159 (*Google France*), [114].

[43] *L'Oréal SA and Others v eBay International AG and Others*, Case C-324/09, 12 July, 2011, ECLI:EU:C:2011:474 (*eBay*), [116].

knowledge that would have allowed a diligent operator to recognize the illegal activity but did not expeditiously act to avoid it from happening, either by disabling the relevant users' access or by removing the infringing artefacts from featuring on the network.

The court has also clarified that the service provided by an Internet website host which comprises the storage of information, is of a more permanent nature compared to the activities of caching and mere conduit; such a host may obtain knowledge of the illegal character of information that it stores at a time subsequent to that when the storage was processed. However, with regard to communication network access providers, while their service transmits information this is not normally continued over any length of time; after the information is transmitted, the provider no longer has any control over that information. This means that, unlike Internet website hosts, a communication network access provider will often not be in a position to take action to remove certain information or disable access to it at a later time.[44] This has an impact on the application of the hosting defence and the fulfilment of the knowledge requirement.

Importantly, the hosting exemption does not apply to online content-sharing service providers by virtue of Article 17(3) of the Directive on Copyright in the Digital Single Market and, thus, may only apply in cases falling outside the scope of this Directive. This effectively disarms a defensive rule that these kinds of providers used to benefit from until the launch of the Digital Single Market Directive and exposes them to a system of primary liability for copyright infringements carried out by their users, unless they obtain authorization, for instance by concluding a licensing arrangement with the relevant rightsholders as stipulated in Article 17(2) of the Directive. This is an instance where the authorial entitlement over acts of communication, or otherwise making works available to the public, has prevailed and a defensive rule was replaced by a requirement to conclude licensing arrangements between content providers and the relevant rightsholders.

Hosting under the Directive on Copyright in the Digital Single Market

The Directive on Copyright in the Digital Single Market imposes a new liability mechanism in cases of unlicensed content and offers a new set of defences available to online content-sharing service providers who have failed to secure authorization from the relevant rightsholders. Although the hosting exemption of Article 14 of the e-Commerce Directive is not available to online content-sharing service providers who fall within the purposes of the Directive on Copyright in the Digital Single Market, there is a defensive mechanism available to such providers that partially corresponds to the hosting exemption, although it does not have a fully overlapping scope. Effectively, online content-sharing service providers are

---

[44] *Tobias Mc Fadden v Sony Music Entertainment Germany GmbH*, Case C-484/14, 15 September 2016, ECLI:EU:C:2016:689 (*Mc Fadden*), [62]–[63].

deprived of the lack of knowledge defence available under the hosting exemption of the e-Commerce Directive, which aligns with the new system of primary liability. They can still escape liability should they be able to demonstrate that they acted expeditiously on receipt of a sufficiently substantiated notice from the rightsholders to disable access to, or to remove from their websites, the notified copyright-protected content.

The liability mechanism envisaged by the Directive on Copyright in the Digital Single Market adopts a complex, threefold approach, in order to determine the applicable liability framework. To put things in the simplest way possible, there are three kinds of liability envisaged: a minimal, an intermediate, and an enhanced liability framework. Each of these mechanisms largely depends on the kind of online content-sharing service provider that has not been able to secure authorization from the relevant rightsholders. Different types of online content-sharing service providers are classified on the basis of popularity, time, and turnover criteria. In particular, popularity criteria are met where the average number of unique visitors exceeds five million monthly, calculated on the basis of the previous year; time requirements are satisfied where the services have been available to the public for three years or more; and turnover criteria are fulfilled where the annual turnover is EUR 10 million or more.[45]

The minimal liability framework covers new online content-sharing service providers (a) whose services have been made available to the public for less than three years, (b) whose annual turnover is below EUR 10 million,[46] and (c) whose average number of monthly unique visitors does not exceed five million. According to the combined application of Articles 17(4) and 17(6), these providers may escape liability for not having secured authorization where they demonstrate that they have made best efforts to obtain an authorization and acted expeditiously upon receiving a sufficiently substantiated notice to disable access to the notified works or other subject matter or to remove those works or other subject matter from their websites. The notice and takedown process corresponds to the liability regime of hosting providers under the e-Commerce Directive, adding one obligation according to which the providers must make their best efforts to obtain prior authorization from rightsholders.

The intermediate mechanism is available for new content-sharing service providers (a) whose services have been made available to the public for less than three years, and (b) whose annual turnover is below EUR 10 million,[47] but (c) whose average number of monthly unique visitors does exceed five million. These providers shall be liable by virtue of the second paragraph Article 17(6) if, in addition

---

[45]   Digital Single Market Directive (Directive (EU) 2019/790), Art. 17(6).

[46]   Calculated in accordance with Commission Recommendation 2003/361/EC of 6 May 2003 concerning the Definition of Micro, Small and Medium-Sized Enterprises (notified under document number C(2003) 1422), OJ L 124, 20 May 2003, 36.

[47]   Ibid.

to the conditions available under the so-called minimal mechanism (i.e. to secure authorization and follow a notice and take down protocol) they do not demonstrate that they have made their best efforts to prevent further uploads of the notified works for which rightholders have provided the relevant and necessary information. This adds yet another layer of responsibility (and cost) for these kinds of service providers, who are likely to resort to the use of fingerprinting technologies in order to filter content bearing a unique electronic signature and to remove unauthorized content algorithmically.

Finally, the enhanced liability framework will be available for those new content-sharing service providers (a) whose services have been made available to the public for three years or more, and/or (b) whose annual turnover is of EUR 10 million or more. In addition to the requirements available for the intermediate liability framework, these providers, to avoid liability, will also have to show that they have made, in accordance with the high industry standards of professional diligence, their best efforts to ensure the unavailability of specific works for which the rightsholders have provided the relevant and necessary information. This requirement, i.e. that the content provider has made its best efforts 'in accordance with the high industry standards of professional diligence' to ensure the unavailability of works, requires an assessment of several factors according to Article 17(5), including but not limited to

(a) the type, the audience, and the size of the service and the type of works or other subject matter uploaded by the users of the service; and
(b) the availability of suitable and effective means and their cost for service providers.

Assessment of this criterion will have to take into consideration the principle of proportionality but many content providers falling within this category will have to implement filtering mechanisms in order to ensure compliance with the law. An example of a service provider that will be governed under the mechanism of enhanced liability is Google's YouTube service, for which Google has already developed a programme called Content ID. Google states that this fingerprinting system will help copyright owners 'to easily identify and manage their content on YouTube.'[48] The application of filtering mechanisms, however, goes against the rule that intermediaries should not be subject to a general monitoring obligation.

No general monitoring obligation
Article 15 of the e-Commerce Directive stipulates that Member States shall not impose a general obligation on providers, when providing the services covered by the

---

[48] For details see <https://support.google.com/youtube/answer/2797370?hl=en-GB>, accessed 11 November 2019.

safe harbours of Articles 12–14 to monitor the information which they transmit or store, nor a general obligation to actively seek facts or circumstances which indicate illegal activity. The second paragraph of this Article allows the discretion of Member States to establish obligations for information society service providers to promptly inform the competent public authorities of alleged illegal activities undertaken or information provided by recipients of their service or obligations to communicate to the competent authorities at their request information which will enable the identification of recipients of their service with whom they have storage agreements. This is a specific obligation that Member States may impose on Internet service providers.[49]

Even though the e-Commerce Directive does not introduce a general obligation to monitor content and in this regard does not place a positive responsibility on Internet service providers, as also affirmed in *eBay*[50] and *McFadden*,[51] this lack of general monitoring obligation is subject to a number of limitations. Recital 48 of the Directive introduces duties of care that can be reasonably expected from Internet service providers in order to detect and prevent certain kinds of illegal activity (with some commentators arguing that this indicative guidance should not be taken into account).[52] Recital 47 makes allowance for a monitoring obligation in cases where injunctions are necessary. This has been discussed by the Court of Justice in *Scarlet*,[53] where it was held that any injunction that would require Internet service providers to actively monitor the content circulated within its platform would be in conflict with the e-Commerce Directive, and Article 15 in particular.

Besides instances where liability for unauthorized acts of communication to the public is more likely to arise, particularly in instances of actual and constructive knowledge, as the *Pirate Bay* case instructs,[54] recent case law of the Court of Justice seems to indicate that some monitoring checks may be necessary in certain contexts. For instance, the court has held that

> when the posting of hyperlinks is carried out for profit, it can be expected that the person who posted such a link carries out the necessary checks to ensure that the

---

[49] For a comment see Pablo Baistrocchi, 'Liability of Intermediary Service Providers in the EU Directive on Electronic Commerce' (2003) 19(1) *Santa Clara Computer & High Technology Law Journal* 126.

[50] *L'Oréal SA and Others v eBay International AG and Others*, Case C-324/09, 12 July 2011, ECLI:EU:C:2011:474 (*L'Oréal*), [139].

[51] *Tobias Mc Fadden v Sony Music Entertainment Germany GmbH*, Case C-484/14, 15 September 2016, ECLI:EU:C:2016:689 (*Mc Fadden*), [87].

[52] Kamiel J. Koelman and Julia Barcelo, 'Intermediary Liability In The E-Commerce Directive: So Far So Good, But It's Not Enough' (2000) 4 *Computer Law & Security Report* 231.

[53] *Scarlet Extended SA v Société belge des auteurs, compositeurs et éditeurs SCRL (SABAM)*, Case C-70/10, 24 November 2011, ECLI:EU:C:2011:771 (*Scarlet*); *Belgische Vereniging van Auteurs, Componisten en Uitgevers CVBA (SABAM) v Netlog NV*, Case C-360/10, 16 February 2012, ECLI:EU:C:2012:85 (*Netlog*).

[54] *Stichting Brein v Ziggo BV and XS4All Internet BV*, C-610/15, 14 June 2017, ECLI:EU:C:2017:456 (*The Pirate Bay*).

work concerned is not illegally published on the website to which those hyper-links lead, so that it must be presumed that that posting has occurred with the full knowledge of the protected nature of that work and the possible lack of consent to publication on the internet by the copyright holder.[55]

Although not directly addressing intermediary liability, GS Media[56] indicates a shift in the way in which the knowledge standard and monitoring obligation are construed in the context of secondary liability. The liability system that governs information society service providers according to the e-Commerce Directive does not outline a framework of strict liability in the sense that knowledge of the wrongdoing is not a requirement and Internet service providers will be held liable if they knowingly violate the rights of third parties. This fault-based system may require either the actual knowledge of Internet service providers in order to impose liability or a level of constructive knowledge, namely some indication that the information society service provider is reasonably presumed to be aware of the relevant infringements. This has a bearing on the applicability of the relevant defence, which arguably requires no monitoring duties to be imposed on Internet service providers.

The Directive on Copyright in the Digital Single Market affirmed the lack of a general monitoring obligation for online content-sharing service providers,[57] unlike earlier versions of the Directive which expressly required online content-service providers to apply filtering mechanisms. This was an aspect that attracted severe criticism from both academics and members of the European Parliament as it would breach one of the key immunities laid down by the e-Commerce Directive. Personal data protection was also seen as an area that could have been affected if earlier versions of the Directive had come to a final vote. In particular, (then numbered as) Article 13(1) of the Parliament's proposal for a Directive on Copyright in the Digital Single Market, entitled 'use of protected content by information society service providers storing and giving access to large amounts of works and other subject matter uploaded by their users', used to read:

> Information society service providers that store and provide to the public access to large amounts of works or other subject matter uploaded by their users shall, in cooperation with rightholders, take measures to ensure the functioning of agreements concluded with rightholders for the use of their works or other subject

---

[55] GS Media BV v Sanoma Media Netherlands BV, Playboy Enterprises International Inc., Britt Geertruida Dekker, Case C-160/15, 8 September 2016, ECLI:EU:C:2016:644 (GS Media), [51].

[56] GS Media BV v Sanoma Media Netherlands BV, Playboy Enterprises International Inc., Britt Geertruida Dekker, Case C-160/15, 8 September 2016, ECLI:EU:C:2016:644 (GS Media).

[57] Digital Single Market Directive (Directive (EU) 2019/790), Art. 17(8).

matter or to prevent the availability on their services of works or other subject matter identified by rightholders through the cooperation with the service providers. Those measures, *such as the use of effective content recognition technologies*, shall be appropriate and proportionate. The service providers shall provide rightholders with adequate information on the functioning and the deployment of the measures, as well as, when relevant, adequate reporting on the recognition and use of the works and other subject matter.[58]

This earlier version of the Article became the source of criticism for imposing extensive duties of care and, more importantly certain monitoring obligations on Internet service providers that host content.[59] This goes beyond Article 15 of the e-Commerce Directive and consistent case law of the Court of Justice, which refrained from imposing filtering, monitoring, and user-identification duties on Internet service providers in cases such as *Promusicae*,[60] *Scarlet*,[61] and *Netlog*.[62] The Court of Justice explained that the purpose was to enhance the freedom to conduct a business, protect customers' data protection, and the freedom to receive and impart information. A clearer outline of filtering mechanism duties was envisaged in the 2017 Commission Communication which stated that, in light of their central role, online platforms should adopt effective proactive measures in order to detect and remove illegal content, rather than merely reacting to relevant notices to take content or other infringing articles down.[63] According to the Commission, 'such voluntary, proactive measures do not automatically lead to the

---

[58] EU Parliament, Proposal for a Directive of the European Parliament and of the Council on Copyright in the Digital Single Market (SWD(2016) 301) (SWD(2016) 302), COM (2016) 593 final, 2016/0280 (COD), Brussels, 14 September 2016, (emphasis added).

[59] Martin Senftleben, Christina Angelopoulos, Giancarlo Frosio, Valentina Moscon, Miquel Peguera, and Ole Andreas Rognstad, 'The Recommendation on Measures to Safeguard Fundamental Rights and the Open Internet in the Framework of the EU Copyright Reform' (2018) 40(3) *European Intellectual Property Review* 149; Martin Husovec, Sophie Stalla-Bourdillon, Eleonora Rosati, Karmen Turk, Christina Angelopoulos, Aleksandra Kuczerawy, and Miquel Peguera, 'An Academic Perspective on the Copyright Reform' (2017) 33(1) *Computer Law and Security Review* 3. Some critical insights are also included in an open letter entitled 'Article 13 Open letter—Monitoring and Filtering of Internet Content is Unacceptable' and signed by fifty-seven human rights and digital rights organizations. See <https://www.liberties.eu/en/news/delete-article-thirteen-open-letter/13194>, accessed 11 November 2019; Julia Reda, 'Civil Liberties Committee joins the opposition against automated censorship machines', 20 November 2017, available at <https://juliareda.eu/2017/11/civil-liberties-censorship-machines/>, accessed 11 November 2019.

[60] *Productores de Música de España v Telefónica de España SAU*, Case C-275/06, 29 January 2008, ECLI:EU:C:2008:54 (*Promusicae*).

[61] *Scarlet Extended SA v Société Belge des Auteurs, Compositeurs et Éditeurs SCRL (SABAM)*, Case C-70/10, 24 November 2011, ECLI:EU:C:2011:771 (*Scarlet*).

[62] *Belgische Vereniging van Auteurs, Componisten en Uitgevers CVBA (SABAM) v Netlog NV*, Case C-360/10, 16 February 2012, ECLI:EU:C:2012:85 (*Netlog*).

[63] European Commission, Communication from the Commission to the European Parliament, the Council, the European Economic and Social Committee and the Committee of the Regions, 'Tackling Illegal Content Online: Towards an Enhanced Responsibility of Online Platforms', Brussels, 28 September 2017, COM (2017) 555 final, [3.3.1].

online platform losing the benefit of the liability exemption provided for in Article 14 of the e-Commerce Directive'.[64] The Commission offered an indicative outline of mechanisms that could be used in order to manage the volume of material that is intermediated by online platforms, focusing on the use of technologies which enable automatic detection and filtering as tools for fighting the online circulation of illegal platforms.[65] These could include metadata filtering, hashing, and finger-printing content, tools of which various larger platforms already make use.

As already mentioned, however, with regard to the threefold mechanism of li-ability applicable under the Directive, certain online content-sharing providers, in particular those subject to the intermediary and enhanced liability framework, may still be *indirectly* obliged to enact monitoring mechanisms in order to demonstrate that they have made their best efforts to prevent further uploads of the notified works. Although this may—technically speaking—not qualify as a general moni-toring duty, but rather as a specific one, many content providers will likely enact fingerprinting technologies in order to manage content within their platforms and be in a position to effectively filter unauthorized content. What is more, content providers falling under the requirements of the enhanced liability mechanism will have to show that they have made, in accordance with the high industry standards of professional diligence, their best efforts to ensure the unavailability of specific works for which the rightsholders have provided the relevant and necessary infor-mation. It is very likely that the interpretation of those high industry standards will require the launch of some monitoring mechanisms in order to filter the content circulated within electronic networks and ensure compliance with the law.

The changing face of online content-sharing service provider liability, especially in light of the shift from secondary liability rules to primary liability at the eleventh hour, has had an effect on the applicability of the network of defensive rules applic-able to online service providers. Instead of reducing the scope of the immunity of Article 15, EU legislators opted to narrow the availability of the hosting defence of Article 14. Arguably, this will have an impact on the modus operandi of on-line content-sharing service providers by increasing transaction costs to secure li-censing arrangements with the relevant rightsholders and reforming the terms and conditions on the use of their platforms. An extremely lengthy, complex, and con-troversial legal provision, Article 17 of the Directive on Copyright in the Digital Single Market, narrows the scope of the permissible activity of hosting providers and brings forward technical legal challenges that will need to be addressed, such as the possibility of enabling fingerprinting and filtering technologies in order to determine which uses are legitimate. The broader negative impact of such a possi-bility would be the change of the Internet as we know it and its replacement with a 'filtered' space that allows the development of a particular set of online companies

---

[64] Ibid.
[65] Ibid., [3.3.2].

and inhibits user freedom to share works that are not comfortably covered by one of the copyright exceptions and limitations, such as parodies, remixes, and possibly memes.

The public interest

The public interest serves both as an objective of copyright and as its internal limit.[66] It requires offering incentives for creativity, whilst ensuring the wide dissemination of copyright-protected materials.[67] In this sense, copyright aspires to promote creativity, dissemination of, and access to, culture and knowledge[68] and, at the same time, it accomplishes its social function through the protection of the public interest, often reflected in copyright exceptions and limitations with an underlying fundamental freedoms rationale.[69]

This receives recognition at the international and the EU level. The WIPO Copyright Treaty (WCT) recognizes, in its Preamble, the need to maintain a balance between the rights of authors and the broader public interest, offering some precise, yet indicative, references to education, research, and access to information. At the EU level, the Information Society Directive also includes the public interest as one of the fundamental principles of law that the proposed harmonization aimed to help implement.[70] A specific illustration of the public interest is offered in Recital 14 of the Information Society Directive, according to which the Directive seeks 'to promote learning and culture by protecting works and other subject matter while permitting exceptions or limitations in the public interest for the purpose of education and teaching.' This balancing exercise between copyright and the public interest has been further developed in *Luksan*, where the Court of Justice indicated that copyright has a relative character, holding that

---

[66] João Pedro Quintais, *Copyright in the Age of Online Access: Alternative Compensation Systems in EU Law* (Alphen aan den Rijn: Kluwer Law International, 2017) 227: 'from a Lockean viewpoint, copyright can always be statutorily restricted if that would be in the public interest'.

[67] Abraham Drassinower, *What's Wrong with Copying?* (Cambridge: Harvard University Press, 2015) 3.

[68] Caterina Sganga, 'Right to Culture and Copyright: Participation and Access' in Christophe Geiger (ed.), *Research Handbook on Human Rights and Intellectual Property* (Cheltenham: Edward Elgar, 2015) 560; European Parliament Resolution of 9 July 2015 on the Implementation of Directive 2001/29/EC of the European Parliament and of the Council of 22 May 2001 on the Harmonisation of Certain Aspects of Copyright and Related Rights in the Information Society (2014/2256(INI)), [25].

[69] João Pedro Quintais, *Copyright in the Age of Online Access: Alternative Compensation Systems in EU law* (Alphen aan den Rijn: Kluwer Law International, 2017) 289; Caterina Sganga, 'Right to Culture and Copyright: Participation and Access' in Christophe Geiger (ed.), *Research Handbook on Human Rights and Intellectual Property* (Cheltenham: Edward Elgar, 2015) 560; see also Jonathan Griffiths and Luke McDonagh, 'Fundamental Rights and European Intellectual Property Law—The Case of Art 17(2) of the EU Charter' in Christophe Geiger (ed.), *Constructing European IP: Achievements and New Perspectives* (Cheltenham: Edward Elgar, 2012) 75.

[70] Information Society Directive (Directive 2001/29), Recital 3.

under Article 17(1) of the Charter of Fundamental Rights of the European Union, everyone has the right to own, use, dispose of, and bequeath his or her lawfully acquired possessions. No one may be deprived of his or her possessions, *except in the public interest and in the cases and under the conditions provided for by law*, subject to fair compensation being paid in good time for their loss. The use of property may be regulated by law in so far as is necessary for the general interest. Article 17(2) provides that intellectual property is to be protected.[71]

Although the public interest is seen as a limitation to copyright as property entitlement, the Directive does not lay down a public interest defence, even though many of the copyright exceptions and limitations are meant to serve the public interest in some specific way. The Directive does not allow Member States to retain exceptions that are not specified and aligned with the three-step test of Article 5(5). This puts into question the applicability of the public interest defence in Member States where it emerged as a doctrinally developed principle and was thereinafter inserted in the statute, such as in the United Kingdom.[72] What is more, the relevant national defences[73] have to be compatible with the three-step test incorporated in Article 5(5) of the Directive, which is not simply a standard for evaluation of the permissibility of exceptions at the legislative level but also a test for the judiciary to apply in order to determine whether a particular use is permissible.[74] It is difficult to see how a general public interest defence can pass the scrutiny of the first step of the test that requires exceptions to be applicable in certain special cases. As Ricketson observes with regard to the international level, 'it would ... be unlikely that any exception could be justified on the basis of an unqualified assertion of "public interest." ' In this context, an unqualified public interest defence may not pass the scrutiny of the first step of the three-step test.[75] This is because the nature and the extent of the public interest needs to be subject to clear delineation, stating specific policy objectives.

[71] *Martin Luksan v Petrus van der Let*, C-277/10, 9 February 2012, ECLI:EU:C:2012:65 (*Luksan*), [68] (emphasis added).
[72] See in this regard Robert Burrell and Alison Coleman, *Copyright Exceptions: the Digital Impact* (Cambridge: Cambridge University Press, 2005) 107; Phillip Johnson, 'The Public Interest: Is it still a Defence to Copyright Infringement?' (2005) 16(1) *Entertainment Law Review* 1.
[73] The UK public interest defence has been criticized as offering 'a dangerous invitation to judicial policy-making'. See Jonathan Griffiths, 'Pre-Empting Conflict - A Re-Examination of the Public Interest Defence in United Kingdom (UK) Copyright Law' (2014) 34(1) *Legal Studies* 7; *Hyde Park v Yelland* [2000] 3 WLR 215 (CA).
[74] For a critical perspective, see Stavroula Karapapa, *Private Copying* (London: Routledge, 2012) 100–2; See *Infopaq International A/S v Danske Dagblades Forening*, Case C-5/08, 16 July 2009, ECLI:EU:C:2009:465, [58]; *Stichting de Thuiskopie v Opus Supplies Deutschland GmbH and Others*, Case C-462/09, 16 June 2011, ECLI:EU:C:2011:397; *Eva-Maria Painer v Standard VerlagsGmbH and Others*, Case C-145/10, 1 December 2011, ECLI:EU:C:2011:798 (*Painer*), [100]–[116], [129]–[149].
[75] Sam Ricketson, WIPO Study on Limitations and Exceptions of Copyright and Related Rights in the Digital Environment, SCCR/9/7 (WIPO, 2003) 75.

Although not available under EU copyright as a defence against allegations for copyright infringement, but as a broader limit to copyright protection, a public interest defence is doctrinally available in some national laws, guiding the assessment of whether an activity is permissible. In certain instances, it is linked to specific considerations, such as the use of works by public libraries and other scientific institutions for the purposes of the public interest.[76] The most notable example is the United Kingdom, where the public interest was originally developed at the judicial level[77] and was later introduced in the 1988 Copyright, Designs and Patents Act (CDPA).[78] There are, however, as we will see, other Member States, such as Italy and Spain, that have resorted to a broader public interest defence to justify instances of potential infringement of moral rights.

In the United Kingdom, the public interest defence was tied to the law of confidentiality to evolve consequently as an independent defence for copyright law. It was first developed in *Beloff v Pressdram*,[79] a case involving claims for copyright infringement and breach of confidence, where Ungoed-Thomas J held that

> public interest, as a defence in law, operates to override the rights of the individual (including copyright) which would otherwise prevail and which the law is also concerned to protect, such public interest, as now recognised by the law, does not extend beyond misdeeds of a serious nature and importance to the country and thus, in my view, clearly recognisable as such

As Griffiths argues,[80] the public interest defence, as developed in *Beloff*, is limited to situations of wrongdoing, in the sense that copyright shall not be enforced with regard to 'iniquitous' works. The broader, fully fledged public interest defence was developed in *Lion Laboratories Ltd v Evans*.[81] This case involved an allegation of infringement of copyright law as well as a claim of breach of confidence. The claimant was a manufacturer of devices for breath-testing alcohol levels who owned the copyright in confidential memoranda which raised doubts on the accuracy of the said devices; he brought proceedings against a national newspaper that got hold of them and intended to publish them. Arguing towards a public interest defence regarding the publication of the memoranda, Griffiths LJ held that:

---

[76] E.g. Copyright Act, Art. 7(j) (Cyprus).

[77] See, e.g., *Initial Services v Putterill* [1968] 1 QB 396 (per Lord Denning, 405) (UK); *Fraser v Evans* [1969] 1 QB 349 (UK).

[78] CDPA 1988, s. 171(3).

[79] *Beloff v Pressdram* [1973] 1 All ER 241 (UK); for a discussion see Robert Burrell, 'Defending the Public Interest' (2000) 22(9) *European Intellectual Property Review* 394, 401.

[80] Jonathan Griffiths, 'Pre-Empting Conflict - A Re-Examination of the Public Interest Defence in United Kingdom (UK) Copyright Law' (2014) 34(1) *Legal Studies* 76.

[81] *Lion Laboratories Ltd v Evans* [1985] QB 526 (UK).

I am quite satisfied that the defence of public interest is now well established in actions for breach of confidence and, although there is less authority on the point, that it also extends to breach of copyright ... I can see no sensible reason why this defence should be limited to cases in which there has been wrongdoing on the part of the plaintiff ... It is not difficult to think of instances where, although there has been no wrongdoing on the part of the plaintiff, it may be vital in the public interest to publish a part of his confidential information.[82]

The defence was said to apply in cases where possible disclosures genuinely served the public interest and where those disclosures would be made to the appropriate authorities instead of the public at large.[83] In this sense, the doctrine evolved as a specific instance of the principle that courts will refuse to enforce claims that are based on wrongdoings.[84]

Soon after the judgment in *Lion Laboratories Ltd v Evans*[85] was issued, the CDPA entered into force, statutorily endorsing a broad public interest defence in 171(3):[86] 'Nothing in this Part affects any rule of law preventing or restricting the enforcement of copyright, on grounds of public interest or otherwise.' The statutorily introduced doctrine was first discussed in *Hyde Park Residence Ltd v Yelland*, where, in the first instance, Jacob J found in favour of the application of the defence with regard to the publication of two still photographs taken from a security video system.[87] However, the Court of Appeal overturned the judgment,[88] with Stuart-Smith LJ holding that the defence in its broader form had no legitimate role in copyright law and interpreting the statutory defence as allowing uses in the public interest in a more limited form. It was noted that a court was entitled to refuse the enforcement of copyright where the work was

(i) immoral, scandalous, or contrary to family life; (ii) injurious to public life, public health and safety, or the administration of justice; (iii) incites or encourages others to act in a way referred to in (ii).[89]

---

[82] Ibid., 550.

[83] Ibid., 537.

[84] See *Gartside v Outram* [1857] 26 LJ Ch 113, 114 (UK); for discussion, see Isabella Alexander, *Copyright Law and the Public Interest in the Nineteenth Century* (Oxford, Portland: Hart Publishing, 2010) 63–79.

[85] *Lion Laboratories Ltd v Evans* [1985] QB 526 (UK).

[86] For discussion, see Robert Burrell, 'Defending the Public Interest' (2000) 22(9) *European Intellectual Property Review* 394, 403; Gerald Dworkin, 'Judicial Control of Copyright on Public Policy Grounds' in Jan Kabel and Gerard Mom (eds), *Intellectual Property and Information Law* (Alphen aan den Rijn: Kluwer Law International, 1998) 137, 142.

[87] *Hyde Park Residence Ltd v Yelland* [1999] EMLR 654 (UK).

[88] *Hyde Park Residence Ltd v Yelland* [2000] 3 WLR 215 (UK). For discussion of the judgment of the Court of Appeal, see Robert Burrell, 'Defending the Public Interest' (2000) 22(9) *European Intellectual Property Review* 394; Rachel A. Yurkowski, 'Is *Hyde Park* Hiding the Truth? An Analysis of the Public Interest Defence to Copyright Infringement' (2001) 32 *Victoria University of Wellington Law Review* 1053.

[89] *Hyde Park Residence Ltd v Yelland* [2000] 3 WLR 215 (UK), [66].

This stemmed from the distinction between copyright infringement—a statutory right accompanied by a number of clearly outlined 'permitted uses'—and breach of confidence as a judicially developed doctrine. Although some specific instances of the public interest were listed in the judgment, Mance LJ, in his concurring opinion, interestingly noted that 'the circumstances in which the public interest may override copyright are probably not capable of precise categorisation or definition.'[90]

Just a few months after the *Hyde Park* judgment was handed down, the defence was subject to consideration in *Ashdown v Telegraph Group Ltd.*[91] The leader of a political party brought proceedings for breach of confidence and copyright infringement against a newspaper for having published a previously unpublished memorandum containing confidential information. In its defence, the newspaper relied on the fair dealing defences available under section 30 of the CDPA and on the common law public interest doctrine, arguing that Article 10 of the European Convention on Human Rights (ECHR)—which had just been incorporated into the UK Human Rights Act—had to be read as requiring a liberal interpretation of defences. Lord Phillips MR accepted that the protection of freedom of expression under the Human Rights Act required that the use of a copyright-protected work has to be permitted, even though it does not fall under the spectrum of the statutorily provided permitted acts. In such cases, where fundamental rights protection would allow the exercise of an activity not elsewhere permitted, the broader defence of public interest could ensure compatibility with the Human Rights Act. Lord Phillips took into consideration earlier case law, concluding that the restrictive construal of the public interest defence in *Hyde Park* was too narrow[92] and that it was not Parliament's intention to endorse the defence in such a limited form. On the basis of the facts at issue, however, fair dealing appropriately accommodated the defendant's freedom of expression and there was no need for section 171(3) to apply.[93] With regard to the scope of the defence, Lord Phillips agreed with Mance LJ that the circumstances where section 171(3) may apply were 'not capable of precise categorisation or definition.'[94] In this light, various commentators have noted that *Ashdown* offers limited guidance in understanding when the exception applies.[95] Hence, it has been argued that—by not offering a workable definition to the defence—*Ashdown* 'effectively killed it off again.'[96]

---

[90] *Hyde Park Residence Ltd v Yelland* [2000] 3 WLR 215 (UK), [83].
[91] *Ashdown v Telegraph Group Ltd* [2001] EWCA Civ 1142 (UK).
[92] Ibid., [21].
[93] See in this regard Michael Birnhack, 'Acknowledging the Conflict between Copyright Law and Freedom of Expression Under the Human Rights Act' (2003) 14 *Entertainment Law Review* 24.
[94] *Ashdown v Telegraph Group Ltd* [2001] EWCA Civ 1142 (UK), [58].
[95] Robert Burrell and Alison Coleman, *Copyright Exceptions: the Digital Impact* (Cambridge: Cambridge University Press, 2005) 94.
[96] Jonathan Griffiths, 'Pre-Empting Conflict - A Re-Examination of the Public Interest Defence in United Kingdom (UK) Copyright Law' (2014) 34(1) *Legal Studies* 76.

In the aftermath of the introduction of the Information Society Directive, which does not leave room for a general public interest defence, case law indicates a slight departure from *Ashdown*. *HRH Prince of Wales v Associated Newspapers Ltd*[97] concerned claims for breach of confidence and copyright infringement as a result of the unauthorized newspaper publication of extracts from the claimant's unpublished journals. The defendant newspaper group argued that the publication of these extracts promoted the public's understanding of important political issues and, as such, it benefits from the fair dealing and public interest defences. On the facts, neither the High Court[98] nor the Court of Appeal[99] could conclude that those defences could apply and in reference to the public interest defence the Court of Appeal held that it was not 'one of those rare cases in which the public interest trumps the rights conferred by the CDPA'.[100] Difficulties with regard to the application of the public interest defence and its unclear scope arose in other cases too, such as *Ashdown - Grisbrook v MGN Ltd*,[101] *Vitof Limited v Altoft*,[102] *Unilever plc v Griffin*,[103] and *BBC, Petitioners*.[104]

Griffiths argues that the persistent refusal of courts to define the scope of the public interest defence may result from a desire to retain space for manoeuvre, but the current uncertainty risks eroding the defence's capacity for principled application.[105] The defence, which arguably faces application difficulties following the strict approach followed by the Information Society Directive (but which still features in section 17(3) of the CDPA), could have been relevant in cases of uses carried out by emergent technologies or in the context of new business models, where copying or other acts restricted by copyright are carried out in the public interest.[106]

In Italy, which has a long-standing tradition in the protection of image rights, the public interest defence was upheld in *CE v RAI*.[107] In this case, the Italian Constitutional Court found that the public display of someone's image on TV does not amount to infringement of Article 96 of the Italian Copyright Act,[108] outlining

---

[97] *HRH Prince of Wales v Associated Newspapers Ltd* [2006] EWHC 522 (Ch) (UK).

[98] *HRH Prince of Wales v Associated Newspapers Ltd* [2006] EWHC 522 (Ch) (UK).

[99] *HRH Prince of Wales v Associated Newspapers Ltd* [2006] EWCA Civ 1776 (UK).

[100] *HRH Prince of Wales v Associated Newspapers Ltd* [2006] EWHC 522 (Ch) (UK), [180].

[101] *Ashdown - Grisbrook v MGN Ltd* [2009] EWHC 2520 Ch (Patten LJ) (UK), [68]–[71]; aff'd on appeal [2010] EWCA Civ 1399 (UK).

[102] *Vitof Limited v Altoft* [2006] EWHC 1678 (Ch) (UK).

[103] *Unilever plc v Griffin* [2010] FSR 33 (Ch) (UK).

[104] *BBC, Petitioners* [2012] HCJ 10 (High Court, Scotland).

[105] Jonathan Griffiths, 'Pre-Empting Conflict - A Re-Examination of the Public Interest Defence in United Kingdom (UK) Copyright Law' (2014) 34(1) *Legal Studies* 76.

[106] See e.g. *Authors Guild, Inc. v Google Inc.*, No. 13-4829-cv (2d Cir. 16 October 2015) (US) and decision of the US Supreme Court on April 2016 declining to review the case, leaving the lower court's decision standing: *Authors Guild, et al. v Google, Inc.*, 15-849 (US).

[107] *C.E. v RAI/Portrait*, Constitutional Court, 24 October 2013 (Italy); an interesting case where the public interest defence may apply concerns a man from Ischia whose image featured in the health warnings on cigarette packs. See Eleonora Rosati, 'Image Rights and the Unauthorized Use of One's Own Portrait on Cigarette Packs' (21 January 2018) *IPKat*.

[108] Law No. 633/1941 (Italy).

moral rights, when such a display is linked to facts or events that are of public interest and/or have taken place in public. The Italian national public broadcasting company (RAI) broadcast images of a group of people standing outside the Milan train station before joining Gay Pride in Rome in 2000 and proceedings were initiated because the claimant's image was recognizable. The claim focused on Article 96, according to which the public display of images amounts to infringement. The court drew a distinction holding that the public interest defence could apply with regard to economic rights, but not to moral rights. In the present case, there was no infringement of the honour or reputation of the claimant as his image was broadcast for a very short time and, at the time, an anonymous crowd surrounded him.

In Spain,[109] a public interest defence was used in a case concerning modifications to a bridge designed by well-known architect Calatrava without his consent or knowledge. Even though the court found that the bridge qualified as a work of art by virtue of Article 10 of the Intellectual Property Act,[110] the court could not uphold that Calatrava's moral right of integrity had been infringed because the modification at issue did not negatively impact on his reputation or legitimate interests, according to Article 14(4) of the Intellectual Property Act. Even though alterations, modifications, or distortions of the work amount to infringement of the integrity right, harm to the author's reputation or legitimate interests cannot be established where the public interest to carry out the modifications prevails. As the court noted, a different outcome may have been reached had the subject of consideration been the conflict of competing private interests.

Although not statutorily offered as a defence to copyright infringement in most EU Member States, with the exception of the United Kingdom, the public interest represents a broader objective, as well as limitation to copyright law that has been discussed in various national cases and is included in some specific exceptions of EU copyright, such as those on research and education.

Abuse of right

Abuse of right is a doctrinal principle that becomes relevant in cases where copyright holders exceed their power of proprietary control, often concerning instances that have not yet been subject to regulation, but which eventually result in conflict between authorial entitlements and other interests, public or private. The prohibition of the abusive exercise of rights may be used as a defence in cases where rightsholders use their entitlement excessively. The rationale is to offer a balance between exclusive rights and user entitlements through a regulatory standard whereby copyright will not encroach on areas that do not fall within the core of the

---

[109] 'Calatrava Bridge', Commercial Court n.1 of Bilbao, 23 November 2007 (Spain).
[110] Intellectual Property Act 20/1992 (Ley de Propiedad Intelectual 20/1992) (Spain).

statutory definition, and the purpose of exclusive rights. In this sense, the principle of abuse of right covers the unreasonable, overreaching, or excessive exercise of copyright or its judicial enforcement.

The prohibition of the abusive exercise of rights is a general legal principle that has not been subject to EU harmonization. There is some case law from the Court of Justice echoing a broadly framed principle of abuse of rights, particularly with regard to the examination of the exhaustion of intellectual property rights[111] and the development of the 'existence/exercise' dichotomy. Relevant cases are *Deutsche Grammophon*[112] and *Musik-Vertrieb Membran*.[113] There is no legislative or judicial trend, however, to be assumed regarding the development of a pan-European abuse of right principle and the way in which the prohibition is outlined in each Member State varies, featuring either in copyright statutes, in competition law provisions or in general principles of civil law that may have application in copyright cases. It is only a few Member States to specifically prohibit the abuse of rights as a general legal concept or as an interpretative standard for the judiciary specifically in the context of copyright. France is the only Member State that expressly prohibits the abuse of economic or moral rights by the heirs of the author in Articles L. 121-3 and L. 122-9 of the Copyright Act[114] and third parties interested in using a work may make a judicial request to gain access.[115] Similar provisions are also available in the Spanish and Portuguese Copyright Acts with regard to the re-publication of out-of-commerce or posthumous works. Refusal from the heirs of the author to authorize or license such a use is not permitted.[116] Elsewhere in Europe, the doctrine has emerged through case law in the context of civil liability[117] or features as a general legal principle in civil codes.[118] Despite its statutory mention, the

---

[111] See in general Stavroula Karapapa, 'Reconstructing Copyright Exhaustion in the Online World' (2014) 4 *Intellectual Property Quarterly* 307; Jens Schovsbo, 'The Exhaustion of Rights and Common Principles of European Intellectual Property Law' in Ansgar Ohly (ed.), *Common Principles of European Intellectual Property Law* (Tübingen: Mohr Siebeck, 2010) 174.

[112] *Deutsche Grammophon* and *Musik-Vertrieb Membran* and *K-tel International*, Case C-78/70, 8 June 1971, ECLI:EU:C:1971:59 (*Deutsche Grammophon*).

[113] *Musik-Vertrieb Membran GmbH and K-tel International v GEMA - Gesellschaft für Musikalische Aufführungs- und Mechanische Vervielfältigungsrechte*, Joined Cases 55/80 and 57/80, 20 January 1981, ECLI:EU:C:1981:10 (*Musik-Vertrieb Membran*).

[114] Nicolas Bouche, *Intellectual Property Law in France* (Alphen aan den Rijn: Kluwer Law International, 2011) 98.

[115] André Lucas and Henri-Jacques Lucas, *Traité de la Propriété Litteraire et Artistique* (Paris: Litec, 2006, 2nd edn) 349, 428; Reto M. Hilty and Sylvie Nérisson (eds), *Balancing Copyright – A Survey of National Approaches* (Berlin Heidelberg: Springer-Verlag, 2012) 21.

[116] Reto M. Hilty and Sylvie Nérisson (eds), *Balancing Copyright – A Survey of National Approaches* (Berlin Heidelberg: Springer-Verlag, 2012) 65, 69.

[117] See indicatively Civil Court Brussels, 4 March 2009, IRDI, 2009, 197 (Belgium); Civil Court of Brussels, 5 January 1996, IRDI, 1996, 97 (Belgium); Commercial Court of Brussels, 26 May 1993, RDC, 1994, 651 (Belgium); Civil Court Brussels, 27 February 1998, A&M, 1998, 143, aff'd by Court of Appeals of Brussels, 18 September 1998 (Belgium).

[118] Examples include Art. 833 of the Italian Civil Code and Art. 281 of the Greek Civil Law. See in general Michael Byers, 'Abuse of Right: An Old Principle, A New Age' (2002) 47 *McGill Law Journal* 389, 392; Joseph Perillo, 'Abuse of Rights: A Pervasive Legal Concept' (1995) 27 *Pacific Law Review* 37.

application of the principle with regard to intellectual property, and copyright in particular, is sporadic and limited.

The common denominator of all these nationally borne elaborations of the principle is their theoretical justification as tools to enable the fair and proportionate exercise of rights that does not hinder the exercise of rights and legitimate entitlements of third parties. This becomes particularly relevant and useful in unregulated or under-regulated areas of the law where excessive claims and entitlements may emerge through the expansive interpretation of the statutory core of rights. With regard to copyright, such excessive claims could impact on a number of third party interests, including consumer welfare, the preservation of rigorous competition in the market, and the enhancement of creativity, innovation, and access to information and knowledge. Determining what falls under the statutorily defined core and teleological rationale of rights is a central factor in understanding whether abusive or excessive derogations from statutory rights have taken place.

Abuse of right in Court of Justice of the European Union decisions

Despite the call for a 'high level of protection' that features in Recitals 4 and 9 of the Information Society Directive[119] that has been deemed as the main goal of harmonization, the Court of Justice has elaborated on facets of a principled prohibition of abuse of rights with a view to offering a balanced approach in cases where the statutory scope of exclusive rights was expansively interpreted, preserving the appropriate exercise of the fundamental freedoms of the EU, and ensuring conformity with the rules and principles of competition law and policy.

Three issues should be noted in this context. First, the objectives of copyright harmonization in the European Union and the objectives of copyright protection do not fully overlap, although they relate to each other. In this sense, a high level of protection of intellectual property is primarily the basis of harmonization, but is also a means for the achievement of broader goals, such as investment in creativity and innovation, growth, and increased competitiveness in European industry. Second, copyright means to serve both economic interests, such as the sustainability of intellectual creations,[120] growth and job creation,[121] and broader

---

[119] It also features in Corrigendum to Directive 2004/48/EC of the European Parliament and of the Council of 29 April 2004 on the Enforcement of Intellectual Property Rights (OJ L 157, 30 April 2004), OJ L 195, 2 June 2004, 16–25, Recital; Directive 2006/116/EC of the European Parliament and of the Council of 12 December 2006 on the Term of Protection of Copyright and Certain Related Rights, OJ L 372, 27 December 2006, 12–18 (Term Directive), Recital 11; and Directive (EU) 2012/28 of the European Parliament and of the Council of 25 October 2012 on Certain Permitted Uses of Orphan Works Text with EEA relevance, OJ L 299, 27 October 2012, 5–12 (Orphan Works Directive), Recital 14.

[120] Term Directive (Directive 2006/116/EC), Recital 11.

[121] Information Society Directive (Directive 2001/29/EC), Recitals 2 and 4; Directive 2009/24/EC of the European Parliament and of the Council of 23 April 2009 on the Legal Protection of Computer

objectives, such as ensuring investment in the creation and dissemination of creative works,[122] access to knowledge, and culture.[123] Third, the framework of protection at the EU level was never meant to be one which outlines absolute rights. Indeed, the guidance offered implicitly sets some inherent limits on rights with regard to the function they mean to serve: for instance, references may be made to 'legitimate profit'[124] or 'appropriate remuneration',[125] indicating a negation of absolute levels of protection.

Bearing these contextual parameters in mind, the cases of the Court of Justice that echo a principle of abuse of right—although not expressly labelled as such—concern the distorted exploitation of copyright and its contradiction with the objectives of the creation of the Internal Market. As such, these cases address issues of parallel trade, the exhaustion of rights,[126] and the development of the so-called 'existence/exercise' dichotomy. Some of these cases, such as *Deutsche Grammophon*[127] and *Musik-Vertrieb Membran*,[128] have been discussed earlier with reference to the exhaustion of the distribution right.[129] In this context, the Court of Justice has determined the limits and appropriate scope of copyright within the requirements arising from the Treaty on the Functioning of the European Union (TFEU),[130] with a view to enhancing the functioning of the Internal Market whilst stopping rightsholders from the disproportional exercise of rights that would inhibit competition and market development.[131]

Programs, OJ L 111, 5 May 2009, 16–22 (Computer Programs Directive), Recital 2; Directive 96/9/EC of the European Parliament and of the Council of 11 March 1996 on the Legal Protection of Databases, OJ L 77, 27 March 1996, 20–8 (Database Directive), Recitals 9, 11–13; Directive 2006/115/EC of the European Parliament and of the Council of 12 December 2006 on Rental Right and Lending Right and on Certain Rights Related to Copyright in the Field of Intellectual Property, OJ L 376, 27 December 2006, 28–35 (Rental and Lending Directive), Recital 8; Term Directive (Directive 2006/116/EC), Recital 11; Corrigendum to Directive 2004/48/EC of the European Parliament and of the Council of 29 April 2004 on the Enforcement of Intellectual Property Rights (OJ L 157, 30 April 2004), OJ L 195, 2 June 2004, 16–25, Recital 1; Directive 2001/84/EC of the European Parliament and of the Council of 27 September 2001 on the Resale Right for the Benefit of the Author of an Original Work of Art, OJ L 272, 13 October 2001, 32–6 (Resale Directive), Recitals 3, 11, 13.

[122]   See indicatively Term Directive (Directive 2006/116/EC), Recital 11.

[123]   See Orphan Works Directive (Directive (EU) 2012/28), Recital 14.

[124]   Enforcement Directive (Directive 2004/48/EC), Recital 21.

[125]   Orphan Works Directive (Directive (EU) 2012/28), Recital 5.

[126]   See in general Stavroula Karapapa, 'Reconstructing Copyright Exhaustion in the Online World' (2014) 4 *Intellectual Property Quarterly* 307; Jens Schovsbo, 'The Exhaustion of Rights and Common Principles of European Intellectual Property Law' in Ansgar Ohly (ed.), *Common Principles of European Intellectual Property Law* (Tübingen: Mohr Siebeck, 2010) 174.

[127]   *Deutsche Grammophon* and *Musik-Vertrieb Membran and K-tel International*, Case C-78/70, 8 June 1971, ECLI:EU:C:1971:59 (*Deutsche Grammophon*).

[128]   *Musik-Vertrieb Membran GmbH and K-tel International v GEMA - Gesellschaft für Musikalische Aufführungs- und Mechanische Vervielfältigungsrechte*, Joined Cases 55/80 and 57/80, 20 January 1981, ECLI:EU:C:1981:10 (*Musik-Vertrieb Membran*).

[129]   In Chapter 3.

[130]   Treaty on the Functioning of the European Union (TFEU), OJ C 326, 26 October 2012, 47–390.

[131]   Christine Godt, 'Intellectual Property and European Fundamental Rights' in Hans-Wolfgang Micklitz (ed.), *Constitutionalization of European Private Law* (Oxford: Oxford University Press, 2014) 210, 213.

Freedom of movement and the specific subject matter of intellectual property
Although not expressly discussing abuse of right, the doctrinal principles that the
Court of Justice developed in cases such as *Deutsche Grammophon*[132] and *Coditel*[133]
outline a balancing mechanism whereby the expansive or disproportionate exercise of rights has to stop towards the fulfilment of policy objectives, fundamental
freedoms, and other public interests. In this regard, this mechanism can be said to
function as a defensive rule when allegations of infringement exceed the core of
exclusive rights.

In *Deutsche Grammophon*,[134] the Court of Justice held that a licensing scheme
that would prevent or restrict the importation of sound recordings, which had already been lawfully marketed in another Member State by the owner himself or
with his consent, was 'repugnant to the essential purpose of the Treaty, which is
to unite national markets into a single market.'[135] In this light, the exhaustion rule
served as a limit to the exercise of the distribution right in order to avoid the conflict of copyright with policy objectives aimed at the creation and functioning of
the Internal Market. The Court of Justice made a distinction between the existence
of intellectual property rights that is covered by the specific subject matter of the
right and not affected by the EU law and the exercise of these rights that can be
subject to restrictions resulting from the Treaty. Depending on the type of intellectual property right (e.g. copyright or trade marks), the concept of the specific
subject matter will vary. The emphasis on the specific subject matter of protection
is important because the purpose of each intellectual property right impacts on the
exercise of rights, their use, and possible abuse.

Other cases have also reiterated the discussion on the specificity of subject
matter. In *Coditel*,[136] the court discussed the essential function of copyright with
regard to the particular characteristics of cinematographic works.[137] The exhaustion rule was not affirmed as the authorial entitlement to request fees for the
showing of cinematographic works, and exploiting them within a particular geographical region, was deemed part of the copyright function with regard to this
category of protected subject matter. As the Court of Justice stated: although the

---

[132] *Deutsche Grammophon* and *Musik-Vertrieb Membran and K-tel International*, Case C-78/70, 8
June 1971, ECLI:EU:C:1971:59 (*Deutsche Grammophon*).

[133] *SA Compagnie Générale pour la Diffusion de la Télévision, Coditel, and Others v Ciné Vog Films and
Others*, Case C-62/79, 18 March 1980, ECLI:EU:C:1980:84 (*Coditel I*); also see *UsedSoft GmbH v Oracle
International Corp*, Case C-128/11, 3 July 2012, ECLI:EU:C:2012:407 (*UsedSoft*).

[134] *Deutsche Grammophon* and *Musik-Vertrieb Membran and K-tel International*, Case C-78/70, 8
June 1971, ECLI:EU:C:1971:59 (*Deutsche Grammophon*).

[135] *Deutsche Grammophon* and *Musik-Vertrieb Membran and K-tel International*, Case C-78/70, 8
June 1971, ECLI:EU:C:1971:59 (*Deutsche Grammophon*), [12].

[136] *SA Compagnie Générale pour la Diffusion de la Télévision, Coditel, and Others v Ciné Vog Films and
Others*, Case C-62/79, 18 March 1980, ECLI:EU:C:1980:84 (*Coditel I*); also see *UsedSoft GmbH v Oracle
International Corp*, Case C-128/11, 3 July 2012, ECLI:EU:C:2012:407 (*UsedSoft*).

[137] *SA Compagnie Générale pour la Diffusion de la Télévision, Coditel, and Others v Ciné Vog Films and
Others*, Case C-62/79, 18 March 1980, ECLI:EU:C:1980:84 (*Coditel I*), [13] and [14].

Treaty Establishing the European Community (now TFEU) prohibits restrictions on the freedom to provide services, it does not include limits on the exercise of certain economic activities that originate from the application of national intellectual property laws.[138] Whereas copyright entails the right to request payment for the exhibition of cinematographic works, the Treaty does not set limits on the geographical region in which such an exhibition is licensed. In this regard, copyright and the relevant licensing agreement have priority over other public policy objectives and the restrictive behaviour of copyright holders is found to be in line with the function of copyright in the Internal Market.

More recent cases that have followed the codification of the exhaustion rule in Article 4(2) of the Computer Programs Directive[139] and Article 4(2) of the Information Society Directive[140] are also indicative of this approach. We have already seen[141] how the Court of Justice has balanced freedom of contract and the exhaustion rule in *UsedSoft*,[142] a case concerning an agreement on the resale of software online, which qualified as a sales contract, not as a license, with the result that the online resale of computer programs would be allowed according to the EU law. As explained in this decision, the proprietors of intellectual property rights would have already obtained remuneration corresponding to the economic value of the work as a result of the first sale.[143] This had the effect that—regardless of the way in which the contract was labelled—it could not include the power to go beyond what was appropriate for the purposes of serving the function of copyright within the broader objectives of the functioning of the Internal Market and the development of electronic commerce. A similar stance was taken in other more recent cases too, such as in *Football Association Premier League* (*FAPL*), where the Court of Justice confirmed that rightsholders cannot 'go beyond what is necessary to ensure *appropriate remuneration*'[144] for the use of their works by use of overly restrictive licensing arrangements. Even though copyright exhaustion was not affirmed in this case, contrary to the suggestion of the Advocate General,[145] the court held that contractual restrictions on the cross-border availability of football matches would artificially partition the Internal Market and would contravene the goals of EU law.

---

[138] Ibid., [15].

[139] Computer Programs Directive (Directive 91/250/EEC).

[140] Information Society Directive (Directive 2001/29/EC).

[141] In Chapter 3.

[142] *UsedSoft GmbH v Oracle International Corp*, Case C-128/11, 3 July 2012, ECLI:EU:C:2012:407 (*UsedSoft*), [45] and [63].

[143] Ibid., [72], [88].

[144] *Football Association Premier League Ltd and Others v QC Leisure and Others and Karen Murphy v Media Protection Services Ltd*, Joined Cases C-403/08 and C-429/08, 4 October 2011, ECLI:EU:C:2011:631 (*FAPL*), [116].

[145] Opinion of Advocate General Kokkot, *Football Association Premier League Ltd and Others v QC Leisure and Others and Karen Murphy v Media Protection Services Ltd*, Joined Cases C-403/08 and C-429/08, 3 February 2011, ECLI:EU:C:2011:43.

The aforementioned cases of the Court of Justice indicate that EU law offers protection to copyright claims to the extent that the exercise of exclusive rights serves the function that the law has ascribed to these rights. This principle-based approach of the court indicates that the function of economic rights does not mean to ensure the maximum benefit that could result from each and every exploitative use of the works,[146] but it does mean that an appropriate reward is necessary to incentivize creativity. This results from judgments where the court considered that appropriate protection reflects the normal exploitation of the work by means of allowing equitable remuneration and a satisfactory share of the market.[147]

Clearer insights on the distinction between desirable exploitative use and abuse of rights, and the balancing exercise, can be drawn from cases that emerge from the encounter of copyright with competition law and policy. The Court of Justice has elaborated on aspects of a broadly conceived principle of abuse of right in cases where disproportionate conduct of copyright holders would affect intercommunity trade and distort competition within the Internal Market.

Competition law and copyright: conflicting or complementary legal orders?

Although intellectual property rights are often considered to be irreconcilable with the objectives of competition law and policy,[148] in that intellectual property rights create 'monopolies' over the exploitation of works and exclude third parties from making use of the protected subject matter without authorization, this is not accurate. Both disciplines have complementary roles within the framework of industrial policy and economic growth, either by encouraging innovation and market entry or by stimulating innovation and creativity through the creation of substitutable goods.[149] Indeed, a central justification underpinning the grant of exclusive rights under copyright is to enhance innovation by offering protection to an author's, or related rightsholder's, creative activity.[150] To this end, copyright

[146] See indicatively in this regard *Football Association Premier League Ltd and Others v QC Leisure and Others and Karen Murphy v Media Protection Services Ltd*, Joined Cases C-403/08 and C-429/08, 4 October 2011, ECLI:EU:C:2011:631 (*FAPL*), [94]; *SA Compagnie Générale pour la Diffusion de la Télévision, Coditel, and Others v Ciné Vog Films and Others*, Case C-62/79, 18 March 1980, ECLI:EU:C:1980:84 (*Coditel I*), [15]–[16].

[147] *Football Association Premier League Ltd and Others v QC Leisure and Others and Karen Murphy v Media Protection Services Ltd*, Joined Cases C-403/08 and C-429/08, 4 October 2011, ECLI:EU:C:2011:631 (*FAPL*), [108]; Also see in this regard, *UsedSoft GmbH v Oracle International Corp*, Case C-128/11, 3 July 2012, ECLI:EU:C:2012:407 (*UsedSoft*), [63]; *Warner Brothers and Another v Christiansen*, Case 158/86, 22 September 1988, ECLI:EU:C:1998:422, [15]–[16]; *Metronome Musik GmbH v Music Point Hokamp GmbH*, Case C-200/96, 28 April 1998, ECLI:EU:C:1998:172; *Musik-Vertrieb Membran GmbH and K-tel International v GEMA - Gesellschaft für Musikalische Aufführungs- und Mechanische Vervielfältigungsrechte*, Joined Cases 55/80 and 57/80, 20 January 1981, ECLI:EU:C:1981:10 (*Musik-Vertrieb Membran*), [10] and [15].

[148] See e.g. Jonathan D. C. Turner, *Intellectual Property and EU Competition Law* (Oxford: Oxford University Press, 2010) 3.

[149] Ariel Ezrachi and Mariateresa Maggiolino, 'European Competition Law, Compulsory Licensing, and Innovation' (2012) 8(3) *Journal of Competition Law & Economics* 595, 596–7.

[150] See in general Steve Anderman, *The Interface Between Intellectual Property Rights and Competition Policy* (Cambridge: Cambridge University Press, 2007) 37.

prevents third parties from free riding on innovative activity and investment, and, at the same time, encourages 'competition by substitution' instead of 'competition by imitation'.[151]

The intersection of intellectual property and competition law is particularly relevant with regard to information society services and high technology industries in the so-called new economy, where technological change and innovation can emerge rapidly. This includes mass digitization projects and other relevant ventures.[152] In this new economy, often referred to as the fourth Industrial Revolution, certain online services are likely to generate 'network effects' in the sense that the value and attractiveness of a platform or a service increases, depending on the number of users.[153] In such a context, a company may abuse its market power reinforced by its intellectual property rights by foreclosing exclusive contracts or refusing to deal or license their products and services. Such practices could have an impact on the stimulation of innovation, research, and development and could entail the risk that network effects become a barrier to entry for competitors, resulting in products and services of inferior quality.

The Court of Justice of the European Union has discussed the intersection of copyright and competition law through the doctrinal dichotomy between the existence and the exercise of intellectual property rights. In *Consten & Grundig*,[154] the court famously stated that the exclusive agreement between Consten and Grundig fell under the prohibition of Article 101 of the TFEU, while indicating that the enforcement of this Article would not interfere with the protection of intellectual property rights under national law. In this light, EU law allows Member States to determine the conditions for the grant of intellectual property rights.[155] At the same time, the existence of intellectual property rights cannot be affected by the provisions of the EU Treaty, whereas the exercise of such rights has to be subject to competition law and the rules regarding the freedom of movement within the European Union.[156] The dichotomy between the existence and the exercise of intellectual property rights has attracted criticism for being artificial and unconvincing;[157] part of this criticism has to do with the inability of the copyright

---

[151] Steve Anderman and Ariel Ezrachi, *Intellectual Property and Competition Law: New Frontiers* (Oxford: Oxford University Press, 2011) 4.

[152] See in general Maurizio Borghi and Stavroula Karapapa, *Copyright and Mass Digitization: A Cross-Jurisdictional Perspective* (Oxford: Oxford University Press, 2013) 92.

[153] See *Microsoft Corp. v Commission of the European Communities*, Case T-201/04, 17 September 2007, ECLI:EU:T:2007:289 (*Microsoft*).

[154] *Établissements Consten S.à.R.L. and Grundig-Verkaufs-GmbH v Commission of the European Economic Community*, Joined Cases C-56/64 and C-58/64, 13 July 1966, ECLI:EU:C:1966:41 (*Consten & Grundig*).

[155] *Keurkoop BV v Nancy Kean Gifts BV*, Case C-144/81, 14 September 1982, ECLI:EU:C:1982:289, [18].

[156] See in this regard *Coditel SA, Compagnie générale pour la Diffusion de la Télévision, and Others v Ciné-Vog Films SA and Others*, Case C-262/81, 6 October 1982, ECLI:EU:C:1982:334 (*Coditel II*), [13].

[157] Valentine Korah, 'The Interface Between Intellectual Property and Antitrust: The European Experience' (2002) 69(3) *Antitrust Law Journal* 801, 805.

holders to control certain activities that fall under the property rights. As Korah acutely observes, 'the existence of a right consists of all the ways in which it may be exercised.'[158]

In more recent rulings, the Court of Justice seems to have reshaped the existence/exercise dichotomy. In *Volvo v Veng*,[159] the court clarified that, even though a design entails the right to prevent third parties from manufacturing and selling products bearing the design without its holder's consent, the exercise of that exclusive right may be subject to limitations on the basis of Article 102 of the TFEU in cases involving abusive conduct from an undertaking that occupies a dominant position in the market. Various commentators have noted that within this emergent jurisprudence it is possible that Article 102 of the TFEU interferes with rights falling under the specific subject matter of an intellectual property right.[160] The development of the concept of 'specific subject matter' of an intellectual property right has been deemed to include, among other things, the right to: decide the placing of a work in the market;[161] authorize the rental of a literary or artistic work;[162] and require fees for public performance.[163] The shift in the court's approach is manifest through its differentiated earlier stance,[164] according to which rights that form the core of the specific subject matter of intellectual property rights are meant to preserve its existence and hence fall outside the scope of the Treaty.[165]

These considerations become relevant in the context of understanding defences against allegations of copyright infringement to the extent that they represent instances where the excessive exercise of copyright may need to be balanced against the objectives of competition law and the interests of third parties that benefit from carrying out a particular use of copyright-protected content. Although not in the form of liability-defeating claims, but in the shape of actionable rights against a

---

[158] Valentine Korah, *An Introductory Guide to EC Competition Law and Practice* (Oxford, Portland, Oregon: Hart Publishing 2004, 8th edn) 292.

[159] *AB Volvo v Erik Veng (UK) Ltd*, Case C-238/87, 5 October 1988, ECLI:EU:C:1988:477, [8]–[9].

[160] See e.g. Sergio Baches Opi, 'The Application of the Essential Facilities Doctrine to Intellectual Property Licensing in the European Union and the United States: Are Intellectual Property Rights Still Sacrosanct?' (2001) 11 *Fordham Intellectual Property Media and Entertainment Law Journal* 409, 453; also see in this regard Steve Anderman and Ariel Ezrachi, *Intellectual Property and Competition Law: New Frontiers* (Oxford: Oxford University Press, 2011) 127–9.

[161] *Musik-Vertrieb Membran GmbH and K-tel International v GEMA - Gesellschaft für Musikalische Aufführungs- und Mechanische Vervielfältigungsrechte*, Joined Cases 55/80 and 57/80, 20 January 1981, ECLI:EU:C:1981:10 (*Musik-Vertrieb Membran*), [25].

[162] *Warner Brothers Inc. and Metronome Video ApS v Erik Viuff Christiansen*, Case C-158/86, 17 May 1988, ECLI:EU:C:1988:242, [13].

[163] *SA Compagnie Générale pour la Diffusion de la Télévision, Coditel, and Others v Ciné Vog Films and Others*, Case C-62/79, 18 March 1980, ECLI:EU:C:1980:84 (*Coditel I*), [14].

[164] *Radio Telefis Eireann (RTE) and Independent Television Publications Ltd (ITP) v Commission of the European Communities*, Joined Cases C-241/91 P and C-242/91 P, 6 April 1995, ECLI:EU:C:1995:98 (*Magill*); *IMS Health GmbH & Co. OHG v NDC Health GmbH & Co. KG*, Case C-418/01, 29 April 2004, ECLI:EU:C:2004:257 (*IMS Health*).

[165] See Christian Ahlborn, David S. Evans, and A. Jorge Padilla, 'The Logic & Limits of the "Exceptional Circumstances Test" in Magill and IMS Health' (2004) 28(4) *Fordham International Law Journal* 1109.

copyright holder, they may be useful in instances where a copyright holder refuses to license the use of their protected materials.

Refusal to license intellectual property rights

According to Article 102(1) of the TFEU, 'any abuse by one or more undertakings of a dominant position within the internal market or in a substantial part of it shall be prohibited as incompatible with the internal market in so far as it may affect trade between Member States'. Even though 'abuse' is not defined, the Article outlines a list of activities that may amount to abuse, including practices:

(a) directly or indirectly imposing unfair purchase or selling prices or other unfair trading conditions;
(b) limiting production, markets or technical development to the prejudice of consumers;
(c) applying dissimilar conditions to equivalent transactions with other trading parties, thereby placing them at a competitive disadvantage;
(d) making the conclusion of contracts subject to acceptance by the other parties of supplementary obligations which, by their nature or according to commercial usage, have no connection with the subject of such contracts.

The Court of Justice has explained that this list is non-exhaustive and in this sense the Commission and national courts have discretion to apply the Article with regard to practices not expressly mentioned in the Treaty.[166] The Commission's guidance paper classifies these abuses as either exploitative or exclusionary.[167] The first category refers to practices where an undertaking in a dominant position exploits its market power at the expense of consumers,[168] whereas the second category concerns conducts whereby a dominant company hinders competition in the market and effectively causes harm to consumers.[169]

The Court of Justice and the General Court have consistently taken the position that the exclusive exercise of intellectual property on a specific product is permitted in primary markets, whereas this goes against competition law—and Article 102 of the TFEU in particular—in cases where the exploitative use is made in secondary

---

[166] See e.g. *Deutsche Telekom AG v European Commission*, Case C-280/08 P, 14 October 2010, ECLI:EU:C:2010:603, [173]; *British Airways plc v Commission of the European Communities*, Case C-95/04 P, 15 March 2007, ECLI:EU:C:2007:166, [57]–[58].

[167] Communication from the Commission, Guidance on the Commission's Enforcement Priorities in Applying Art. 82 of the EC Treaty to Abusive Exclusionary Conduct by Dominant Undertakings, OJ C 45/2, 24 February 2009, [7].

[168] John Temple Lang, 'Monopolisation and the Definition of "Abuse" of a Dominant Position under Article 86 EEC Treaty' (1979) 16 *Common Market Law Review* 345.

[169] *Post Danmark A/S v Konkurrencerådet*, Case C-209/10, 27 March 2012, ECLI:EU:C:2012:172 (*Post Danmark*), [20]; *Hoffmann-La Roche & Co. AG v Commission of the European Communities*, Case C-85/76, 13 February 1979, ECLI:EU:C:1979:36 (*Hoffman-La Roche*), [91].

markets or related products.[170] For instance, companies have been required to license their intellectual property rights in cases which involve innovative technologies that have become the standard practice in the market;[171] or where such technologies have become indispensable for competitors towards the development of new products.[172] In light of the jurisprudence of the European Court, the decisive criterion in determining abuse is whether the allegedly infringing practice takes place in a primary or secondary market, especially where the use of complementary products has become the norm in that particular market. Another key consideration is the expansive notion of the subject matter that receives protection under intellectual property law. These considerations impact on the breadth of the defensive rules that rely on the abusive exercise of rights through refusals to license copyright-protected content, and such defensive rules may become more relevant as licensing online content tends to become the norm. This is especially so after the Directive on Copyright in the Digital Single Market requested online content-sharing service providers to secure authorization from the relevant rightsholders in order to host content online.[173]

Refusal to supply

Under the general principle of freedom of contract, companies in a market economy are free to choose their trading partners and enter into contractual relationships with them.[174] What is more, companies may invoke various reasonable explanations in order to refuse to enter into a licensing agreement, including, for instance, reasons having to do with insolvency that may causes disruptions to the company's production. Refusal to license intellectual property rights can be seen as a subcategory of general claims against refusal to supply.[175] Commercial practices that may amount to refusal to license intellectual property rights, including licenses of copyright-protected content, may include the refusal to offer information that is required for purposes of interoperability, providing access to facilities or networks, or licensing intellectual property rights. Such instances are very likely to be in breach of Article 102 of the TFEU. Other less straightforward cases include

---

[170] Steve Anderman and Hedvig Schmidt, *EU Competition Law and Intellectual Property Rights: The Regulation of Innovation* (Oxford: Oxford University Press, 2011) 85–6.

[171] *Microsoft Corp. v Commission of the European Communities*, Case T-201/04, 17 September 2007, ECLI:EU:T:2007:289 (*Microsoft*).

[172] *Radio Telefis Eireann (RTE) and Independent Television Publications Ltd (ITP) v Commission of the European Communities*, Joined Cases C-241/91 P and C-242/91 P, 6 April 1995, ECLI:EU:C:1995:98 (*Magill*).

[173] Digital Single Market Directive (Directive 2019/790), Art. 17.

[174] See Communication from the Commission, Guidance on the Commission's Enforcement Priorities in Applying Art. 82 of the EC Treaty to Abusive Exclusionary Conduct by Dominant Undertakings, OJ C 45/2, 24 February 2009, [75]. See also *Bayer AG v Commission of the European Communities*, Case T-41/96, 26 October 2000, ECLI:EU:T:2000:242, [180].

[175] Hans Henrik Lidgard, 'Application of Article 82 EC to Abusive Exclusionary Conduct – Refusal to Supply or License' (2009) 4 *Europarättslig Tidskrift* 694.

licensing agreements containing excessive or merely unreasonable terms that make the contract unacceptable *ab initio* or that cause disproportionate delays in negotiations. In principle, Article 102 shall be breached in cases where a dominant company refuses to offer third parties information, goods, or facilities that are essential to maintain effective competition in the market.

Despite the fact that copyright law offers rightsholders the discretion to decide whether or not they wish to authorize the use of their works, in exceptional circumstances rightsholders may be under an obligation to license certain rights to third parties. Indeed, the copyright holders' refusal to license the use of their protected works or other subject matter may leave no alternative for third parties than to seek a compulsory license. However, such an option would come into conflict with the exclusive nature of intellectual property rights. The regulation of a possible conflict takes place through the 'essential facilities' doctrine that applies in cases where a company makes use of its market power to refuse access to a facility that is essential in order for a competitor to enter the market.[176] This doctrine was first applied in the context of copyright in *Magill*,[177] where the refusal of an Irish broadcasting organization to license its copyright-protected TV programme schedules to a weekly magazine was found to amount to an abuse of the broadcaster's dominant position. The decision of the Commission was upheld by both the Court of First Instance and the Court of Justice on the basis of Article 86 of the Treaty (now Article 102 TFEU). According to the Court of Justice, three conditions led to this conclusion which effectively develop the doctrine of abusive conduct resulting in refusal to license intellectual property rights: (a) the owner is the only source of the indispensable raw material for a new product, but refuses to provide such material and hence prevents the offer of the new product, of which there is consumer demand but no substitute, (b) there is no objective justification for that refusal, and (c) the owner of the new material reserves the secondary product market for themselves, thus excluding competition in the relevant market.[178] A refusal to license by a rightsholder in a dominant position amounts to abuse to the extent that it hinders the marketing of a new product with possible consumer demand and blocks competitors

---

[176] On the application of this doctrine to search engines see Frank Pasquale, Geoffrey A. Manne, James Grimmelmann and Eric Goldman, 'Is Search now an "Essential Facility"?' in Berin Szoka and Adam Marcus (eds), *The Next Digital Decade: Essays on the Future of the Internet* (Washington DC: TechFreedom, 2010) 401.

[177] *Radio Telefis Eireann (RTE) and Independent Television Publications Ltd (ITP) v Commission of the European Communities*, Joined Cases C-241/91 P and C-242/91 P, 6 April 1995, ECLI:EU:C:1995:98 (*Magill*). For a discussion on the doctrines of refusal to licence in the context of intellectual property rights see Mariateresa Maggiolino, *Intellectual Property and Antitrust: A Comparative Economic Analysis of US and EU Law* (Cheltenham and Northampton: Edward Elgar, 2011) 141.

[178] See to this effect *Radio Telefis Eireann (RTE) and Independent Television Publications Ltd (ITP) v Commission of the European Communities*, Joined Cases C-241/91 P and C-242/91 P, 6 April 1995, ECLI:EU:C:1995:98 (*Magill*).

from entering secondary markets.[179] The test developed in *Magill* does not only look at consumer welfare as an objective of competition law, but also elaborates on the concept of the specificity of subject matter and the essential function of exclusive rights under copyright. Exclusive rights have to be exercised proportionately to avoid conflict with competition law and principles.[180] In this light, competition law may serve as an external limit to disproportionate copyright claims, develop a defensive rule, and make allowances for certain uses by declaring that copyright holders ought to step back from overreaching claims.

The starting point for any consideration under Article 102 of the TFEU is that the company should hold a dominant position in the market. According to EU competition law, dominant companies have a special responsibility to avoid disruptions or distortions to competition. Subsequent decisions, such as *IMS Health*,[181] have affirmed the validity of the three *Magill* conditions in assessing abusive conducts when licensing is refused and the Commission clarified in *Microsoft*[182] that they are not cumulative criteria in that not all of these three conditions are required in the assessment of a particular conduct.

The first *Magill* element stipulates that a refusal to licence may be deemed abusive where the relevant right is indispensable raw material for the creation of a new product. This may include a new tool for indexing and search of content, an automated process for text mining, an algorithm enabling content processing and generation of links, or user interfaces for easier navigation through digital materials.[183] *IMS Health* instructs that refusal to offer access to digital content will be anticompetitive only where the licensee means to offer goods that are not of a different nature that correspond to consumer needs that are not satisfied by goods and services already on the market.[184] This is within the main objectives of competition policy, namely to allow for 'competition by substitution' rather than 'competition by imitation'.[185] Regarding the second *Magill* requirement, *IMS Health* stipulates that the refusal to be abusive should not be objectively justified. Such an objective

---

[179] *Radio Telefis Eireann (RTE) and Independent Television Publications Ltd (ITP) v Commission of the European Communities*, Joined Cases C-241/91 P and C-242/91 P, 6 April 1995, ECLI:EU:C:1995:98 (*Magill*), [54]–[56].

[180] See *IMS Health GmbH & Co. OHG v NDC Health GmbH & Co. KG*, Case C-418/01, 29 April 2004, ECLI:EU:C:2004:257 (*IMS Health*).

[181] For instance in *IMS Health GmbH & Co. OHG v NDC Health GmbH & Co. KG*, Case C-418/01, 29 April 2004, ECLI:EU:C:2004:257 (*IMS Health*), [38].

[182] All three conditions were met in *Microsoft Corp. v Commission of the European Communities*, Case T-201/04, 17 September 2007, ECLI:EU:T:2007:289 (*Microsoft*), [712].

[183] See in this regard Maurizio Borghi and Stavroula Karapapa, *Copyright and Mass Digitization: A Cross-Jurisdictional Perspective* (Oxford: Oxford University Press, 2013).

[184] See Opinion of Advocate General Antonio Tizzano, *IMS Health GmbH & Co. OHG v NDC Health GmbH & Co. KG*, Case C-418/01, 2 October 2003, ECLI:EU:C:2003:537, [62]; upheld by the decision of *IMS Health GmbH & Co. OHG v NDC Health GmbH & Co. KG*, Case C-418/01, 29 April 2004, ECLI:EU:C:2004:257 (*IMS Health*), [48]–[49].

[185] Steve Anderman and Ariel Ezrachi, *Intellectual Property and Competition Law: New Frontiers* (Oxford: Oxford University Press, 2011) 4.

justification could include furnishing proof that the license would impact on incentives to innovate. As regards the third *Magill* requirement, the refusal should have the likely effect of excluding competition in a secondary market. A secondary market of content could include, for instance, a search engine, a text mining tool, a news aggregator, or a media monitoring service—all of which require extracting materials from another source in order to subsist. Refusal to license the use of content in such secondary markets may be in excess of proportionate copyright claims and amount to anticompetitive conduct.

Both competition rules and copyright law are premised on the same aspiration, namely to offer incentives for innovation and to develop market structures for the creation and dissemination of new works. It is for these reasons that the Court of Justice, in order to discuss the relationship between the two legal disciplines, has formulated a test that takes into account the broader aims and objectives that each means to serve. In this context, the central criterion is deemed to be the development of new products and services in the sense that behaviours that would hinder creativity, innovation, and placement of new products in the market would contravene the broader objectives that competition principles and copyright law mean to serve. These considerations explain why abuse of right is treated differently in cases which deal with the disproportionate exercise of copyright that may impact on freedom of movement. Considerations that have to do with innovative business strategies, and the broader purposes that copyright law means to serve, have resulted in decisions that could create structures for more innovation in the market and possibly the creation of new or secondary markets. An example includes *UsedSoft* and its outcome, namely the possibility that second-hand markets for used software can be legally created.

Consumer law

With the emergence of e-commerce and online licenses regarding the use of digital content, consumer law has become highly relevant in order to regulate the intersection between expansive claims of the rightsholders and user entitlements. Such contractual agreements, which often include standard licensing terms,[186] are regulated by the Consumer Rights Directive[187] which outlines an obligation to offer consumers specific information regarding digital content, including the possibility that technological protection measures have been applied and how these may impact on interoperability with various devices.[188] Even though consumer law could

---

[186] See in this regard Lucie Guibault, 'Individual Licensing Models and Consumer Protection' in Kung-Chung Liu and Reto M. Hilty (eds), *Remuneration of Copyright Owners: Regulatory Challenges of New Business Models* (Berlin/Heidelberg: Springer, 2016) 207.

[187] Directive 2011/83/EU of the European Parliament and of the Council of 25 October 2011 on consumer rights, amending Council Directive 93/13/EEC and Directive 1999/44/EC of the European Parliament and of the Council and repealing Council Directive 85/577/EEC and Directive 97/7/EC of the European Parliament and of the Council Text with EEA relevance (Consumer Rights Directive), OJ L 304, 22 November 2011, 64–88.

[188] Ibid., Arts 5(1)(g), 5(1)(h), 6(1)(r), 6(1)(s).

offer a response regarding users' reasonable expectations on the use of online content, it may not serve to establish users' claims against copyright holders for contractually restricting the availability of a copyright exception. We have seen that with regard to remunerated exceptions, for example, and private copying in particular, it has not been possible for consumers to succeed in a claim that private copying is a user right;[189] it has, however, been possible to rely on consumer law claiming that the application of anti-copying measures was not clearly visible to consumers of CDs.[190]

Abuse of right and the fragmented exceptions and limitations

At a broader level, the set of copyright exceptions and limitations available in the various Directives does not offer safeguards in order to protect the interests of users in cases where the rightsholders exercise their rights disproportionately or excessively. Many Member States do not consider exceptions and limitations to confer enforceable user rights[191] and this proves problematic where the benefit of a copyright exception might be technologically restricted or contractually overridden. Because exceptions are not considered mandatory against contractual terms restricting their scope, and because the Court of Justice has developed the principle of strict interpretation of copyright exceptions and limitations,[192] it is very difficult to see how such a rigid system can accommodate new and emergent uses of copyright-protected works, some of which may involve the use of freely available content, such as hyperlinks or thumbnails. In *Svensson*,[193] as we have seen, linking was found to be lawful simply because the communication was not addressed to a new public, not because it does not altogether amount to an act of communication to the public.[194] Linking, however, is an indispensable activity for the functioning of the Internet and electronic communications.

[189] See e.g. *Fnac Paris v UFC Que Choisir et autres*, Court of Appeal Paris (Cour d'appel Paris), 20 June 2007 ('*Phil Collins*') (France); *Mr X and UFC Que Choisir v Warner Music France and FNAC Paris*, Paris District Court, 10 January 2006 ('*Phil Collins*') (France).

[190] *Studio Canal et al v S. Penguin and Union Federale des Consommateurs Que Choisir*, Cour de Cassation, 19 June 2008, No. 07-142777 (France); *Studio Canal et al v S. Penguin and Union Federale des Consommateurs Que Choisir*, Paris Court of Appeal, 4 April 2007, Gaz. Pal. 18 July 2007 No. 199, 23 (France); *Studio Canal et al v S. Penguin and Union Federale des Consommateurs Que Choisir*, Cour de Cassation, 1st civil section, 28 February 2006, Case No. 549, Bull. 2006 I No. 126, 115 ('*Mulholland Drive*') (France).

[191] Reto M. Hilty and Sylvie Nérisson (eds), *Balancing Copyright – A Survey of National Approaches* (Berlin Heidelberg: Springer-Verlag, 2012) 1–78; it is only few Member States (e.g. Belgium and Portugal, also the United Kingdom in part) that declare exceptions mandatory. See Lucie Guibault, *Copyright Limitations and Contracts: An Analysis of the Contractual Overridability of Limitations on Copyright* (The Hague, London, Boston: Kluwer Law International, 2002).

[192] See *Infopaq International A/S v Danske Dagblades Forening*, Case C-5/08, 16 July 2009, ECLI:EU:C:2009:465 (*Infopaq*), [56].

[193] *Nils Svensson and Others v Retriever Sverige AB*, Case C-466/12, 13 February 2014, ECLI:EU:C:2014:76 (*Svensson*).

[194] European Parliament, Committee on Legal Affairs, Draft Report on the Implementation of Directive 2001/29/EC of the European Parliament and of the Council of 22 May 2001 on the Harmonisation of Certain Aspects of Copyright and Related Rights in the Information Society, 15 January 2015, 2014/2256(INI), point 15.

Lack of flexibility, despite references to general legal principles, such as fairness in the balancing of conflicting rights was also visible in *Bonnier Audio*[195] where the 'fair balance' between copyright and users' privacy did not preclude national laws permitting Internet service providers to disclose the IP addresses of users who were allegedly infringing copyright.[196] Such an assessment of fair balancing may amount to a variety of results depending on the context and, in this light, cannot lead to safe and consistent conclusions. Relying on *FAPL*, the Court of Justice in *Painer* stressed the need to achieve a fair balance between freedom of expression and copyright in order to 'enable the effectiveness of the exception thereby established to be safeguarded and its purpose to be observed.'[197]

Assessing fairness in the context of establishing a balance of interests takes into consideration the status of intellectual property as a fundamental right by virtue of Article 17(2) of the Charter of Fundamental Rights of the European Union, along with the corresponding lack of ascribed limitations to this right in the Charter. This has resulted in reinforcing the protection offered to copyright holders without setting an interpretative tool to assess their limits, despite the fact that abuse of rights is expressly prohibited in Article 54 of the Charter. According to this Article:

> Nothing in this Charter shall be interpreted as implying any right to engage in any activity or to perform any act aimed at the destruction of any of the rights and freedoms recognised in this Charter or at their limitation to a greater extent than is provided for herein.

The national evolution of the prohibition of abuse of right

Various national courts have resorted to general legal principles[198] and contract law provisions[199] in order to address abusive, excessive, or disproportionate behaviour on behalf of the rightsholders. Indeed, cases involving emergent uses of copyright-protected materials cannot be appropriately dealt with by the extreme

---

[195] *Bonnier Audio AB et al. v Perfect Communication Sweden AB*, Case C-461/10, 19 April 2012, ECLI:EU:C:2012:219 (*Bonnier*).

[196] Note the Parliament's contradictory approach in Proposal for Directive: EU Parliament, Proposal for a Directive of the European Parliament and of the Council on Copyright in the Digital Single Market (SWD(2016) 301) (SWD(2016) 302), COM (2016) 593 final, 2016/0280 (COD), Brussels, 14 September 2016.

[197] *Eva-Maria Painer v Standard VerlagsGmbH and Others*, Case C-145/10, 1 December 2011, ECLI:EU:C:2011:798 (*Painer*), [133], also [134]–[135].

[198] Supreme Court, Civil Chamber, Sentencia n 172/2012, 3 April 2012 (Spain).

[199] See 'Vorschaubilder I', Supreme Court (Bundesgerichtshof) 29 April 2010, I ZR 69/08 (Germany), available in German at <http://www.bundesgerichtshof.de>, accessed 11 November 2019; 'Vorschaubilder II', Supreme Court (Bundesgerichtshof), 19 October 2011, I ZR 140/10 (Germany); Jena Court of Appeal (Oberlandesgericht Jena), 2 U 319/07, 27 February 2008, *Kommunikation und Recht* 2008, 301 (Germany).

specificity of the current legal framework and, at the same time—unless general principles of law are taken into consideration—it is difficult to block certain behaviours that depart from the statutory framework and attempt to colonize grey areas in favour of proprietary claims.

As we have seen, France is one of the few Member States to expressly exclude abuse of right in its Copyright Act.[200] There is a judicial trend, however, not to exceed the boundaries that the law has very narrowly set. This is despite the fact that the French Supreme court has elaborated on the theoretical framework underpinning the principle of abuse of right that exceeds the strict contours of the Copyright Act. In *Chiavarino*,[201] the French Supreme court held that the exercise of the moral right of withdrawal was abusive because its purpose was to obtain higher remuneration, whereas the purpose of moral rights is to protect non-pecuniary interests. The ruling was premised on the normative underpinning of proportionality. With regard to economic rights, similar arguments have been developed in *Sté TF1 v Sté Editions Montparnasse*,[202] where the French Supreme court deemed a licensing practice to amount to abuse of copyright and not normal exercise of exclusive rights.[203] Bearing links to the concept of normal exploitation embedded within the three-step test,[204] the concept of the normal exercise of right serves as a normative standard in understanding the appropriate scope of rights, placing the focus on the function and purpose of rights within the legal framework. In this sense, the exercise of rights that goes beyond the normal exploitation of the work may be seen as abusive or disruptive conduct. This is important in order to understand the synergies between exclusivity and permissibility.

The Spanish doctrine of *ius usus inocui* may also be seen as a ground to regulate overreaching behaviours on behalf of the rightsholders. The doctrine was upheld in *Megakini.com v Google Spain*,[205] where the claimant sought to stop Google from exhibiting snippets of their work and claimed damages for copyright infringement. In assessing the legitimacy of Google's caching service, the Spanish Supreme Court[206] interpreted the three-step test through the lens of constitutionally safeguarded 'societal goals'[207] and general principles of law, including good

---

[200] Intellectual Property Act (Code de la Propriété Intellectuelle), Arts L.121-3 and L. 122-9.

[201] Supreme Court, 1st Civil Division, 14 May 1991, 89-21.701, 151 RIDA 1992, 273 (France).

[202] Supreme Court, Commercial Division, 26 November 2003, 00-22.605, Bulletin 2003 IV, No. 178, 195 (France).

[203] Ibid., 197.

[204] Information Society Directive (Directive 2001/29/EC), Art. 5(5); Intellectual Property Act (Code de la Propriété Intellectuelle), Art. L. 122–5 (penultimate paragraph). The French Constitutional Council concluded that the Information Society Directive requires the application of the exceptions to be subordinated to the three-step test: Constitutional Council, Decision 2006–540 DC, 27 July 2006 (France).

[205] Supreme Court, Civil Chamber, Sentencia n 172/2012, 3 April 2012 (Spain); for a comment see Raquel Xalabarder, 'Spanish Supreme Court Rules in Favour of Google Search Engine ... and a Flexible Reading of Copyright Statutes?' (2012) 2 *JIPITEC* 162, available at <https://www.jipitec.eu/issues/jipitec-3-2-2012/3445/xalabarder.pdf>, accessed 11 November 2019.

[206] Ibid.

[207] Spanish Constitution, Art. 33.

faith,[208] prohibition of abusive exercise of rights,[209] and innocuous use, a Roman principle which favours fairness in activities that do not harm one party, but may benefit another.[210] Proceedings started in 2006 when a website owner objected to the unauthorized copying and making available of contents of his website in the Google Cache Service. Three kinds of unauthorized use were identified. First, Google's robots made some initial copies of content for indexation purposes. These were not put into question as the plaintiff himself accepted the necessity of this kind of copying for the very existence of search engines and the application of Article 31.1 of the Spanish Copyright Act (implementing Article 5(1) of the Information Society Directive). Second, there was copying of content featuring snippets from the plaintiff's websites following the main link on the main search results page. Although the plaintiff claimed this amounted to infringement, the Court of Appeal rejected this argument, finding the use to be *de minimis* and hence not impacting on copyright. The third kind of use that was identified concerned the cached webpage. There was no exception to clearly exempt this use from infringement and its legality was put in question, particularly in reference to the fact that the cached content was made available to the public. According to the Court of Appeal,[211] the caching safe harbour[212] could not apply, and equally inapplicable were the relevant exemptions for search engines[213] and the temporary copying exception. The latter is meant to cover only the reproduction right, thus does not extend to activities of making content available to the public, as was the case in *Megakini.com*. Despite the fact that none of the aforementioned defences were applicable, the Court of Appeal held that the use in question did not amount to copyright infringement[214] as it was temporary, incidental, and minimal. The court applied the three-step test available under Article 40 of the Spanish Copyright Act as an interpretative tool for the appropriate scope of intellectual property rights, instead of a legislative guide towards the construal of available defences. It also reverted to the doctrine of *ius usus innocui*, a principle that traditionally applies to cases of real property, arguing that this principle should also apply in copyright cases—and not just in real property cases. Applying this principle, the Court of Appeal concluded that Google's activity did not amount to infringement because it did not harm the right of the plaintiff.

---

[208] Civil Code, Art. 7.1 (Spain).

[209] Civil Code, Art. 7.2 (Spain).

[210] The maxim reads: '*quod tibi non nocet et alii prodest, non prohibetur*'.

[211] Provincial Audience of Barcelona, s. 15, 17 September 2008 (Spain).

[212] Law of Information Society Services and Electronic Commerce (*Ley de Servicios de la Sociedad de la Información y de Comercio Electrónico*) (LSSI), Art. 15 (Spain), also see e-Commerce Directive (Directive 2000/31/EC), Art. 13.

[213] LSSICE, Art. 17 (Spain).

[214] The Appeals Court decision affirmed the ruling reached at first instance: Juzgado Mercantil No. 5 de Barcelona, 30 March 2007 (Spain).

Affirming the decision of the Court of Appeal, the Spanish Supreme court held that it is necessary to examine the lawfulness of the activities on the basis of statutory provisions and general legal principles. Even though the cached copies and copied fragments of linked websites could not benefit from the temporary copying exception, the Supreme Court offered a positive interpretation of the three-step test in light of general principles of law. These principles include general constitutional norms, good faith, prohibition of abusive exercise of rights, and *use innocuous*, as a natural limit to the abusive exercise of rights. In this sense, the three-step test was read through a principle-based approach, which can overcome the abusive exercise of copyright that may result from the strict interpretation of copyright exceptions. *Ius usus innocui* is a Roman law principle that has been developed with regard to real property rights, serving as a natural limit against the excessive or unjustified exercise of property right[215] and allowing a third party to benefit from a use that does not harm the owner of the property right.

An interesting aspect of the doctrine is that it does not qualify *stricto senso* as a limitation of a right for the very reason that there is no right, as such, over the objects or the uses to which it applies. It is an external limit, however, which ensures that exclusivity shall not be overreaching, rather it frames and refines the appropriate scope of rights in order to avoid abusive proprietary conducts, while making allowances for advantageous uses that do not impact on the property right. The Spanish decisions in *Google Cache* have brought the doctrine of innocuous use into copyright, giving it the shape of a defence against allegations of infringement. Because in real property this principle introduces a positive entitlement in the form of a right—and not as mere permission or limitation to a right—the generalization of its application in copyright law could result in shaping a European version of fair use.[216]

The doctrine of abuse of right has also been applied in other continental jurisdictions on different legal bases and with varying outcomes. In Belgium,[217] it emerged from a general clause against civil liability and was developed through case law to cover the unjustified or excessive exercise of rights that goes beyond their statutory function. A similar stance is taken by Greek courts that rely on the general civil law prohibition of abuse of right,[218] complemented by the principles of fairness and proportionality. The doctrine has been used at least twice in reference

[215] On the background of the development of the doctrine see Maurizio Borghi and Stavroula Karapapa, *Copyright and Mass Digitization: A Cross-Jurisdictional Perspective* (Oxford: Oxford University Press, 2013) 41.

[216] Ibid., 43.

[217] See indicatively Civil Court Brussels, 4 March 2009, IRDI, 2009, 197 (Belgium); Civil Court of Brussels, 5 January 1996, IRDI, 1996, 97 (Belgium); Commercial Court of Brussels, 26 May 1993, RDC, 1994, 651 (Belgium); Civil Court Brussels, 27 February 1998, A&M, 1998, 143, aff'd by Court of Appeals of Brussels, 18 September 1998 (Belgium).

[218] Civil Code, Art. 281.

to copyright. Greek Courts have ruled against a co-author's refusal to authorize the commercial exploitation of a work[219] and have also dismissed a belated claim challenging the validity of a license, inducing the licensee to believe that the agreement was valid.[220] Germany[221] and the Netherlands[222] have also elaborated on the prohibition of abuse of right but cases have been sporadic. In Germany, the doctrine has been elaborated in conjunction with cases of implied license, discussed in Chapter 5.[223]

The national approaches on the application of abuse of right have been fragmented and diverse and the EU stance taken by the Court of Justice has not been conducive towards a more coherent approach. However, the prohibition of abusive exercise of rights has the merit of flexibility that the rigid system of copyright exceptions and limitations at the EU level lacks. Understood either as fairness and proportionality in the context of the disruptive exercise of rights or as abuse of dominance in the context of competition law claims, the prohibition of abuse of rights stands as a mechanism for ensuring the balance between conflicting interests and the appropriate exercise of rights.

The consideration of this general legal principle becomes extremely important in the online context, where new business models and innovative services may emerge. Such business growth may not be clearly exempt from infringement through the framework of available exceptions and limitations. At the same time, the intersection of technological protection measures and the exercise of copyright exceptions and limitations, together with the issue of contractual overridability, have not been sufficiently addressed. This has been interpreted as offering the possibility for expansive interpretations of the scope of copyright,[224] including the possibility of restricting access to works instead of merely offering regulatory approaches towards their use.[225] In such under-regulated, grey areas the doctrine of

---

[219] Multimember Court of First Instance of Athens (Πολυμελές Πρωτοδικείο Αθηνών), No. 2028/2003 (Greece); One-Member Court of First Instance of Athens (Μονομελές Πρωτοδικείο Αθηνών), No. 276/2001 (Greece); Multimember Court of First Instance of Thessaloniki (Πολυμελές Πρωτοδικείο Θεσσαλονίκης), No. 13300/2004 (Greece).

[220] One-Member Court of First Instance of Athens (Μονομελές Πρωτοδικείο Αθηνών), No. 36247/1999 (Greece).

[221] CA Jena, MMR 2008, 408 [413] (Germany).

[222] Supreme Court, 20 October 1995, NJ 1996, 682, s. 3.10(Netherlands).

[223] Although fairness and proportionality in the exercise of rights may be discussed on the basis of consumer law regarding unfair contractual terms, abuse of right tends to receive broader attention with regard to competition law and the abuse of dominant position. There have indeed been numerous national decisions regarding refusal to license as abusive conduct. The most relevant are: BGH NJW-RR 2009, 1047, 1049 (Germany); Supreme Court, Commercial Division, 4 December 2001, Bulletin 2001, IV, No. 193, 185 (France).

[224] See also Thomas P. Heide, 'Copyright, Contract and the Legal Protection of Technological Measures - Not "the Old Fashioned Way": Providing a Rationale to the 'Copyright Exceptions Interface' (2003) 50 *Journal of the Copyright Society of the U.S.A.* 315; Séverine Dusollier, 'Technology as an Imperative for Regulating Copyright: from the Public Exploitation to the Private Use of The Work' (2005) 6 *European Intellectual Property Review* 201, 202.

[225] Stavroula Karapapa, *Private Copying* (London: Routledge, 2012) 144.

abuse of right, and insights drawn from it, offer a principled approach whereby the appropriate scope of right and availability of permitted uses can be determined.

Even though abuse of right has been developed on a non-systematic, sporadic basis, it forms the core of a defence against excessive authorial claims and serves as a balancing act between authorial and public/private interests. Its consistent application could make it an additional tool to address distortive uses of copyright[226] and an external to copyright law ground that can ensure fairness and proportionality in the exercise of copyright. Because it is a general legal principle of considerable flexibility and breadth of coverage, it could be used as a regulatory standard applicable with regard to grey areas, such as those where innovation and technological growth can spur.

Conclusion

Defences that are available on grounds that are extraneous to copyright are based either on other legal disciplines, such as e-commerce protection, or on general legal principles, such as the public interest and the general prohibition of the abuse of right. These represent an important body of defensive rules as they indicate that in the encounter of copyright with other legal orders, external to copyright considerations that which not be expressly reflected in the framework of copyright exceptions and limitations may prevail. These external defences are an essential component for understanding the scope of permissible copyright use on the Internet and the contours of the public domain more broadly. Internet service provider liability and the defences to it have been subject to EU harmonization on the basis of the parallel application of two Directives, namely the e-Commerce Directive and the Directive on Copyright in the Digital Single Market. The complex mechanism of liability governing online content-sharing service providers by virtue of the Digital Single Market Directive, and the joint application of the provisions available under both Directives, is questionable as it introduces primary liability for service providers that marks a dramatic shift from the theory and principles of tort law and established norms of EU law. At the same time, it narrows down the defensive framework governing the activities of online content-sharing service providers by depriving them of the hosting exemption of the e-Commerce Directive and implying that specific monitoring duties may have to be launched to ensure compliance with the new Directive, despite the fact that no general monitoring duty is imposed on intermediaries. This is likely to increase transaction

---

[226] Caterina Sganga and Silvia Scalzini, 'From Abuse of Right to European Copyright Misuse: A New Doctrine for EU Copyright Law' (2017) 48(4) *International Review of Intellectual Property and Competition Law* 405.

costs, have an impact on the development of new services and methods of content circulation, and possibly change the Internet as we know it.

At the same time, the viability of broader defences residing in the application of general legal principles, such as the public interest or the prohibition of the abusive exercise of rights, is dubious. This is because such defences are either not compatible with existing legal norms, e.g. national public interest defences may not be compatible with the Information Society Directive and the three-step test, or are subject to sporadic and non-harmonious application by the relevant Member States, resulting in limited instances of permissible use that cannot have a more general application in the online context. This has the effect of narrowing down the potential benefit of defensive rules premised on general legal principles that work towards the preservation of a rigorous public domain. The affirmation of such broader principles is likely to be rather limited. However, the general legal principle that prohibits the abusive exercise of rights has the potential to fine-tune copyright for the sake of achieving its objectives and to set the boundary between exclusivity and permissibility in unregulated or under-regulated areas.

10

Conclusion

The taxonomic project carried out in this book offers a holistic account of the defensive rules available to attack allegations of copyright infringement. Defences against infringement are viewed as an organic whole and a system of rules that has the capacity to acquit a defendant from infringing liability. In the fourth industrial revolution, where innovative copy-reliant services and business models constantly emerge, enhancing public welfare, on one hand, and challenging the limits of copyright, on the other, such a contextual approach is essential in order to ascertain the breadth of permissible use. It can serve to unveil overlaps and possible 'gaps' in defensive rules, ascertain the scope of permissibility, and evaluate the adaptability of the law towards technological change. This is particularly so in EU copyright, which tends to offer a rigid approach by laying down broadly framed exclusive rights and proprietary entitlements, and narrowly construed and strictly interpreted defences. In this sense, the discussion does not merely focus on substantive defences against infringement in the form of copyright exceptions and limitations, permitted uses, and other user privileges, but also invites an examination of the large body of broadly conceived rules that serve a defensive role in practice by negating the existence of infringing liability.

An initial distinction of defensive rules is made on the basis of the way in which they attack allegations of copyright infringement. Drawing insights from tort law and theory, two main kinds of defence, broadly conceived, are identified in copyright: negations of the elements of infringement, namely arguments supporting the absence of infringement, and rationale-based defences, i.e. defensive rules claiming that there is a judicial justification or public policy explanation for a given conduct. From a judicial perspective, defensive rules in a broad sense may either deny one or more of the elements in which the claimant sues or bring forward a justification or explanation for an allegedly infringing conduct. When successful, such defences affirm the absence of infringement. The second broad category of defences has a supervening force and, in order to exempt a defendant from infringement, they set forth justifications for a given conduct. In this sense, they are rationale-based and, when successful, can exempt a defendant from infringing liability, despite an initial finding that the elements of infringement were met.

At a second level, the anatomy of defensive rules is determined on the basis of their intrinsic characteristics and theoretical grounding. Once this secondary distinction is made it is easier to identify aspects in which the various defensive rules collide and develop normative insights on their legal nature and function within

Defences to Copyright Infringement. Stavroula Karapapa, Oxford University Press (2020). © Stavroula Karapapa.
DOI: 10.1093/oso/9780198795636.001.0001

copyright. Denials of elements of infringement may attack different aspects of the claimant's entitlement, such as subsistence of copyright, scope of exclusive rights, or authorization to carry out a given activity. Rationale-based defences are distinguished on the basis of the kind of justification that is brought forward to explain why an allegedly infringing use should be permitted, which may be premised on a fundamental human rights underpinning or a public policy objective or on grounds that are external to copyright, such as e-commerce protection, competition law, or general legal principles.

The discussion offers positivist and normative insights into law and doctrine and an argument is made in favour of a principle-based approach towards defensive rules that could inform future law and policy making. The taxonomy demonstrates that defensive rules that negate the elements of infringement in which the claimant sues have tended to become more and more narrow in recent years. It has been shown that recent legislative and judicial trends adopt an expansive approach towards the construal of subject matter protected by copyright. Although infringement negating claims are not supervening defences and attack the existence of—at least one of—the elements of infringement, they call for reconsideration of the way in which subsistence requirements and the scope of rights are legislatively drafted and judicially interpreted. Almost every activity carried out with regard to a work or other subject matter amounts prima facie to infringement. In this sense, exclusivity becomes the norm, which may then be subject to limitations.

Liability-defeating rules that consist of negations of subsistence requirements function as defences in a broad sense and have the underlying effect of challenging the existence of the requirements for liability. In this regard, denials of the elements of infringement can be seen as challenges to causation and negations of liability, rather than supervening defensive rules bringing forward justifications or excuses for a particular conduct. When successful, they indicate the absence of infringement. There are numerous cases from the Court of Justice indicating that the scope of copyright protection is not absolute and that exclusive rights are subject to internal scope limitations. Scope limitations define the scope of exclusivity and breadth of protection, determine the nature of the rights, and outline the availability of entitlements that copyright grants on the protected subject matter. As with pleas which deny liability because copyright does not subsist in a specific work or other subject matter, scope limitations deny liability because a particular activity does not fall within the remit of right. In this light, although they serve as liability-defeating claims, they cannot qualify as supervening defences. The reason is that, just as with defensive claims targeting subsistence, scope limitations negate the existence of elements of infringement in which the claimant sues and, if successful, affirm that the defendant has not committed copyright infringement. Although these limitations can be regarded as defences in a broad sense, they are not exceptional grounds on which liability is defeated, but essential understandings of what falls within and outside the scope of rights.

It has been demonstrated that the temporary copying exception, currently incorporated in Article 5(1) of the Information Society Directive and organically listed as a copyright exception, does not serve as a supervening rule in *stricto sensu* as the majority of copyright exceptions and limitations do, and in this regard resists strict classification. Albeit an exception, and indeed the only exception that is compulsory for Member States to implement into their national laws under this Directive, the exception allowing temporary copying has the merit of serving as a scope limit to the reproduction right. This emanates from the historical principles and interpretative guidance on the function of this exception within the copyright system which indicate that the temporary copying exception means to frame the limits of the reproduction right, offer a clearer definition of its scope, and lower the level of generality in which the right is drafted. At the same time, the defence is compulsory for Member States to implement and as a matter of fact it is the only compulsory exception included within the Information Society Directive. Finally, the Court of Justice has affirmed that Article 5(1) is a derogation from the reproduction right, with the result that the conditions making out the temporary copying exception ought to be subject to strict interpretation.[1] In this regard, the temporary copying exception can, and should, be understood as serving both as a scope limitation to an exclusive right and as an exemption from infringement.[2] In light of the foregoing considerations, it is argued that the temporary copying exception can be understood as setting a scope limitation to the reproduction right in order to allow determination of the kinds of temporary copying that are covered by the right and those which remain outside its scope.

Denials of the elements of infringement have also affirmed internal limits within the scope of rights, such as the newly introduced concept of the 'new public' with regard to the right of communication to the public. This doctrinal rule which was developed through the case law of the Court of Justice and repeats some national approaches and legal principles, such as the UK 'monopoly test' discussed in Chapter 3, serves a defensive function in cases where the re-use of copyright-protected content does not reach an audience outside of the one that copyright holders had in mind when initially making the work available to the public. Although heavily criticized[3] and demonstrating a degree of judicial activism

---

[1] *Infopaq International A/S v Danske Dagblades Forening*, Case C-5/08, 16 July 2009, ECLI:EU:C:2009:465 (*Infopaq I*), [56] and [57]; *Football Association Premier League and Others*, Joined Cases C-403/08 and C-429/08, 4 October 2011, ECLI:EU:C:2011:631 (*FAPL*), [162]; *Public Relations Consultants Association Ltd and Newspaper Licensing Agency Ltd and Others*, Case C-360/13, 5 June 2014, ECLI:EU:C:2014:1195 (*Meltwater*), [23].

[2] See in this regard, the reasoning developed in the decision of the UK Supreme Court: *Public Relations Consultants Association Limited (Appellant) v The Newspaper Licensing Agency Limited and Others (Respondents)* [2013] UKSC 18, [36].

[3] See e.g. Association Littéraire et Artistique Internationale (ALAI), 'Opinion on the Criterion "New Public", Developed by the Court of Justice of the European Union (CJEU), Put in the Context of Making Available and Communication to the Public' (17 September 2014) available at http://www.alai.org/en/assets/files/resolutions/2014-opinion-new-public.pdf, accessed 11 November 2019.

from the Court of Justice, this doctrinal principle may help refine the scope of the broadly construed right of communicating works to the public and serve a defensive function in certain instances.

The copyright holders' consent, express or implied, is at the heart of the nature of the authorial right 'to authorize or prohibit' acts falling within the scope of exclusivity. Claiming that such consent was given, if successful, has the capacity to acquit a defendant from infringing liability. Implied consent has gained significance on the Internet as a defence against allegations of infringement, particularly in cases of 're-use' of protected content without express permission. The pleas forwarded by such a defensive rule do not aspire to defeat liability by offering an explanation for a particular conduct, but attack the nature of rights which represent a system of permissions and focus on the claim that the copyright holder's conduct should be interpreted as indicating the offer of permission. The principle of implied consent, as developed in recent case law, has the potential to offer clarity with regard to the permissibility of certain online activities. In particular, the way in which this principle has evolved in German jurisprudence[4] and recent cases of the Court of Justice, notably *Svensson*,[5] could infuse a degree of flexibility in the determination of which uses should be permitted and which should not, to the effect that, depending on the context, certain activities will be exempt from infringement where the copyright holder's conduct implies that they had allowed a certain activity to be carried out.

Although the concept of protected subject matter and exclusive rights are broadly construed both in statutory and judicial language, leaving very few opportunities for denials of infringing liability to succeed, supervening defensive rules, outlined mostly through copyright exceptions and limitations, are very narrowly drafted in legislation and strictly interpreted by courts. This does not seem to generate the desirable 'balance' in the copyright framework, which is one of the stated objectives of copyright protection and EU harmonization under various Directives.[6] Hence, it calls for a reconsideration of the development of supervening

---

[4] See e.g. '*Vorschaubilder I*', Supreme Court (Bundesgerichtshof) 29 April 2010, I ZR 69/08, 14–15 (Germany), available in German at <http://www.bundesgerichtshof.de>, accessed 11 November 2019; '*Vorschaubilder II*', Supreme Court (Bundesgerichtshof), 19 October 2011, I ZR 140/10 (Germany); Court of Appeal of Jena (Oberlandesgericht Jena), 2 U 319/07, 27 February 2008, *Kommunikation und Recht* 2008, 301 (Germany).

[5] *Nils Svensson and Others v Retriever Sverige AB*, Case C-466/12, 13 February 2014, ECLI:EU:C:2014:76 (*Svensson*).

[6] Directive 2001/29/EC of the European Parliament and of the Council of 22 May 2001 on the Harmonisation of Certain Aspects of Copyright and Related Rights in the Information Society, OJ L 167, 22 June 2001, 10–19 (Information Society Directive), Recital 31 (affirmed in various cases such as *Funke Medien NRW GmbH v Federal Republic of Germany*, C-469/17, 29 July 2019, ECLI:EU:C:2019:623 (*Funke Medien*), [32]; *Pelham GmbH, Moses Pelham, Martin Haas v Ralf Hütter, Florian Schneider-Esleben*, Case C-476/17, 29 July 2019, ECLI:EU:C:2019:624 (*Pelham*), [32]); Directive (EU) 2019/790 of the European Parliament and of the Council of 17 April 2019 on Copyright and Related Rights in the Digital Single Market and Amending Directives 96/9/EC and 2001/29/EC, OJ L 130, 17 May 2019, 92–125 (Digital Single Market Directive), Recitals 6, also 21, 61, 70, 75.

defences which are gaining increased relevance in the online context that is characterized by technological advancement and the development of innovative services and business models.

Substantive defences are judicial, doctrinal, or policy explanations of infringing liability. They do not negate elements that construe copyright infringement, but go around relevant allegations by explaining why a certain activity should be exempt from infringement. Often, these defensive rules find their justificatory basis on grounds that bring into question the relationship of copyright with other legal orders. These include both justifications on the use and re-use of protected materials for reasons which fall under the umbrella of fundamental human rights, and explanations of infringement for reasons of public policy. They may also originate in fields of law that are external to copyright and, in this sense, form grounds for defeating liability that do not feature in copyright statutes. In this sense, substantive defences are judicial invitations to look into the relationship of copyright with other legal orders and, in so doing, offer a judicial explanation for activities that touch upon the scope of copyright, but which are sufficiently justified to remain outside infringing liability. Defensive rules that serve as supervening defences, i.e. claims that have the capacity to justify infringement or offer a policy explanation for it, are all rationale-based and, if successful, have a supervening force. The relevant rationales may emerge from different legal orders, whether or not these have been institutionalized within copyright law.

An important part of copyright exceptions and limitations are defensive rules that find their justificatory basis on fundamental human rights, such as freedom of speech and freedom of the media. In this book they are referred to as a speech entitlements. They represent instances where copyright encounters freedom of speech or freedom of press and regulate the possible conflict that may arise between these legal orders. Defendants can benefit to the extent that the relevant copyright exceptions and limitations allow, but they cannot invoke the relevant fundamental freedoms independently. Speech entitlements promote the production of new copyright works and authorship and, in this regard, they represent defensive rules that are inherent within the very purposes of copyright protection. Typical examples of such speech entitlements are reproductions by the press for the reporting of current events, quotations for criticism or review, and uses for the purpose of caricature, parody, or pastiche. They also include the enablement of access to works for specific groups, such as disabled individuals.[7]

---

[7] Broader accessibility to copyright-protected content has been one of the priorities at the EU level. In implementation of the Marrakesh Treaty, the Directive on Permitted Uses for Disabled Individuals enlarged the scope of permissible uses carried out by, or on behalf of, disabled individuals. See Directive (EU) 2017/1564 of the European Parliament and of the Council of 13 September 2017 on Certain Permitted Uses of Certain Works and Other Subject Matter Protected by Copyright and Related Rights for the Benefit of Persons who are Blind, Visually Impaired or Otherwise Print-Disabled and Amending Directive 2001/29/EC on the Harmonisation of Certain Aspects of Copyright and Related Rights in the Information Society, OJ L 242, 20 September 2017, 6–13.

A problematic aspect of these copyright exceptions and limitations is that their scope remains relatively narrow and their status against contractual overridability is not settled at the EU level.[8] This could be viewed as an obstacle to the creation of new authorship involving use of pre-existing materials, especially in the online context, where use of protected content may be subject to technological access controls or restrictive contractual terms. What is more, the numerous and strictly interpreted internal limits of the relevant copyright exceptions and limitations narrow the scope of permissible use and the applicability of the relevant defences.

The taxonomy indicates that speech entitlements may need to be rethought and strengthened in line with the objectives of copyright law and EU harmonization. It has been argued that speech entitlements ought to have the normative force of imperative rules on the basis of their theoretical premise and function within the copyright system. Speech entitlements are manifestations of fundamental human rights, and although relevant defences should not be used in excess of the relevant copyright exceptions and limitations embodying them,[9] by invoking for instance the relevant fundamental freedoms directly they are meant to promote new authorship and the objectives of copyright. It is claimed that copyright cannot unreasonably limit what it itself is about. For instance, certain kinds of works, such as parodies or book reviews, necessitate the copying of pre-existing works by their own very nature. In this regard, speech entitlements ought to be compulsory against contractual override and enforceable against the courts in instances where such entitlements are restricted through excessive copyright claims. First, making allowance for such uses of protected works is in line with copyright principles and the very rationale of encouraging new authorship. Second, speech entitlements are manifestations of fundamental rights and as such they should not be left at the discretion of the copyright holders to authorize or prohibit, to the extent that the conditions of the relevant copyright exceptions and limitations are met. In this regard, it is claimed that speech entitlements ought to be strengthened by being declared compulsory against contractual restrictions and being enforceable before the courts to the extent that the law specifically permits.

Equally important in the copyright system are uses of copyright-protected works that are allowed in furtherance of public policy objectives. These are activities that are primarily available to institutional users, such as educational establishments, libraries, and archives, or to specific sets of end users, such as scientific researchers. Unlike speech entitlements, public policy defences have been subject to intensive steps of harmonization at the EU level in recent years. There have been a number of legislative initiatives aiming to enlarge the scope of permissible activities carried out by certain institutional users or other end users in the online

---

[8] See e.g. the 2014 UK copyright reform.
[9] *Funke Medien NRW GmbH v Federal Republic of Germany*, C-469/17, 29 July 2019, ECLI:EU:C:2019:623 (*Funke Medien*), [64].

context. The Information Society Directive contains a good set of exceptions and limitations with a public policy rationale. At a more specific level, the Orphan Works Directive[10] regulates the use and re-use of orphan works at the EU level and, although not ideal, develops certain principles and ways in which cultural institutions in Europe can extract value from the digitization of such materials. Importantly, the Directive on Copyright in the Digital Single Market[11] has introduced certain new exceptions reflecting public policy objectives and has enlarged the scope of some of the existing ones. The new exceptions make allowances for modern methods of teaching provision, exempt from infringement new methods of carrying out research, such as text mining and data analytics, and enable the extraction of value from the plethora of works that are currently out of commerce. Despite the efforts made at the legislative level, law and policy making has not overcome the rigidity of the defensive rules under EU copyright law and efforts to enhance innovation and growth on the Internet through a rigorous framework of copyright exceptions and limitations have been very limited in terms of their efficacy.

Public policy privileges do not offer a justification of a defendant's conduct in the sense that a defendant cannot claim that they carried out a particular activity with a view to meet a given public policy objective. What they do is offer an explanation as to why a particular conduct should be permissible and thus exempt from infringement. This body of defences, which is a form of a supervening claim, places the use and re-use of copyright-protected content at the heart of political, societal, and economic considerations, including the proper functioning of the Internal Market and EU harmonization objectives. Although resting on the furtherance of goals that lie outside the core of copyright, such objectives are often deemed so paramount that the relevant copyright exceptions are declared imperative against possible contractual restriction.[12] The recent legislative reform at the EU level unveiled the need to clarify the conditions under which this kind of defence will be set as imperative against restrictive contractual terms as there seems to be no common denominator as to what makes a copyright exception compulsory against contractual override. In EU copyright, it is not clear why some exceptions are declared compulsory against contractual override and why others are not, nor what the decisive factor is in making such a distinction.

A body of defensive rules that qualify as substantive defences, i.e. liability supervening claims, are activities that, to be permitted, are premised on the

---

[10] Directive (EU) 2012/28 of the European Parliament and of the Council of 25 October 2012 on Certain Permitted Uses of Orphan Works Text with EEA relevance, OJ L 299, 27 October 2012, 5–12 (Orphan Works Directive).

[11] Digital Single Market Directive (Directive 2019/790).

[12] For instance, according to the Directive on Copyright in the Digital Single Market, the exceptions on text mining for scientific research, online teaching activities, and preservation of cultural heritage are declared imperative against contractual restriction. See Digital Single Market Directive (Directive 2019/790), Art. 7(1).

requirement that the copyright holders are fairly remunerated for the relevant permitted use. Such remunerated exceptions include private copying, reprography, and the reproduction of broadcasts that are made by social institutions pursuing non-commercial purposes. The reason why these exceptions are subject to remuneration, specifically referred to in the Information Society Directive as 'fair compensation', is that the permitted activities are expected to cause harm to the copyright holders. Even though the Court of Justice has ruled on the concept of fair compensation, especially with regard to private copying,[13] it has not elaborated on the impact of compensation on the legal nature of the permitted activities. National case law indicates that, although remunerated, the relevant copyright exceptions do not generate user rights for the benefit of end users.[14] Because fair compensation is linked to the concept of harm, remunerated exceptions are often seen as an intermediary form of entitlement for the copyright holders in the form of a statutory license, whereby exclusive rights give way to a permitted use under the specific conditions established by law. The permitted activities do not, however, represent instances that merely restrict the relief available to claimants where liability has been established. Instead, these are activities the exercise of which is essential for the accomplishment of certain policy objectives and, because they broaden user freedom, remuneration is a compromise solution for copyright holders and users of protected works alike.

Remunerated exceptions is an area on which future legislative reform may meaningfully expand on. It has been demonstrated that such defensive rules often operate on the basis of a statutory license; instead of offering users a right to carry out an activity they have paid for, they represent derogations from exclusive rights

---

[13] *Padawan SL v Sociedad General de Autores y Editores de España (SGAE)*, Case C-467/08, 21 October 2011, ECLI:EU:C:2010:620; (*Padawan*); *Stichting de Thuiskopie v Opus Supplies Deutschland GmbH*, Case C-462/09, 16 June 2011, ECLI:EU:C:2011:397 (*Opus*); *Martin Luksan v Petrus van der Let*, Case C-277/10, 9 February 2012, ECLI:EU:C:2012:65 (*Luksan*); *Verwertungsgesellschaft Wort (VG Wort) v Kyocera and Others and Canon Deutschland GmbH and Fujitsu Technology Solutions GmbH and Hewlett-Packard GmbH v Verwertungsgesellschaft Wort*, Cases C-457/11 to C-460/11, 27 June 2013, ECLI:EU:C:2013:426 (*VG Wort*); *Amazon.com International v Austro-Mechana Gesellschaft zur Wahrnehmung mechanisch-musikalischer Urheberrechte Gesellschaft mbH*, Case C-521/11, 11 July 2013, ECLI:EU:C:2013:515 (*Amazon*); *Copydan Bândkopi v Nokia Danmark A/S*, Case C-463/12, 5 March 2015, ECLI:EU:C:2015:144 (*Copydan*); *Hewlett-Packard Belgium SPRL v Reprobel SCRL*, Case C-572/13, 12 November 2015, ECLI:EU:C:2015:750 (*Reprobel*).

[14] Indicatively see *Studio Canal et al v S. Penguin and Union Federale des Consommateurs Que Choisir*, Cour de Cassation, 19 June 2008, No. 07-142777 (France); *Studio Canal et al v S. Penguin and Union Federale des Consommateurs Que Choisir*, Paris Court of Appeal, 4 April 2007, *Gaz. Pal.* 18 July 2007 No. 199, 23 (France); *Studio Canal et al v S. Penguin and Union Federale des Consommateurs Que Choisir*, Cour de Cassation, 1st civil section, 28 February 2006, Case No. 549, Bull. 2006 I No. 126, 115 ('*Mulholland Drive*') (France); Supreme Court (Cour de cassation), No. 07-18778, 27 November 2008 ('*Phil Collins*') (France); *Fnac Paris v UFC Que Choisir et autres*, Court of Appeal Paris (Cour d'appel Paris), 20 June 2007 ('*Phil Collins*') (France); *Mr X and UFC Que Choisir v Warner Music France and FNAC Paris*, Paris District Court, 10 January 2006 ('*Phil Collins*') (France); *L'ASBL Association Belge des Consomateurs Test Achats v La SA EMI Recorded Music Belgium et al*, Tribunal of First Instance of Brussels, 2004/46/A, 27 April 2004 (Belgium); *L'ASBL Association Belge des Consommateurs Test Achats v La SA EMI Recorded Music Belgium et al*, Brussels Court of Appeal, 9 September 2005, Case 2004/AR/1649 (Belgium).

making allowance for a particular activity on condition that copyright holders receive fair compensation. This is an area which lawmakers may wish to explore in the search for compromise solutions in the use of copyright-protected works in the online context, particularly with reference to certain mass users of protected materials such as copy-reliant businesses. Such a solution would have the merit of enhancing the scope of permissible use on the Internet without depriving copyright holders of the fair remuneration that would correspond to the use and re-use of their works online.

A final body of permitted activities is premised on grounds external to copyright law, or rooted in general legal principles. These include competition law, e-commerce protection, or general principles of law, often embodied in civil law codes or legal doctrine. Not all of these permitted activities have been subject to harmonization at the EU level, nor do they cover a wide range of permissible use. They do, however, offer alternative grounds for ensuring the preservation of a rigorous public domain. Examples include defences available to Internet service providers for infringements carried out by their users, including defences for hosting, caching, and 'mere conduit'. Recent changes in EU copyright have arguably limited the scope of defences available to Internet service providers and have launched a framework of primary liability for online content-sharing service providers, which is unprecedented at the EU level. This is expected to increase Internet service providers' transaction costs and possibly lead to the introduction of filtering mechanisms on the content uploaded by end users. It is yet another instance where the scope of permissible use has been narrowed down and one that has particular relevance to the development of copy-reliant services in the online context. Other defensive rules find their justificatory ground in competition law and include, for instance, the doctrines of refusal to license, or abuse of dominant position. Although limited in terms of their applicability, these defensive rules gain significance in the context of online uses of copyright-protected content. General legal principles available under national laws may also be invoked in certain instances, offering a principled justification as to why a particular conduct is permissible.

Such a justification could be the public interest or the doctrine of the 'abuse of right'. The public interest has been used in some Member States as a defensive rule but may be found in conflict with the three-step test in the aftermath of the implementation of the Information Society Directive. The principle of abuse of right is a judge-made doctrine that offers an external-to-copyright explanation on why infringement has not taken place in cases where copyright holders bring forward abusive, excessive, or disproportionate claims and do not allow third parties to carry out certain activities with regard to protected works. This could include, for instance, the refusal to license the use of copyright-protected materials. The general principle prohibiting the abusive exercise of rights qualifies as a defence in a broad sense to the extent that it can be used to defeat claims of infringing liability.

But it also demonstrates one of the instances in which copyright encounters other legal orders, such as competition law or general commercial law. The principle prohibiting the abusive exercise of rights represents yet another area that seems to have the potential to infuse fairness in the context of permissible copyright use at the judicial level. Although not subject to EU harmonization, and having been only sporadically discussed in EU and national case law, this doctrine could fine-tune the lawfulness and permissibility of certain online uses and lead to the dismissal of excessive or disproportionate copyright claims. There is national case law indicating that this legal principle can be used with regard to copyright and, although often finding its root in general principles of civil law, can serve as a tool which balances the interests involved in the use and re-use of copyright-protected content. Notably, this principle can be relevant to the development of new business models and copy-reliant technologies, especially with regard to the refusal to license copyright-protected content.[15]

Both denials of infringement and rationale-based defences, despite some legislative attempts to enlarge the breadth of permissible use, especially with reference to online uses and new business models, have not effectively enlarged the availability of permissible uses and what is often referred to as the public domain. Instead, the framework governing permissible uses and defensive claims under EU copyright becomes more and more narrow and specifically delineated by the effect of the applicable legislation and judicial reasoning. This results in a situation whereby more and more permissible use is governed by licensing arrangements and there are very limited instances where use and re-use of protected content is permissible without the prior express consent of the copyright holders. It has been demonstrated that this rigid legislative approach has resulted in long lists of narrowly defined instances of permissible use, whilst exclusivity is defined in open-ended and general terms. The legislative framework is also characterized by its complexity and technicality as defensive rules are legislatively drafted on the basis of what amounts to a normal exploitation of protected content at the time of the law-making process. At the same time, judicial reasoning is governed by the broad understanding of exclusive rights and the principle of strict interpretation of defensive rules, notably copyright exceptions and limitations, leaving very narrow scope for the available defences.

---

[15] Although it can be claimed, in principle, that the principle which prohibits the abusive exercise of rights could qualify as a scope limitation, such a claim would have to be an external rather than an internal limit to the scope of exclusive rights. It can also be claimed that it is no such limitation at all on the basis that excessive claims from the copyright holders are not a 'right' that can be subject to limitations thereinafter. In either case, the logic of the taxonomy does not insist that each specimen should be placed in one category or another, especially in cases where the specimen is a legal doctrine. There is no way to account for legal development in the course of which a doctrine has moved from one category to another or to reflect the composite nature of a doctrine and as a result, flexibility in classifying doctrinal principles is required.

Overlaps, gaps, and the limits of permissibility

The classification unveils instances where the various defensive rules overlap. An example includes allegations of infringement on the basis that the defendant took part of a copyright-protected work. In cases such as this a defendant may either negate infringing liability by arguing that the portion taken is not sufficient in order for infringement to be established—a defence which arguably becomes rather limited in the aftermath of *Infopaq*[16]—or justify the said conduct on the basis of a copyright exception or limitation, e.g. the quotation exception or any other purpose-specific limitation to copyright that may be applicable. Within the framework of copyright exceptions and limitations there are further possible instances of overlap between defensive rules. For instance, the remunerated exception of reprography may coincide with educational exceptions or other public policy exceptions, such as those available to libraries and archives. The remunerated exception allowing private copying could overlap with the exceptions on research and private study, although the latter have an arguably narrower scope.

Defensive rules available to specific sets of institutional users such as libraries and archives can also overlap in some regards and in this respect allow for the permissibility of a variety of activities. In such cases, gaps between the various permissible activities may become more relevant than overlaps in that numerous activities related to the online context may not be sufficiently covered by the existing legal framework. This is particularly so when the permitted activities are designed on the basis of current trends in technology and the business sector and are not sufficiently flexible or technologically neutral in order to accommodate emergent uses of protected works that serve the public interest and align with the purposes of copyright and the objectives of EU harmonization.

Clearly some of the 'gaps' in the legislative drafting of defensive rules are meant to remain within the scope of the entitlement of the copyright holders. Not all of these 'gaps', however, are meant to fall, by default, within the system of exclusive rights and there may well be instances of permitted use that have escaped legislative attention, primarily due to the fact that copyright exceptions and limitations are drafted on the basis of technological advances and business trends that are contemporaneous to legislative reform, but which are not necessarily forward-looking. Drafting narrowly framed copyright exceptions and limitations has the disadvantage of leaving the impression that everything that is not expressly permitted falls, by default, within the system of copyright exclusivity and remains outside the framework of permissibility. Emergent uses, which are enabled through technological evolution but are not contemporaneous to legislative drafting, are bound to be excluded from permissibility before the political will matures, and

---

[16] *Infopaq International A/S v Danske Dagblades Forening*, Case C-5/08, 16 July 2009, ECLI:EU:C:2009:465 (*Infopaq I*).

thus may be subject to legislative reform years after their emergence. Examples include copyright exceptions and limitations available for cross-border teaching activities. Although such uses were technologically feasible for many years before the Directive on Copyright in the Digital Single Market was launched, educational institutions were bound by copyright norms and, being risk-averse in their majority, were discouraged from making full use of the technological tools at hand for the purposes of their teaching provision. This is to say that narrow legislative drafting means that certain uses that are in line with policy objectives and copyright principles remain outside the framework of defensive claims for several years before making their way into the framework of permissibility.

The need for broader, more flexible, and stronger defences: objectives, principles, and perspectives

The current framework of defensive rules under EU copyright does not seem appropriate to achieve the policy objectives stated in the various Directives on copyright law. The reasons for this rest on the rigidity of the system, its complexity (especially in the aftermath of the Directive on Copyright in the Digital Single Market), the broad definition of rights as opposed to the narrow drafting and strict interpretation of copyright exceptions and limitations, and the legal nature of this latter set of defensive rules.

An argument that is often made in copyright literature is that the current legal framework needs to be more flexible in order to accommodate the breadth of modern activities that have significant public benefits, but which cannot be safely covered by the available defences.[17] Discussion centres around the value of an open-ended norm in the form of a test for judicial interpretation of whether a particular activity is permitted or not. Proponents of such a judicial test draw inspiration from the fair use test that is applicable in the United States, arguing towards the introduction of a similar, open-ended judicial standard at the EU level.[18] The benefits of such a rule rest in broader fairness considerations that the judiciary is called to take into account when asked to determine the lawfulness of a given activity for the purposes of copyright protection. Such a judicial test is deemed

---

[17] P. Bernt Hugenholtz and Martin Senftleben, 'Fair Use in Europe: In Search of Flexibilities' (2001) Institute for Information Law, Vrije Universiteit, Amsterdam; P. Bernt Hugenholtz, 'Flexible Copyright: Can the EU Author's Rights Accommodate Fair Use' in Ruth L. Okediji (ed.), *Copyright Law in an Age of Limitations and Exceptions* (New York: Cambridge University Press, 2017) 275; also see Robert Burrell and Allison Coleman, *Copyright Exceptions: The Digital Impact* (Cambridge: Cambridge University Press, 2005); Christophe Geiger, '"Fair Use" through Fundamental Rights in Europe: When Freedom of Artistic Expression allows Creative Appropriations and Opens up Statutory Copyright Limitations' (2018) Center for International Intellectual Property Studies (CEIPI) Research Paper No. 2018-09.

[18] See e.g. P. Bernt Hugenholtz and Martin Senftleben, 'Fair Use in Europe: In Search of Flexibilities' (2001) Institute for Information Law, Vrije Universiteit, Amsterdam.

to generate a degree of flexibility as it cannot be superseded by technological advancement and can make allowance for activities that narrowly framed defensive rules cannot accommodate.

Discussions which argue in favour of the introduction of an open-ended norm such as a fair use styled test urge for the transformation of the three-step test—as the existing international norm that determines the permissibility of certain uses at the legislative stage—into a test suitable for assessment by the judiciary.[19] This test states that legislators of countries bound by the international instruments that provide the test ought to confine limitations and exceptions to exclusive rights to (a) certain special cases, which (b) do not conflict with a normal exploitation of the work, and (c) do not unreasonably prejudice the legitimate interests of the rights holders. Although the test was historically introduced in international instruments as a tool for legislative use, Article 5(5) of the Information Society Directive lays it down as a test for judicial application.[20] However controversial,[21] this shift in the function of the test at the EU level could mean that the test has the potential to serve as Europe's fair use test. The main proponent of construing a judicial test on the basis of the three-step test is the Wittem Group. According to their proposal, the suggested test will complement four sets of exceptions listed under Articles 5(1) to 5(4), falling under diverse justificatory grounds, including uses with minimal economic significance; uses for the purpose of freedom of expression and information; uses permitted to promote social, political, and cultural objectives; and uses for the purpose of enhancing competition. The proposed test reads as follows:

> Any other use that is comparable to the uses enumerated in art. 5.1 to 5.4(1) is permitted provided that the corresponding requirements of the relevant limitation are met and the use does not conflict with the normal exploitation of the work and does not unreasonably prejudice the legitimate interests of the author or rightholder, taking account of the legitimate interests of third parties

In the initial discussions on the Directive on Copyright in the Digital Single Market, the European Parliament had also called for 'flexibility in the interpretation of exceptions and limitations in certain special cases that do not conflict with the normal exploitation of the work and do not unreasonably prejudice the legitimate interests of the author or rightsholder.'[22] This proposal, which was welcomed with

---

[19]   See e.g. the proposal of the Wittem Group: see Wittem Group, 'European Copyright Code', <http://www.copyrightcode.eu>, accessed 11 November 2019, Art. 5.5. The 'three step test' is an international instrument featuring in the Berne Convention, the World Intellectual Property Organization Copyright Treaty, and the Agreement on Trade-Related Aspects of Intellectual Property Rights that lays down the parameters of what should be permitted at the legislative level in the various Member States.

[20]   Stavroula Karapapa, *Private Copying* (London: Routledge, 2012) 99 et seq.

[21]   This is so because it sets yet an extra condition for the permissibility of exceptions and limitations.

[22]   European Parliament, Committee on Legal Affairs, Draft Report on the Implementation of Directive 2001/29/EC of the European Parliament and of the Council of 22 May 2001 on the

enthusiasm by academia,[23] did not make its way into the Directive on Copyright in the Digital Single Market. Instead of adopting an open norm, the Directive introduced a set of copyright exceptions which are not only characterized by their high degree of specificity, but also their extreme complexity. In the aftermath of the launch of the Directive on Copyright in the Digital Single Market, the introduction of a flexible norm remains less likely, at least in the near future, even though such a policy option would have arguably offered a more efficient mechanism in accommodating modern uses of copyright-protected works, particularly those that are not envisaged by current statutory language, but which are beneficial to society, conform with copyright principles, and align with the objectives of creativity, innovation, and business growth.

The approach towards the permissibility of certain copyright uses under EU copyright would benefit from the infusion of certain key principles and values, which align with, or even stem from, the rationale for copyright protection but also broader themes, such as legislative drafting and the objectives of the Internal Market. This will enable accommodation of uses of protected content without authorial permission in instances that align with the objectives of copyright protection and EU harmonization.

At the legislative level, future reform could be framed around rules that are sufficiently flexible and technologically neutral to embrace advances in technology and development of new business models, but which are also simple, clear, and effective.[24] The recent launch of the Directive on Copyright in the Digital Single Market unveiled the complexity of the defensive rules currently available which are lengthy, spread across a number of legislative instruments, and drafted in rather technical legal terms. Such exhaustive lists of closely defined exceptions enhance the rigidity of the current legal framework and its adaptation to technological advancements, emergent business models, or novel creative practices. Unlike exclusive rights which are drafted in open-ended and technologically neutral terms, copyright exceptions and limitations cover narrowly defined acts and refer to specific technologies that enable copying. This

---

Harmonisation of Certain Aspects of Copyright and Related Rights in the Information Society, 15 January 2015, 2014/2256(INI), point 13.

[23] P. Bernt Hugenholtz, 'Flexible Copyright: Can the EU Author's Rights Accommodate Fair Use' in Ruth L. Okediji (ed.), *Copyright Law in an Age of Limitations and Exceptions* (New York: Cambridge University Press, 2017) 275.

[24] 'Community legislative acts shall be drafted clearly, simply, and precisely' (Interinstitutional Agreement of 22 December 1998 on common guidelines for the quality of drafting of Community legislation, 1999/C 73/01, OJ EC C 73/1, 17 March 1999, Art. 1); also see Agreement on the Quality of Drafting: 'Clear, simple, and precise drafting of Community legislative acts is essential if they are to be transparent and readily understandable by the public and economic operators. It is also a prerequisite for the proper implementation and uniform application of Community legislation in the Member States' (Interinstitutional Agreement of 22 December 1998 on common guidelines for the quality of drafting of Community legislation, 1999/C 73/01, OJ EC C 73/1, 17 March 1999, preamble (1)).

system can be seen as creating an imbalanced framework, one that generates injustice for end users. Drafting copyright exceptions with a view to retaining some degree of flexibility could overcome the rigidity and fragmentation of the current legal framework and leave enough room for national judges to develop interpretations on the basis of the purpose underpinning each defensive rule. One such possibility could include a fair use styled exception, possibly through an appropriate rewording of the three-step test in this regard, as has already been suggested in the literature.

Another possibility could be to introduce an open norm covering emergent uses of copyright-protected content, subject to the conditions of the three-step test. In this regard, such an open rule would allow judges discretion in determining the permissibility of a use that law making could not foresee at the time of legislative drafting and also have the merit of being sufficiently specific in order to qualify as a certain special case in line with the three-step test. Such a rule would allow principle-based considerations to be taken into judicial consideration, in line with the principle of strict interpretation that has been developed by the Court of Justice[25] but also the broader perspective of technological advances that have a positive effect on public welfare. A rule allowing the judiciary to examine such cases without being limited to the strictly enumerated rules embodied in copyright exceptions and limitations, in line with established principles of copyright law, could arguably overcome the rigidity of the currently narrowly framed scope of copyright exceptions and limitations. Such a principle-based approach would require taking into consideration the objectives of copyright law from the perspective of established legal principles and stated objectives of copyright protection. A purposive construal of rationale-based defences would infuse judicial examinations with a degree of flexibility that the current drafting of defensive rules is missing.

At the same time, the current legal framework is too complex, with long lists of rather detailed and technically drafted copyright exceptions and limitations that are spread across a number of legislative instruments, mostly Directives. Introducing a single copyright instrument to include the relevant legal provisions could offer a solution. But simplicity as a principle that could govern future legislative reform could also address the design of each defensive rule as such. Indeed, as affirmed in the Agreement on the quality of drafting:

> clear, simple, and precise drafting of Community legislative acts is essential if they are to be transparent and readily understandable by the public and economic

---

[25] See e.g. *Stichting Brein v Jack Frederik Wullems*, Case C-527/15, 26 April 2017, ECLI:EU:C:2017:300 (*Filmspeler*), [61]–[62]; *Infopaq International A/S v Danske Dagblades Forening*, Case C-5/08, 16 July 2009, ECLI:EU:C:2009:465 (*Infopaq I*), [55]; *Infopaq International A/S v Danske Dagblades Forening*, Case C-302/10, 17 January 2012, ECLI:EU:C:2012:16 (*Infopaq II*), [26].

operators. It is also a prerequisite for the proper implementation and uniform application of Community legislation in the Member States.[26]

Simplicity is here suggested as complementing legal certainty and clarity in the law. It may possibly be achieved with a higher degree of specificity in the scope of exclusive rights and a parallel rethinking of the scope of permitted use.

Finally, for the purposes of ensuring a rigorous system of copyright protection that aligns with its theoretical underpinnings and the drivers of legal protection, a stronger role for the end user would be beneficial. There can be no 'balance' in the copyright framework[27] unless users are empowered with a set of enforceable rights, i.e. unless like is compared with like. Even though, for the sake of establishing and maintaining a balanced framework within EU copyright, as per the objectives of the various Directives on copyright law, it would have been opportune to introduce user rights, namely rules that can be enforced before courts on the user's initiative (possibly via specific rules in copyright or consumer law), there is currently no such thing under EU copyright law. We have seen that there have been sporadic judicial affirmations that exceptions serve as defences against infringing liability, but not as fully fledged user rights,[28] with the effect that users have neither the right nor the entitlement to claim that their benefit in carrying out a particular permitted use has been restricted by copyright holders, either contractually or technologically. Although the legal tradition of EU copyright does not seem supportive of the creation of defensive rules taking the shape of user rights,[29] this could be an aspect

---

[26] Interinstitutional Agreement of 22 December 1998 on common guidelines for the quality of drafting of Community legislation, 1999/C 73/01, OJ EC C 73/1, 17 March 1999, preamble (1).

[27] Directive 2001/29/EC of the European Parliament and of the Council of 22 May 2001 on the Harmonisation of Certain Aspects of Copyright and Related Rights in the Information Society, OJ L 167, 22 June 2001, 10–19 (Information Society Directive), Recital 31 (affirmed in various cases such as *Funke Medien NRW GmbH v Federal Republic of Germany*, Case C-469/17, 29 July 2019, ECLI:EU:C:2019:623 (*Funke Medien*), [32]; *Pelham GmbH, Moses Pelham, Martin Haas v Ralf Hütter, Florian Schneider-Esleben*, Case C-476/17, 29 July 2019, ECLI:EU:C:2019:624 (*Pelham*), [32]); Directive (EU) 2019/790 of the European Parliament and of the Council of 17 April 2019 on Copyright and Related Rights in the Digital Single Market and Amending Directives 96/9/EC and 2001/29/EC, OJ L 130, 17 May 2019, 92–125 (Digital Single Market Directive), Recitals 6, also 21, 61, 70, 75.

[28] *Studio Canal et al v S. Penguin and Union Federale des Consommateurs Que Choisir*, Cour de Cassation, 19 June 2008, No. 07-142777 (France); *Studio Canal et al v S. Penguin and Union Federale des Consommateurs Que Choisir*, Paris Court of Appeal, 4 April 2007, *Gaz. Pal.* 18 July 2007 No. 199, 23 (France); *Studio Canal et al v S. Penguin and Union Federale des Consommateurs Que Choisir*, Cour de Cassation, 1st civil section, 28 February 2006, Case No. 549, Bull. 2006 I No. 126, 115 ('*Mulholland Drive*') (France); Supreme Court (Cour de cassation), No. 07-18778, 27 November 2008 ('*Phil Collins*') (France); *Fnac Paris v UFC Que Choisir et autres*, Court of Appeal Paris (Cour d'appel Paris), 20 June 2007 ('*Phil Collins*') (France); *Mr X and UFC Que Choisir v Warner Music France and FNAC Paris*, Paris District Court, 10 January 2006 ('*Phil Collins*') (France); *L'ASBL Association Belge des Consomateurs Test Achats v La SA EMI Recorded Music Belgium et al*, Tribunal of First Instance of Brussels, 2004/46/A, 27 April 2004 (Belgium); *L'ASBL Association Belge des Consomateurs Test Achats v La SA EMI Recorded Music Belgium et al*, Brussels Court of Appeal, 9 September 2005, Case 2004/AR/1649 (Belgium); contra *CCH Canadian Ltd v Law Society of Upper Canada*, 2004 SCC 14 (CCH) (Canada).

[29] Unlike, for instance, Canada where user rights have been affirmed in *CCH Canadian Ltd v Law Society of Upper Canada* [2004] 1 SCR 339, 2004 SCC 13 (Canada).

for future legislative consideration. Perhaps the most suitable defensive rules that could function as rights of the users are speech entitlements, which represent and enable the exercise of the very principles on which copyright itself is premised. Such an affirmation could enhance the development of a rigorous public domain where innovation and creativity can flourish, and an environment that is constitutive towards the preservation of the copyright balance as a fundamental notion on which rights and their exceptions are constitutive aspects of a single judicial order.

Bibliography

Afori, O., 'Implied License: An Emerging New Standard in Copyright Law' (2008) 25 *Santa Clara Computer and High Technology Law Journal* 275.

Ahlborn, C., Evans, D. S., and Padilla, A. J., 'The Logic & Limits of the "Exceptional Circumstances Test" in Magill and IMS Health' (2004) 28(4) *Fordham International Law Journal* 1109.

Allgrove, B. and Ganley, P., 'Search Engines, Data Aggregators and UK Copyright Law: A Proposal' (2007) 29(6) *European Intellectual Property Review* 227.

Anderman, S., *The Interface Between Intellectual Property Rights and Competition Policy* (Cambridge: Cambridge University Press, 2007).

Anderman, S. and Ezrachi, A., *Intellectual Property and Competition Law: New Frontiers* (Oxford: Oxford University Press, 2011).

Angelopoulos, C., 'Beyond the Safe Harbours: Harmonising Substantive Intermediary Liability for Copyright Infringement in Europe' (2013) 3 *Intellectual Property Quarterly* 253.

Angelopoulos, C., *European Intermediary Liability in Copyright* (Kluwer Law International: Information Law Series, 2016).

Arezzo, E., 'Hyperlinks and Making Available Right in the European Union – What Future for the Internet after Svensson?' (2014) 45(5) *International Review of Intellectual Property and Competition Law* 524.

Arnold, R. and Rosati, E., 'Are National Courts the Addressees of the InfoSoc Three-Step Test?' (2005) 10(10) *Journal of Intellectual Property Law & Practice* 741.

Association Littéraire et Artistique Internationale (ALAI), 'Opinion on the Criterion "New Public", Developed by the Court of Justice of the European Union (CJEU), Put in the Context of Making Available and Communication to the Public' (17 September 2014), available at <http://www.alai.org/en/assets/files/resolutions/2014-opinion-new-public.pdf>, accessed 11 November 2019.

Axhamn, J. and Guibault, L., 'Cross-border Extended Collective Licensing: a Solution to Online Dissemination of Europe's Cultural Heritage?' (2012) Amsterdam Law School Research Paper No. 2012-22, available at <https://ssrn.com/abstract=2001347>, accessed 11 November 2019.

Baistrocchi, P., 'Liability of Intermediary Service Providers in the EU Directive on Electronic Commerce' (2003) 19(1) *Santa Clara Computer & High Technology Law Journal* 126.

Barron, A., 'Kant, Copyright and Communicative Freedom' (2012) 31 *Law and Philosophy* 1.

Bechtold, S., 'Directive 2001/29/EC (Information Society Directive) of the European Parliament and of the Council of 22 May 2001 on the Harmonisation of Certain Aspects of Copyright and Related Rights in the Information Society' in Dreier, T. and Hugenholtz, P. B. (eds), *Concise European Copyright Law* (Alphen aan den Rijn: Kluwer Law International, 2006) 343, 371.

Beebe, B., 'An Empirical Study of U.S. Fair Use Opinions, 1978-2005' (2008) 156 *University of Pennsylvania Law Review* 549.

Benabou, V. L., 'Patatras! À Propos de la Décision du Conseil Constitutionnel du 27 Juillet 2006' (2006) 20 *Propriétés Intellectuelles* 240.

Bently, L. and Aplin, T., 'Whatever Became of Global Mandatory Fair Use? A Case Study in Dysfunctional Pluralism' in Frankel, S. (ed.), *Is Intellectual Property Pluralism Functional?* (Cheltenham: Edward Elgar, 2018) 8.

Besen, S. and Kirby, S. N., 'Private Copying, Appropriability, and Optimal Copying Royalties' (1989) 32 *Journal of Law and Economics* 255.

Birnhack, M. D., 'Acknowledging the Conflict between Copyright Law and Freedom of Expression under the Human Rights Act' (2003) 14(2) *Entertainment Law Review* 24.

Borghi, M., 'Chasing Copyright Infringement in the Streaming Landscape' (2011) 42(3) *International Review of Intellectual Property and Competition Law* 1.

Borghi, M., 'Copyright and Truth' (2011) 12(1) *Theoretical Inquires in Law* 1.

Borghi, M. and Karapapa, S., 'Non-Display Uses of Digital Works: Google Books and Beyond' (2011) 1(1) *Queen Mary Journal of Intellectual Property* 21.

Borghi, M. and Karapapa, S., *Copyright and Mass Digitization: A Cross-Jurisdictional Perspective* (Oxford: Oxford University Press, 2013).

Borghi, M. and Karapapa, S., 'Contractual Restrictions on Lawful Use of Information: Sole-Source Databases Protected by the Back Door?' (2015) 37(8) *European Intellectual Property Review* 505.

Borghi, M., Erickson, K., and Favale, M., 'With Enough Eyeballs All Searches are Diligent: Mobilizing the Crowd in Copyright Clearance for Mass Digitization' (2016) 16(1) *Journal of Intellectual Property* 135.

Borghi, M., Ferretti, F. and Karapapa, S., 'Online Processing Consent under EU Law: A Theoretical Framework and Empirical Evidence from the UK' (2013) 21 *International Journal of Law and Information Technology* 1.

Borghi, M., Montagnani, M. L., Maggiolino, M., and Nuccio, M., 'Determinants in the On-Line Distribution of Digital Content: an Exploratory Analysis' (2012) 3(2) *European Journal of Law and Technology* 1.

Bouche, N., *Intellectual Property Law in France* (Alphen aan den Rijn: Kluwer Law International, 2011).

Bradshaw, D., 'Copyright, Fair Dealing and the Mandy Allwood Case: the Court of Appeal Gets the Max out of a Multiple Pregnancy Opportunity' (1999) 19(5) *Entertainment Law Review* 125.

Burrell, R., 'Defending the Public Interest' (2000) 22(9) *European Intellectual Property Review* 394.

Burrell, R. and Coleman, A., *Copyright Exceptions: The Digital Impact* (Cambridge: Cambridge University Press, 2005).

Buydens, M. and Dusollier, S., 'Les Exceptions au Droit d'Auteur dans l'Environnement Numérique: Evolutions Dangereuses' (2001) 9 *Communication – Commerce Electronique* 13.

Calabresi, G. and Melamed, A. D., 'Property Rules, Liability Rules, and Inalienability: One View of the Cathedral' (1972) 85(6) *Harvard Law Review* 1089.

Chapdelaine P., *Copyright User Rights: Contracts and the Erosion of Property* (Oxford: Oxford University Press, 2017).

Christie, A. F., 'Maximizing Permissible Exceptions to Intellectual Property Rights' in Kur, A. and Mizaras, V. (eds), *The Structure of Intellectual Property Law: Can One Size Fit All?* (Cheltenham: Edward Elgar, 2011) 121.

Cohen, J., 'The Place of the User in Copyright Law' (2005) 74 *Fordham Law Review* 347.

Coleman, J. L., *The Practice of Principle: In Defence of a Pragmatist Approach to Legal Theory* (Oxford: Oxford University Press, 2001).

Cornish, W., 'European Community Directive on Database Protection' (1995) 21(1) *Columbia VLA J Law & the Arts* 1.

Crews, K. D., 'Study on Copyright Limitations and Exceptions for Libraries and Archives: Updated and Revised' (Geneva: WIPO, 2008; revised in 2014; updated and revised in 2015).

Cruquenaire, A., 'Electronic Agents as Search Engines: Copyright-Related Aspects' (2001) 9 *International Journal of Law and Information Technology* 327.

Dahlmanns, G., 'Reprography and Copyright' (1974) 2 *International Journal of Law Libraries* 55.

Derclaye, E., 'The Court of Justice Interprets the Database Sui Generis Right for the First Time' (2005) 30 *European Law Review* 420.

Derclaye, E., 'Copyright does not Protect the Taste of Cheese' (2018) *The Conversation*, available at http://theconversation.com/copyright-law-does-not-protect-the-taste-of-cheese-108356, accessed on 11 November 2019.

Derclaye, E. and Favale, M., 'Copyright and Contract Law: Regulating User Contracts: The State of the Art and a Research Agenda' (2010) 18(1) *Journal of Intellectual Property Law* 65.

Dietz, A., 'Private Study and Research; Disabilities; Education; Libraries and Archives' in Baulch, L., Green, M., and Wyburn, M. (eds), *ALAI Study Days – The Boundaries of Copyright: Its Proper Limitations and Exceptions* (Sydney: Australian Copyright Council, 1999) 95.

Drassinower, A., 'Sweat of the Brow, Creativity, and Authorship' (2003–4) 1 *University of Ottawa Law & Technology Journal* 105.

Drassinower, A., 'Authorship as Public Address: on the Specificity of Copyright vis-à-vis Patent and Trade-Mark' (2008) 1 *Michigan State Law Review* 1999.

Drassinower, A., 'Exceptions Properly-So-Called' in Gendreau, Y and Drassinower, A (eds), *Langues et Droit d'Auteur / Language and Copyright* (Montreal: Carswell & Brussels: Bruylant, 2009) 205.

Drassinower, A., 'From Distribution to Dialogue: Remarks on the Concept of Balance in Copyright Law' (2009) 34(4) *Journal of Corporation Law* 991.

Drassinower, A., 'Subject Matter, Scope and User Rights in Copyright Law' (2015) 67 *Studies in Law, Politics and Society Special Issue: Thinking and Rethinking Intellectual Property* 59.

Drassinower, A., *What's Wrong with Copying?* (Cambridge, MA: Harvard University Press, 2015).

Durantaye, K. de la, 'Orphan Works: A Comparative and International Perspective' in Gervais, D. J. (ed.), *International Intellectual Property: A Handbook of Contemporary Research* (Cheltenham: Edward Elgar, 2015) 190.

Dusollier, S., 'Exceptions and Technological Measures in the European Copyright Directive of 2001: An Empty Promise' (2003) 34(1) *International Review of Intellectual Property and Competition Law* 62.

Dusollier, S., 'Technology as an Imperative for Regulating Copyright: from the Public Exploitation to the Private Use of The Work' (2005) 6 *European Intellectual Property Review* 201.

Dusollier, S., Poullet, Y., and Buydens, M., 'Copyright and Access to Information in the Digital Environment' (2000) XXXIV(4) *Copyright Bulletin* 4.

Dworkin, G., 'Judicial Control of Copyright on Public Policy Grounds' in Kabel, J. and Mom, G. (eds), *Intellectual Property and Information Law* (Alphen aan den Rijn: Kluwer Law International, 1998) 137.

Easterbrook, F. H., 'Intellectual Property is Still Property' (1990) 13 *Harvard Journal of Law and Public Policy* 108.

Elkin-Koren, N., 'Copyright in a Digital Ecosystem: A User Rights Approach' in Okediji, R. L. (ed.), *Copyright Law in an Age of Limitations and Exceptions* (New York: Cambridge University Press, 2017) 132.

European Copyright Society, Opinion on the Reference to the CJEU in Case C-466/12 (15 February 2013) Svensson.

Ezrachi, A. and Maggiolino, M., 'European Competition Law, Compulsory Licensing, and Innovation' (2012) 8(3) *Journal of Competition Law & Economics* 595.

Ficsor, M., *The Law of Copyright and the Internet: the 1996 WIPO Treaties, their Interpretation and Implementation* (Oxford: Oxford University Press, 2002).

Ficsor, M., *Guide to the Copyright and Related Rights Treaties Administered by WIPO and Glossary of Copyright and Related Rights Terms* (Geneva: WIPO, 2003).

Ficsor, M. J., '*Svensson*: Honest Attempt at Establishing Due Balance Concerning the Use of Hyperlinks – Spoiled by the Erroneous "New Public" Theory' (2015) available online at <http://www.copyrightseesaw.net>, accessed 11 November 2019.

Firth, A. and Pereira, B., 'Exceptions for Libraries and Archives' in Stamatoudi, I. (ed.), *New Developments in EU and International Copyright Law* (Alphen aan den Rijn: Kluwer Law International, 2016) 2.

Fischman Afori, O., 'Proportionality: A New Mega Standard in European Copyright Law' (2014) 45(8) *International Review of Intellectual Property and Competition Law* 889.

Garnett, K., Davies G., and Harbottle, G. (eds), *Copinger and Scone James on Copyright* (London: Sweet and Maxwell, 2009, 15th edn).

Geiger, C., 'From Berne to National Law, via the Copyright Directive: The Dangerous Mutations of the Three-Step Test' (2007) 29(12) *European Intellectual Property Review* 486.

Geiger, C., '"Fair Use" through Fundamental Rights in Europe: When Freedom of Artistic Expression allows Creative Appropriations and Opens up Statutory Copyright Limitations' (2018) Center for International Intellectual Property Studies (CEIPI) Research Paper No. 2018-09.

Geiger, C. et al., 'Declaration A Balanced Interpretation Of The "Three-Step Test" In Copyright Law' (2010) 1 *JIPITEC* 119.

Geiger, C. et al., 'Limitations and Exceptions as Key Elements of the Legal Framework for Copyright in the European Union – Opinion of the European Copyright Society on the Judgment of the CJEU in Case C-201/13 *Deckmyn*' (2015) 46(1) *International Review of Intellectual Property and Competition Law* 46.

Geist, M., 'The Canadian Copyright Story: How Canada Improbably Became the World Leader on Users' Rights in Copyright Law' in Okediji, R. L. (ed.), *Copyright Law in an Age of Limitations and Exceptions* (New York: Cambridge University Press, 2017) 169.

Gendreau, Y., 'Chapter 2: Exceptions for Education and Research' in Stamatoudi, I. (ed.), *New Developments in EU and International Copyright Law* (Alphen aan den Rijn: Kluwer Law International, 2016) 56.

Ginsburg, J., 'The Concept of Authorship in Comparative Copyright Law' (2003) 52 *DePaul Law Review* 1063.

Ginsburg, J. C., 'Fair Use for Free, or Permitted-but-Paid?' (2014) 29 *Berkeley Technology Law Journal* 1383.

Godt, C., 'Intellectual Property and European Fundamental Rights' in Micklitz, H-W (ed.), *Constitutionalization of European Private Law* (Oxford: Oxford University Press, 2014) 210.

Goold, P. R., 'Unbundling the "Tort" of Copyright Infringement' (2016) 102 *Virginia Law Review* 1833.

Goudkamp, J., *Tort Law Defences* (Oxford: Hart Publishing, 2013).

Griffin, J., 'The Interface Between Copyright and Contract: Suggestions for the Future' (2011) 2(1) *European Journal of Law and Technology*, available at <http://ejlt.org/article/view/23/110>, accessed 11 November 2019.

Griffiths, J., 'Copyright Law after Ashdown—Time to Deal Fairly with the Public' (2002) 3 *Intellectual Property Quarterly* 240.

Griffiths, J., 'The "Three-Step Test" in European Copyright Law - Problems and Solutions' (2009) *Queen Mary School of Law Legal Studies Research Paper* No. 31/2009, available at <https://ssrn.com/abstract=1476968>, accessed 11 November 2019.

Griffiths, J., 'Pre-Empting Conflict - A Re-Examination of the Public Interest Defence in United Kingdom (UK) Copyright Law' (2014) 34(1) *Legal Studies* 7.

Griffiths, J., 'Fair Dealing after Deckmyn - The United Kingdom's Defence for Caricature, Parody or Pastiche' in Richardson, M and Ricketson, S (2017) *Research Handbook on Intellectual Property in Media and Entertainment* (Cheltenham: Edward Elgar, 2017) 64.

Griffiths, J. and McDonagh, L., 'Fundamental Rights and European Intellectual Property Law - The Case of Art 17(2) of the EU Charter' in Geiger, C. (ed.), *Constructing European IP: Achievements and New Perspectives* (Cheltenham: Edward Elgar, 2012) 75.

Guibault, L., *Copyright Limitations and Contracts: An Analysis of the Contractual Overridability of Limitations on Copyright* (The Hague/London/Boston, MA: Kluwer Law International, 2002).

Guibault, L., 'The Reprography Levies Across the European Union' (March 2003) IvIR, University of Amsterdam, available at <https://www.ivir.nl/publicaties/download/reprography_levies.pdf>, accessed 11 November 2019.

Guibault, L., 'Individual Licensing Models and Consumer Protection' in Liu, K-C and Hilty, R. M. (eds), *Remuneration of Copyright Owners: Regulatory Challenges of New Business Models* (Berlin/Heidelberg: Springer, 2016) 207.

Guibault, L. et al., 'Study on the Implementation and Effect in Member States' Laws of Directive 2001/29/EC on the Harmonisation of Certain Aspects of Copyright and Related Rights in the Information Society' (2007) Report to the European Commission.

Haftke, M., 'Pro Sieben Media AG v Carlton UK Television Ltd [1999] 1 WLR 605 (CA)' (1999) 10(4) *Entertainment Law Review* 118.

Harding, I., 'Is NLA v Meltwater the End of Browsing?' (2012) 7(7) *Journal of Intellectual Property Law and Practice* 525.

Hargreaves, I., *Digital Opportunity: A Review of Intellectual Property and Growth, An Independent Report* (May 2011).

Harrison, R., 'Pastiched-Off' (1998) 9(5) *Entertainment Law Review* 181.

Hart, M., 'The Legality of Internet Browsing in the Digital Age' (2014) 36(10) *European Intellectual Property Review* 630.

Heide, T., 'Copyright, Contract and the Legal Protection of Technological Measures – Not "the Old Fashioned Way": Providing a Rationale to the "Copyright Exceptions Interface"' (2003) 50 *Journal of the Copyright Society of the USA* 315.

Heide, T. P., 'Copyright in the EU and U.S.: What "Access Right"' (2001) 48(3) *Journal of the Copyright Society of the U.S.A.*, 363.

Helberger, N., 'It's not a Right, Silly! The Private Copying Exception in Practice' (7 October 2004) *INDICARE Monitor*.

Helfer, L. R., Land, M. K., Okediji, R. L., and Reichman, J. H., *The World Blind Union Guide to the Marrakesh Treaty* (Oxford: Oxford University Press, 2017).

Hilty, R. M. and Nérisson, S. (eds), *Balancing Copyright – A Survey of National Approaches* (Berlin Heidelberg: Springer-Verlag, 2012).

Hohfeld, W. N., 'Some Fundamental Legal Conceptions as Applied in Judicial Reasoning' (1913) *Yale Law Journal* 16.

Hohfeld, W. N., 'Fundamental Legal Conceptions as Applied to Judicial Reasoning' (2017) 26 *Yale Law Journal* 710.

Hugenholtz, P. B., 'Caching and Copyright: the Right of Temporary Copying' 22(10) (2000) *European Intellectual Property Review* 482.

Hugenholtz, P. B., 'Flexible Copyright: Can the EU Author's Rights Accommodate Fair Use' in Okediji, R. L. (ed.), *Copyright Law in an Age of Limitations and Exceptions* (New York: Cambridge University Press, 2017) 275.

Hugenholtz, P. B. and Okediji, R. L., 'Conceiving an International Instrument on Limitations and Exceptions to Copyright; Final Report (2008), https://www.ivir.nl/publicaties/download/limitations_exceptions_copyright.pdf, accessed 11 November 2019.

Hugenholtz, P. B. and Senftleben, M., 'Fair Use in Europe: In Search of Flexibilities' (2001) Institute for Information Law, Vrije Universiteit, Amsterdam.

Hugenholtz, P. B., Guibault, L., and van Geffen, S (2003) *The Future of Levies in a Digital Environment* (Amsterdam: Institute for Information Law (IViR), 2003).

Hugenholtz, P. B. et al (2006) *The Recasting of Copyright and Related Rights for the Knowledge Economy* (Amsterdam: IvIR, 2006).

Hughes, J., 'Size Matters (or Should) in Copyright Law' (2005) 74 *Fordham Law Review* 575.

Husovec, M., 'The End of (Meta) Search Engines in Europe?' (2014) Max Planck Institute for Innovation and Competition Research Paper, No. 14-15.

Husovec, M., *Injunctions Against Intermediaries in the European Union: Accountable but not Liable* (Cambridge: Cambridge University Press, 2017).

Husovec, M., Stalla-Bourdillon, S., Rosati, E., Turk, K., Angelopoulos, C., Kuczerawy, A., and Peguera, M., 'An Academic Perspective on the Copyright Reform' (2017) 33(1) *Computer Law and Security Review* 3.

Hutcheon, L., *A Theory of Parody: The Teachings of Twentieth-Century Art Forms* (Urbana: University of Illinois Press, 1985).

IFPI, 'The WIPO Treaties: "Making Available" Right' (March 2003).

Janssens, M-C and Tryggvadóttir, R., 'Facilitating Access to Orphan and Out-of-Commerce Works to Make Europe's Cultural Resources Available to the Broader Public' in Stamatoudi, I. (ed.), *Copyright and the Digital Agenda for Europe: Current Challenges for the Future* (Athens: Sakkoulas Publications, 2015) 27.

Johnson, P., 'The Public Interest: Is it Still a Defence to Copyright Infringement?' (2005) 16(1) *Entertainment Law Review* 1.

Kant, I., 'On the Wrongfulness of Unauthorized Publication of Books' in Gregor, M. J. (ed.), *Immanuel Kant: Practical Philosophy* (Cambridge: Cambridge University Press, 1998).

Kant, I., 'The Metaphysics of Morals' in Gregor, M. J. (ed.), *Immanuel Kant: Practical Philosophy* (Cambridge: Cambridge University Press, 1998).

Karapapa, S., 'Padawan v SGAE: A Right to Private Copy?' (2011) 33(4) *European Intellectual Property Review* 252.

Karapapa, S., *Private Copying* (London: Routledge, 2012).

Karapapa, S., 'A Copyright Exception for Private Copying in the United Kingdom' (2013) 35(3) *European Intellectual Property Review* 129.

Karapapa, S., 'Reconstructing Copyright Exhaustion in the Online World' (2014) 4 *Intellectual Property Quarterly* 304.

Karapapa, S., 'The Requirement for a "New Public" in EU Copyright Law' (2017) 1 *European Law Review* 63.

Karapapa, S., 'Article 30(3) of the International Convention on the Rights of Disabled Persons' in Bantekas, I., Stein, M., and Anastasiou, D. (eds), *Commentary on the International Convention on the Rights of Disabled Persons* (Oxford: Oxford University Press, 2018) 888.

Karapapa, S., 'The Press Publishers' Right in the European Union: An Overreaching Proposal and the Future of News Online' in Bonadio, E. and Lucchi, N. (eds), *Non-Conventional Copyright: Do New and Atypical Works Deserve Protection?* (Cheltenham: Edward Elgar, 2018) 316.

Karapapa, S., 'Exhaustion of Rights on Digital Content under EU Copyright: Positive and Normative Perspectives' in Aplin, T. (ed.), *Research Handbook on Intellectual Property and Digital Technologies* (Cheltenham: Edward Elgar, 2019) 481.

Karnell, G., 'Extended Collective License Clauses and Agreements in Nordic Copyright Law' (1985–6) 10 *Columbia-VLA Journal of Law & the Arts* 73.

Kernochan, J. M., 'The Distribution Right in the United States of America: Review and Reflections' (1989) 42 *Vanderbilt Law Review* 1407.

Klass, N. and Rupp, H., 'EUROPEANA, ARROW and Orphan Works: Bringing Europe's Cultural Heritage Online' in Stamatoudi, I. (ed.), *EU Copyright Law: A Commentary* (Cheltenham: Edward Elgar, 2014) 946.

Kleinschimdt, B., 'An International Comparison of ISP's Liabilities for Unlawful Third Party Content' (2010) 18(4) *International Journal of Law and Information Technology* 332.

Koelman, K., 'Fixing the Three-Step Test' (2006) 28(8) *European Intellectual Property Review* 407.

Kohler, J., *Das Autorrecht: eine Zivilistische Abhandlung; zugleich ein Beitrag zur Lehre vom Eigenthum, vom Miteigenthum, vom Rechtsgeschäft und vom Individualrecht* (Jena: Fischer, 1880).

Korah, V., 'The Interface Between Intellectual Property and Antitrust: The European Experience' (2002) 69(3) *Antitrust Law Journal* 801.

Korah, V., *An Introductory Guide to EC Competition Law and Practice* (Oxford, Portland, Oregon: Hart Publishing, 2004, 8th edn).

Koskinen-Olsson, T., 'Collective Management in the Nordic Countries' in Gervais, D. J. (ed.), *Collective Management of Copyright and Related Rights* (Alphen aan den Rijn: Kluwer Law International, 2006) 257.

Kretschmer, M., 'Private Copying and Fair Compensation – Study II: Empirical Effects on Copyright Levy Schemes', A Report for the UK Intellectual Property Office (2011) available at <www.cippm.org.uk/ publications/comparative-study-of-copyright-levies-in-europe.html>, accessed 11 November 2019.

Kretschmer, M. et al., 'The Relationship between Copyright and Contract Law' (2010) 4 *Strategic Advisory Board for Intellectual Property Policy* 85.

Kretschmer, M. et al., 'The European Commission's Public Consultation on the Review of EU Copyright Rules: a Response by the CREATe Centre' (2014) 36(9) *European Intellectual Property Review* 547.

Kur, A., 'Of Oceans, Islands, and Inland Water - How Much Room for Exceptions and Limitations Under the Three-Step Test?' (2008) Max Planck Institute for Intellectual Property, Competition & Tax Law Research Paper Series, No. 08-04.

Lagarde, L. and Ang, C., 'Parody in the UK and France: defined by humour?' (24 March 2016) *Practical Law*.

Lang, B., 'Orphan Works and the Google Book Settlement: An International Perspective' in Grimmelmann, J. (ed.), (2010) D is for Digitize *55 New York Law School Law Review* 111.

Latman, A., 'Fair Use of Copyrighted Works' (1960) Study no 14, Copyright Law Revision, Studies Prepared for the Subcommittee on Patents, Trademarks and Copyrights, S. Comm. in the Judiciary, 86th Cong. 3.

Leistner, M., 'The German Federal Supreme Court's Judgment on Google's Image Search—A Topical Example of the "Limitations" of the European Approach to Exceptions and Limitations' (2011) 42(4) *International Review of Intellectual Property and Competition Law* 417.

Lemley, M. A., 'Romantic Authorship and the Rhetoric of Property' (1997) 75 *Texas Law Review* 873.

Lepage, A., 'Overview of Exceptions and Limitations to Copyright in the Digital Environment' (January–March 2003) *E-Copyright Bulletin*, UNESCO.

Leval, P., 'Toward a Fair Use Standard' (1990) 103 *Harvard Law Review* 1105.

Litman, J., 'Fetishizing Copies' in Okediji, R. L. (ed.), *Copyright Law in an Age of Limitations and Exceptions* (New York: Cambridge University Press, 2017) 107.

Lucas, A., 'International Exhaustion' in Bently, L., Suthersanen U., and Torremans P. (eds), *Global Copyright Three Hundred Years Since the Statute of Anne, From 1709 to Cyberspace* (Cheltenham: Edward Edgar Publishing, 2010) 304.

Lucas, A. and Lucas, H-J, *Traité de la Propriété Littéraire et Artistique* (Paris: Litec, 2004, 3rd edn).

McDonagh, L., 'Headlines and Hyperlinks: UK Copyright Law Post-Infopaq - Newspaper Licensing Agency Ltd and Others v Meltwater Holding BV and Other Companies' (2011) 1(2) *Queen Mary Journal of Intellectual Property Law* 184.

Madison, M. J., 'A Pattern-Oriented Approach to Fair Use' (2004) 45 *William & Mary Law Review* 1525.

Montagnani, M. L. and Borghi, M., 'Positive Copyright and Open Content Licences: How to Make a Marriage Work by Empowering Authors to Disseminate Their Creations' (2007) 12 *International Journal of Communications Law and Policy* 244.

Moyse, P-E, *Le Droit de Distribution: Analyse Historique et Comparative en Droit d'Auteur* (Cowansville, Québec: Les Editions Yvon Blais, 2007).

Netanel, N. W., 'Copyright and the First Amendment: What *Eldred* Misses – and Portends' in Griffiths, J. and Suthersanen, U. (eds), *Copyright and Free Speech: Comparative and International Analyses* (Oxford: Oxford University Press, 2005) 129.

Netpop Research, 'Defining "Non-Commercial": A Study on How the Internet Population Understands "Non-Commercial Use"' (September 2009) Creative Commons Corporation.

Newman, C. M., 'What Exactly are you Implying? The Elusive Nature of the Implied Copyright License' (2014) 32(3) *Cardozo Arts and Entertainment Law* 501.

Niggemann, E., 'National Libraries and Copyright in the Digital Age - the German Situation for Orphan Works and Out-of-Print Works' (2012) 23 *Alexandria: The Journal of National and International Library and Information Issues* 125.

Opi, S. B., 'The Application of the Essential Facilities Doctrine to Intellectual Property Licensing in the European Union and the United States: Are Intellectual Property Rights Still Sacrosanct?' (2001) 11 *Fordham Intellectual Property Media and Entertainment Law Journal* 409.

Parchomovsky, G. and Stein, A., 'Intellectual Property Defences' (2013) 113 *Columbia Law Review* 1483.

Pasquale, F., Manne, G. A., Grimmelmann, J., and Goldman, E, 'Is Search now an "Essential Facility"?' in Szoka, B. and Marcus, A. (eds), *The Next Digital Decade: Essays on the Future of the Internet* (Washington DC: TechFreedom, 2010) 401.

Patry, W., *The Fair Use Privilege in Copyright Law* (Washington, DC: Bureau of National Affairs, 1995, 2nd edn).

Phillips, J., 'Fair Stealing and the Teddy Bears' Picnic' (1999) 10(3) *Entertainment Law Review* 57.

Pihlajarinne, T., 'Setting the Limits for the Implied License in Copyright and Linking Discourse – the European Perspective' (2012) 43(6) *International Review of Intellectual Property and Competition Law* 700.

Posner, R., 'When is Parody Fair Use?' (1992) 21 *Journal of Legal Studies* 67.

Quintais, J. P., *Copyright in the Age of Online Access: Alternative Compensation Systems in EU Law* (Alphen aan den Rijn: Kluwer Law International, 2017).

Rahmatian, A., *Copyright and Creativity: The Making of Property Rights in Creative Works* (Cheltenham/Northampton: Edward Elgar, 2011).

Ramalho, A., *The Competence of the European Union in Copyright Lawmaking: A Normative Perspective of EU Powers for Copyright Harmonization* (Cham: Springer, 2016).

Reichman, J. H. and Samuelson, P., 'Intellectual Property Rights in Data' (1997) 50 *Vanderbilt Law Review* 51.

Reinbothe, J., 'Chapter 11: Private Copy Levies' in Stamatoudi, I (ed.), *New Developments in EU and International Copyright Law* (Alphen aan den Rijn: Kluwer Law International, 2016) 298.

Ricketson, S., WIPO Study on Limitations and Exceptions of Copyright and Related Rights in the Digital Environment, SCCR/9/7, WIPO, 5 April 2003.

Ricketson, S. and Ginsburg, J., *International Copyright and Neighbouring Rights* (Oxford: Oxford University Press, 2006, 2nd edn).

Riordan, J., *The Liability of Internet Intermediaries* (Oxford: Oxford University Press, 2016).

Rosati, E., 'The Orphan Works Directive, or Throwing a Stone and Hiding the Hand' (2013) 8 *Journal of Intellectual Property Law & Practice* 303.

Rosati, E., ('Copyright in the EU: In Search of (In)Flexibilities' 2014) 9(7) *Journal of Intellectual Property Law & Practice* 585.

Rosati, E., *Copyright and the Court of Justice of the European Union* (Oxford: Oxford University Press, 2018).

Rose, M., *Parody: Ancient, Modern and Post-Modern* (Cambridge: Cambridge University Press, 1993).

Rosén, J., 'Chapter 12: How Much Communication to the Public is "Communication to the Public"?' in Stamatoudi, I. (ed.), *New Developments in EU and International Copyright Law* (Alphen aan den Rijn: Kluwer Law International - Information Law Series, Volume 35, 2016) 331.

Sag, M., 'Copyright and Copy-Reliant Technology' (2009) 103 *Northwestern University Law Review* 1607.

Samuelson, P., 'Google Book Search and the Future of Books in Cyberspace' (2009) 94 *Minnesota Law Review* 1308.

Samuelson, P., 'Justifications for Copyright Limitations and Exceptions' in Okediji, R. L. (ed.), *Copyright Law in an Age of Limitations and Exceptions* (New York: Cambridge University Press, 2017) 12.

Samuelson, P., 'Unbudling Fair Uses' (2009) 77 *Fordham Law Review* 2537, 2540.

Samuelson, P., 'Justifications for Copyright Limitations and Exceptions' in Okediji, R. L. (ed), *Copyright Law in an Age of Limitations and Exceptions* (New York: Cambridge University Press, 2017), 12.

Schack, H., *Urheber- und Urheberverstragsrecht* (Tübingen: Mohr Siebeck, 5 Auflage, 2010).

Schauer, F., 'Exceptions' (1991) 58 *University of Chicago Law Review* 871.

Schovsbo, J., 'The Exhaustion of Rights and Common Principles of European Intellectual Property Law' in Ohly, A. (ed.), *Common Principles of European Intellectual Property Law* (Tübingen: Mohr Siebeck, 2010) 174.

Schulze, F., 'Resale of Digital Content such as Music, Films or eBooks under European Law' (2014) 36(1) *European Intellectual Property Review* 9.

Senftleben, M., 'The International Three-Step Test: A Model Provision for EC Fair Use Legislation' (2010) 1(2) *Journal of Intellectual Property, Information Technology and E-Commerce Law* 67.

Senftleben, M., Angelopoulos, C., Frosio, G., Moscon, V., Peguera, M., and Rognstad, O. A., 'The Recommendation on Measures to Safeguard Fundamental Rights and the Open Internet in the Framework of the EU Copyright Reform' (2018) 40(3) *European Intellectual Property Review* 149.

Seshadri, R., 'Bridging the Digital Divide: How the Implied License Doctrine Could Narrow the Copynorm-Copyright Gap' (2007) *II UCLA Journal of Law and Technology* 1.

Sganga, C., 'Right to Culture and Copyright: Participation and Access' in Geiger, C. (ed.), *Research Handbook on Human Rights and Intellectual Property* (Cheltenham: Edward Elgar, 2015) 560.

Sganga, C., 'Say Nay to a Tastier Copyright: Why the CJEU Should Deny Copyright Protection for Taste (and Smells)' (2019) 14(3) *Journal of Intellectual Property Law & Practice* 187.

Sganga, C. and Scalzini, S., 'From Abuse of Right to European Copyright Misuse: A New Doctrine for EU Copyright Law' (2017) 48(4) *International Review of Intellectual Property and Competition Law* 405.

Shaheed, F., 'Report of the Special Rapporteur in the Field of Cultural Rights: Copyright Policy and the Right to Science and Culture', United Nations Human Rights Council Document A/HRS/28/57, 24 December 2014.

Sherman, B., 'What is a Copyright Work?' (2010) 12(1) *Theoretical Inquiries in Law* 99.

Sieman, J. S., 'Using the Implied License To Inject Common Sense into Digital Copyright' (2007) 85 *North Carolina Law Review* 885.

Sims, A., 'The Public Interest Defence in Copyright Law: Myth or Reality?' (2006) 28(6) *European Intellectual Property Review* 335.

Sirinelli, P., 'Exceptions et Limites aux Droit d'Auteur et Droits Voisins' Atelier sur la mise en œuvre du Traité de l'OMPI sur le droit d'auteur, *Les Frontières du droit d'auteur: ses limites et exceptions*, Geneve, 6–7 December 1999.

Smith, H. E., 'Intellectual Property as Property: Delineating Entitlements in Information' (2007) 116 *Yale Law Journal* 1742.

Spence, M., 'Intellectual Property and the Problem of Parody' (1998) 114 *Law Quarterly Review* 594.

Spoor, J. H., 'General Aspects of Exceptions and Limitations: General Report' in Baulch, L., Green, M., and Wyburn, M. (eds), *Les Frontières du Droit d'Auteur: ses Limites et Exceptions* (Cambridge: Ed. Australian Copyright Council, 1999) 27.

Stamatoudi, I., 'Text and Data Mining' in Stamatoudi, I. (ed.), *New Developments in EU and International Copyright Law* (Alphen aan den Rijn: Kluwer Law International, 2016) 251.

Sterk, S. E., 'Rhetoric and Reality in Copyright Law' (1996) 94 *Michigan Law Review* 1197.

Strowel, A., *Droit d'Auteur et Copyright: Divergences et Convergences* (Paris: Bruylant and L.G.D.J., 1993).

Strowel, A. and Hanley, V., 'Secondary Liability for Copyright Infringement with regard to Hyperlinks' in Strowel, A. (ed.), *Peer-to-Peer File Sharing and Secondary Liability in Copyright Law* (Cheltenham: Edward Elgar, 2008).

Suthersanen, U. and Frabboni, M. M., 'The Orphan Works Directive' in Stamatoudi, I. and Torremans, P. (eds), *EU Copyright Law: A Commentary* (Cheltenham: Edward Elgar, 2014) 653.

Synodinou, T-E, 'The Lawful User and a Balancing of Interests in European Copyright Law' (2010) 41(7) *International Review of Intellectual Property and Competition Law* 819.

Synodinou, T-E, 'The Principle of Technological Neutrality in European Copyright Law: Myth or Reality?' (2012) 34(9) *European Intellectual Property Review* 618.

Temple Lang, J., 'Monopolisation and the Definition of "Abuse" of a Dominant Position under Article 86 EEC Treaty' (1979) 16 *Common Market Law Review* 345.

Thorne, C. D., 'The Alan Clark Case – What it is; What it is Not' (1998) 20(5) *European Intellectual Property Review* 194.

Treiger-Bar-Am, L. K., 'Kant on Copyright: Rights of Transformative Authorship' (2008) *Cardozo Arts and Entertainment Law Journal* 1059.

Triaille, J-P, 'La Question des Copies "Cache" et la Responsabilité des Intermédiaires: Copiepresse c. Google, Field v. Google' in Strowel, A. and Triaille, J-P (eds), *Google et les Nouveaux Services en Ligne* (Bruxelles: Larcier, 2008).

Triaille, J. P. et al., Study on the Application of Directive 2001/29/EC on Copyright and Related Rights in the Information Society 253, 2013, available at < https://op.europa.eu/en/publication-detail/-/publication/9ebb5084-ea89-4b3e-bda2-33816f11425b >, accessed 11 November 2019.

Turner, J. D. C., *Intellectual Property and EU Competition Law* (Oxford: Oxford University Press, 2010).

Van Gompel, S., 'Unlocking the Potential of Pre-existing Content: How to Address the Issue of Orphan Works in Europe?' (2007) 38(6) *International Review of Intellectual Property and Competition Law* 669.

Vinje, T., 'Copyright Imperilled' (1999) 21 *European Intellectual Property Review* 192.

Von Lewinski, S. (2007) 'Mandatory Collective Administration of Exclusive Rights—A Case Study on its Compatibility with International and EC Copyright Law', January–March 2007, UNESCO, *e-Copyright Bulletin.*

Von Lewinski, S. and Reinbothe, J., 'The WIPO Treaties 1996: Ready to Come into Force' (2002) 24(4) *European Intellectual Property Review* 199.

Vousden, S., 'Innoweb, Search Engines and Engineering Legitimacy in EU law' (2014) *Intellectual Property Quarterly* 280.

Walter, M. M. and Von Lewinski, S., *European Copyright Law: A Commentary* (Oxford: Oxford University Press, 2010).

Wanrooij, W., 'Remuneration Systems for Private Copying in Europe' in Báldy, P. (ed.), *Creators' Rights in the Information Society* (KJK-Kersov legal and business publishers (with the assistance of the Hungarian Patent office): Budapest, 2003) 371.

Weinreb, L., 'Copyright for Functional Expression' (1998) 111 *Harvard Law Review* 1149.

Westcamp, G., 'The Implementation of Directive 2001/29/EC in the Member States, Part II' (February 2007) Queen Mary Intellectual Property Research Institute, Centre for Commercial Law Studies.

Wiseman, L., 'Chapter 8: Making Copies: Photocopying and Copyright' in Sherman, B. and Wiseman, L. (eds), *Copyright and the Challenge of the New* (Alphen aan den Rijn: Kluwer Law International, 2012) 198.

Wittem Group, 'European Copyright Code' (2010) <http://www.copyrightcode.eu>, accessed 11 November 2019.

Xalabarder, R., 'Spanish Supreme Court Rules in Favour of Google Search Engine... and a Flexible Reading of Copyright Statutes?' (2012) 2 *JIPITEC* 162, available at <https://www.jipitec.eu/issues/jipitec-3-2-2012/3445/xalabarder.pdf>, accessed 11 Nov. 2019.

Yen, A. C., 'Restoring the Natural Law: Copyright as Labor and Possession' (1990) 51 *Ohio State Law Journal* 517.

Index